CW01667219

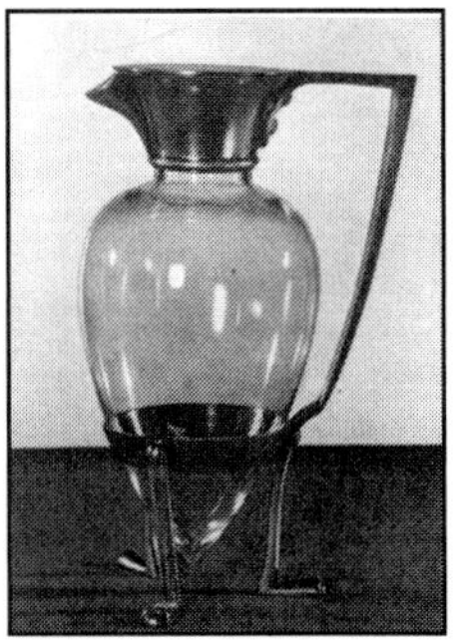

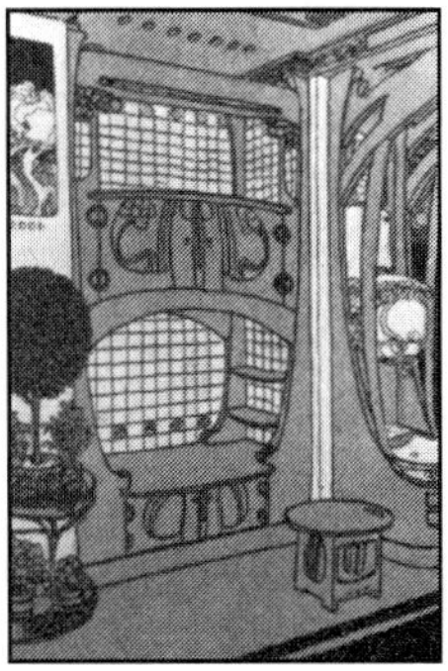

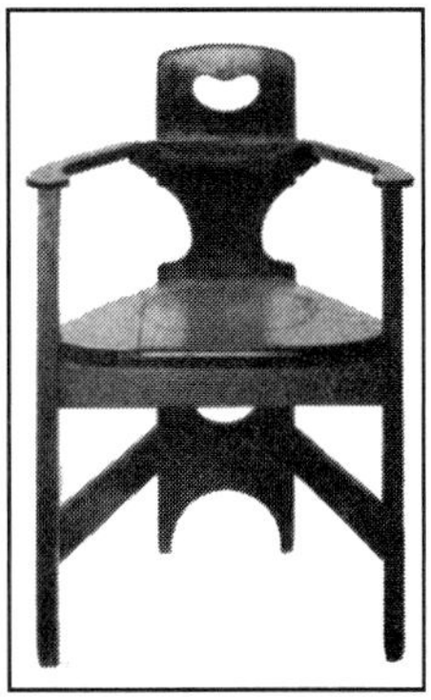

The Art Nouveau Style

A Comprehensive Guide with 264 Illustrations

Stephan Tschudi Madsen

Translated by Ragnar Christophersen

Dover Publications, Inc.
Mineola, New York

Bibliographical Note

This Dover edition, first published in 2002, is an unabridged republication of *Sources of Art Nouveau*, translated by Ragnar Christophersen, originally published by H. Aschehoug, Oslo, Norway, in 1956.

Library of Congress Cataloging-in-Publication Data

Tschudi-Madsen, Stephan, 1923–
[Sources of art nouveau]
The art nouveau style: a comprehensive guide with 264 illustrations / Stephan Tschudi Madsen; translated by Ragnar Christophersen.
p. cm.
Originally published: Sources of art nouveau. Oslo, Norway : H. Aschehoug, 1956.
Includes bibliographical references and index.
ISBN 0-486-41794-8 (pbk.)
1. Art nouveau—Europe. 2. Art, European—19th century. 3. Art, European—20th century. I. Title.

N6757.5.A78 T78 2002
709'.03'49—dc21 2001047763

Manufactured in the United States of America
Dover Publications, Inc., 31 East 2nd Street, Mineola, N.Y. 11501

In memory
of the late Professor
Anders Bugge

CONTENTS

PREFACE

My thanks are due to a great many individuals and institutions who have assisted me in my work, in one way or another, but here, I should like to express my profound gratitude to those institutions which provided the basis without which my investigations could never have been carried out. First and foremost the Norwegian Research Council for Science and the Humanities, who have constantly assisted me and made this publication possible, the University of Oslo, through the granting of Proprietær Øverland and his wife's bequest for investigations on the Continent, and the British Council, with a scholarship to Great Britain. I should also like to express my gratitude to H. Aschehoug & Co. (W. Nygaard) who have published this book. My thanks are also due to the Department of Circulation at the Victoria and Albert Museum, London, whose entire staff, led by Peter Floud, gave me full access to the results of their research work.

Finally I feel greatly indebted to Dr. Thomas Howarth who not only encouraged me, but has taken the pains to read through the manuscript, and willingly suggested valuable improvements.

Oslo, September 1955.

Stephan Tschudi Madsen.

INTRODUCTION

In recent years the architecture and applied art of the latter half of the nineteenth century have gradually engaged the interest of art historians, particularly through the medium of exhibitions and publications. The time is ripe to submit this period to study, not only because it can now be seen in sufficient perspective to emerge with greater clarity, but because several of the artists, and those who knew them, are still alive and can provide useful information.

Interest has so far been concentrated mainly on that part of the development which has contributed directly to the Modern Movement and the style of our own age. All the varied forms of expression within the architecture and applied art of the nineteenth century based on previous styles and the historical *Einleben*— to use a neutral term, Historicism—have, however, so far been neglected. Nevertheless this development too deserves to be dealt with. The objects that have come down to us from this period are expressions of a mode of thinking and feeling basically different from ours. Whether they evoke revulsion or enthusiasm, it is impossible to remain indifferent to the philosophy and artistic ideals of this age, now receding into history.

The Art Nouveau style, both in time as well as in its development, may be placed midway between Historicism and the emergence of the Modern Movement. And yet—with a few exceptions—it has suffered the same fate as the rest of the latter half of the nineteenth century. One is often inclined to judge with the eyes of one's own age, but if Historicism or Art Nouveau is evaluated with the aesthetic yardstick of the twentieth century, the verdict will of necessity be based on false premisses, for the reason that the artists of that age strove to attain ideals which were the opposite of those of our own age. If we are to attempt to evaluate the age and its objects, we must be familiar with the peculiar feeling for form of the nineteenth century and be capable of appreciating it. The term "function" and its application alone give some idea of the gulf that separates the two ages: during the latter half of the nineteenth century function was expressed through decoration—in the first half of the twentieth century it is expressed through construction.

Before proceeding to an evaluation, however, the facts must be marshalled, the formal development must be investigated, and the material presented and placed in relation to the other currents which were operating in the contemporary development.

The object of this thesis is to investigate the background of Art Nouveau, and to discover how and why the style arose, as well as which formal elements contributed to shape it. It is proposed also to determine how it developed, and subsequently declined, and finally an attempt will be made to place the style in its proper European context.

Owing to the great quantity of material from the period which has been preserved, it has proved necessary at all times to make a selection based essentially on an aesthetic appraisal as well as on the standard of workmanship shown, except where special considerations of the history of art have overruled these principles. The basis for an aesthetic appreciation rests not on the standards of our own century, but on principles which have crystallised in Europe's centuries-old tradition of handicrafts, while at the same time an attempt has been made to adapt the selection to the nineteenth century's own special scale of values, thus ensuring the inclusion of objects typical of their age, and imbued with its spirit.

In the preparation of this study investigations have been made in Great Britain, France, Belgium, Holland, as well as in Germany and Austria. These geographical limitations were self-imposed, as the basis and origin of this style may be found in the countries bordering on the English Channel. Neither Italy, Russia, nor the Balkans made any significant contributions to the origin of the style, while the Scandinavian countries only contributed to a very slight extent. For this reason the last mentioned countries have not been dealt with since they made no notable contribution to the development of the style or created any independent Art Nouveau of their own. The same also seems to apply to America.

In order to provide the proper background for the style, and to appreciate its position, it has been necessary to contrast it with the general contemporary development in architecture and applied art. It has proved necessary to deal with movements which formally speaking have little to do with Art Nouveau, e.g. the Arts and Crafts Movement and the Gothic Revival. But these were trends, each in its own way contributing to the origin of the style and its development. Without this wider background Art Nouveau would appear an isolated phenomenon.

It has thus appeared natural to work within a framework comprising architecture and applied art. Despite the temptation to include reviews from contemporary philosophy and drama, and vivid cultural-historical sketches from the Gay Nineties, other branches of art have not been allowed to intrude except where they contribute directly to the main purpose of the study.

In view of the various aspects evinced by Art Nouveau in the various countries, and the many names and shapes it assumed, it is essential first of all to analyse the style itself, as it appeared in full flower around the year 1900. Only through the mature works of the leading artists is it possible to establish the ideal which the style set up and to clarify the national characteristics and the elements on which it is based. By a formal analysis of this nature we shall discover forms and conditions which will frequently help to reveal the origins.

After having clarified the different aspects of Art Nouveau proper, the second part deals with the trends leading up to the style, and establishing its premisses. Advancing into the wilderness of Historicism an attempt is made to find out from where some of the form elements come, which constitute Art Nouveau.

One way of dealing with the problem of the origin of Art Nouveau would have been a chronological investigation, proceeding year by year, of a relatively large geographical area. But in an attempt to arrive at a closer assessment of the various trends involved, and present them as clearly as possible, the attempt has been made to trace each movement or current in turn, though the shortcomings of this method are obvious. In dealing with the development of Art Nouveau there were also several possible methods of approach. At the risk of some chronological repetitions it has nevertheless been decided to deal with each country in turn, and the historical biographical approach may safely be adapted to a geographical subdivision.

The order in which the various countries have been described has been determined in part one by the desire to throw as much light as possible on the salient differences between the various national varieties of Art Nouveau. In part three, however, the sequence has been varied, mainly to show how the style arose and how it spread.

While part one and two are mainly concerned with analyses of form, the third part deals with the development of the style in various countries as well as its decline; this part is adapted to a more historical-biographical method, based *inter alia* upon the series of exhibitions which constitute the chronological backbone necessary for any investigation of the second half of the nineteenth century. These exhibitions, together with contemporary periodicals, provide the most important mirror of the age.

During the hectic decade from 1890 to 1900 about one hundred periodicals connected in various ways with applied art were started, and these furnish us with the broad basis for a close study of stylistic development.

In order to provide as authentic sources as possible, quotations from the artists themselves have to a large extent been used. As representative a selection of quotations as possible has been made, with a view to covering their views and opinions, and in practically every case the quotation is rendered in the form in which the artist actually gave it. This enables us not only to obtain a more vivid picture of the age, but also places us in more intimate contact with the artist.

The main emphasis of this study is placed on work produced in the cultural area bordering on the Channel, with somewhat less emphasis on the Germano-Austrian sphere. There are three reasons for this: first of all, the development of Art Nouveau was most pronounced in the Channel area, while Austria and Germany only joined the movement later, and it was here quickly blended with elements that were essentially foreign to it. Secondly, in Austria and Germany the style was more closely linked only to the two-dimensional form. Thirdly and finally, the *Jugend*-style, from the point of view of the history of art, has been more thoroughly documented and written about than the Art Nouveau of the other countries. For this reason, as far as Austria and Germany are concerned, there were more ample facilities for working on the basis of earlier investigations, and the work is here less independent.

Many illustrations have been included in order that this work may give as representative a picture as possible of the phenomenon, and in the hope that it may be of assistance to other investigators and provide a *point d'appui* for any scholar whose opinions may differ on this subject.

Finally, it is hoped that the historical facts here adduced may serve to throw some light on this unique stylistic phenomenon in the history of European art.

Part I

ART
NOUVEAU
FULLY
DEVELOPED

National Aspects

FRANCE

Floral and Fashionable

French Art Nouveau had two centres, the Nancy school, with its founder Emile Gallé (1846–1904) and the artists who worked around him in King Stanislaus' venerable university town; next there was the group of artists working for the cosmopolitan and energetic little Hamburger Sigfried Bing, in Paris—as well as a number of entirely independent artists also working in Paris.

For the Paris Exhibition of 1900 Gallé made a worktable of ash and walnut, with marquetry of various woods,[1] representing his mature style (fig. 1). On the side of the vertical part of the table are a number of stalk motifs, as well as circles placed freely on the surface of the wood. An inscription, "Travail est Joie," is also found in marquetry. Gallé's speciality is inlay work, varying from plant motifs to verses by Baudelaire inset in the surface, and his decoration is invariably developed two-dimensionally, as can also be seen in the lowest vertical part of the table. The floral motifs flow and undulate rhythmically in a linear interplay between the legs; it is a decoration envisaged in *one* plane. The table as a whole is not a new type: both its construction and the design of the legs are traditional, while the rich moulding derives from the latter half of the nineteenth century.

Gallé's use of inscriptions is typical of his literary attitude, and "Travail est Joie" might well stand as a motto for his varied achievements as well as his artistic attitude: the object is not to express function through the construction—as some of his contemporaries maintained—no, a piece of

1 Cat. No. 1986–1900. Victoria and Albert Museum, London.

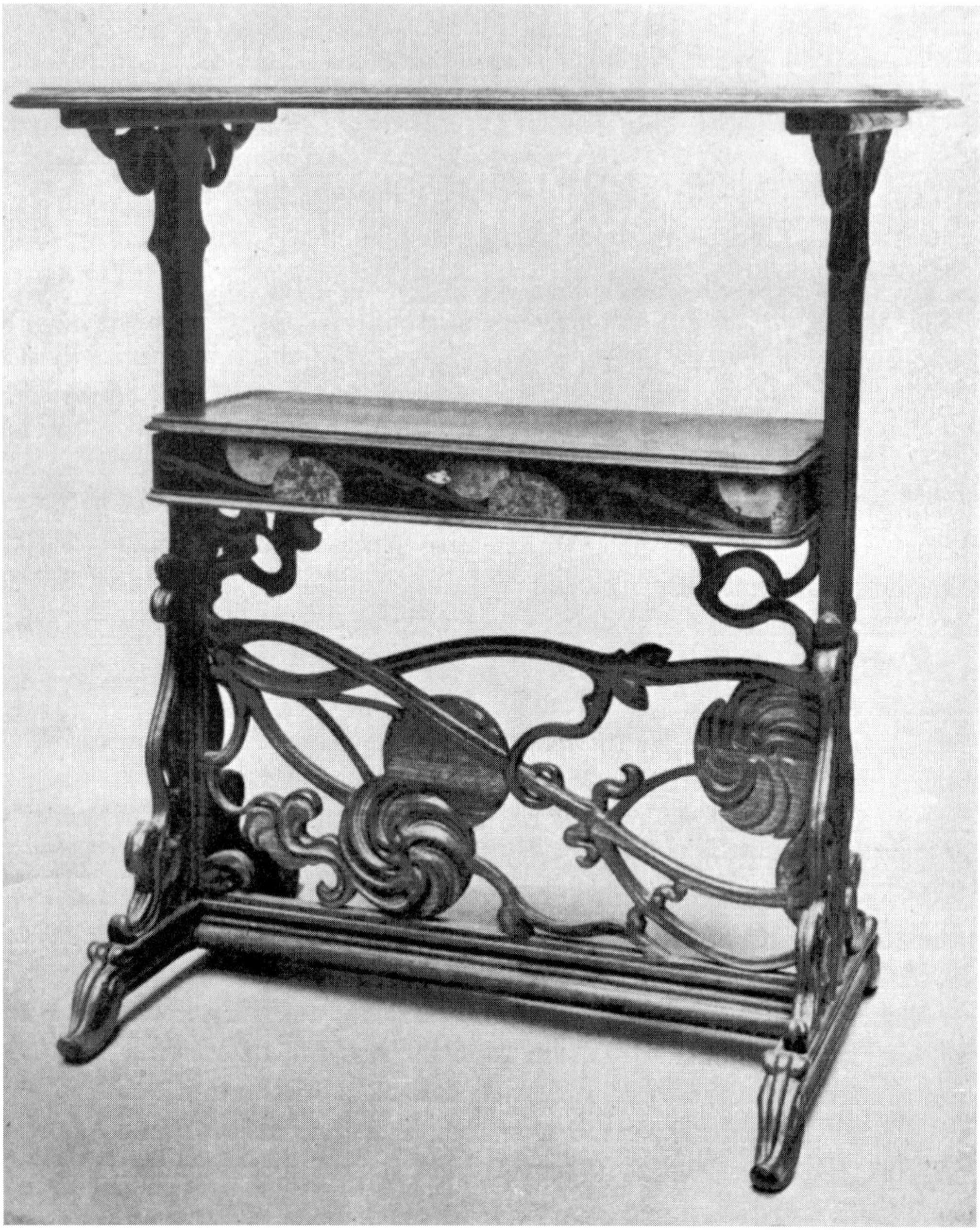

Fig. 1. Gallé: Work table of ash and walnut with marquetry in various woods. Inscription: *Travail est Joie*. 1900.
Victoria and Albert Museum. Crown Copyright reserved.

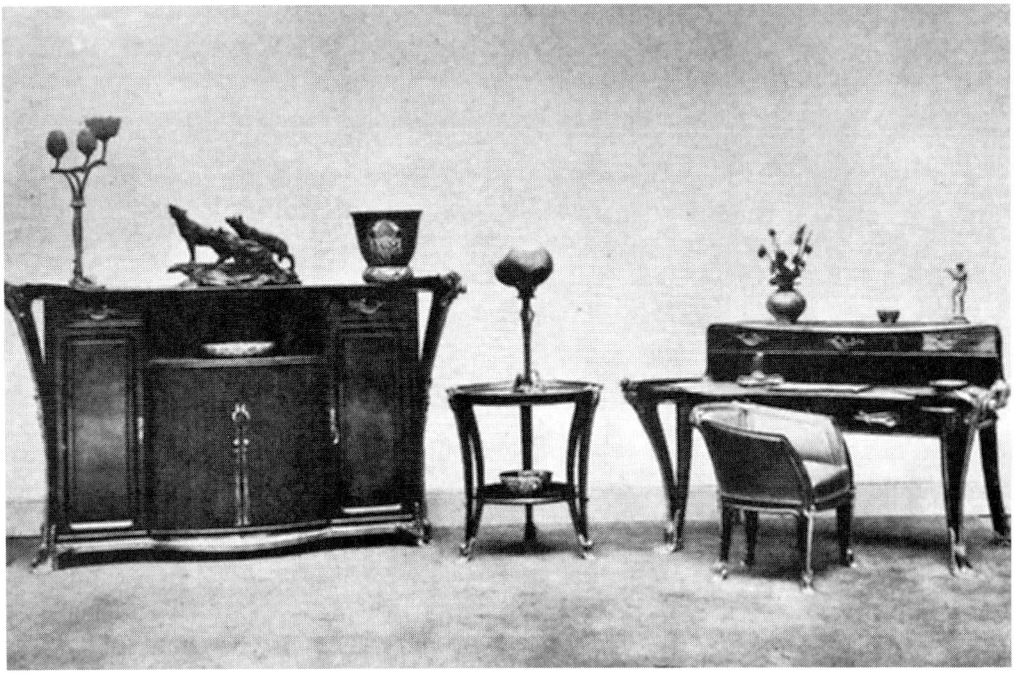

Fig. 2. Majorelle: Cabinet de Travail. «Nénuphars». Mahogany fitted with brass gilt. 1900.

furniture should convey a *Stimmung*, and its aims should find expression through its decoration.

Furthermore, the decoration should provide incitement and a moral—as in the case of the inscription above—giving symbolical expression to the idea of the furniture, or inducing an aesthetic experience beyond what is innate in the piece of furniture itself. "Pour bannir le symbole du décor, il faudrait chasser du firmament notre satellite."[2]

The leading furniture-producer of the Nancy school was Louis Majorelle (1859–1926). In 1902 Majorelle designed a *cabinet de travail* entitled *Nénuphars* (fig. 2),[3] from the name given to the sacred white Egyptian water-lily which is the basic motif of this piece of furniture. The suite is representative, not only of Majorelle, but also of the Nancy school: it is

2 E. Gallé, Le Décor Symbolique, lecture delivered May 17, 1900, at l'Académie de Stanislas, Nancy, *Ecrits pour l'Art*, Paris 1908, p. 219. "In order to banish the symbol of the decoration it would be necessary to chase our planet from the firmament."

3 *Majorelle Frères & Cie.—Meubles d'Art*, Nancy n. d., pl. 92.

symmetrical and more or less traditional in construction, while all ornaments are asymmetrical. While the mahogany is polished smooth, with its mouldings and profiles, the gilt flowers and leaves are contrasted with the smooth surfaces of the wood. A special feature of this suite is the design of the corners, whose sole object is to be decorative. Together with the deep flutings in the legs and the lavish use of gold, the somewhat ponderously designed corners have a marked similarity with Louis XV. The central section of the sideboard also curves out slightly; the chair is the French fauteuil type adapted to the new style. The sides, which are gently curved, terminate in rounded corners with gilt water-lily motifs—leaves and flowers opening out to enfold the legs and corners of the chair.

In contrast to Gallé's two-dimensional decoration Majorelle's is far more plastic: while Gallé's line is at times elegiac, Majorelle's is frequently dynamic.

The *Maison Huot*, 92–93bis Quai Claude Lorrain, Nancy (fig. 3), designed by the leading architect of the Nancy school, Emile André (1871–1933), was completed in 1903. Taken as a whole, this house presents a medieval effect, with its tall roof and projecting cornices, as well as the Gothic pointed gables, but below the cornice the medieval or Gothic impression ends: here, the form-language of the Nancy school is clearly in evidence. The decoration, instead of being spread across the facade—of smooth and unornamented sandstone—is confined to the doors and windows. But to make up for this the element concerned has been given over entirely to ornamentation. The decoration is on the whole of a floral nature, being constructed of stalks, leaves, and single flowers—in the case of the door of fir twigs and cones—which twine round the apertures like a tendril. But the floral elements have also taken complete possession of the actual structure of windows and doors, and in the door the iron grille, the mullion, and the framework conform to the same stalk-like rhythm. The mullions are entirely original in shape, springing out from the central transom like growing branches, and giving the top part of the window a characteristic onion shape.

Other noteworthy features of the facade are the Moorish-type window and the small projections and decoratively-shaped depressions in the wall,

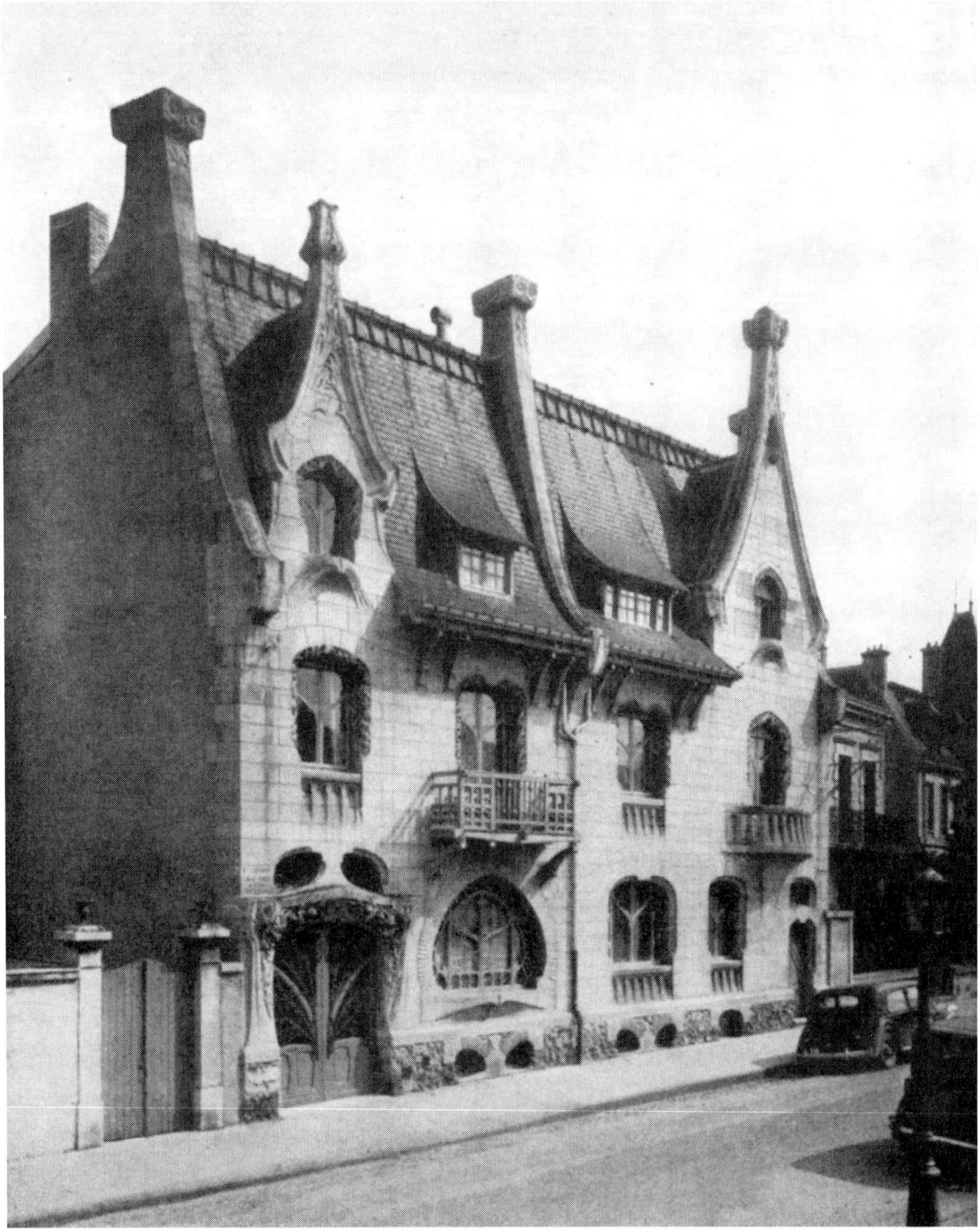

Fig. 3. E. André: Maison Huot, 92—93 bis, Quai Claude Lorrain, Nancy. 1902—1903.
Courtesy of Jacques André.

which bear witness to a plastic conception of the surface, striving for a three-dimensional effect. There is not a single sharp angle in the whole facade, all corners being smoothed off. The house represents no special constructional ideas or any striving towards rationalism.

Even with such different artists as Gallé and Majorelle the Nancy school nevertheless shows certain peculiar features which distinguish it from all other types of Art Nouveau. The artistic attitude of the Nancy school is based entirely on Nature and exploits its motifs—especially flowers—without any special stylisation. The Nature-inspired decoration tends to spread over the entire object, literally enfolding it in its floral embrace. The Rococo predilection for asymmetry and for a *vue d'ensemble* are important factors in the decoration. A literary touch of a symbolical nature is especially noticeable, and this found expression in frequent use of inscriptions, and was referred to in the language of the furniture-designer as *meuble parlant*. The signing of pieces of furniture and inlay work are also special features of the Nancy school. In architecture the link with the French tradition is represented by a neo-Gothic manner bearing all the hallmarks of Art Nouveau.

The Parisian Art Nouveau is lighter and more austere than that of the Nancy school: the decoration is often confined to a single square, and though it takes its inspiration from Nature, it is more stylised and at times even abstract. In 1900 Eugène Gaillard designed a *canapé* executed in rosewood by Bing[4] (fig. 4). This piece is remarkable for its simple faintly-curved lines and discreet decoration. With its narrow mouldings it has a light and airy, somewhat prim, appearance, with the decoration unerringly placed on the rounded corners and the arm-rests. The actual décor consists of freely-adapted leaves which wind their way gracefully out of the flutings, clinging in low relief to the actual shape of the *canapé*. The decoration is so discreet that the noble rosewood gives the essential decorative effect. The upholstery is pale blue and dove grey.

[4] Cat. No. A.18302. Musée des Arts Décoratifs. Paris.

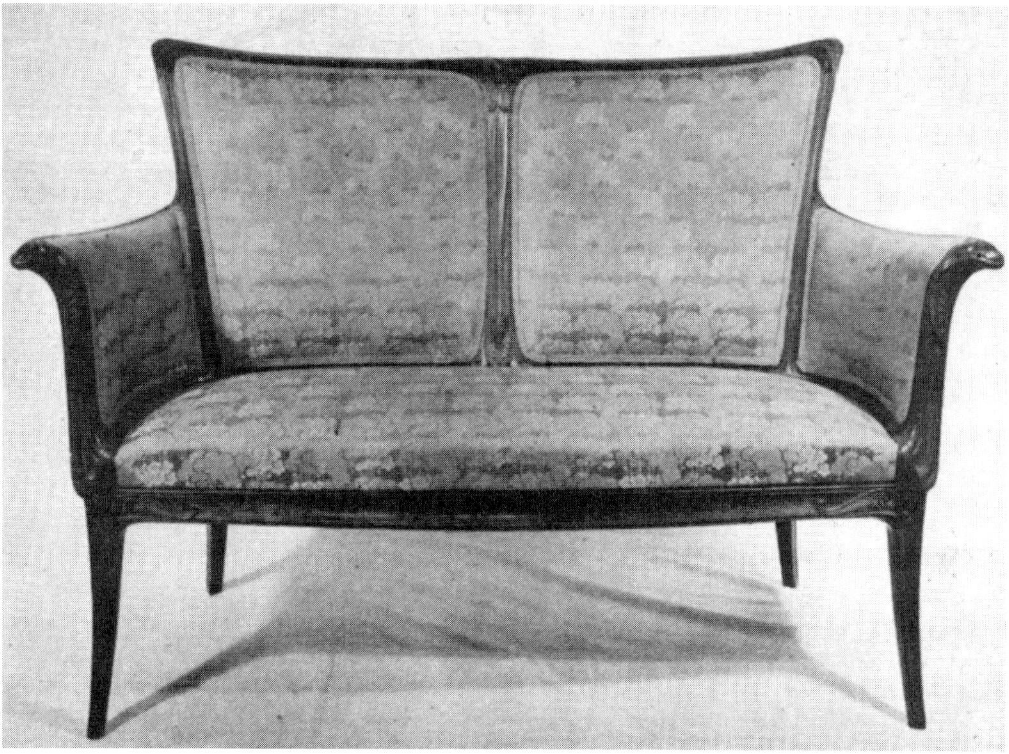

Fig. 4. Gaillard: Canapé of pallisander covered with light grey and blue silk. 1900.
Musée des Arts Décoratifs, Paris. Copyright reserved.

This exquisite piece from 1900 seems to embody some of the best features of French eighteenth century furniture-making, with its light and airy elegance. So perfect is the rhythm of all the separate elements and curves, and so subtly attuned, that any change—even of the tiniest curve—would seem to affect the whole piece and destroy its harmony.

Georges de Feure's (1868–1928) *canapé* and chair from the same year, also executed by Bing[5] (fig. 5), are constructed in the same way as Gaillard's piece—viz. a divided backpiece, upholstered arm-rests, and a small seat. While all the lines in Gaillard's piece were curved, we find here a contrast between the arched top section and the straight bottom part. All the woodwork is gilt, in conformity with the best traditions of the eighteenth- and

[5] Cat. No. 1042. Det Danske Kunstindustrimuseum, Copenhagen.

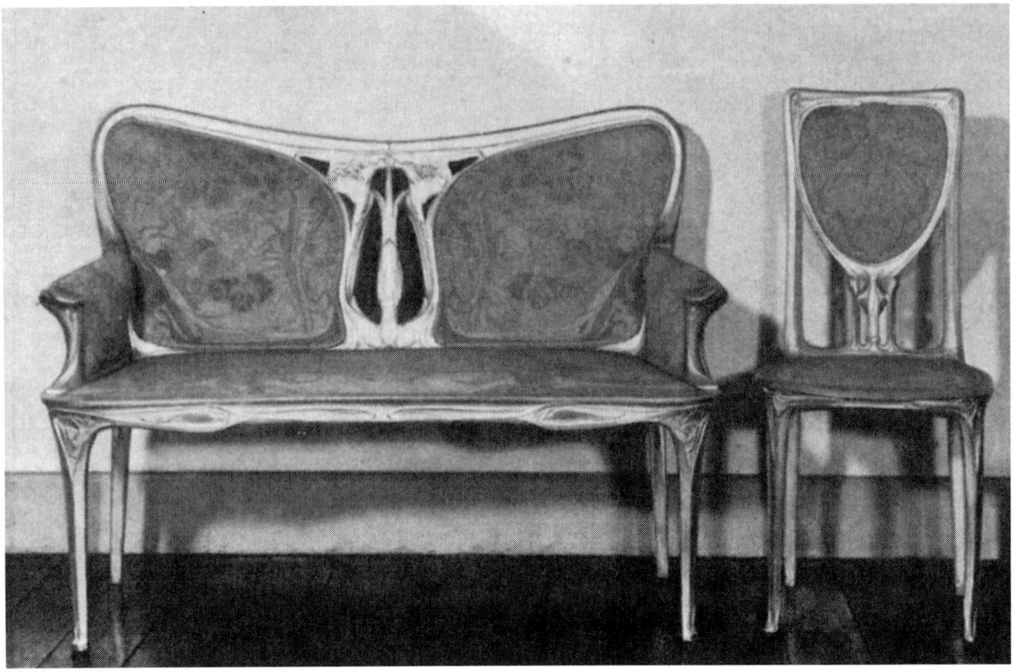

Fig. 5. de Feure: Canapé and chair of gilt wood. 1900.
Det Danske Kunstindustrimuseum, Copenhagen. Copyright reserved.

nineteenth-century Rococo. The decoration consists of abstract plant shapes, with a few fancy-flowers à la water-lily. All the woodwork is included in the decorative system, and in the back the germinating motif is visible.

In the Parisian Art Nouveau school few architects are better known for their fantasies than Hector Guimard (1867–1942), the designer of the decorative subways of the Metro stations. His designs for Le Castel Béranger, 16 Rue de la Fontaine, Paris 1894–98, are also very characteristic. In the panels in the dining-rooms in this block of flats (fig. 6),[6] Guimard has allowed the abstract ornament full rein to develop freely according to his fancy. There are no shapes here which can be derived from nature, or which are of a symbolical character. The most essential characteristics of the entirely asymmetrical lines with their faintly plastic modelling, are their pliancy and the sense of powerful movement which they convey:

[6] H. Guimard, *Le Castel Béranger,* Paris 1899, pl. 17.

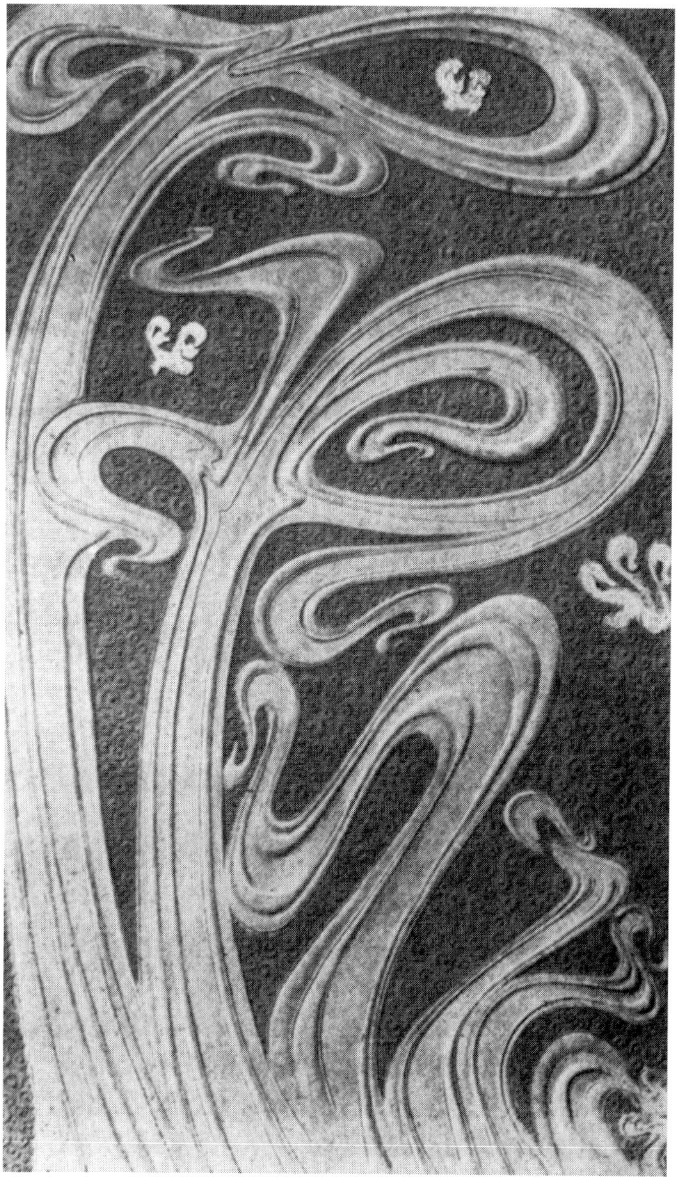

Fig. 6. Guimard: Decorative panel for the dining-room, Le Castel Béranger, 16. Rue de la Fontaine, Paris. 1894—98.

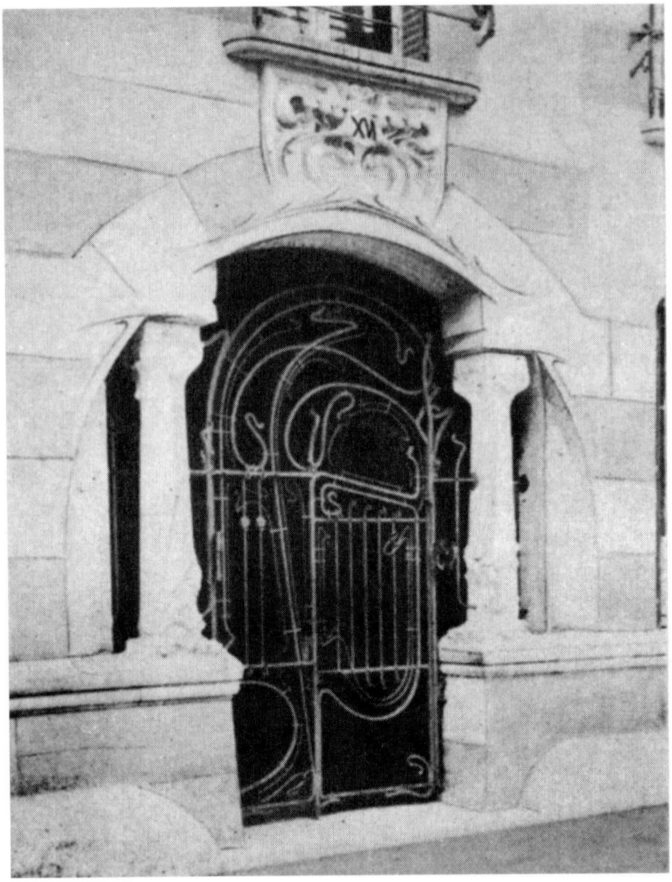

Fig. 7. Guimard: Main entrance, Le Castel Béranger, 16. Rue de la Fontaine, Paris. 1894—98.

gentle curves alternate with sudden violent twists, reminding us almost of a curling whiplash.

The same qualities come to the fore when he makes use of ornamentation in a somewhat larger format and in an architectural connection. In the actual entrance (fig. 7)[7]—the building's main decorative piece—Guimard has allowed this style to unfold with great decorative forcefulness. In a semi-circular gateway, flanked by columns with floral capitals and motifs, wrought iron is allowed to curve in an abstract linear pattern. The vivid interplay of line is markedly asymmetrical, and yet so beautifully

7 *Ibid.*, pl. 4.

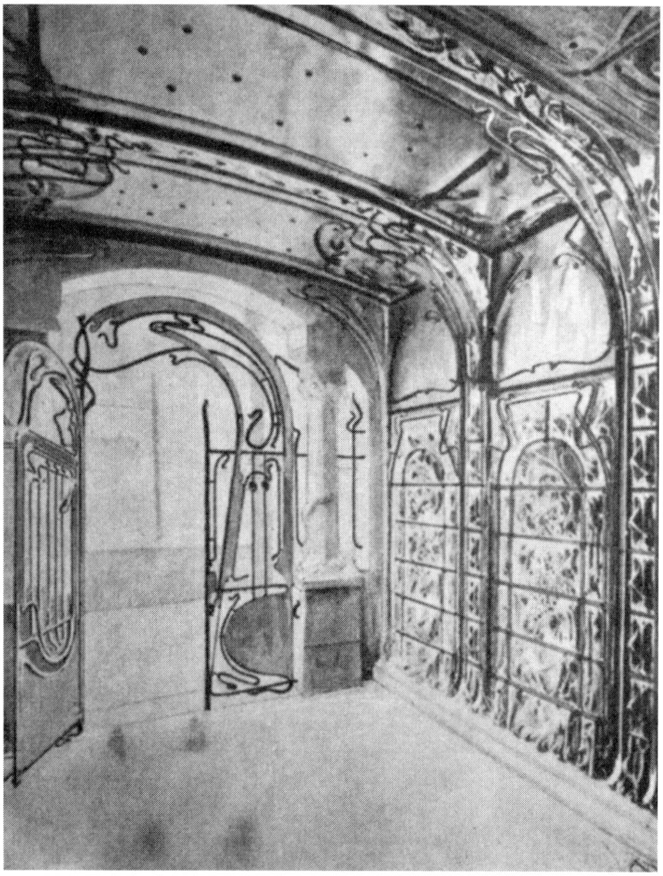

Fig. 8. Guimard: Main entrance from inside, Le Castel Béranger, 16. Rue de la Fontaine, Paris. 1894—98.

balanced that the total effect is one of harmony—excellently inset between the ponderous stone masses on either side. The principle underlying his line is throughout the same: long, gentle curves culminating in a tense climax and a retroflex movement.

The keystone of the gateway is a plastic ornament reminding us of the "gristle" ornamentation of Louis XV.

In the entrance (fig. 8)[8] the style has invaded the whole interior, and here we are completely under the spell of Art Nouveau. The iron construction, the polychrome faience tiles of the walls, the ceiling decorations,

8 *Ibid.*, pl. 5.

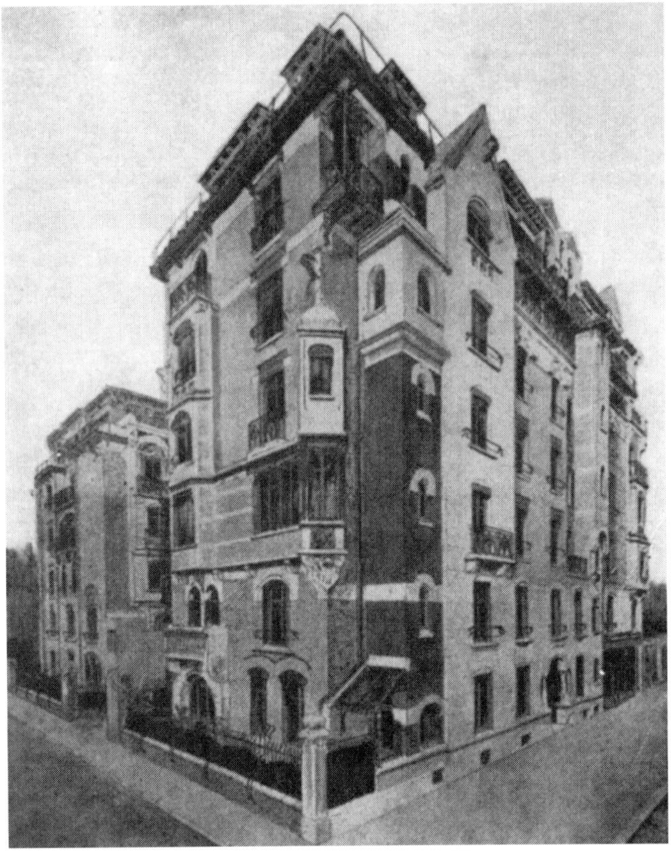

Fig. 9. Guimard: Le Castel Béranger, 16 Rue de la Fontaine, Paris. Not altered. 1894—98.

everything is subjected to the sophisticated interplay of line and wanton use of material of French Art Nouveau. The unique portal in this way acts as a transition from an interior which is at once original and free from tradition to a relatively conventional exterior.

Architecturally the building contains all the features of the 1880's (fig. 9),[9] the facade itself being constructed of three different materials: red and green brick, sandstone, and millstone. This vivid play of colour is in some places further enhanced by horizontal bands of sandstone, which in a way soften the highly irregular and original construction of the facade. Furthermore the actual body of the building is dealt with in a remark-

9 *Ibid.*, pl. 1.

ably plastic way, certain parts being made to project, others to recede; while bays, balconies, and projections strike an asymmetrical note.

While the facade as a whole presents nothing new or revolutionary—being typical of the hectic polychrome treatment and the vivid modelling so familiar to us from the 1870's and 1880's—it is in the details that we encounter the new style. Guimard's artistic temperament, which finds its clear expression in the facade, though in more traditional form, is given free rein when he fashions in wrought-iron, faience, wallpaper, and other decorative fittings.

*

The French Art Nouveau, being primarily a decorative style, linked up with the interior and fittings, only occurs to a limited extent in architecture—and then merely decoratively. Nor does there appear to be any constructive seeking or treatment of constructive problems in French Art Nouveau.

Furthermore, in its French guise, the style shows certain traditional features—elements from earlier styles such as Gothic and Louis XV, while both gilt and mountings, and traditional solutions of types are exploited. On the whole it is based on Nature, and its motifs are plastically conceived, for in its very nature French Art Nouveau is three-dimensional.

In the single ornament, as well as in the object as a whole, French Art Nouveau at its best shows a grace and refinement of line which places it side by side with the work executed in France in the eighteenth century.

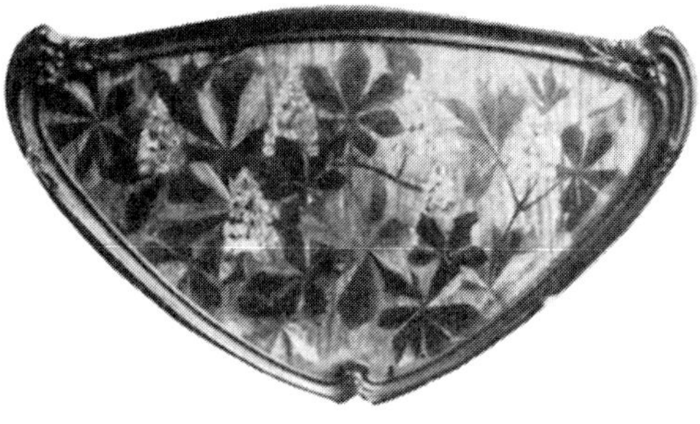

Vignette. E. André: Detail from a screen for the Vaxelaire storehouse, Nancy. Mahogany with marquetry of various woods. 1901.
Courtesy of Jacques André.

SCOTLAND*

Linearism and Symbolism

The style which corresponds in Great Britain to the Art Nouveau of the Continent had its centre in Glasgow, with the architect Charles Rennie Mackintosh (1868–1928) as its leading exponent. The other three artists who form the Glasgow group are Herbert McNair and the sisters Margaret and Francis Macdonald—"the Four," as they have often been called.

The fundamental decorative principle of the school, and one of Mackintosh's fundamental artistic *points de départ*, was the decorate value of the line. The mirror from about 1903[1] (fig. 10) which Mackintosh designed for the *Room de Luxe* in the Willow restaurant in Sauchiehall Street in Glasgow, illustrates a number of his outstanding decorative qualities. The mirror is built up of intersecting vertical and horizontal lines, together with separate surfaces which are egg- or drop-shaped. The lines are given peculiar tension by their deviation from regular forms: the straight line is not quite straight, as one would expect, but is slightly curved, while the circle is not perfectly round but appears to have been inflated, until it has acquired a slightly unsymmetrical ellipsoidal form. In this Mackintosh always manages to retain an unresolved tension-factor in the irregular shapes. Time and again he makes use of the onion shape, or the egg, or the drop, the split bud or cell form, the thin line with a circle at one end, and the "flexed knee joint." All these elements are formally speaking closed, not open or sprawling—and in their small deviations from customary shapes they give the impression of breathing, budding, or being alive.

This two-dimensional decorative style is then transferred in a few selected places to the very simple pieces of furniture, such as in the cupboard from 1902[2] (fig. 11). Its cornice is rigid and simple, with no mouldings

* For this chapter, as well as for the chapter about Scotland in the third part of the book, the author would especially like to express his indebtedness to Thomas Howarth for his kindly help.

1 The Glasgow School of Art. The mirrors, still in the room, are illustrated in T. Howarth, *Charles Rennie Mackintosh and the Modern Movement,* London 1952, pl. 57A. (The mirror is shown upside-down in the catalogue of the Zurich Exhibition, *Um 1900. Art Nouveau und Jugendstil,* Zurich 1952, pl. 6, and in a number of periodicals.)

or any traces of tradition. The large door-panel is quite bare, with a slight curve in its lower edge to break the otherwise rigid line. A very characteristic feature is the colour—the whole cupboard being executed in ivory-white, at that time a rather unusual colour for furniture, and typical of Mackintosh's bright and airy bedroom interiors. On opening the cupboard (fig. 12) the characteristic decoration is revealed. Against a pearl-grey background stands the slender figure of a woman enveloped in a white robe with a pink "rose-ball" in her hands. There is a refined colour-scale in the clearly delimited surfaces.

However, we can pursue the style of the Glasgow group still further from the ornament itself via the piece of furniture, to the entire interior.

In 1901 Mackintosh took part in a competition arranged under the auspices of the *Zeitschrift für Innendekoration*, the subject of the competition being to design, with all interior decorations, a house for an art-lover, the so-called *Haus eines Kunstfreundes*. The winning design was submitted by H. M. Baillie Scott, with Mackintosh second, and Leopold Bauer third. The designs were published in 1902 by that indefatigable promoter of art, Alexander Koch of Darmstadt, under the title of *Meister der Innenkunst*.

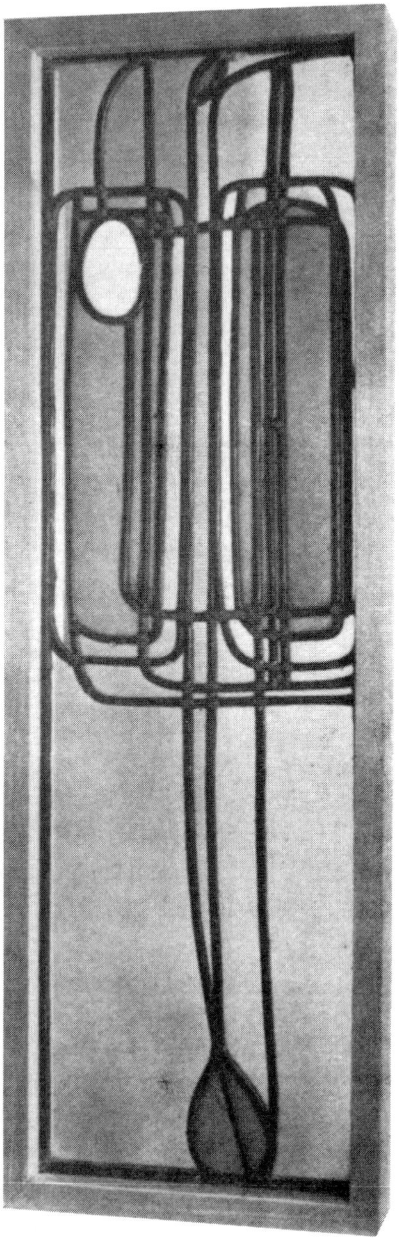

Fig. 10. Mackintosh: Mirror inlaid with stained glass for the *Room de Luxe*, Willow Restaurant, Glasgow. About 1903.
Courtesy of the Glasgow School of Art, Glasgow. Victoria and Albert photo. Crown Copyright reserved.

[2] The Glasgow School of Art, Glasgow. The Cabinet was exhibited at the Turin Exhibition, 1902.

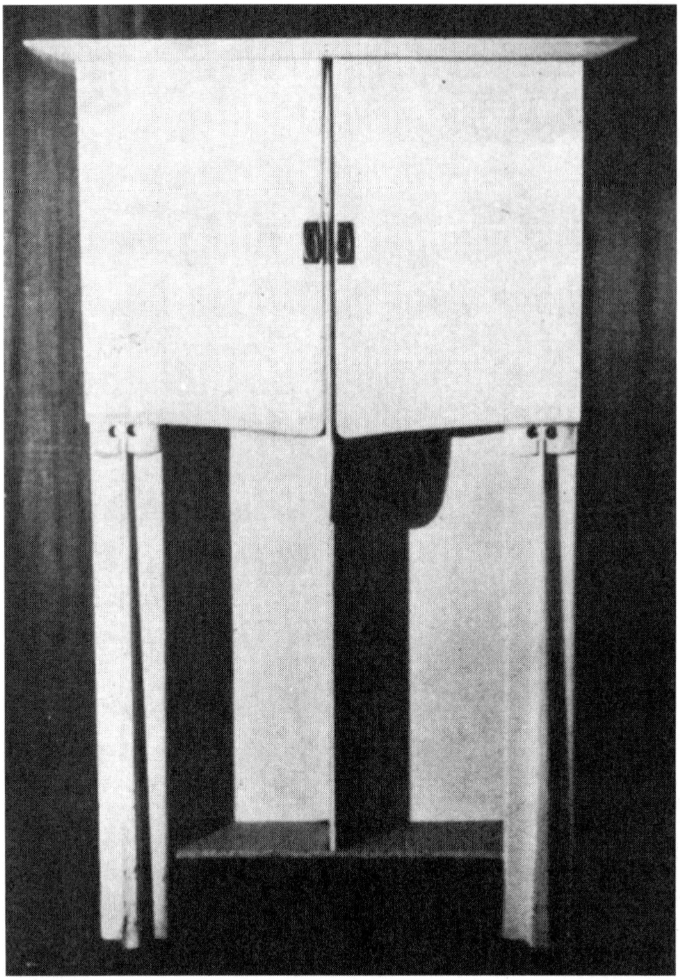

Fig. 11. Mackintosh: Cabinet, white enamelled wood. About 1902.
Courtesy of the University of Glasgow, and of Thomas Howarth.

Fig. 12. Mackintosh: Cabinet opened, the doors inlaid with opaque coloured glass in white, dark blue and pink. About 1902.
Courtesy of the University of Glasgow, and of Thomas Howarth.

Fig. 13. Mackintosh: Music-hall for *Haus eines Kunstfreundes* competition. 1901.

The music-cum-reception room is the most important part of this house (fig. 13).[3] Mackintosh's project is decorated in a colour-scale which has all the delicate fragility of porcelain: roofs, walls, floor, are in pearl-grey and ivory, with occasional highlights of silver, pale green, pink, and mauve. The panels between the windows and the wall at the end of the room are the work of Margaret Macdonald, but so uniform is the style that they merge imperceptibly with the rest of the room. If the expression

[3] C. R. Mackintosh, *Haus eines Kunstfreundes. Meister der Innenkunst, II,* Darmstadt 1901. Introduction by H. Muthesius, pl. 8.

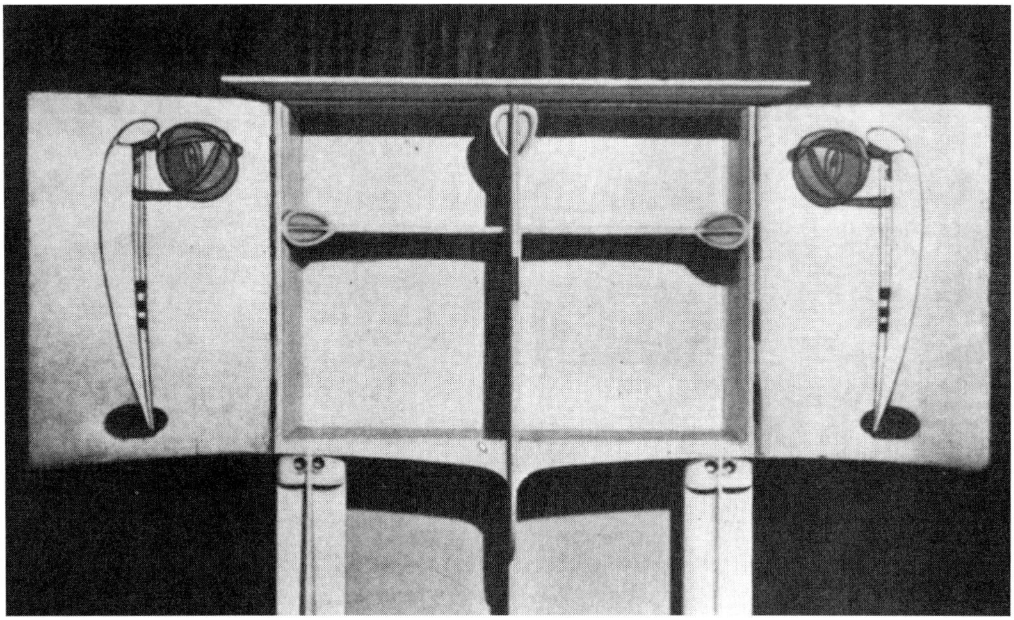

Fig. 12.

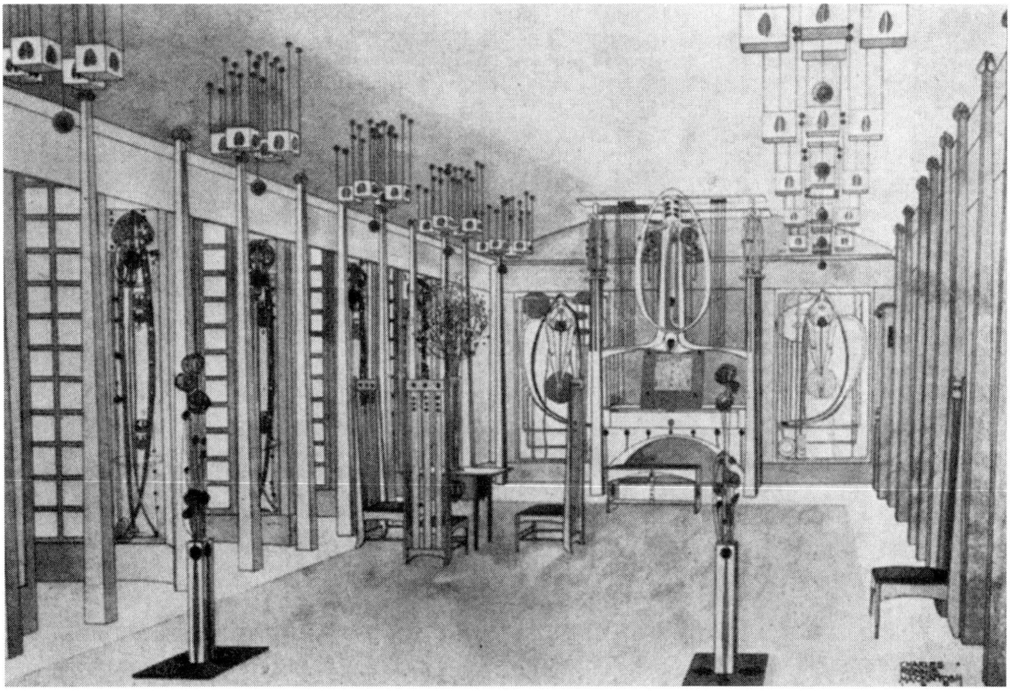

Fig. 13.

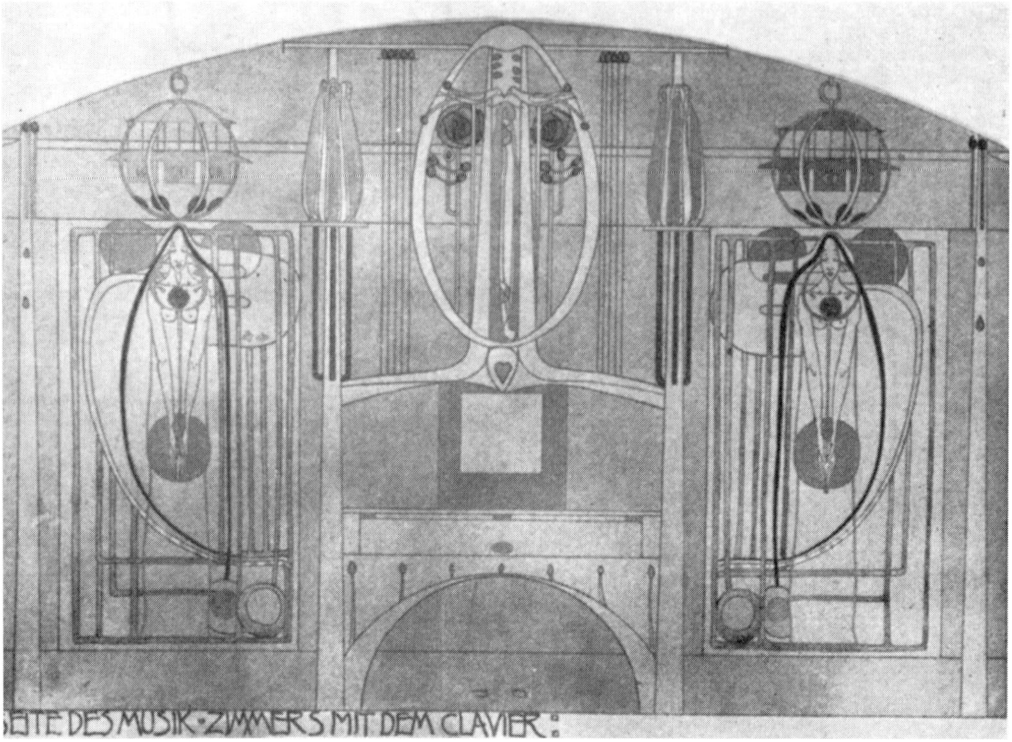

Fig. 14. Margaret Macdonald: Wall decoration for *Haus eines Kunstfreundes* competition. 1901.

"feminine interior decoration" calls up any associations at all, then it must be this graceful linearism and range of delicate, carefully controlled hues.

The room has been conceived as an entity, all the component parts being subordinate to the main decorative conception, and fusing to such an extent that they cannot exist apart from one another.

The end wall with the piano (fig. 14),[4] with the linear play in the pastel colours, reveals the most important elements in the decoration of the Glasgow school. As a whole the wall is notable for its vertical effect, having rows of parallel lines, which shoot out of the ground like growing stalks, covering the surface. But mixed in with this rippling tracery of lines we come across the egg-shape with its asymmetrical tensed arch. Within this interplay of lines the separate motifs are placed: we find the woman with

[4] *Ibid.*, pl. 9.

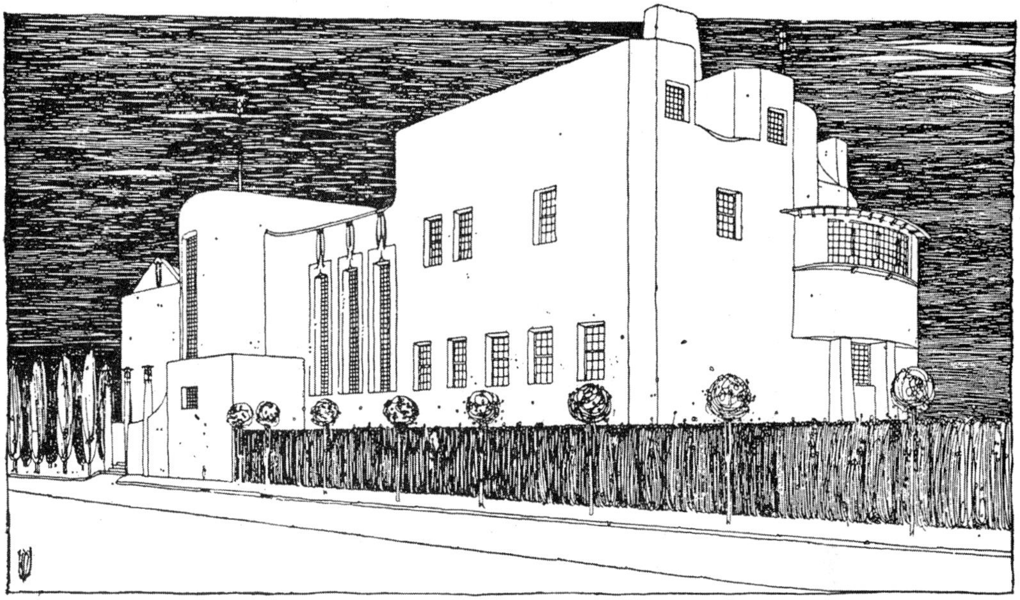

Fig. 15. Mackintosh: *Haus eines Kunstfreundes* competition. View from the North-West. 1901.

the sad countenance holding the rose between her breasts, her hair streaming out in a wide curve and almost enclosing her; or we find her enclosed within the egg-shape, part-concealed by her mantle—or the women are joined together in threes to Egyptian capitals. But everything is subordinate to clear definite decorative principles; there is no striving for an effect of depth or illusion, everything is stylised and simplified.

But does Mackintosh introduce this style into his architecture? No, but it is nevertheless of interest to analyse his design for the *Haus eines Kunstfreundes*, because here we are face to face with the young architect's purest intentions. In *Haus eines Kunstfreundes* (fig. 15)[5], he operates with masses and blocks just as freely as he composes in two dimensions with flat surfaces and lines. In this system of blocks the total impression is softened by gently rounded projections, bays, and corners. One has a sense almost of a musical note ringing out in the proportion of the masses and echoing in the pliant stepping of the west facade towards the main block. An important feature in the building is the way it terminates without a cornice, a feature

5 *Ibid.*, pl. 6.

which makes greater demands on a firm clear contour, and which thus helps to create a closed architectural effect. The somewhat closed appearance of the building is emphasised by the large bare surfaces, where a special architectural effect is achieved by the functionally-conditioned and asymmetrical placing of the windows. This light asymmetry can be traced from the smallest decorative detail to the positioning of the surface and the distribution of the masses.

Added to this is his careful treatment of the surface, only three small decorative fields being allowed to intrude between these large plane surfaces. Every single architectural element in itself acts as an ornament where it stands against the plane surface, acquiring its own aesthetic value by virtue of the contrast between broken and unbroken surface.

The Glasgow group operates with a different colour-scheme from that used by contemporary French interior artists and decorators. The Scottish artists make use of a light pastel-like colouring—olive, pink, mauve, silver, and white. French Art Nouveau artists to a certain extent used the same colour-scale, but where the Scots used ivory the French used a bluish milky-white—where the Glasgow group employed mauve, the Parisian prefered violet—where the Briton selected silver, a de Feure or a Majorelle would choose heavy gilt. Mackintosh also painted some pieces of furniture white, as well as whole interiors, which at that time would have been quite inconceivable on the Continent. It should be noted, however, that Mackintosh sometimes descends to a very deep-toned colour-scale, e.g. in his dining-room interiors.

Just as the use of pale colours breaks with ordinary tradition, so we also find unusual furniture shapes, new table constructions, and high-backed chairs. Just as mouldings are excluded in furniture, the bay is dispensed with in architecture, thus increasing the effect of the large smooth surfaces.

*

Mackintosh, as well as the other members of his group, approach decorative art with a two-dimensional style without illusory or perspective effects. The French school often prefer a medium relief in their decoration, but this is not the case with the Glasgow group. Here we find the stencilled pattern design, or else marquetry and entirely two-dimensional principles are used.

While the French school as a whole was not literary in its decoration, the Scottish school was to a very high degree. If we get down to the single decorative element—which in France might either be a flower or a dragonfly—we shall not find the concrete and relatively complicated natural forms in the Scottish school, but simple, stylised figures such as the root, germs, and buds, eggs and hearts, which contain quite different and more symbolistic ideas. The Scots are bound by no tradition either in pattern design, furniture-making, or interior decorating. Their ornaments are originally based on flowers or plants but transformed to simplified, rigidly-closed symbolical forms, with a marked tendency to verticalism.

The furniture shapes are entirely free from historicism, and in their originality they are at times subtly refined with highly exaggerated single features such as the back of the chair, and the square capital-like terminations of upright parts. Hand in hand with the group's pliant form-language goes a frequent use of geometrical form, especially the square. These two style-forms flourish side by side in Mackintosh's work, without either merging or disturbing one another.

A distinction between Scottish and French Art Nouveau which is difficult to define, but nevertheless significant, is the rhythm of the line, and the tense form of the curvature. The French rhythm is a whiplash rhythm, a powerful shape producing abruptly contrasted and dynamic movements. Not so in Glasgow, where the curves flow more smoothly, and where the line as a rule is less abruptly bent, but by contrast longer, which helps to produce an effect of greater restfulness. For this reason the tension factor in the line is reduced. Here the line does not fling its final rhythm into space, but recoils, enclosing the form, thus appearing more controlled, less dynamic and temperamental than on the other side of the Channel.

In England the revival of interest in the minor arts grew into an Arts and Crafts Movement, and while attempts were made both in Scotland and in France—in fact all over the Continent—to achieve a complete

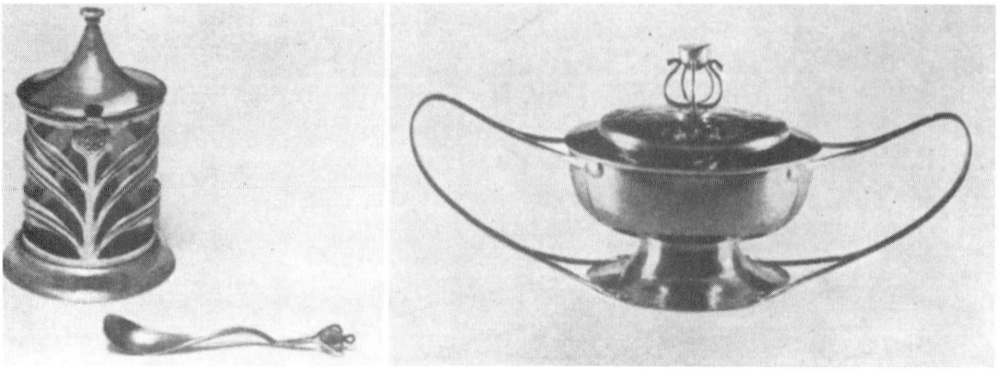

Fig. 16. Ashbee: Silverwork, the Guild of Handicraft, London. Mustard jar. P. P. Basle. 1900. Bowl, Kunstgewerbemuseum, Zürich. 1903.
From *Um 1900*.

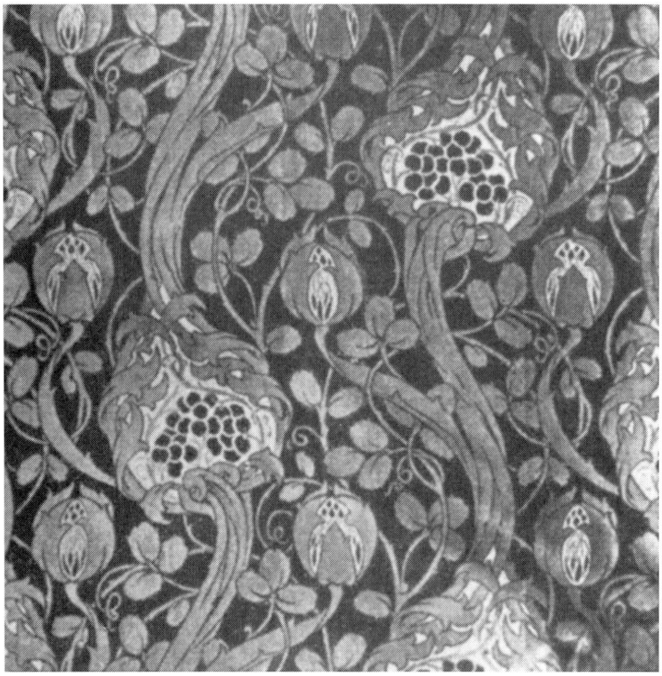

Fig. 17. Liberty & Co: Silk material for furniture. About 1900.

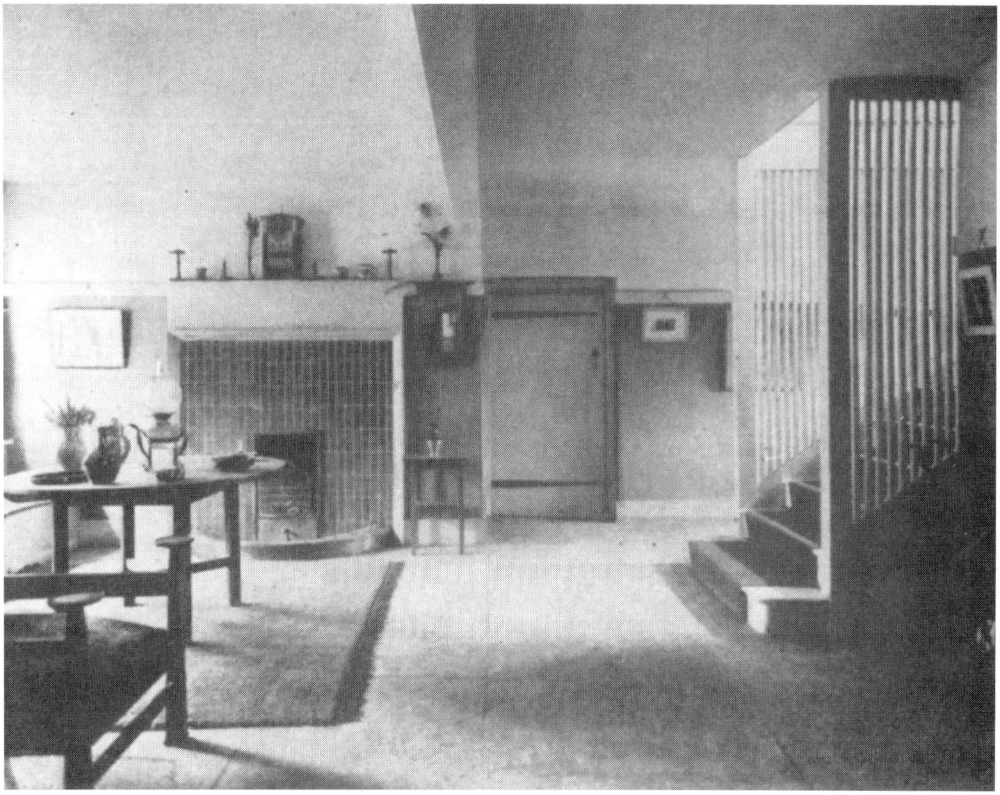

Fig. 18. C. F. A. Voysey: The Orchard, Chorley Wood, Buckinghamshire. 1899.

revolution of applied art, the English movement always remained far more conservative. Though the characteristic ornamentation of the movement was based on the plant form, and its object was to free furniture—and interior decoration—from the grip of Historicism, this occurred consciously on traditional grounds, intimately bound up with the best in English furniture-making, especially the rustic. Rational and constructive furniture design played a much more important role than decoration and its problems.

Though one cannot speak of an independent English Art Nouveau, there can on the other hand be found an Art-Nouveau-like decoration in metal, textiles, and book illustration (figs. 16 and 17).[6] This decoration is

[6] C. R. Ashbee: Silverwork, the Guild of Handicraft, London. Liberty and Co.: Textile of silk for furniture. Illustrated in J. Hoffmann jr. *Der Moderne Stil,* vol. II, Stuttgart, 1900, pl. 53, fig. 6.

derived from plants and flowers, highly stylised in form. The distinguishing mark of this English style is a regular, graceful undulating rhythm which is just as far removed from the French, with its powerfully contrasted movement, as it is from the Scottish with its linear asymmetry. The essence of the English Art Nouveau-like style around the year 1900 is that in relation to the Scottish and all the Continental style, it may be said to be symmetrical in detail as well as in the whole. In view of the important part played by the asymmetrical element in Art Nouveau, as well as the absence of the tendril—which remained a basic motif in English decorative art—Ashbee's and Liberty's work can hardly be described as Art Nouveau.

*

Important sources of Art Nouveau are to be found in England, but the English Art Nouveau-like style has less interest to the art historian in relation to the work of other countries during the same period—nor is it of any real significance when seen in relation to the Arts and Crafts Movement, and the work which England's leading architects did during these years (fig. 18).

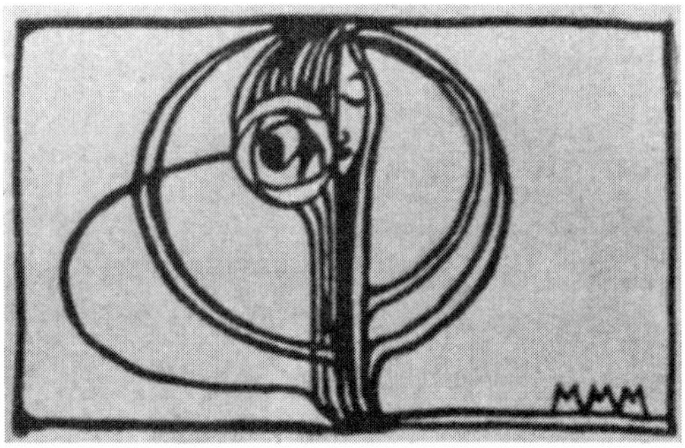

Vignette. Margaret Macdonald: Vignette, *Ver Sacrum*. 1901.

BELGIUM

Dynamic Abstractions

Unlike the Scottish Art Nouveau, the Belgian style has several aspects, each of them formed by an outstanding artist. The first and most important Art Nouveau artist in Belgium was Victor Horta (1861–1946), who was at the same time Belgium's leading architectural personality at the turn of the century.

One of the houses he designed in which his conception of style found its very best expression was the *Hotel Aubecq*, 520 Avenue Louise, Brussels, completed in 1900, and demolished 1949–50 (fig. 19). The *Hotel Aubecq*, a corner house, was a two-storey building with a mansard roof. What immediately strikes us is the markedly plastic treatment of the masses, with the bay projecting from the recessed niches, a sculptural treatment of the architectural element in the spirit of Baroque—or rather neo-Baroque. In contrast to Mackintosh, who terminates his buildings with a firm and rigid contour-line, Horta allows the body of the building to end in a disintegrated and varied interplay of masses and lines. The contrast to the polychrome house next door in a neo-Renaissance style, with its austere lines, is also characteristic enough. Apart from the plastic conception of form and the asymmetry there are no further points of similarity with Mackintosh's architecture. Horta has nothing of Mackintosh's ascetic treatment of the surface: in his case the surface ripples with its ornamentation of motifs in the neo-Gothic and neo-Rococo spirit. The window-frames in the *Hotel Aubecq* are slightly rounded above, and here and there small C-like motifs are to be found (fig. 20). In accordance with the principles of Art Nouveau Horta seeks to avoid right-angles, sharp corners, and rectangular areas, using instead gentle curves, rounded joints, and many-sided and irregular shapes.

In designing his doors and windows and their ornamentation Horta is quite ruthless in his attitude to the material and its special qualities, subduing it completely and endowing it with the rhythm of Art Nouveau. In the asymmetrically constructed central part one can see how he lets the

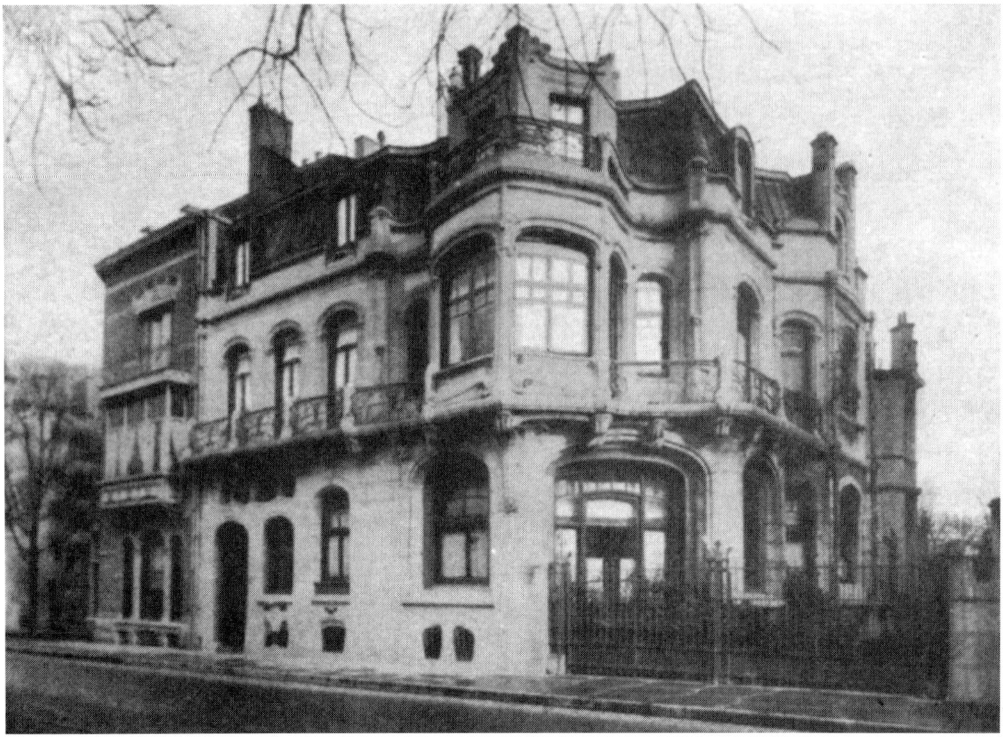

Fig. 19. Horta: Hotel Aubecq, 520 Avenue Louise, Brussels. 1899—1900. Pulled down 1949—50.
Courtesy of J. Delhaye.

ornamentation spring out of the very surface of the stone; the stone mullions of the window are arched in the same rather ponderous rhythm, the wooden fillet-work is then forced to follow the curvature of the stone, and the wrought iron chimes in as the third instrument in this highly-mixed but well-attuned musical solution. In the doorway to the *Hotel Solvay*, 224 Avenue Louise, Brussels, 1895–1900, brass also swells the orchestra (fig. 21). His striving to fuse the various elements and material into a plastic synthesis becomes apparent in the upper part, where the woodwork is formed like a whip handle, from which the ironwork issues in its pliant lines—but no naturalistic forms are allowed to reveal directly the innermost source of inspiration of this organic ornamentation—everything has been abstracted into a linear rhythm. Everything is ruthlessly subjected to the same decorative laws, glass, stone, lead, and wood. "Lorsque tout est

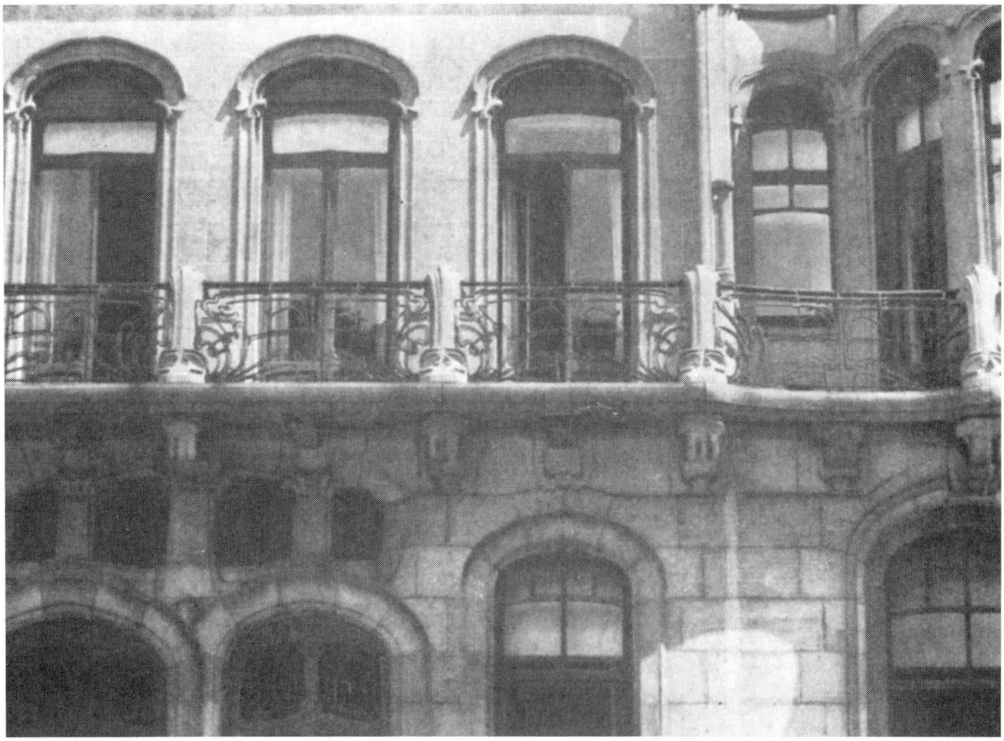

Fig. 20. Horta: Hotel Aubecq, 520 Avenue Louise, Brussels. 1899—1900. Pulled down 1949—50.
Copyright A. C. L. Brussels.

simple et aisé, il crée la difficulté pour la vaincre et la résoudre. Il fait gémir et hurler la matière. Conclusion: C'est un Titan."[1]

In Belgium too the 1890's present a powerful reaction against the interior decoration of Historicism: the picturesque lack of planning and the romantic individuality of a piece of furniture—both in their placing as well as in their shape—are forced to give way to the uniform space-décor of Art Nouveau. In the *Hotel Solvay* (fig. 22) Horta fuses all the parts into a whole—every single element, from the violet-like flowers and stalks of the lamp to the coils of the ceiling decoration and the softly rounded panels. The unified conception of space which was created during the Rococo,

[1] Letter from the architect J. J. Eggericx, who for some years worked as Horta's pupil, to the author, April 4, 1953. "When everything is simple and easy he creates difficulty in order to overcome it and solve it. He makes the material groan and howl. Conclusion: He is a Titan."

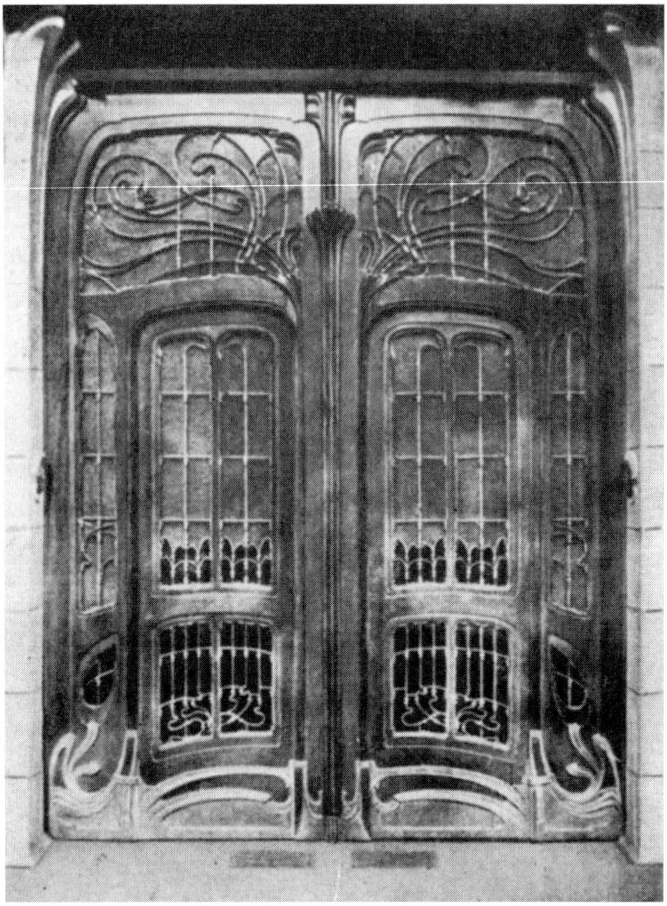

Fig. 21. Horta: Main entrance, Hotel Solvay, 224 Avenue Louise, Brussels. 1895—1900.

only to disappear under Romanticism, has been restored. The elements of Rococo have already been seen, and it is not surprising that we find them most richly represented in the interior.

If we examine the single little object we shall find that this too is subject to the same dynamic and plastic laws (fig. 23).[2] Even when Horta keeps to the two-dimensional plane, as for example in the grilles, his dynamic feeling for form emerges in the asymmetrical and exuberant lines with the characteristic contrasting movements such as we have seen in France. However abstract his form may be, it is nevertheless interesting

[2] In Hotel Solvay, 224 Avenue Louise, Brussels.

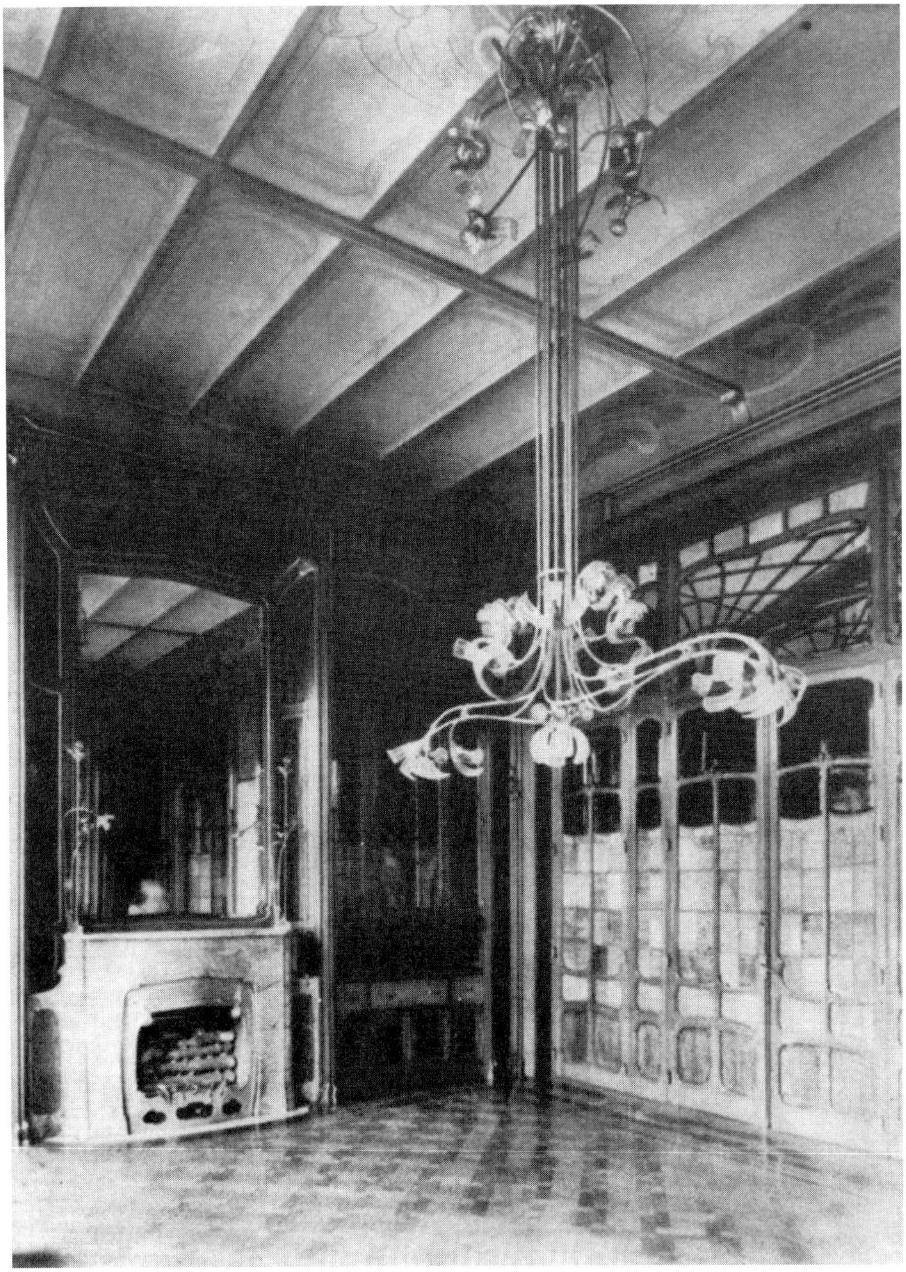

Fig. 22. Horta: Dining room, Hotel Solvay, 224 Avenue Louise, Brussels. 1895—1900.

Copyright A. C. L. Brussels.

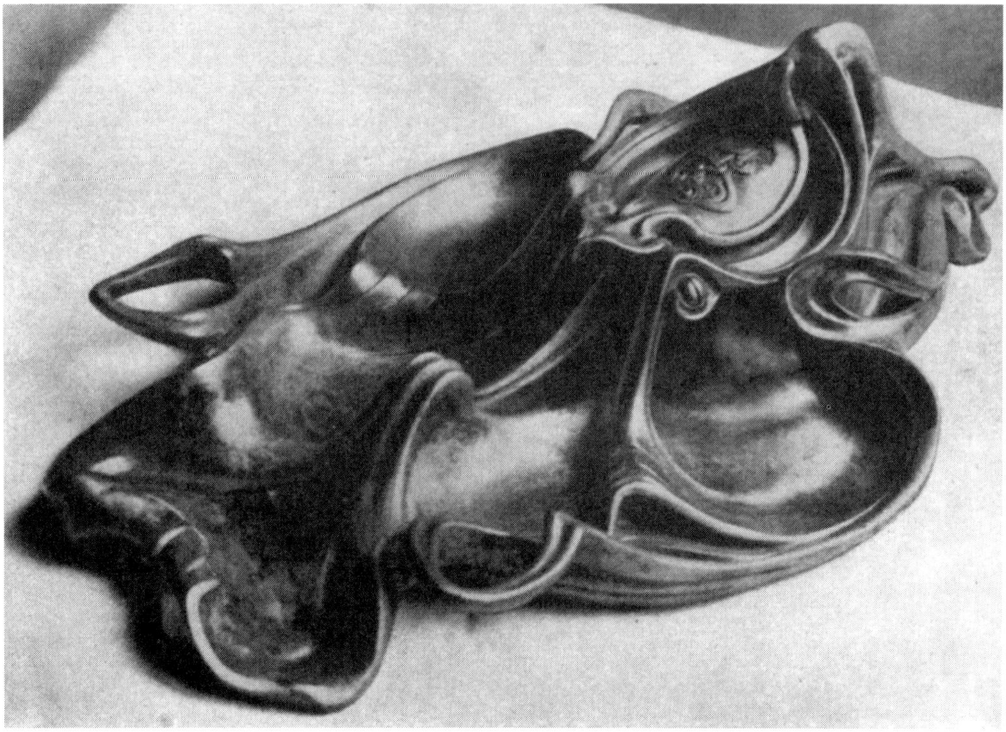

Fig. 23. Horta: Inkstand for Hotel Solvay, 224 Avenue Louise, Brussels. 1895—1900.
Copyright A. C. L. Brussels.

to note that his lines and shapes practically always spring from a central point, like stalks growing from a root.

While Horta represents the dynamic Belgian Art Nouveau, often with an extra touch of refined asymmetry, we shall find an entirely new conception of form in the work of Gustav Serrurier-Bovy (1858–1910).

He is more frugal in his treatment of furniture; nor does he show anything of the great architect's plastic and emotional form-language either in his total effect or in his details. His constructive strivings emerge in the cupboard he designed in 1898[3] (fig. 24). One of his most typical characteristics is his lavish use of stays and supports, which are placed in great abundance both where they are needed and where they are not. These stays have a rather peculiar form, being always diagonally placed in the

[3] H. van de Velde, Gustav Serrurier-Bovy, *Zeitschrift für Innendekoration*, vol. XIII, 1902, pp. 41–68.

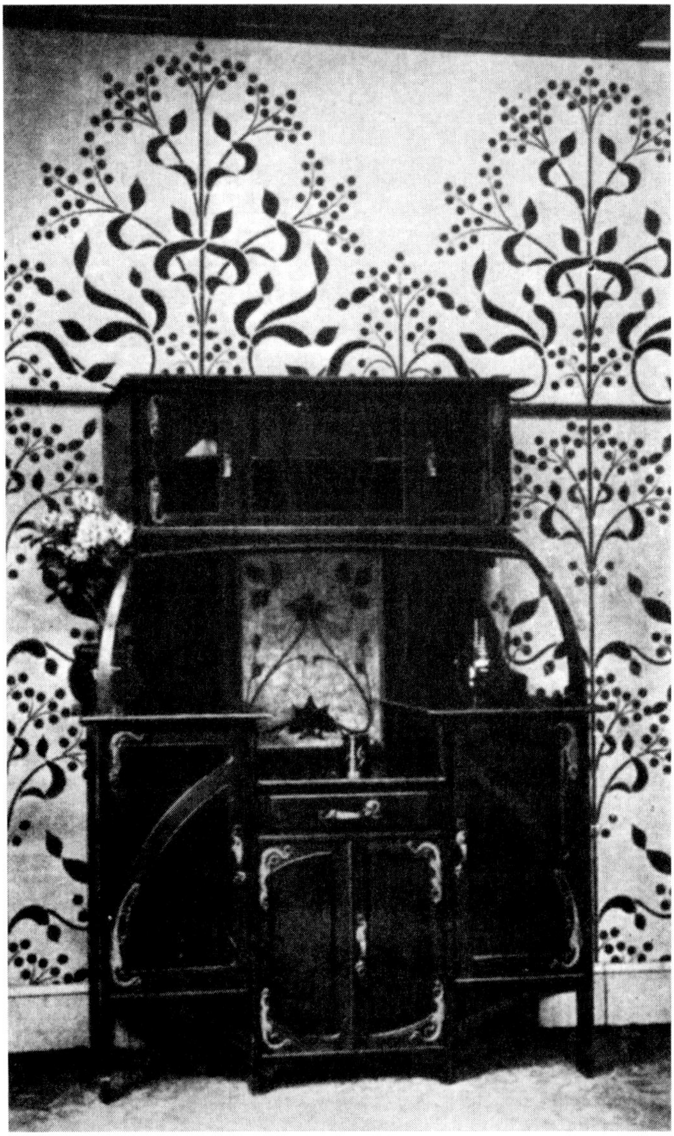

Fig. 24. Serrurier-Bovy: Cabinet. 1898.

panel and slightly curved. They give the effect of enclosing the cupboard in a series of arches, which frame it and point inwards. This effect is very characteristic of Serrurier-Bovy's furniture, and helps to give it a ponderous and closed form. Sometimes there is a horseshoe-shaped Moorish arch running round and enclosing the whole cupboard.

All these stays are furthermore adorned with fittings which show the most fantastic twirls, reminding us most of all of Celtic ornamentation from around the year A.D. 800 to 1000. These fittings coil round bolts and keyholes, and their effect is all the greater because the wood is otherwise quite unadorned. He operates with a conscious interplay between ornament and surface—an interplay which the Scottish school too at times also mastered so unerringly. There are also other features of Serrurier-Bovy, seen in the cupboard, which suggest that the searchlight should be turned on the British Isles in order to see things in their full context. Both the marked emphasis of the constructive element and the simple character of the whole piece of furniture, apart from the Celtic-like ornament, makes it a highly interesting task to try to trace the connection between the two countries—between Belgian handicrafts renaissance and the Arts and Crafts Movement in Great Britain.

His subdivision, with several planes, and the subsequent division into storeys, intended for the placing of flowers, vases, and *bric-à-brac*, is typical, though here it is very simple in form. All the above-mentioned characteristics can be found in his furniture, but only rarely do we find them all so well combined as here.

Belgium's third important Art-Nouveau artist, Henry van Velde (1863–), occupies stylistically a position between the two already mentioned. In his details he has all Horta's asymmetrical, abstract, and dynamic form-language, as can be seen for example in the inkwell from 1898[4] (fig. 25), while his furniture reveals more of Serrurier-Bovy's constructive striving. In the writing-desk from 1898[5] (fig. 26) there is an outer limit which gives this piece of furniture its special qualities, this outer limit being shaped like a band—partly in *entrelac*—which practically speaking encircles the whole writing-desk. The outer edges slope inwards, which further increases the impression we get that the desk is enclosed in itself. In addition we find a wanton but decorative treatment of all the constructive elements, independent of the special quality of the material, such as we notice in the work of Horta. But what tends to upset our impression of the whole is that all these

[4] Cat. No. N.K. 162—1900. Nordenfjeldske Kunstindustrimuseum, Trondheim.
[5] Cat. No. N.K. 144—1900. Nordenfjeldske Kunstindustrimuseum, Trondheim.

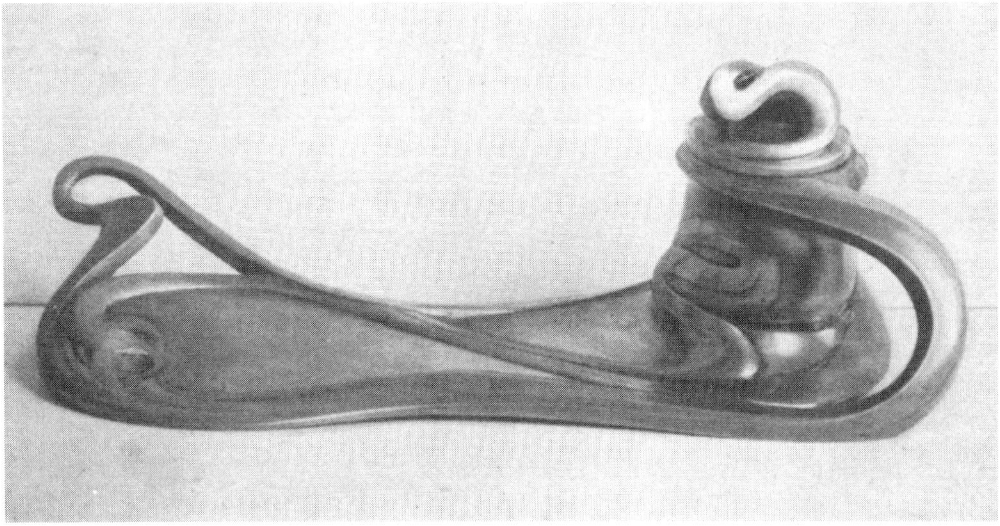

Fig. 25. Van de Velde: Inkstand, brass. 1898.
Nordenfjeldske Kunstindustrimuseum, Trondheim. Copyright reserved.

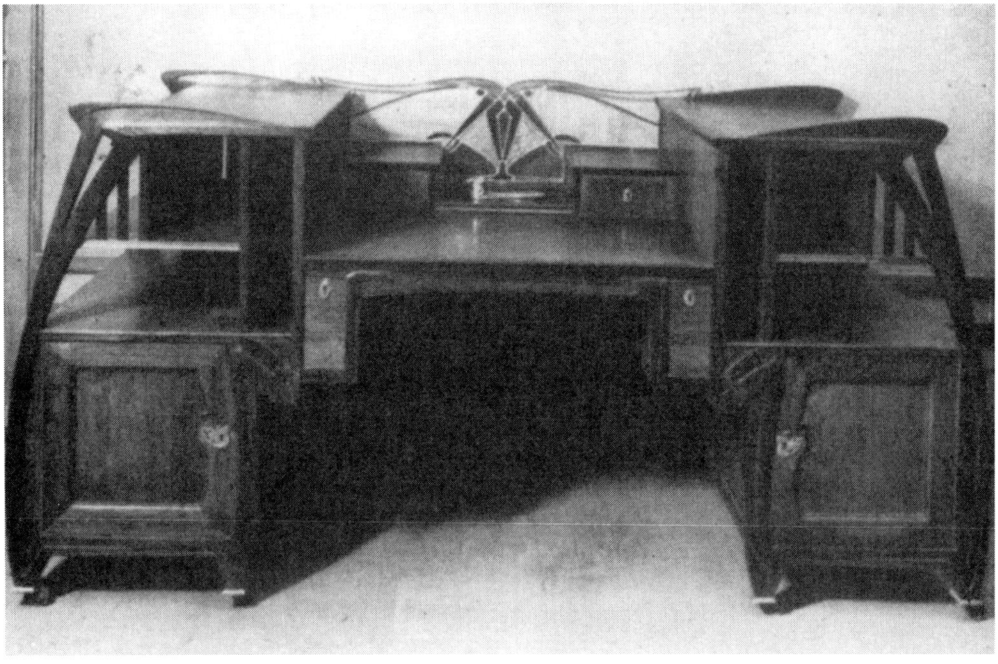

Fig. 26. Van de Velde: Writing table, jacaranda. Executed in Uccle, near Brussels. About 1898.
Nordenfjeldske Kunstindustrimuseum, Trondheim. Copyright reserved.

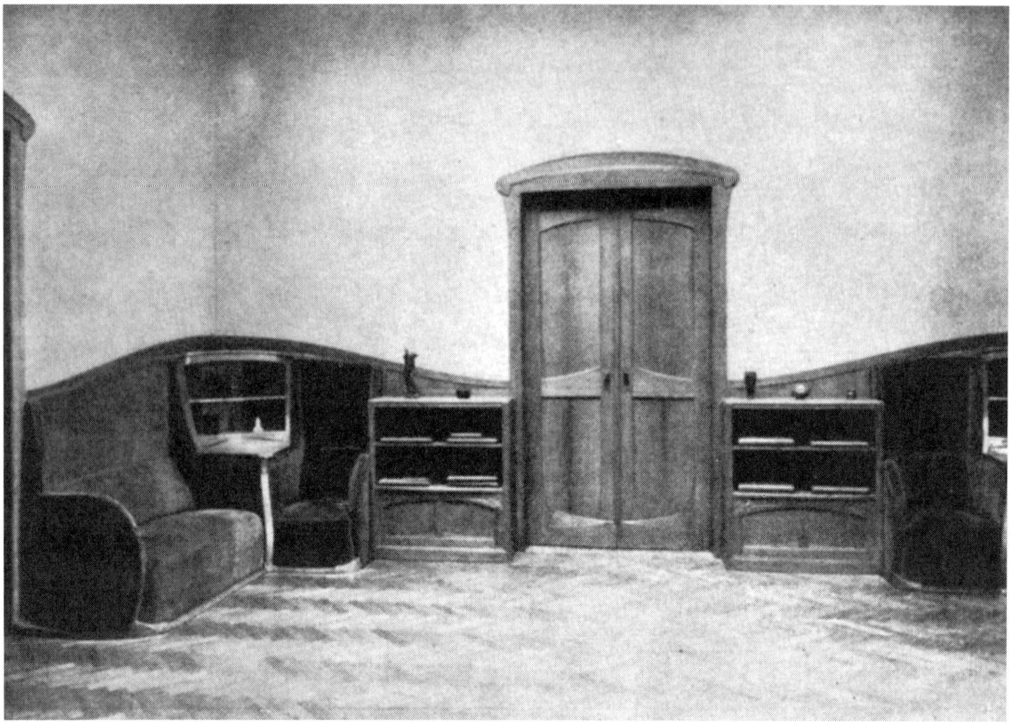

Fig. 27. Van de Velde: Interior. The Folkwang Museum, Folkwang, Germany.

fluctuating lines constantly meet and are broken by a marked rectilinearism. With all its small right-angled shelves and drawers and spaces of a purely Japanese character, a great number, as it were, of small collisions occur in the constructive rectilinearism and the decoratively undulating Art Nouveau.

In the interiors in the museum in Folkwang, Germany, the interplay between the straight lines and the slight curves, as well as the panels, are similarly a characteristic feature, but the essential peculiarity about the interior is its unity. The individual pieces of furniture in the room are fused together—sofa, table, shelf, and door being still further linked together by the undulating line of the panel (fig. 27).[6]

Belgian Art Nouveau represents two trends, viz. the plastic and dynamic decorative style on the one hand, and a markedly constructive and

[6] *Zeitschrift für Innendekoration*, vol. XIII, 1902, p. 283.

austere striving on the other hand. The first trend is similar to its counterpart in France in a certain traditional stylistic connection, and furthermore the run of the line makes the same use of countermovement.

The second trend, as represented by Serrurier-Bovy, has more in common with Great Britain. The decoration is very modest, and in no way subdues the furniture. The problems lie first and foremost in the constructive sphere; van de Velde has elements of both trends.

Nevertheless it might prove fruitful to compare the Belgian style as a whole with the Art Nouveau in the other two countries. While the Scottish style is marked by a refined linearism, and the French is gracefully budding, the Belgian is energetic and powerful, giving a far more ponderous impression, while at the same time it is much more three-dimensional than the other two. While the French artists on the one hand made the floral background quite clear, and enhanced the organic line with Nature's small flowers and leaves, as an easily recognisable feature to help us on our road, and while the Scots on the other hand presented the natural form in an abstract way, while at the same time enveloping it in a symbolical guise, with the Belgians neither natural shape nor symbolism occurs, even though the decoration provides associations from the growing power of a plant stem. The ornamentation becomes entirely abstract.

With van de Velde, who brings Belgian Art Nouveau to Germany, we approach the German-Austrian cultural sphere, but in connection with developments in the Channel countries it seems natural first to look at Holland.

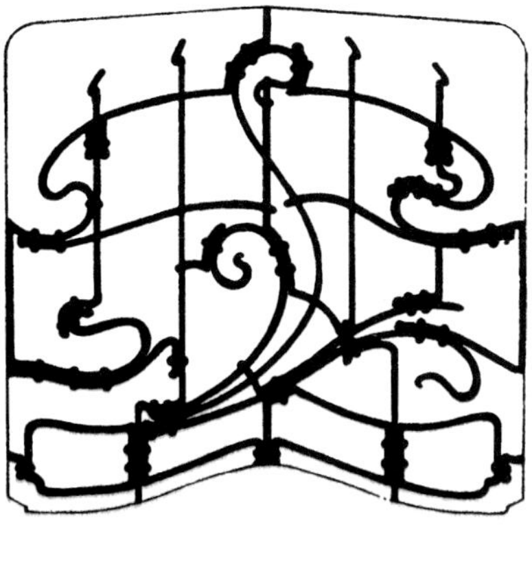

Vignette. Horta: Railing, wrought iron, 25 Rue Americaine, Brussels. 1898.

HOLLAND

Two-dimensional Orientalism

Holland has no Art Nouveau of the kind we have seen in the preceding countries, no luxurious and refined fashionable style as in France, none of the Scots' linear and symbolical verticalism, and certainly none of the dynamic capers of the neighbouring country.

For centuries Holland's stylistic development has been bound up with that of England, and the outstanding feature of Dutch artists, in their conscious efforts to liberate themselves from Historicism, is the great similarity with the English Arts and Crafts Movement. With their sober approach to the furniture-maker's art, the Dutch at a very early stage seized the essential features of this movement and made their own contribution to the European phase.

In furniture, and architecture, Holland is relatively untouched by the main stream of Art Nouveau, and has its own special development which is essentially so different from the other countries in Europe. But in the art of the illustrators and painters there are several basic features which have much in common with Art Nouveau, and might even justify the designation "Dutch Art Nouveau."

T. Nieuwenhuis' (1866–?) calendar from 1896 provides us with one of the best examples (fig. 28).[1] In perfect harmony with the linear rhythm of the nineties the snakes twine in irregular coils around the gorgeous bird of the 1880's and 1890's—the peacock—completely enclosing it. Those portions of the page which are not filled with this are covered with floating jellyfish and worm-like scrolls.

Equally characteristic of Dutch book art in this style is the periodical vignette from the same year[2] (fig. 29), designed by the architect de Bazel. Here, however, all the forms are abstract; and as so frequently is the case in batik-pattern the flat surfaces terminate in trunklike twirls. De Bazel's book illustrations and woodcuts are, apparently, executed with complete

1 *Dekorative Kunst,* vol. I, 1898, p. 19.

2 *De Houtsneden van K.P.C. de Bazel,* with an introduction by J.L.M. Lauweriks, Amsterdam, 1925, pl. 32.

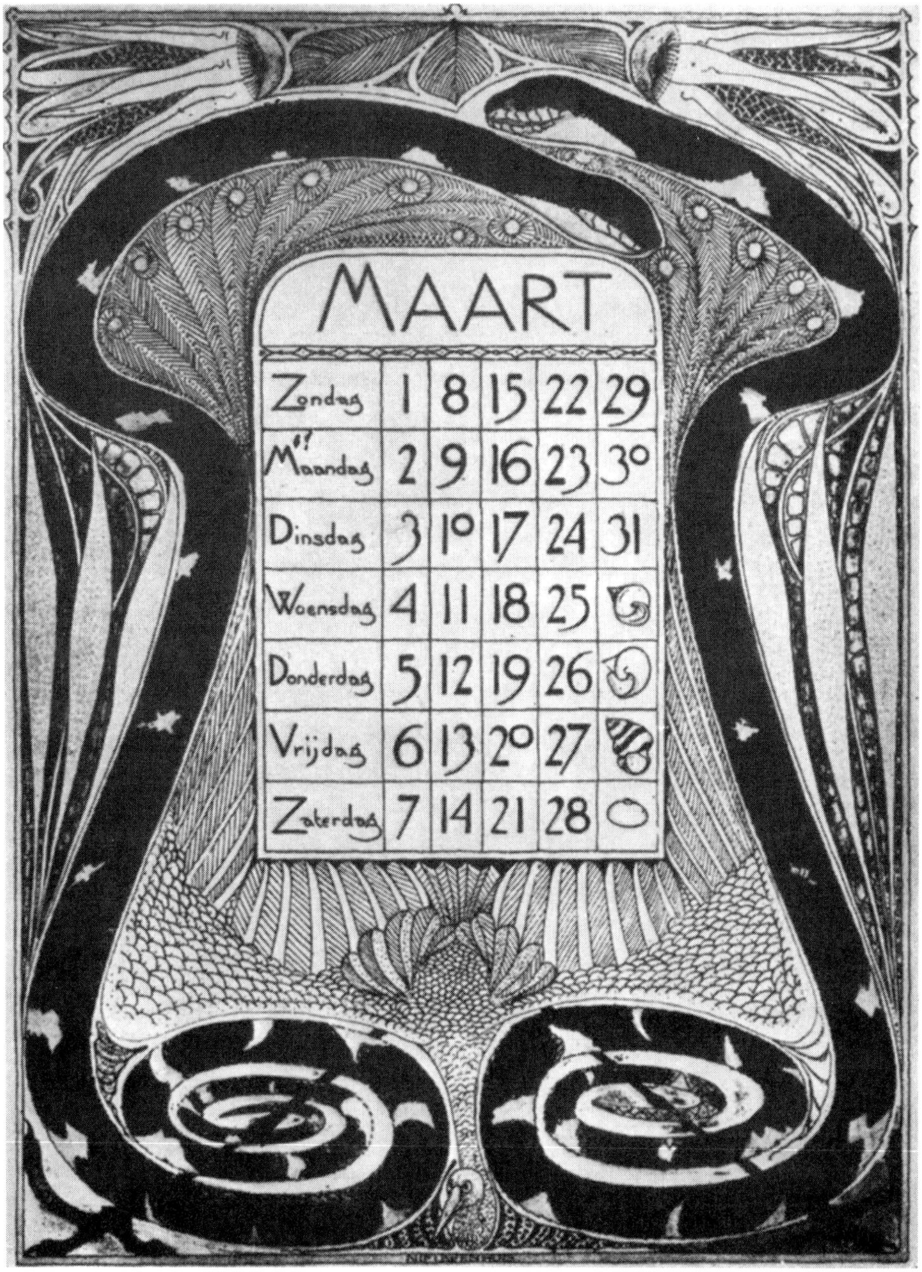

Fig. 28. Nieuwenhuis: Illustrated page from a calendar. 1896.

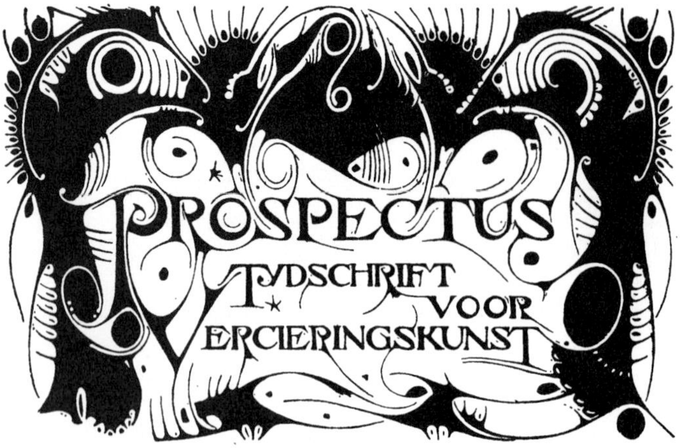

Fig. 29. de Bazel: Heading for periodical. 1896.

balance and symmetry, but on closer examination it will be seen that they are constructed according to the most minute and imaginative asymmetry.

One of the leading artists who worked within this movement was the painter and designer Gerrit Willem Dijsselhof (1866–1924), who as early as 1890, with his so-called "Dijsselhofkamer"—now in the Gemeente Museum, The Hague—had evinced a complete liberation from Historicism, and a seeking for the same ideals which marked the Arts and Crafts Movement. In 1894 he designed a screen of unpainted oak with a pattern in batik technique[3] (fig. 30). Along the edge of the screen, the straws wave to and fro, entwined with long thin leaves. While we do not exactly find the typical whiplash rhythm, nevertheless in these leaves, and in all these tense birds' necks and birds' bodies, we have a cult of the same linear ideal which we found in the other contemporary European artists. Holland's leading decorative artists came no closer to what we associate with Art Nouveau. This does not, of course, take into account second-rate work or slavish imitations of the Art Nouveau of other nations.

The most reasonable explanation of Holland's position is probably that Holland had moved away from Historicism without external aid, as indeed had England. Moreover Holland's most advanced architect, H. P. Berlage (1856–1934), not only guided the development in his own country into new channels, but was, himself, one of the European pioneers of the Modern

[3] Cat. No. 115/B174. Stedelijk Museum, Amsterdam.

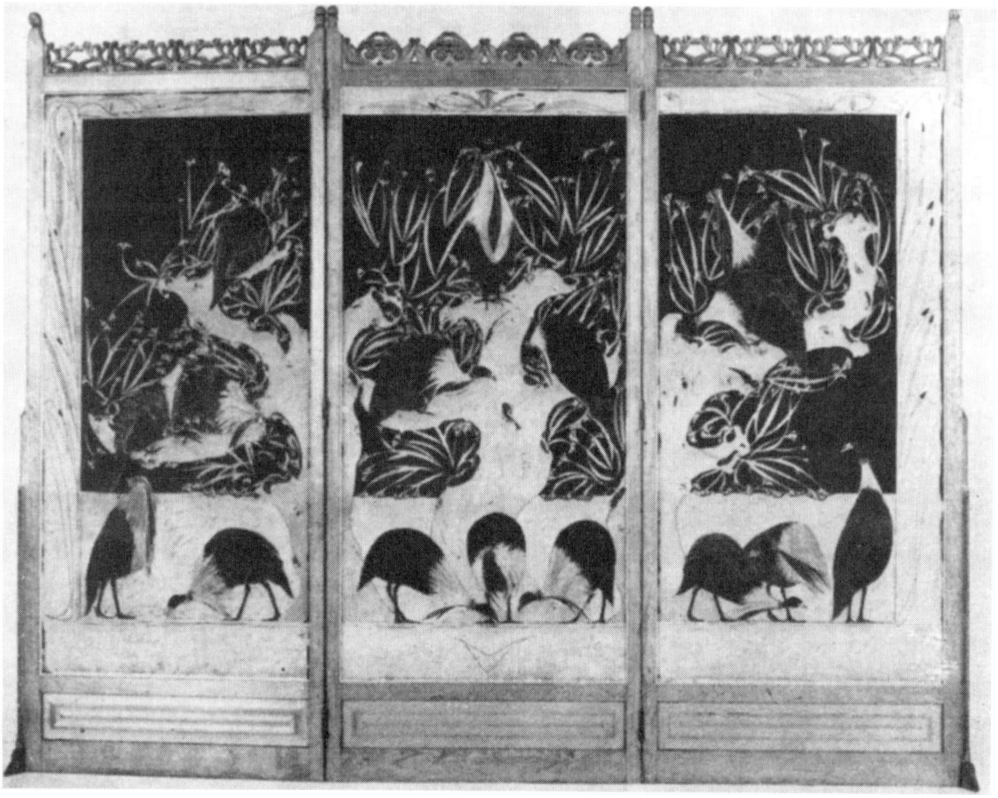

Fig. 30. Dijsselhof: Screen. Unpainted oak and textile printed in batik-technique. 1894.
Stedelijk Museum, Amsterdam. Copyright reserved.

Movement. In his work a special source of inspiration, far removed from Art Nouveau, emerged: the basic principles of Egyptian, Assyrian and Norman architecture; but it is interesting to see how the Egyptian palmettes are translated into the linear rhythm of the eighteen-nineties (fig. 31).

Berlage's furniture from about the year 1900[4] (fig. 32) is characteristic of this age. Here the simple matt-polished jacaranda wood appears in an exceedingly simple and clean-lined construction, accentuated by the uprights which are faintly reminiscent of English style. Every piece of furniture, rectilinear in its construction, has a simple closed form, and is almost Egyptian in appearance. The batik-printed velour cover has un-

[4] Cat. No. N.M. 1–53, N.M. 3–53. Gemeente Museum, The Hague. (n. d.)

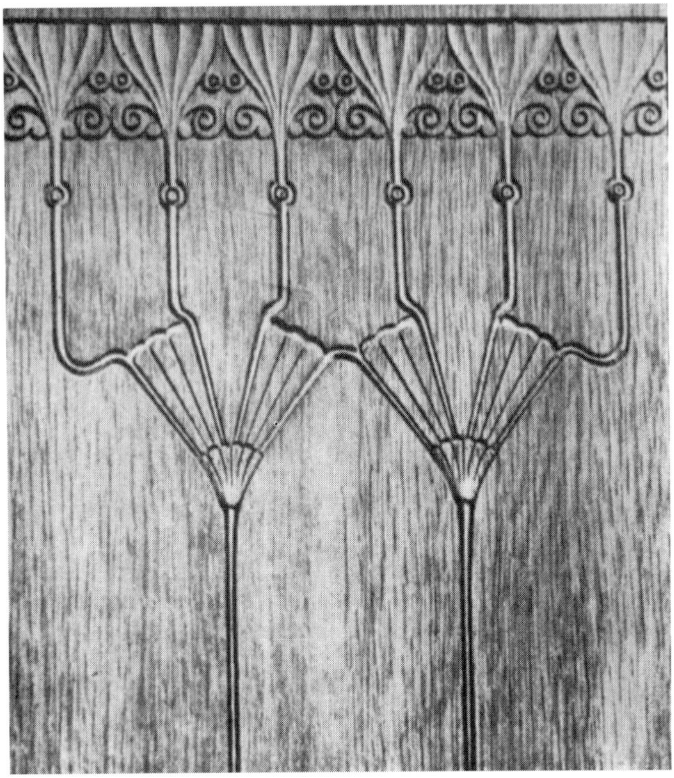

Fig. 31. Berlage: Decorated panel. The Exchange Building, Damrak, Amsterdam. Unpainted oak. 1898—1903.

mistakably Art Nouveau motifs, but even these are Scottish rather than Continental in character, thanks to the vertical parallelism.

Otherwise Dutch Art Nouveau, on such rare occasions as we come across it, is closely related to the art of book design and painting, and coincided at the beginning of the eighteen-nineties with artists such as Toorop, Lemmen, Thorn-Prikker, and Finch. As this is of more importance to the very earliest development, it seems more convenient to deal with it elsewhere.

Taken as a whole it may be said that the liberation from Historicism and a seeking for new ideals and a new form-language, found their solution in Holland in a different manner from the other countries. The extremes of Art Nouveau were avoided, and a more sober national line was pursued, similar to the trend in England. This process, which stylistically may be

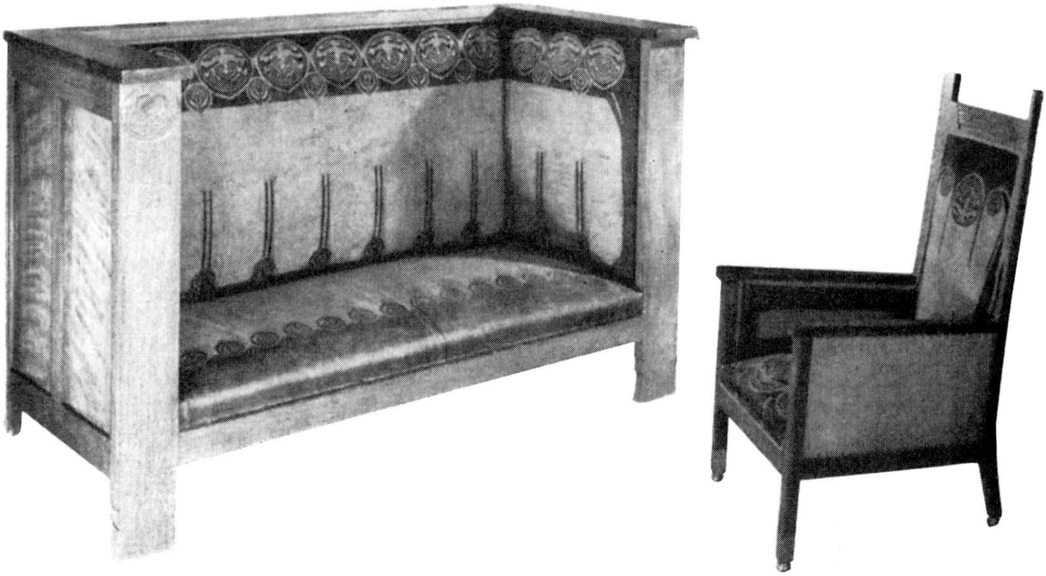

Fig. 32. Berlage: Sofa and armchair. Jacaranda with textile cover printed in batik-technic. Gemeente Museum, The Hague. Copyright reserved.

said to have its root in the interest in the Dutch neo-Renaissance, was of such a nature that not only did Art Nouveau fall outside its scope, but even such general European style-trends as neo-Baroque and neo-Rococo were destined to play a subordinate role. As far as connections with England are concerned, the natural course would seem to be to look for direct links, on the assumption that the same preconditions may have operated in both countries.

*

The tendencies of Dutch Art Nouveau made their appearance very early, though they never came to full fruition; its most important features are a marked two-dimensional decorative effect, a flat treatment which is anti-illusionist and anti-perspective. Furthermore, in the linear rhythmic interplay of Art Nouveau we frequently come across a striking, almost bristling, scroll, unlike anything we encounter anywhere else. Dutch Art Nouveau is occasionally abstract but is never dynamic as across the border—it is not floral like the French, but uses long narrow fishes and long-necked animals, snakes, and jellyfishes. It tends to be asymmetric in detail and symmetric in its conception, and the various motifs do not overflow the surface, engulfing the object.

One is tempted to look for the origin of this Art Nouveau, whose typical features seem to have so little in common with that of Western Europe, and which is so markedly flat in its appearance—in Orientalism and book decoration.

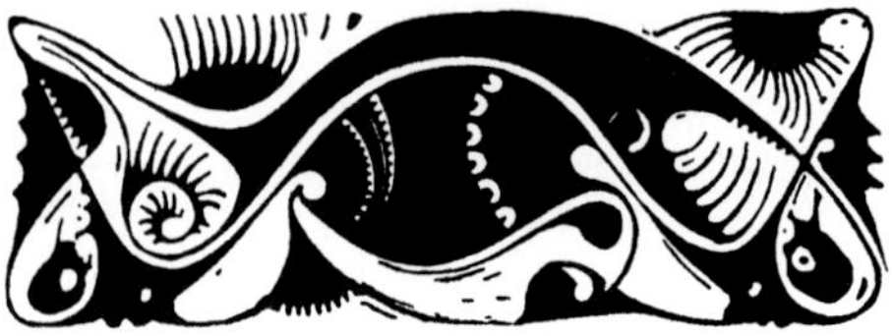

Vignette. De Bazel: Vignette. 1896.

GERMANY

Flowers and Construction

The mature and fully-developed German Art Nouveau—the Jugend style—had two main centres, one in Munich, in a milieu of painters and graphic artists; the other among a group of artists who worked in Darmstadt under the patronage of the Grand-Duke Ernst Ludwig of Hesse. The latter group had strong links with Austria, the Viennese school and its architects.

Otto Eckmann (1865–1902), who belongs to the Munich group, is the foremost floral artist of German Art Nouveau. In his floral book illustrations he represents all the qualities innate in Jugend. The vignettes he designed for the periodical *Pan* from 1896 (fig. 33)[1] are completely stylised, the natural

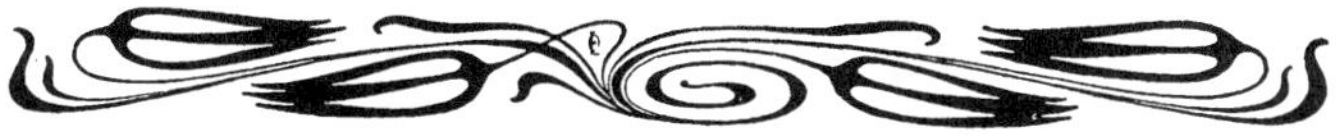

Fig. 33. Eckmann: Vignette for *Pan*. 1896.

form being subordinate to the decorative poise and yet in the movement of the stalk which shoots out on each side, he has conveyed a sense of Nature's budding force. His plant motifs are usually entirely two-dimensional, but in his tulip- and poppy-like flowers there is often a three-dimensional effect. The special feature of his decorative linear rhythm—and something which is so typical of the Jugend style—is the pronounced thickening of the line in all curves. This is the two-dimensional artist's method of expressing dynamic concentrated strength, just as the Belgians and the Frenchmen found a convenient three-dimensional expression. At its best in the work of Eckmann this play of line often has a peculiarly heavy, coarse effect, despite its many subtle curves.

Eckmann is just as asymmetrical in his details and symmetrical in his total composition as for example the Dutchman de Bazel, but unlike their

[1] Vignette for *Pan*, vol. I, 1896–97, p. 21.

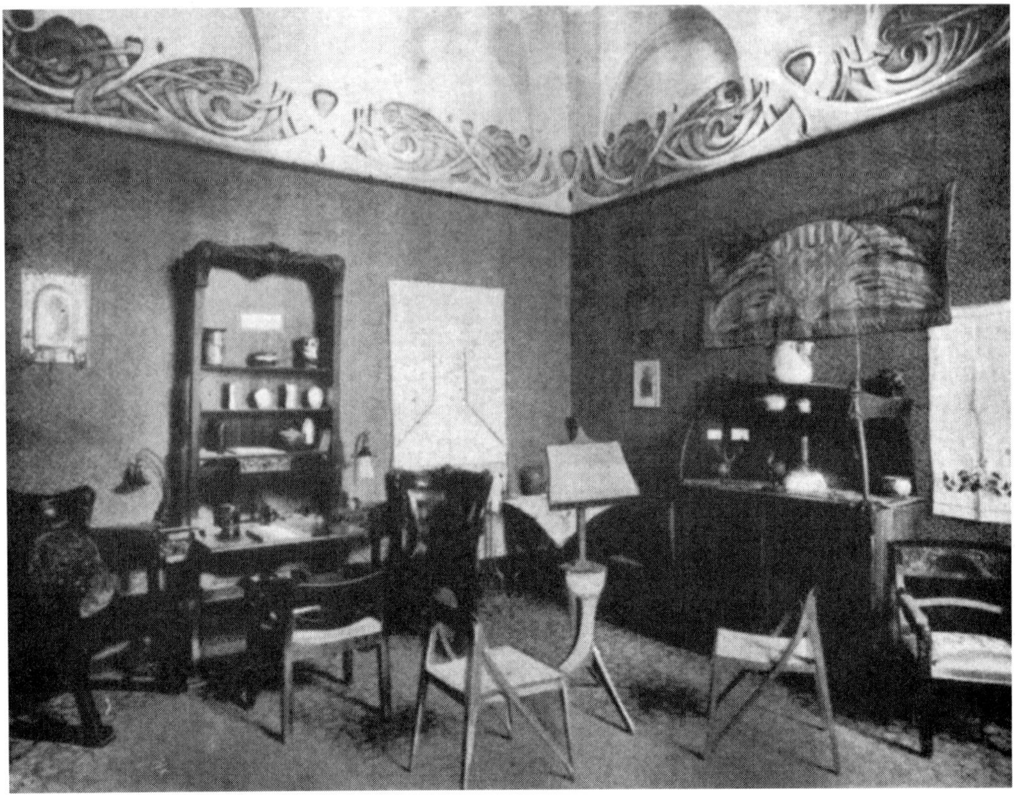

Fig. 34. Riemerschmid: "Salle Riemerschmid".
Paris Exhibition. 1900.

Western neighbours the Germans use a more compact arrangement: there is nothing sprawling or protruding beyond the closed and fixed area, but merely space surrounding the ornament. Eckmann always retains his flair for the two-dimensional, and his natural playground is to be found in the pages of a book.

In the *Salle Riemerschmid* at the Paris Exhibition in 1900 (fig. 34)[2] we find several of the artists of the Munich school represented: Hermann Obrist (1863–1927) by his embroideries in rectilinear as well as curved floral motifs; Bernhard Pankok (1872–) by his chair and dresser with its simple curved parts (on the right). The simple motifs in the interior, firmly placed in certain carefully-selected spots, and in no way tending to occupy

2 *La Décoration et l'Ameublement à l'Exposition de 1900,* Paris 1901, vol. I, pl. 45.

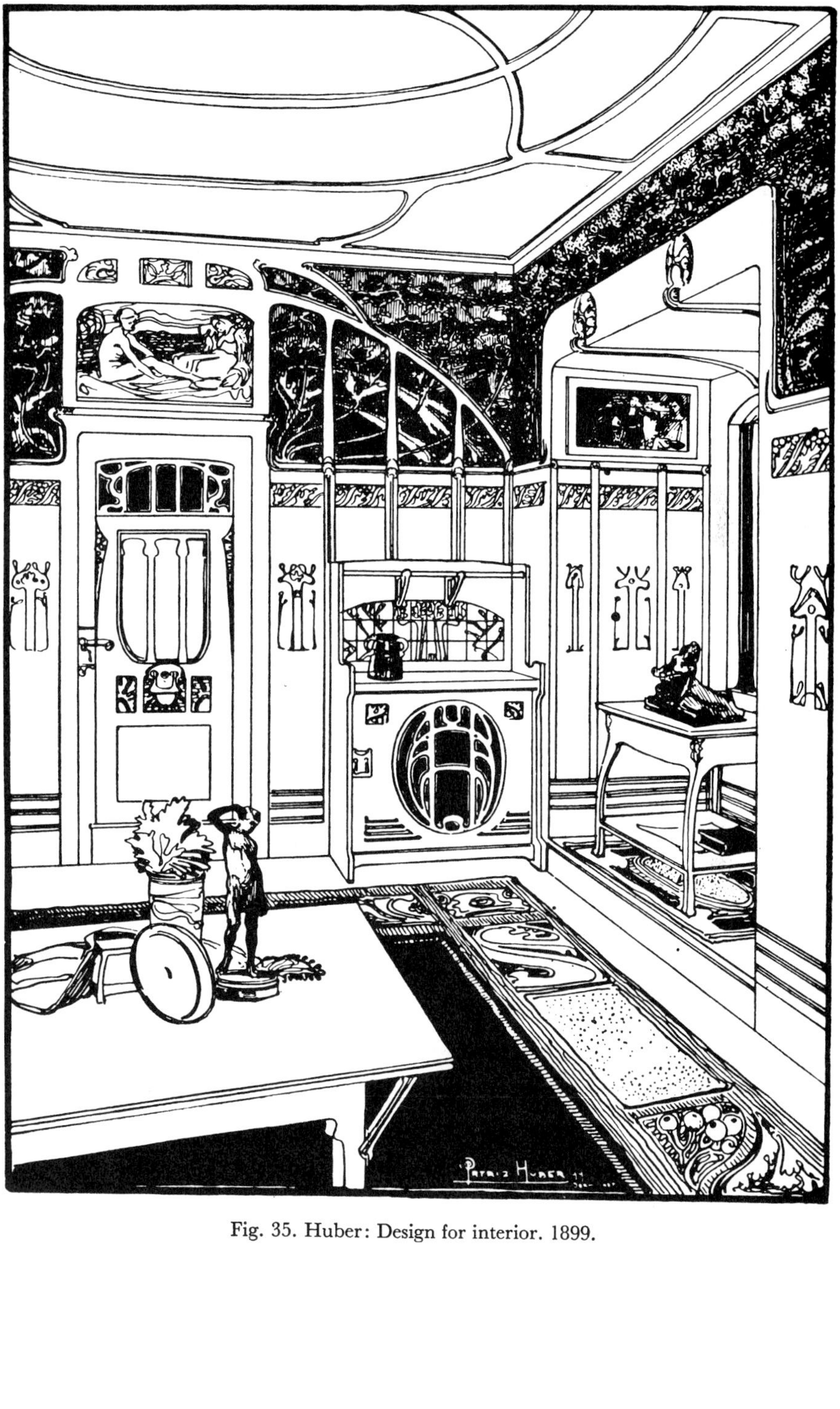

Fig. 35. Huber: Design for interior. 1899.

the surface, may suggest that the vignette has been transferred from the pages of a book to a piece of furniture. While the main shapes of the furniture are straight and almost heavily proportioned, all the minor parts show a penchant for soft curves and a wavy line.

The other pieces shown are the work of Richard Riemerschmid (1868–), whose furniture is still more ponderous. In his work too the floral motifs are placed with great firmness—the flowers being cut, and imprisoned within a square field. The marked austerity and the constructive simplicity which we encounter in practically every object, remind us of the Arts and Crafts Movement and the Modern Movement rather than of Art Nouveau. In Riemerschmid's ceiling frieze, on the other hand, the Jugend style rings out unmistakably, and here typical features have been dealt with in typical fashion: we find the scroll motif in *entrelac* in the form of a frieze. The other leading artists working in Munich were Peter Behrens (1868–1940), August Endell (1871–1925) and Bruno Paul (1874–).

The activity of the Darmstadt group comes somewhat later in time than that of the Munich school, and is dominated by Peter Behrens and the Austrian Olbrich (1867–1908),[3] who thus links Germany and Austria together, interpretating the form-language of the Vienna school in Germany. In the work of Patriz Huber (1878–1902), one of the most characteristic of the Darmstadt artists, we find the style in full flower, e.g. in the interior he designed in 1899 (fig. 35).[4]

The whole room shows stylistic unity, but what distinguishes this interior from the Munich one, is a more airy appearance. This is due partly to the colouring in which the interior is conceived, but also to the rows of thin vertical lines and other component parts which enhance this effect. Another characteristic feature is the large arcs. We have the impression that the free rhythm of the lines is always arrested by verticals or horizontals. The floral details are not as natural in shape as in the Munich school, and they are often so stylised that they appear as an abstract pattern, though the contact with Nature is never entirely lost. But as in Munich, Scotland, and in Holland, the single ornament is firmly placed

3 Olbrich will be dealt with in the next chapter.

4 *Zeitschrift für Innendekoration*, vol. XI, 1900, p. 49.

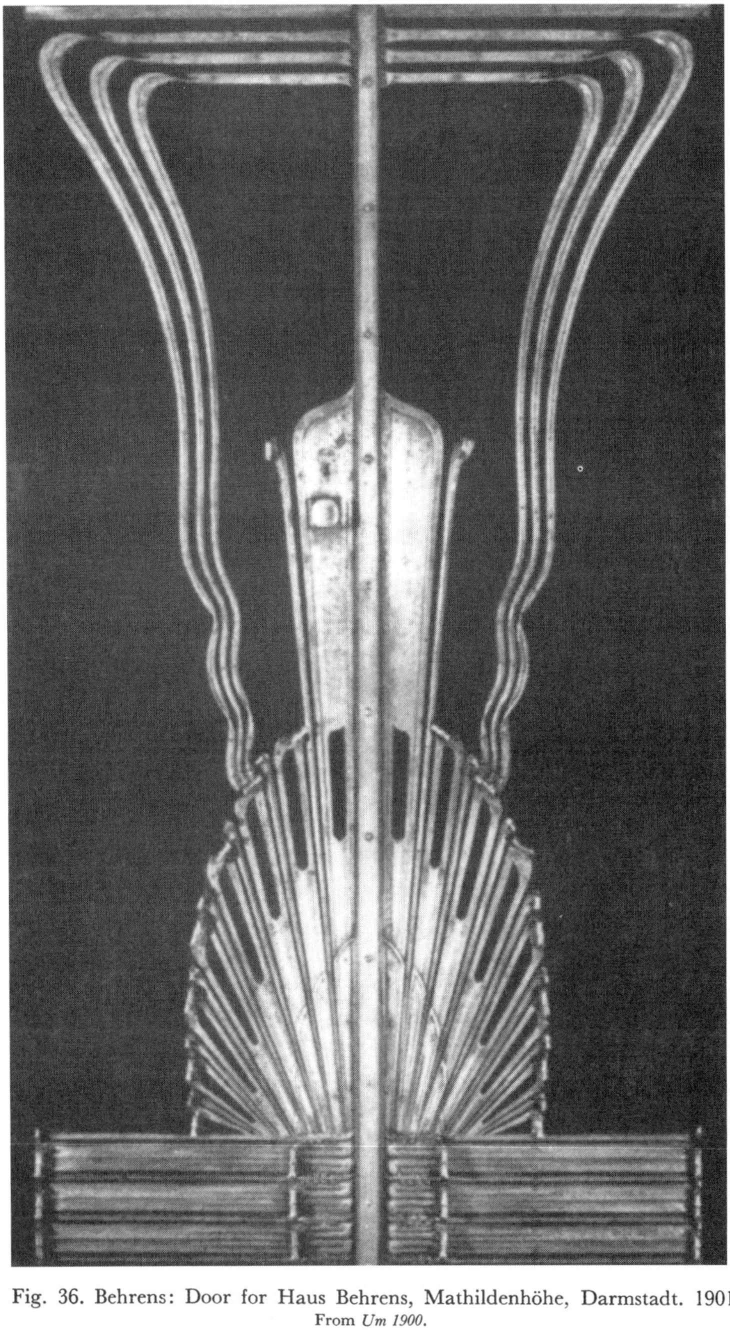

Fig. 36. Behrens: Door for Haus Behrens, Mathildenhöhe, Darmstadt. 1901.
From *Um 1900*.

on the surface, frequently framed or confined to panels, as for instance in the tall narrow wallpanels with the linear flower-like motif.

The leading German in the group was Peter Behrens, who worked in Munich until 1899, and who built his famous *Haus Behrens* in Darmstadt in 1901. There are not so many traces of the Jugend style in his work: as in the case of so many Germans his contribution lies outside this style, and wherever it appears it is moderated and associated with a system of parallel and straight lines which shows little in common with the vigorous evolutions we have encountered in the grille treatment in other countries (fig. 36). We are face to face with a symmetrical decorative treatment, where the wrought iron literally ripples in a linear flow of line, and whose most essential characteristic is the marked rigidity of composition and detail. The other artists forming the Darmstadt group, "*Die Sieben*," were Hans Christiansen, the sculptors Ludwig Habich, Rudolf Bosselt and the designer and painter Paul Bürck.

*

An essential feature of German design is its striving towards a constructive form which at times is translated into an Art Nouveau-like constructivism, with ample use of arched struts and rectilinear components. Together with the blunt arches, which have none of the pliancy and grace we find in other countries, this gives the style a somewhat ponderous effect. On the other hand the extensive use of right-angles emphasises its austerity. The single motif, unlike what we find in the Franco–Belgian sphere—but in common with the Anglo–Dutch—is securely anchored in the surface, frequently enclosed in sharp lines. The scroll-like entrelac motif is also typical of Germany. In the more commercial and somewhat simpler versions of this style the rather "plump" thickening of all curves and coils, which gives the line a paste-like effect, was specially developed. This applies both to the floral as well as to the abstract version of the style. These two versions are to be found, clearly separated, in the work of the leading artists. The German artists are always far more preoccupied with the flower than with its stalk, the latter dissolving in an abstract interplay.

The German style shows no elements from previous styles, as was the case in France and Belgium. The constructional striving, the two-dimensional treatment and the vignette-like placing of the floral and the abstract motifs inevitably suggest that the precursors of this style are to be found in England, Austria and Belgium.

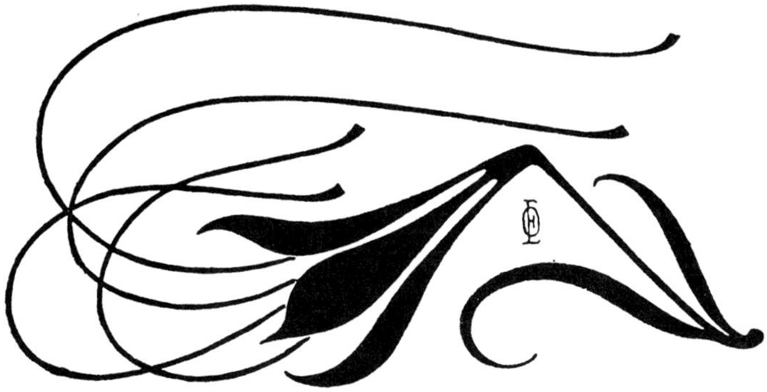

Vignette. Eckmann: Vignette for *Pan*. 1896.

AUSTRIA

Geometric Linearism

Austrian Art Nouveau is indissolubly associated with Vienna, and with the architects Josef Hoffmann (1870-) and Joseph Olbrich (1867–1908).

Olbrich's interior for the Paris Exhibition in 1900 (fig. 37)[1] is enclosed in a horseshoe-shape arch, and the wavy panel runs right round the whole room, giving unity to the various components. The ceiling is furnished with thin ribs which run in parallel lines from one end to the other. In the corner a flame motif billows across the walls, perhaps a symbolical reminder of the functions of the hearth. A closer investigation of the various decorative elements shows that they consist of almost circular roses and fruits, which are frequently so stylised that nothing is left except an abstract interplay of line. The ornamentation is clearly disposed on the surface, and having its fixed limits, never overflows. There is no tendency for the ornamentation to take possession of the furniture: instead the room as a whole is subordinate to a decorative *vue d'ensemble*. The thin parallel wavy lines on the cupboard accentuate its light and graceful air, while the table and the chairs are soberly undecorated with an air of Rococo.

A visitor to the Paris Exhibition of 1900 who walked straight from Olbrich's room to the interior shown by the *Wiener Kunstgewerbeschule*[2] would in the latter have encountered all over the walls Hoffmann's elegant and slender linear rhythms—thin vertical and horizontal lines, constantly crossing and thus forming squares.

His interior design from 1900 (fig. 38)[3] shows the large horseshoe-shaped arch which Olbrich was so fond of using. In this case it has almost the appearance of an iron construction, and its soft lines harmonise perfectly with the window-niche. The decoration, with its soft lines, is well in keeping with this form-language, but where these lines reach the ceiling they appear to collide with a different world of forms. Here everything is austerely and

1 *Zeitschrift für Innendekoration*, vol. XI, 1900, p. 149; see also J. Olbrich, *Ideen von Olbrich*, Vienna 1900, p. 53.

2 Illustrated in *Das Interieur*, vol. I, 1900, pp. 123–25.

3 *Ibid.*, vol. I, 1900, pl. 7.

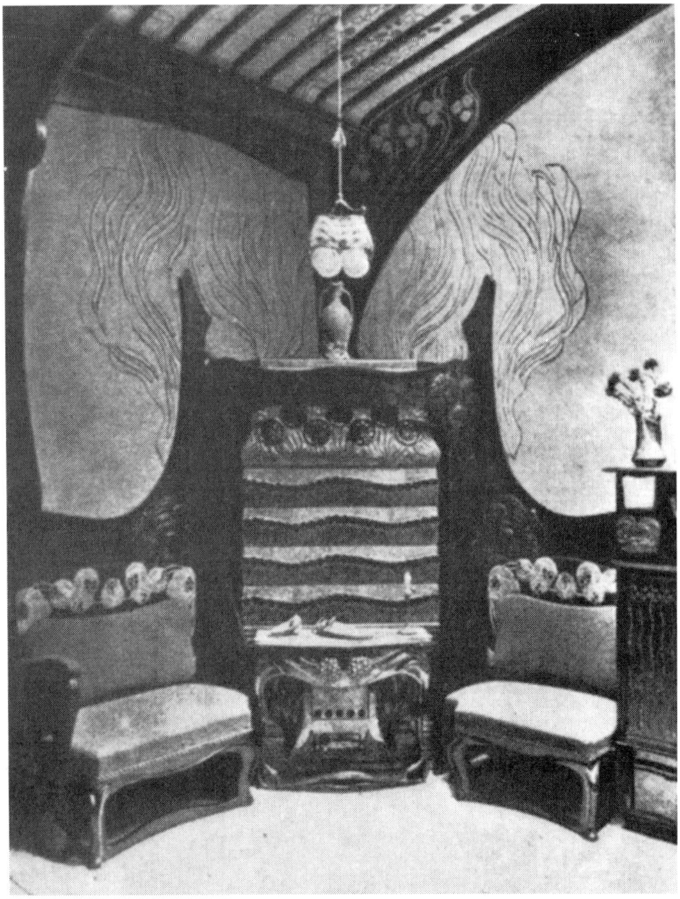

Fig. 37. Olbrich: Corner of the Austrian Section.
Paris Exhibition 1900.

rigidly rectilinear, an effect which is heightened not least by the parallel lines, cut off at right-angles, giving it a touch of classicism. Everything is subordinated to a strict ornamental order, and the motifs he uses are the Glasgow-like bud or bean, Olbrich's clusters of circles and flowers, and finally the little square, which was the decorative element he made most use of during these years, and which he chose to decorate the window.

The impression, however, would not be complete if merely confined to his two-dimensional creations and fantasies, so let us consider a completely designed room by Hoffmann. In 1900 he completed his villa for Gustav

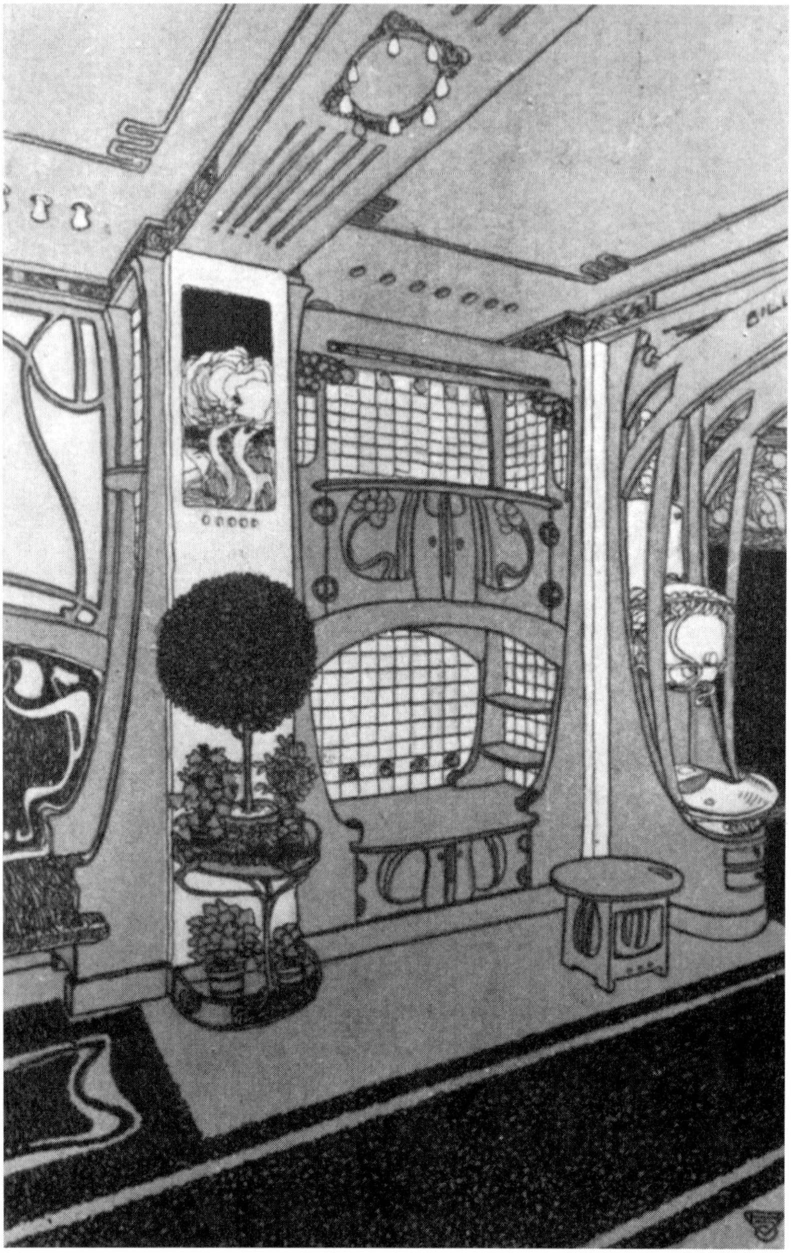

Fig. 38. Hoffmann: Design for interior. 1900.

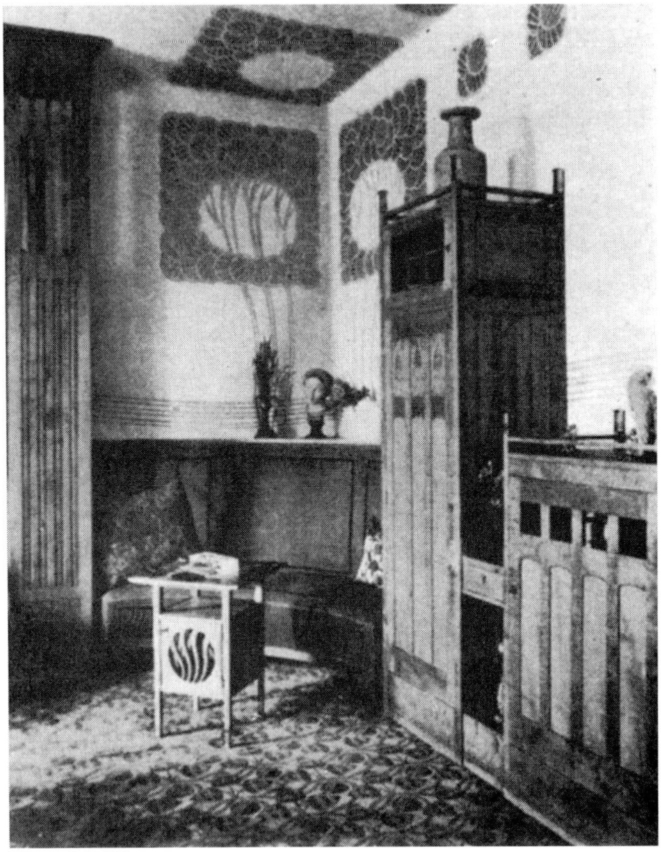

Fig. 39. Hoffmann: Sitting-room in Gustav Pollak's Villa, Atzgersdorf. 1899—1900.

Pollak in Atzgersdorf (fig. 39).[4] This sitting-room exudes an air of austerity and a rigidity in all its forms which is emphasised by the lavish use of thin parallel mouldings and lines. The surfaces of the furniture are without decoration, and only in a few panels is the stylised flower-motif admitted. The sofa in the corner emphasises the simple form-language. Otherwise we encounter such well-known motifs as the square (in the cupboard), the circle with its flame-motif (in the table), and both happily united in a tree-like motif on the wall. It is doubtful whether we can describe this as Art Nouveau: the ornaments certainly represent an Austrian form of

4 *Ibid.*, vol. I, 1900, pl. 141.

Art Nouveau, but the furniture in itself has little in common with Art Nouveau. The name which best covers it is the one which was used by its contemporaries, viz. the Secession style.

Together with the bud, the flame-filled circle, the tree with the clusters of circles, and the square, we also find a classical elegance, reminiscent of Louis XVI, which together with the pronounced linearity contributes to the refined and subtle character which is typical of the Austrian version of the European Art Nouveau style. Last but not least, where others stylised Nature, or preferred abstractions, the Austrians made use of geometric forms.

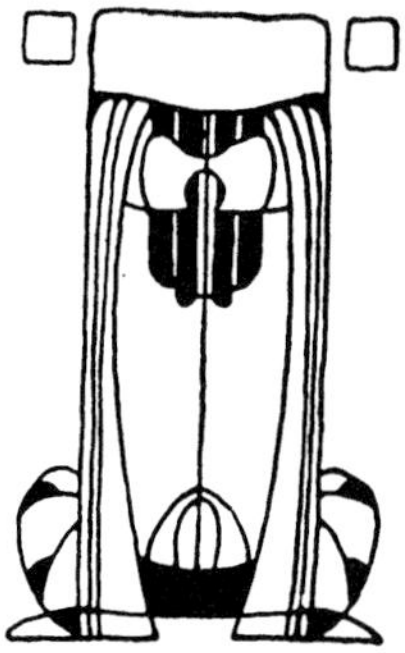

Vignette.
Hoffmann: Vignette for
Ver Sacrum. 1900.

Part II

ORIGINS

Name and Conception

So far we have considered Art Nouveau exclusively within the realms of decorative art and architecture—but before proceeding it is necessary to deal briefly with the problem of its spread in sculpture and painting.

When a series of special decorative forms arise in a number of countries at about the same time, such as occurred in the eighteen-nineties, this must be an expression of certain tendencies latent in the age, and it is natural to assume that these formal features will also appear in other branches of art. Some of these features did in fact appear both in sculpture and painting, though in the case of sculpture they were rather sporadic and somewhat apart from the significant sculptural trend.[1] But we do find a tendency to a confined and gently undulating contour as a reaction against the neo-Baroque and Impressionistic conception of form of the eighteen-nineties.[2] Certain purely decorative features, naturally, also appear in the shape of the plinth and the like, especially the sliding movement in the lower portion, which often gives the impression that the plinth is supporting the weight of the monument and transmitting it to the ground. Most of the Art Nouveau features in sculpture are not primarily of sculptural interest, and are hardly sufficient to form the basis for a fruitful discussion about an Art Nouveau school in sculpture.

A reason why Art Nouveau's conception of form plays such a subordinate role in sculpture around the turn of the century is that in so many

1 A. Brenna, Jugendstilen i norsk og europeisk skulptur, lecture delivered at the University of Oslo, March 1951. MS.

2 *Idem,* Reaction against Neo-Baroque and Impressionism in the 1890's, *Form og komposisjon i nordisk granittskulptur 1909–1926,* Oslo 1954, pp. 207 sq.

countries the style was linear and two-dimensional in its essence, and consequently had no opportunity of influencing plastic and three-dimensional art. And yet the fact remains that several of the designers who worked with the plastic arts created markedly sculptural Art Nouveau.

In painting[3] the state of affairs is quite different, because here it was much easier to introduce some of the elements of this style. In Germany the term "*Jugendstil*" has also been used in painting, principally as a label for German post-Impressionism.[4] But Fritz Schmalenbach maintains[5]—in common with Nikolaus Pevsner[6]—that the term "Art Nouveau" arose in decorative art, and belongs first and foremost to this genre. Furthermore Jugendstil in painting only refers to purely external and formal features, as Fritz Schmalenbach also points out,[7] while at the same time he draws attention to the fact that it was not until 1914 that the expression *Jugendstil* was used in painting.[8]

For the above-mentioned reasons, and furthermore in order to arrive at a clear limitation, we shall therefore mostly deal with the decorative arts, and the handicrafts, only introducing sculpture, painting and architecture when these arts help us to understand the origins, or influenced the development.

From the point of view of form analysis, what we have called Art Nouveau has nothing in common with what in recent research is called the Modern Movement. This trend, which made a clean sweep, ruthlessly removing all ornaments, and allowing a construction and a rational form to emerge, paid full attention to the exploitation and special qualities of the material, coupled with honesty in the use of it, though without in any way neglecting aesthetic considerations. This revolutionary theory of architecture took shape in the latter half of the nineteenth century, and in inti-

3 F. Schmalenbach, Jugendstil in der Malerei, *Jugendstil. Ein Beitrag zu Theorie und Geschichte der Flächenkunst,* Würzburg 1935, pp. 138–48.

4 E. Michalski, Die Entwicklungsgeschichtliche Bedeutung des Jugendstils, *Repertorium für Kunstwissenschaft,* vol. XLVI, 1925, Berlin-Leipzig, pp. 133–49.

5 F. Schmalenbach, *op. cit.,* p. 138.

6 N. Pevsner, *Pioneers of Modern Design,* New York 1949, pp. 56 sq.

7 F. Schmalenbach, *loc. cit.*

8 *Ibid.*

mate contact with the latest technical inventions, its first monuments being raised at the end of the century and around the turn of the century.

It is not difficult to find fault with the term "Modern Movement," because all movements are modern when they start, and the name is to a large extent conditioned by an attitude which is stamped by a special epoch. But scholars such as Sigfried Giedion, Henry-Russell Hitchcock, Thomas Howarth, Nikolaus Pevsner, and Bruno Zevi have in their work given international approval to this term.

Another movement which spread at about the same time as Art Nouveau and the Modern Movement was the Arts and Crafts Movement. The latter, in contrast to the two other international trends, is an English phenomenon, but like Art Nouveau is linked to applied art. This movement represents a renaissance in English applied art and industrial art which came into being with William Morris. The movement acquired more fixed forms in the eighteen-eighties, when a number of organisations were started, and the actual idea finds expression in the name of the oldest of these organisations, the Century Guild: a renaissance in the spirit of the Middle Ages, but rooted in the current century. In a number of other countries the revolt against Historicism was launched, though it was conducted on a different basis, and without the background of organisations such as those founded in England.

What occasionally confuses the issue is that certain artists and architects who participated in the Modern Movement, and as far as the English were concerned contributed to the Arts and Crafts Movement, were also capable of working in pure Art Nouveau. Gradually, as each trend acquired its more or less special character, these naturally tended to fuse.

For those artists who were the central figures in the conflicts of the day it was not always easy to make a clear distinction between the various parallel trends, and still more difficult to recognise what would be the style of the future—what was to become the basis of the architectural nad aesthetic ideology of the twentieth century, and what was merely a passing phenomenon.

As Art Nouveau gradually spread and attained popularity, it was given a host of terms and names—a phenomenon which as a matter of fact is symptomatic of the striving of that age for an acceptable stylistic conception. Among the more popular names are *Paling stijl* (paling = Flemish: Eel), which was the name it quickly acquired in Belgium, as well as *Style Nouille*, which was the soubriquet Paul Morand gave it.[9] Names such as *Mouvement belge* and *Ligne belge* are expressive rather of a national Belgian consciousness, and furthermore we get names such as *Style 1900* and *Modern Style*,[10] the latter alluding to the connection with England.

In 1901 van de Velde mentions names such as *Veldescher Stil, Stil van de Velde,* but also notes that in Dresden and Berlin his work was called *Schnörkelstil,* and *Bandwurmstil,* while the *Kölnischer Zeitung* called it *Wellenstil.*[11] Other German nicknames were *belgischer Bandwurm, gereizter Regenwurm,* and *moderne Strumpfbandlinien,*[12] while the term *Jugendstil* soon replaced names such as *neu-Stil* and *neudeutsche Kunst.*[13] The German name is taken from the lively and ribald periodical *Jugend,* the first copies of which circulated in Munich in January 1896. Here we find Otto Eckmann delighting his readers with his floral Art Nouveau vignettes, in company with a number of other artists with definite Art Nouveau leanings, and three or four years after the founding of this periodical the term *Jugendstil* had taken root and was being used in applied art.[14]

It was hardly surprising that the style was also named after certain artists, as mentioned above in the case of van de Velde, and we find names such as *Style Horta* and *Style Guimard.*[15]

In Austria the corresponding stylistic phenomenon was covered by the name *Secessionsstil* or *Sezessionsstil,* a term which can trace its origin back to the union of radical Viennese painters and Viennese sculptors which was founded in 1897 under the name of *Wiener Sezession.*[16]

9 P. Fierens, La Belgique et l'Architecture moderne, *La Vie Artistique,* Brussels 1937, p. 509.

10 For the first three names, cf. M. Schmitz, *l'Architecture Moderne en Belgique,* Brussels 1937. *Modern Style* is still in use in Belgium as the proper term for Art Nouveau. Recently used by P. L. Flouquet, Surréalisme et Architecture, *La Maison,* Brussels, vol. VIII, No. 11, 1952, pp. 340–44.

11 H. van de Velde, *Renaissance im Kunstgewerbe,* Berlin 1901, Neue Ausgabe, p. 81 sq.

12 F. Schmalenbach, *op. cit.,* p. 30.

13 R. Graul, *Die Krisis im Kunstgewerbe,* Leipzig 1901, p. 46.

14 Fr. Ahler-Hestermann, *Stilwende Aufbruch der Jugend um 1900,* Berlin 1941, p. 8; F. Schmalenbach gives the year 1899, *op. cit.,* p. 17.

15 Information kindly given by Madame Horta to the author May 1953.

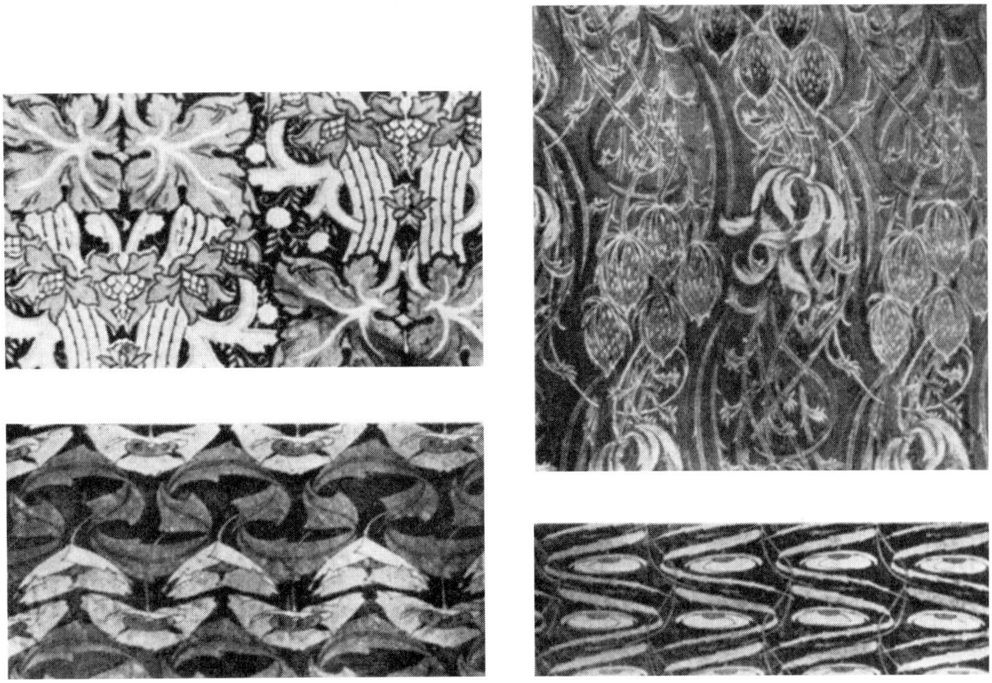

Fig. 40. Printed silk textiles from Liberty & Co. London. 1900.

The French author Edmond Goncourt gave the style the celebrated name of *Yachting Style* as early as 1896,[17] while in Italy the style was occasionally called the *Stile Inglese*,[18] though the commonest designation was *Stile Liberty* after the firm of Liberty and Co. in London. As Nikolaus Pevsner and Clay Lancaster have already pointed out, it was this firm's predilection for a bright colour-scheme and their constant interest in new designs, that accounts for this term[19] (fig. 40).[20] Frank P. Higgins, writing in 1895, says:

16 H. Pudor, *Das Moderne in Kunst und Kunstgewerbe, I, Secessionsstil und modernes Kunstgewerbe,* Leipzig 1903; P. Schultze-Naumburg, Der "Sezessionsstil," *Der Kunstwart,* Munich, vol. XV, 1901–02, No. 1, p. 326.

17 The year van de Velde's furniture and design were on show for the first time in Paris. Van de Velde mentions that Goncourt made some notes in his diary when he visited the exhibition: H. van de Velde, *Renaissance im Kunstgewerbe,* Berlin 1901, Neue Ausgabe, p. 18.

18 *The Journal of Decorative Art,* vol. XXI, 1901, p. 237.

19 N. Pevsner, *Pioneers of the Modern Movement,* 1st ed., London 1936, p. 114; C. Lancaster, Oriental Contribution to Art Nouveau, *The Art Bulletin,* vol. XXIX, 1952, p. 302.

20 J. Hoffmann jr., *Der Moderne Stil,* Stuttgart 1900, vol. II, pl. 37, figs. 1–4.

"It is known to the veriest tyro connected with the silk industries of the world how closely identified the name of Mr. Lasenby Liberty has become with the wonderful studies in advance of the British silk trading during late years."[21] Arthur Liberty himself says "at this time the name Liberty was the quintessence of Fashion in London, . . . one also dressed à la Liberty."[22]

The name of Liberty was also well known in France: The designer Ernest Duez writes in 1895, "Voilà que les acheteurs se précipitent en foule chez Maple et Liberty. Ils ont raison, puisqu'ils trouvent là des meubles et des étoffes qu'ils ne voient encore nulle part ailleurs . . . ."[23]

The name of Liberty became identified with the English renaissance in industrial design—Liberty himself was a friend of several of the men in the Arts and Crafts Movement—and since Art Nouveau and the Arts and Crafts Movement at that time might have been regarded as one and the same,[24] it is not surprising that a confusion of ideas and terms took place. This is still easier to understand when we remember that Liberty also produced textiles and silver in the Art Nouveau style—the silver was inter alia presented under the name of "Cymric Silver."

Modern research[25] has retained the term "Stile Liberty," in common with "Jugend" in Germany.[26]

When Julius Hoffmann jr. published his reproductions in Stuttgart in 1899 he called it *Der Moderne Stil.* It is one of the most important sources of information on Art Nouveau, containing between two and three thousand illustrations, a great many of which are English. The very name of the periodical is characteristic enough, and also corresponds to a French name for the style, for in the early days the Frenchmen called it *Modern Style,* thus

21 F. C. Higgins, *British Warehouseman,* London, February 1895, p. 26.

22 A. S. Liberty, Easter Art in London, unpublished, Liberty & Co., Regent Street, London.

23 H. Nocq, Tendances Nouvelles. *Enquête sur l'évolution des industries d'art,* Paris 1896, pp. 37 sq. "Crowds of buyers are hurrying off to Maple and Liberty's. They're quite right, for there they will find furniture and materials that they wont see anywhere else."

24 See note 36.

25 I. Cremona, Discuro sullo Stile Liberty, *Sele Arte,* No. 3, 1952, pp. 15–22; A. Pica, Revisione del Liberty, *Emporium,* vol. XCIV, No. 560, August 1941; G. Dorfles, *Barocco nell'architectura Moderna,* Milan 1951. (With an illustration of Liberty & Co.'s main-entrance at the Paris Exhibition 1900, p. 43.)

26 F. Schmalenbach, *op. cit.;* F. Ahler-Hestermann, *op. cit.*

expressing the idea that the movement was English in its origins. "One says Modern Style," a French connoisseur of applied-art problems writes in 1901, "in order to remind oneself of the British origin."[27] Emile Gallé, too, used the name,[28] and likewise Emile Bayard in the last volume of his series *l'Art de reconnaître les Styles.*[29]

It is significant, however, that in France there was a change in nomenclature of the movement after Sigfried Bing had opened his shop round about Christmas 1895 in Paris, with the orange-coloured sign which Arsène Alexandre, the editor of the *Revue des Arts Décoratifs,* described as follows: "Au-dessus des deux énormes bouquets de soleil en ronde bosse, brutalement agrandis après une nature littérale, sans goût et sans style, se lisent ces deux mots, d'une délicieuse modestie: *l'art nouveau*" *[sic].*[30]

As the French fashioned their own style out of Art Nouveau, and the shop gradually increased in popularity, it became the name of the style in France. In this connection it may be of interest to hear what Bing himself has to say about the name: "L'Art Nouveau à sa naissance n'avait aucune prétention de passer à l'honneur d'un terme générique. Ce fut modestement le titre d'un établissement ouvert comme point de ralliement, à toutes les jeunes ardeurs anxieuses de manifester la modernité de leurs tendances."[31]

In the late eighteen-nineties the name Art Nouveau became the customary one in France, apart from more flippant names used by the man-in-the-street, such as *Style Métro,* containing a reference to Hector Guimard's iron railings designed for the Underground stations in Paris, or *style rastaquouère,*[20] which means "foreign adventure." Characteristically

27 R. Graul, *Die Krisis im Kunstgewerbe,* Leipzig, 1901, p. 25.

28 E. Gallé, Le Mobilier contemporain orné d'après la nature, *Ecrits pour l'art,* Paris 1908, pp. 237–76. The article published in *Revue des Arts Décoratifs,* Nov/Dec. 1900, and in *La Lorraine,* vol. XIX, 1901.

29 E. Bayard, *Le Style Moderne,* Paris 1912. He seems here to use "Modern Style" for "Art Nouveau" and "Style Moderne" for "the Modern Movement."

30 *Le Figaro,* Paris, December 28, 1895. "Above the two enormous sun orioles with their round discs, violently exaggerated, without taste and style, can be read these two words with their delightful modesty: *art nouveau.*"

31 René Puaux, *George de Feure,* Paris n.d. (1902), p. 2. "At its birth Art Nouveau made no claim to rising to the distinction of a generic term. It was simply the name of an establishment opened as a rallying point for all the keen young people anxious to demonstrate the modernity of their tendencies."

enough the highly-reputable periodical *l'Ameublement* no longer called Art Nouveau furniture "*Genre Anglais,*" but "*Art Nouveau.*"[32]

It was of course only reasonable to expect that this name would establish itself, because the term so completely reflects the age and its strivings. For half a century people had searched for a new style. In 1849 John Ruskin (1819–1900) wrote: "A day never passes without our hearing our English architects called upon to be original and to invent a new style . . ."[33]; and as early as 1836 August W. N. Pugin (1812–52) had warned his readers of the danger.[34] In cultural circles in France in the eighteen-seventies and eighteen-eighties the hope—and the demand—for a new art is constantly expressed. Van de Velde speaks in 1894 of an Art Nouveau *[sic]*[35] which is to come, by which he means a complete artistic revival. This was the dominant mood in the eighteen-nineties: In the midst of *la décadence* and the *fin de siècle Stimmung,* people were striving energetically to attain a renaissance, a new form-language—an *Art Nouveau* and a new *Jugend,* with all the wealth of symbolism contained in these words.

In *The Eighteen-Nineties* Holbrook Jackson draws attention to the interest in "the New." There seems to have been an insatiable yearning for everything that was new, and we get movements such as New Paganism or New Hedonism, while *The Picture of Dorian Grey* was characterised as New Voluptuousness. Oscar Wilde himself wrote about the New Remorse in *The Spirit of the Lamp.* Turning over the pages of *Punch* and other contemporary magazines one is constantly coming across allusions to "new" movements and ideas—New Humour, New Women, New Realism, New Drama—and we find periodicals such as *The New Ages* and *The New Review.* In common with all these names, and expressing the same spirit and tendency of the age, the New Art—l'Art Nouveau—comes into being.

In England this term was used to describe decorative art as early as 1896[36]—though at that time it implied the Continental trend. In the same

32 *l'Ameublement,* 1900, pl. 3393, 3394. Fanciful Portechapeau in a sort of Rococo-Art-Nouveau, entitled "Modern Style." Same expression used on the cover. In the following numbers only "Art Nouveau" used.

33 J. Ruskin, *The Seven Lamps of Architecture,* London 1849, Chapter VII, § 4.

34 A. W. N. Pugin, *Contrasts,* 2nd edition, London 1841, p. 30 sq.

35 H. van de Velde, *Déblaiement d'Art,* Brussels 1894, p. 18.

36 "Now, eight years after, Paris has an 'Arts and Crafts'—l'Art Nouveau." The Arts and Crafts Exhibition, *The Studio,* vol. IX, 1896–97, p. 50.

year Victor Champier writes: "... n'est-il pas evident que cette expression *d'Art nouveau*, n'a contre elle que sa trop prétensieuse précision? . . . Elle indique simplement un effort, . . . ne convient-il pas de l'accepter, cette expression d'*Art nouveau*, et de lui donner droit d'entrée désormais dans les discussions?"[37]

This in fact happened, and after the Paris Exhibition of 1900 and the spread of the style, this term became the usual one. German-speaking countries proved an exception, as here the name *Jugend* was used—and is still used—both in two-dimensional art as well as in three-dimensional applied art. After the period became the subject of investigation by art historians, especially English and American, the name *Art Nouveau*—essentially confined to applied art—appears to have been generally accepted.

37 V. Champier, Les expositions de *l'Art nouveau*, *Revue des Arts Décoratifs*, vol. XVI, 1896, p. 3. " . . . is it not obvious that this expression *Art Nouveau* has only one thing against it: its unduly pretentious precision? It simply indicates an effort, . . . should we not accept it, this expression *Art Nouveau*, and give it the right of entry from now on to our discussions?"

Historicism[1]

On the basis of the analysis of form which has been made of Art Nouveau in various countries, it has been possible to arrive at the characteristics of this style, and these in turn enable us to trace the origins of the style and the conditions under which it arose. The latter are legion, and occasionally vary from one country to another, but some at least are common to the whole of Western Europe, and played their part in creating the same soil in which the style could grow.

In the widest sense it was Historicism which indirectly gave rise to the new style. From about 1820 to 1890 all the styles in Western Europe had been copied, transformed, and recreated; and furthermore towards the end of the century impulses had also been felt from other parts of the world. We may say that the nineteenth century was a repository for the artistic ideas of all countries and all other centuries. At the time it can hardly have been envisaged that this search for inspiration and this copying of other styles was in itself to become a typical stylistic phenomenon.

1 *GENERAL:* K. Scheffler, *Das Phänomen der Kunst. Grundsätzliche Betrachtungen zum 19. Jahrhundert,* Munich 1952; *idem, Verwandlungen des Barocks in der Kunst des Neunzehnten Jahrhunderts,* Vienna 1947; St. Tschudi Madsen, C. Hopstock, *Stoler og Stiler,* Oslo 1955.

ARCHITECTURE: D. Joseph, *Geschichte der Baukunst des 19. Jahrhunderts,* vol. I–II, Leipzig 1910; H. Muthesius, *Stilarchitectur und Baukunst. Wandlungen der Architectur im XIX. Jahrhundert und ihr heutiger Standpunkt,* Mülheim–Ruhr, 1902. ENGLAND: H. Casson, *An Introduction to Victorian Architecture,* London 1948; H. S. Goodhart-Rendel, *English Architecture since the Regency: An Interpretation,* London 1953; H.-R. Hitchcock, *Early Victorian Architecture in Britain,* vol. I–II, New Haven 1954; W. Randolph, *A Century of English Architecture,* London 1939; The Royal Institute of British Architects, *One Hundred Years of British Architecture, 1851–1951,* London 1951; R. Turnor, *Nineteenth Century Architecture in Britain,* London 1950. GERMANY: F. Schumacher, *Strömungen in deutscher Baukunst seit 1800,* Leipzig 1936. DENMARK: K. Millech, *Danske Arkitekturstrømninger 1850–1950* (*Danish Architectural Tendencies, 1850–1950*), Copenhagen 1952. SWEDEN: G. Lindahl, *Høgkyrkligt Lågkyrkligt Frikyrkligt i svensk arkitektur 1800–1950,* Stockholm 1955; R. Josephson, *Svensk 1800-tals arkitektur, "Arkitektur", 1922, appendix to Teknisk Tidskrift,* Stockholm, vol. LII, 1922.

DECORATIVE ART: GENERAL: R. Wellman, *Victoria Royal. The Flowering of a Style,* New York 1939. ENGLAND: M. Flower, *Victorian Jewellery,* London 1951; St. Tschudi Madsen, *Victoriansk Dekorativ Kunst* (*Victorian Decorative Art*), Nordenfjeldske Kunstindustrimuseums Årbok 1952 (Yearbook 1952), Trondheim 1953, pp. 9–92; N. Pevsner, *High Victorian Design,* London 1951; J. Steegman, *Consort in Taste,* London 1950. FRANCE: H. Clouzot, *Le style Louis-Philippe—Napoleon III,* Paris 1939; H. Clouzot, *Des Tuileries à Saint Cloud, l'Art décoratif du second empire,* Paris 1925. HOLLAND: H. Baaren, G. C. Schubad, *Het meubel en het interieur in de negentiende en twintigste eeuw,* Deventer 1951. AUSTRIA: M. Zweig, *Zweites Rokoko,* Vienna 1924.

It is easy to understand that the leading men of the age regarded developments with fear and contempt, and that in every country nearly all the periodicals dealing with arts and crafts worked intensely in order to break away from a historically-minded development. Thanks to their efforts a revival was ushered in, but the views of this pioneering and challenging generation are untenable today. As far as possible these events have to be considered objectively, avoiding the pitfall of regarding Historicism as a process of valueless imitation carried out by a few generations—it should be regarded as an independent expression of the age, as a phenomenon belonging to the realms of art history and which deserves to be seen in a wider context.

A study of the history of art through the ages shows that men have turned back to the styles of previous periods, and from Greek art to Roman art A.D. 500 runs a protracted development of classical waves, continuing through Byzantinism, the Carolingian renaissance, Ottonian renaissance, Proto-Renaissance, and right up to the Renaissance itself. All the way along our road we shall find constantly retrospective tendencies—e.g. in Louis XVI and the Empire during Classicism—the same phenomenon is reflected in every country: the form-language of previous ages is imitated, copied, and transformed.

Two external circumstances were destined to a special degree to increase this re-creation, *Einlebung*, and imitation of earlier styles in the nineteenth century: first of all the Industrial Revolution[2] and the changes in the social structure which accompanied it, and the fact that a great many everyday things were now being industrially produced, without the co-operation of an artist, for a large new purchasing public.

In the second place the great progress made by Medieval archeology and historical research during the Romantic period—which was later in the nineteenth century assisted by the results of research into the history of art—directly influenced the development of Historicism.

Historicism is both an indirect precondition which contributes to the rise of Art Nouveau, and furthermore it contributes purely formal elements, which fused with it.

2 F. D. Klingender, *Art and the Industrial Revolution,* London 1947.

THE GOTHIC REVIVAL[1]

The first return to a non-Classical style took place with the Gothic revival, a general European phenomenon[2] whose deepest roots are to be found in England, though in France too there is also a more or less continuous Medieval tradition.[3] The Gothic revival was developed in close association with Romanticism and the historical outlook, in time finding expression in a style which on the Continent is called neo-Gothic. The first period is remarkable for its fanciful and picturesque romanticism, after which the movement develops in the direction of a more scientifically archaeological phase, stimulated by an interest in restoration and—especially in the case of England—by the strong religious movements of the age.[4] The leading personality in this period was August Welby Pugin (1812–52). After the neo-Gothic style had dominated English church architecture in the eighteen-twenties and eighteen-thirties, Pugin and Barry built *the Houses of Parliament* in London, the most important of all non-ecclesiastical buildings erected in this style. It was started in 1836, but not completed till after Pugin's death.

Side by side with the development of Medieval research and the intensification of restoration, in the eighteen-forties, -fifties, and -sixties, the neo-Gothic flourished in ecclesiastical architecture all over Europe. It also played an important role in secular architecture, not least in official buildings—town halls, railway stations, fire stations, and the like.

About 1850 the Gothic revival underwent a change. After Karl Friedrich Schinkel (1781–1841) had introduced bricks in the *Bauakademie*

1 A. Addison, *Romanticism and the Gothic Revival,* New York 1938; K. Clark, *The Gothic Revival,* London 1928; C. L. Eastlake, *A History of the Gothic Revival,* London 1872.

2 St. Tschudi Madsen, Romantikkens Arkitektur. En almeneuropeisk oversikt med særlig henblikk på nygotikken. Thesis for M.A., University of Oslo, unpublished, the University Library, Oslo.

3 P. Léon, La Renaissance de l'architecture gothique, *La Revue de Paris,* Paris, July 1913, vol. XX, pp. 115–33.

4 The Church Building Society, founded 1818; the Oxford Movement, started in 1833; The Cambridge Camden Society, active from 1840, and shortly afterwards The Oxford Society for Promoting the Study of Gothic Architecture, with the Archbishop of Canterbury and John Ruskin as members.

(Building Academy) in Berlin in 1832–35, and after William Butterfield's (1814–1900) use of polychrome material and brick in All Saints' Church, Margaret Street, London, 1849–58, both these features became general. In addition to this we get John Ruskin's (1819–1900) literary activity about 1850, *The Seven Lamps of Architecture*, 1849, and *The Stones of Venice*, 1851–53. In the first of these he propounds his basic architectural ideas, while the second is a paean of praise to Gothic architecture in general and to Italian Gothic architecture in particular.

After the eighteen-fifties neo-Gothic became more polychrome, and one of the reasons for this is almost certainly the results of research into polychrome architecture, as well as the steadily increasing interest in Byzantine architecture at this time. At the same time neo-Gothic ideals, throughout Europe, were pushed further back in time.[5] From now on it was Norman and Byzantine architecture which provided models and sources of inspiration. The most important works of this period are Leon Vaudoyer's (1783–1872), *Notre Dame de Marseille* in Roman-Byzantine style, which was started in 1852 but not completed when he died; then we have Auguste Vaudremer's (1829–1914) churches in Paris—*St. Pierre de Montrouge*, completed in 1873, and *Notre Dame d'Ateuil*, completed ten years later. Not least important among the churches built in this style was Paul Abadier's (1812–84) *Sacré Coeur*, Paris, commenced in 1874 and not completed until after his death. In England the Roman-Catholic *Westminster Cathedral*, London, designed by John Bentley (1839–1902), commenced in 1895 and completed in 1903, and with its horizontal polychrome decoration resembling Vaudoyer's church in Marseilles, is the most important monument. Among the most important contributions made by the Germans in this sphere Heinrich von Schmidt's (1850–1928) work in Munich and Gabriel von Seidl's (1848–1913) Church of *St. Anna*, 1889–99, in the same town, are outstanding examples. Art historians and architects were now working hand in glove and the periods mentioned had just been added to the steadily increasing sphere of interest of art history.[6]

5 F. Schumacher also draws attention to this in his *Strömungen in deutscher Baukunst seit 1800*, Leipzig 1936, p. 68.

6 F. de Dartein, *Etude sur l'architecture Lombarde et sur les Origines d'Architecture Romano-Byzantine*, 1865.

In applied art the neo-Gothic wave passed quickly. In France it was over already in 1835–40, only surviving to any marked extent as a Restoration style in the work of Viollet-le-Duc (1814–79). In England it was strongly represented at the Great Exhibition in 1851, thanks to Pugin. The last important monument was George Street's (1824–81) *Law Courts* in London, 1868–74, but the style had already received its official *coup de grâce* when Sir George Gilbert Scott's (1811–78) neo-Gothic drawings for the *Foreign Office*, Whitehall, London, were rejected and Classical plans approved instead by the House of Commons in 1861.

But in the same year that the neo-Gothic style was dethroned from its position in profane architecture, its basic principles and its architectural doctrine—as formulated by Pugin and developed by Ruskin—made its appearance in a new form and acquired a new actuality. When young William Morris (1834–96) on a day in January 1856 entered the office of the Gothic revivalist, George Street, to commence his training as an architect, he met Philip Webb (1831–1915), who was three years his senior, and in these neo-Gothic surroundings a friendship was formed which was to result some years later in Webb's *The Red House*, 1859–60, and to the foundation in 1861 of the firm of Morris, Marshall, Faulkner and Co., Fine Art Workmen in Painting, Carving, Furniture and the Metals, whose object was to renew decorative art on a Medieval basis.

Morris's forerunners were Pugin and Ruskin. The basis of Pugin's architectural doctrine has been laid down in *The True Principles of Pointed Architecture*, 1841, where the author's views are set forth more clearly than they are in *Contrasts*.[7]

"*First, that there should be no features about a building which are not necessary for convenience, construction, or propriety; second, that all ornament should consist of enrichment of the essential construction of the building.*"—"In pure architecture the smallest detail should *have a meaning or serve a purpose;* and even the

A. Le Dion's extensive writings on the same subject in the 'sixties; in the 'eighties he edited *l'Architecture Romane*. Among others J. J. Bourassée and the German H. Otto, author of *Geschichte der romanischen Baukunst in Deutschland*, 1885.

7 Full title: *Contrasts; or a Parallel between the noble Edifices of the Fourteenth and Fifteenth Centuries, and Similar Buildings of the present day: shewing the Present Decay of Taste*, London 1836. Second edition in 1841; his theories are here more developed, especially those concerning social matters.

construction itself should *vary with material employed*, and the design should be adapted to the material in which they are executed."[8] He developed this doctrine on the basis of careful investigation of Gothic architecture, making not less than fifteen study tours on the Continent, and he summed up his own contribution in these words: "My writings, much more than what I have been able to do, have revolutionised the taste of England."[9]

Ruskin's architectural ideology conforms in part with Pugin's; in *The Seven Lamps of Architecture* he says *inter alia:* " . . . That building will generally be the noblest, which to an intelligent eye discovers the great secrets of its structure."[10]

His teaching contains more of ideologic philosophy, and is general in its application. Some of his most important ideas find expression in the chapter *The Nature of Gothic* in *The Stones of Venice*, where he has formulated three basic principles:

1. Never encourage the manufacture of any article not absolutely necessary in the production of which *invention* has no share.
2. Never demand an exact finish for its own sake, but only for some practical work or noble end.
3. Never encourage imitation or copying of any kind, except for the sake of preserving records of great works.

Young William Morris developed these ideas. What Ruskin's chapter on the *Nature of Gothic* meant to him can be understood from the way in which he expresses it in one of the very first of the 35 lectures he delivered in the years 1877–94.[11] This chapter of Ruskin's which proved so important to his contemporaries, was also one of the very first things printed by Morris in the Kelmscott Press in 1892.

8 A. W. Pugin, *True Principles of Pointed Architecture,* London 1841, p. 1.

9 Letter to John Hardman, Ph. B. Stanton, Some Comments on the Life and Work of Augustus Welby Northmore Pugin, *The Journal of the Royal Institute of British Architects,* vol. LX, 2, 1952, pp. 53 sq.

10 J. Ruskin, *The Seven Lamps of Architecture,* London 1849, chap. II, § 7.

11 W. Morris, The Decorative Arts and their Relation to Modern Life and Progress, lecture delivered before the Trades' Guild of Learning, 1878, published under the title The Lesser Arts, *Hopes and Fears for Art,* London 1882, p. 5.

Both in relation to Nature as a source of inspiration, in the struggle against the machine, against each and every form of imitation, and in relationship to genuineness of material, honesty in construction, the origin of art and the consideration of architecture as the Mother of all the arts, as well as the social aims and conditions of art—in every respect Morris was the bearer of these ideas of Ruskin's. As in the case of Ruskin his artistic views are founded on a belief in the Middle Ages. Furthermore, Morris's philosophy was based entirely on the joy of the creative process and the demand for honesty in production, with the very same love of the Middle Ages and its relationship to art and the artist. " . . . Today there is only one style of architecture on which it is possible to found a true living art . . . and that that *[sic]* style is Gothic Architecture."[12]

Viollet-le-Duc, enthusiastic admirer of the Gothic as he was, also formulated his ideas in a number of luminous lectures. With Gallic clarity and with the constructive ability of the trained architect, he submitted his rational principles and his programme in *Les Causes de la Décadence de l'Architecture.*[13] But like Pugin—and unlike Morris—he did not translate his principles into work which could remain as a pattern to others. On the other hand the influence of his writings can hardly be overestimated.

Though the main principles in the development of artistic theory from Pugin to Morris remained the same,[14] a very marked development took place in furniture-making and the decorative arts, stronger and more radical perhaps than in any other artistic genre at this time. If, for example, we consider the chair designed by Pugin for Windsor Castle, 1828–30,[15] with its mixture of Classicism and late Gothic, with its decoration applied in gold, or the enormous ten-foot cabinet which he designed for the Exhibition in 1851,[16] or even the simple table, about 1850,[17] (fig. 41), and

12 *Idem, Gothic Architecture,* lecture delivered 1889 for the Arts and Crafts Exhibition Society, London 1893, p. 58 sq.

13 E. E. Viollet-le-Duc, *l'Entretiens sur l'Architecture,* Paris 1863–72, vol. I, pp. 321–84.

14 Apart from Ruskin's social theories, which Morris developed further. A. Bøe, *From Gothic Revival to Functional Form. A Study in Victorian Theories of Design,* Oslo. In print.

15 H. Clifford Smith, *Buckingham Palace, Its Furniture, Decoration, and History,* London 1931, ill. p. 148; Victoria and Albert Museum, *Catalogue of an Exhibition of Victorian and Edwardian Decorative Arts,* London 1952, p. 14.

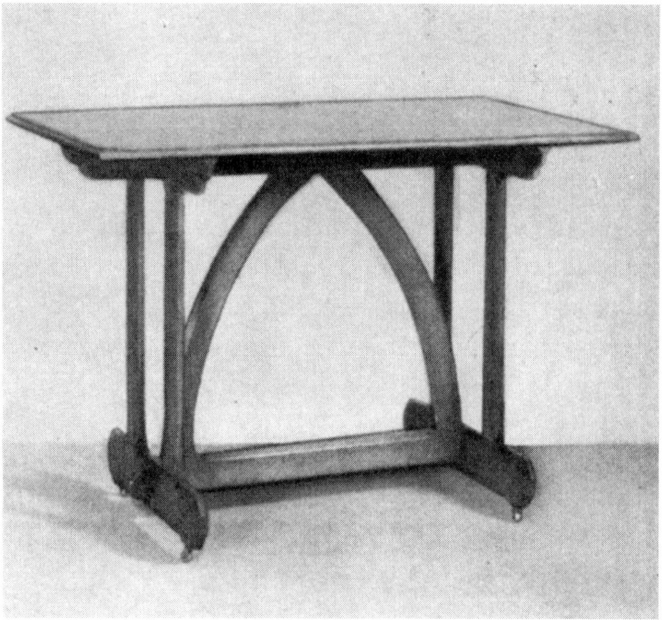

Fig. 41. Pugin: Table, oak.
About 1850.
Courtesy of Canon B. Morris. Victoria and Albert Museum photo. Crown Copyright reserved.

compare these with Webb's table from 1858–59[18] (fig. 42), we shall observe an essential difference.

The Middle Ages are reflected, not in the decoration, neither in the curve of an arch nor in any ornamental detail which has been glued or painted on, but in the simple and vigorous construction, the honest treatment of the material, a sparing use of decoration, and a general impression of solidity. There is still no proof that Morris designed furniture[19], but

16 H. Gibbs-Smith, *The Great Exhibition 1851,* London 1950, ill. p. 124, fig. 177; Victoria and Albert Museum, *op. cit.,* p. 14, No. C 5.

17 Probably made originally for Canon Luck, Victoria and Albert Museum, *op. cit.,* p. 14, No. C 4, Canon B. Morris.

18 Victoria and Albert Museum, *op. cit.,* p. 41, No. I 2. Dr. D. C. Wren, Kelmscott Manor, Lechlade. Said to be the first piece of furniture he ever designed. Originally in the possession of William Morris.

19 Mackail mentions that Morris made some sketches, J. W. Mackail, *The Life of William Morris,* I–II, London 1899, The World's Classic Ed., London 1950, p. 116. A. H. Mackmurdo says that the furnishing at 17 Red Lion Square was designed by Webb, A. H. Mackmurdo, The History of the Arts and Crafts Movement, chap. VI, William Morris and his Circle. Unpublished, kindyl lent by Miss C. McQueen. Morris' daughter, May Morris, relates that Webb took care of the furnishing of the interior, "and Morris helping with the planning of house and garden," M. Morris, *William Morris. Artist, Writer, Socialist,* I–II, Oxford 1936, vol. I, p. 13.

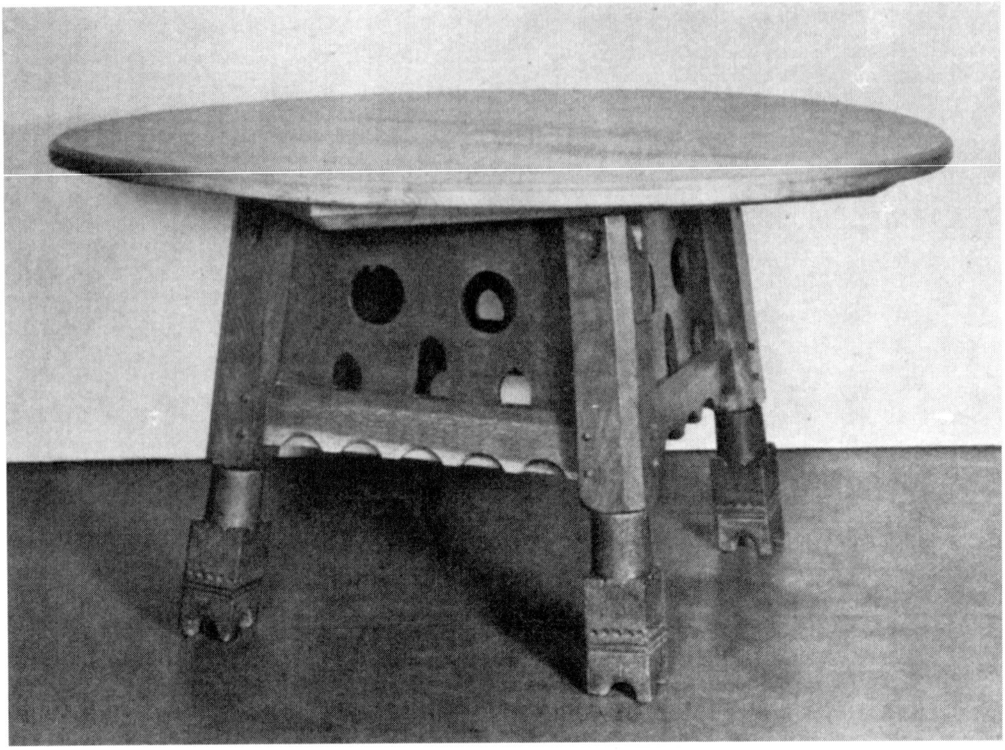

Fig. 42. Webb: Circular table, oak. 1858—59.
Courtesy of D. C. Wren. Victoria and Albert Museum photo. Crown Copyright reserved.

there can hardly be any doubt that furniture of this character was in his mind. In 1857 he settled in 17 Red Lion Square, London, where he was frequently visited by his friends Dante Gabriel Rossetti, Burne Jones, and Philip Webb during the years from 1857 to 1860. They have given us amusing descriptions of the interior fittings, and we know for example that the chairs were "such as Barbarossa might have sat in," and that there were "tables and chairs like incubi and succubi." Rossetti also speaks of a round table "as firm and heavy as a rock," and the general impression we get is quite clearly that the furniture was intensely medieval.[20]

Morris was in search of other values in the Middle Ages than those

20 J. W. Mackail, *The Life of William Morris,* I–II, London 1899, the World's Classic Ed., London 1950, pp. 116 sqq.

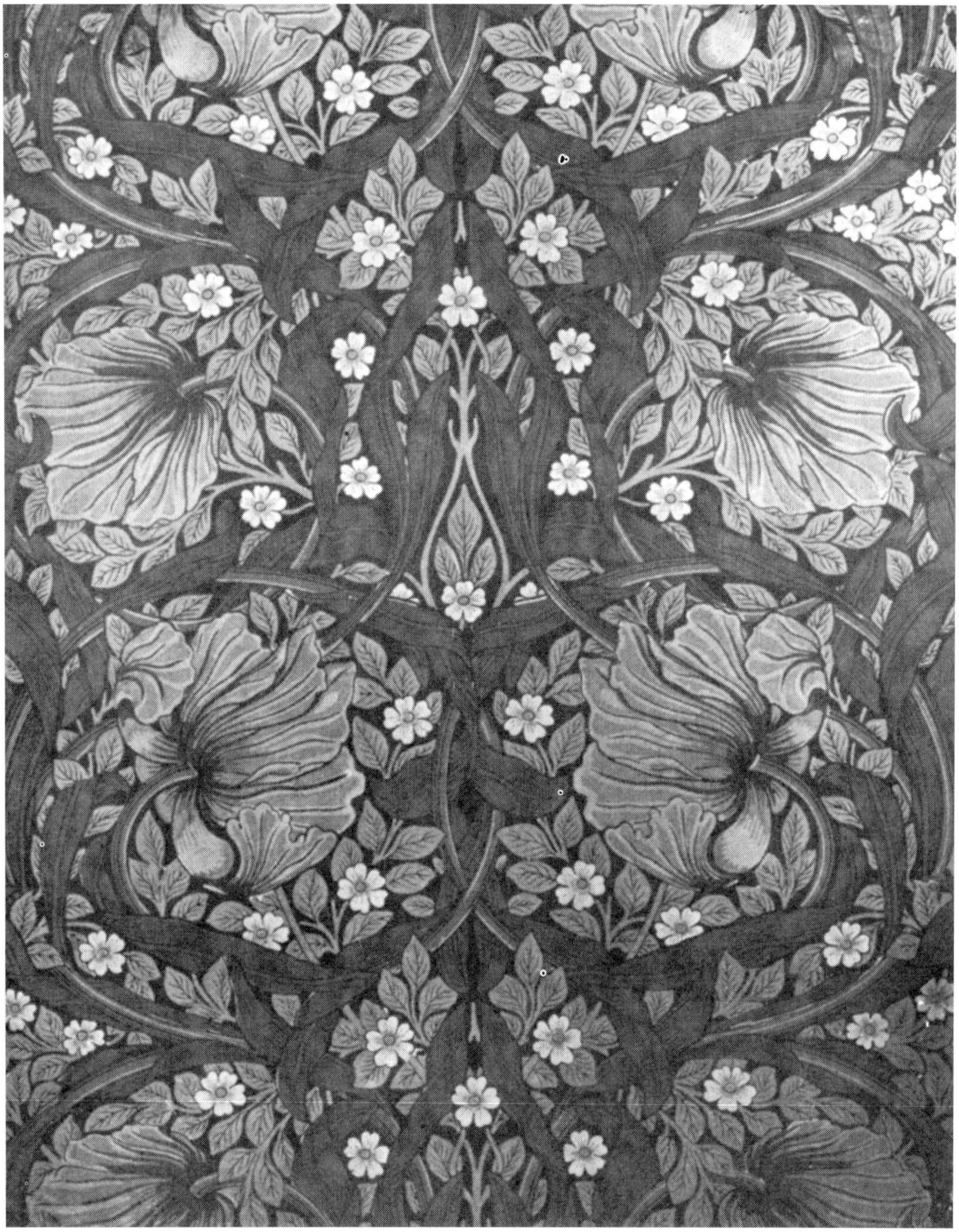

Fig. 43. Morris: "Pimpernel". Wallpaper. 1876.
Victoria and Albert Museum photo. Crown Copyright reserved.

sought by the adherents of neo-Gothic. He was not committed to a pursuit of more and more modern motifs, but strove to adapt himself to its spirit and re-create it through a more intimate contact between artist and artisan.

Morris has no formal importance as far as Art Nouveau is concerned. If we examine his wallpapers, which he started designing in 1861, and the textiles, with which he worked from 1879, we shall find that his two-dimensional art rests on three principles: 1. two-dimensional treatment of the motif, with only two main planes: the plane of the pattern and the neutral background plane. 2. large patterns, with a large interval between each repeat. 3. a quiet regular rhythm. As his rhythm always has the calm line of the acanthus, and is never irregular or whiplash (fig. 43), his art is always essentially different from Art Nouveau; even when his stalks run in *entrelac* or diagonally, they are no more like Art Nouveau than the advanced German pattern from 1836 (fig. 44).[21]

In England the three leading personalities of the Gothic revival were Pugin, Ruskin, and Morris; and it was largely due to Morris—who directly continued and developed their doctrine—that a revival occurred in English applied art. The Gothic revival, as developed by Morris, is the forerunner and the actual basis of the Arts and Crafts Movement: without this foundation of knowledge and understanding of the Middle Ages the further development of the movement would have been impossible, and it is in the ranks of the Arts and Crafts Movement that we find the proto-Art Nouveau artists. Among the men of the Gothic revival and the Arts and Crafts Movement we shall also encounter later on an attitude to Nature and a floral interest which coincides with that of the Art Nouveau artists.

From the point of view of formal analysis there is no inner connection between neo-Gothic and Art Nouveau, but the form-language of neo-Gothic occasionally fuses with that of Art Nouveau, as in some French designs for benches, 1898, where Art Nouveau merges both with neo-Gothic and neo-Norman[22]. In E. Bagués's furniture from the Paris Exhi-

21 *Vorbilder für Fabrikanten und Handwerker,* auf Befehl des Ministers für Handel, Gewerbe und Bauwesen, herausgegeben von der technischen Deputation für Gewerbe, vol. II, Fortsetzung. Berlin 1836. Contributors: Schinkel, Mauch, Boetcker. The author is here indebted to Dr. Elias Cornell.

22 Julius Hoffmann Jr., *Der Moderne Stil,* vol. I, 1899, pl. 100, figs. 1–5.

Fig. 44. German pattern. 1836.
Courtesy of E. Cornell.

bition of 1900[23] (figs. 45–46) we also encounter a mixture of Norman arches and Gothic pillars à la Art Nouveau. In the Nancy school we likewise find this fusion, as in Emile André (1871–1933) and his Maison Huot, 92 Quai Claude Lorrain, Nancy, 1902–03 (fig. 3). This purely external similarity was, in France as well, an expression of a more profound interest in the Middle Ages. We also come across it in the writings of Viollet-le-Duc, but it finds its expression, too, in the younger generation, among the

23 Cat. No. 1995–1900, 1993–1900. Victoria and Albert Museum.

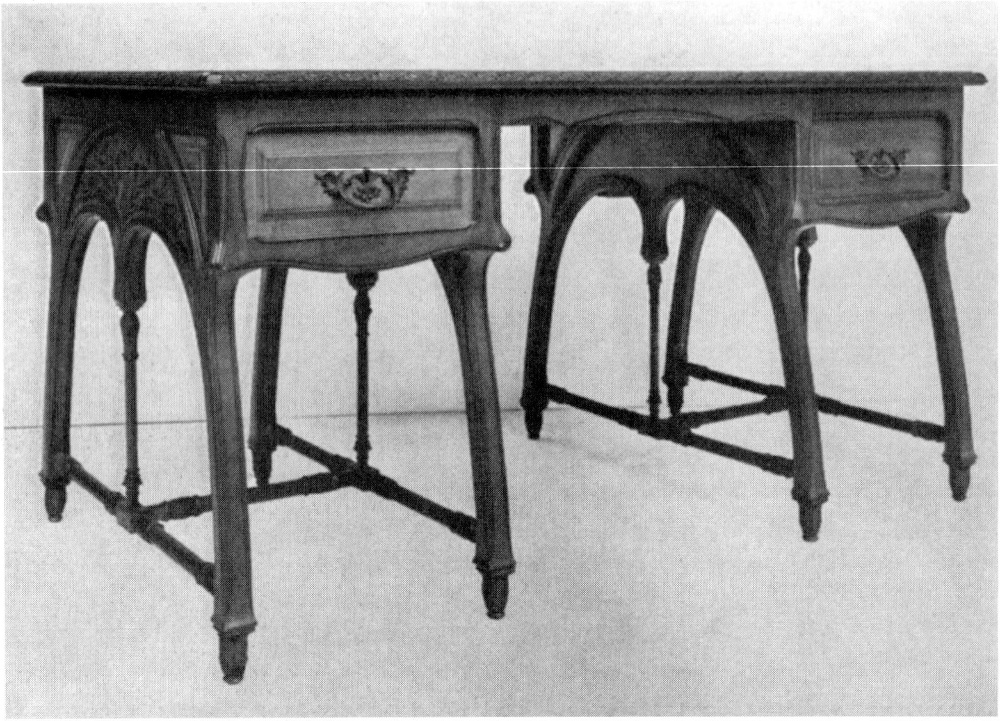

Fig. 45. Bagués: Writing table. Pearwood with mountings of gilted brass.
Victoria and Albert Museum. Crown Copyright reserved.

pure Art Nouveau artists. In 1895 Eugène Grasset (1841–1917) writes that a return must be made to the Middle Ages, not to copy it, but that it is necessary to "*étudier le Moyen-Age pour en tirer le bon sens . . .*"[24] F.-R. Carabin and Ch. Carpentier also express the same attitude.[25]

In Belgium we find it in the work of Victor Horta, where his neo-Gothic form-language in iron enters into a sort of marriage of convenience, on a constructive basis, with Art Nouveau.[26]

24 H. Nocq, *Tendances Nouvelles. Enquête sur l'evolution des industries d'Art.* Paris 1896, p. 14. The questions for the *enquête* were published in the *Journal des Artistes,* Paris, September 1894. "study the Middle Ages in order to extract their common-sense . . ."

25 *Ibid.,* pp. 19, 43.

26 6 Rue Paul-Emile Janson; 224 Avenue Louise; Maison de Peuple, Place van de Velde; all of them in Brussels.

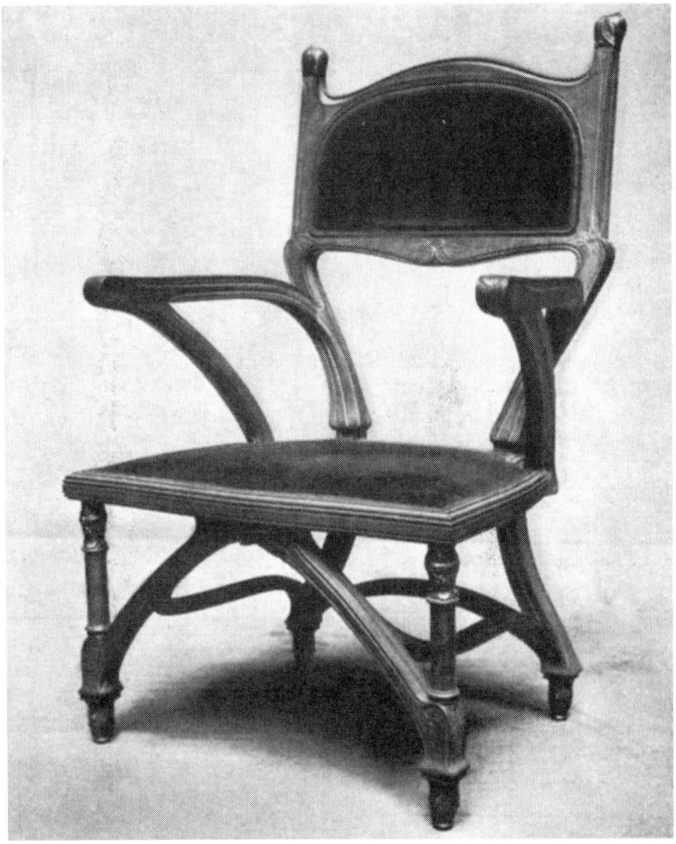

Fig. 46. Bagués: Chair.
Pearwood.
Victoria and Albert Museum.
Copyright reserved.

Van de Velde speaks in 1901 of the importance of Gothic to the renaissance in applied arts, and points to the main difference between the English and Belgian conception of the medieval style. According to the Belgian, the English artists were only concerned with the external beauty of Gothic, while his own countrymen were "von der schöpferischen Seite ihrer Schönheit, von ihrem hohen, und reiner Vernunft entspringendem und offensichtlichem Grundgedanken eingenommen."[27]

A sentence of this kind could only have been uttered in the heat of battle, when it was impossible to enjoy a complete survey, and may be explained by the somewhat self-conscious, and not entirely unassuming,

27 Van de Velde, *Renaissance im Kunstgewerbe,* Berlin 1901, Neue Ausgabe, p. 72, para 2; "entranced by the creative side of its beauty, springing from its pure and lofty reason and readily apparent basic idea."

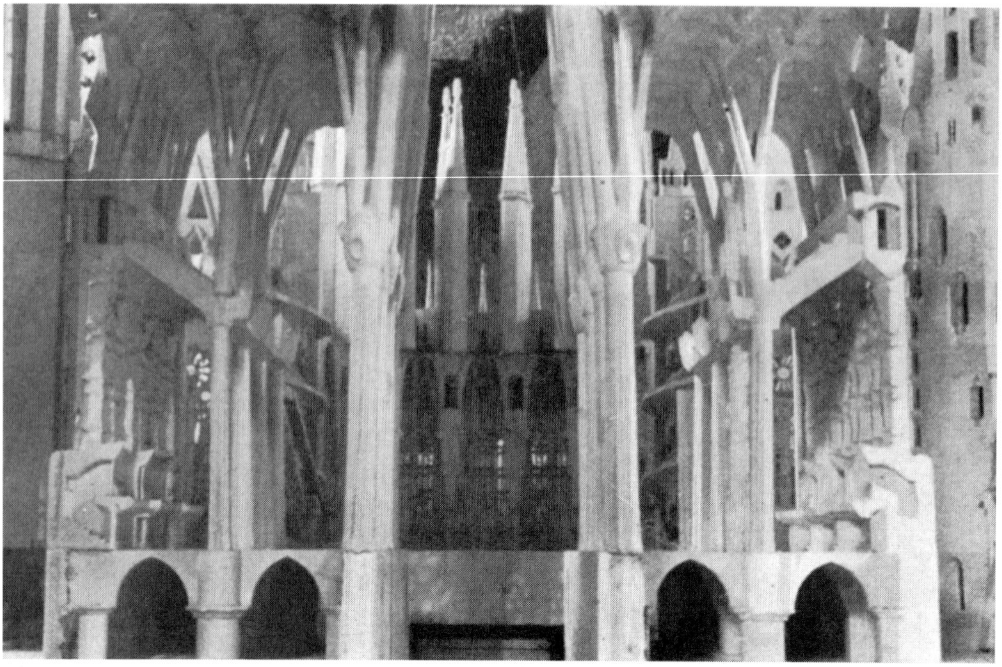

Fig. 47. Gaudí: Model for Sagrada Familia, Barcelona, 1882—1900.
Courtesy of Andreas Bugge, Oslo.

attitude which van de Velde maintained at that time towards himself and the "veldescher stil." But it does give us a clear idea of the importance of Gothic.

In England, where the Gothic revival was so firmly established, the situation was somewhat different. We hardly ever find a similar fusion, and the natural explanation is that Art Nouveau never really took root there, and that the principles of the Gothic revival were fully applied in the Arts and Crafts Movement. Meanwhile, we shall see later on how the last stylistic offshoot of the medieval movement—the Celtic style—coincided with Art Nouveau in Great Britain.

As far as Germany is concerned, K. Scheffler, the expert on the nineteenth century, goes comparatively far in his attitude to the influence of Gothic on Art Nouveau, and maintains that "Dieses sich gegenseitige Durchdringen von Formen des 15. und 18. Jahrhunderts gibt dem Jugend-

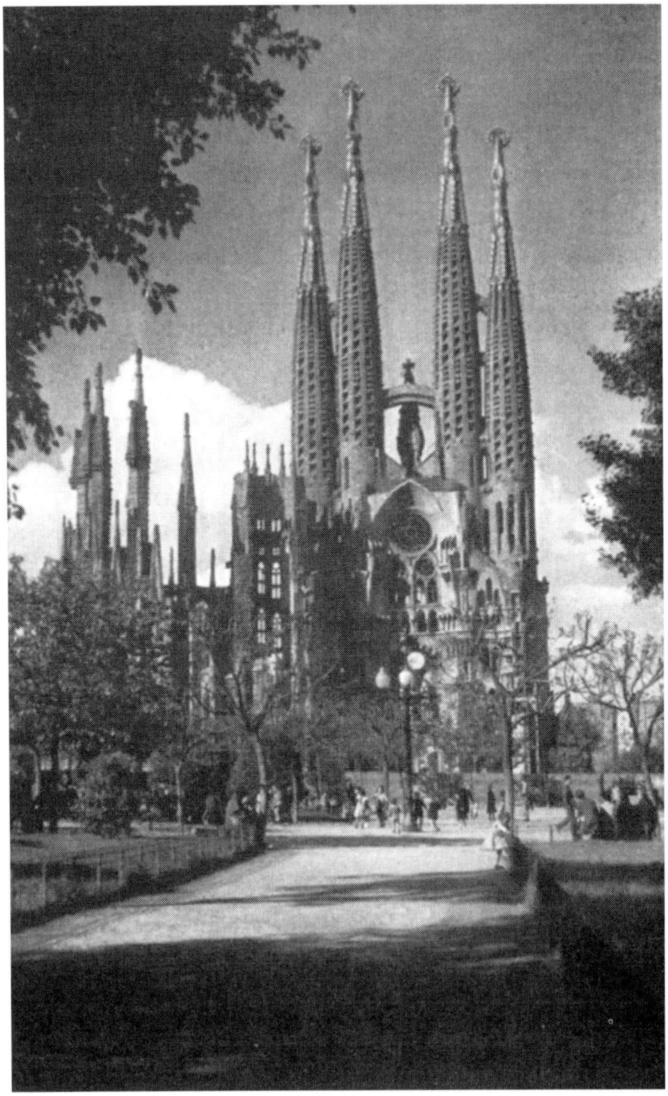

Fig. 48. Gaudí: Sagrada Familia, Barcelona, 1882—1900.
Courtesy of Andreas Bugge, Oslo.

stil-Ornament jedoch etwas Dezidiertes."[28] In this connection he is thinking more of the Baroque form-conception of late-Gothic than of any direct or constructively-conditioned association with Art Nouveau. As early as

28 K. Scheffler, *Verwandlungen des Barocks in der Kunst des Neunzehnten Jahrhunderts,* Vienna 1947, p. 191. "This mutual penetration of the forms of the 15th and 18th centuries gives the Jugend style nevertheless a decided quality."

1899 he pronounced: "Auch die Gotik ist ein Element van de Veldescher Kunst," and what is even more interesting, is van de Velde's verification of it.[29]

Antonio Gaudí y Cornet (1852–1926) on the other hand fits in perfectly in this context. In 1882 the foundation-stone of his masterpiece, *La Sagrada Familia,* was laid in Barcelona.[30] The crypt was built between 1884 and 1887, the apse from 1891 to 1893, while most of the facade was ready by 1900. The church has not yet been completed (figs. 47, 48, 49, 68). This building represents a free and imaginative remodelling of Gothic. Here the inner similarity of form which exists between late Gothic and Baroque rings out unmistakably in neo-Gothic and neo-Baroque. Gaudí is in reality the only artist who has completely fused these very different style-elements, and succeeded in producing a consistent unity.

André Calzada mentions Ruskin's doctrines in connection with Gaudí's architecture, and adds that he also had constructive ideas in mind, and sometimes succeeds in getting near the intentions of Viollet-le-Duc.[31]

J. J. Sweeney supports both these assumptions,[32] and in this connection it is interesting to hear what Gaudí himself says of Gothic: "The Gothic is sublime, but incomplete; it is only a beginning, stopped outright by the deplorable renaissance . . . Today we must not imitate, or reproduce, but *continue* the Gothic, at the same time rescuing it from the flamboyant."[33]

*

It would be wrong to over-estimate the importance of the Gothic revival in connection with the origins of the Art-Nouveau style, but of the many concomitant factors it is the one which goes furthest back, and indirectly it plays a very fundamental role, while its ideas and search for sound principles in many ways coincide with those of the new style. The Art Nouveau architects joined the Gothic revivalists in their search for new trends in architecture and construction. It may be assumed that this

29 See notes 17 and 18, next chapter.

30 P. Boada, *El templo de la Sagrada Familia,* Barcelona 1929. For the best illustrations: A. Cirici-Pellicer, *La Sagrada Familia,* Barcelona 1950; *Expiatory Temple of the Holy Family,* Barcelona 1952.

31 A. Calzada, *Historia de la Arquitectura Española,* Barcelona, 1933, pp. 418 sqq.

32 J. J. Sweeney, Antonio Gaudí, *The Magazine of Art,* New York, May 1953, pp. 195–205.

33 Quoted by Marius-Ary Leblond, Gaudí's French admirer, J. J. Sweeney, *loc. cit.,* p. 196.

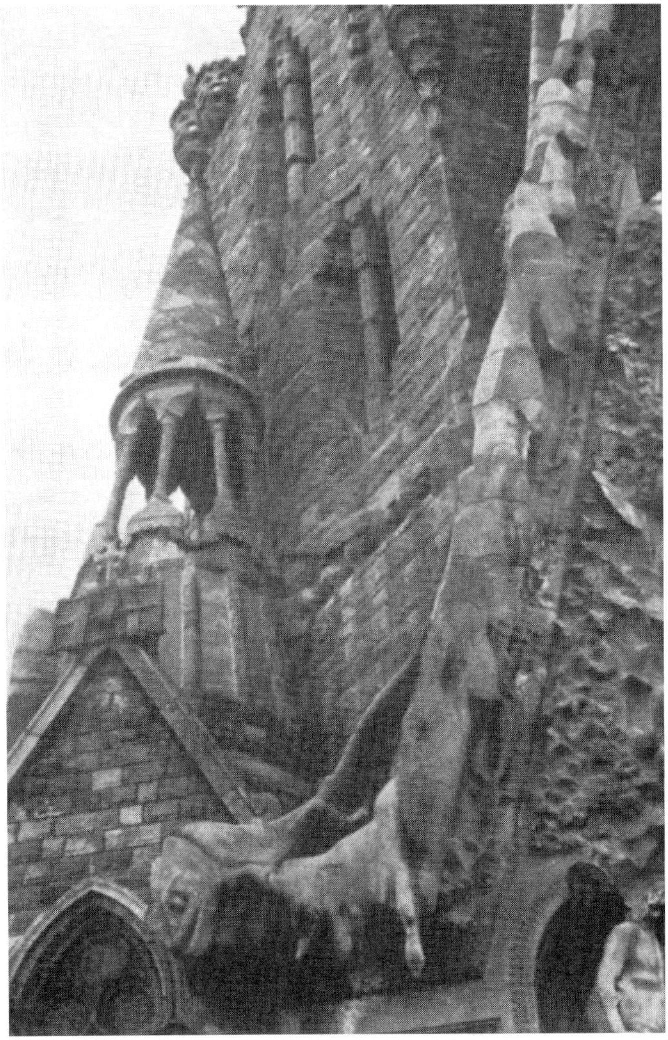

Fig. 49. Gaudí: Detail from Sagrada Familia, Barcelona. 1882—1900.
Courtesy of Andreas Bugge, Oslo.

explains how Gothic features fuse with Art Nouveau, mostly in constructive parts, and often in iron.[34] Though there may not be any deeper common features, from the point of view of formal analysis, the Gothic revival is of fundamental importance in understanding the age, both the Arts and Crafts Movement, the Modern Movement, and Art Nouveau.

[34] See chapter on Iron.

The generation which stood on the threshold of the new century recognised this. In 1893 Morris's pupil John Sedding (1838–91) says: "Our Gothic Revival has been a solid, not a trifling transient piece of Art History. It has enriched the crafts by impetus and initiation. It has endued two generations of art-workers with passion. It has been the health-giving spark—the ozone of modern art."[35] In the columns of *The Craftsman* and *The Studio* at about the turn of the century we find the same: " . . . it is through the Gothic Movement with all its failings that we have come to a newer and better class of work."[36]

NEO-ROCOCO[1]

Among the other period styles of Historicism neo-Rococo is the oldest. In its essence and expression it differs widely from the Gothic revival: while the latter was a movement which arose in the same way as neo-Classicism in the latter half of the eighteenth century, and like it became an expression of a deep-rooted movement and a fresh cultural outlook, neo-Rococo was not a movement in that sense of the word: it was a stylistic expression of a search for something new—a fashion which flourished from approximately 1835–40 until it was superseded by Napoleon III's classicism in the 1860's.

And yet its appearance was neither entirely sudden nor entirely accidental. Just as in its origins Rococo is a French style, so likewise is neo-Rococo. When Louis XVIII assumed power with the Restoration (1815–24), there was a genuine Bourbon on the throne, a prince who was the grandson of the Rococo king Louis XV, and who had grown up in Versailles in the most typical Rococo milieu. It was hardly surprising that, as a reaction

35 J. D. Sedding, Our Art and Industries, *Art and Handicraft,* London 1893, p. 142.

36 "Mr. G.," The Revival of English Architecture, *The Studio,* vol. VII, 1896, p. 24. In *The Craftsman,* vol. I, No. 6, 1902, under the title *The Gothic Revival,* by an anonymous author: "The final lesson of the Gothic Revival has not yet been taught, for the influence of the movement is still felt wherever there is an impetus towards an art which shall be maintained by the encouragement, the wise criticism and the love of the whole body social."

1 M. Zweig, *Zweites Rokoko,* Vienna 1924.

against Napoleon's Empire—and as though to emphasise that an old tradition was coming into its own,—he also reintroduced Rococo. The oldest French neo-Rococo furniture is from this period.[2]

Just as French influence dominated the Austrian Rococo, so it did in the case of neo-Rococo.[3] In her book *Zweites Rococo* Marianne Zweig refers to neo-Rococo ornaments from 1830,[4] and also mentions that occasionally one comes across objects which, though belonging to the Classical period, are unmistakably Rococo.[5] This is in itself quite natural, and is merely due to time-lag. Similar trends undoubtedly apply in other countries.[6]

In the case of Germany the Biedermeier style had already developed a form which deviated markedly from austere Classicism, and forms a smoother transition to neo-Rococo.

Speaking quite generally it may be said that neo-Rococo gives way to neo-Classicism in the eighteen-sixties and to neo-Renaissance in the eighteen-seventies, to reappear a second time in the nineteenth century, in a somewhat coarser and more violent form-language, together with the neo-Baroque of the eighteen-eighties and eighteen-nineties.

Neo-Rococo contained form-elements far more favourable to a combination with Art Nouveau than the neo-Gothic. It shows a plastic treatment of the whole as well as of the details, and often a well-nigh bombastic fashioning of each separate element. It lacks the elegance of Rococo, but has the same sense of the asymmetrical, sometimes in the details and at times in the whole.[7]

Asymmetry is one of the essential features of Art Nouveau, and it is not unlikely that this search for outer balance combined with asymmetry of composition, may in part be due to the influence of neo-Rococo. However,

2 Information given by M. Raymond Koechlin, Union Centrale des Arts Décoratifs, Paris, to M. Zweig. M. Zweig, *op. cit.*, p. 17, ill. of a fauteuil and a settee in neo-Rococo from the Restoration.

3 M. Zweig, *op. cit.*, p. 4.

4 *Ibid.*, p. 7, ill. p. 8.

5 *Ibid.*, p. 4.

6 The English characteristic neo-Rococo objects in the Victoria and Albert Museum, Cat. No. 472–73/1864, M.26–26a/1943, 5718–5718a/1901, 62/1905, are all before 1820. Whether they are late Rococo or early neo-Rococo need not be discussed here.

7 A more precise analysis of the difference between Rococo and neo-Rococo may be found in M. Zweig, *op. cit.*, p. 19, St. Tschudi Madsen, C. Hopstock, *Stoler og Stiler*, Oslo 1955, pp. 123–25.

the most important reason is probably the asymmetry of Japanese work. Just as the Orient had been one of the main sources of inspiration for Rococo, so it was to be for Art Nouveau. It may be said, therefore, that, as far as asymmetry was concerned, Japan influenced Art Nouveau both directly and indirectly. We shall later deal with its direct importance, while the indirect may be said to have come through Rococo and neo-Rococo.

In as much as Rococo and neo-Rococo both reached the finest flower of their fruition in France, it seems reasonable to trace the most important influence of neo-Rococo on Art Nouveau to this cultural area.

It is in Nancy that we find the most intimate connection between neo-Rococo and Art Nouveau. Nancy is the capital of the ancient county of Lorraine, and under Counts François and Leopold the town was lavishly decorated in the eighteenth century, though it was not until the arrival of Stanislas Leszczynski (reign 1735–66)—*le bien faisant*—that Nancy really acquired its peculiar beauty and architectural greatness. In the artistic regime of the former Polish King, Emmanuel Héré (1698–1771) was allowed to give free reign to his talents, and some of France's noblest Rococo squares were designed by him, while some of the outstanding grille-works of the eighteenth century took shape around Lamour's fountains—all created in honour of the Rococo king.

It is hardly surprising that neo-Rococo should have established itself here, and it is easy to understand why the artists who lived and worked here should carry on the proud traditions of their native town. Subsequently when the artistic revival and flowering took place in the eighteen-nineties with the rise of the Nancy school, the motifs of neo-Rococo in their turn made their appearance, fusing with the form-elements of the new style.

Emile Gallé is the creative force and founder of the Nancy school, reviving the artistic life of Nancy on foundations of Nature, and with Nature as his source of inspiration. But neo-Rococo was also to be a concomitant element, having just come into fashion in the eighteen-eighties and -nineties for the second time. In one of his very earliest works we find Rococo influences,[8] though these were to find clearer and more varied expression

[8] Cabinet in the possession of Madame Perdrizet-Gallé, Nancy; not dated, but said to be one of his first works. Information given to the author April 1953.

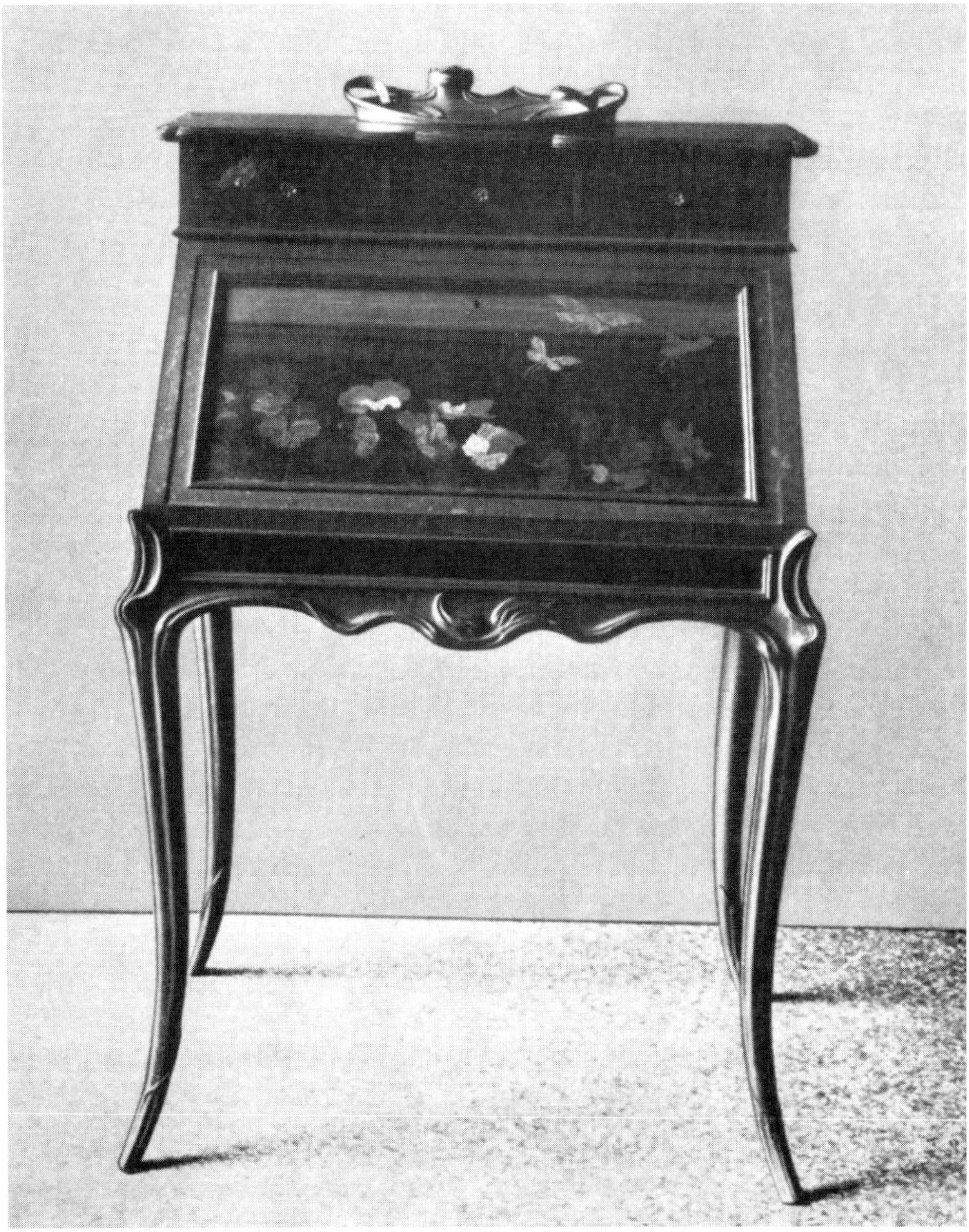

Fig. 50. Gallé: Lady's writing table. Nut with marquetry of various woods. 1900.
Det Danske Kunstindustrimuseum, Copenhagen. Copyright reserved.

at a subsequent date. This is perhaps most evident in the lady's *écritoire* from 1900[9] (fig. 50). In its elegant and frail effect it is Rococo, and certain parts, especially the lower section with the legs and the undulating lines, also remind us instinctively of Rococo. A detail like the flame-motif in the middle of the top rail, with its asymmetry and its C-shape, is also an imaginative re-creation of Rococo. The upper part of the desk on the other hand is more traditional in appearance—being rectilinear and having narrow mouldings. But there is no part that leaves us in any doubt that this is Art Nouveau—and a product of the Nancy school: the soft, curly features do not belong to the Rococo, and the inlay work with its plant and butterfly motifs immediately proclaims that this piece of furniture was made in Lorraine. The quality of the inlay and its very nature are such that it can only have been the work of Emile Gallé.

Another of the leading furniture designers of the Nancy school, Louis Majorelle, also reveals features from the magnificent and somewhat ponderous style of his native town. The two styles which were dominant in French furniture design in the eighteen-eighties and eighteen-nineties were Louis XV and furthermore a more Classic trend of Louis XVI or Napoleon III—ignoring for the moment the neo-Renaissance aspect of the dining-room suite. Majorelle worked in both these styles[10]—this came quite naturally to him as his father, Auguste Majorelle, founded his workshop in 1860, and his son worked here, chiefly reproducing period furniture.[11] But as was only reasonable it was with Rococo that he worked most before passing over to Art Nouveau.[12] As he continued working in Art Nouveau, he introduced more and more of the features of Rococo, and there is something of the weight and pounderousness of Louis XV in his *Nénuphars* (fig. 2), something of the same delight in ornament to be found in all the brass fittings, as well as a touch of Louis XV rhythm in the legs. The Rococo

9 Cat. no. 1023.1900. Det Danske Kunstindustrimuseum, Copenhagen.

10 Photographs of his furniture in la Musée des Beaux Arts, Nancy, Nos. 279, 404, and 136. All pre-1900.

11 Paul Juyot, *Louis Majorelle. Artiste décorateur-maître ébéniste,* 1926, pp. 2–3. Information also given by Louis Majorelle's son, Jean Majorelle, to the author, April 1953.

12 E.g. J. Hoffmann, *Der Moderne Stil,* Stuttgart 1899, vol. I, pl. 95, fig. 4. See also Les Meubles de Louis Majorelle, *La Lorraine,* vol. XIX, 1901, pp. 74–80. Information also given by Jean Majorelle to the author, April 1953.

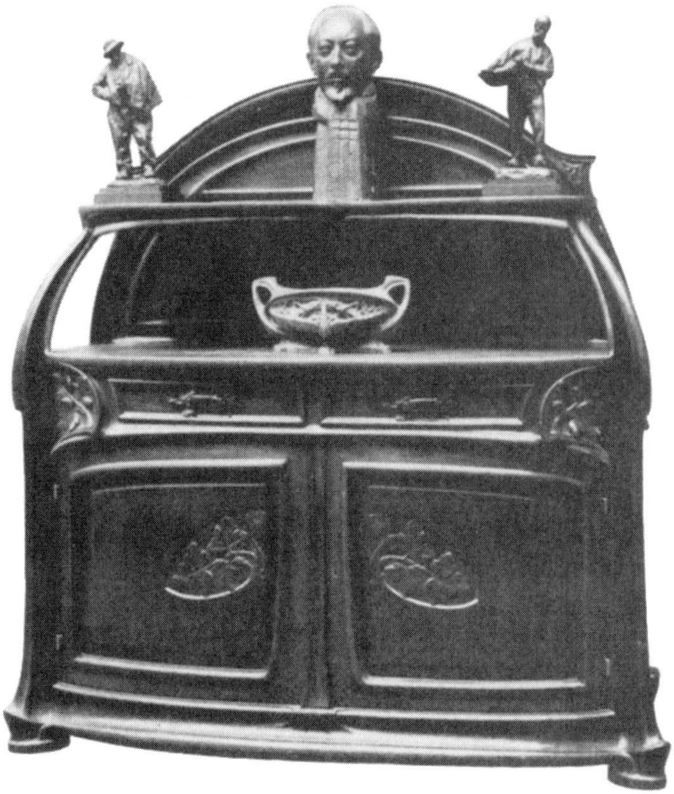

Fig. 51. Vallin: Sideboard. Mahogany. About 1901.
Musée des Beaux-Arts, Nancy. Copyright reserved.

elements could hardly have been less directly used, but sometimes we find a relic of period left—a suggestion rather than an imitation,—sometimes only a Rococo-like groove which usually runs along legs and edges.

Rococo or neo-Rococo features are also encountered in the work of other designers from the Nancy school: Eugène Vallin's furniture[13] (fig. 51) is in its entire conception so markedly Art Nouveau-neo-Rococo, even though we miss the flowers and the C-motifs. Vallin also worked a great deal with Rococo during his earlier years, and among other things he carried out a certain amount of restoration work for *les Monuments Historiques.*[14] Rococo features can be found even in the work of the less-

13 Musée de l'Ecole de Nancy, Galeries Poirel. Catalogue: *Ville de Nancy Galeries Poirel. Musée de l'Ecole de Nancy,* Nancy 1935.

14 Information given by Eugène Vallin's son, Auguste Vallin, to the author, April 1953.

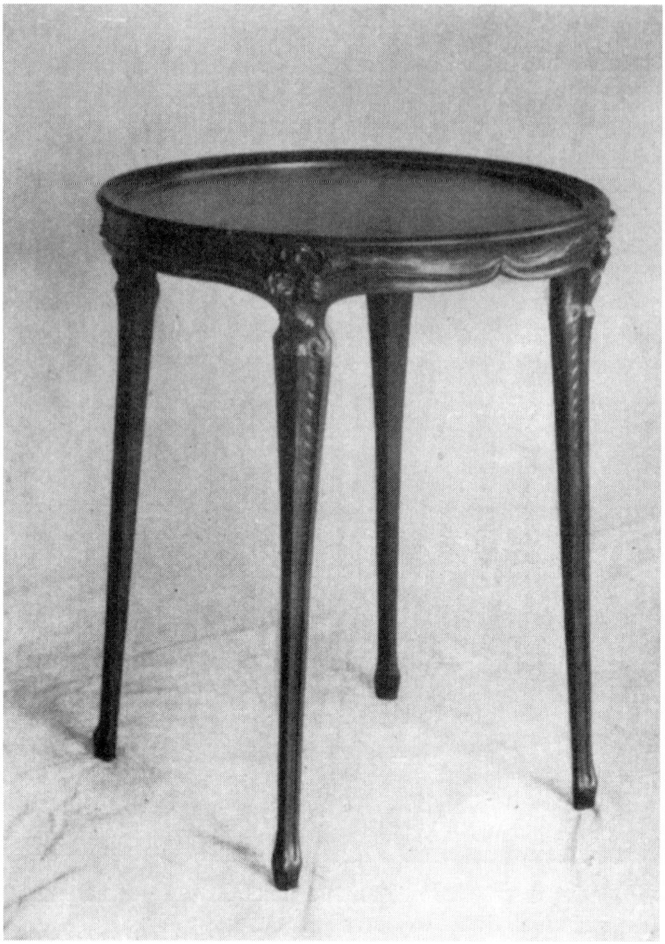

Fig. 52. E. André: Table. Probably mahogany. 1900. Courtesy of Jacques André.

famous architects, as in 24 Rue Lionnois, Maison Bergeret, designed by Weisenburger round about the year 1900. The leading architect of the Nancy school, Emile André, shows the traditional features in a table from 1900[15] (fig. 52), but at the same time we notice how the undulations of Art Nouveau have fused with the details. The chair, also from 1900[16] (fig. 53), is one of the very best examples of how Art Nouveau has merged

15 Photographs given by Emile André's son, Jacques André, to the author, April 1953. Dated negatives in his archives.

16 As note 15.

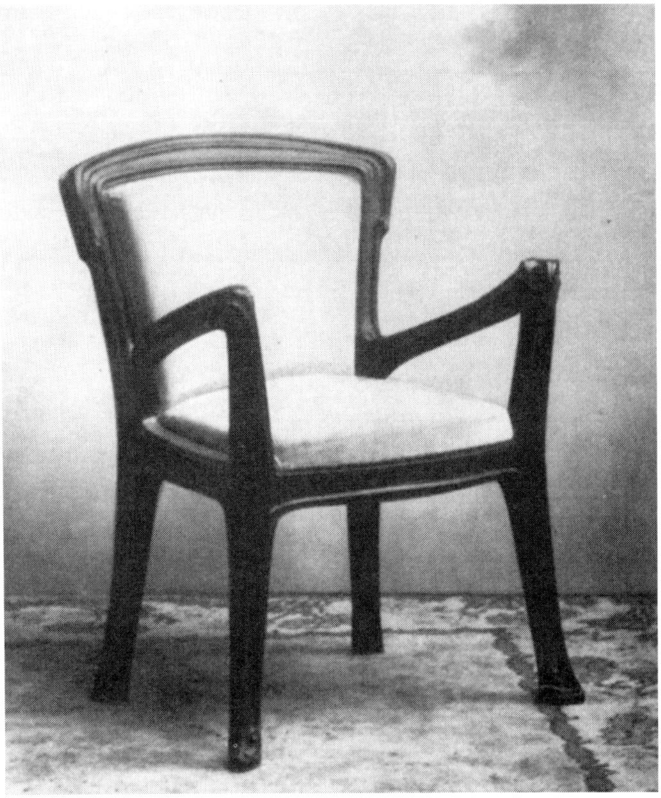

Fig. 53. E. André: Chair. Probably mahogany. 1900.
Courtesy of Jacques André.

completely with the Rococo-neo-Rococo tradition. This chair in an amazing way combines power and weight with elegance, and can be placed side by side with the best that French furniture designers achieved in the Art-Nouveau style.

In the general conception of form and interior there is an obvious parallel between Rococo and Art Nouveau. It is not always so easy to put one's finger on the various reasons—to a very large extent this is purely a matter of feeling—but we have for example Art Nouveau's predilection for the lighter colours and its pastel shades, together with its frequent use of flowers, such as we see in Nancy, especially in the work of Gallé. However, a more essential agreement is to be found in Art Nouveau's introduction of a unified conception of interior, such as occurred under Rococo.

In Paris and in Belgium the neo-styles never played the same role in determining form as the Rococo did in Nancy—these styles were merely loosely related to Art Nouveau. But in the work of Victor Horta we constantly find neo-Rococo features in the detail. The fireplace in the dining-room for A. Solvay, 1900 (fig. 22), is almost Rococo, but fits in beautifully, even though the room has been furnished in a consistent Art Nouveau style, down to the smallest detail. A feature of this kind shows that these two styles had a common conception of form, for no other style could so easily have been adapted to this interior.

Already in 1899 K. Scheffler drew attention to Rococo's importance to Art Nouveau, and in the *Deutsches Wochenblatt* he wrote: "Es bedarf aufmerksamer Augen, um das Rokoko durch die Werke der Modernen und vor allem durch van de Veldes Kunst spielen zu sehen; hat man es jedoch bemerkt, so wird es unabweisbar, und man freut sich dann, dass die Tradition den modernen architektonischen Künsten nicht fehlt," adding "Auch die Gotik ist ein Element van de Veldescher Kunst. Wiederum eine Tradition. Aber im Gegensatz zur ersten, ganz bewusst angewandt."[17]

This view agrees entirely with the conclusion already arrived at, and it is worth noting van de Velde's own comment to Scheffler's observations: "Dies ist richtig, es ist besonders richtig für das, was über den Geist der gotischen Kunst gesagt wurde . . . ."[18]

In the house in the Boulevard Berthier, Paris, designed by X. Schollkopf for the popular music-hall singer of the eighteen-nineties Yvette Guilbert,[19] (fig. 54), we find one of the most amusing mixtures not only of neo-Rococo and Art Nouveau, but also of neo-Gothic. Here we have characteristically Gothic pillars entwined by plants and flowers, here too we find typically Rococo frills and undulating—even rippling—C-motifs, and a host of asymmetric devices—all half-fused in a gliding floating Art

17 *Deutschen Wochenblatt,* 1899, p. 408. "Sharp eyes are required to see the Rococo behind the works of the moderns, and above all in the art of van de Velde; once it has been spotted, however, it is undeniable, and one is glad that the tradition of modern architectural art does not fail," . . . "Gothic too is an element in the art of van de Velde. Once again a tradition, but, in contrast to the first, consciously applied."

18 H. van de Velde, *Renaissance im Kunstgewerbe,* Berlin 1901, Neue Ausgabe, p. 96. "This is right, it applies especially to what has been said about Gothic art . . ."

19 Ch. Saunier, l'Hotel de Mme Yvette Guilbert, *l'Art Décoratif,* vol. III, part 1, 1900–01, pp. 190–97. Information also given to the author by H. Bugge Mahrt.

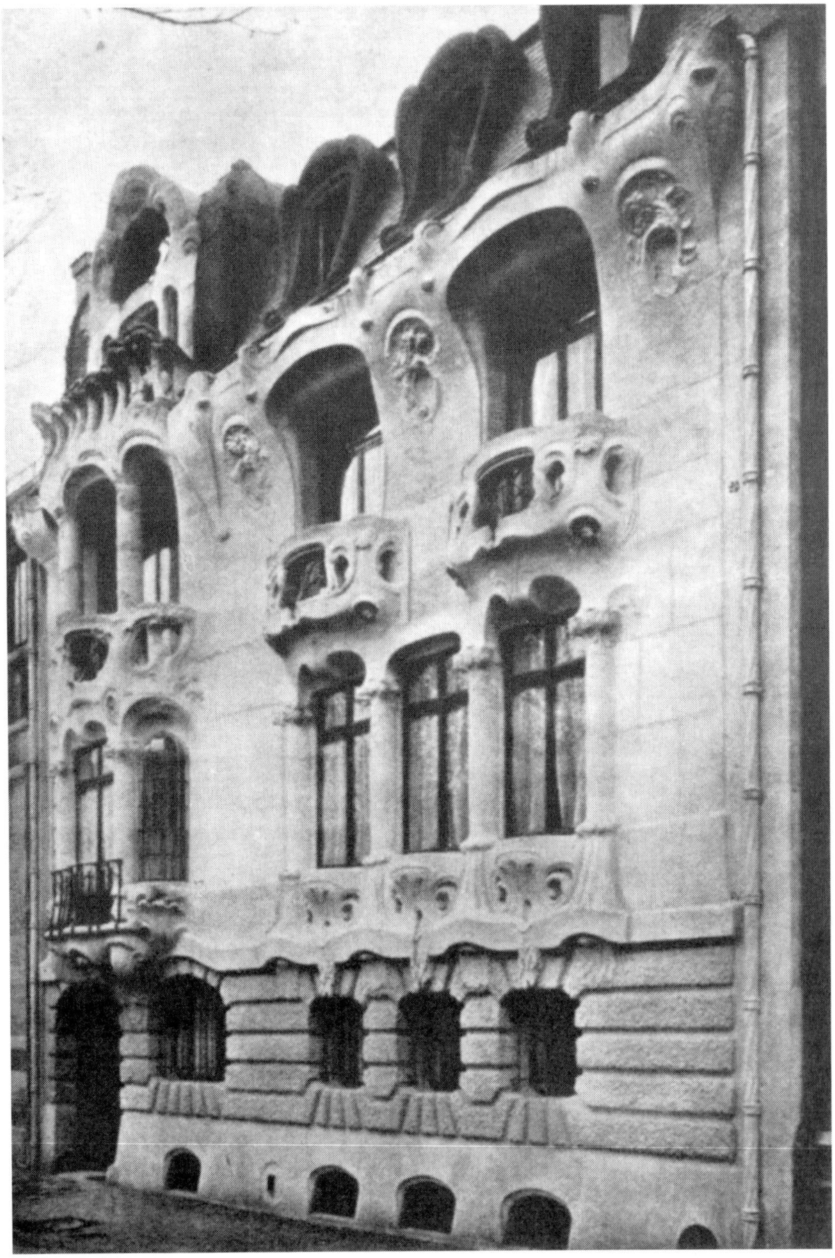

Fig. 54. Schollkopf: Hotel Madame Guilbert, 23 bis Boulevard Berthier, Paris. 1900. Pulled down.

Nouveau rhythm. Art Nouveau is most characteristically represented in the windows of the top floor. Yvette Guilbert's house has a facade in which every style plays its own instrument with wanton abandon—and yet orchestrated to produce an Art Nouveau symphony. The result is a music-hall turn featuring an architectural can-can.

But this house also contains elements of another of the stylistic trends of the eighteen-eighties and eighteen-nineties. The details are admittedly neo-Rococo cast in the style of Art Nouveau, but as a whole the facade, architecturally speaking, is an expression of neo-Baroque, with a pronounced light-and-shade effect, with its deep niches and projecting balconies, its rustic plinth, and a roof of asymmetrical design. Apart from all this the house has precisely the plastic and dynamic effect of contrast which is so typical of neo-Baroque. This conception of form far exceeds what we have seen of the plastic conception of neo-Rococo, and points towards one which is worth examining more closely, in connection with Art Nouveau.

*

The influence of Rococo and neo-Rococo on Art Nouveau is mainly limited to France and Belgium, and is especially dominant in Nancy. The elegant use of flowers and the naturalistic way in which they are arranged—not common to Art Nouveau in general—may have been stimulated by this trend, and may partly explain how French Art Nouveau at times came close to a pure imitation of Nature. The sense of asymmetry and the use of pastel shades may also derive from Rococo and neo-Rococo. These influences fuse with those of Japanese art—a feature common to both Art Nouveau and Rococo.

NEO-BAROQUE[1]

While the influence of neo-Rococo on Art Nouveau was limited to the detail, the influence of the neo-Baroque applies as well to the architectural *vue d'ensemble* of the plastic conception. Neo-Baroque developed especially in France and Flanders from the eighteen-seventies and beyond, and in this

[1] K. Scheffler. *Verwandlungen des Barocks in der Kunst des neunzehnten Jahrhunderts,* Vienna 1948.

part it enjoyed a position corresponding to that of the neo-Renaissance in Germany. Already as early as 1860 Jakob Burckhardt had written *Die Kultur der Renaissance.* In 1868 W. Lübke wrote *Geschichte der Renaissance Frankreichs*, in 1873 his *Geschichte der Deutschen Renaissance* was published, and in 1877 *Der Formenschatz der Renaissance* started publication, while in 1880 A. Hauser published his *Stil-Lehre der Architektonischen Formen der Renaissance.* Gradually, too, Baroque engaged the attention of scholars, and in 1887 C. Gurlitt wrote *Geschichte des Barockstils in Italien*, the next year Heinrich Wölfflin's *Renaissance und Barock* appeared, and in 1889 Gurlitt published his *Geschichte des Barockstiles und des Rokoko in Deutschland.* In Germany the development of the neo-Renaissance and neo-Baroque seems to be intimately bound up with the growth of research into the history of art.

Neo-Rococo, which survived into the eighteen-fifties—and in the case of Germany into the eighteen-sixties[2]—was then superseded by neo-Renaissance, which flourished in Germany in the eighteen-seventies, stimulated by the wave of nationalism which followed the war of 1870–71, with the Munich Exhibition of 1873 as an important *point de départ.* Neo-Baroque then flourished in Europe during the eighteen-eighties and eighteen-nineties, though its origins in France can be traced back to the eighteen-sixties, while in Holland its influence is negligible.[3]

In France the chief monuments in this style were the work of Charles Garnier (1825–98), who built the *Opéra de Paris*[4] between 1861 and 1875. It is no mere coincidence that the supreme achievement of this whole movement should have been a theatre building. There is something pathetic about this style in its violent light-and-shade effects, and something theatrical in its lavish use of superficial architectural effects—polychrome marble, polished metal, and ornate stairs illumined by countless twinkling globes. It is also significant that among other great examples of this style

2 *Ibid.,* p. 158.

3 This is due to the fact that the Dutch adhered more closely to the neo-Renaissance than most other countries. It was a style which had strong traditions in Holland, and was regarded as peculiarly national. Holland's leading architect in the latter half of the nineteenth century, until the inception of the Modern Movement, P. J. H. Cuypers (1827–1921), also set his seal on the age with this monumental neo-Renaissance buildings the *Rijksmuseum,* 1877–85, the *Railway Station,* 1881–89, and the *General Post Office,* completed in 1898, all of them in Amsterdam.

4 C. Garnier, *Le Nouvel Opéra,* Paris 1881.

are Garnier's *Theatre* and *Casino de Monte Carlo*, 1878, and Charles Girault's (1851–1921) *Arc de Triomphe* in the Parc Cinquantenaire in Brussels, 1905, as well as his *magnum opus*, the exhibition building, *Petit Palais*, in Paris, 1897–1900.

In Germany the supreme monument in this style is Paul Wallot's (1841–1912) *Reichstag* building in Berlin, 1884–94, while Belgium can boast Europe's largest neo-Baroque building, the *Palais de Justice*, in Brussels, by Joseph Poelaert (1817–79), commenced in 1862 and not completed until four years after his death. In England a similar development took place: Elizabethan, which was very popular, was superseded in the eighteen-seventies by simple Queen Anne architecture, thanks mainly to Richard Norman Shaw (1831–1912), after which there was a further development in the direction of the so-called Free Classic in the eighteen-eighties and eighteen-nineties, corresponding more or less to Continental neo-Baroque. But as in England, France, Germany, and Belgium, the pioneer architects at this time were preoccupied with very different problems!

The most important stylistic feature of neo-Baroque is its plastic and markedly three-dimensional treatment. It operates with a violent light-and-shade effect, of which perhaps the outstanding example is the *Palais de Justice* in Brussels. Bold cornices and deep incisions seem at times to transform the surface into a veritable battlefield between light and shade. Not only do the details emphasize the vigorous treatment, but even the actual mass of the building is subjected to the same plastic treatment. The wings at the corners project markedly, while deep balconies and projecting bays are other fundamental features of this neo-Baroque architecture.

The conception of form did not apply only to architecture, but can also be encountered in applied art, and with its markedly plastic effect the style was eminently suitable for sculpture, and it is in sculpture that neo-Baroque first fuses with early Art Nouveau.

In the work of the English sculptor Alfred Gilbert[5] (1854–1934) neo-Baroque features occur in such a way that they are of interest in connection

[5] J. Hatton, Alfred Gilbert, R.A. The Easter Art Annual, *The Art Journal*, 1903, pp. 1–32, with 47 illustrations of his early works; I. Macallister, *Alfred Gilbert*, London, 1929; A. Bury, *Shadow of Eros*, London 1952.

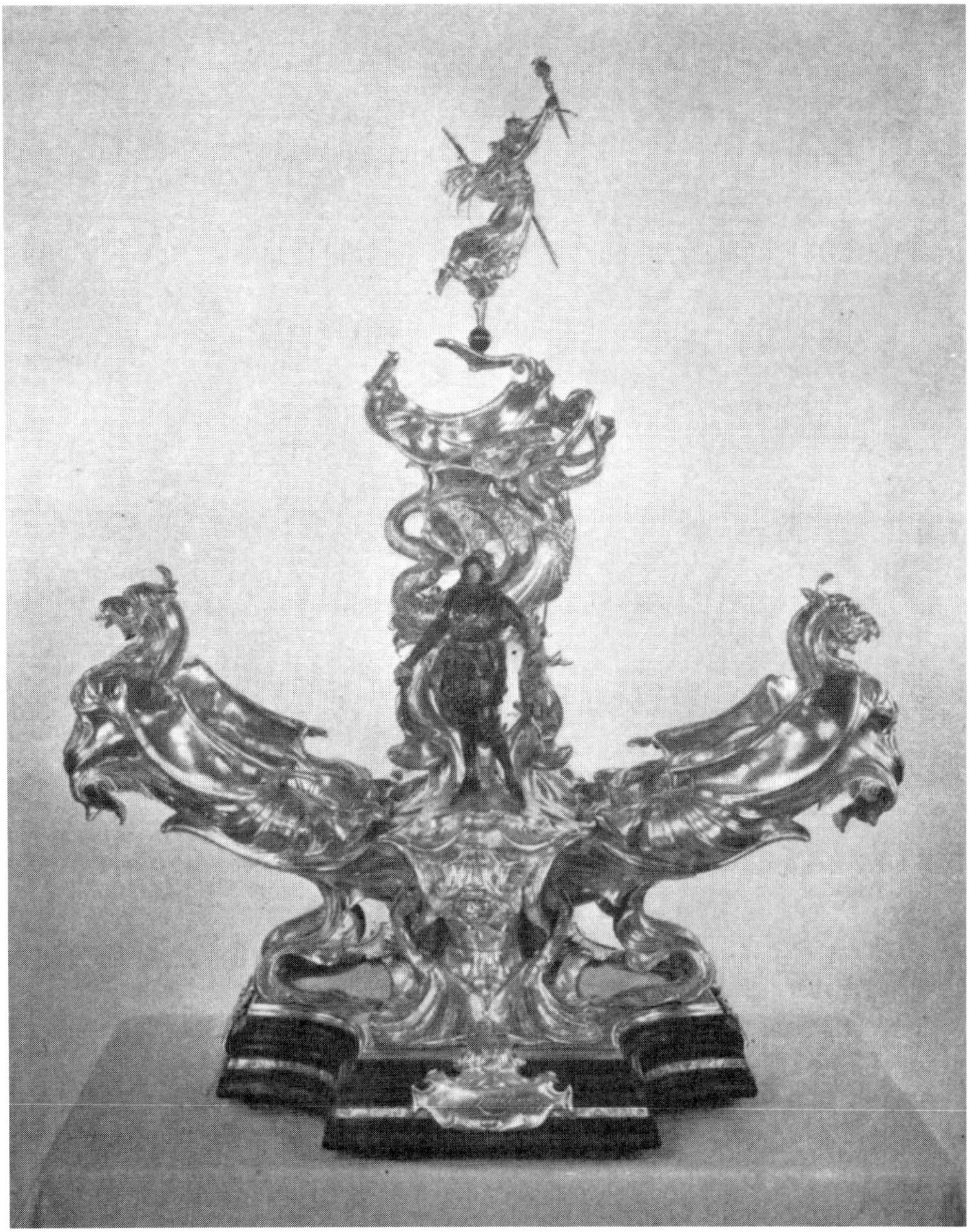

Fig. 55. Gilbert: Epergne of silver, parcel-gilt, mounted with mother-of-pearl and geological specimens. 1887.
Courtesy of Lord Chamberlain. Victoria and Albert Museum photo. Crown Copyright reserved.

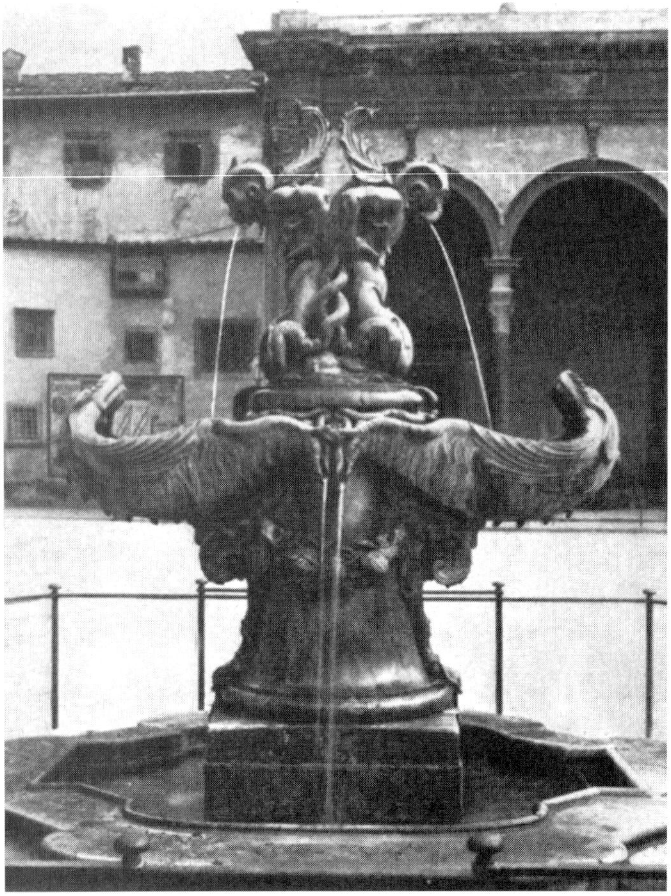

Fig. 56. Tacca: Fountain at Piazza della Annunziata, Florence. Bronze. 1629.
Mansell collection copyright.

with Art Nouveau. Trained on the Continent, he came into contact with Baroque at an early period, and his interest was directed towards Michel Angelo and Benevenuto Cellini; especially the latter, however, whose skill as a goldsmith Gilbert was anxious to emulate. It was in fact the latter's mannered blend of realism with imaginative ornamentation that was to prove the hallmark of Gilbert's decorative works.

For Queen Victoria's Jubilee Gilbert executed a splendid epergne[6] (fig. 55) in silver. The individual figures stand heroically unmoved in the

6 Victoria and Albert Museum, *Catalogue of an Exhibition of Victorian and Edwardian Decorative Arts*, London 1952, p. 116, No. W 2.

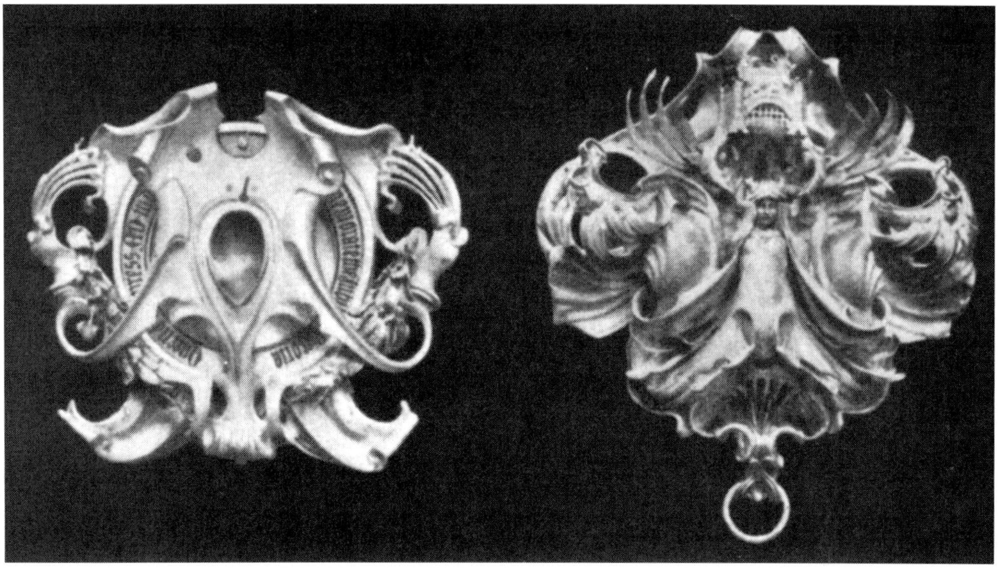

Fig. 57. Gilbert: Front and back centre of the Badge of the Preston chain in course of execution. 1888—92.

midst of serpents, hissing lizards, snorting monsters, and sprawling fish, symbolising the unity of the British Empire.

In its structure this piece is entirely Baroque, with very pronounced indentations and projections, dynamic movement, and violent light-and-shade effects. In the innate Naturalism of the lobster-like motifs and the many curves and undulations, and not least in its structure, this piece is reminiscent of sculpture cast in the mould of the highly mannered early Baroque, especially that of Benevenuto Cellini (1500–71). This epergne can also be stylistically compared with e.g. Pietro Tacca's (1577–1640) fountain for the Piazza della Annunziata in Florence from 1629 (fig. 56). And yet, despite these likenesses, the epergne bears the hallmark of the new style, with its soft undulations and many lines, and not least with its supple rhythm.

It was especially in his jewellery and ornamental work that Gilbert foreshadowed Art Nouveau: he says himself of the difficulties he encountered in ornamental work in 1884–85: "Being unwilling to copy or steal the method of ornament I had so strangely neglected, I set myself a new task,

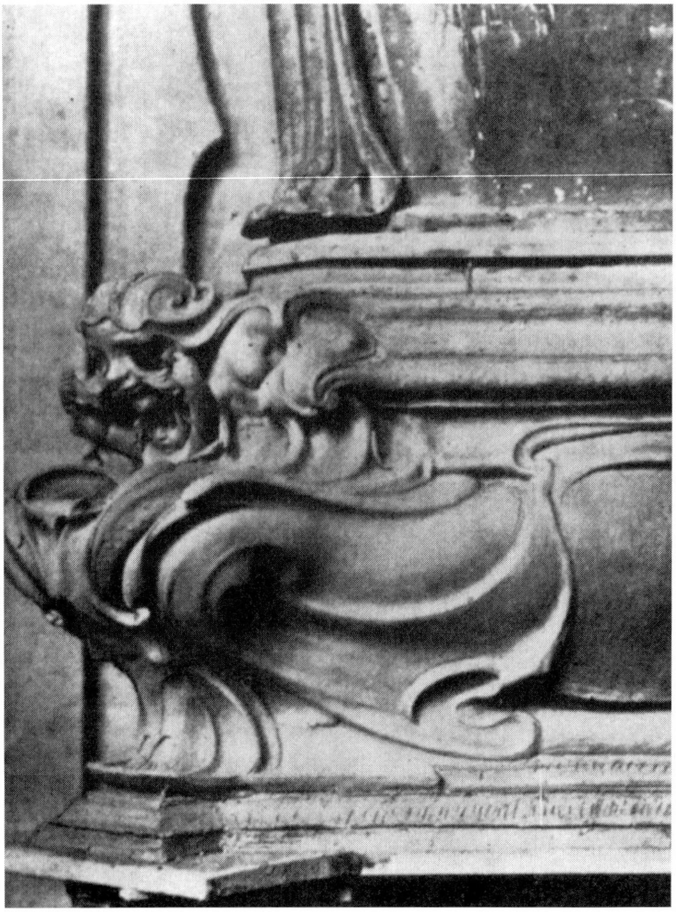

Fig. 58. Detail of the basis of the John Howard Memorial, Bedford, in course of execution. 1892—93.

the hardest task of my life, which some day may bear fruit."[7] In 1892 he executed the Preston Chain (fig. 57),[8] where we once again encounter that peculiar blend of the style of past centuries and the passing fashion of a decade, though here the inspiration is clearly Baroque rather than Art Nouveau. In a number of details, for example in the Memorial Font to the son of the fourth Marquess of Bath, in the corners of the casket to Baron Huddleston, and in the plinth of the memorial to John Howard, Bedford, 1893–94 (fig. 58), the same tendencies can be traced.

[7] J. Hatton, *op. cit.*, p. 11.

[8] Figs. 57, 58 both illustrated in J. Hatton, *op. cit.*, pp. 6 and 7.

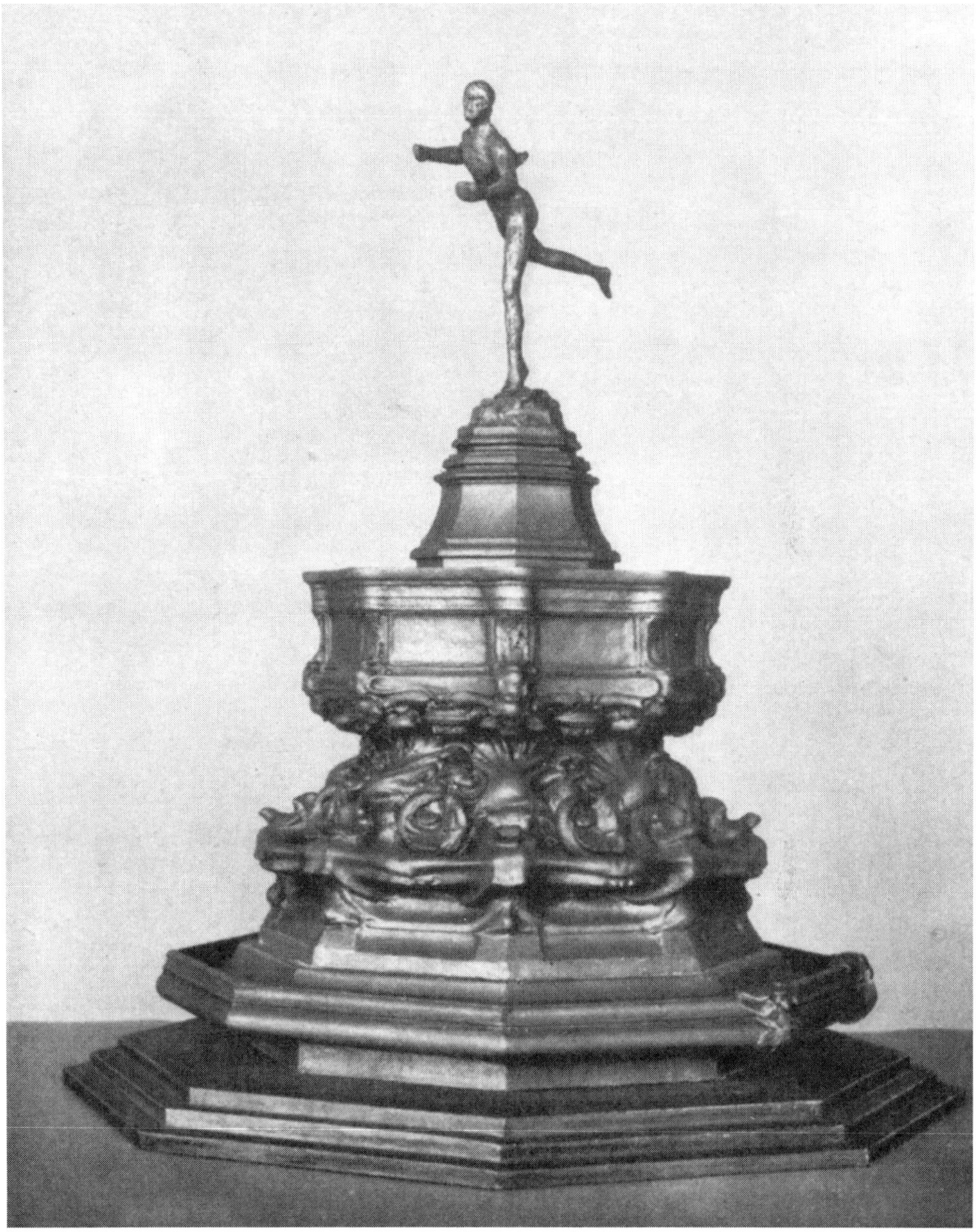

Fig. 59. Gilbert: Working model for the Shaftesbury Fountain. Bronzed plaster on wood. Between 1887—1893.
Courtesy of the Museum Art Gallery, Perth. Victoria and Albert Museum photo. Crown Copyright reserved.

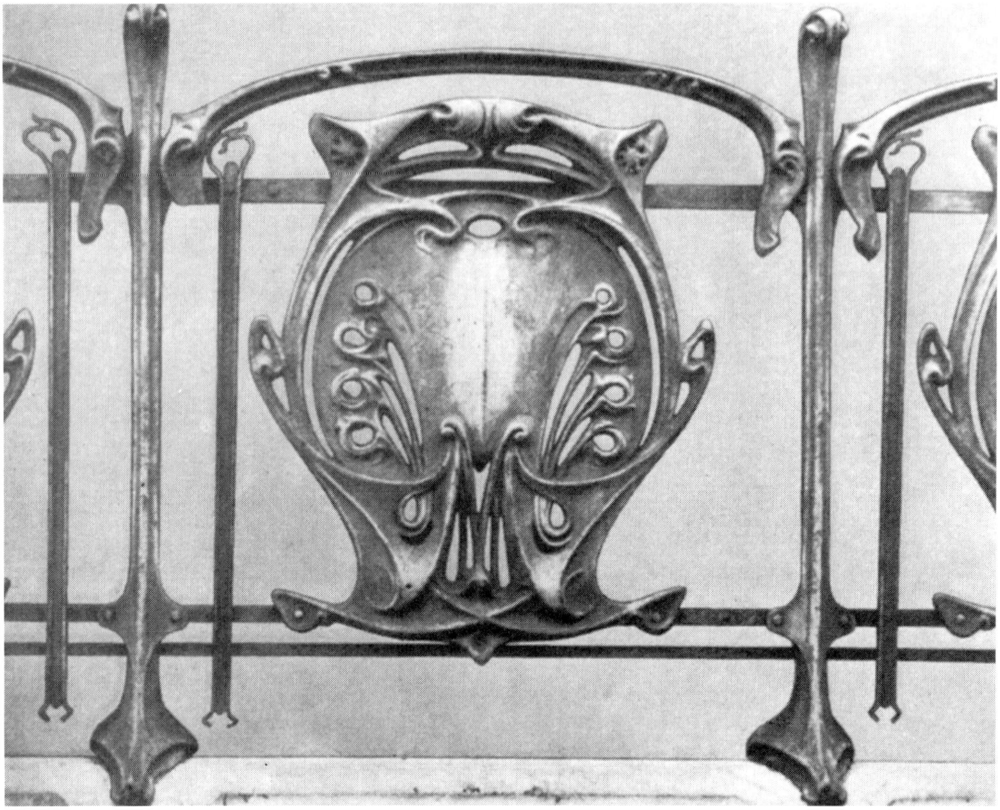

Fig. 60. Guimard: Detail of the railing for the Metropolitan Underground, Paris. Cast iron, painted green. 1899—1900. Courtesy of A. Brenna, Oslo.

The *magnum opus* of the Art-Nouveau-neo-Baroque of the eighteen-nineties, however, is the Shaftesbury Memorial Fountain in Piccadilly Circus, London, 1893 (fig. 59)—the world-famous statue which is popularly known as the Eros statue. At the foot of the octagonal basin there is a teeming welter of "gristle"- and crayfish-like figures, fishes, and helmeted heads in the typical scaly finish of neo-Baroque and Art Nouveau.

In Alfred Gilbert's ornaments we have the forerunners of Hector Guimard's Metro phantasies 13 years later. It is curious to reflect that it was an Englishman—though he had been trained in Paris and Rome—who first effected a fusion of two elements, of which one was, and the other was to remain, relatively unfamiliar in Britain.

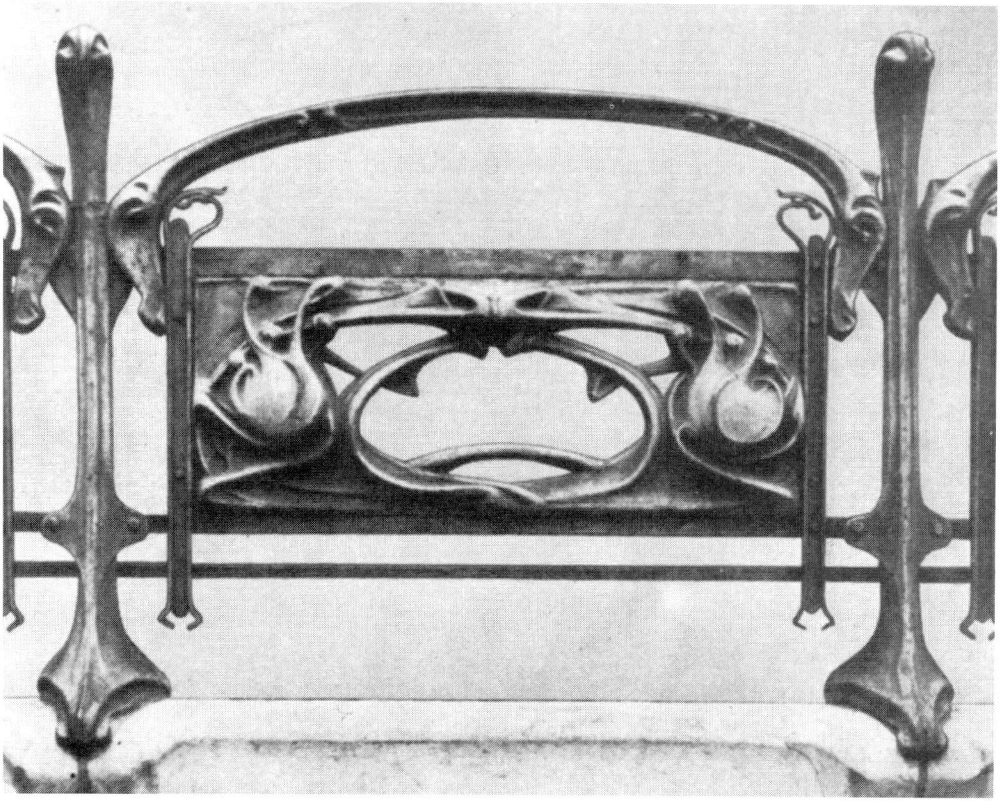

Fig. 61. Guimard: Detail of the railing for the Metropolitan Underground, Paris. Cast iron, painted green. 1899—1900. Courtesy of A. Brenna, Oslo.

Though the background was a different one, it was likewise within the sphere of decorative art that neo-Baroque and Art Nouveau were to fuse in France. As in England, it is only occasionally found in architecture. Yvette Guilbert's house may be said to show a complete fusion of the *vue d'ensemble* of neo-Baroque and Art Nouveau, while at the same time the style merges in its details with neo-Rococo. This house was only an isolated phenomenon: as far as the external architecture was concerned neo-Baroque took refuge in a majestic Classicism, leaving Art Nouveau to deal with the interior. Guimard's Castel Béranger, 1894–98, is probably the best example of this[9] (figs. 6–9).

9 H. Guimard, *Castel Béranger,* Paris 1899; G. Soulier, *Etudes sur le Castel Béranger,* Paris 1899.

Apart from this Guimard is the creator of the most typical fusion of neo-Baroque and Art Nouveau, as can be seen everywhere in Paris in the iron decorations of the Metro stations (figs. 60 and 61), like the scales of fantastic lizards and sea-monsters side by side at all subway entrances and exist. Gilbert's and Guimard's motifs can clearly be traced back to the same models, but while Gilbert has a little more of the sixteenth- and seventeenth-century cartouche in his ornaments, Guimard's imagination is even more vivid, and created some of the most interesting ornaments of Art Nouveau. This difference is quite natural: Guimard was working in a later phase of the style, when the artist had to a greater extent broken away from his source of inspiration. But common to them both is the retention of the symmetrical construction of the ornament.

The plastic conception of applied art was so important to some of the contemporary artists that practically everything they executed was modelled in advance. The Nancy architect Emile André, for instance, actually modelled the prototype for his chairs. The photo showing the chair on the pedestal furnishes an interesting proof of this[10] (figs. 62, 63). A chair was not constructed—it was modelled, and it is hardly surprising that the ornament and the total effect were plastic.

In Belgium the neo-Baroque ideas of form is most vigorously expressed in the work of Victor Horta, where it is lavishly represented both in architecture and applied art. The house 520 Avenue Louise, Brussels, 1900, which was demolished in 1949–50, was one of the most typical (figs. 19 and 20), but the Art Nouveau details do not invade its external architecture, even though the ornately curved projecting parts with their window-frames very nearly do so. In applied art his Art Nouveau phantasies are the product of his sculptural and neo-Baroque conception of form (fig. 23). As far as the architectural details are concerned—and this also applies to all the details of the houses he built—it is characteristic of his sculptural attitude that every single detail was first modelled by himself, before being cast in plaster and hewn out of stone or formed in metal.[11]

Pure Art Nouveau architecture seldom got further than the drawing-

10 Negatives in the archives of Jaques André, Nancy.

11 Victor Horta's collection of details in plaster, Musée Cinquantenaire, Brussels.

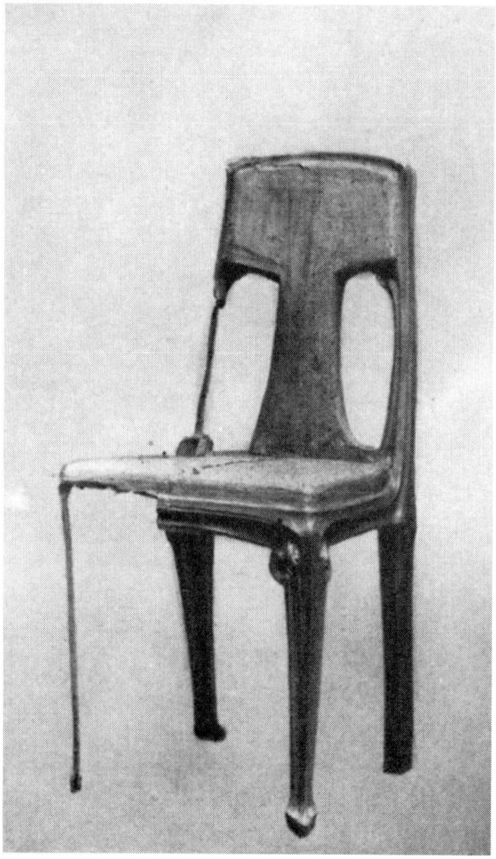
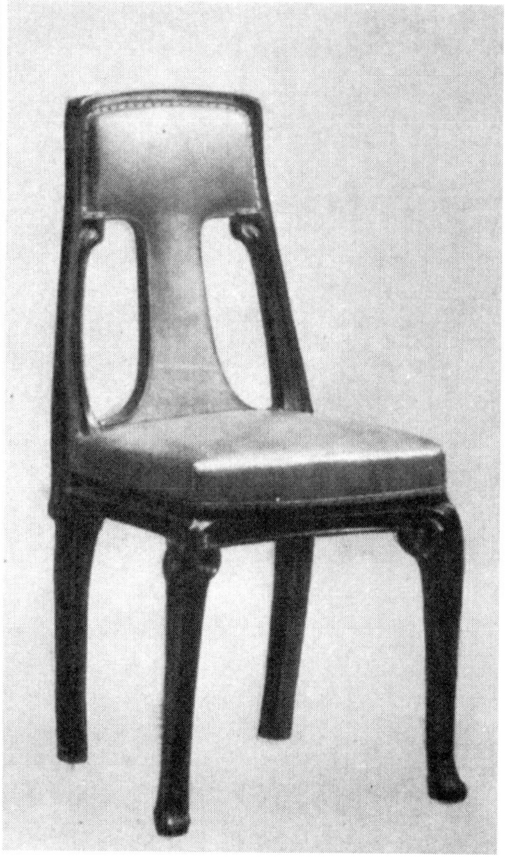

Figs. 62, 63. André: Chair under modelling and the finished chair. About 1901.
Courtesy of Jacques André, Nancy.

board: this applies both to Germany and England. Josef Hoffmann's (1870–) sketch for an entrance gateway from 1898[12] (fig. 64) shows precisely this fusion of the plastic conception of neo-Baroque, and the undulating lines of Art Nouveau. Characteristically enough he also tried his hand at the same time at a sort of faintly Egyptian neo-Baroque.

Charles Rennie Mackintosh was another artist who, in common with

12 *Ver Sacrum,* vol. I, 1898, July, p. 14.
13 *Ibid.,* vol. I, 1898, July, p. 15.

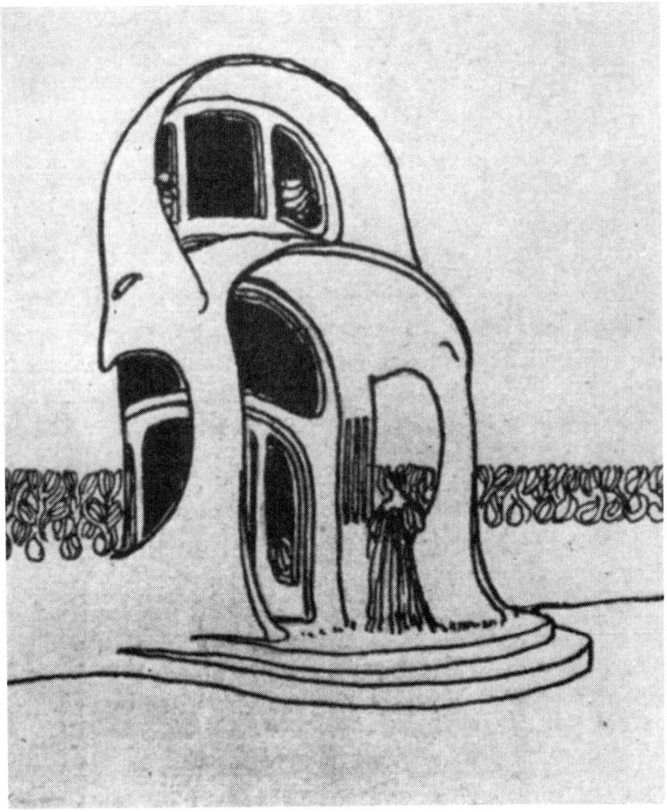

Fig. 64. Hoffmann: Sketch for an entrance. 1898.

Hoffmann, made neo-Baroque designs at the very beginning of his career,[14] but only a few years later he submitted his designs for *Haus eines Kunstfreundes*, 1900,[15] where his conception of the actual body of the building first and foremost is advanced modern, but also agrees with the plastic sense of form of neo-Baroque. At the same time the building has a smoothly rounded and compact contour, undoubtedly a result of the marked interest in the late nineties of the closed conception of form (fig. 15).

No artist, however, fused neo-Baroque together with Art Nouveau to the same extent as Henry van de Velde (1863–). Karl Scheffler has de-

14 T. Howarth, *Charles Rennie Mackintosh and the Modern Movement*, London, 1952, pp. 8, 14. Mackintosh may also have been working on the designs for the Royal Insurance Building, Glasgow, 1894, pl. 19, fig. C.

15 *Meister der Innenkunst. Charles Rennie Mackintosh. Haus eines Kunstfreundes*. Foreword by H. Muthesius. Darmstadt. 1902.

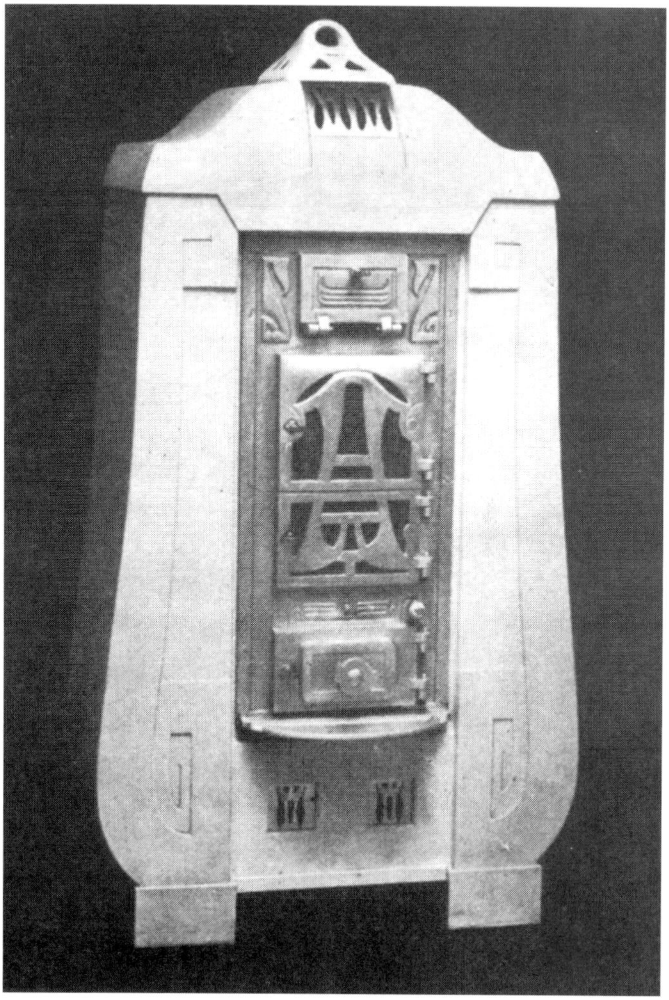

Fig. 65. Van de Velde: Stove. 1904.

voted a good deal of attention to this problem, and calls it *Jugendstil-barock.*[16] It is not surprising that van de Velde and his circle, round about the year 1900, failed to realise all the impulses to which they were subject. If he realised the Gothic and the Rococo influences, nothing was said of Baroque, but if we look at van de Velde's stove from as late as 1904 (fig. 65), with its heavy ponderous Baroque-like volutes, the neo-Baroque impulses are obvious. In one of his *chefs-d'oeuvre* from this period—the large writing-desk

[16] K. Schefler, *op. cit.,* Chapter IX. Der Jugendstil-Barock, pp. 186–194.

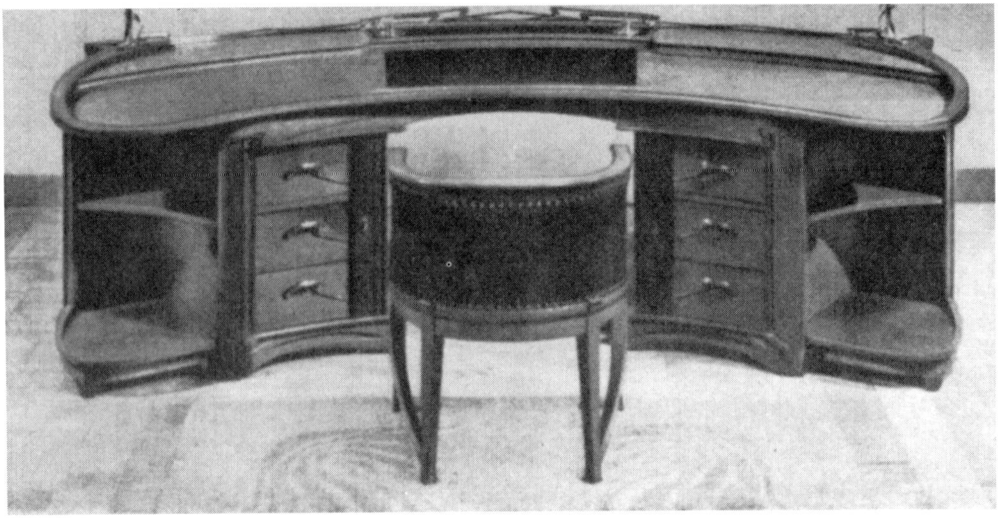

Fig. 66. Van de Velde: Writing table for J. Meier-Graefe. Probably 1897.
From *Um 1900.*

designed for J. Meier-Graefe, probably 1897[17] (fig. 66), all the qualities of this mixed style appear. When it was shown at the exhibition *Um 1900* together with Ferdinand Hodler's *Der Tag*, 1900, these two constituted a unity which Johannes Itten aptly describes as follows: "It (the writing-desk) merged with Ferdinand Hodler's *Tag* into a formal and imaginary unit of dynamic force."[18] Van de Velde may not have been among the first to fuse the formal elements of neo-Baroque and Art Nouveau, but he was among those who continued longest to do so. When van de Velde designed the Museum Hall for the German Applied Art Exhibition in Dresden in 1906, the style he chose was a pompous neo-Baroque-Art Nouveau. There were "gilt" and stucco frames supported by marble columns, bulging grisle and theatrical tinsel, blending here and there with a rectilinearism which had constructive associations.[19] The senior officer's comment—"Etwas für exklusive Leute"—was just as characteristic as the exclamation of the two peasant girls: "Wie scheen!"[20] It was in the same town that,

17 Drawings of details of the writing-table appeared in *Pan,* vol. III, 1897, No. 4, pp. 260–64.

18 Kunstgewerbemuseum Zürich, *Um 1900. Art Nouveau und Jugend,* Zürich 1952, p. 38.

19 K. E. Osthaus, *van de Velde. Leben und Schaffen des Künstlers,* Hagen in Weimar, 1920, ill. p. 49.

20 *Ibid.,* p. 54 sq. "Something for exclusive people." "How luvly!"

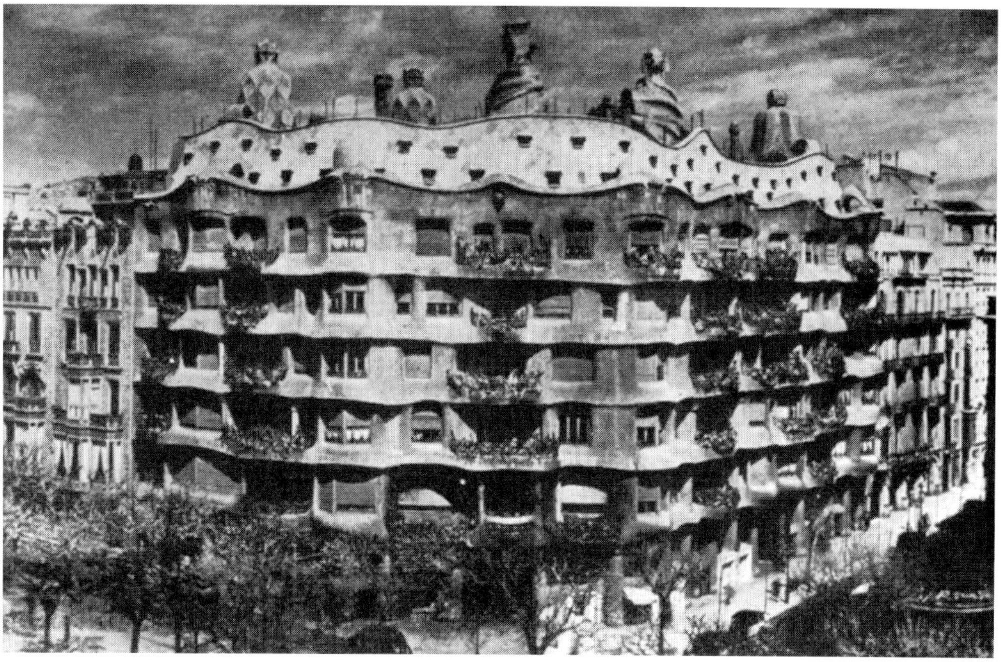

Fig. 67. Gaudí: Casa Mila, Barcelona. About 1905.

nine years previously, he had garnered his first laurels in Germany for his austere and constructive applied art.

It may be an advantage to consider Antonio Gaudí y Cornet's (1852–1926) architectural work about the turn of the century, in relation to neo-Baroque feeling and form. His mature style, as we find it in his *Casa Mila*, Barcelona, 1905–07 (fig. 67), exactly expresses Hoffmann's phantasies (fig. 64), but only a Gaudí could have created them. With its pronounced light-and-shade effect and the markedly plastic shape of the facade plane, it forms a complete fusion of Art Nouveau and neo-Baroque on a huge scale. This is a form of neo-Baroque in which the conception of style appears unadorned, while the ornamentation of Art Nouveau is confined to limited fields of flat pattern. The structure and material are completely subordinated to the soft rounded forms of Art Nouveau, with long undulating lines and flowing planes. It would prove a thankless task to attempt to explain the top part of the house, with all its details, or to assign it to any

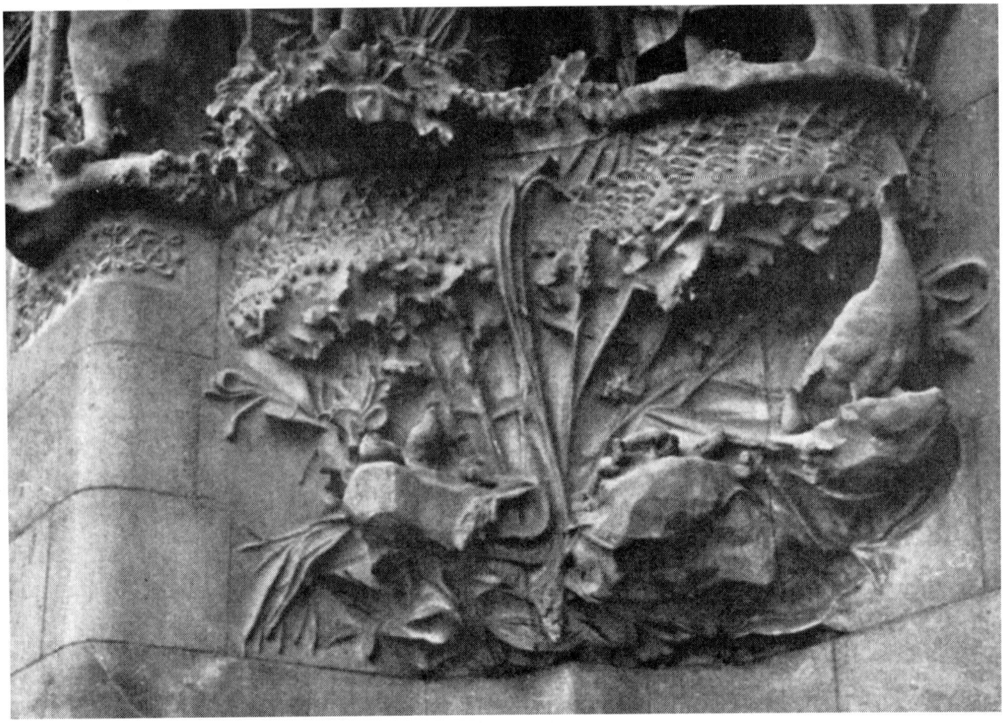

Fig. 68. Gaudí: Detail from Sagrada Familia, Barcelona. 1882—1900.
Courtesy of Andreas Bugge, Oslo.

style—it is nothing but an artist's free imaginative play with forms which the Surrealists were the first to appreciate to their full extent a generation later.[21] Other buildings in the same style are the Casa Guëll, 1885–89,[22] the church in Guëll Park, 1898, as well as the maze and lodge in the Guëll Park.

For a fuller understanding of Gaudí we should mention yet another factor, which explains his world of forms, viz. the marked naturalism which is most in evidence in his details (fig. 68). Summing up Gaudí's chief characteristics, and assigning him to his place in history, we may say that

21 Salvador Dali, Apparitions aerodynamiques des être-objets, *Minotaure*, Paris, 1936, No. 6, pp. 33–34. P. L. Flouquet, Surréalisme et architecture. A propos de Gaudí y Cornet, *La Maison*, vol. VIII, no. 11, pp. 340–44.

22 J. J. Sweeney dates it somewhat earlier, 1883, J. J. Sweeney, Antonio Gaudí, *The Magazine of Art*, New York, May 1953, pp. 195–205.

he is one of the most imaginative artists who succeeded in fusing most of the elements of the nineteenth century in a decorative and architectural whole.—He brought together, in the supple form-world of Art Nouveau, the constructive seeking of neo-Gothic, the plastic feeling for form of neo-Baroque, and the most fanciful naturalism.

*

If we consider the influence of neo-Baroque on Art Nouveau as a whole, we shall find that it is one of the factors principally responsible for the form language of the style. It is quite natural that the architects and other artists who had been trained in neo-Baroque, and who lived and worked in an age permeated with this style, were unable completely to liberate themselves from its conception of form. They proceeded to develop it, even though they abandoned the external form-language of neo-Baroque.

Summing up we may say that neo-Baroque may be considered as the most important source of Art Nouveau's plastic conception of form in the French cultural sphere.

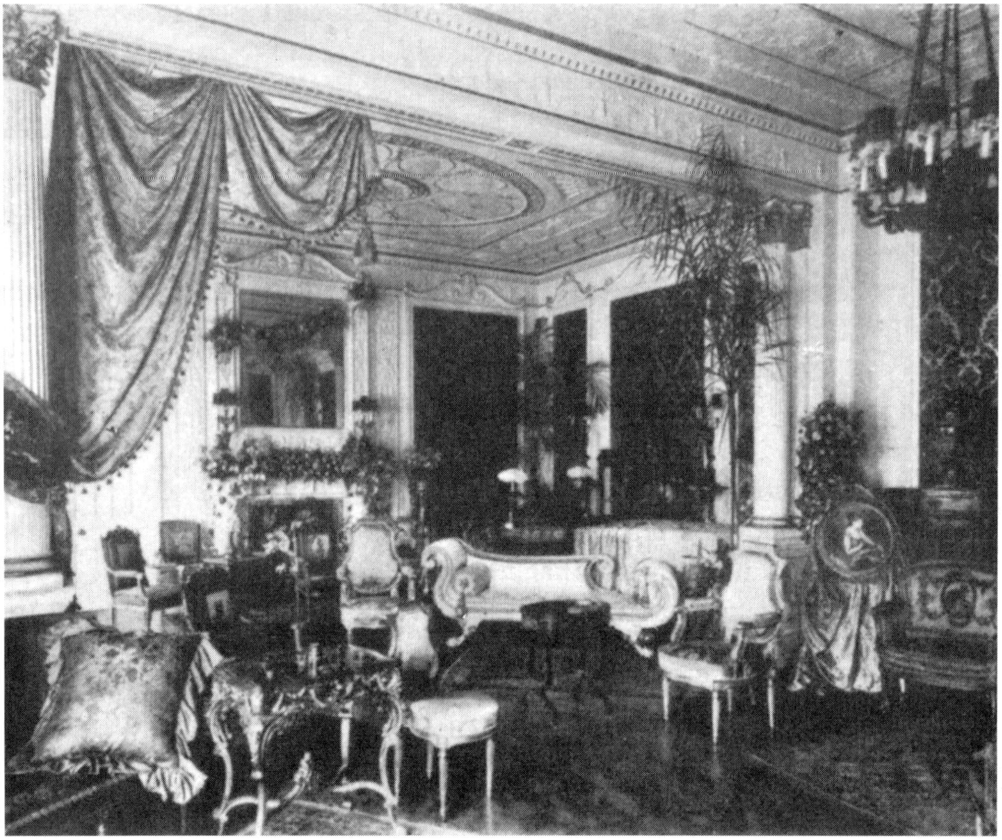

Fig. 69. Interior from Grosvenor Square, London. 1880's.
Victoria and Albert Museum photo. (No. 185-1926.) Crown copyright reserved.

Formal Reaction

The interior decoration of Historicism was largely a continuation of Romanticism: the room was filled with objects freely spread around, often asymmetrical and "picturesquely" placed. Not least typical is the oblique position of the various objects—from the piano to the sofa and the chairs. Each object speaks its own language; it is the reign of the single object. A feature of this kind of interior was the great many curtains and draperies.[1]

[1] H. Clouzot, *Des Tuileries à Saint-Cloud. L'Art décoratif du second empire,* Paris 1925, pp. 96 sq. Suites of furniture in one style, especially dining-rooms, and bed-rooms, were of course still produced.

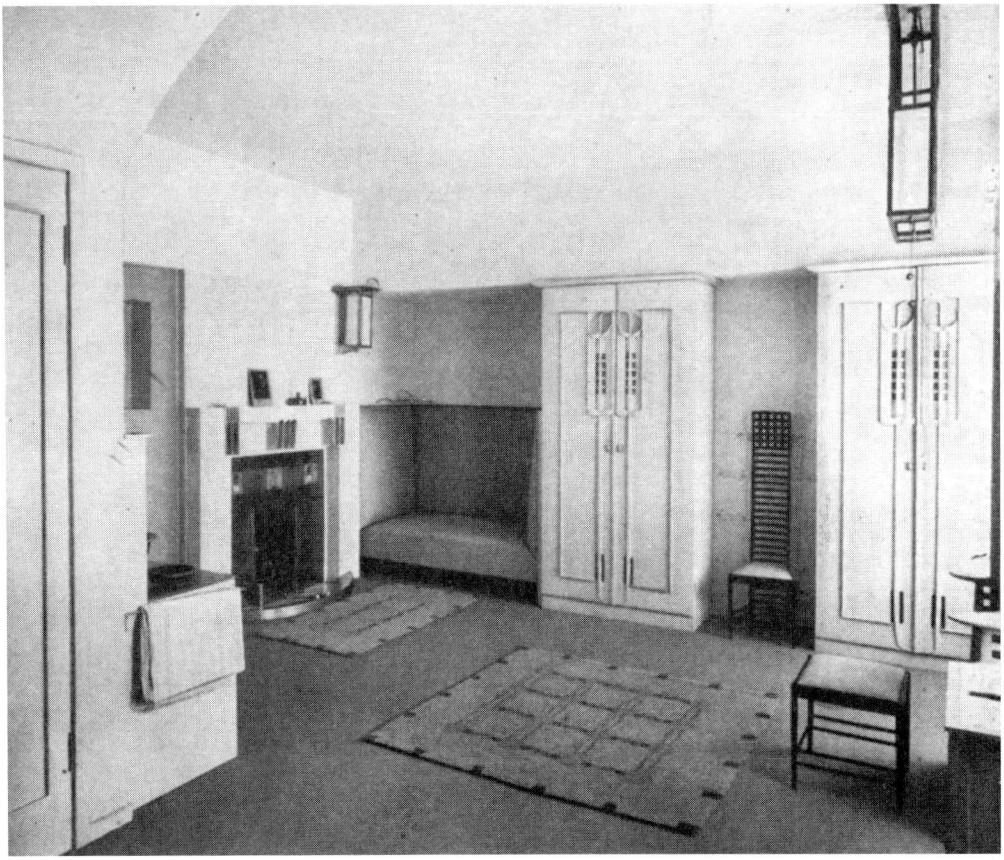

Fig. 70. Mackintosh: Bedroom in the Hill House, Helensburgh. 1902—03.
Bedford Lemere Copyright.

This tended to make the interior relatively dark, while the large upholstered furniture accentuated the heavy effect (fig. 69).

The Art Nouveau interior (fig. 70) is on the whole bright, and the various objects are subordinate to a decorative *vue d'ensemble.* In their attempt to fuse the interior to a single unity, Mackintosh, van de Velde, and Hoffmann all went so far as to build furniture into the room as an integral part of the whole (figs. 13 27, 39, 70,). Each part exists not in and by itself, but only by virtue of the part it plays in the whole: a piece of furniture or object of any other style would completely upset the artistic

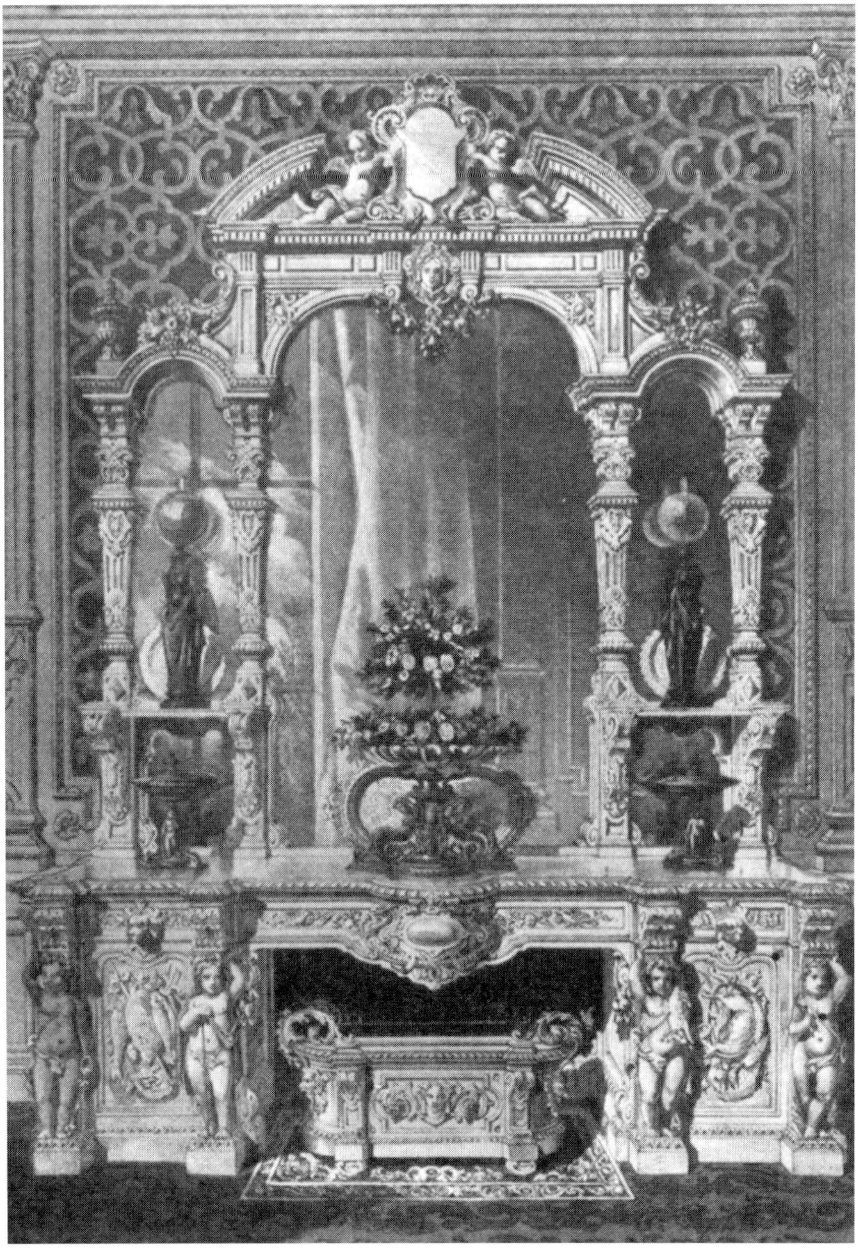

Fig. 71. E. Prignot: Sideboard in carved oak. 1851. "The style of the work is a happy adaptation fo the English revival of antique art most generally known under the name of Elizabethan, and there is much taste displayed both in the selection and carrying out of the various ornamental details." The Great Exhibition, class XXVI, No. 126.

effect of unity. This is Art Nouveau's most important contribution to the art of interior decoration, and it is an expression of its synthetic attitude.

The same applies to the individual piece of furniture: here too the form conception of Art Nouveau is equally diametrical in relation to Historicism (figs. 71 and 72).[2] In the furniture of Historicism one component part is added to another, and the total composition of each piece is additive. The contours are restless, angular, indented, serrated—bristling. In Art Nouveau furniture the separate parts are forged so as to fuse with the whole: the form-language is synthetic. The contours are firm and closed, with no projecting pieces, everything being smoothed out in a fixed and continuous outline. The topheaviness of the eighteen-fifties and -sixties, has now disappeared completely. Instead we often find the lower part of the furniture splayed. This tendency can also be

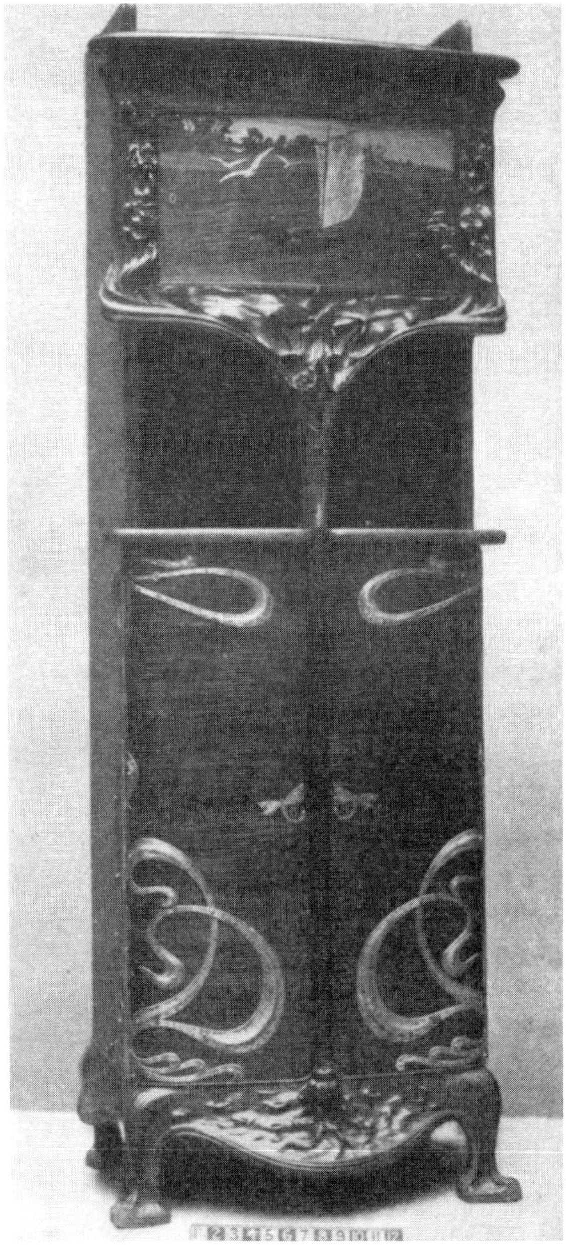

Fig. 72. Majorelle: Cabinet, veneered with coromandel, burr, walnut; marquetry in various woods. Signed *L. Majorelle, Nancy.* 1900. Victoria and Albert Museum photo. Crown Copyright reserved.

[2] 71. The Great Exhibition. Class XXVI, No. 126; 72. Cat. no. 1997–1900, Victoria and Albert Museum, London.

traced in architecture and sculpture, especially where the plinth is modelled and takes on the appearance of a soft or viscous material.

With regard to decorative characteristics the hallmark of Historicism is an ornamental delight which seems to be quite sincere, and at times is almost overwhelming. The form of the object is subordinate to the decoration, and the surface covered with ornaments, be they neo-Baroque, -Rococo, -Renaissance, or fashioned according to any other style. The individual ornaments themselves are lost in the violent, total decorative effect. What matters is neither the design of the ornament itself nor its position, but its mass; it is a decorative *horror vacui*-principle (fig. 73).

Art Nouveau, on the other hand, subjects the individual ornament to the most meticulous treatment, and presents it against a plain background, so that its effect can be fully appreciated. The Art Nouveau designer, in fact, aims to bring out the ornament's artistic relationship to its background. In this respect, too, Art Nouveau created new effects which had not been achieved for generations. Art Nouveau also strove to place an ornament according to its function. The ornament was to be logical: in this connection van de Velde has the following remark to make about the new ornamentation:

"Diese Ornamentik ist vor allem notwendig, sie entsteht aus dem Gegenstande, mit dem sie verbunden bleibt, sie weist auf seinen Zweck oder seine Bildungsweise hin, sie hilft ihm, sich der Aufgabe, die ihm zufällt, seiner Nützlichkeit noch mehr anzupassen."[3] He says furthermore that an object can only be beautiful "wenn alle seine Einzelheiten, aller Schmuck seinen Daseinszweck bereichern."[4]

The Art Nouveau artists were consistent in their synthetic conception of form, right down to the single ornament (figs. 74 and 75). The pliant, round, and closed form contrasts sharply with the gristly, angular, and open. The difference lies in an entirely new attitude to pattern design. A two-dimensional surface demands a two-dimensional decorative prin-

[3] H. van de Velde, *Renaissance im Kunstgewerbe,* Neue Ausgabe, Berlin 1901, pp. 102 sq. "This ornamentation is above all necessary, it arises from the object, remains associated with it, indicating its purpose or its method of construction helping it to adapt itself still more to the object to which it is assigned, its usefulness."

[4] *Ibid.,* pp. 72 sq. When all its details and all its ornamentation enrich its "raison d'être."

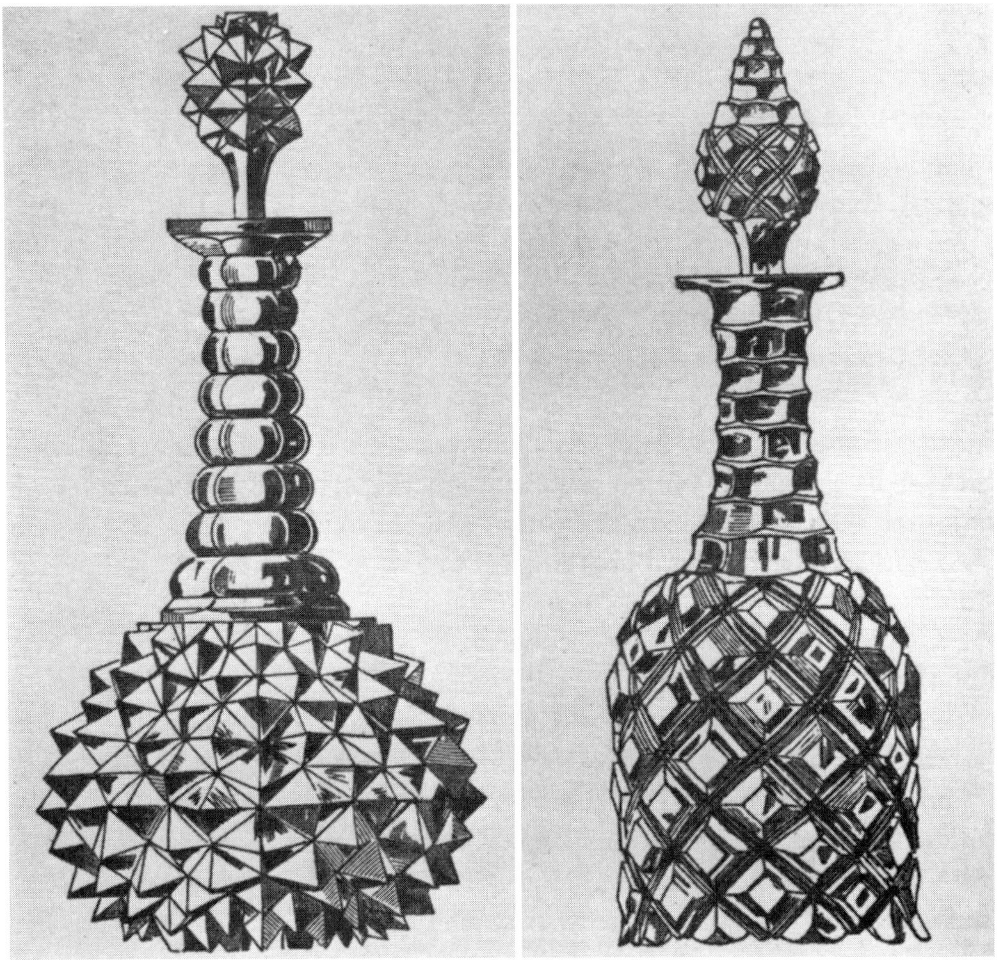

Fig. 73. Richardson: Crystal glass. 1851. The Great Exhibition, class XXVI, No. 14.
Victoria and Albert Museum photo. Crown Copyright reserved.

ciple, and for this reason the plastic and three-dimensional conception of form has to give way. The former naturalistic shape gave way to a stylised and simplified shape, and the three-dimensional and illusionary to a two-dimensional effect.

However, it is not only within the realm of form development itself taht we find a swing of the pendulum towards contrary decorative principles: this also applies to colour schemes. The eighteen-seventies and

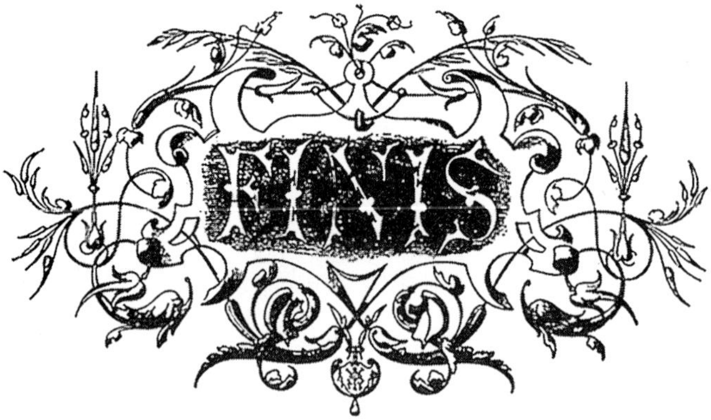

Fig. 74. Vignette from *the Art Journal. Illustrated Catalogue for the Great Exhibition.* 1851.

eighteen-eighties preferred a somewhat darker range of colours in their interior decoration to the harsh scale of the eighteen-fifties and eighteen-sixties with their deep-blue and bright-yellow, livid red, and grass green. The eighteen-seventies and eighteen-eighties were in this respect the "dark decades."

On the basis of 330 dated colour samples from the latter half of the nineteenth century[5] it is possible, in general outlines, to get an impression of the colour scale of the eighteen-seventies and eighteen-eighties. The colours were just as saturated as previously, but no longer so pure, being frequently mixed with black or brown. Furniture was often painted black, while wallpapers and furniture materials were almost bound to have a touch of black.[6] Red was superseded by ox-blood, dark blue became violet, yellow became orange, and green became grey-green. The 1889 Exhibition in Paris seems to mark a culminating point in colour development in the latter half of the nineteenth century.[7]

Towards the turn of the century a radical change takes place: the unified colour scheme makes its appearance, black is excluded, and instead

5 The colour samples were included in an *Exhibition of Victorian and Edwardian Decorative Arts,* 1952, Victoria and Albert Museum.

6 St. Tschudi Madsen, Victoriansk Dekorative Kunst, *Nordenfjeldske Kunstindustrimuseums Årbok,* 1952, Trondheim 1953, p. 54.

7 Roger Marx, one of the best-known art critics at the time in France, asserts that the polychromy, very typical at the exhibition of 1889, derives from the Far East. R. Marx, *La Décoration et l'art industriel à l'exposition universelle de 1889*, Paris 1890.

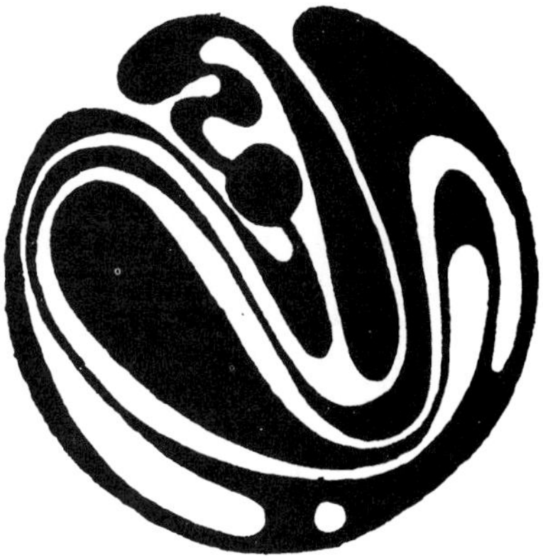

Fig. 75. Moser: Vignette for *Ver Sacrum*. 1899.

white becomes dominant. Purple fades to mauve, ox-blood to pink, and green becomes apple green or a pale olive, while brown tends towards beige, and blue to pale blue, and in addition we get a whole range from grey and pale grey to milk-white.

As the rich and striking colours faded away, to be replaced by pastel hues, the interest in gold and gilt decorations passed. The light silver effect toned better with the pale colour scheme, and silver and light blue thus replaced the more ponderous combination of gold and deep red.

*

The Gothic revival, neo-Rococo, and neo-Baroque contributed to shape Art Nouveau—each in its own way—one with its theory, the other with its application to details, and the third with its conception of form. It may appear strange, therefore, to assume that Art Nouveau was a reaction against these very styles. But on account of the interest in what was new, and the earnest desire to make a break with all the styles of Historicism, it would be natural, too, for this reaction to find formal expression.

In fact there is no objection to the assumption that, in a general and conscious formal reaction, certain elements of a previous stylistic conception can survive—almost unconsciously.[8] But this contributory factor must not blind us to a most essential point, viz. that Art Nouveau had the force of an "anti"-movement, and was filled with reaction against previous gener-

[8] K. Scheffler, *Verwandlungen des Barocks in der Kunst des neunzehnten Jahrhunderts*, Vienna, 1947, p. 187.

ations. Morris reacted violently against what he called "the imitation of an imitation of an imitation," Voysey spoke about "the tyranny of styles," and Hankar about "le sacro-sainte Renaissance," while Horta states quite frankly that the trend was a reaction.[9] Since Art Nouveau's formal conception and colour scheme are direct contrasts to those of preceding periods, one may be permitted to assume that a formal reaction was an essential contributory factor.

The very fact that the style was an "anti"-movement in so many ways, and a reaction, conditions its form-language, and discloses one of its weaknesses. It reacts violently against formal expression, of which it possesses elements, and its quest for the new becomes a desperate pursuit of the new for its own sake. One tends to lose sight of the conception of style and come dangerously close to mere fashion.

But as a part of the reaction, one of the most important features of the style was developed: the synthetic conception of form and the unity of expression.

[9] V. Horta, *L'Architecture Moderne,* Brussels 1926, p. 23 (Lecture given at "La séance publique de la classe des Beaux-Arts de l'Académie royale de Belgique," November 29, 1925).

Arts and Crafts Movement

In the last third of the nineteenth century there was a strong movement in all the countries in Europe, initiated by a number of official organisations, to renew the arts and crafts. It was in England and France that the work of dealing systematically with these problems first began—both countries with a wealth of artistic traditions, and old and reputable arts and crafts to maintain. On the whole these two countries set the pattern that was followed by the other European countries.

As early as about the middle of the 19th century responsible persons in France and in England set to work to improve the relationship between industry and the artist. In both countries the solution was based on the setting up of retrospective and contemporary museums, an improvement in art training, an increase in the number of exhibitions, as well as a more intimate co-operation between artist and artisan. A special feature of the movement in England was the establishment of guilds to raise the general standard of design by enlisting the co-operation of artists and craftsmen.

In France[1] the *point de départ* was the great exhibition in London in 1851. After the dangers which this heralded had been clearly envisaged, a number of reports and accounts were published which further helped to open the eyes of Frenchmen. The designer Charles Clerget, who had been one of the delegates at the exhibition, made an appeal in 1852 to the *Comité Centrale des Arts Appliqués à l'Industrie* to help put things right by setting up a museum of applied art. The sculptor Klagmann also handed in a report in the same year, in which he proposed that an institution should be founded with the object of arranging periodical exhibitions of applied art, while at the same time he emphasized the lack of contact between artists and artisans. Chabal Dussurgey agitated in the same year for the founding of a school of applied art.

1 *Rapport Général sur l'Exposition de 1851,* Paris 1852; L. Laborde, *De l'Union des Arts et de l'Industrie,* Paris 1856; Ph. de Chennevières, *Souvenirs d'un Directeur des Beaux-Arts,* vols. I–II, Paris 1885; *l'Union Centrale des Arts Décoratifs. Palais du Louvre. Pavillon de Marsan. Actes Constitutifs. Status. Notice Historique. Membres Fondateurs.* Paris n.d.; L. Bénédite, France, in R. Graul, *Die Krisis im Kunstgewerbe,* Leipzig 1901, pp. 21–38.

The suggestions contributed by these three did in fact constitute a fully-developed programme for museums, exhibitions, and training capable of solving the problem. This was followed in 1856 by Leon Laborde's rousing call to arms—*De l'Union des Arts et de l'Industrie*, and in 1858 the *Société du Progrès de l'Art Industriel* was formed, two exhibitions of applied art being given under its auspices in 1861 and 1863.

The next stage in the development in France was also linked to a world exhibition. During the exhibition of 1863 in Paris a number of exhibitors, critics, and artists joined hands—with the approval of the Emperor Napoleon III, and formed the *Union Centrale des Beaux-Arts appliqués à l'Industrie*. The French were quick to acknowledge the progress which the English had made during the preceding decade, and realised their own weakness. The report of the organising committee contained among other things the following passage: "L'industrie anglaise en particulier, très arriérée au point de vue de l'art, lors de l'Exposition de 1851, à fait depuis quelques années des progrès prodigieux, et, si elle continue à marcher du même pas, nous pourrions être bientôt dépassés."[2]

On July 24, 1864, the association was constituted, with the aim of founding a retrospective museum, a contemporary museum, a library, courses, and competitions, and already in the same year a museum was opened, while exhibitions were arranged in 1865, 1869, 1874, and 1876.

Side by side with this organisation another, no less important, was gradually developed, viz. the *Société du Musée des Arts Décoratifs*, which was founded in 1877, thanks largely to the efforts of the Duc de Chaulnes. Its primary object was to acquire a museum collection, and after four years it was possible to exhibit the first collection.

In both these circles, however, the disadvantages of having two separate organisations, both working for the same objects, were realised, and in 1880 an amalgamation took place, the new society being called the *Union Centrale des Arts Décoratifs*, receiving state authorisation on May 15, 1882, and having as its organ the *Revue des Arts Décoratifs*.

2 *l'Union Centrale des Arts Décoratifs. Palais du Louvre. Pavillon de Marsan.* Paris n.d., p. 38. "English industry in particular, artistically backward, has made prodigious strides since the Exhibition of 1851, and if this rate is maintained we shall soon be left behind."

At the World Exhibition in 1889 Gallé was one of the exhibitors, and it was immediately clear, not only that applied art had made great progress, but that there was a need for a special *salon* of decorative art, and ever since 1891, the year in which the *Musée des Arts Décoratifs* was founded, there has been an annual exhibition of decorative art in the *Salon des Champs de Mars*. Here men like Delaherche, Gallé, Dampt, Charpentier, Cheret, and Chaplet, painters and sculptors, used to meet. In 1893 Chennevières reorganised the collection of decorative art in the Luxembourg Museum, and made purchases of contemporary art, while in 1895 the *Société des Artistes Françaises* was founded, with a certain national air in harmony with the trend of the eighteen-nineties. It was here that René Lalique made his début in 1895.

The development in England was more or less on the same lines: the basis was provided by the private enterprise of foreseeing and practical-minded art-lovers, and also by the establishment of art schools and museums. But a most essential difference between the English Arts and Crafts Movement[3] and the French Movement is that the former was more associated with the Middle Ages—not its form but its spirit.

As early as 1824 all schools of art in France had been placed under the jurisdiction of the *Ministère d'Instruction Publique des Beaux-Arts*, thus ensuring that the actual artistic training should be comparatively fixed and moulded by tradition. In England the development was rather different, as discussed in Alf Bøe's interesting study *From Gothic Revival to Functional Form.*

Sporadic attempts at guiding the movement into proper channels had been made by various local organisations,[4] while in 1835–36 a parliamentary committee[5] was set up for the purpose of investigating art education. Its

[3] A Survey of the Arts and Crafts Movement—its history and development—has not yet been written. The following publications are among the important sources: T. J. Cobden Sanderson, *The Arts and Crafts Movement,* London 1905; W. Crane, Ideals in the Art of the Arts and Crafts Movement, *Ideals in Art,* London 1905, pp. 1–34; H. P. Horne, The Century Guild, *The Art Journal,* vol. VII, 1887, pp. 295–98; A. H. Mackmurdo, History of the Arts and Crafts Movement, unpublished, The archives of Connie McQueen; *idem,* The Guild Flag's Unfurling, *The Hobby Horse,* No. 1, 1884, pp. 2–13; D. Newton, Arts and Crafts, *World Review,* January 1953, pp. 28–32; O. L. Triggs, *Chapter in the History of the Arts and Crafts Movement,* Chicago 1902.

[4] *Birmingham College of Arts and Crafts,* founded 1821; *Nottingham College of Arts and Crafts,* 1843.

[5] For further information about the development before the Great Exhibition, cf. A. Bøe, "Govern-

findings resulted in 1837 in the setting up of the *Normal School of Design*, which in 1849 had as many as 16 branches.

In 1847–49 reports were issued by the New Parliamentary Committee, and gradually there was an increase of activity both in private and official quarters. In 1849 the *Journal of Design* was started by R. Redgrave and H. Cole—men who were both destined to play an important role in shaping the new course of English applied art. But it was not until after the Great Exhibition in 1851 that the problems relating to the training of applied artists, as well as a satisfactory production of applied art, were fully realised.

Already in 1847 Cole had founded *Summarly's Art Manufactures*, and although this attempt to associate leading painters and sculptors directly with the applied art industry only lasted for three years, it constituted a clearly expressed desire to raise the level of English applied art. The severe criticism and reaction which were a sequel to the Great Exhibition[6] were also soon to bear fruit. In 1852 the *Department of Practical Art* was set up, though its name was changed after one year to the *Department of Science and Art*, and at the same time the *Victoria and Albert Museum* was founded, on the assumption that a great deal of its activity should be based on teaching.

As was only to be expected Ruskin was actively committed to this movement, and together with the pre-Raphaelites D. G. Rossetti, F. Madox Brown, and E. Burne Jones and others, he taught in the *Working-man's Guild* in Oxford, founded in 1854. 400 reprints of Ruskin's chapter the *Nature of Gothic* from his *Stones of Venice* were distributed at the opening meeting.[7]

In 1875 Ruskin founded the *St. George's Guild*, an association which in its social structure is of minor interest in this connection, but is interesting in that the guild's form was inspired by the Middle Ages.

The most important single contributor, however, was William Morris. The year after he had moved into *Red House* in 1860, newly married and

mental Reform," Part I, *From Gothic Revival to Functional Form. A Study in Victorian Theories of Design*, Oslo. In Print.

6 Universal Infidelity in Principles of Design, *The Journal of Design and Manufactures*, vol. V, 1851, pp. 158–61; R. Redgrave, Supplementary Report on Design, *Reports of the Juries*, London 1852; N. Wornum, The Exhibition as a Lesson in Taste, *The Art Journal*, Illustrated Catalogue to the Exhibition 1851, pp. I***-XXII***.

7 A. H. Mackmurdo, History of the Arts and Crafts Movement, p. 31, The archives of Connie McQueen.

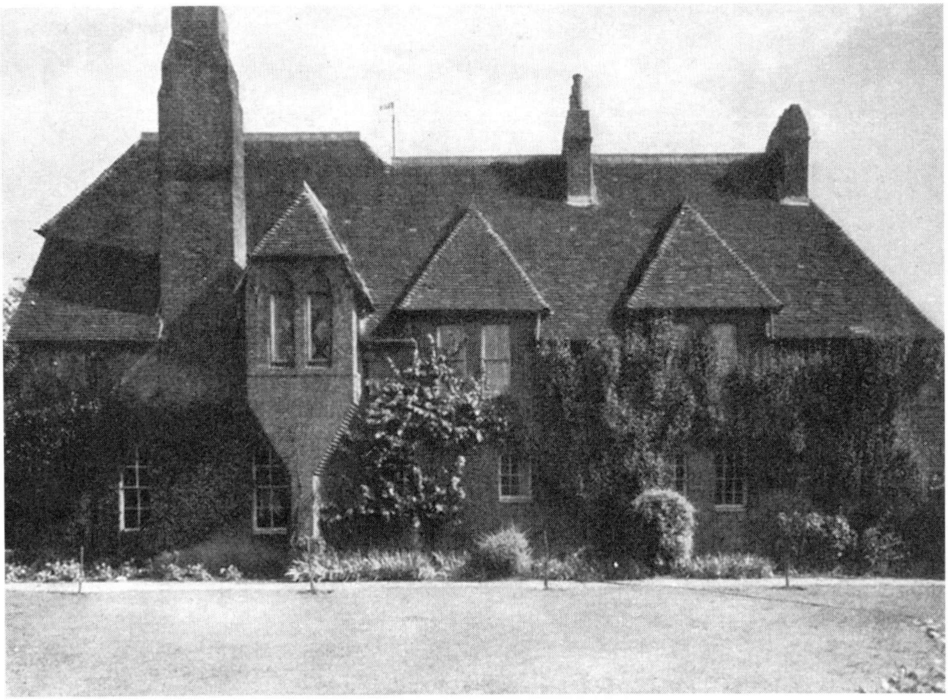

Fig. 76. Webb: Red House, Bexley Heath, Kent. 1859—60.
National Buildings Record Copyright.

full of optimism, his firm took concrete shape, with offices in 8 Red Lion Square, close to the house where he and his companions had lived during their gay student days. *Red House*, its architecture, interior fittings, as well as the men who worked there, are all important factors in the history of nineteenth-century art, and of basic importance to the Arts and Crafts Movement (figs. 76, 77, 78).

Here, in almost rural surroundings worked William Morris, Philip Webb, the pre-Raphaelites Ford Madox Brown and Edward Burne Jones—and occasionally Dante Gabriel Rossetti—as well as the shrewd mathematician Charles J. Faulkner. The seventh member of the firm was Peter Paul Marshall, a friend of Madox Brown, originally an engineer, but like the others intensely interested in arts and crafts.

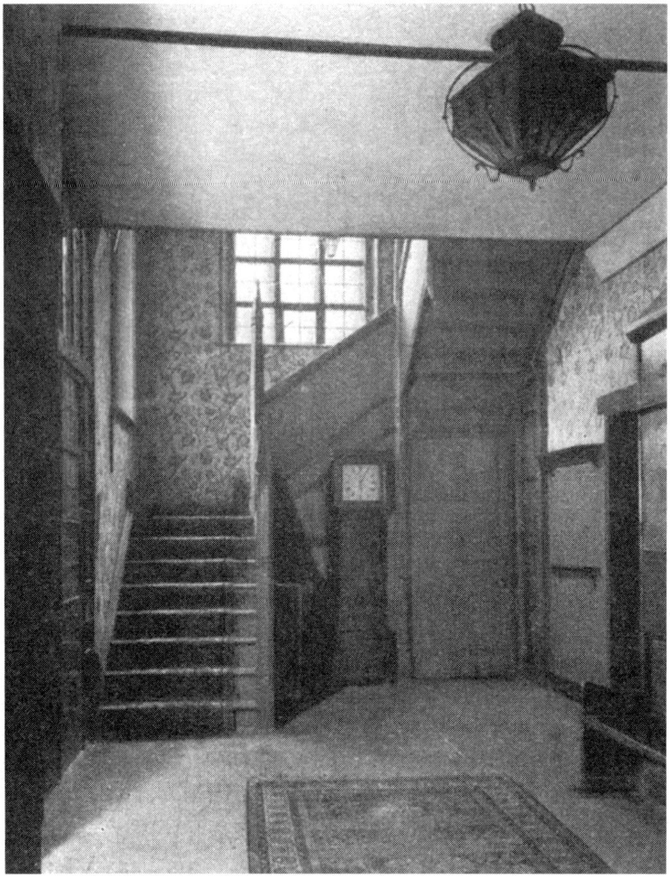

Fig. 77. Webb: The Hall.
Red House, Bexley Heath, Kent.
1859—60.
National Buildings Record Copyright.

From Morris's doctrine and his entire attitude we know that simplicity, honest craftsmanship, and co-operation between artist and artisan became the watchword of the day, inspired by a profound admiration for the arts and crafts of the Middle Ages, and in violent reaction to the taste of the age: "Only in a few isolated cases . . . was there anything then to be bought ready-made that Morris could be content with in his house. Not a chair, or table, or bed; not a cloth or paper hanging for the walls; nor tiles to line fireplaces or passages; nor a curtain or a candlestick; nor a jug to hold wine or a glass to drink it out of, but had to be reinvented . . ."[8]

[8] J. W. Mackail, *The Life of William Morris,* I-II, London 1899, The World's Classics ed. London 1950, p. 147.

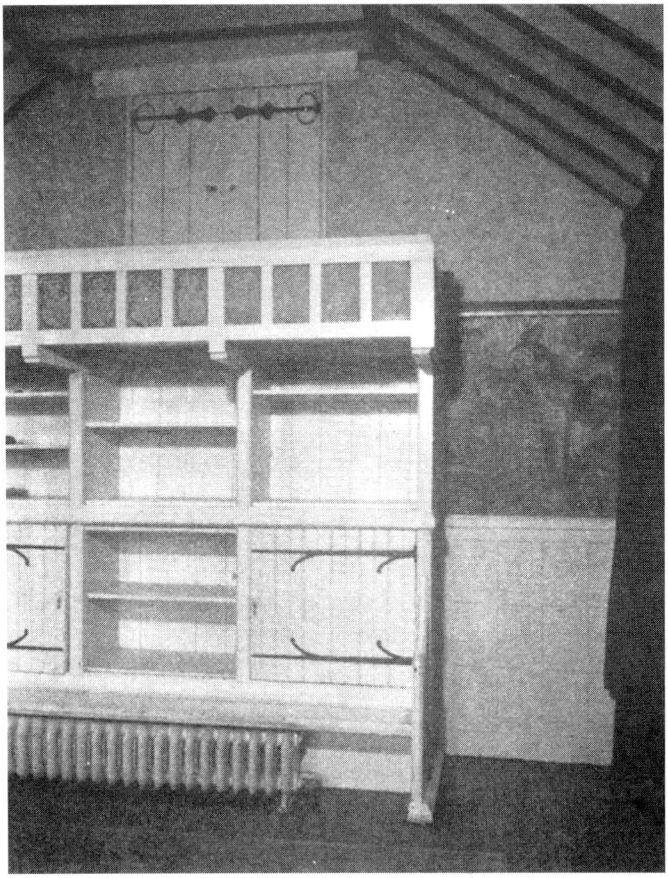

Fig. 78. Webb: Interior.
Red House, Bexley Heath, Kent.
1859—60.
National Buildings Record Copyright.

But already in 1865 Morris was forced, for financial reasons, to relinquish Red House and leave his palace of art—as he calls it in his letters to Burne Jones—and the firm now moved to 26 Queen Square, London. In 1875 the firm was reorganised as *Morris & Co.*, and 1881 the workshops were moved to Merton Abbey. In 1877 and right up to the nineteen-twenties the firm of Morris & Co. had showcases in Oxford Street, but in 1940 it went into voluntary liquidation. As the firm survived until well into the twentieth century, so its influence spread well beyond the contemporary age.

From the eighteen-seventies Morris and his movement seemed to be having a clear influence on contemporary taste and trends, and by now the firm had taken part in international exhibitions, while its production comprised practically every branch of applied art.

The generation born around the year 1850—Arthur Mackmurdo in 1851, Walter Crane and Lewis Day in 1845, Selwyn Image in 1849, C. F. Annesley Vosey in 1857, as well as the somewhat younger Herbert Horne, born 1864, and Charles R. Ashbee, 1863—are all in some way or other associated with Ruskin and Morris or the Gothic Revival. And it was this handful of enterprising men who were to start the Arts and Crafts Movement, and became the leading lights in the various organisations which the movement fostered.

Of these organisations the oldest was *The Century Guild*, founded in 1882 with the object—as expressed in its statutes—"to render all branches of art the sphere no longer of the tradesman, but of the artist. It would restore building, decoration, glass-painting, pottery, wood-carving and metal to their right place beside painting and sculpture. In other words, the Century Guild seeks to emphasise the Unity of Art and by thus dignifying Art in all of its forms, it hopes to make it living, a thing of our own century and of the people." The Guild owed its inception to the enterprise of Mackmurdo and Image, and in 1884 Mackmurdo joined forces with Horne in publishing the *Hobby Horse* (fig. 79). In the same year a number of artists who where in the habit of meeting at the house of Crane ever since 1881 formed themselves into an organisation called *The Art Workers Guild*, with Crane and Day as its leading originators. The two last-mentioned were also actively engaged in the *Arts and Crafts Exhibition Society*, both at its inception in 1888 and its subsequent development. A smaller organisation, the *Home Arts and Industries Association*, was founded in 1885, and here too Mackmurdo was actively engaged. In 1888 both the *Guild and School of Handicraft* and the *National Association for the Advancement of Art and its Application to Industry* were founded, the former on the initiative of Ashbee, while in the second Mackmurdo and Crane were active members from the start.

Thus it may be seen that all these organisations recruited their members from, and largely owed their inception to the initiative of, a small clique of enterprising men.

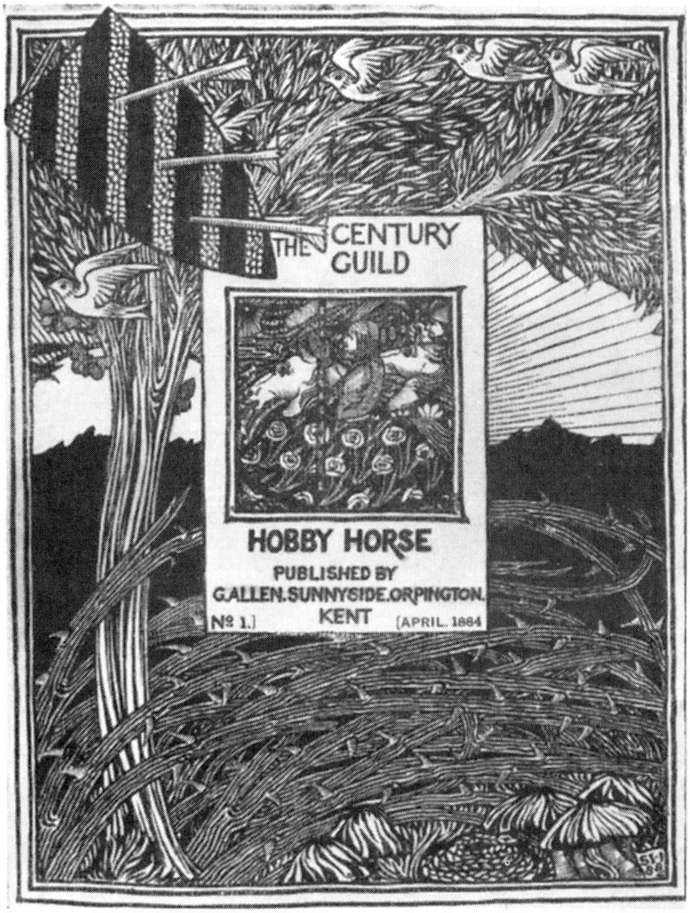

Fig. 79. Image: Cover for *the Hobby Horse*. 1888.

In this milieu of Gothic revivalists, naturalists and theoreticians—a milieu which was alive to the simple and the genuine, where a Ruskin or a Morris could provide a source of inspiration—we shall find the first linear and floral English Art Nouveau, created by Crane and Dresser.

*

The Arts and Crafts Movement is, in the widest sense of the word, the most important contribution to the entirely new trend in applied art both in Great Britain and on the Continent—and yet at the same time a factor which must be taken into consideration in the purely formal development of Art Nouveau.

English Proto-Art Nouveau

Since the term Art Nouveau is associated with a Continental movement in the 1890's, it would be rather misleading to apply the same label to English trends about twenty years earlier. It is possible to trace a whole chain of dated works right up to the middle of the 1890's—not all Art Nouveau, but possessing several of the most important elements of this form-language and directly foreshadowing the later international style. The best solution seems to be to call this earlier English stylistic phenomenon proto-Art Nouveau. This label is, of course, only intended to apply to style-tendencies and is not meant to describe a period or a movement.

By studying close on one hundred books illustrated by Walter Crane (1845–1915),[1] from 1863 to the time of his death, it is possible to trace a change of style about 1870. His first books, such as *The New Forest*, 1863, and *Sing a Song of Sixpence*, 1865, contain pen drawings with use of light and shade, no special contours, but characterised by a thin searching line, such as we also find in *The Old Courtier*, 1865–68. But in *King Luckie-Boy's Party*, from 1870, the light-and-shade modelling has been markedly reduced. He works with a fixed monochrome background, the various colour planes being largely of the same shade and surrounded by a fixed black contour. In his two children's books, *Picture Book* and *New Toy Book*, both from 1873, the contrast between his light pen style with the many Gothic details, as well as his shading in some of the drawings (in the former), are in marked contrast to the simple unmodelled surfaces with the fixed contour line (in the latter). The outline is clear, and the actual run of his line starts to acquire a value of its own, such as we also see in *Lines and Outlines—Mrs. Mundu at Home*, 1875. The title in itself is indicative!

In wallpaper design a fixed background, clearly differentiated planes and clean contours were not usual at that time. By 1875 Crane had acquired

[1] Lewis F. Day, An Artist in Design, *Magazine of Art*, vol. X, 1886–87, pp. 95–100; The Art of Walter Crane, Notes by the Artist, *The Art Journal*, The Easter Art Annual, vol. L, 1898, pp. 1–32, Otto v. Schleinitz, *Walter Crane*, Leipzig, 1902, P. G. Konody, *The Art of Walter Crane*, London, 1902, Walter Crane, *An Artist's Reminiscences*, London 1907. Horniman's file, V. & A., London.

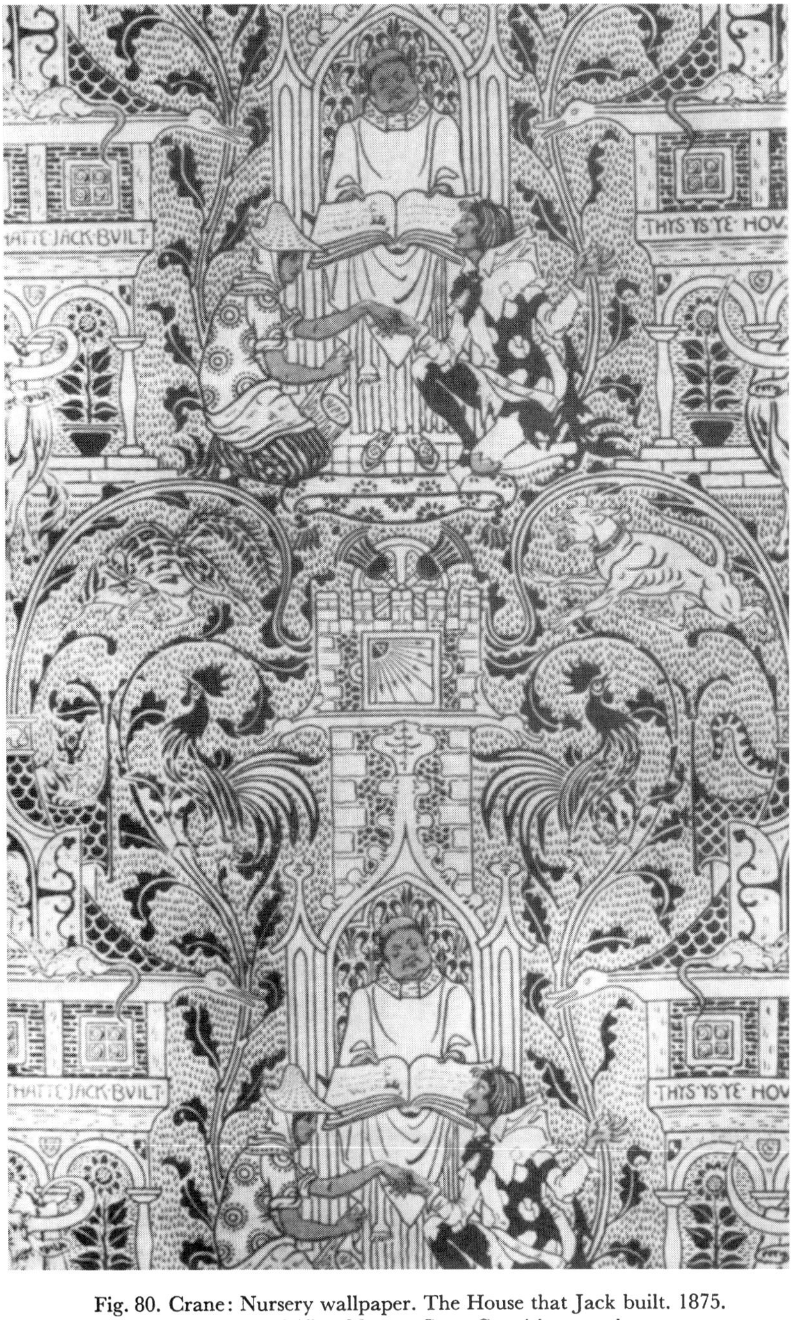

Fig. 80. Crane: Nursery wallpaper. The House that Jack built. 1875.
Victoria and Albert Museum. Crown Copyright reserved.

these qualities in his pattern design, as might be seen in *Bo-Peep*, *Boy Blue*, *Queen of Hearts*, *The Sleeping Beauty*, *Iris and the Kingfisher*, *The House that Jack Built*[2] (fig. 80), all nursery wallpapers, and many of them having the same title and subject-matter as we find in his children's books.

What strikes us in his nursery wallpapers from 1875[3] (fig. 81) is the growing rhythm and the wealth of floral ornamentation. Every single figure seems to be enclosed in a world of creepers which possess a flamelike and whiplike rhythm. This is still more marked in *The House that Jack Built* (fig. 80): here the rhythm of the plant stems runs off into a distended and clearly designed arch which terminates abruptly. This arch, with its long flowing lines and its energetic termination, is precisely one of the formal characteristics of the Art Nouveau style—and at the same time essentially different from the contemporary tendril coils.

Morris's pattern design was one of the forerunners of Crane's art, as the latter himself has pointed out,[4] but in one respect he differs from his great predecessor—Morris's tendril composition is always symmetrical, even when he builds up his pattern with the help of diagonal rhythmic stems, as in *The Wild Tulip*, *The Bruges*, *The Wandle* and *The Way*. Crane's tendril, on the other hand, is asymmetric, and shows a characteristic reflex movement where it terminates.

This is what is new and fundamental in Crane's linear form of expression. On a floral basis Crane developed a stylistic element which was to prove one of the outstanding characteristics of the Art Nouveau style, and which, 25 years later, was so aptly described as "a swirl and a blob."[5]

A few years later Christopher Dresser (1834–1904)[6] designed his wine-jug,[7] 1875 (fig. 82). At the time Dresser was associated with the Linthorpe

2 Cat. No. E. 2292–1932. Victoria and Albert Museum.

3 Cat. No. E. 4043–1915. Victoria and Albert Museum.

4 W. Crane, Of Wall Paper, *Arts and Crafts Essays,* London 1893, pp. 52–62.

5 *Journal of Decorative Art,* vol. XXI, 1901, p. 237.

6 The Work of Christopher Dresser, *The Studio,* vol. XIV, 1898, pp. 104–113; obituary, *The Builder,* December 10, 1904, p. 134; N. Pevsner, Christopher Dresser, Industrial Designer, *The Architectural Review,* LXXXI, 1937, pp. 183–86. The illustrations from his sketchbooks in this article, are the only ones extant; the remainder were lost during the war 1939–45.

7 Victoria and Albert Museum, *A Catalogue of an Exhibition of Victorian and Edwardian Decorative Arts,* London 1952, p. 35, No. H.18.

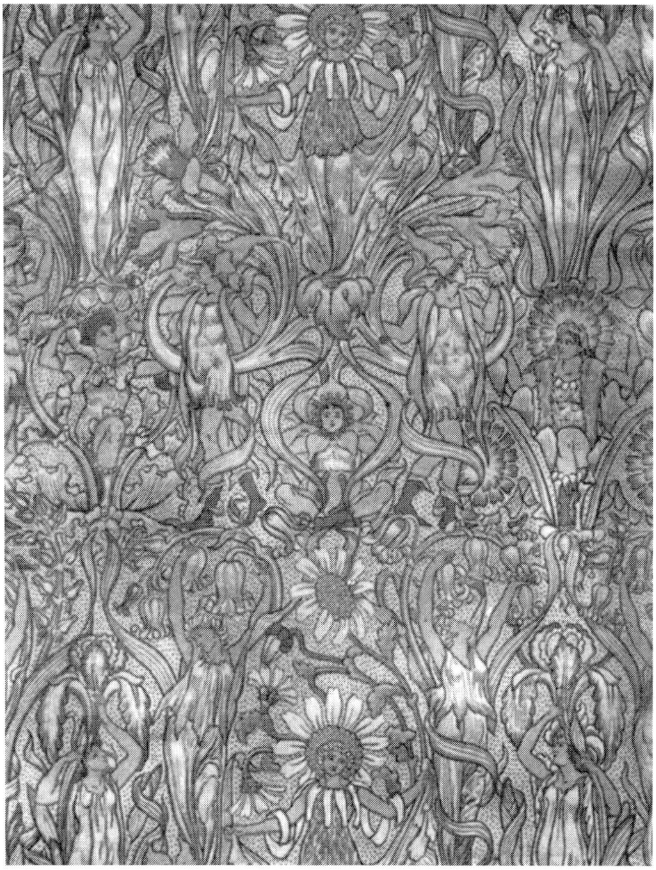

Fig. 81. Crane: Nursery wallpaper. 1875.
Victoria and Albert Museum. Crown Copyright reserved.

Pottery in the capacity of art adviser, and at the same time he was busy recording his theories in writing. He had been made art editor of *The Furniture Gazette*, was engaged in founding the *Art Furnisher's Alliance*, and at the same time was writing a series of articles for *The Technical Educator*, from 1870, articles which were subsequently expanded and published in book form in 1880. In its revolutionary simplicity this jug occupies a place apart from contemporary work—including the bulk of Dresser's own work. In it we find none of the bristling contours of contemporary applied art, nor the *horror vacui:* instead form and function have fused in a unity which may with good reason be admired by a child of the twentieth century.

Even the functionalistic yardstick of our own age can without a doubt be applied to this work of art, and it satisfies all the demands. But at the same time it can be regarded from an angle which is less conditioned by an age or a period, and we simply enjoy the pure glass and silver, which harmonise so excellently in their texture, finding beauty in the graceful play of line, the firm contours, and the vigorous curvature. The rhythmical design of the handle itself has a curvature which is characteristic of a man with Dresser's aesthetic delight in the curvilinear, while we feel the impression of great power which he strove to convey, and for which he found his inspiration in "luxuriant tropical vegetation, the spring growth, and in certain bones of birds which are associated with flight and strength."[8] His aims are expressed in picturesque but clear language, and his realisation of these intentions shows the same intellectual clarity, simplicity of structure and truthfulness of construction.[9] The legs, too, contain the same energetic termination which is so readily adaptable, while the swirl and the blob are never far away.

Crane's and Dresser's works are by no means Art Nouveau, though they do contain elements which were to form an essential part of the style of the eighteen-nineties. It is no coincidence that it is precisely in the work of these theoreticians, both with a marked penchant for the linear, the latter a botanist, and the former risen from the ranks of the pre-Raphaelites, that we find those first features that were to become so popular and such basic features of a stylistic form-language.

An investigation of the form-language of other leading artists will gradually reveal more and more features of the same character.

We next find proto-Art Nouveau in the work of one of the leading personalities of the Arts and Crafts Movement, Arthur H. Mackmurdo (1851–1942),[10] and in his circle.

8 Chr. Dresser, Principles in Design, III, *Technical Educator,* vol. I, 1870, p. 121.

9 *Ibid.,* X, vol. I, p. 378.

10 V. Aymer, Mr. Arthur H. Mackmurdo and the Century Guild, *The Studio,* vol. XVI, 1899, pp. 183–192; N. Pevsner, A Pioneer Designer, Arthur H. Mackmurdo, *The Architectural Review,* vol. LXXXIII, 1938, pp. 141–43; *idem Pioneers of Modern Design,* New York, 1949, pp. 91 sqq.; Edw. Carter, Obituary in *the Journal of the Royal Institute of British Architects,* April 1942, pp. 94 sq.; Archives and files in the William Morris Gallery, Walthamstow; collections of Miss Connie McQueen and Miss Elinor Pugh.

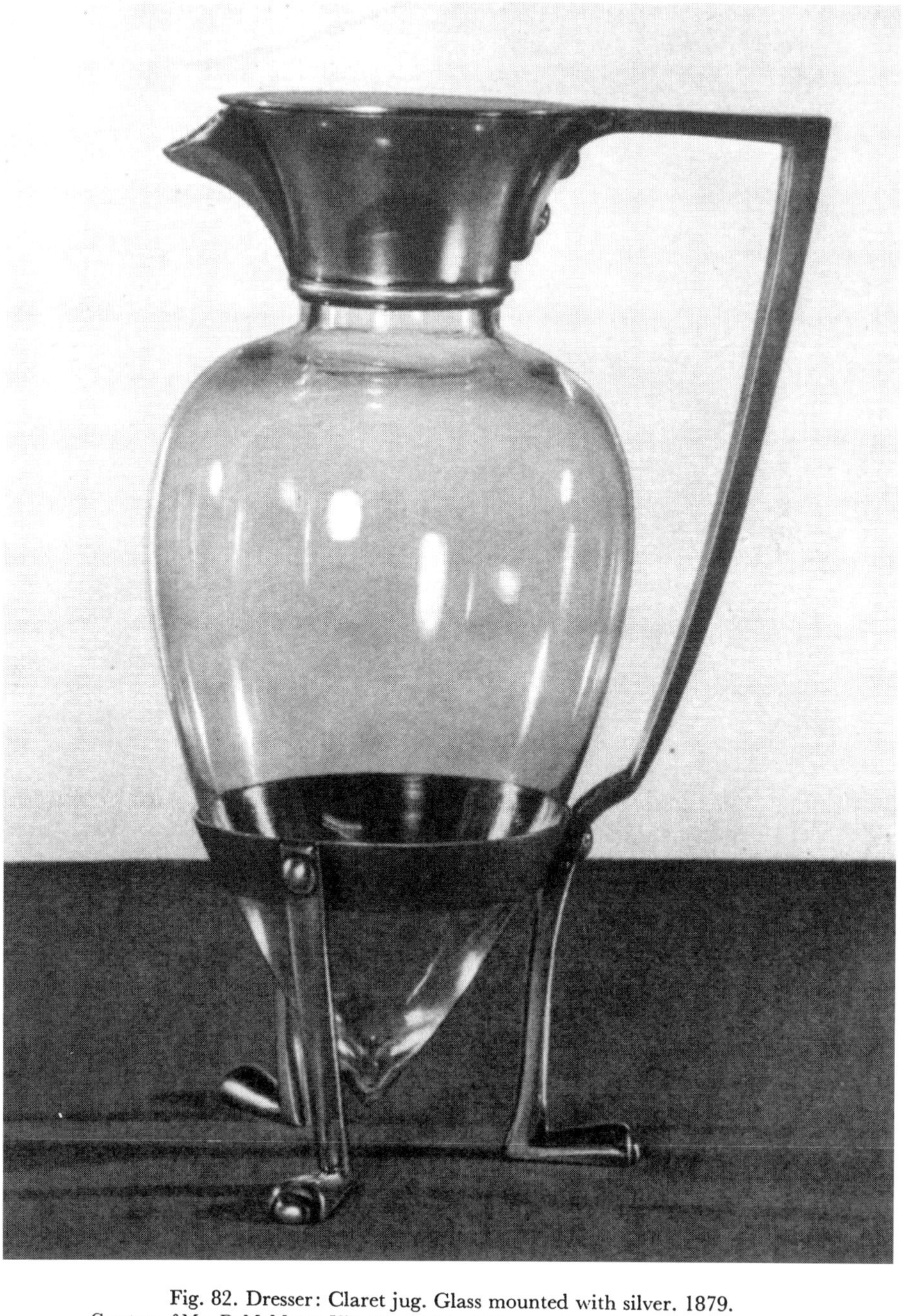

Fig. 82. Dresser: Claret jug. Glass mounted with silver. 1879.
Courtesy of Mrs. D. M. Mayer. Victoria and Albert Museum photo. Crown Copyright reserved.

After working as a pupil of the neo-Gothic artist James Brooks, Mackmurdo attended Ruskin's lectures, and accompanied him in 1874 to Italy, remaining there till 1876. In Florence the energetic young man fell out with the municipal authorities on the subject of the restoration of the cathedral, and the upshot was that he was prevented from working in peace at his sketches in the streets. In 1877, back in England, he was one of the prime movers in founding the *Society for the Protection of Ancient Buildings* in the same year. In 1878 he was back in Florence, in 1879 he visited Switzerland, returning to Italy in 1880. During all these travels, apart from the ordinary run of sketches, commonly undertaken by a student of architecture, he made a great many studies of Gothic and Romanesque tendrils and their floral details, as well as a whole series of naturalistic studies of plants, flowers, buds, and stalks.[11]

When he returned to England in 1881 he designed the chair with the highly characteristic proto-Art Nouveau back (fig. 151). The *point de départ* for all these twirls, which remind us of drifting seaweed, is entirely floral, and this floating stalk motif was to become one of his favourites in the eighteen-eighties.[12] The motif also has the reflex coil which gives it added power and an effect of elasticity.

In other respects the chair is traditionally English, not least in the outline of the back, and is remarkable for its simplicity, which is a feature of nearly all of his furniture. Most striking in its simplicity is the desk designed in 1886[13] (fig. 83), a work of great importance to the history of furniture design thanks to its lack of period features. This is no copy, but a piece of furniture which possesses its own particular style; it points not only in the direction of the eighteen-nineties, but foreshadows the Modern Movement and the twentieth century.

In the *Peacock* wallpaper,[14] 1882 (fig. 84), we find a floral motif with the same floating, seaweed-like character. On closer analysis, however, we shall find that the name is well chosen, because, apart from the leaves with their incessant coils, its pattern is based on the symbol of the aesthetic

11 Sketches and drawing books, William Morris Gallery, Walthamstow.

12 E.g., used as a carved motif on cabinet, No. G.9, William Morris Gallery, Walthamstow,

13 Cat. No. G.5, William Morris Gallery.

14 Cat. No. F.39, William Morris Gallery, Walthamstow; Victoria and Albert Museum, *op. cit.,* L 18a.

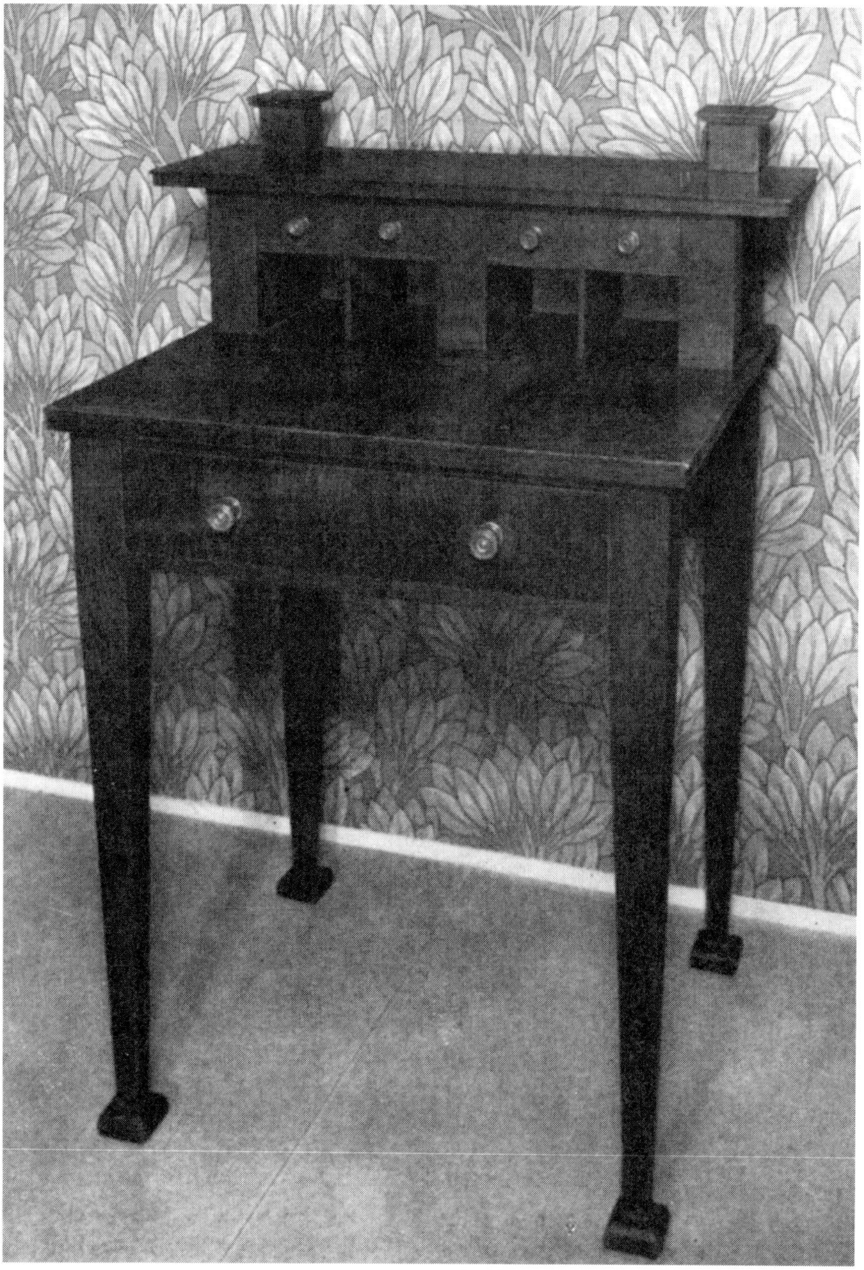

Fig. 83. Mackmurdo: Writing table. Oak. 1886.
William Morris Gallery, Walthamstow. Victoria and Albert Museum photo. Crown Copyright reserved.

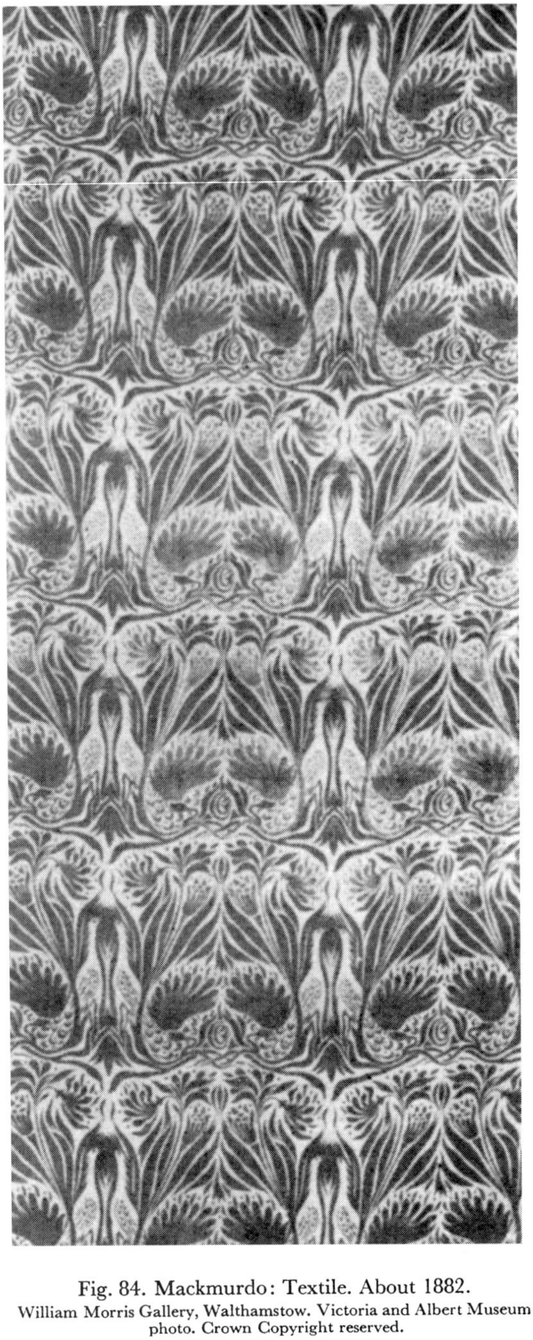

Fig. 84. Mackmurdo: Textile. About 1882.
William Morris Gallery, Walthamstow. Victoria and Albert Museum photo. Crown Copyright reserved.

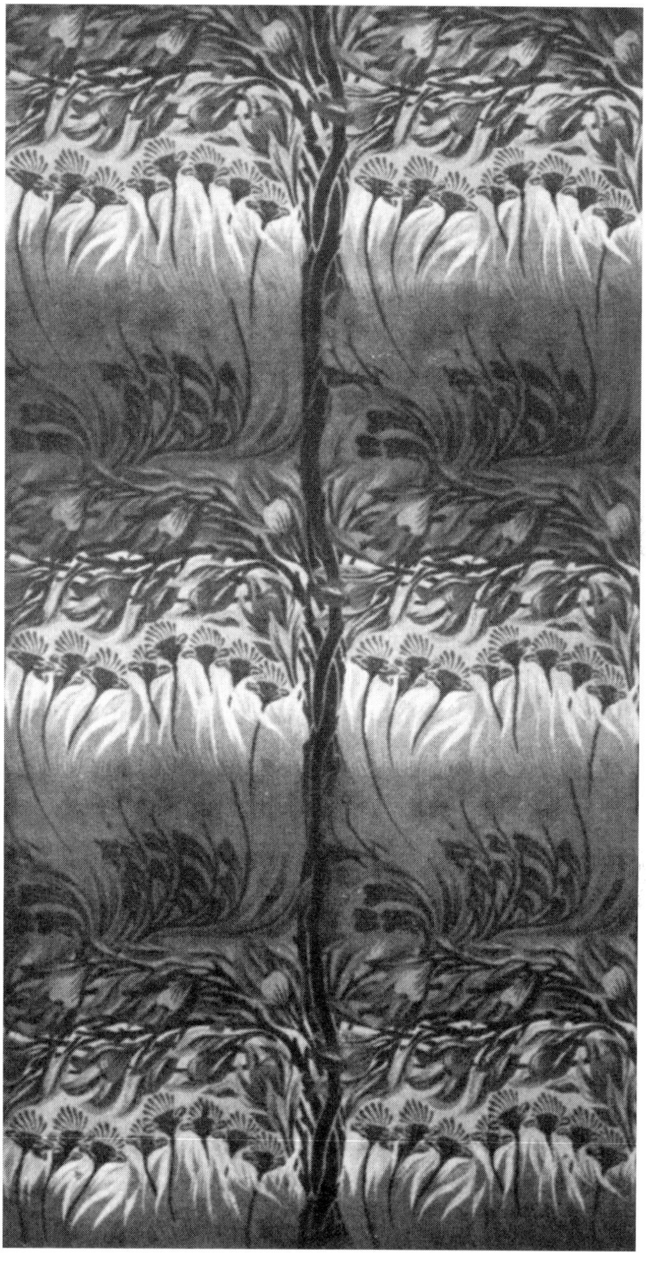

Fig. 85. Mackmurdo: Tapestry hanging. About 1882.
Courtesy of Miss Elinor M. Pugh.

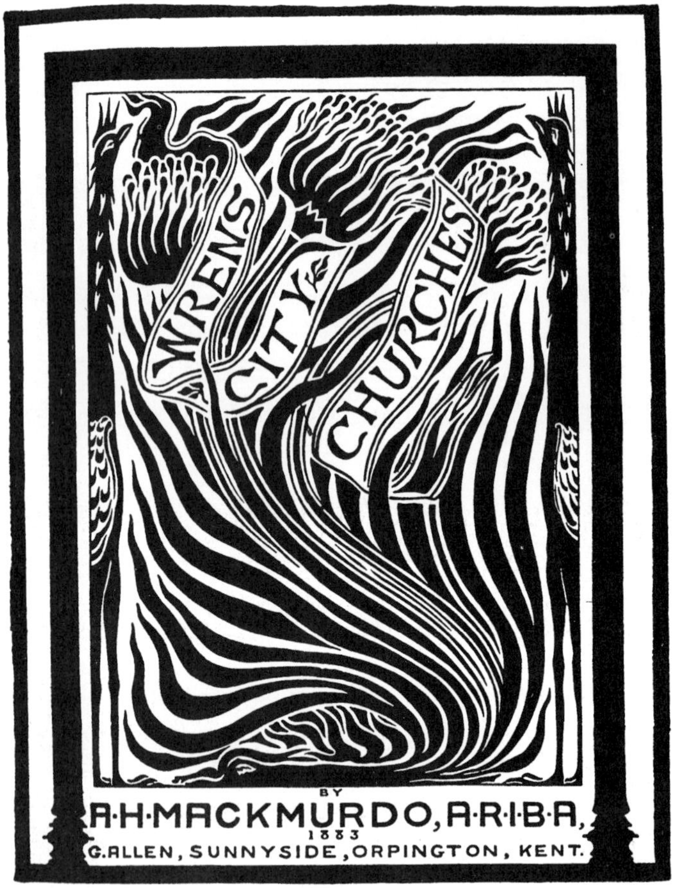

Fig. 86. Mackmurdo: Cover for *Wren's City Churches*. 1883.

movement, the peacock, with two of these birds facing one another antithetically, while between their tail-feathers and a petal we find the initials C.G., standing for the Century Guild, entwined. This is emblematic of a textile design of 1882. In the same year Mackmurdo designed the Tapestry Hanging[15] (fig. 85). Here too the basic motif is floral, and in its restless rhythm and whirling movement it repeats in more lively fashion the formal elements we have already noted. The general colour impression is brown, with a dark brown occasionally tending to violet in one direction and shading off into pale beige in the other. The flowers are deep blue and brownish-violet.

15 In the possession of Miss Elinor Pugh.

When Mackmurdo designed the cover for his book *Wren's City Churches*, 1883 (fig. 86), he used the same floral motif, and while the three surrounding peacocks have little bearing on the plant stalks, it is still more difficult to find any association between the cover and the contents. Mackmurdo merely uses the cover to give expression to his decorative talent, and combines in a perfectly natural way a motif which was popular at the time with the composition which at the moment was nearest to his heart. In 1884 he designed the wallpaper "*Thorn motif on butterfly ground*"[16] (fig. 87). Once again we find this rhythmic curve, a swirl and a blob. In the embroidered screen[17] from the same year (fig. 88) the motif is more flame-like, while his imaginative flower and colours are the same and correspond with the impression we have of his colour range. It was not until the eighteen-nineties that it tended to become lighter.

It was not only in two-

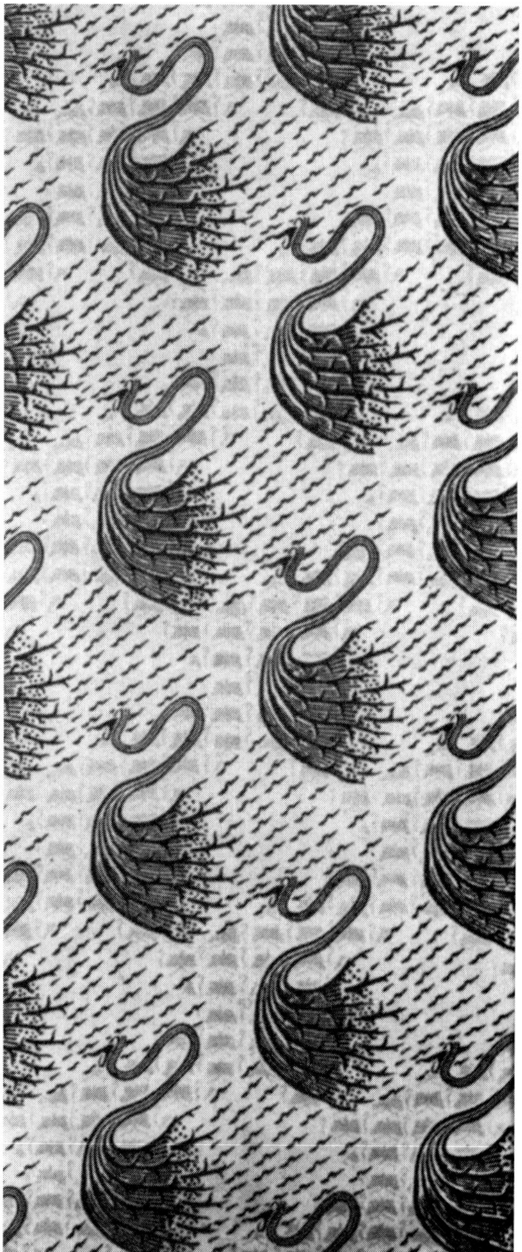

Fig. 87. Mackmurdo: Textile. About 1884.
William Morris Gallery, Walthamstow. Crown Copyright reserved.

16 Cat. No. F.99, William Morris Gallery, Walthamstow; Victoria and Albert Museum, *op. cit.*, L.18b.

17 Cat. No. G.17, William Morris Gallery, Walthamstow; Victoria and Albert Museum, *op. cit.*, L.4.

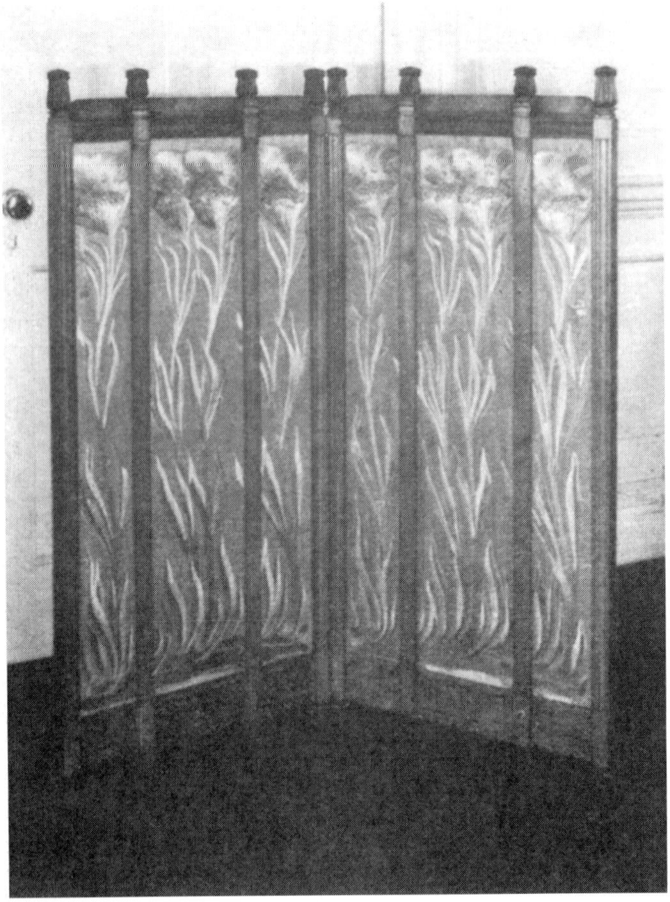

Fig. 88. Mackmurdo: Screen. Satinwood with panels embroidered in silks and gold thread. 1884.
William Morris Gallery, Walthamstow. Crown Copyright reserved.

dimensional pattern-design, however, that Mackmurdo developed his peculiar special decorative talents. They may be seen again in a brass lampstand[18] (fig. 89) from 1884. We recognise the stalk-like floral motif executed on the top part in *repoussé*, while the long flowing rhythm of the legs sweep up from the robust foot. But what makes this piece of work proto-Art Nouveau rather than Art Nouveau—and typical of Mackmurdo—is the refined moulding of the rims, so characteristic of Mackmurdo's furniture and of his enthusiasm for the early Italian Renaissance generally.

18 Made by the Century Guild. Exhibited in Manchester 1887. Colchester and Essex Museum. Illustrated mounted in *The Studio,* vol. XVI, 1889, p. 191.

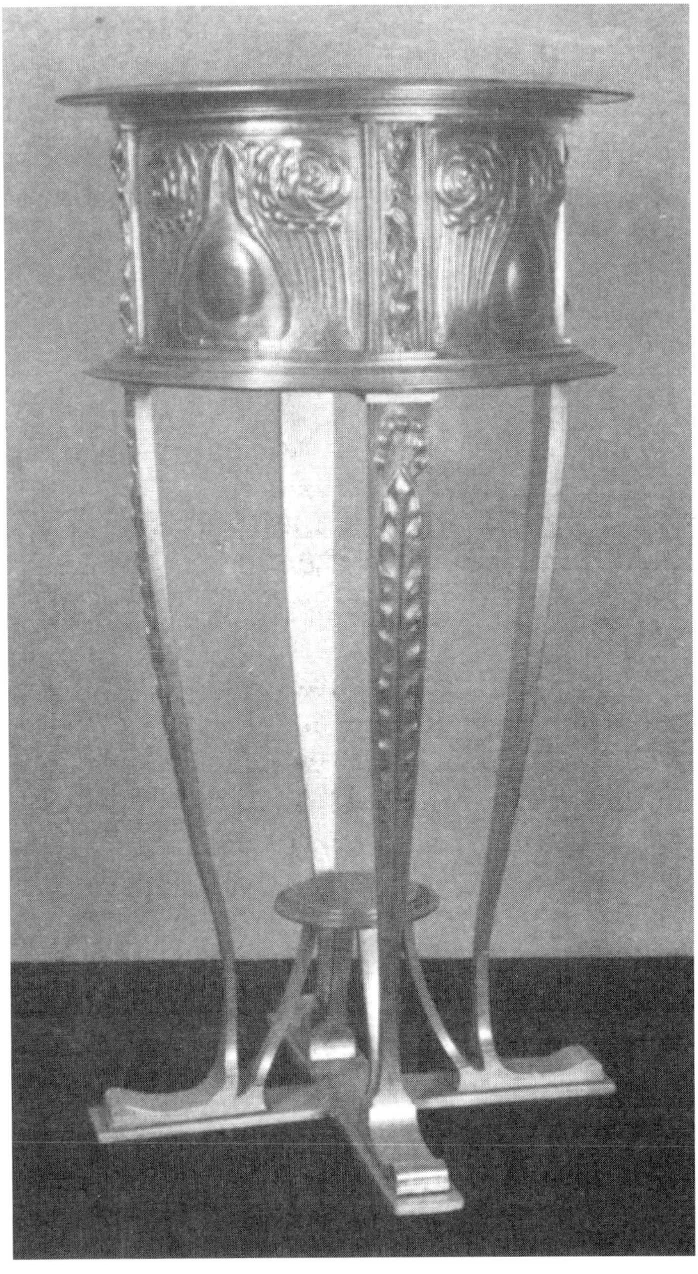

Fig. 89. Mackmurdo: Standing lamp. Repousée brass. 1884.
The Colchester and Essex Museum. Crown Copyright reserved.

And yet it would be wrong, on the basis of the above, to conclude that Mackmurdo's decoration is exclusively floral proto-Art Nouveau.

His furniture from the eighteen-eighties has an air of the Florentine early Renaissance; the best example of this seems to be a cupboard from 1880[19], but in other respects the simplification and execution of this work are so entirely Mackmurdo's own that it is a far cry from the ordinary neo-Renaissance of the age. But the most important impulse he received in Italy was the idea of the ideal union of artist and artisan in the Middle Ages and in the Renaissance.

In Mackmurdo's architectural work the significant characteristic again is the simplicity of construction which was so evident in the desk. Gradually, however, he abandoned architecture in order to devote himself to political and social activities, and after 1904 he rarely worked as an architect. His last major work, Great Ruffins, Wickham Bishops, Witham, Essex, commenced in 1904 and completed about ten years later in a moderate neo-Renaissance, has no historical significance.[20] As he says himself: "In his later years through his study of the work of Sir Christopher Wren, he had a strong leaning to the early Italian Renaissance, exemplified in the works of Sansovino and Alberti."[21]

Closely associated with Mackmurdo and the Arts and Crafts Movement was Selwyn Image (1849–1930),[22] a highly cultivated and versatile individual, and co-founder with Mackmurdo of the Century Guild. Together with Clement J. Heaton (1861–1940), and Herbert Percy Horne (1864–1916), these two formed the core of the Guild.

Among Image's work we also find various sketches and wallpaper designs, made immediately preceding and just after 1880, which might be described as proto-Art Nouveau.[23] In his neat and delicate work, as for

19 *Ibid.*, illustrated p. 185.

20 Information and photos, Miss Elinor Pugh's collection.

21 A. H. Mackmurdo, Monography, MS., p. 4, Miss C. McQueen's collection.

22 Biography in William Morris Gallery, Walthamstow, file 192/4; Selwyn Image and A. H. Mackmurdo, *The Weekend Review,* August 6, 1932, p. 162; *Selwyn Image Letters,* London 1932, edited by A. H. Mackmurdo; The Work of Mr. Selwyn Image, *The Studio,* vol. XIV, 1898, pp. 3–10.

23 Selwyn Image's drawings, 1879–82, I–III, Central School of Arts and Crafts Library, London County Council.

example in the inlay for a box by Mackmurdo, 1884, and in a pin-cushion,[24] he uses a floral and linear rhythm which is closely akin to Mackmurdo's (fig. 79), as well as a similar range of colours.

*

English proto-Art Nouveau foreshadowed the Continental movement, but remained an English phenomenon—an off-shoot of the Arts and Crafts Movement with emphasis on linear and floral decoration. It was in the milieu of the late pre-Raphaelite illustrators and designers that English proto-Art Nouveau came into being, and for this reason it is two-dimensional in character and largely confined to a flat surface, and to books. It was floral in inspiration and linear in essence, and it seems natural therefore to seek its origin in the contemporary cult of plant and line.

24 The former in Colchester and Essex Museum; the latter Cat. No. M.6., in William Morris Gallery, Walthamstow.

The Cult of Plant and Line

It was among the leaders of the Arts and Crafts Movement and those who created the proto-Art Nouveau, that England's outstanding art theoriticians were to be found. Their theories leading up to the Modern Movement are discussed in Nikolaus Pevsner's important writings[1]; in connection with Art Nouveau it is the designer's attitude to Nature and his aesthetic theories which are of special interest.

About the middle of the 19th century principles of naturalism, both in painting and sculpture as well as in decorative art, were firmly established. As early as 1828 Davis Ramsay Hay had published *Laws of harmonious colouring adapted to Interior Decoration,* in which he maintained that inspiration and models must be sought among plants and flowers—among Nature's shapes. As we approach the middle of the century the naturalistic method of reproduction becomes more and more general among artists, and the dependence on Nature more direct. In the announcements of the Summerly group, about 1850, we read that ornaments and details must be taken "as directly as possible from Nature."[2]

In metal-work T. Spencer's invention of the electrolytic process of plating[3] in 1837 undoubtedly stimulated naturalism, as it was now possible, in the simplest way, to achieve a perfectly naturalistic reproduction of any object. Among all the styles of Historicism Naturalism was also represented, e.g. in Grainger & Co.'s earthenware (fig. 90). The graceful way in which the plants encircle the corpus, the reed-shaped leaves with their willowy rhythm, and not least the functional role allotted to certain shapes of plants, remind us of the style of the eighteen-nineties. But the exact imitation, the lack of abstraction of natural shapes, and the way in which the decoration

1 N. Pevsner, William Morris, C. R. Ashbee und das zwanzigste Jahrhundert, *Deutsche Vierteljahrsschrift für Literaturwissenschaft und Geistesgeschichte,* vol. XIV, 4, 1936, Halle 1936; *idem, Pioneers of the Modern Movement,* London 1936; new and extended edition, *Pioneers of Modern Design,* New York 1949.

2 A. Bøe, *From Gothic Revival to Functional Form. A Study in Victorian Theories of Design,* Oslo. In Print. MS. p. 74.

3 G. W. Yapp, Electro-Metallurgy and Plating, *Metal-Work,* I–II, London 1877, vol. I, pp. 64–72.

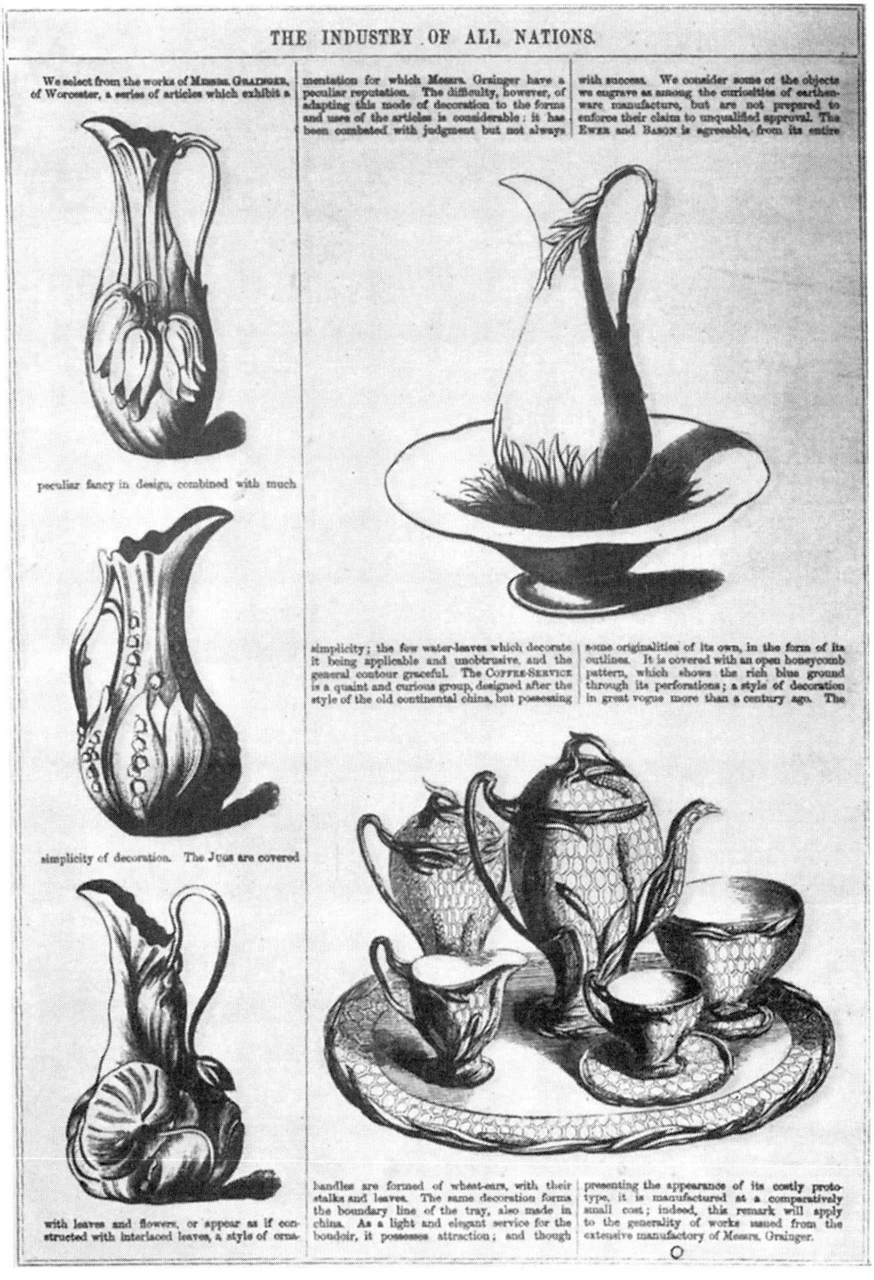

THE INDUSTRY OF ALL NATIONS.

We select from the works of MESSRS. GRAINGER, of Worcester, a series of articles which exhibit a peculiar fancy in design, combined with much simplicity of decoration. The JUGS are covered with leaves and flowers, or appear as if constructed with interlaced leaves, a style of ornamentation for which Messrs. Grainger have a peculiar reputation. The difficulty, however, of adapting this mode of decoration to the forms and uses of the articles is considerable: it has been combated with judgment but not always with success. We consider some of the objects we engrave as among the curiosities of earthenware manufacture, but are not prepared to enforce their claim to unqualified approval. The EWER and BASON is agreeable, from its entire simplicity; the few water-leaves which decorate it being applicable and unobtrusive, and the general contour graceful. The COFFEE-SERVICE is a quaint and curious group, designed after the style of the old continental china, but possessing some originalities of its own, in the form of its outlines. It is covered with an open honeycomb pattern, which shows the rich blue ground through its perforations; a style of decoration in great vogue more than a century ago. The handles are formed of wheat-ears, with their stalks and leaves. The same decoration forms the boundary line of the tray, also made in china. As a light and elegant service for the boudoir, it possesses attraction; and though presenting the appearance of its costly prototype, it is manufactured at a comparatively small cost; indeed, this remark will apply to the generality of works issued from the extesive manufactory of Messrs. Grainger.

Fig. 90. Earthenware by Grainger & Co. Class XXXV. No. 46. The Great Exhibition. 1851.
Victoria and Albert Museum photo. Crown Copyright reserved.

tends to spread over the whole article, tells us that this is 1851 and not 1891 or 1901.

Ruskin's teaching about Nature was based on an intimate knowledge of it: in his view nature was the source of inspiration of all art, and should be studied in detail, as we can read, more especially in parts V–VII of *Modern Painters*. His relationship to Nature was marked by deep love, and had in it something almost of religion. According to Ruskin, God had established certain shapes in Nature, "and all noble ornamentation is the expression of man's delight in God's work."[4] There is no scope here for recreation or abstraction, " . . . all most lovely forms and thoughts are directly taken from natural objects."[5] Morris's relations are not religious but his entire doctrine springs from the same basic idea. He gives a more theoretical expression of his views on Nature in his lectures, but as an artist he developed Ruskin's doctrine, maintaining that the artist must not copy Nature, but recreate it, and yet without losing its freshness. Lewis Day has expressed this in a very charming way: "He did not ask so much that ornament should be like Nature, as that it should lead one's thoughts out of doors."[6]

With Owen Jones, the most interesting theoretician on colouring in the middle of the century, one already notes a reaction against the imitation of Nature. With his knowledge of the ornamentation of the East he clearly saw the importance of stylisation and simplification. In his book *On the True and the False in the Decorative Arts*, 1863, he sounds a warning note: "I called upon attention to the demoralizing influence of imitating Nature so directly as is the custom of the present day."[7] His colour doctrine, too, is by no means naturalistic, but conditioned by aesthetic-psychological factors.[8]

Apart from the social aspect the radical demands for simplicity which Morris developed—together with his views on Nature and its relation to ornament—were continued and developed by men like John Sedding[9]

4 J. Ruskin, *The Stones of Venice*, London 1851–53, vol. I, Chapter II, §14.

5 *Idem, The Seven Lamps of Architecture*, London 1849, Chapter IV, §3.

6 L. Day, William Morris and his Decorative Art. *The Contemporary Review*, London, vol. LXXXIII, 1903, p. 790.

7 O. Jones, *On the True and the False in the Decorative Arts*, I–II, London 1863, vol. I, p. 46.

8 *Ibid.*, pp. 48–69.

9 J. P. Cooper, The Work of J. Sedding, *The Architectural Review*, 1897–98, pp. 35–41, 62–77, 125–33,

(1838–91), Lewis Day[10] (1845–1910), Charles R. Ashbee, Charles Annesley Voysey, as well as Mackmurdo, Crane, Dresser, and Image.

Sedding, an enthusiastic pupil of Morris, developed the view on the relationship between the machine and applied art, diverging on this point from the views of Morris and Ruskin by his positive attitude, as expressed so clearly in his book *Art and Handicraft*.[11] He also expresses his views of Nature and its relation to art, in a chapter entitled *Design*. "Nature," he says, "is, of course, the groundwork of all art, even ours; but it is not to Nature at first-hand that we go." " . . . drop this wearisome translation of old styles and translate Nature instead."[12]

Ruskin's pupil Selwyn Image maintained the same attitude to Nature. "Learn your business in the schools, but go out to Nature for your inspiration. Return again and again and for evermore, to Nature."[13] But he also realises that "Fine Art . . . is not the counterfeit of Nature, but another world of imaginative creation out of the raw material of Nature supplying it with symbols."[14] Lewis Day is not notably original as a theorist, but shows the same phase of the development, away from an imitative reproduction of Nature, towards an abstract and refashioned interpretation in his book *Nature in Ornament*, 1892.

As we have already seen it was Mackmurdo who, though he was perhaps the least able writer of them all, nevertheless gave renewed strength to these views of Nature and the demand for simplicity. It is characteristic that it was he who started *The Art for Schools Association*, "to awaken the interest of children in the beauties of Nature,"[15] as he himself expressed it. This attitude to Nature seems to have been one of the important forerunners of both Art Nouveau and the rational doctrine. In his article *Nature in Ornament* Mackmurdo writes " . . . there will thus be one character-

188–95, 235–43, 278–80; H. Wilson, J. P. Cooper, *In Memoriam of J. D. Sedding*, London 1891; John D. Sedding, *British Architect*, vol. XXXV, 1895, pp. 289–91.

10 D. M. Ross, *Lewis Foreman Day, Designer and writer on Stained Glass*, Cambridge 1929.

11 J. Sedding, Our Arts and Industries, lecture delivered at the Liverpool Art Congress, 1888, *Art and Handicraft*, London 1893, pp. 114–49.

12 *Idem*, Design, *Arts and Crafts Essays*, London 1893, pp. 408 sqq.

13 S. Image, On Designing for the Art of Embroidery, *Arts and Crafts Essays*, London 1893, pp. 418 sq.

14 *Ibid.*, On Art and Nature, *The Hobby Horse*, vol. I, No. 1, 1884, pp. 16–18.

15 A. H. Mackmurdo, Monography, MS., p. 7; Miss C. McQueen's collection.

istic in each work, wherever and whenever it may be produced, namely, a strict conformity with all organic structure . . . ."[16]

With the designer and writer Christopher Dresser we move still further from the imitative attitude to Nature, approaching the symbolical. His conception of Nature has been formulated with all the systematic and intellectual circumspection of a botanist. Trained as a botanist at the University of Jena, it was not until about 1860 that he first started work as an industrial designer and a writer on art-theory. Of Nature-study he says: "If a week is not too long to spend in the consideration of a simple leaf, how long should we meditate upon a flower? Say a month."[17] All his doctrine and principles, as laid down in *The Art of Decorative Design*, *Development of Ornamental Art*, and in the article *On Decorative Art*,[18] all published in 1862, are based on a botanical *vue d'ensemble*, and are supported by botanical examples. The interesting point, however, is that he warns his readers against an unduly accurate imitation of Nature in the ornament itself, declaring that the source of inspiration must be used with care and after conscious revision.

Dresser then develops his curvilinear aesthetics on a logical and geometrical basis.

"Curves," he says, "will be found to be more beautiful as they are subtle in character:

1. The arc is the least beautiful of curves; being struck from one centre its origin is instantly detected, and the mind requires that a line, the contemplation of which shall be pleasureable, must be in advance of its knowledge, and call into activity its investigative powers.
2. A portion of the bounding-line of an ellipse is more beautiful as a curve than the arc, for its origin is less apparent, it being struck from two centres.
3. The curve which bounds the egg-shape is more subtle than the elliptic curve, for it is struck from three centres.

16 *Idem.*, Nature in Ornament, *The Hobby Horse*, vol. VII, 1892, p. 64.

17 Christopher Dresser, *The Art of Decorative Design*, London 1862, p. 23.

18 *Idem*, On Decorative Art, *The Planet*, London, No. 1, Jan. 1862, pp. 123–35.

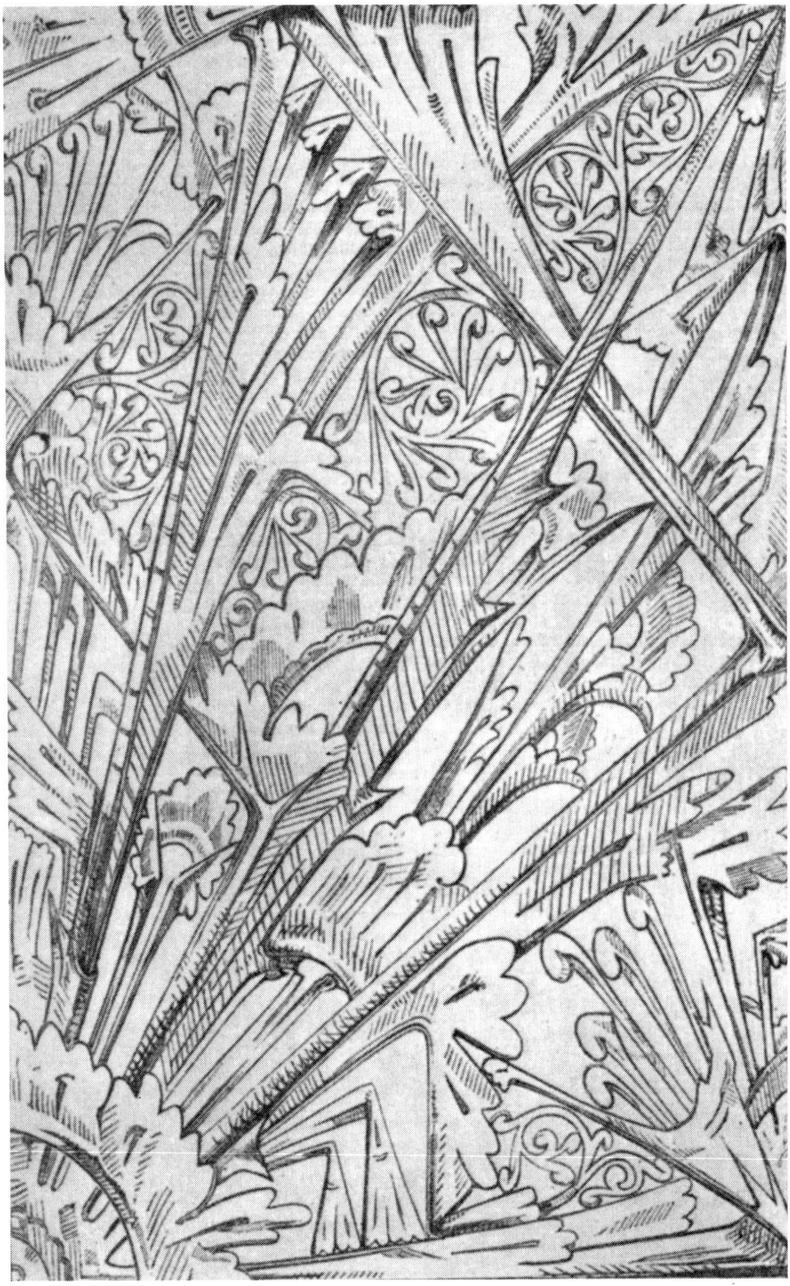

Fig. 91. Dresser: Illustration in *Technical Education*, 1870.

4. The curve bounding the cardioid is more beautiful still, as it is struck from four centres."

In the same way he continues with the parabolic and hyperbolic curves, until he reaches the chain curve.[19]

In other words, the beauty of the curve increases with the complexity of its origin. Dresser seeks the beautiful line in what he calls pliant and energetic curvature. This aesthetic outlook, however, in all its mathematical logic is intimately bound up with his Nature views. He rediscovers the *line of life* in Nature, best expressed in young palms, and tropical vegetation, for here is the energetic curve and the linear rhythm he seeks.[20] Of proportions he says: "Proportions, like the curve, must be of a subtle nature."[21]

Dresser's views on decorative design can be summed up in his demand for Beauty—of which his curvilinear aesthetics are an essential part—his demand for Power, and his demand for Utility. The demand for Power in design can best be illustrated by his own drawing (fig. 91)[22] and the accompanying text:

" . . . I have sought to embody chiefly the one idea of power energy, force, or vigour, as a dominant idea; and in order to do this, I have employed such lines as we see in the bursting buds of spring, when the energy of growth is at its maximum, and especially such as are to be seen in the spring growth of a luxuriant tropical vegetation; and I have also availed myself of those forms which we see in certain bones of birds which are associated with the organs of flight, and which give us an impression of great power, as well as those which we observe in the powerful propelling fins of certain species of fish."[23]

With regard to utility his doctrine is developed largely on the basis of his botanical views. "In vegetable Nature the utmost regard to fitness is manifested."[24] He is constantly repeating that "an object must fitly

19 *Idem,* General Principles of Ornament, *Development of Ornamental Art,* London 1862, pp. 3–16; *Idem,* Curves, *The Art of Decorative Design,* London 1862, pp. 95–101.

20 *Idem, The Art of Decorative Design,* London 1862, pp. 98 sq.

21 *Idem, Development of Ornamental Art,* p. 13.

22 *Idem,* Principles in Design, III, *The Technical Educator,* vol. I, 1870, p. 121.

23 *Ibid.,* p. 121.

24 *Idem, The Art of Decorative Design,* p. 117.

answer the purpose for which it has been originated." This is concisely expressed in his sentence "Utility must precede beauty."[25] In this connection he refers to Pugin. It is interesting to note, especially in connection with English Art Nouveau, his insistence that lines should not cross one another. "There must be a graceful flowing of line out of line."[26]

To a certain extent Art Nouveau and the rational attitude of the Modern Movement both had their *points de départ* in an attitude to Nature—one trend developing the flower, the stem and the rhythm, i.e. the ornament, the other the fitness, the logic and the structure, i.e. the construction. In the work of the botanist Dresser it is on a floral basis that the special side of the aesthetics of the Art-Nouveau style is developed, a generation before the same aesthetic rules are established on the Continent. Moreover at times he showed a rational and constructive feeling for form which also went far beyond his age. One would, however, be disappointed if one expected to find his doctrine applied with the same precision and consistency as his theory. It must be realised that his art theory was largely symbolical and literary in character, not least his reflections on Power in design and his strange speculations on associations in decoration. The bulk of his production springs from these ideas and from period styles, lavishly decorated, and it is only occasionally that he shows the radical form we might expect on the basis of his theories.

Nevertheless his place in the development of art theory is symptomatic of the age, with its literary and symbolical trends, providing a link with Pugin, and at the same time continuing the development as far as to the constructive and rational doctrines at the end of the century.

Dresser was not the only person who maintained a symbolical and constructive attitude to Nature, with the emphasis on the line. Jones is touching on the same problem, when, in *On the True and the False in the Decorative Arts*, he maintains that "junctions of curved lines with curved, or of curved with straight, should be, as in Nature, tangential to each other."[27] But he went further in his constructive and aesthetic theories,

25 *Idem, Development of Ornamental Art,* pp. 9, 83 sq.; *The Art of Decorative Design,* p. 137; Principles in Design, *The Technical Educator,* vol. I, 1870, pp. 312, 378.

26 *Idem, The Art of Decorative Design,* p. 101.

27 O. Jones, *op. cit.,* p. 34, repeated p. 46.

and in his views on the relationship between construction and ornamentation—also set forth in 1863—he goes far beyond his time.

If we now turn to the designer and book-illustrator Walter Crane, and examine his art theories, we shall find that he too is interested in the line, and its emotional powers of expression. It is the most essential factor in his art, and the most important point in his aesthetics. "Hence LINE is all-important. Let the designer, therefore, in the adaptation of his art, lean upon the staff of *line*—line determinative, line emphatic, line delicate, line expressive, line controlling, and uniting."[28]

It is no coincidence that he opens his book *Ideals in Art* with a tribute to William Blake and his expressive linear rhythm. Crane distinguishes between imitative and constructive design, which in turn corresponds to his conceptions informal and formal, with which he associates accidental and organic Beauty. We must first pass through the imitative stage, and then continue to the constructive or formal. Of pattern design he says "Our love of Naturalism may induce us to work up our details, our leaves and flowers, to view with natural appearance in full light and relief, until we find we are losing the repose and sense of quiet planes essential to pattern work. . . ."[29] Crane also dwells on the expressive power of the line, not least its expression of movement. "The wave-line, indeed, may be said not only to suggest movement, but also to describe its direction and force. It is, in fact, the *line of movement*."[30] (fig. 92). But Crane is selective in his attitude to the lines offered by Nature and—as we might expect—is constantly on the lookout for lines which ". . . are essential to the character and structure. They are organic lines, in short. They mean life and growth."[31] Furthermore he says of the innate aesthetic value of the line: "It does not require us to stop and think . . . to appreciate the rhythmic silent music which the more formalised and abstract decorative design may contain, quite apart from the forms it actually represents."[32]

28 W. Crane, Design in Relation to Use and Material, *The Claims of Decorative Art,* London 1892, p. 93. Lecture delivered before the National Association for the Advancement of Art, 1889, *Transactions of The Art Congress,* Edinburgh, 1889, pp. 202–220.

29 *Idem, The Bases of Design,* London 1898, p. 253.

30 *Idem, Line and Form,* London 1900, pp. 12–16, pp. 155 sqq.

31 *Ibid.,* pp. 135 sqq.

32 *Ibid.,* p. 32.

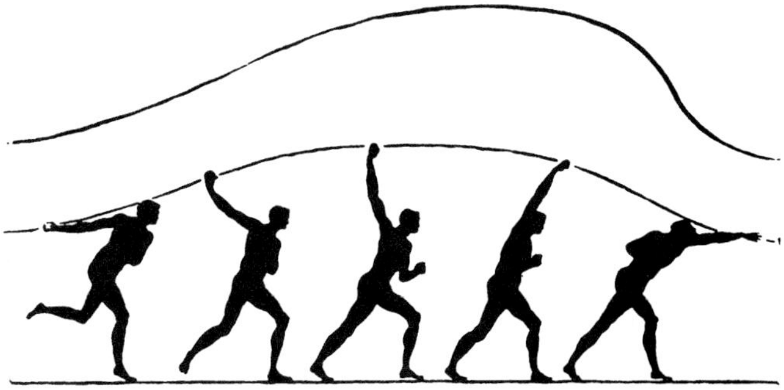

Fig. 92. Crane: Illustration from *Line and Form*. 1900.

Crane formulated these theories in the years 1888 to 1893.[33]

With the architects Ashbee and Voysey the development moves right over to the Modern Movement and the architectural principles of the 20th century. Voysey confirms the development as we have seen, and with him the Tyranny of Styles, as he called it, is at an end: "This regard of utility is the basis of beauty."[34] His views on Nature represent the final point in the development towards abstraction and symbol: "To go to Nature is of course to approach the fountainhead, but . . . before a living plant a man must go through an elaborate process of selection and analysis. The natural forms have to be reduced to mere symbols."[35]

Towards the end of the century the interest in flowers and plants also found expression in a number of theoretical publications, not only in England, but to an equally large extent on the Continent; among the oldest were Ruprich-Robert *Flore Ornementale*, 1865–69, A. Seder, *Die Pflanze in Kunst und Gewerbe*, 1886, to be followed by a whole series: V. Cherbuliez's *l'Art et la Nature* in 1892, F. Moser's *Handbuch der Pflanzen Ornamentik* in 1893, F. Luthmer's *Blüthenformen als Motive für Flächenornament*, 1893, M. Meurer's *Pflanzenformen*, 1895, A. Trenter's *Pflanzen Studien* in 1899, with Grasset's *La Plante et ses applications ornementales* in 1899 as one of the most important. Other works included J. Buchert's *Fleurs de Fantaisies*, 1900, M. P. Verneuil's *Etude de la Plante, son application aux industries d'art*, 1900, A. M. Mucha's

33 First published in the *Magazine of Art*, 1888, under the title *The Language of Line*, and *ibid.*, 1893, under the title *Design*.

34 An Interview with Mr. C. F. A. Voysey, *The Studio*, vol. I, 1893, p. 236.

35 *Ibid.*, p. 234.

Documents décoratifs, *Panneaux décoratifs*, *études des applications de fleurs*, etc., in 1902, and *Formenwelt aus dem Naturreiche*, Leipzig, undated. The interest is also maintained for a while in the 20th century in works such as G. Kolb's *Von der Pflanze zum Ornament*, in 1902, A. Keller's *La Décor par la Plante. l'Ornement et la Végétation: Theorie décorative et Applications industrielles*, M. P. Verneuil's *Encyclopédie artistique et documentaire de la plante*, 1904–08, and Lewis Day's *Nature in Ornament*, 1908–09.

Just as Naturalism had established a firm foothold in the United Kingdom in the third quarter of the century, so it had done on the Continent.

Roger Sandoz and J. Guiffrey also mention in their *Etude documentaire, 1798–1912* on *Arts appliqués et industries d'art aux expositions*, that there were plans made for an important exhibition, *l'Exposition de la Plante*, in 1889, but the projects were rejected, being too vast. The idea of such an exhibition indicates, however, the marked interest in the problem in the most important organisation in France, *l'Union Centrale*, which indeed had launched the idea.

In France we also find the first Art Nouveau-like plant motifs within the Naturalistic school. In 1867 Felix Bracquemond (1833–1914)[36] executed a plate[37] (fig. 93)—after devoting himself mainly to pottery from the eighteen-sixties on—using a decoration with a linear rhythm based on plant shapes which approximate to those of Art Nouveau. Bracquemond maintains as a matter of fact that it is necessary to transform Nature—as he himself has clearly done—but insists nevertheless: "Les œuvres où il y a le plus d'art sont celles, quelle que soit leur destination, qui se rapprochent le plus de la nature."[38] But he adds, a little later, "il faut, pour constituer une œuvre d'art, autre chose que la reproduction exacte de la nature."[39] And, as though to explain the decoration on his plate, we have the following: " . . . ce qui dans l'art est geste, mouvement, trait, expression des êtres, disposition des choses, devient *lignes* dans l'œuvre d'art."[40]

36 A. de Lostalot, M. Felix Bracquemond, peintre graveur, *Gazette des Beaux Arts*, vols. XXIX, XXX, 1884, pp. 420, 517, 155.

37 Cat. No. D.16823. Musée des Arts Décoratifs, Louvre, Paris.

38 J. M. Bracquemond, *Du Dessin et de la Couleur*, Paris, 1885, p. 218. "The works where there is most art are those, whatever their ultimate aim, which come closest to Nature."

39 *Ibid.*, p. 223, "something more than an exact reproduction of Nature is required to make a work of art."

40 *Ibid.*, p. 132, "what in art is gesture, movement, feature, expression of beings and disposition of things becomes *lines* in the work of art."

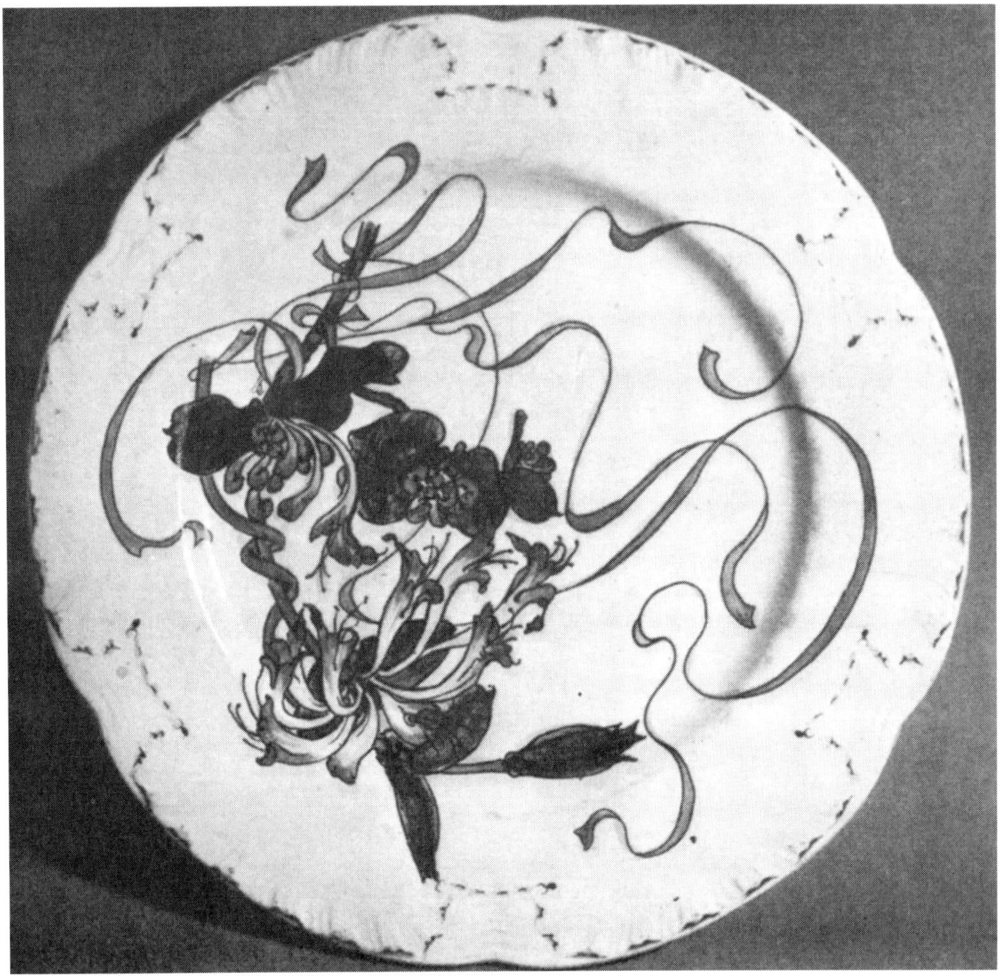

Fig. 93. Bracquemond: Plate, earthenware. Manufactured by de Bailuet & Co. 1867.
Musée des Arts Décoratifs, Louvre, Paris. Copyright reserved.

Henri Vever's (1854–1942)[41] coffee service[42] (fig. 94), which he showed at the Exhibition in 1889[43], also has a naturalistic decoration,

41 R. Plantagenet, Des bijoux nouveaux, *l'Art Décoratif,* vol. IX, 2, 1907, pp. 37–40; H. Vever, *La Bijouterie Française au XIXe siècle,* I–III, Paris 1906–08, vol. III; Some recent examples of the jeweller's art in France, *The Studio,* vol. XXIII, 1903, pp. 25–33.

42 Don Vever, January 17, 1930, Musée des Arts Décoratifs, Louvre, Paris.

43 V. Champier, *Les Industries d'art à l'exposition universelle de 1889,* Paris 1903, pl. 80.

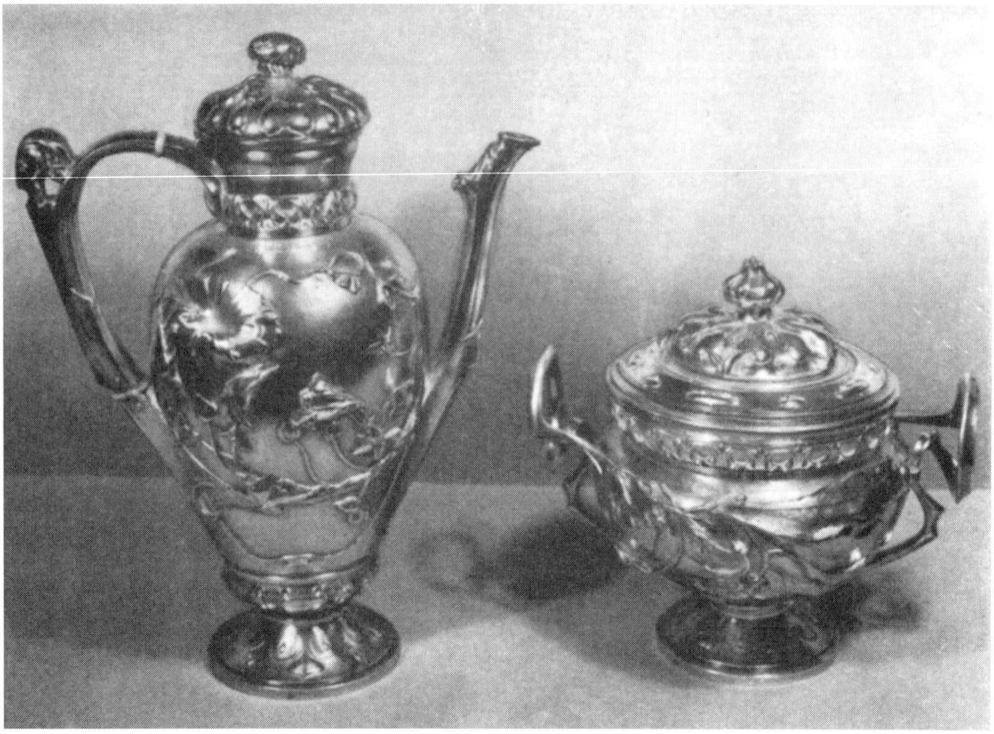

Fig. 94. Vever: Coffee pot and sugar bowl. Silver, repousée. 1889.
Musée des Arts Décoratifs, Louvre, Paris, Copyright reserved.

which may remind us slightly of Bracquemond's, not least in the completely asymmetrical and stalk-shaped handles of the sugar-bowl, which stick out as though they were part of the decoration. However, the traditional main shape of the actual corpus clearly tells us that as yet the artist has not reached what we could call Art Nouveau.

France's most outstanding Naturalist, within the realm of decorative art, is nevertheless Emile Gallé (1846–1904), who, like Vever, made his break-through at the Paris Exhibition of 1889. From his youth his interest had centred in Nature, and he commenced studying botany, but interrupted his studies to start a pottery workshop in 1874, together with his father, after he had visited England. Nevertheless he always remained an ardent lover of Nature, writing scientific articles on horticulture, and devot-

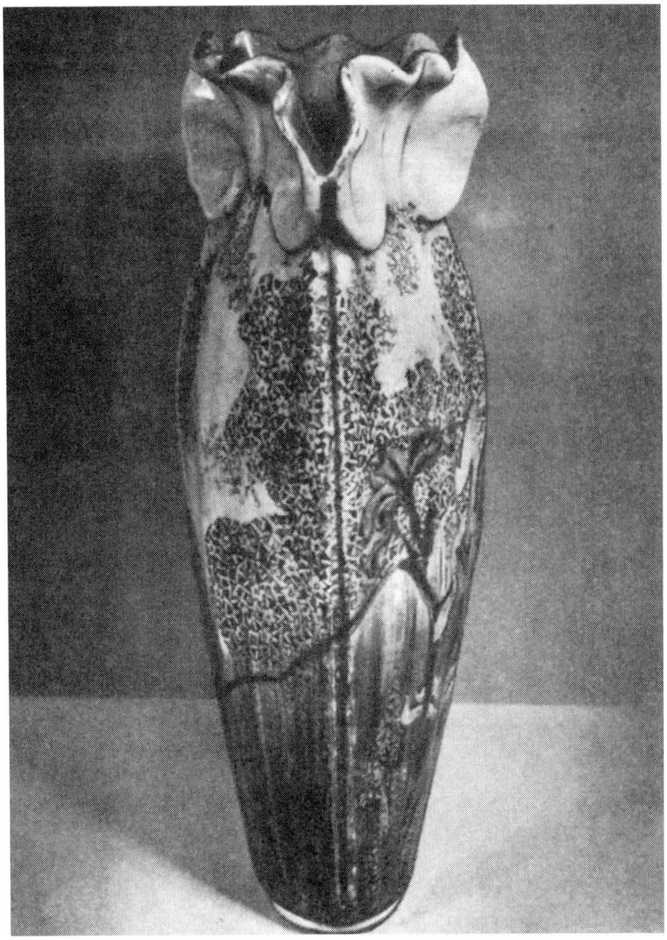

Fig. 95. Gallé: Vase, earthenware. 1893.
Musée des Arts Décoratifs, Louvre, Paris. Copyright reserved.

ing his leisure time to the extensive garden which surrounded his beautiful residence in the Avenue de Garenne in Nancy—"Sa maison de Nancy n'est qu'un atelier dans les roses."[44] Above the door to his studio hung his slogan: "Nos racines sont au fond des bois—au bord des sources, sur les mousses."[45]

Gallé's decorative principles are entirely founded on a study of Nature, and his form is more naturalistic that than of the great majority of his con-

44 J. Gillet, Emile Gallé, Le Poème du Verre, *La Revue Hebdomadaire,* Paris, vol. XIX, 1910, October 8, pp. 153–72 (p. 163) "His house at Nancy is nothing but a studio among the roses."

45 Information kindly given by Madame Perdrizet-Gallé to the author, April 1953. "Our roots are in the depth of the woods—on the bank of streams, on the mosses."

temporaries. He allows flowers and leaves to retain their illusionistic effect, without being converted to two-dimensional principles, even though he occasionally approaches them. His motifs are therefore as a rule three-dimensional in effect, even in the two-dimensional plane, and often with the emphasis on the linear: "Les formes fournies par les végétaux s'adoptent tout naturellement aux ligneaux."[46]

At the beginning of his career as an artist, however, his art was based more on tradition than it was inspired by Nature. It is therefore not surprising to find him covering the inside of the door in the large neo-Renaissance buffet with his naturalistic inlay work. This consists of oak-leaves and oak twigs, in a rhythm which is not exactly Art Nouveau, though it is markedly linear, with elegant coils and undulations.[47] His vase[48] (fig. 95), too, is not what we usually associate with Art Nouveau, though it is by no means traditional in form, having a closed firm contour, and a floral decoration which is partly illusionistic and partly pattern-like.

It might be interesting in this connection to take a look at Gallé's theories and principles for furniture design:

1. Un meuble doit être fait pour servir. . . . Il faut donc qu'elle soit accessible à tout et suffisament solide.
2. Il faut que la construction réponde à la destination de l'œuvre, au matériel d'exécution, et celle-ci aussi simple, aussi logique que possible.
3. Il faut que cette saine construction ne soit masquée par rien et qu'elle reste bien évidente.

   La décoration comprend:

4. Les galbes des membrures organiques, colonnes, supports, poutrelles, pieds et bras de fauteuils, le bâti en un mot.
5. Les morceaux d'ornament superficiel destinés à ajouter au meuble des significations de details et des utilités, des agréments particulier."[49]

And for this ornamentation he recommends plants. An interesting thing

[46] E. Gallé, Le Mobilier Contemporaine, orné d'après la nature, *Revue des Arts Décoratifs,* vol. XX, 1900, pp. 333–41 (p. 341). Later published in *La Lorraine,* Nancy, vol. XIX, 1901, pp. 33–35. "The shapes provided by plants are easily adopted to lines."

[47] Musée des Beaux Arts, Nancy. The door only, exhibited at the exhibition *Um 1900,* Zürich 1952.

[48] Cat. No. A.7649. Musée des Arts Décoratifs, Louvre, Paris.

[49] E. Gallé, *op. cit.* 1. "A piece of furniture should be made to serve. . . . For this reason it must be acces-

about Gallé in this connection is that, like Dresser a generation before him, his rational principles are the result of his thorough knowledge of botany.

In 1895 another of the artists of the Nancy school, Jean Dampt, expressed his views on Nature as follows: "Toujours et toujours l'art est l'essence de la nature épuré, affinée synthétisée, à travers un tempérament d'artiste, que doit, non la copier, mais la transformer, la styliser."[50] But before they went thus far, these artists took their study of Nature very seriously, Dampt for instance undertaking studies on the growth of plants and leaves.[51] Dampt's theory agrees perfectly with the advanced contemporary English theory, and is an expression of the common fundamental decorative principles of the 1890's.

Nancy was not only the main centre of decorative Naturalism, Nature was also widely and generally recognised by other artists, and one of the lesser-known Parisian artists, George Auriol, says in 1895: "Il faut admirer la nature de toutes ses forces, l'étudier sans cesse, et recueillir un à un, comme des trésors, les admirables conseils dont elle est si prodigue."[52]

In the work of Carlos Schwabe (1866–1915), painter, illustrator, and poster-artist, we find as early as 1891 a Naturalism which can only be described as Art Nouveau[53] (fig. 96). It is a far cry from Vever's silver service and Bracquemond's plate, because Schwabe in his linear and asymmetrically constructed tendril coils contains the essentials of Art Nouveau, while the two others, though they based their work on the same decorative conception, have not yet achieved the same pliant whiplash rhythm.

sible to all and sufficiently solid. 2. The construction must correspond to the purpose of the work, to the material in which it is executed, and should be as simple and logical as possible. 3. This sound construction must not be masked by anything and must remain quite obvious. The decoration comprises: 4. The curves of the organic structure, columns, supports, beams, legs and arms of armchairs, in a word the construction. 5. Pieces of superficial ornament which aim to add to the piece of furniture some significant details and uses or particular embellishments."

50 H. Nocq, *Tendances Nouvelles, Enquête sur l'évolution des industries d'art,* Paris 1896. The questions published at the end of 1894. "Always, always art is the essence of Nature refined, purified and synthesised, through the medium of an artist's temperament which should not copy it but transform it and stylise it."

51 V. Champier, *Documents d'atelier,* Paris 1898, pl. XII.

52 H. Nocq, *op. cit.,* p. 63. "One must study Nature with all one's might, study it ceaselessly, and gather one by one, like treasures, the admirable pieces of advice which she provides so lavishly."

53 *l'Evangile de l'Enfance de notre Seigneur Jésus Christ,* Paris, n. d. Illustrated by Carlos Schwabe, Chapter XV, 16–18. It is only in the ornaments we find these advanced illustrations; the rest is more conventional.

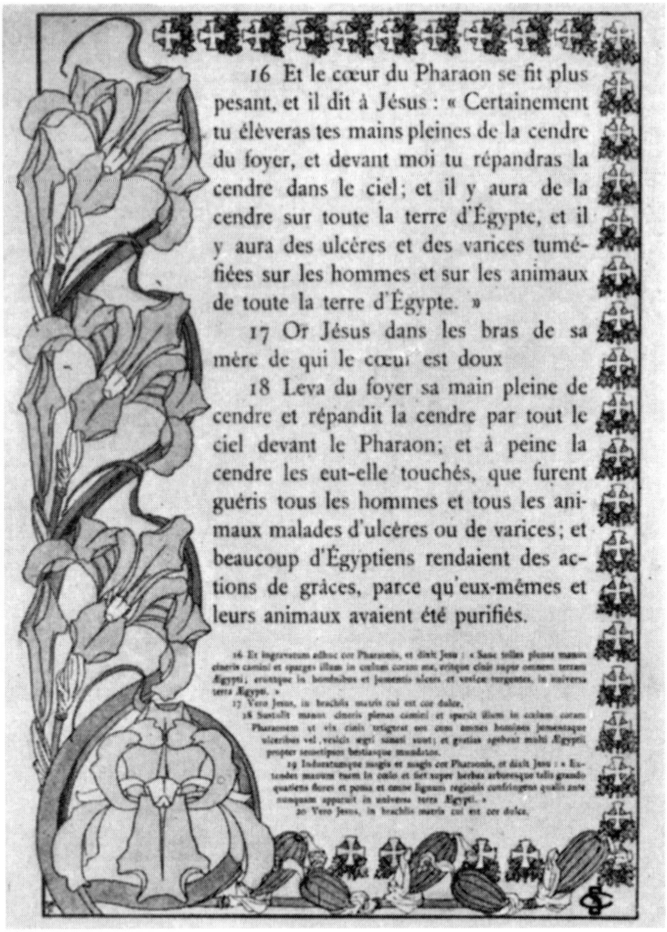
16 Et le cœur du Pharaon se fit plus pesant, et il dit à Jésus : « Certainement tu élèveras tes mains pleines de la cendre du foyer, et devant moi tu répandras la cendre dans le ciel; et il y aura de la cendre sur toute la terre d'Égypte, et il y aura des ulcères et des varices tuméfiées sur les hommes et sur les animaux de toute la terre d'Égypte. »

17 Or Jésus dans les bras de sa mère de qui le cœur est doux

18 Leva du foyer sa main pleine de cendre et répandit la cendre par tout le ciel devant le Pharaon; et à peine la cendre les eut-elle touchés, que furent guéris tous les hommes et tous les animaux malades d'ulcères ou de varices; et beaucoup d'Égyptiens rendaient des actions de grâces, parce qu'eux-mêmes et leurs animaux avaient été purifiés.

Fig. 96. Schwabe: Book illustration in *L'Evangile de l'Enfance de notre Seigneur Jésus Christ.* 1891.

The leading theorist and naturalist outside the Nancy school was Eugène Grasset (1845–1917)—France's Walter Crane, a versatile artist, interested in flowers, and an assiduous illustrator and writer, like his English contemporary. When Grasset illustrated his *Histoire des Quatre Fils Aymon* in the years 1879–83, one of his main sources of inspiration was Japanese, but flowers and leaves, in a rhythm which is naturalistically arranged, occupy a broad place. Whether a full-page illustration, similar to the one shown (fig. 97), is the result of Japonism or Floralism, is a somewhat subtle question, and is really of not very great importance. The inter-

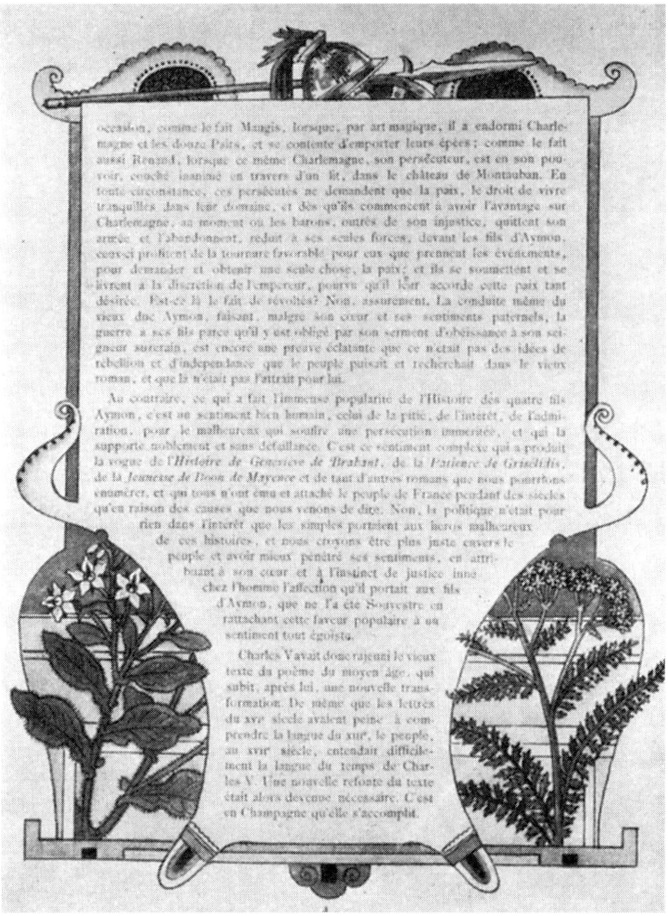
occasion, comme le fait Maugis, lorsque, par art magique, il a endormi Charlemagne et les douze Pairs, et se contente d'emporter leurs épées; comme le fait aussi Renaud, lorsque ce même Charlemagne, son persécuteur, est en son pouvoir, couché inanimé en travers d'un lit, dans le château de Montauban. En toute circonstance, ces persécutés ne demandent que la paix, le droit de vivre tranquilles dans leur domaine, et dès qu'ils commencent à avoir l'avantage sur Charlemagne, au moment où les barons, outrés de son injustice, quittent son armée et l'abandonnent, réduit à ses seules forces, devant les fils d'Aymon, ceux-ci profitent de la tournure favorable pour eux que prennent les événements, pour demander et obtenir une seule chose, la paix; et ils se soumettent et se livrent à la discrétion de l'empereur, pourvu qu'il leur accorde cette paix tant désirée. Est-ce là le fait de révoltés? Non, assurement. La conduite même du vieux duc Aymon, faisant, malgré son cœur et ses sentiments paternels, la guerre à ses fils parce qu'il y est obligé par son serment d'obéissance à son seigneur suzerain, est encore une preuve éclatante que ce n'était pas des idées de rébellion et d'indépendance que le peuple puisait et recherchait dans le vieux roman, et que là n'était pas l'attrait pour lui.

Au contraire, ce qui a fait l'immense popularité de l'Histoire des quatre fils Aymon, c'est un sentiment bien humain, celui de la pitié, de l'intérêt, de l'admiration, pour le malheureux qui souffre une persécution imméritée, et qui la supporte noblement et sans défaillance. C'est ce sentiment complexe qui a produit la vogue de l'*Histoire de Geneviève de Brabant*, de la *Patience de Griselidis*, de la *Jeunesse de Doon de Mayence* et de tant d'autres romans que nous pourrions énumérer, et qui tous n'ont ému et attaché le peuple de France pendant des siècles qu'en raison des causes que nous venons de dire. Non, la politique n'était pour rien dans l'intérêt que les simples portaient aux héros malheureux de ces histoires, et nous croyons être plus juste envers le peuple et avoir mieux pénétré ses sentiments, en attribuant à son cœur et à l'instinct de justice inné chez l'homme l'affection qu'il portait aux fils d'Aymon, que ne l'a été Souvestre en rattachant cette faveur populaire à un sentiment tout égoïste.

Charles V avait donc rajeuni le vieux texte du poème du moyen âge, qui subit, après lui, une nouvelle transformation. De même que les lettrés du XVIe siècle avaient peine à comprendre la langue du XIIe, le peuple, au XVIIe siècle, entendait difficilement la langue du temps de Charles V. Une nouvelle refonte du texte était alors devenue nécessaire. C'est en Champagne qu'elle s'accomplit.

Fig. 97. Grasset: Book illustration for *l'Histoire des Quatre Fils Aymon*. 1879—83.

esting thing is that it was made at that time, and we have as much justification as in the case of the English artists of speaking of a proto-Art Nouveau, though in France it was only represented by some single phenomena.

Some years later Grasset expressed his views on Nature as follows: "La Nature, voilà le livre d'art ornementale qu'il faut consulter."[54] Two years later, in 1897, he stated in an article on the Art Nouveau style: "Nous n'avons q'une chose à faire, *consulter l'usage présent*, *l'utilité* des objets et les orner au moyen des formes puisées dans la nature, en tenant compte de

[54] H. Nocq, *op. cit.*, p. 15. "Nature, that's the handbook of design one should consult."

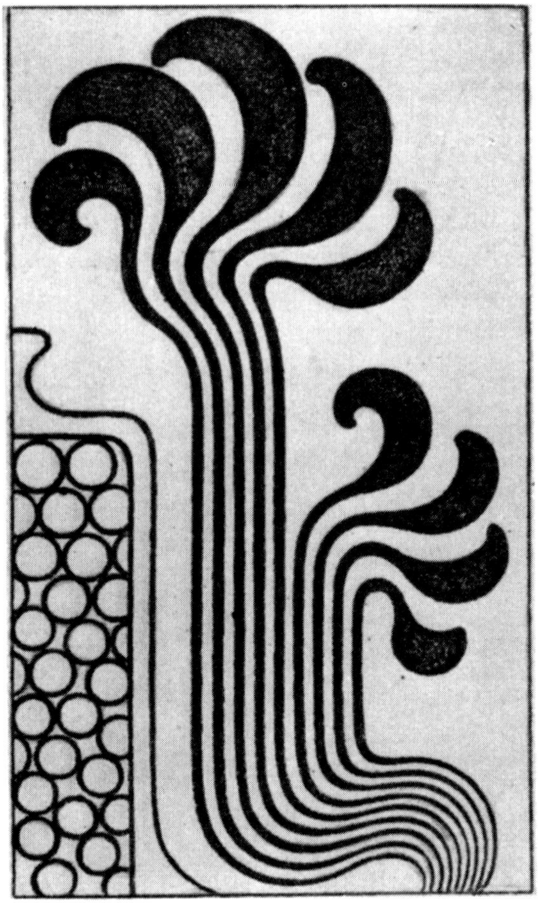

Fig. 98 a. Grasset: Illustration from *Méthode de Composition*. 1905.

la matière employée."[55] Two years later, in 1899, he published his work *La Plante et ses applications ornementales*, and in 1905 his *Méthode de composition ornementale* appeared.

In the latter work he says that: " . . . toute courbe donne l'idée du mouvement et de la vie . . . le tracé de la courbe doit être plein, arrondi, fermé et harmonieux comme une tige pleine de jeune sève."[56] He tried to

[55] E. Grasset, *l'Art Nouveau*. Conférance faite à l'Union Centrale des Arts Décoratifs le 11 avril 1897. Published in *Revue des Arts Décoratifs*, vol. XVII, 1897, pp. 129–44, 182–200 (pp. 16 sq.). "We have only one thing to do: consult present usage, the utility of objects, and ornament them with the help of shapes taken from Nature, taking into account the material used."

[56] *Idem, Méthode de composition ornementale*, Paris 1905, vol. II, p. 7. "Every curve gives the idea of move-

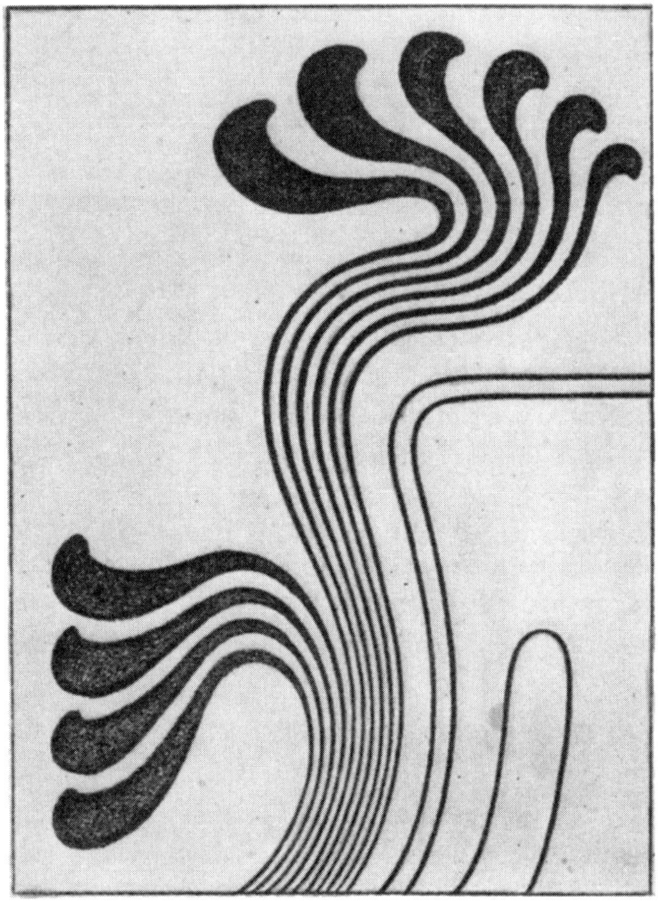

Fig. 98 b. Grasset: Illustration from *Méthode de Composition.* 1905.

put this ideal into practice, as we can see in one of his illustrations[57] (fig. 98a). The text runs as follows: "La figure montre deux faisceaux réunis par leurs racines dont une partie est rectiligne, alors que dans la figure suivante (fig. 98b) le même système est observé avec des courbes harmoniques. On voit ici que le mouvement des racines peut jouer un rôle ornemental important et que chaque masse de faisceaux devient un motif au bout d'une tige."[58]

ment and life . . . the trace of the curve should be full, rounded, firm and harmonious like a stalk full of young sap."

57 *Ibid.,* vol. II, ill. 265.

58 *Ibid.,* vol. II, p. 211. "The figure shows two bundles joined by the roots, one part of which is recti-

What distinguished French theory about the decorative arts from the English, was that the Frenchmen never raised the question of eliminating the decoration but strove to find a new solution to their problems on the basis of Nature. "Le but de l'art ornementale est donc, comme son nom l'indique, *d'orner* les objets fabriqués, de nus qu'ils sont en construction pure, deviennent comme habillés pour le plaisir de l' œil."[59] There is no question of doing without decoration. Grasset's views on decoration are the result of a desire to conceal the construction, and for that reason he belongs to the 19th century and not to the Modern Movement, and precisely because he cultivates the stem rather more than the flower he belongs not to the eighteen-eighties, but to the eighteen-nineties, and is for that reason such a typical Art Nouveau artist.

The same applies to the Belgian Victor Horta: "Je laisse la fleur et la feuille, et je prends la tige."[60] In the case of Hector Guimard too it is clear that Nature was the model he used and that Nature was his source of inspiration: "Nature is a big book from which we can draw inspiration, and it is in that book that we must look for principles, which when found have to be defined and applied by the human mind according to human needs." But he also says that Nature points to the material itself as inspiration for decorative forms.[61]

Perhaps it is the principles in Nature, after all, which have put him on the track of the original form-language we find in his decorations for

linear, while in the following figure (fig. 94b) the same system is seen in harmonious curves. It can be seen here that the movement of the roots can play an important ornamental role and that each mass of bundles becomes a motif at the end of a stalk."

59 *Ibid.*, vol. I, p. XXI. "The aim of ornamental art, as its name suggests, is to *ornament* the things that are manufactured . . . devoid as they are of pure construction, they may become clothed for the delight of the eye."

60 E. Bayard, *le Style Moderne, l'art de reconnaître les Styles,* Paris 1919, p. 100. "I leave the flower and the leaf, and I take the stalk."

61 H. Guimard, An Architect's Opinion of "L'Art Nouveau," *Architectural Record,* vol. XII, No. 2, 1902, p. 127. This quotation is from J. Grady, Nature and the Art Nouveau, *the Art Bulletin,* vol. XXXVII, No. 3, p. 188. Cf. E. Bayard's view on Guimard, E. Bayard, *op. cit.*, p. 102. "Puisque, dans la nature, un objet quelconque a toujours une forme adéquate à sa destination, c'est dans la matière même qu'il nous faut chercher la forme décoratif. C'est ainsi que nous devenons des créateurs—et non en calquant la nature, ce qui est un non-sens." "Since, in Nature, any object always has a shape adequate for its purpose, it is in the material itself that we must look for the decorative form. It is in this way that we become creators—and not by tracing Nature, which is nonsense."

the underground stations. The decorative possibilities of iron may have inspired him, Nature may have contributed with growing and undulating forms, while the Baroque conception of form has given the peculiar stamp (figs. 60–61).

As far as France is concerned the verdict of the two contemporary art critics Leonce Bénédite and Gustav Soulier seems to sum up the situation adequately: in 1900 they stated that nothing was more characteristic of the age than the widespread use of the form-elements which had been acquired as a result of a plant analysis.[62]

Regarding Gaudí and his way of expressing Nature (fig. 68), so typical of him, James Grady puts it very aptly in this way:

"With architecture he recreates the sea in the center of Barcelona. The stone walls are moving waves, the balconies are seaweed and foam in iron, and living plants mingle with the metal leaves until it is difficult to separate them. Interior ceilings are sandy beaches after the tide has receded. The gates to the inner courts are coral forms, and the courts are splashed with blue, green, and purple, grottoes opening onto the sunny strand of the street. This is done not by a direct use of natural shapes but by an architectural impressionism."[63]

*

In France as well as in Great Britain we have seen how the attitude to Nature contributed to the development of Art Nouveau. James Grady who is the first to point to the importance of Nature on Art Nouveau states that "Art Nouveau was the culmination of Nature as an aesthetic expression, and it came appropriately at the end of the century."[64] Nature was one of the many important factors, not only in structural conception but also in ornamental development, and is one of the keys necessary to understand the Art Nouveau artists. But as the process of stylisation and selection of natural forms proceeded, differences began to appear: in Scotland Nature became abstracted to a symbolical ornament of subordinate importance and with little or no connection with the construction. In

62 R. Graul, *Die Krisis im Kunstgewerbe,* Leipzig, 1901, p. 37.

63 J. Grady, Nature and the Art Nouveau, *The Art Bulletin,* vol. XXXVII, No. 3, p. 189.

64 J. Grady, *loc. cit.,* p. 188.

France abstraction proceeded along different lines: in the direction of a symbolical rationalism of essential importance and linked up with the construction. Generally it may be said that England and Scotland cultivated the flower and the root, France the stalk. The use of structure as an aesthetic expression in itself may partly be derived from this interest in Nature.

If we consider Horta's fellow-countryman van de Velde, who has been regarded as the creator and theoretical founder of Art Nouveau, quite apart from his relationship to the Modern Movement, we shall see that he is probably the most ardent writer of Art Nouveau at the turn of the century, the most theoretical of all theorists, and the most vociferous propagandist of the ideas which were latent in the age.

It we examine his personal contribution to the development of the theory of art, the results will be somewhat more meagre than his numerous and forceful words might lead us to believe. His first official pronouncements on the subject of art were in the form of the five lectures he delivered at the *Institut des Hautes Etudes*, a department of the University in Brussels, during the years 1894–95.[65] These contain very little that is new, beyond what had already been said by the others. His bibliography clearly shows whence his ideas derive, including as, it does, six of Morris's lectures, five of his other works, Walter Crane's *Claims of Decorative Art*, and Lewis Day's *Principles of Everyday Art* and *The Anatomy of Pattern*, as well as *The Studio*-editor, Gleeson White's *Practical Design*. In his first publication, *d'Eblaiement d'art*, 1894,[66] and his articles in *l'Art Moderne*, he also shows a good knowledge of contemporary English art and philosophy, and agrees entirely with the younger generation of English art-philosophers in their attitude to the machine and their social conception of art, but, to an even greater extent than they did before him, he emphasised that "l'Utilité seul peut régénérer la beauté."[67]

65 H. van de Velde, *Cours d'Art d'Industrie et d'Ornamentation.* Extension Universitaire de Bruxelles, Brussels 1895.

66 In *Renaissance im Kunstgewerbe,* Neue Ausgabe (new edition), Leipzig 1901, p. 74, he gives the impression that the book was written in 1889, but no credence can be placed in it as the statement lacks any real foundation in fact. On p. 65 of the same book he says that in 1889–90 he was unable to undertake any sort of intellectual activity because of illness.

67 *Idem, Cours d'Art d'Industrie et d'Ornamentation,* fifth lesson, 1895. "Utility alone can regenerate beauty."

Van de Velde's spiritual predecessors are obvious enough, and he states as much on several occasions subsequently, and yet van de Velde deviates from the general conception of his age in two essential points, first of all in his views on the relation of the ornament to the construction. Unlike the French, he maintains that the function of the ornament is not to decorate, but to "structurer," to use his own words: "Les rapports entre cet ornement 'structurel et dynamographique' et la forme ou les surfaces, doivent apparaître si intimes, que l'ornement semble avoir 'determiné' la forme" [*sic*].[68]

Secondly, he has a markedly anti-Naturalistic attitude: "La moindre faiblesse sentimentale, la moindre association naturalistique menacent l'éternité de cet ornement."[69] He could hardly have put it more clearly: the ornament should be abstract, and his attitude is in every way the complete opposite of the English one, and also of the French attitude with its "exécuter *pour servir*, et orner *pour plaire*."[70]

Even though he differs markedly from his contemporary on these two points, van de Velde is strongly linked to the most essential of the contemporary trends: the cult of the line. Sometimes he expresses it in most philosophical terms, and sometimes in terse sentences such as: "Eine Linie ist eine Kraft" (a line is a force).

With van de Velde the role of Nature has been played out, in every aspect: the line is all, worshipped in its every aspect: abstract, symbolical, ornamental and structural.

68 *Idem, Les formules de la beauté architectonique moderne,* Brussels 1923; pp. 64 sqq. Essays written between 1902–12. "The relations between this 'structural and dynamographic' ornament and the form or the surfaces, should appear so intimate that the ornament seems to have 'determined' the form."

69 *Ibid.,* p. 66. "The least sentimental weakness, the least naturalistic association, weakens the lasting nature of this ornament."

70 E. Gallé, *op. cit.* "Execute *to serve* and decorate *to please.*"

Japanese and Oriental influence[1]

After Commodore Perry's visit to Uraga Bay with a force of steam propeller-driven man-o'-wars and 560 officers and other ranks, the first official agreement between America and Japan was concluded in 1854, and on July 4, 1859, the commercial treaty took effect, to be followed by similar treaties with other nations.

In 1862 Japan participated for the first time in a World Exhibition in London, and the firm of Farmer and Rogers dealt with the sale of the Japanese exhibits after the exhibition was over.[2] In the same year Edward William Godwin[3] (1833–86) furnished his house in 21 Portland Square in a simple Japanese style with plain colours and simple Japanese prints on the wall.[4] In the course of 1863 and shortly afterwards Whistler completed his Japanese-inspired pictures, *The Lange-Leizen—of the Six Marks. The Golden Screen, The Balcony*, and *La Princesse du Pays de la Porcelaine.* William M. Rossetti states that "the 'Japanese mania' began in our quarters towards the middle of 1863," and continues: "It was Mr. Whistler who first called my brother's attention to Japanese art."[5] There is little doubt that Whistler was responsible for introducing "the blue and white" from Paris to London, and in the course of the 1860's and 1870's this fashion gathered impetus.

Farmer and Rogers' Oriental Warehouse closed down in 1874, but

1 L. Gonse, l'Art Japonais et son Influence sur le Goût Européen, *Revue des Arts Décoratifs,* vol. XVIII, 1898, pp. 97–116; C. Lancaster, Oriental Contribution to Art Nouveau, *The Art Bulletin,* New York, vol. XXXIV, 1952, pp. 297–310; *idem.,* Japanese Buildings in the United States before 1900, *The Art Bulletin,* New York 1953, vol. XXXV, No. 3, pp. 217–225; *idem.,* Oriental Forms in American Architecture 1800–70, *The Art Bulletin,* New York, 1947, vol. XXIX, pp. 183–93; J. Lowry, *Japanese Influence on Victorian Design,* lecture delivered December, 1952, Victoria and Albert Museum, London (unpublished).

2 John Lowry, *The Japanese Influence on Victorian Design,* December 1952 (unpublished), Victoria and Albert Museum, London.

3 D. Harbron, *The Conscious Stone. The Life of Edward William Godwin,* London 1949; H. Montgomery Hyde, Oscar Wilde and his Architect, *The Architectural Review,* vol. CIX, 1951, pp. 175–76.

4 D. Harbron, *op. cit.,* pp. 32 sq.

5 William M. Rossetti, *Some Reminiscences,* I—II, London 1906, vol. I, p. 276. See also E.R. and J. Pennel, *The Life of James William McNeill Whistler,* I—II, London 1908, vol. I, p. 116.

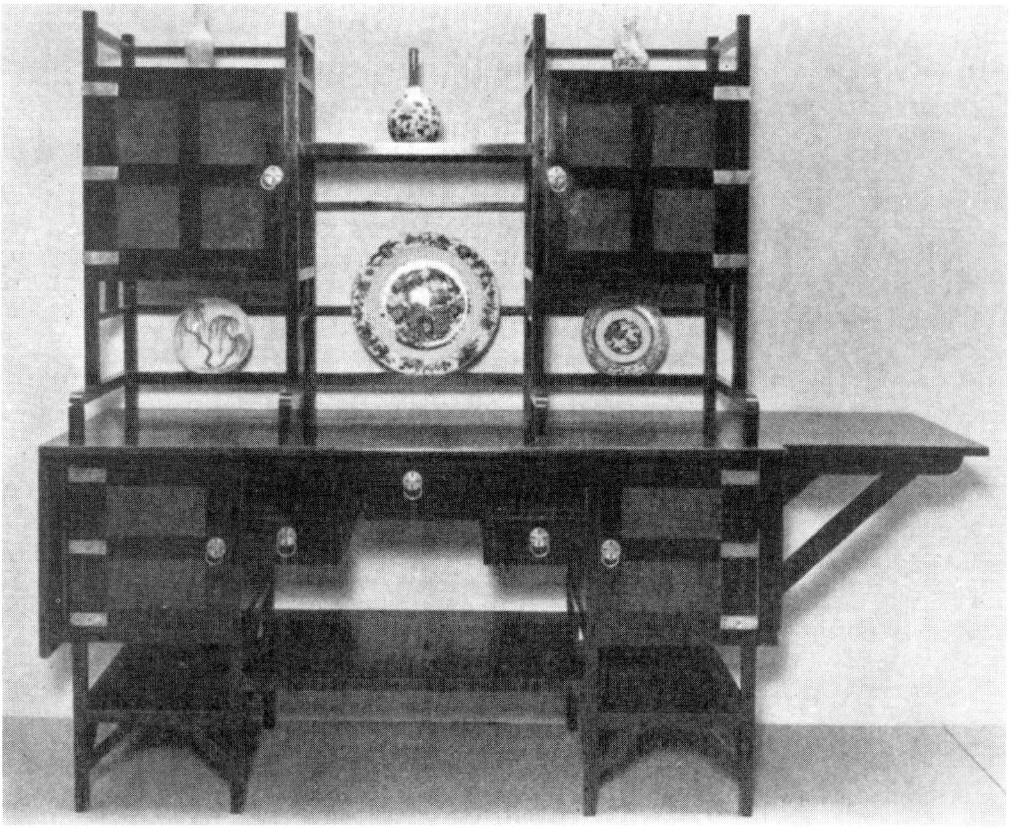

Fig. 99. Godwin: Sideboard, ebonised wood with silver-plated fittings and "embossed leather" paper panels. About 1877.
Victoria and Albert Museum. Crown Copyright reserved.

young Arthur Lasenby Liberty (1843–1917), who had been manager of the firm from 1862, realising how important it was to satisfy the demand for Oriental textiles, opened his East India House in 1875 in Regent Street in London, a modest undertaking which originally had only three employees and from which the firm of Liberty & Co., Ltd. is descended. Liberty himself visited Japan in 1888–89.

Throughout the 1860's and right up to the 1890's the interest in Japan was stimulated by a great many books and articles. The first of these was Cornwall's *Two Journeys to Japan*, 1859, while Owen Jones's *Examples of*

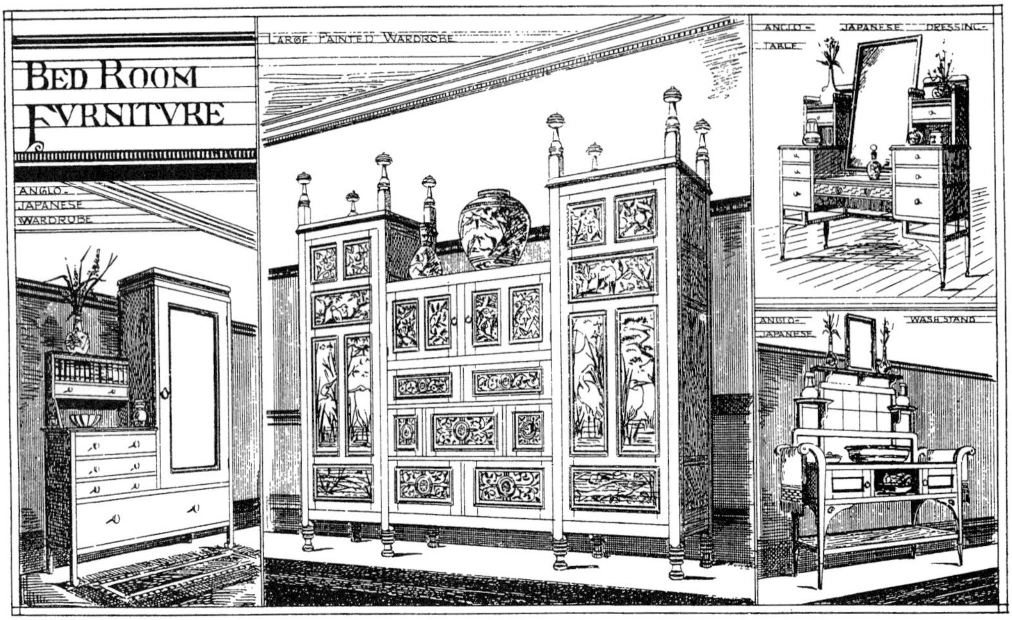

Fig. 100. Godwin: Illustration from *Art Furniture*. 1877.

Chinese Ornaments, 1867, should also be mentioned in this connection. These were followed in rapid succession by R. Alcock's *Art and Art Industries in Japan*, 1878, Th. W. Cutler's *A Grammar of Japanese Ornament and Design*, 1880, and, in the same year, D. H. Moser's *Book of Japanese Ornamentation, composing Designs for the use of Signpainters, Decorators, Designers, Silversmiths, and many other purposes.* In 1882 came the publication of Dresser's *Japan, its Architecture, Art, and Art Manufactures*, in 1884 G. A. Audsley's *The Ornamental Arts of Japan*, in 1883 L. Gonse wrote the French opus *l'Art Japonais*, and in 1886 appeared E. S. Morse's *Japanese Houses and their Surroundings.* This interest continued through the 1890's, and in 1892 the Japan Society was founded, for the benefit of those interested in Japanese art, while *The Studio* devoted a great deal of attention to the subject from the year 1893.

At the same time as Farmer and Rogers held their sale of Japanese exhibits in London, 1862–63, Madame de Soye opened her shop *La Porte Chinoise* in the Rue de Rivoli, Paris. The interest which French painters

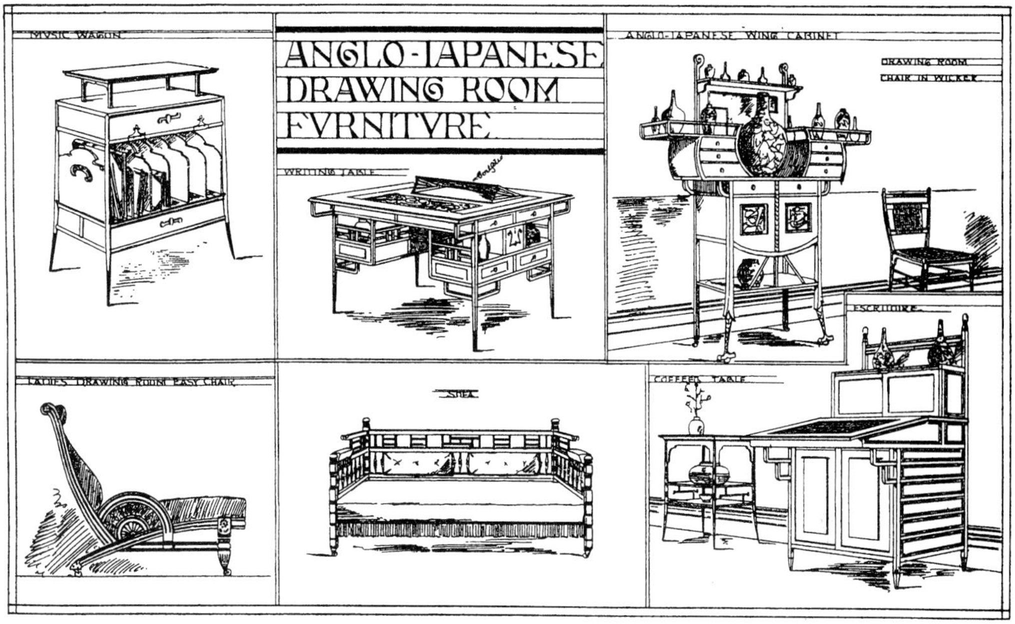

Fig. 101. Godwin: Illustration from *Art Furniture* 1877.

evinced for Japan and Orientalism is sufficiently well known[6], but as Clay Lancaster mentions, "designs comparable to the English hardly appeared before the 1870's on the Continent."[7]

Apart from this information on the rise of Japanese and Oriental influence, Clay Lancaster mentions a number of reasons why Oriental art was one of the paramount influences upon Art Nouveau: he points out that three of the outstanding supporters of Art Nouveau, S. Bing, Tiffany, and Liberty, were all collectors of Oriental art, and furthermore that in the age of Historicism there was a romantic urge for luxuries and exoticism, as exemplified in the Viennese bohème Hans Makart, who "imported soft Eastern cushions and bedecked everything with carpets, Indian shawls, Persian textiles," and it is probably right to connect the exoticism of Romanticism with the same interest in this period, as there is every indication that the tradition was continued uninterrupted from the 18th

6 Inter alia referred to in G. Duthuit's *Chinese Mysticism and Modern Painting,* Paris 1936.

7 C. Lancaster, Oriental Contribution to Art Nouveau, *The Art Bulletin,* New York, vol. XXXIV, 1952, p. 302.

century. Clay Lancaster also points out that the European countries "were examining Eastern Arts as a by-product of the new imperialistic pride in territorial possessions, particularly England that of India, France that of Indo-China and the Netherlands that of Java."[8]

Generally speaking the features of Orientalism which were to have the greatest significance for Art Nouveau, were a more sophisticated and refined attitude to interior decoration and applied art. Trends in furniture design were influenced by three or four elements essentially typical of Japanese and Oriental influence: first of all the simple, fragile structure—the peculiarly Oriental construction which is conditioned by the use of bamboo and manilla—was copied with ordinary European materials to produce correspondingly light and rectangular construction, as for example in Godwin's sideboard[9] (fig. 99), which was executed in the same year as he published his *Art Furniture, with hints and suggestions on domestic furniture and decoration*, 1877.[10] This includes a great many pieces of furniture in what he calls *Anglo–Japanese*, all notable for the same rectilinear construction (figs. 100, 101). The same penchant for constructive elements is also a typical feature of George Walton's[11] (1867–1933) table[12] from 1898 (fig. 102).

This rectilinear style was assiduously cultivated by Paul Hankar (1859–1901), who was especially influenced by Oriental art. This characteristic motif was given full rein in his own house, 71 Rue de Facqz, Brussels, completed in 1893, and rectilinearism became one of his most important decorative motifs (fig. 103).

It is possible that this special interest in the rectilinear may be attributed to Japanese influence and a conscious striving for simple construction. In the hands of Austrian architects it acquires an added touch of refinement and eventually only exists as a decorative motif in itself.

8 C. Lancaster, *loc. cit.*, pp. 304 sq.

9 Victoria and Albert Museum, *Catalogue of an Exhibition of Victorian and Edwardian Decorative Arts*, London 1952, p. 56, K 1.

10 Recently discussed by Nikolaus Pevsner, Art Furniture, *The Architectural Review*, vol. CXI, 1952, pp. 43–50.

11 N. Pevsner, George Walton, His Life and Work, *The Journal of the Royal Institute of British Architects*, vol. XLVI, 1939, pp. 537–48; T. Howarth, *Charles Rennie Mackintosh and the Modern Movement*, London 1952, pp. 233–39.

12 Victoria and Albert Museum, *op. cit.*, p. 97, R 42, Kodak Ltd.

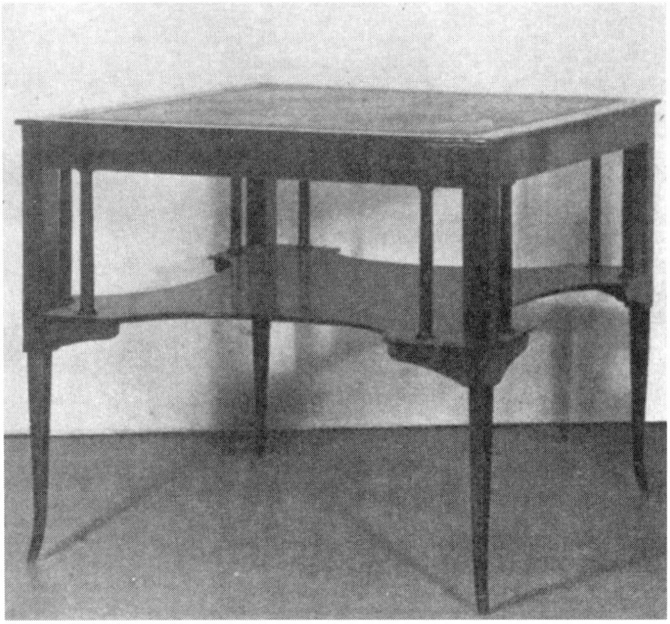

Fig. 102. Walton: Table, mahogany, top covered with leather. About 1898.
Courtesy of Kodak Ltd., London. Victoria and Albert Museum photo. Crown Copyright reserved.

Secondly ornamentation is sparingly employed, and when it is used it contrasts effectively and clearly with the smooth surface which forms its background. An ornament used in this way obtains a decidedly refined effect.

In this connection the influence of Japan coincides with the formal reaction against the decorative *horror vacui* of Historicism, and while its influence can hardly be overestimated, it is probably an exaggeration to suggest that its trends also had a direct bearing on the polychromy of the 1880's and 1890's, as some people have maintained.[13]

In addition to this there is an asymmetrical conception both of the interior itself as well as of the individual piece of furniture, and furthermore the circular or horseshoe-shaped arch which is also due to Moorish influence.

The first two of these features are opposed to the contemporary decorative principles; the two last-mentioned are part of the Oriental tradition which goes back even further. All four features, however, were to set their seal on the style of the nineties.

13 See *Formal Reaction*, note 7.

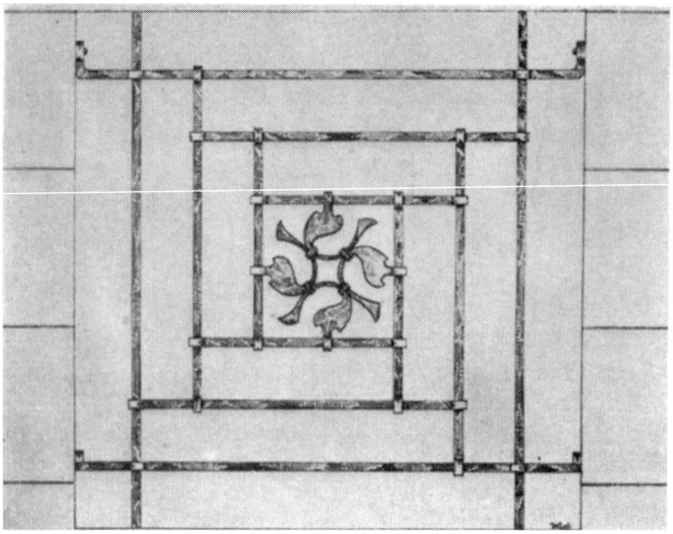

Fig. 103. Hankar: Grating for basement window. 71 Rue de Facqz, Brussels. Forged iron. 1893.

It was, however, in the realm of decorative pattern design that the Oriental and Japanese influence was most obvious, as may be seen in Bruce J. Talbert's[14] (1838–1881) wallpaper from 1877[15] (fig. 104).

One of the features of Japonism which the illustrators of the 1880's and 1890's most eagerly exploited, was the apparently random placing of ornaments and decorative sections. Parts of plants, flowers, and reeds were placed loosely round about the side, separated by oblique lines, semi-circles, and straight lines, and the text was then inserted with a corresponding artistic freedom, often asymmetrically, intimately bound up with the décor in a manner which was highly unorthodox at the time. Both Godwin and Grasset, for instance, used vertical text.[16] These features were the basic forerunners of the kind of art which was to come into being in the poster art of the 1890's.

An English artist who adopted the Japanese ideas and transformed them to an artistic language, was the young and receptive Aubrey Beards-

14 Obituary in *The Cabinet Maker and Art Furnisher,* vol. II, July 1881; L. F. Day, Victorian Progress in Applied Design, *The Art Journal,* June 1887, pp. 185–202.

15 Cat. No. E. 1842–1934, Victoria and Albert Museum.

16 E. Godwin, *Art Furniture,* London 1877, the cover; Grasset, cover for *Histoire des Quatre Fils Aymon,* Paris 1883 (fig. 121).

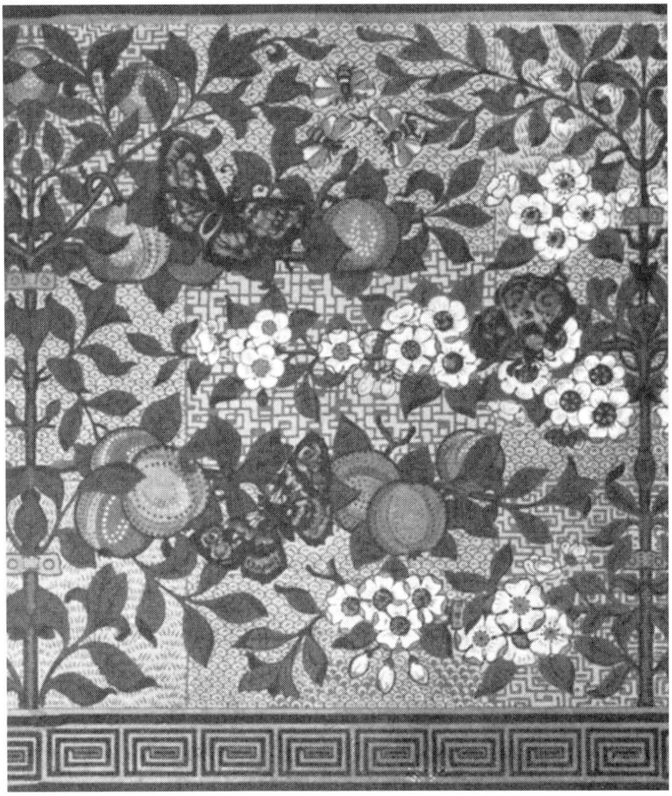

Fig. 104. Talbert: Wallpaper, dado and filling. Handprinted. 1877.
Victoria and Albert Museum. Crown Copyright reserved.

ley. He did not only pick up single elements, but acquired the Japanese spirit and thus created his own personal expression.

The floral aspects of Japanese art readily accorded with the taste of the age, but it was a great innovation that its two-dimensional nature was adopted by eliminating the background plane.

French painters came into touch with Japonism at an early date: as early as 1856 Bracquemond had, quite by chance, stumbled on Japanese prints. While the influence of Japan in decorative art was to be greatest in England—in the introduction to Otto Eckmann's *Dekorative Entwürfe* from 1897 comes the statement that the English are the only people who have been able to adopt Japanese art—it was in painting in the 1860's and 1870's that it came to its fullest fruition in France. Ernest Chesneau's book *Le*

Japon à Paris, 1878, together with his lectures on Japanese art in the *Union Centrale des Arts Décoratifs*, gave art-lovers an added interest.

In poster art its principles also enjoyed great triumphs, and in the art of illustration one of France's most important books in the latter half of the 19th century was illustrated under marked Japanese influence (fig. 105). The illustrations to *Histoire des Quatre Fils Aymon* were executed by Grasset in the years 1879–83, (figs. 97, 121) and it is hard to imagine how they could have acquired the form they did without Japanese influence and the principles of two-dimensional art.

As far as the Nancy school is concerned it might be interesting to mention the special and direct way in which Japonism was introduced here. In 1885 a Japanese by the name of Takasima came to Nancy to study botany at the *Ecole Forestier*. He was in addition a "*savant-artiste*," and made friends with Vallin and Gallé. There is every reason to believe that the presence of Takasima helped to increase the interest in Japan and Japanese art.[17] After the exhibition in 1889 E. de Vogue, writing about Gallé, said: "Bénissons le caprice du sort qui a fait naître un Japonais à Nancy."[18]

In common with England, France, and Belgium, Holland too had direct connection with the East, and like all the other nations in Europe at the time the Dutch attempted to solve the problems of Historicism on a national basis by creating and developing a feeling of style which was at one and the same time new and national, and for this reason, as already mentioned, they went back in architecture to the Dutch Renaissance, as shown by the doyen of Dutch architects in the latter half of the 19th century, P. J. H. Cuypers, in a number of his monumental buildings.

In decorative art they sought their inspiration in a source which in one respect was national, and was in fact the only exotic one that was used, viz. the art of Java, the centuries-old Dutch colony, where Dutch governors had resided ever since the year 1510. Java's own special type of two-dimensional art is batik. It is frequently built up of flaming and irregular

[17] Information kindly given by Auguste Vallin to the author, April 1953.

[18] E. de Vogue, *Remarques sur l'Exposition de 1889*, Paris 1889. "Let us bless the whims of fate which caused a Japanese to be born in Nancy." By "naître" de Vogue does not mean the literal sense of the word. He is, of course, referring to Gallé. T. was born in Japan.

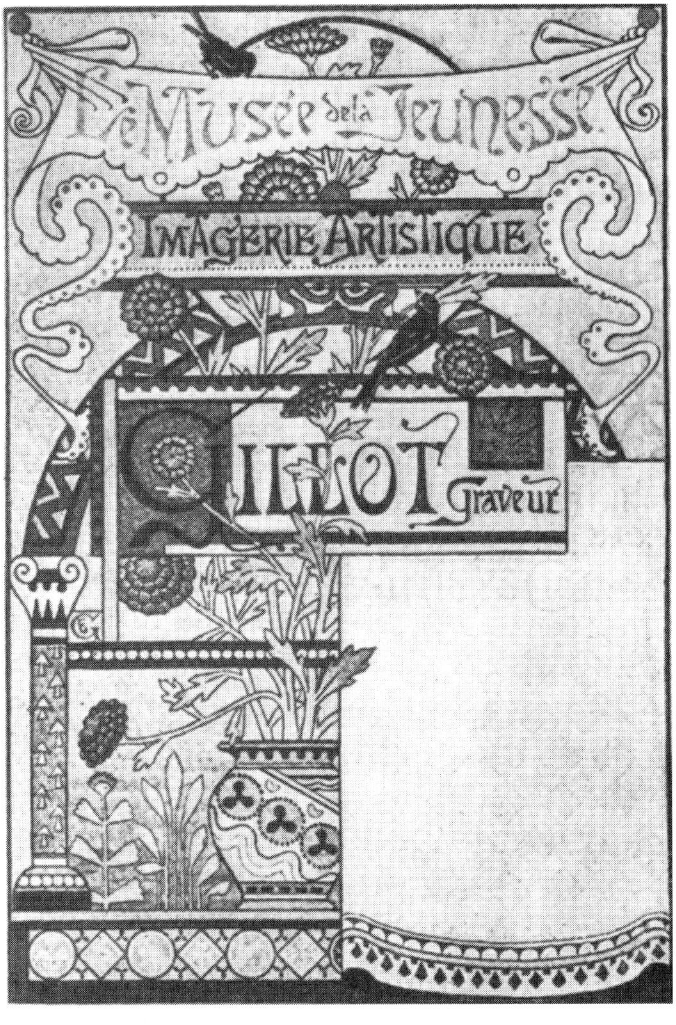

Fig. 105. Grasset: Cover for an illustrated journal. 1884.

shapes, often with thin, linear projections like the antennæ of an insect[19] (figs. 106, 107).

Just as the Belgian Wolffers introduced ivory from the Belgian Congo as a fashionable material, so the Dutchman T. A. C. Colenbrander introduced the Javanese batik technique, both in porcelain and in textile work.

19 G. P. Rouffaer, H. H. Juynboll, *Die Batik-Kunst in Niederländisch-Indien und ihre Geschichte,* I–III, Utrecht 1899–1914, vol. II, pls. 6, 31.

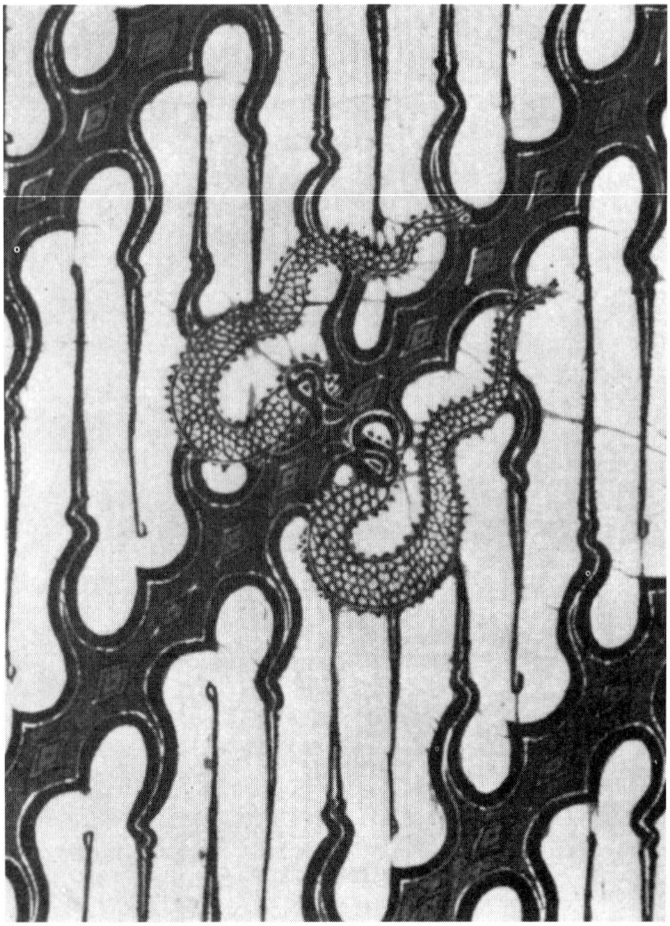

Fig. 106. Parang-rusak pattern. Batik. Jogjakarta, Java. G. P. Rouffaer & H. H. Juynboll: *Die Batik-Kunst in Niederländisch-Indien und ihre Geschichte,* Utrecht. 1899–1944. vol. II. pl. 6.

From the point of view of form this ancient technique has a number of features which rendered it eminently suitable to the stylistic temper of the nineties. Owing to the fact that certain parts of the wool material are covered with a layer of wax, and consequently will not take the imprint of the dye-stuff when the textiles are coloured, it gives a markedly flat pattern, with fixed contours and clear lines, essentially two-dimensional and unnaturalistic, with flowers and leaves stylised and abstracted, and subordinated to the rhythm of line. The neo-Impressionists and Synthetists to some extent strove to achieve the same aesthetic effect, and also went back to Oriental art.

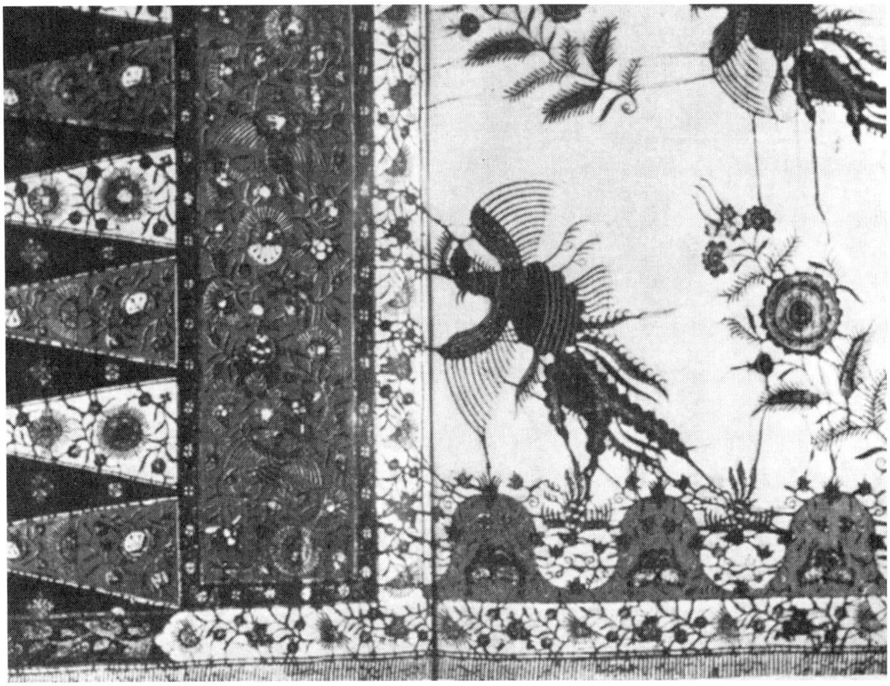

Fig. 107. Mêrak-mibêr-pattern. Batik. Surabaja, Java. G. P. Rouffaer & H. H. Juynboll: *Die Batik-Kunst in Niederländisch-Indien und ihre Geschichte,* Utrecht. 1899–1944. vol. II. pl. 31.

By the middle of the 1880's T. A. C. Colenbrander had launched his batik-inspired work[20] (fig. 108). "Colenbrander hat den grossen Verdienst, die praktische Verwendbarkeit des exotischen Elementes sofort erkannt zu haben," says an article, *Das Neue Ornament der jungen Holländer.*[21] The painter Johan Thorn Prikker worked at carpet designs, inlay, and decorated materials, as well as in batik technique,[22] and the same also applies to C. A. Lion Cachet. He relates that it was about the year 1890 that he learnt the batik technique on linen from Dijsselhof. He transferred his design from this material onto other surfaces, parchment, bookbindings, and finally to furniture.[23]

20 From l. to r.: Cat. No. M.K. 109a, M.K. 108, M.K. 109b, Gemeentemuseum, The Hague.

21 *Dekorative Kunst,* No. 7, vol. I, 1898, pp. 1–28 (p. 10). "Colenbrander's great merit is that he realised the practical application of the exotic element."

22 *Ibid.,* p. 12.

23 C. A. Lion Cachet, Voorwerpen van gebatikt perkament, *Maandblad voor beeldende Kunsten,* vol. I, 1924, pp. 108–13.

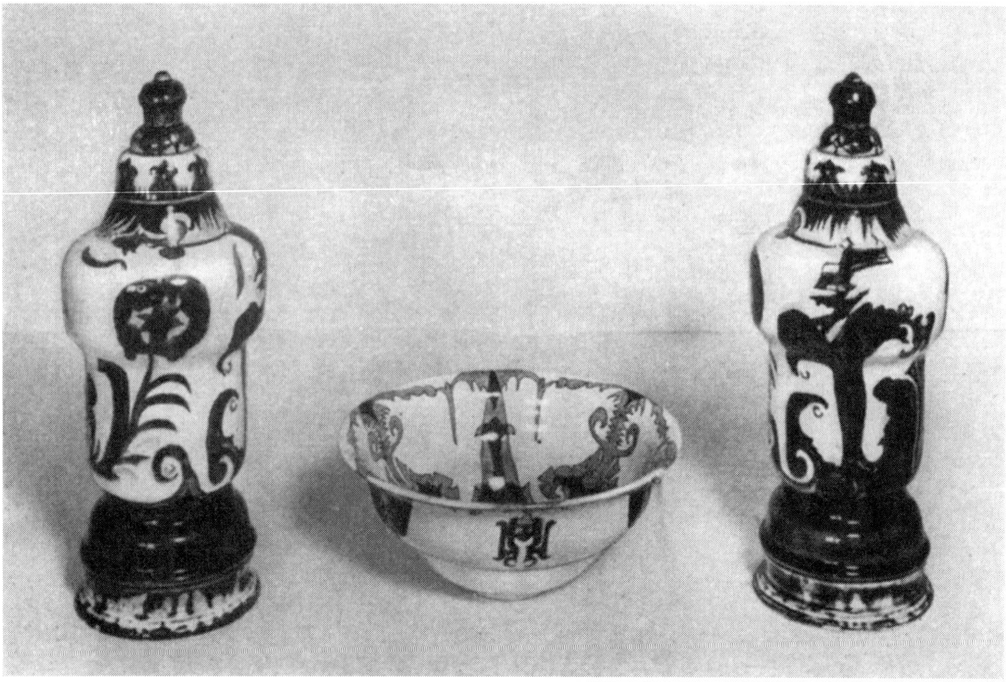

Fig. 108. Colenbrander: Earthenware. Blue-black and dark-brown on cream yellow. 1886.
Gemeentemuseum, The Hague. Copyright reserved.

Willem Dijsselhof was the foremost of these Oriental-inspired artists, and his *magnum opus*, the so-called Dijsselhof Room from the years 1891–92, is decorated with materials in batik technique similar to what we saw in his screen (fig. 30). Writing in 1898 a critic said of Dijsselhof: "Der exotische Einfluss springt bei allen Dijsselhofschen Werken in die Augen; man kan leicht verfolgen, dass er in seinen Holzschnitten von persischen Ornamenten beeinflusst ist, während er in seinen Stoffen – auch er fertigt Batiks – mehr chinesischen und japanischen Eindrücken folgt."[24]

We find the same characteristic Orientalism in the work of Agatha Wegerif-Gravesteyn. Her velour-chiffon panneau[25] (fig. 109) is built up

[24] Das Neue Ornament der jungen Holländer, *Dekorative Kunst,* No. 7, vol. I, 1998, pp. 14 sq. "In all Dijsselhof's work the exotic influence is apparent. It is easy to trace the influence of Persian design in his woodcuts, while in his materials—he also worked in batik—he tends rather to follow Chinese and Japanese impressions."

[25] Ct. No. M.K. 7–53, Gemeentemuseum, The Hague.

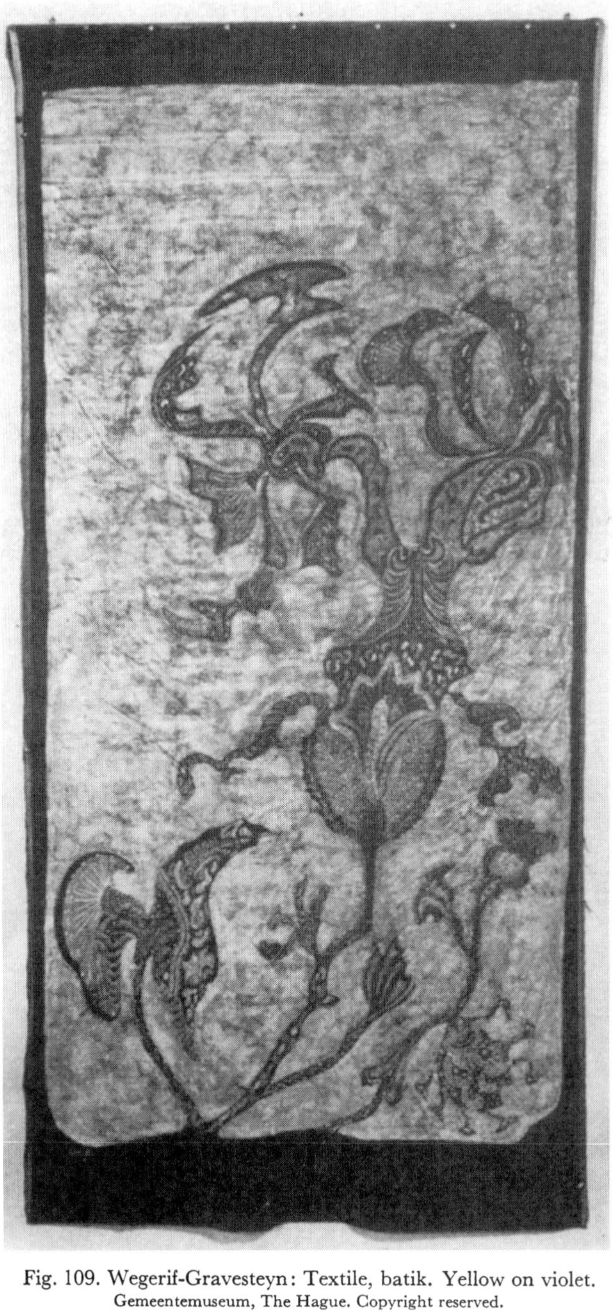

Fig. 109. Wegerif-Gravesteyn: Textile, batik. Yellow on violet.
Gemeentemuseum, The Hague. Copyright reserved.

of similar elements as August Endell's facade decoration for the *Elvira Studio,* Munich, 1897–98. The Japanese influence in Germany and Austria, like most of the other factors determining the origins of Art Nouveau, arrived much later.

Clay Lancaster also convincingly demonstrates in his article the similarity between one of the plates in the publication on Bing's collection of Japanese art, showing a bird on a nelumbium plant, on one side, and Endell's asymmetric, spindrift- and dragon-like facade ornament for the Elvira Photographische Atelier, 13 to 14 years later, on the other.[26]

The interest in Egypt falls outside the scope of Orientalism in its narrower sense, but it is nevertheless an important factor at this time, playing a not unimportant role in architecture.

The interest in Egyptian art was especially prominent in the 1880's and 90's, and Margaret Flower mentions Sarah Bernhardt's great role as Cleopatra in 1890 as symptomatic of this interest. Egyptian jewels and trinkets, *porte-bonheur* (lucky charms), and the like were used to an increasing extent, and as might have been expected the large illustrated works which were published not only expressed this interest in things Egyptian, but helped to stimulate it. Among the most important was W. M. Flinders Petrie's *Egyptian Decorative Arts,* in 1895. Architects and artists, such as for instance Emile André and Eugène Grasset, bent their steps towards Egypt instead of making the traditional study tour in Italy. It was above all the search for a simple and monumental form of expression which inspired these ideals. Berlage's *Exchange,* Damrak, Amsterdam, 1898–1903, where the only ornamentation on the facade is a Norman, an Assyrian, and an Egyptian head side by side is symptomatic enough.

Decorative art was only to a certain extent directly influenced by Egyptian art even though Berlage's panel (fig. 31) is an interesting example, as also some of de Bazel's woodcuts e.g. *The Victory* from the illustration to *De Tocht der Argonauter* from 1894 (fig. 110), and the top of a cupboard by J. L. M. Lauweriks (1864–1932).[27]

26 C. Lancaster, *loc. cit.,* p. 307, figs. 9, 11.

27 Illustrated in J. de Jong: *De Nieuwerichting in de kunstnijverheid in Nederland,* Rotterdam 1929, pl. 18. More detailed illustrations in *Wendingen,* No. 8, vol. X, 1929, p. 12; it is here dated 1895.

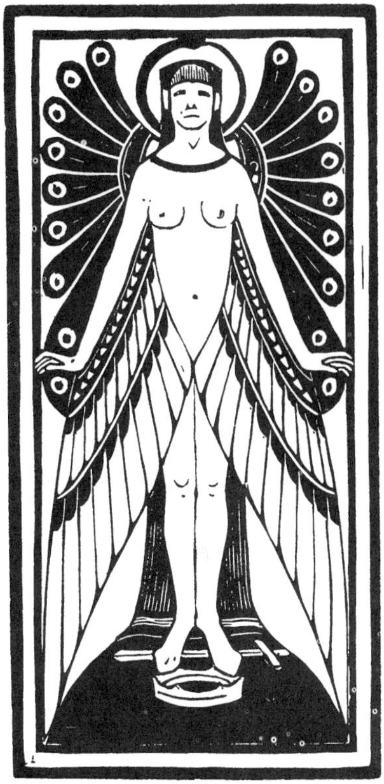

Fig. 110. De Bazel: Victory. Illustration from *De Tocht der Argonauter*. 1894.

Regarding the Glasgow School, Thomas Howarth points out that the murals in the luncheon-room in Buchanan Street have something in common with Egyptian decorative work"—an impression conveyed by the employment of stylized trees reminiscent of the lotus, and the ubiquitous peacock motive."[28] In Glasgow the Graeco–Egyptian decorative schemes of Alexander Thomson, may also be mentioned as typical of the age as well as Gleeson White's suggestion that "the Four" should have been influenced by Egyptian Art —a suggestion which they, however, strongly denied.[29]

The interest in Turkish, Persian, Moorish, and Indian decorative art went hand in hand with the craze for Orientalism. The artist who grew weary of European styles could always fetch his impulses from more distant civilisations. The popularity of these more ephemeral fashions is often connected with historical events at the time. Thus the heroic struggle of the Turks in the 1870's resulted in a wave of sympathy sweeping over Europe which lead to an interest in everything Turkish, while Indian jewellery became fashionable after Queen Victoria had been crowned Empress of India in 1876.[30]

Historicism was undoubtedly generally inspired by these distant cultures and their art, as was Art Nouveau (figs. 111–112). Their most important direct contribution to Art Nouveau was the large semi lune-shaped arch and the Moorish arch which has already been mentioned. It

28 T. Howarth, *Charles Rennie Mackintosh and the Modern Movement,* London 1952, p. 127.

29 For this information the author is indebted to Thomas Howarth. Gleeson White, Some Glasgow Designers and their Work, *The Studio,* vol. XI, 1897, pp. 86–100, pp. 227–36, vol. XII, 1898, pp. 47–51, vol. XIII, 1898, pp. 12–25 (vol. XI, 1897, pp. 88 sq.).

30 M. Flower, *Victorian Jewellery,* London 1951, p. 30.

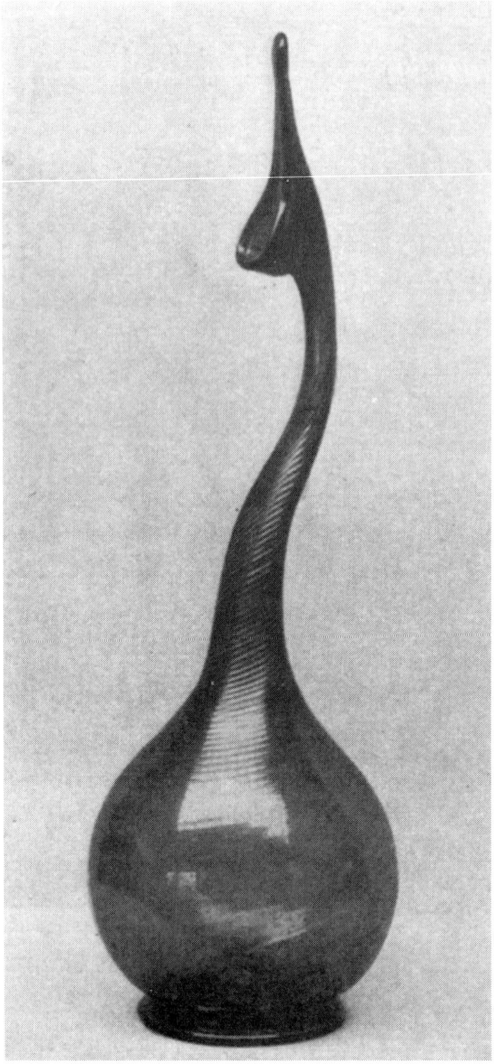

Fig. 111. Persian perfume spray. Glass.
Victoria and Albert Museum. Crown Copyright reserved.

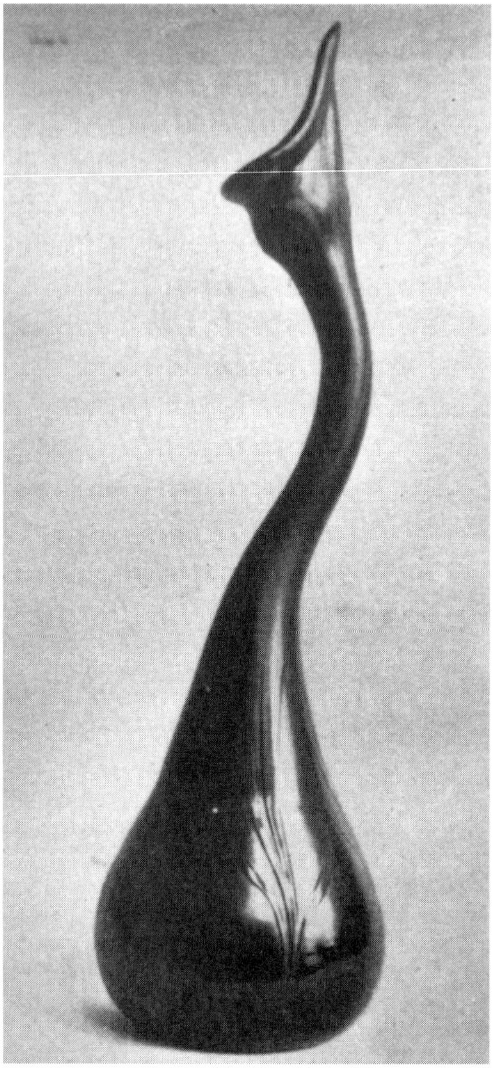

Fig. 112. Tiffany: Vase. Coloured glass. 1897.
Nationalmuseum, Stockholm. Copyright reserved.

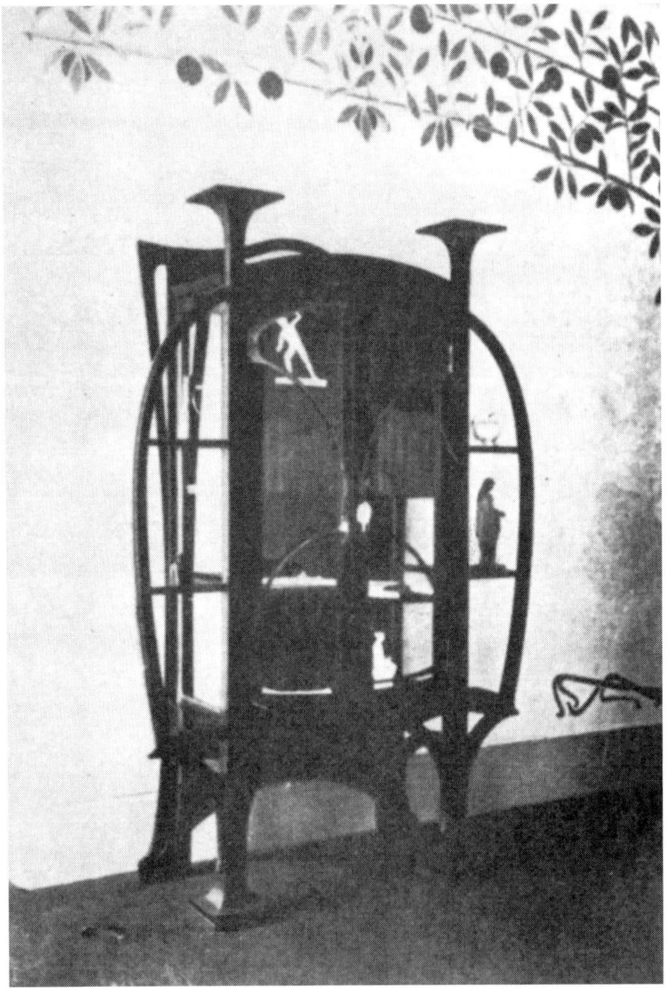

Fig. 113. Serrurier-Bovy: Cabinet with glass doors. 1900.

has been encountered in German and Austrian art, e.g. as exploited by Olbrich and Huber (figs. 35, 37, 38), while in Belgium it was a favourite motif, especially with Paul Hankar and Paul Serrurier-Bovy (fig. 113).[31]

*

Indirectly the Japanese influence led to a more sophisticated attitude to interior decoration and applied art, with a special feeling for the light

31 H. van de Velde, Gustav Serrurier-Bovy, *Zeitschrift für Innendekoration,* vol. XIII, 1902, p. 61.

and airy. Furthermore there is an interest in simple and rectilinear construction. The influence of Japanese decorative art also led to a greater understanding of ornament and background, of two-dimensional effect and also asymmetrical conception of detail as well as of the whole. Last but not least the artist learned the value of the elegant and refined use of line. The influence of Oriental and Japanese art was on the line of inspiration and not of imitation.

In conclusion, and to give a contemporary estimate of the influence of Japanese art, it might be interesting to quote Marcel Bing's final pronouncement in the chapter on Japan in Richard Graul's book, *Die Krisis im Kunstgewerbe*, 1901:

"So haben einige Künstler geglaubt, in verschiedenartigen Linienkombinationen eine neue Quelle der Ornamentation oder gar die verlorenen Prinzipen des modernen Stils zu finden. Diese Versuche scheinen ein wenig inspiriert zu sein von der graziösen Wellenbewegung japanischer Linienführung, die in glücklicher Weise das lineare Ornament beeinflusst hat. Ohne Zweifel hat die Zeichnung in den dekorativen Künsten eine Bereicherung durch neuartige Linienverschlingungen und Mäanderspiele erfahren und eine Manier ausgebildet, in der man etwas von der reizenden Weichheit und dem gesunden dekorativen Verstand der orientalischen Motive derart wiederfindet."*

* "Thus some artists believed they could find a new source of ornamentation, or even the lost principles of modern style, in various linear combinations. These attempts seem to have been inspired to a certain extent by the graceful wary movement of Japanese line, which has so happily influenced linear ornament. Without a doubt drawing has in the decorative arts experienced an enrichment in new kinds of linear coils and developed a manner, in which can be found something of the charming pliancy and sound decorative understanding of oriental motifs."

Celtic Revival

Grasset's illustration to *Histoire des Quatre Fils Aymon*, executed in the years 1879–83 (figs. 97, 121), contains certain features reminiscent of Celtic *entrelac* ornamentation or the linear rhythm which is to be found in the ornamentation of the late migrations. This is no coincidence, but an expression of a stylistic tendency which borrowed some of its impulses from the ornamentation of the Celts, and of the Vikings. In some countries it was not only a stylistic tendency, but a movement which left behind lasting impressions in a great many cultural spheres.

With the growing historical interest which developed in a great many countries under the stimulus of Romanticism, and which often took a national turn, it was hardly surprising that in Scandinavia writers and artists should have turned for inspiration to the years of national greatness in the Viking epoch. This cult of the Viking age goes right back to the beginning of the 19th century, reaching its peak in the era of national romanticism, especially in Norway, in the 1840's and 1850's. In decorative art the first signs of this movement can be found as far back as the 1830's and 1840's (fig. 114), and in its general European context this movement may be regarded as a national and special offshoot of the Gothic revival. Stylistically it is often referred to as the "dragon style," but as the Gothic revival drew to a close, the dragon style continued to develop, and when the Gothic revival and its Continental aspect, Neo-Gothic, died away in the 1890's, the dragon style continued to flourish in Scandinavia side by side with the Celtic revival in the British Isles.

The ornamental design of the architect Henrik Bull (1864–1952), the most Art Nouveau influenced designer in Norway, shows how the dragon style and Art Nouveau sometimes fuse in a perfect ornamental symbiosis (fig. 115). Scandinavia has contributed little or nothing internationally to the origin and development of Art Nouveau, but this dragon-style-Art

1 St. Tschudi Madsen, Dragestilen. Honnør til en hånet stil, *Vestlandske Kunstindustrimuseums Årbok*, Bergen 1952, pp. 19–62.

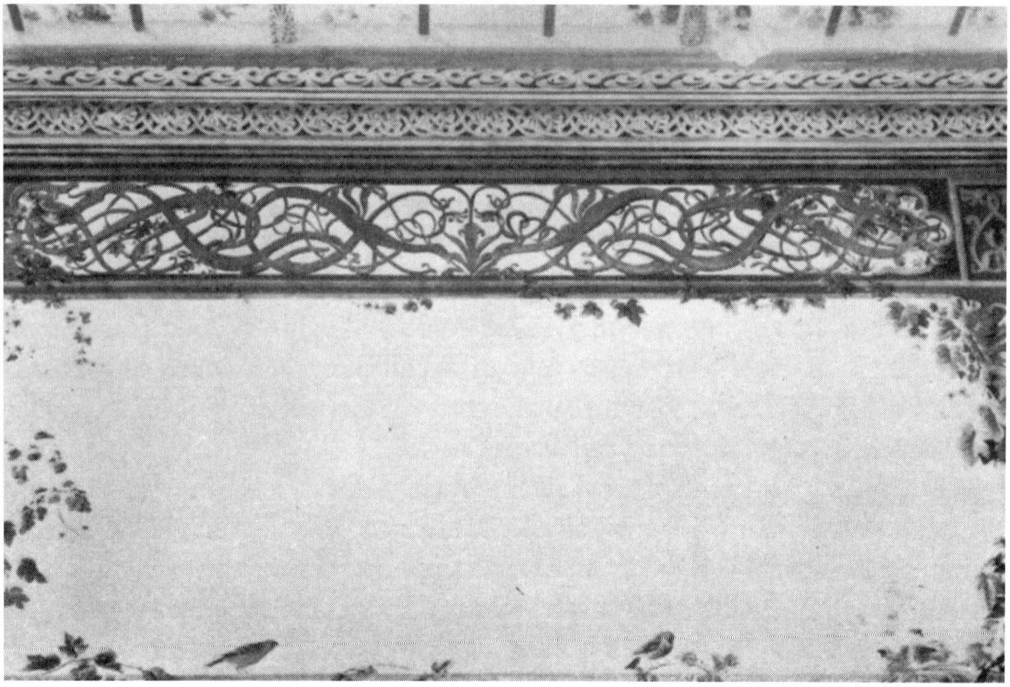

Fig. 114. Flintoe: Painted frieze. The Royal Palace, Oslo. 1841.
K. Teigen Copyright.

Nouveau constitutes a special phenomenon, which artistically speaking can be compared with the other European styles. Because Norway was regarded as the home and the most important creator of this dragon style[2], and presumably because this style coincided at the time with the Celtic movement in England, and in its form-language with Art Nouveau, the Victoria and Albert Museum purchased two dragon-style chairs in 1900[3]—and though they were not particularly representative of Scandinavian wood carving or of the dragon style, they were at any rate Norwegian enough, and had been furnished with the sufficient number of dragons. The Musée des Arts Décoratifs also purchased a bench in the same style.[4] The following

2 Norwegian architectural and decorative contributions at the international exhibitions were from the 1870's and onwards more or less moulded on the lines of the dragon style.

3 Cat. No. 4–1901, Victoria and Albert Museum, London (made by Borgersen, Oslo). Illustrated St. Tschudi Madsen, Stiltendenser omkring 1905, *Bonytt*, Oslo, vol. XV, 1955, p. 109.

4 Cat. No. D. 20741, Musée des Arts Décoratifs, Louvre, Paris (made by Krafft).

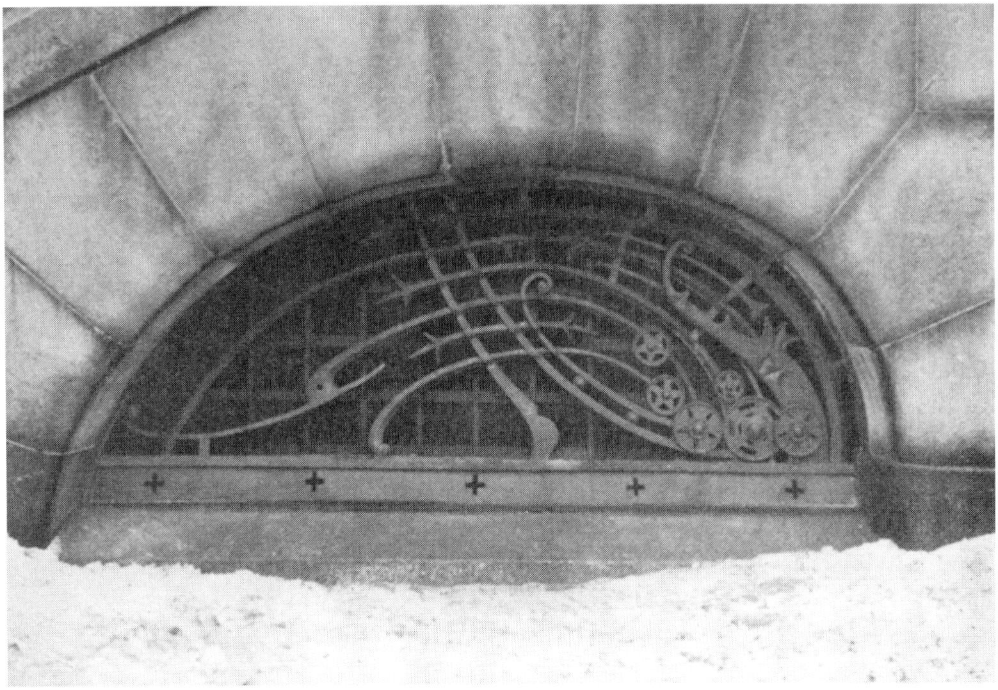

Fig. 115. Bull: Grating for cellar window. Forged iron. 1902.
Historisk Museum, Oslo. K. Teigen Copyright.

year, in 1901, the Victoria and Albert Museum purchased copies of two Norwegian Norman chairs, the Tyldal Chair and Blaker Chair.[5] All these purchases may be said to have represented the contemporary interest in this style round about the year 1900, a style which was considered Norwegian and an original contribution to the trends of the age. Similarly we also find several articles and reproductions of Norwegian furniture with Norman ornamentation in contemporary periodicals, e.g. both in *The Studio*[6] and in *The Art Worker's Quarterly.*[7]

In their wider implications and in their historical context the dragon style and the ornamentation which found expression during the Celtic

5 Cat. No. 916–1901, 915–1901, Victoria and Albert Museum, London. They may have been bought in 1900.

6 J. Romilly Allen, Early Scandinavian Wood-Carvings, *The Studio,* vol. X, 1897, pp. 11–20, vol. XII, 1898, pp. 82–90.

7 *The Art Worker's Quarterly,* vol. I, 1902, pp. 110 sq., pls. 4, 6.

revival in Great Britain will take their place naturally as part and parcel of the contemporary search for non-Classical ideals, a search which developed retrogressively, from neo-Gothic back to neo-Norman, and via the dragon style and the style of the migrations, until by the end of the century inspiration is sought from the distant sources of Assyrian, Babylonian, and finally Egyptian art. The dragon style and the neo-Celtic style are therefore in the widest sense of the word a phase in the regressive stylistic development of Historicism.

As the Celtic Revival coincided towards the end of the century with Art Nouveau, it might be of interest to examine it a little more closely.

Hand in hand with the enthusiasm for the Middle Ages and the interest in historical research went the interest in Nordic archaeology, and in Great Britain people became alive to the remarkable art and ornamentation of the Celts. The earliest known example of Irish illuminated manuscripts, is the famous *Gospel Book of Durrow*, about 650–700; the *Book of Lindisfarne* is a little later. The *Book of Kells* dates from about 800, but it may well compete in fame with the two first mentioned. These three books were already familiar, and were accorded an increasing measure of attention, while Queen Victoria herself went so far in her interest that she added her own autograph to the last mentioned of these medieval manuscripts.

In 1850 the Tara Brooch was found, and it is hardly surprising that Celtic ornamentation should have been eagerly adopted by silversmiths and goldsmiths and by book illustrators.

At the Exhibition in 1851, we find brooches, bracelets, neckchains, pins, and rings executed by James West & Son, Dublin, "copied from antique Irish ornaments."[8] It is more than probable that these were in the "Byzantine" or "runic style," as Celtic ornamentation was also called in those days.[9]

When the next exhibition was held, on Irish soil, in Dublin in 1853, a great deal of silverwork in the Irish style was on show, including a copy

8 *Official and Descriptive Illustrated Catalogue of the Great Exhibition,* I–III, London 1851, vol. II, class 23, No. 15.

9 In 1863 Henry O'Neill writes: "Archaeologists term Byzantine all ornamental art which prevailed throughout Europe from the age of Constantine to the period of the Renaissance," H. O'Neill, *The Fine Arts and Civilization of Ancient Ireland,* London 1863, p.l. "Runic" is used by G. W. Yapp, *Metal Work,* I–II, London 1877, vol. I, second part, pl. XLVII.

of the Tara Brooch,[10] executed by Messrs. Waterhouse of Dublin, who with J. West were the leading craftsmen working in this style.

In the 1840's, '50's and '60's George Petrie and Henry O'Neill published their works on Irish archaeology, and in 1863 O'Neill states that "among the branches of manufactures which have, within the last years, made great progress in Ireland, that of brooches and other personal ornaments in imitation of the old Irish models, holds an important place."[11]

H. H. Armsted's cup from 1860 may be said to be one of the very earliest works, independently conceived, in the Celtic style. It has been said of it that "the design is quite novel in style and treatment . . ." and furthermore that "such a work of art could scarcely have been produced in this country ten years earlier."[12]

This statement and the examples already mentioned make it natural to place the beginning of the Celtic revival in English silverware to about the year 1860.

William Morris's interest in old Nordic culture is familiar enough: he had already made two visits to Iceland when in the autumn of 1872 he started to translate some of the sagas. Three years later appeared *Sigurd the Volsung*. But as early as 1861 his firm had made a cabinet of inlay work with unmistakably Celtic-inspired initials on the lid, with serpents coiling in entrelac and biting one another.[13]

The archaeological and scientific work was followed by books of a more popular nature, such as Edward Sullivan's *Facsimilies of National Manuscripts of Ireland*, 1874–84, and Celtic ornaments invade the realm of magazines and pattern books.[14]

In Robert Newbery's *Gleanings from Ornamental Art*, 1863, there were already plates of Anglo–Saxon, Celtic, and Irish patterns; and Dresser speaks of Celtic ornaments in his *Modern Ornamentation*, 1886.

In her book *Victorian Jewellery* Margaret Flower mentions the Celtic

10 Illustrations in the Illustrated Catalogue of the Exhibition of Art Industry in Dublin, *The Art Journal*, London 1853, p. 39.

11 H. O'Neill, *The Fine Arts and Civilization of Ancient Ireland*, London 1863, p. 49.

12 G. W. Yapp, *Metal Work*, I–II, London 1877, vol. I, first part, pl. V.

13 Cat. No. W.10–1927, Victoria and Albert Museum, London.

14 G. W. Yapp, *op. cit.*, vol. I, second part, pls. VII, XXX, XLVII; *Decoration*, London 1881, vol. I–II; Th. K. Abbott, *Celtic Ornaments from the Book of Kells*, London 1892–95.

influence in the 1860's in brooches and bracelets,[15] and the well-known goldsmith Alessandro Castellani, author of *Antique Jewellery and its Revival,* 1862, in describing his impressions from the Paris Exhibition in 1878, mentions that there were three main trends within the art of the goldsmith and the silversmith, first the Scottish, inspired by the traditional jewellery of Anglo-Saxons and Celt, and then the two other trends, one geometrically inspired and the other classically inspired.[16]

Whether the term Byzantine, Runic, Anglo–Saxon, Celtic, or Irish is used, the meaning is the same, and the source of inspiration is to be found in the Irish book illustrations and goldsmiths' art between the years 650 and 1100. The elements most frequently adopted are the asymmetrical conception, the *entrelac* motif, the dragon or the serpent, the linear twisting coils, and the principle that the decoration should be kept in one plane, raised above the background plane.

In fact the Celtic revival was political, literary, and artistic in character, and Ireland was its natural centre. In the 1890's William B. Yeats was its literary spokesman, and Holbrook Jackson in *The Eighteen-Nineties* points out that it was not until Yeats's *The Wanderings of Oisin, and Other Poems,* 1889, that the real Celtic revival began, to be followed by works such as *The Countess Kathleen,* in 1892, and *The Celtic Twilight,* in 1893. H. Jackson also mentions Grant Allen's article in *The Fortnightly Review,* 1891, in which he gave the impression that the Celtic influence dominated the field of artistic activity.[17]

The foremost connoisseur of the Glasgow School, Thomas Howarth, has pointed out in *Charles Rennie Mackintosh and the Modern Movement* that this resurgence of national spirit also found expression in Scotland, and emphasises its influence on the Glasgow School.[18] Among other works Mackintosh was responsible for a gravestone which Thomas Howarth describes as "full of Celtic spirit."[19]

15 M. Flower, *Victorian Jewellery,* London 1951, p. 134.

16 *Ibid.,* p. 30.

17 H. Jackson, The Discovery of the Celt, *The Eighteen-Nineties,* London 1913, pp. 178–89.

18 Thomas Howarth, *Charles Rennie Mackintosh and the Modern Movement,* London 1952, pp. 229 sq. and footnote 1, p. 231.

19 *Ibid.,* p. 183.

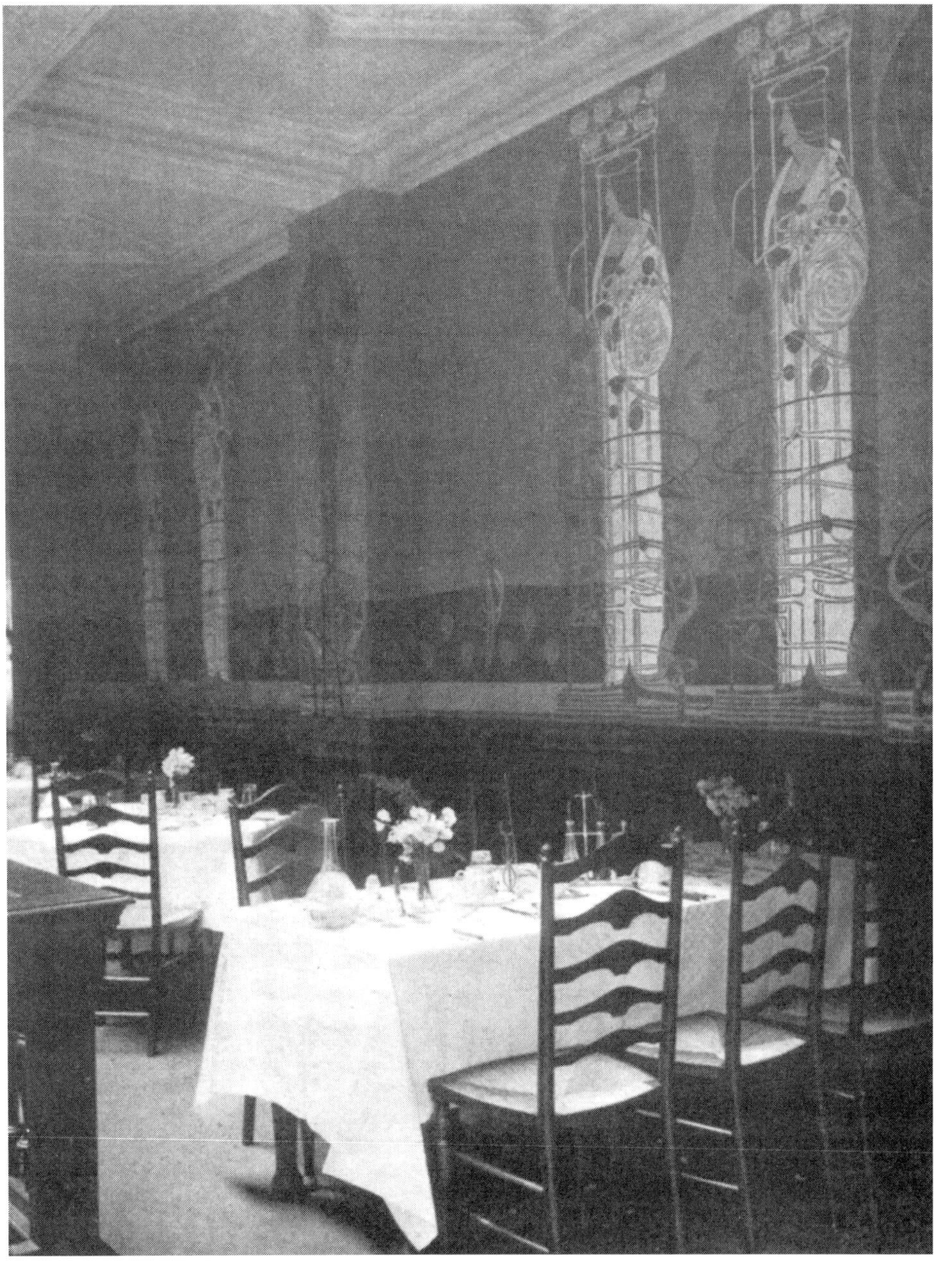

Fig. 116. Mackintosh: Wall decoration. Buchanan Street Tearoom, Glasgow. 1897.

Mackintosh's tall and willowy women in the Buchanan Street Tearoom, Glasgow (fig. 116) from 1897, are also surrounded by *entrelac* motifs which, more than anything else, resemble the Scandinavian animal ornamentation from the beginning of the 11th century, but with this difference, that Mackintosh has omitted the small dragon-heads, and given it an extra touch of the Art Nouveau whiplash.

The most typical feature of this revival in Scotland is the periodical *Evergreen*, four numbers of which appeared in the years from 1895–97, with Patrick Geddes (1854–1932), scientist, socialist, and philosopher, as its editor and prime mover. The first number contained articles such as *The Awakenings in History* and *The Scots Renaiscence*, and poems such as *Anima Celtica* by John Duncan:

> The visioned stories read, the book is closed—
>   The Past has been and shall not be again.
> She dreams; . . . Yet comes to her, disarmed, deposed,
>   A wide new kingdom in the minds of men.[20]

It would be difficult for more melancholy and yearning—more Celts, swords, and dragon-coils—to be contained within the narrow compass of a single page than Duncan succeeded in doing in his illustration to this poem. The illustration to *The Norland Wind*[21] (fig. 117) also gives an excellent picture of the style. It is possible to see how incunabula have inspired the illustrator, and how the waving rhythm and line of the 1890's fuses with the Celtic-inspired ornamentation. The result is a *vue d'ensemble* which is typically Art Nouveau.

At the same time the periodical also dealt with topics from abroad, especially from France, and we find articles such as *La littérature Nouvelle en France* and a reproduction of Paul Serusier's *Pastorale Bretonne*. Great emphasis was placed on the graphic outlay and several of the initials were pure Celtic. Some of the illustrations clearly reveal the influence of Beardsley, especially in the case of Duncan, and the female types that recur are filled with a melancholy and tristesse which would only have been possible

20 *Evergreen*, vol. I, 1895, p. 106.

21 *Ibid.*, vol. I, p. 109.

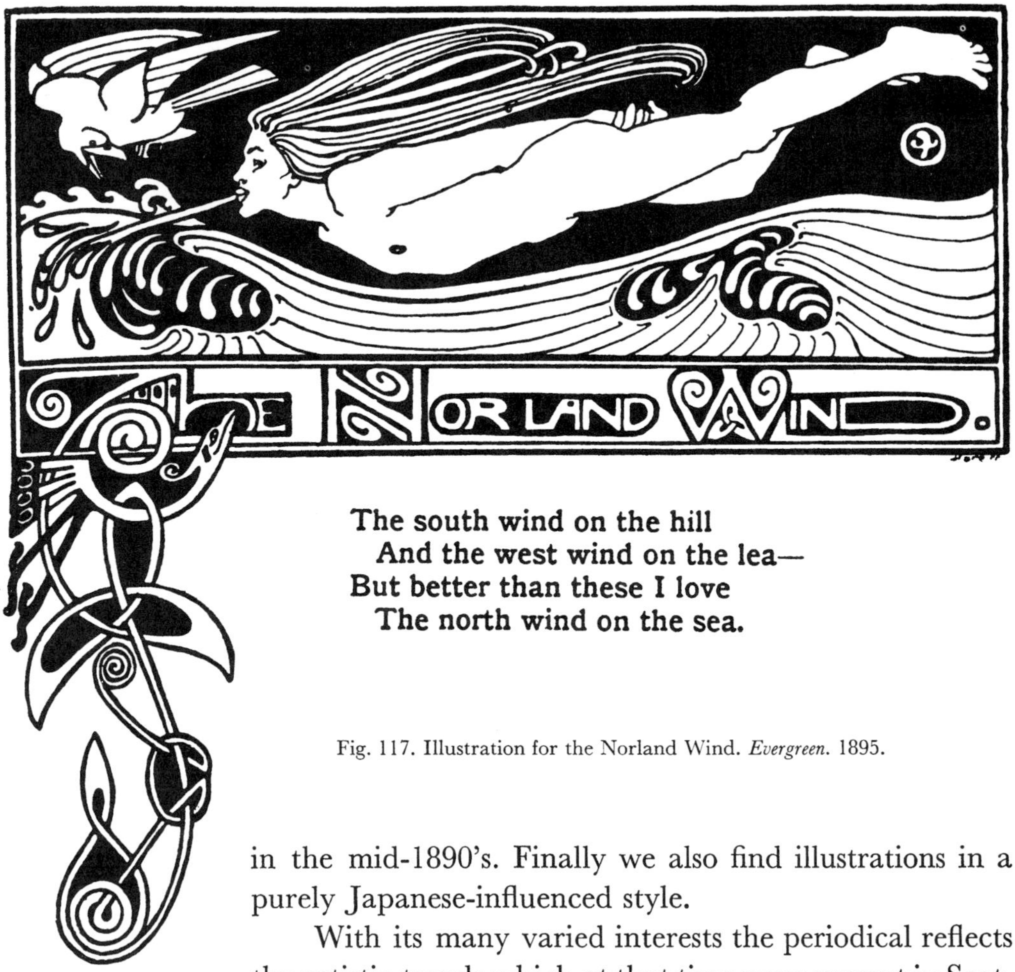

Fig. 117. Illustration for the Norland Wind. *Evergreen*. 1895.

in the mid-1890's. Finally we also find illustrations in a purely Japanese-influenced style.

With its many varied interests the periodical reflects the artistic trends which at that time were current in Scotland, and it is interesting to note that it was in Scotland that a British Art Nouveau was to take shape—Scotland, where the soil had been well prepared with nationalism and the desire for an independent form of expression, and where the interest in Celtic art, with its coils and linear rhythm, was waiting to be exploited.

In England, too, but not to that extent, we also find the interest in Celtic art in the 1890's, and, characteristically enough, in silver. One of the most fashionable jewellers of the age, Alexander Fisher (1864–1936),[22]

22 F. Miller, The Art of an Enameller, and of Mr. Alex Fisher in particular, *The Art Journal,* 1898, pp. 263–67.

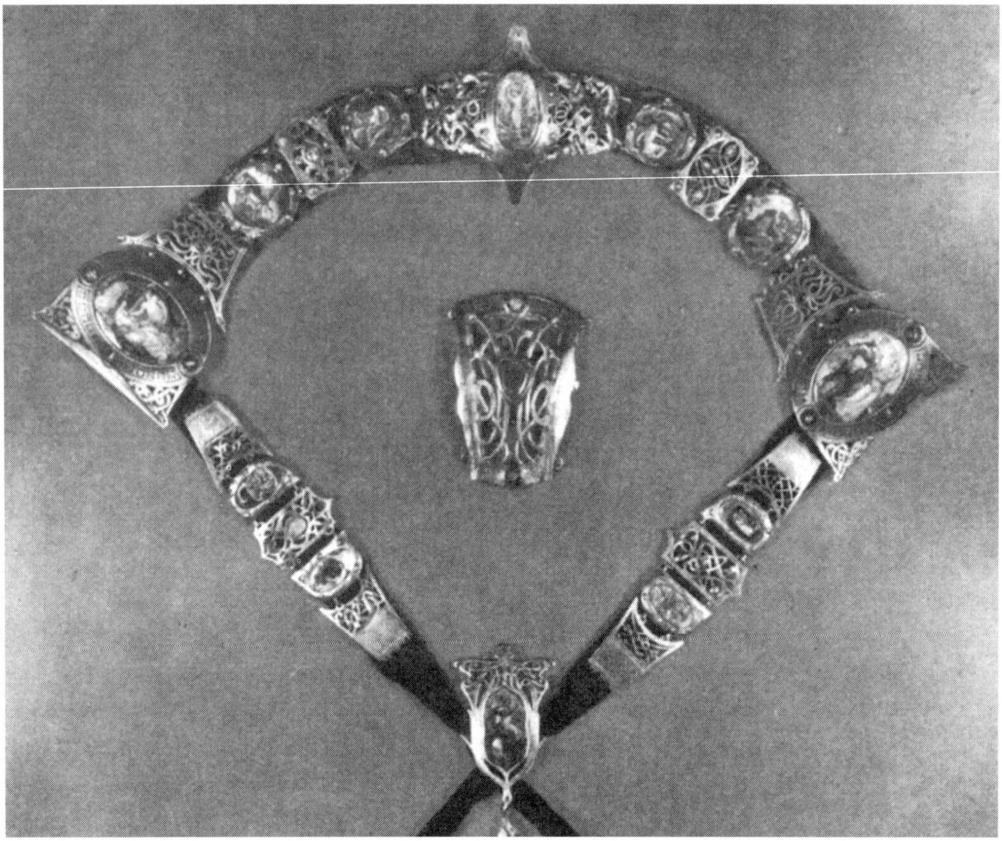

Fig. 118. Fisher: Girdle, decorated with scenes from Wagnerian operas. 1893–96. Victoria and Albert Museum. Crown Copyright reserved.

executed between 1893 and 1896 a buckle[23] (fig. 118), which also shows Celtic features. The *entrelac* motif, too, proved especially popular at this time.

The ever-vigilant Arthur Liberty adopted the style in 1900, and issued a catalogue in which he introduced it under the name of "Cymric Silver" (figs. 119–120).[24] "The especially interesting feature of this new school," says the introduction, "is its complete and unmistakable differentiation from all other descriptions of modern silverwork."[25] In view of the search

23 Cat. No. M.10–1943, Victoria and Albert Museum.

24 Liberty & Co. Ltd., London, "*Cymric Silver*," pl. 37.

25 *Ibid.*, p. 4.

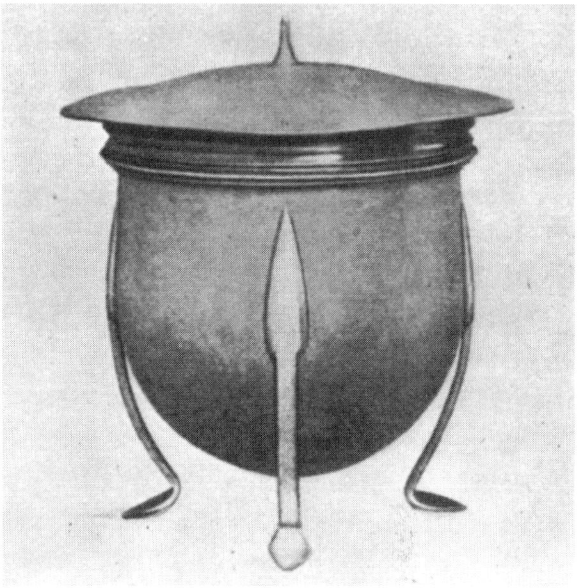

Fig. 119. Illustration from A. Liberty's catalogue. *Cymric silver*. 1900.

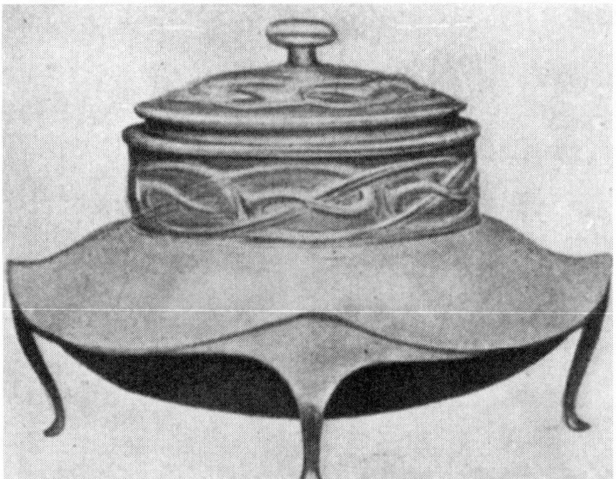

Fig. 120. Illustration from A. Liberty's catalogue. *Cymric silver*. 1900.

of the age for new stylistic forms, it was hardly surprising that an enterprising businessman should launch this style, the more so as it was admired at the time for its good simple form. "But 'Cymric Silver', although original and initiatory of a new school of work, is suggestive of a more remote era than this (Tudor days) and simplicity is the keynote of its design."[26]

Liberty's launching of this style is the last important result of the neo-Celtic tendency, and is an expression of the formal fusion of the stylistic elements of Art Nouveau and the Celtic. The last fashionable design he produced in the style was the *Tudric Pewter*, in 1903, with an ornamentation of approximately the same character and derived from the same source of inspiration.

In France Grasset was the foremost representative of this style. When he composed illustrations to *Histoire des Quatre Fils Aymon*, that fabulous tale from the time of Charlemagne, popularised all over France through the medieval poem of Renaud de Montauban—it was only natural that he should give his illustrations a "local colour" in harmony with the story. This work is perhaps the most outstanding expression in France, during the last half of the 19th century, of a conscious effort to raise the level of book-illustration. Ornaments and drawings bear in their details the influence of the period of the great migrations (fig. 121).

As we have already seen, Grasset had several sources of inspiration. Japanese influence and floral features are subtly blended as well. Grasset is a good example of how the various impulses of the 1880's and 1890's fuse in such a way that it is not always possible to distinguish them, to form a new and independent form of expression.

During the Exhibition in 1889 considerable interest was also shown in Celtic design, and M. Germain Babst delivered several lectures on the work of the Celtic goldsmiths, describing the work in its modern form as "bijoux barbare."[27]

Anton der Kinderen's (1859–1929) illustrations for *Gysbrecht van Amstel*, 1893, assumes a similar position in Dutch book-art, as *Histoire des Quatre Fils Aymon* in French, both with regard to its historical subject, its general

26 A. L. Baldry, The Growth of an Influence, *The Art Journal,* February 1900, pp. 45–49; Arthur Stuart Liberty, *Easter Art in London,* stencil, London 1952, p. 5.

27 *Revue des Arts Decoratifs,* vol. X, 1889–90, p. 160.

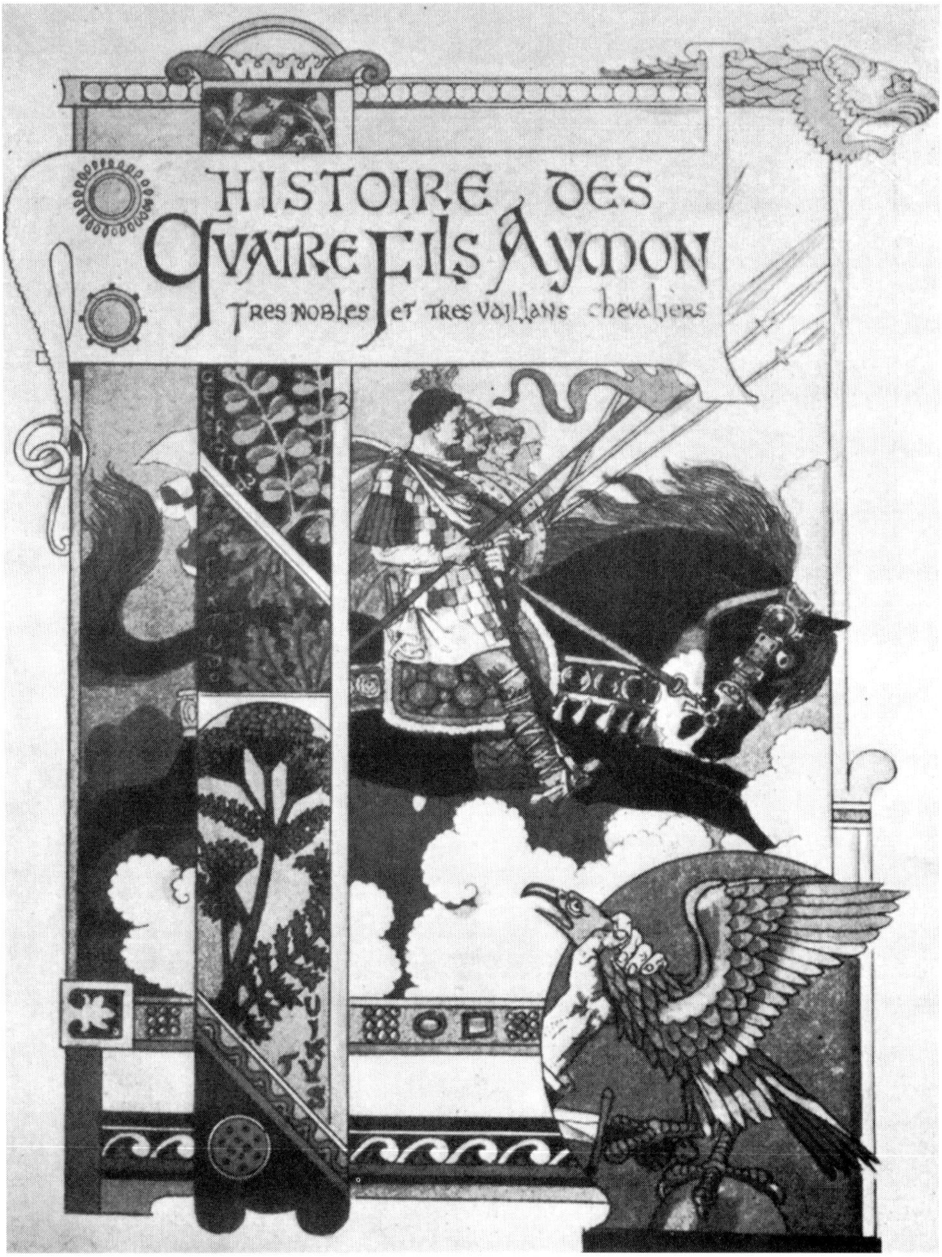

Fig. 121. Grasset: Cover for *Histoire des Quatre Fils Aymon*. 1879–83.

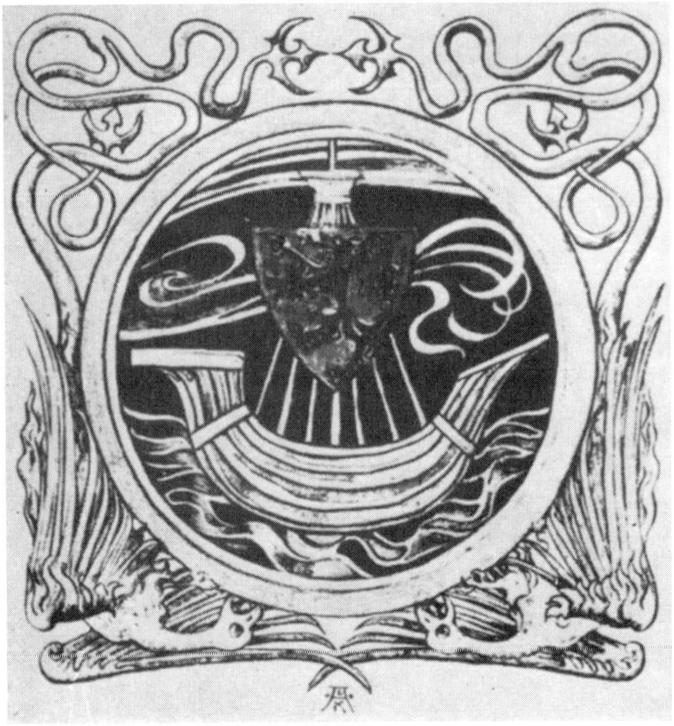

Fig. 122. Der Kinderen: Vignette for *Gysbrecht van Amstel*. 1893.

layout, and its illustrations. Whether the inspiration for the vignette (fig. 122) actually has anything to do with Celtic style, is difficult to decide, but in the outer frame we have the serpent-shaped *entrelac* motif in a rhythm which approximates to Art Nouveau. But a glance at the cloud and wind motifs inside the circle will reveal a much more marked Art Nouveau character. This has nothing to do with the Celtic style, but concerns rather the book illustrators and painters of the age, and their importance to the origins of Art Nouveau.

*

The influence of the Celtic revival on Art Nouveau should not be overestimated: geographically speaking it is a somewhat limited phenomenon, being confined to Scandinavia and Scotland and Ireland. The neo-Celtic style was also quite naturally more confined to special fields: the art of the silversmith and of the book-illustrator. Only in Norway and Sweden was it of any importance to furniture making, interior design or architecture.

But the linear rhythm in the decorative works of the Celtic Revival may have helped to prepare the ground for Art Nouveau, and it may be assumed that the use of the *entrelac* motive in Art Nouveau is explained by the influence of the Celtic revival. Characteristically enough it was in book design—between the pages of richly decorated books—that some of the earliest Art Nouveau features were to appear. Both directly, through form, and indirectly by the increasing interest in artistically decorated and illustrated books, the Celtic revival has thus contributed to the origin of Art Nouveau. When the two styles fuse into an ornamental symbiosis in the hands of gifted artists, a new and nordic aspect of Art Nouveau emerges.

Iron

Throughout the architectural and constructional development of the 19th century—from Napoleon's command that the temple for his *Grande Armée* should be built of stone and iron until the time when the Eiffel Tower was completed in 1889—there was a considerable increase in the use of iron construction. One of the principle questions discussed by architects and designers in the 1880's and 1890's was to what extent the iron should be visible. Everyone recognised the qualities and possibilities of iron, but should the construction stand naked and revealed, or should it be a skin of period style? Ruskin, one of the first to realise the possibilities of iron, maintained that iron construction is not architecture in the real sense of the word, and his well-known dictum runs: iron "may be used as a *cement*, but not as a *support*" [*sic*].[1] Viollet-le-Duc, on the other hand, is entirely in favour of a visible use of iron construction, as shown in his *Entretiens sur l'Architecture*, 1863–72, but as an ardent admirer of neo-Gothic he gave it a Gothic form. Just as stone and wood served the logical constructions of the Middle Ages, so iron was to serve that of the 19th century.[2] Fig. 123[3] shows how he plays with the Gothic shapes between the constructional elements. By replacing the Gothic foliage with leaves from his own imagination, he created a rhythm which is entirely in the spirit of Art Nouveau. Viollet-le-Duc's

[1] J. Ruskin, *The Seven Lamps of Architecture,* London 1849, Chapter II, § 10. Ruskin was interested in problems connected with iron, and touches on them several times in his writings. But as he grew older he changed his opinion. In the edition of 1880 of *The Seven Lamps of Architecture* he makes reservations on his statement made in 1849: The iron ". . . has changed our merry England into the Man in the Iron Mask." (II § 12). It seems that he had no real understanding of the possibilities of iron, and he demanded that it should be disguised—rather on symbolistic lines, as for instance in Blackfriars Bridge, London. He proposes ". . . vast winged statues of bronze folding their wings, and grasping the iron rails with their hands or monstrous eagles, or serpents holding with claw or coil. . . . Thousands of grotesque or lovely thoughts would have risen before him, and the bronze forms, animal or human would have signified either in symbol or in legend . . . the purpose of their work. . . ." "An inquiry into some of the conditions at present affecting the study of Architecture in our schools" (1865), *Papers and Transactions of the Royal Institute of British Architects,* Session 1864–65, pp. 139–56 (141).

[2] E. E. Viollet-le-Duc, "Sur la construction des bâtiments," *Entretiens sur l'Architecture,* I–II, Paris 1863–72, vol. II.

[3] *Ibid.,* vol. II, p. 130.

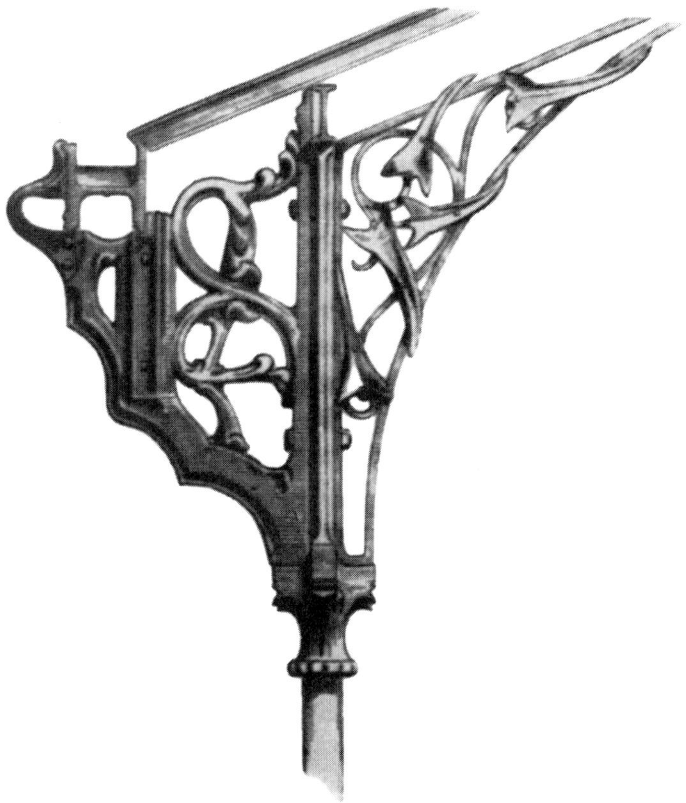

Fig. 123. Viollet-le-Duc: Illustration from *Entretiens sur l'Architecture*. 1872.

decoration—e.g. as shown in fig. 123—has nothing to do with the actual iron construction: it is "padding" in the form of imaginative iron leaves, a result of the desire of the 1870's to decorate, as well as being a striving for a new form of expression. Characteristically enough there is not a single sentence dealing with the decoration of it: Viollet-le-Duc is merely preoccupied with the construction.

The decoration between the supporting and supported elements of his illustration in the chapter *Sur la construction des bâtiments* (fig. 124)[4] has the same rhythm and makes the same combined effect, suggesting a realisation of Christopher Dresser's theories from the same period. Viollet-le-Duc has apparently tried to find a form with a pliant rhythm which represents the qualities of iron, and his interesting decorative innovation may

[4] Ibid., vol. II, p. 126.

be regarded as a structural symbol on a par with Dresser's. As he says himself:

" . . . il lui (the iron) faut trouver les formes qui conviennent à ses qualités et à sa fabrication; nous devons le montrer, et chercher ces formes convenables jusqu'à ce que nous les ayons trouvées . . . . Mieux vaut, pour des architectes, se livrer à cette recherche, dût-elle produire des premiers essais incomplets au point de vue de l'art, que de passer son temps à élever des façades en pastillages."[5]

The discussion about iron continued unabated well into the 1890's, and it was especially in Belgium, where hopes for a new architecture were strongly linked up with iron, that the problem was most debated. In 1893 L.A. wrote in *l'Emulation*, the vigilant organ of the Society of Belgian Architects: "Le fer est bien de notre siècle; pourquoi ne l'emploie-t-on pas d'une manière judicieuse dans toutes les constructions nouvelles? Avec le mélange d'autres matériaux, on arriverait à créer un *style* [*sic*]."[6] On the other hand Charles Garnier, writing in the same periodical, asserted that "le fer est un moyen, ce ne sera jamais un principe."[7] His countryman Eugène Grasset states on the same occasion: "On ne rêve que ferraille . . . cette architecture en fer est horrible, parce qu'on a la sotte prétention de vouloir tout montrer . . . l'Art est précisement né du besoin *d'habiller l'utile pur* [*sic*], qui est toujours repugnant et horrible. Voilà ce qu'ignorent nos modernes ferrailleurs."[8]

5 *Ibid.*, vol. II, p. 106. ". . . it should find the forms which suit its qualities and its fabrication. We should show it, and seek these suitable forms until we have found them. It would be better for architects to devote themselves to this search, even if it were to produce first attempts which are artistically incomplete, than to spend one's time setting up lozenge-pattern facades."

6 L.A., l'Architecture au XIXe siècle, *l'Emulation*, vol. XVIII, 1893, pp. 111–112; also in *l'Art Moderne*, vol. XIII, 1893, p. 106. "Iron certainly belongs to our century; why isn't it used in a judicious way in all the new constructions? With the mixture of other materials one would succeed in creating a style."

7 Charles Garnier, le Style Actuel, *l'Emulation*, vol. XVIII, 1893, pp. 161–167. "Iron is a medium, it will never be a principle."

8 E. Grasset, l'Architecture Moderne jugée par Eugène Grasset, *ibid.*, vol. XXI, 1896, pp. 58–59. "People dream of nothing but ironwork . . . this iron architecture is horrible, because people are filled with the stupid pretence of wanting to show everything. . . . Art has been born precisely from the need *to clothe the purely useful* [*sic*] which is always repugnant and horrible. That's something our modern wrought-iron workers don't know."

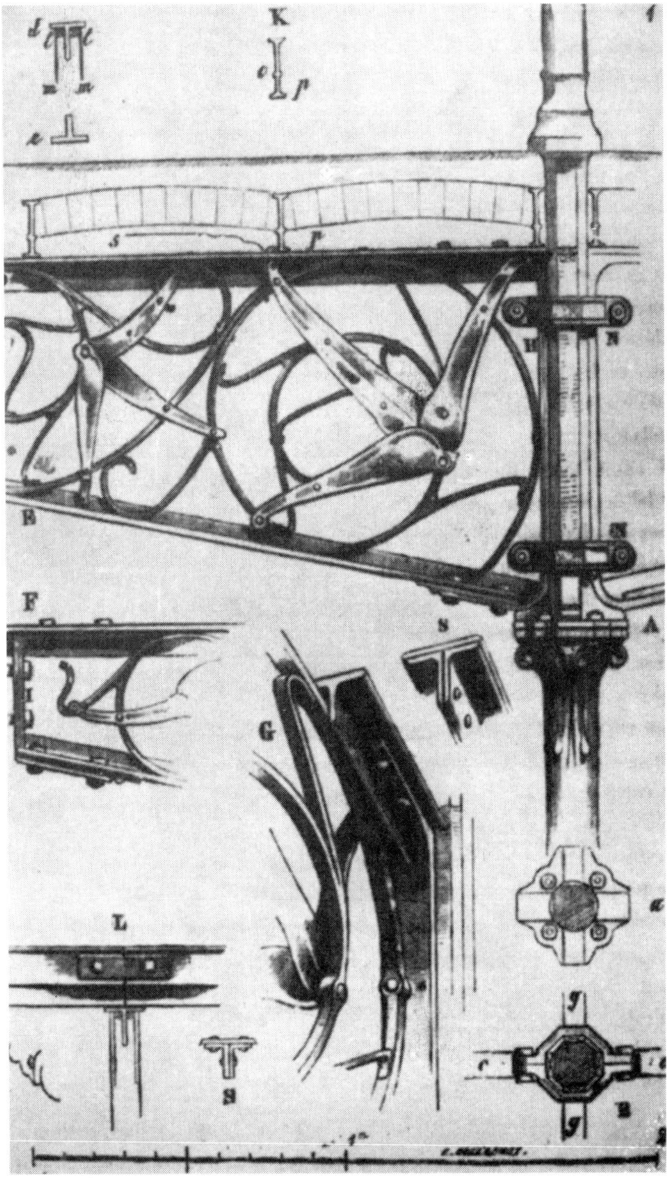

Fig. 124. Viollet-le-Duc: Illustration from *Entretiens sur l'Architecture*. 1872.

In Belgium the young radical architects demonstrated both the constructive and decorative qualities of iron. Iron and its construction were the incarnation of the belief in, and hope of, a new and liberating era in architecture; iron was experimented with more than any other material, and there was an intense search for new forms. It was therefore in this material that some of the earliest examples of Art Nouveau are to be found. Already in 1889 Paul Hankar (1861–1901) designed an iron grille for No. 83 Chaussée le Charleroi, Brussels (fig. 125),[9] where both the iron flowers and leaves possess a curvature and a flow of line which can only be described as Art Nouveau. It is in no way remarkable that the interest in plants and flowers should be translated into terms of iron—this has been done at all times. The first hesitant Art Nouveau forms in Belgium were evolved from plant forms in iron, and Hankar's isolated attempts were soon to be followed by Horta's some three years later.

The first house Horta built after several years of study, was No. 6 Rue Paul-Emile Janson, Brussels, 1892–93, formerly 12 Rue de Turin, and here, in the *chef d'oeuvre* of Continental Art Nouveau, we also find iron translated into the forms of Art Nouveau (fig. 126). Of this Sigfried Giedion says in his inspiring book, *Space, Time and Architecture*: "What are these lines but the unrolled curls and rosettes that are to be found under the eaves of so many Belgian railway stations? They have simply stripped off their Gothic or Renaissance clothing."[10]

But what about the interplay of stylized stems and stalks, painted on the wall (fig. 262)—do they also derive from the Belgian Railways?

Certainly not when we find iron, too, fashioned according to the designs of Art Nouveau, we must be careful not to assume that this is in fact the origin of the style. On the contrary we have seen that Horta had a predilection for forming all materials according to the same formal principles, quite independent of the qualities of the material.

The next important building in Brussels with the use of iron—and glass —where Art Nouveau was adapted, is Horta's *Maison du Peuple*, Place Emile van der Velde, 1896–99. The construction has nothing to do with

9 *l'Emulation,* vol. XVIII, 1893, pl. 35. Drawings dated 1889.

10 S. Giedion, *Space, Time and Architecture. The Growth of a new Tradition,* London 1946, pp. 224 sq.

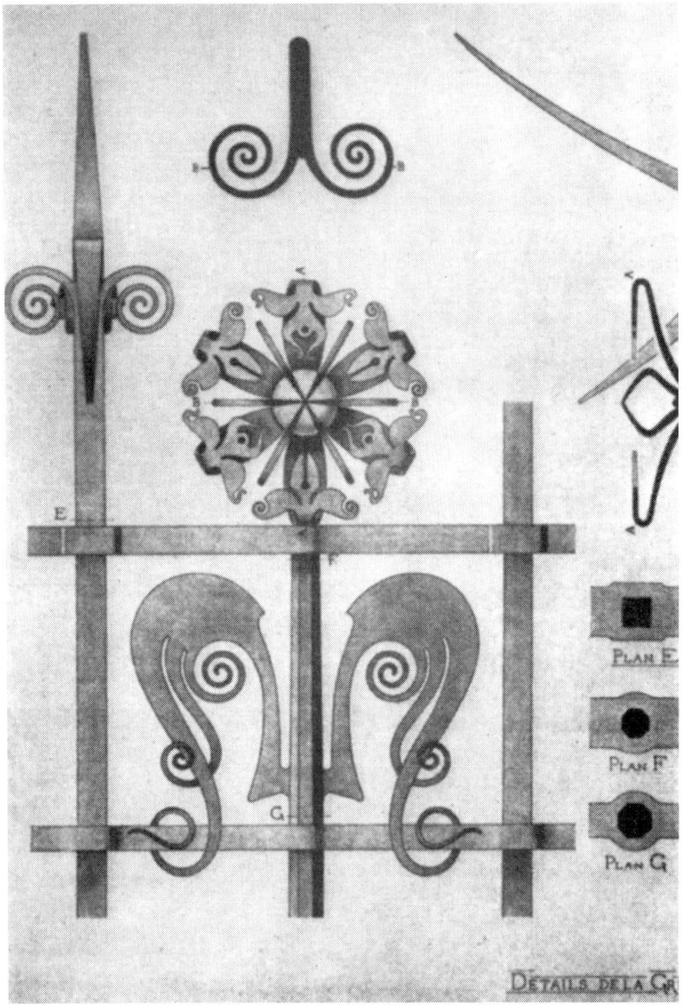

Fig. 125. Hankar: Grating for basement window. 83 Chaussée le Charleroi, Brussels. 1889.

Art Nouveau, the style is confined to ornamentation: elaborated grills and elegant entrances. A few Art Nouveau-like Gothic columns in less important stairways are typical; they pretend to be constructive, but are in fact purely decorative.[11] In the other houses where Horta used iron in the facades, it is always disguised with Gothic-like forms, as it also is in the Old England House, Rue Montagne de la Cour, by Paul Saintenoy, 1899–1902, where

11 The author is indebted to the architect J. J. Eggericx who directed his attention to them.

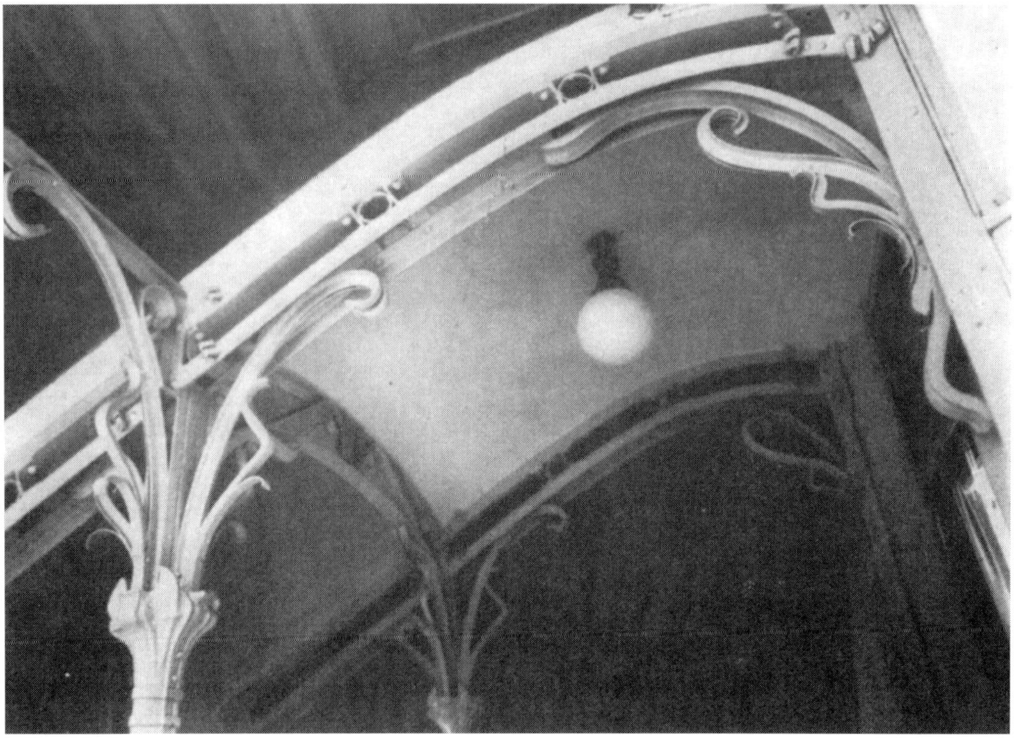

Fig. 126. Horta: Decorated iron construction in 6 Rue Paul Emile Janson, Brussels. 1892–93.

Gothic-like columns with small Art Nouveau details form the constructive elements in a facade of iron and glass.

*

As already mentioned, the striving for sound construction was an important part of the program of the advanced Gothic revivalists. When the exposed iron construction is used, the form-language often fuses with Gothic or Art Nouveau details. Viollet-le-Duc's place in the history of modern architecture can hardly be overestimated, and it seems as if his importance to Art Nouveau too is greater than might be expected. Both his designs in proto-Art Nouveau, his interest in structure as expression, and his direct influence on Horta are interesting. Of Horta we know that he was well acquainted with Viollet-le-Duc's writings, and the *Dictionnaire raisonnée d'Architecture* was his bible.[12] Horta's bold use of iron,[13] as well as his Gothic and undulating details, may well be inspired by the great French architect. But the iron constructions of Belgian architects, especially those of Horta, do not become Art Nouveau as a result of the construction, but because the architects wanted to apply the Art Nouveau style—which is conditioned by a number of factors—on iron as well as on other materials. It was generally thought that the use of iron would lead to a new architecture; and as the new style emerged, it was applied to iron, and fused with construction and ornament.

The influence of iron on Art Nouveau was on the one hand limited to its decorative possibilities as a source of inspiration. Beautiful flowers, stems and stalks—and even columns and stretchers— thus took form, from the early nineties, in iron and wrought iron. But one question is essential in the relation between Iron and Art Nouveau: the influence of structure. The interest in structure as an architectural expression in itself was connected with the development of iron construction, and the Art Nouveau theoreticians were as well preoccupied with the aesthetic value of structure. It would be difficult to trace or divide these sources any further, but it may be said with certainty that Art Nouveau developed the use of structure as expression to the most refined degree in iron as well as in other materials.[14]

It may be said to be less certain, but more fascinating, to suggest that the influence of iron construction on Art Nouveau was less important than the structural expression of Art Nouveau upon the development of modern architecture.

12 Information given to the author by J. J. Eggericx, April 1953.

13 See note 26, *The Gothic revival.*

14 Recent research supports this, cf. J. Grady, Nature and the Art Nouveau, *The Art Bulletin,* vol. XXXVII, 1955, pp. 187–192, (192).

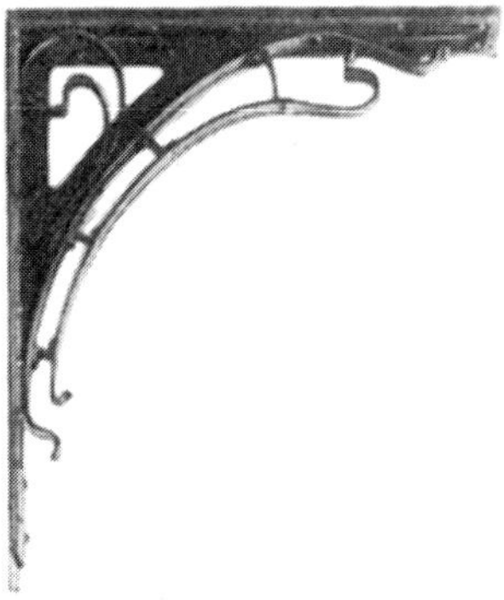

Fig. 127. Horta: Detail of iron construction and decoration. Maison du Peuple, Brussels. 1896–99.

*The Pre-Raphaelite Movement**

The bonds uniting painting, literature, and decorative art in various countries during the latter half of the 19th century are numerous and hard to disentangle. The pre-Raphaelite periodical *The Germ*, four numbers of which appeared in 1850, aimed to combine the Arts and Letters in one harmonious whole, and its subtitle is, characteristically enough, *Thoughts towards Nature in Poetry, Literature, and Art.* Morris formulated these aims in his own way: "If a chap can't compose an epic poem while he's weaving tapestry, he had better shut up, he'll never do any good at all,"[1] and Rossetti's famous remark has precisely the same tendency: "The man who has any poetry in him ought to be a painter; the next Keats ought to be a painter." All the pre-Raphaelites, Rossetti, Hunt, Burne Jones and Madox Brown, designed furniture and textiles, or contributed in some other way to design,[2] and Henry Cole's attempts to bring new impulses into applied art were also based on a more intimate collaboration between the artist and the artisan. The younger artists who belonged to the late pre-Raphaelite school, men such as Walter Crane, George Heywood Sumner (1853–1940), as well as designers such as Herbert P. Horne (1864–1916) and Selwyn Image (1849–1930), all contributed in their youth to the development of decorative art, and the architect Mackmurdo, who in his youth had worked for Whistler,[3] regarded himself nevertheless as the bearer of the pre-Raphaelite principles.[4] Mention should also be made of the painter Frank Brangwyn (1867–), who designed a number of textiles for Bing in Paris. One of the most significant ideas in the latter half of the 19th century was that of uniting all the arts. In France the *Union des Beaux Arts appliqués à l'Industrie*, has already been mentioned, and the energetic Marquis

* The author would like to thank Ronald Alley, Tate Gallery, London, for reading through this and the following chapter.

1 J. W. Mackail, *William Morris and his Circle,* Oxford 1907, p. 12.

2 The Green Room, 1867, Victoria and Albert Museum, London. See also Victoria and Albert Museum, *Catalogue of an Exhibition of Victorian and Edwardian Decorative Arts,* London 1952, pp. 38–52.

3 E. Carter, Arthur Mackmurdo, *Journal of the Royal Institute of British Architects,* vol. IL, April 1942, pp. 94 sq.

4 Notes in Miss Eleanor Pugh's collection.

Philip de Chennevière, with his talent for administration—he founded the Modern Applied Arts section in the Musée Luxembourg—even went so far that he made no distinction between pure and applied arts.[5]

A considerable number of the French Art Nouveau artists had originally been painters, e.g. de Feure, Grasset, Majorelle—the last-mentioned made his debut as a painter—while Charpentier and Jean Dampt were sculptors. On the other hand the painters were no less interested in the applied arts, e.g. Toulouse-Lautrec, Redon, Schwabe the illustrator, and not least Gauguin, who also did a certain amount of pottery[6] besides his wood carvings. Gauguin believed firmly in a new decorative art, and was the only one among thirty artists and designers who replied positively and affirmatively when Henri Nocq asked them in 1894 whether there really was a new style and whether they believed in it.[7] One of Gallé's most important artistic principles was also based on this equality between the arts; and with the exhibition of pottery side by side with painting and sculpture in 1891 at the Champs-de-Mars, this new idea may be said to have been officially established. Gradually this idea of equality spread among the artists, and in 1895 the painter Henri Rivière declared: "Une belle table est tout aussi intéressante qu'une statue ou un tableau."[8]

In Belgium, too, the idea was eagerly accepted: after *Les XX*, a group of artists, had been formed early in 1884—without any special programme, but as a radical spur to Belgian art in the 1880's and 1890's—concerts were soon included in the programme, and in 1891 Gauguin exhibited two large vases.[9] In 1892 Delaherche exhibited pottery, and van de Velde embroidery designs; in 1893 there were two rooms full of decorative art, including a tea-table by Finch, various minor objects by Charpentier, as well as embroidery by van de Velde.[10] By 1894 it was clear to

5 P. de Chennevière, *Souvenirs d'un Directeur des Beaux Arts,* vol. I–II, Paris 1885.

6 A. M. Berryer, Apropos d'un vase de Chaplet décoré par Gauguin, *Bulletin des Musées Royaux d'Art et d'Histoire,* No. 1–2, Jan–Apr., 1944, Brussels, pp. 13–27. Mug, shape of a head, signed "P. Go. 94," Dagfin Werenskiold, Oslo.

7 H. Nocq, *Tendances Nouvelles, Enquête sur l'évolution des industries d'art,* Paris 1896, pp. 67–69. First published in *Journal des Artistes,* Paris, Sept. 1894.

8 *Ibid.,* p. 60. "A beautiful table is just as interesting as a statue or a picture."

9 O. M. Maus, *Trente Années de lutte pour l'art: 1884–1914,* Brussels 1926, p. 115.

10 *Ibid.,* pp. 145 sqq.

one and all that applied art had come to stay in the exhibitions of *Les XX*, and Octave Maus complained that it took up too much of his time.[11] Van de Velde, like his friend Finch, the painter, had shown more and more interest in decorative art from 1892 on, and in 1894 he delivered a lecture on Camille Lemonnier's (1833–1891) thesis *l'Egalité de tous les arts, décoratifs et autres.*[12]

The interest was just as lively in Holland, where the painters joined eagerly in the new applied-art movement—Georges Lemmen, Johan Thorn Prikker and Lion Cachet; and Dijsselhof had already finished his famous interior in 1892.

It was in Austria and Germany that the relationship between pictorial artist and decorative art was most striking. Here the whole Secession Movement had emanated from the ranks of pictorial artists, and here Art Nouveau took shape "on paper," and also remained essentially in the two-dimensional plane. Otto Wagner's two pupils, Josef Hoffmann and Joseph Olbrich, were practically speaking the only architects who joined the movement, and both also worked as painters and illustrators in their youth. Because the principle of equality was being debated at the time, they nearly all worked as decorative designers in some way or other—Kolo Moser, Peter Behrens, Otto Eckmann, Karl Koepping, Hermann Obrist, Bernhard Pankok, Bruno Paul, and Richard Riemerschmid.

Among the mainsprings of Art Nouveau, painting is probably the most recent and the most tangible. Painting is not so much one of the sources of this style, but rather the most important concomitant factor in its development. The same tendencies which are to be found in painting are therefore traceable in the illustrations, vignettes, and ornaments of the painters—decorative art bears within it the qualities of painting, reflecting its problems and characteristics.

Painting is an important part of the cultural form of expression of the age, illustrating its development and reflecting the ideas. This applies especially to painting in the latter half of the 19th century, because it is so intimately associated with literary trends, and at times even becomes literary itself.

11 *Ibid.*, p. 134.
12 *Ibid.*, p. 179.

Thus in a remarkable way painting, literature, and design are woven together. It is therefore necessary to penetrate into the spirit of the age and see whether it is possible to find—more or less directly—traces which painting and literary tendencies may have given to the decorative art of the age. Wilde's interest in design is symptomatic; on his tour in America in 1882 he lectured on subjects such as *The English Renaissance*, *Art and the Handicraftsman*, and *Art Decoration*.[13]

In England the Aesthetic Movement was the radical school in all branches of art.[14] Algernon Swinburne—King of the Aesthetic Poets, as William Hamilton called him—was intimately associated with the pre-Raphaelites, and had dedicated his drama "*The Queen Mother*" to the poet and painter Rossetti, and "*Laus Veneris*" to Burne Jones, who in turn gave one of his pictures the self-same title.

With Swinburne's *Poems and Ballads*, 1866, the *l'art pour l'art* movement is introduced in England, and in 1877 and 1895 it received its official apologia at the trials of James Whistler and Oscar Wilde respectively, where, to a certain extent, the same arguments—and a great deal of wit—were employed.

Those who were fortunate enough to visit London's most fashionable theatre, the Savoy Theatre, any time between April 23, 1881, and November 22, 1882, would have enjoyed a delightful and catchy parody on the Aesthetic Movement. In William Gilbert's libretto *Patience* Bunthorne sums up the qualities necessary "if you're anxious for to shine in the high Aesthetic line":

Be eloquent in praise
Of the very dull old days
    Which have long since passed away,
And convince 'em if you can,
That the reign of Good Queen Anne
    Was Culture's palmiest day.

13 All lectures given during the winter and spring of 1882. The last bears the subtitle: *The Practical Application of the Principles of the Aesthetic Theory of Exterior and Interior House Decoration, With Observations Upon Dress and Personal Ornaments.* (Also called *Decorative Art in America* and *House Decoration.*)

14 W. Hamilton, *The Aesthetic Movement in England,* London 1882; W. Gaunt, *The Aesthetic Adventure,* London 1945.

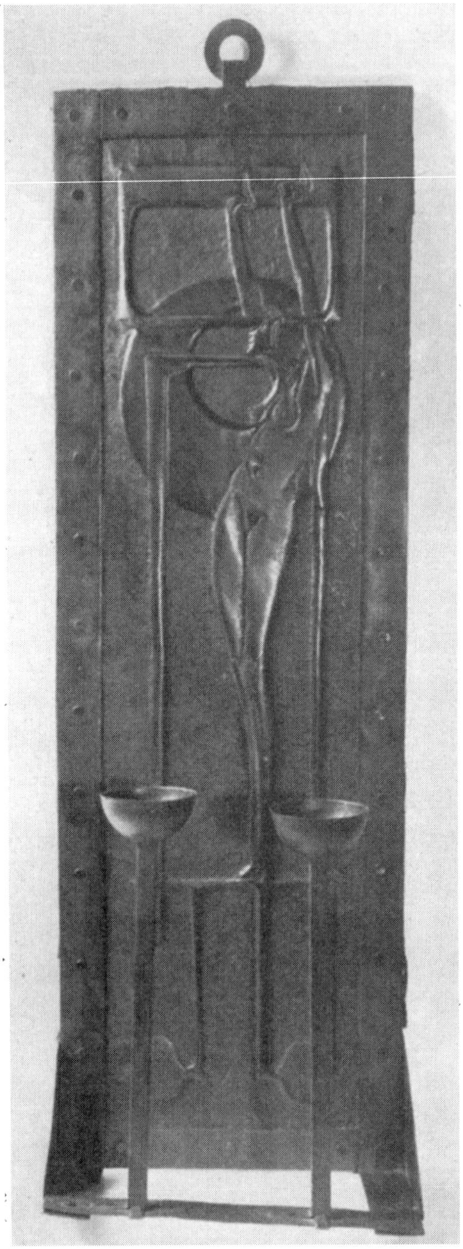

Fig. 128. Margaret and Frances Macdonald: One of a pair of Sconces. Beaten brass. About 1897.

Glasgow Museum and Art Gallery, Glasgow. Victoria and Albert Museum photo. Crown Copyright reserved.

Of course you will pooh-pooh,
Whatever's fresh and new,
And declare it's crude and mean,
For Art stopped short
In the cultivated court
Of the Empress Josephine.

Then a sentimental passion
Of a vegetable fashion
Must excite your languid spleen,
An attachment à la Plato
For a bashful young potato,
Or a not-too-French French bean;
Though the Philistines may jostle,
You will rank as an Apostle
In the High Aesthetic band,
If you walk down Piccadilly
With a poppy or a lily
In your medieval hand.

The symbols of the Aesthetic Movement, the lily, the peacock, and the sunflower were well known and popular, not least in decorative art, where they play an important part from the beginning of the 1870's and right up to the 20th century. Of the significance of these symbols William Hamilton says that one "may surely suppose Purity, Beauty, and Constancy: are they not adequately expressed to the mind's eye . . . , in the lily, the peacock, and the sunflower?"[15]

[15] W. Hamilton, *op. cit.*, p. 138.

Both in the Continental "spleen" and the British mood of "fin-de-siècle" —it was part of the etiquette that the phenomenon should be described in a foreign language—conceptions such as *décadence*, *beauté maudite*, *enfant perdu*, *le beau dans l'horrible*, and *nostalgie de la boue* were familiar and cherished terms. The men of the age were Wilde, Whistler, Verlaine, Beardsley, Baudelaire, Rimbaud and Swinburne—not to mention Nietzsche.

It was indeed a far cry from the bourgeois "Gay Nineties" and the artists' *tristesse*, such as we find it reflected in the countless weeping and suffering female figures.

The development of the female ideal can also be regarded as part of this *fin-de-siècle* mood. We are familiar with the pre-Raphaelite woman from Deverell's *Twelfth Night*, Millais' *Ophelia*, and Hunt's *Valentine and Sylvia*, and from nearly all Rossetti's pictures from 1852 to 1862. In all these pictures one and the same girl stood model, the girl from the hat shop in Leicester Square, Elizabeth Siddal. We find Jane Burden as the model for William Morris's *La Belle Iseult* and Rossetti's *Guinevere*. In 1859 Morris married Jane, and in the following year Rossetti contracted his tragic marriage with Elizabeth. Delicate and frequently subject to illness, she died in 1862, only 29 years old.

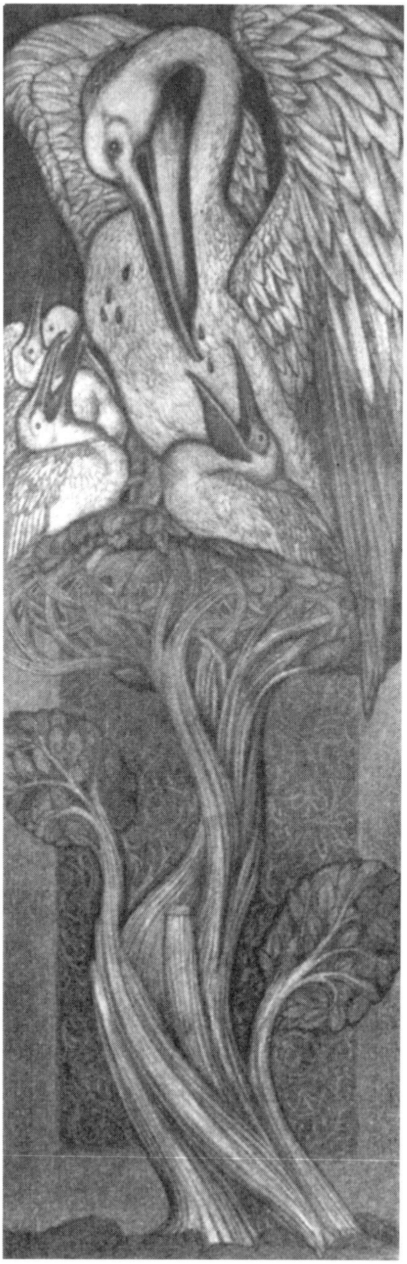

Fig. 129. Burne Jones: Pastel. Blue, violet. brown. 1881.

William Morris Gallery, Walthamstow. Crown Copyright reserved.

These were the two women who helped to inspire the pre-Raphaelite female face, with its greenish-blue eyes, full of melancholy, and half-closed by heavy lids, and the sensual, slightly protruding upper lip, with its peculiar curve. It is an expressive female face, framed in a profusion of copper-coloured locks; the head is tilted back slightly, and has an air of resigned suffering, while the curvature of the long swanlike neck is continued in the draperies of her garments.

This female type recurs in the 1890's: with Beardsley she becomes slightly morbid and diabolical in the illustrations to *Morte d'Arthur*, 1891, and *Salomé*, 1894. The artists of the Glasgow school develop her sophistication still further, at the same time increasing the expressive elements, and allowing the sadness of the *fin-de-siècle* mood free play in the linear streams of tears.

There is an uninterrupted sequence running from the pre-Raphaelites enthusiasm for Botticelli's lines via Walter Crane's linear aesthetics to Beardsley's elegant play with surfaces and curves and to the whiplash linear rhythm of the Glasgow artists.

The suffering, and often symbolically exploited woman in the art of the Glasgow school (fig. 128)[16] is no new creation, but a direct continuation of the late pre-Raphaelite development.

Burne Jones's pastel *The Pelican*, 1881[17] (fig. 129), shows several of the characteristic features, viz. his very marked predilection for the narrow upright format, combined with a vertical linearism. In addition there is often a serpentine and wavy use of line. All these features were to become important elements in the decorative art of the Glasgow school.

In Crane's books *The Sirens Three*, 1886, and *Echoes of Hellas*, 1887, not only is the line markedly proto-Art Nouveau, but the figures themselves are rhythmically placed in whiplash curves, not to mention their garments. Nevertheless, Walter Crane's mosaic cartoon, the graceful emblematic figure of *The Air*[18] (fig. 130) is a most characteristic design of the mid-1880's. The cartoon is nothing more nor less than a realisation of his theory on the

16 Margaret and Frances Macdonald, one of a pair of sconces. The Glasgow Museum and Art Gallery, Glasgow.

17 Cat. No. D.14, William Morris Gallery, Walthamstow, London.

18 Illustrated in Lewis Day, An Artist in Design, *The Magazine of Art*, vol. X, pp. 186–87, (p. 99).

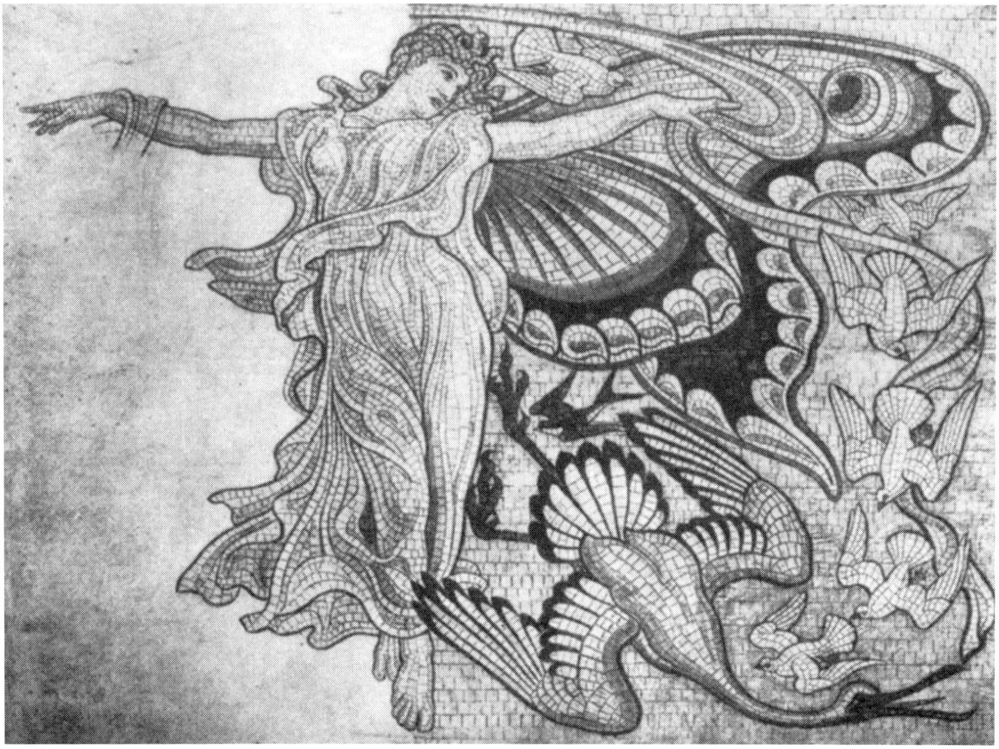

Fig. 130. Crane: Sketch for mosaic. 1886–87.

line of movement—presented in a clear linear *régie* with the usual predilection for ornithological elements so characteristic of English decorative artists in general and of Walter Crane in particular.

His wave-rhythm also lives on in his floral book illustrations, in *Flora's Feast*, 1888, and *Queen's Summer, The Tourney of the Lily and the Rose*, 1891. With these two books he created a prototype for "*le Chevalier de Fleur*"—a figure arising naturally from his medieval Romanticism and his sprightly floralism.

In the painting *Neptune's Horses*, water-colour 1892, in oil 1893, *The Waves*, 1894, and *The Rainbow and the Waves*, 1894, this wave rhythm is also expressed, as the titles themselves suggest.

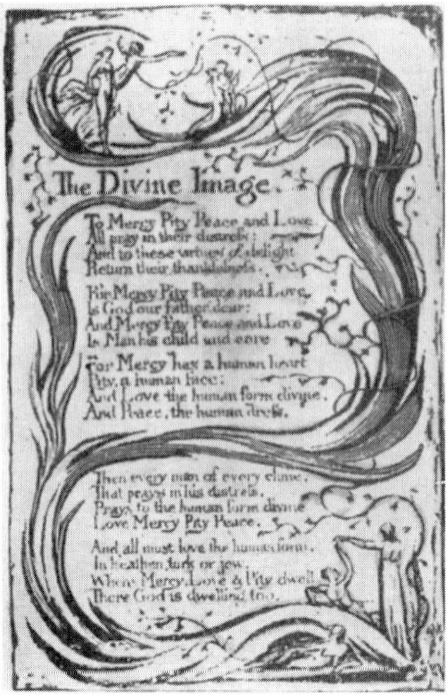

Fig. 131. Blake:
Illustration from the *Songs of Innocence*. 1789.
From Crane's *Ideals in art*. 1905.

An Art Nouveau-like rhythm of this kind has, of course, occurred previously in the history of art, but it has never been a form of expression common to a group of artists, at one and the same time—in other words what we mean by style. It has been a purely sporadic phenomenon.

In England a sporadic phenomenon of this kind, which stylistically is closer to Art Nouveau than any other, is to be found in the poet and draughtsman William Blake (1757–1827). It was hardly surprising that English artists were interested in Blake, for in his work they found several of their own problems expressed more than half a century before their own time. William Blake was now the centre of study: poet, painter, mystic, and symbolist all in one, he possessed precisely those qualities capable of inspiring the age. Selwyn Image acquired several collotype reproductions of his drawings,[19] and delivered two lectures on William Blake.[20] It is also symptomatic that Crane reproduced one of Blake's illustrations to the *Songs of Innocence and Experience* in his book *Ideals in Art* (fig. 131). In the circle of artists constituting *The Century Guild* the interest in Blake was considerable: he was continually discussed and illustrated in *The Hobby Horse*, and in No. 5, 1887, no less than three essays are devoted to Blake. Aubrey Beardsley

19 Blake's designs for *The Book of Job*, 1826, some of them very close to Art Nouveau in style, in S. Image's file, William Morris Gallery, Walthamstow, London. Reference should here also be made to the painter Johann Heinrich Füssli (1741–1825). He was a contemporary of Blake, born in Switzerland but lived in England. Especially in his drawings the same expressive and wave-like rhythm is to be found, for instance in "*Hex*" and "*Das verrückte Käthchen*" (ill. in A. Federmann, *Johann Heinrich Füssli. Dichter und Maler 1741–1825*, Zurich 1927, pl. 20–21). It is not possible to trace any direct influence on the pre-Raphaelites, although this might well be possible. I am here indebted to James Grady who mentioned Füssli to me in this connection.

20 *The Place of Blake in English Art*, *The Woodcuts of Bewick and Blake.*

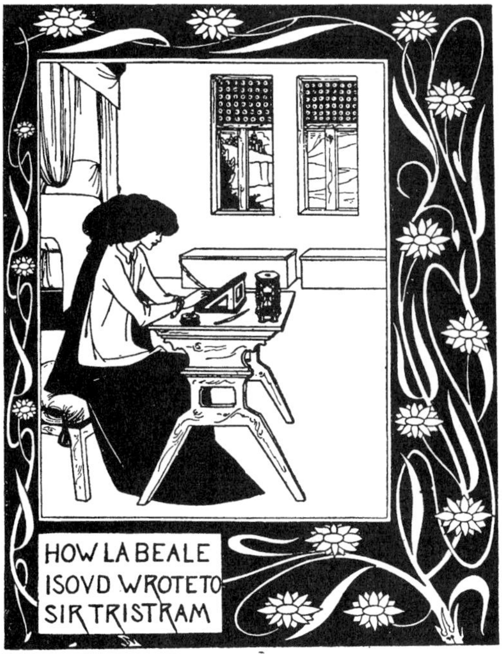

Fig. 132. Beardsley: Illustration from *Morte d'Arthur*. 1892.

was also influenced by Blake, and to the delight of one of his friends, the book-dealer Frederick H. Evans, one of his drawings was clearly inspired by Blake's *Piping down the Valleys Wild.*[21] Aubrey Beardsley[22] (1872–98) was England's most brilliant illustrator at this time. Apart from a few months at the Westminster Art School he could boast of no real art training, but the visits he paid to Burne Jones's studio and to Morris in the Kelmscott Press made a very considerable impression on this receptive young man. In fact some of his earliest drawings even aroused Morris's indignation, owing to their similarity with the designs of the Kelmscott Press.[23] Beardsley slipped elegantly and easily into the linear style of the age; with emphasis on the line he transformed the Japanese refinement to a personal style and became a true representative of the *New Voluptuousness* of the 1890's.

In 1892, in his early twenties, Beardsley started his illustrations of Thomas Malory's *Morte d'Arthur*, a medieval romance which was completed in 1469. These illustrations contain, however, none of the medieval spirit: Beardsley was, in fact, heard to boast that he had never taken the trouble to read the book.[24]

But there is plenty of the plant interest of proto-Art Nouveau in evidence, e.g. in the full-page illustration of Isolde[25] (fig. 132), which shows

21 T. Malory, *Le Morte d'Arthur*. Reproductions of eleven designs omitted from the first edition of *Morte d'Arthur,* London 1927; foreword by Aymer Vallance, p. 14.

22 *The Early Works of Aubrey Beardsley,* London 1899; *The Later Works of Aubrey Beardsley,* London 1900.

23 T. Malory, *op. cit.,* pp. 14 sq.

24 *Ibid.,* p. 14.

25 T. Malory, *Morte d'Arthur,* London 1893, vol. I, p. 384.

her sitting surrounded by sunflowers. In the chapter vignettes symbols of the Aesthetic Movement are continually cropping up, occasionally combined as in fig. 133,[26] where the lines of the peacock's throat are gracefully re-echoed in the dazzling head against a background of sunflowers. The touch of Art Nouveau in Beardsley's work also appears in other vignettes, and is at times so striking that one is reminded of Hector Guimard's underground stations in Paris (fig. 134).[27]

Even before the book had been published Whistler's good friend, Joseph Pennel, had written an article about him in the opening number of *The Studio*,[28] and with Beardsley's association with *The Yellow Book* periodical, 1894–95, and *The Savoy*, in 1896, his fame was assured. His style developed and consolidated, and with simple means—thin lines, dots, and black-and-white surfaces—he was able to dispense with any illusion of depth in creating a brilliant two-dimensional art.

With Beardsley's maturity of style, which is known to us from a great many of the works he produced between 1894–98, he had brought the style of the late pre-Raphaelite Movement to a triumphant artistic climax.

Only one other artist needs to be mentioned in this connection, the relatively unknown Robert Burns[29] (1869–1926), who was also a painter, and who as far back as 1891 had executed the typically proto-Art Nouveau design *Natura Naturans*[30] (fig. 135). The half-closed eyes, the long wavy hair, the convulsively expressive movement of the hand, familiar to us from the Macdonald Sisters' sconce (fig. 128), is intimately associated with late pre-Raphaelite art, as well as containing certain elements of Japanese style, clearly emphasised in the breakers. It is interesting to note that this drawing must have been carried out at the time he was studying at the *Académie de Lecluse* in Paris between 1890 and 1892.

This linearism, which was such an essential feature of contemporary painting and illustration, was the most immediate source of inspiration of

26 *Ibid.*, vol. I, p. 307.

27 *Ibid.*, vol. I, p. 59.

28 J. Pennel, A New Illustrator: Aubrey Beardsley, *The Studio*, vol. I, 1893, pp. 14–19.

29 J. L. Caw, *Scottish Paintings 1620–1908*, London 1908; *The Studio*, vol. XXXVII, 1906, pp. 25, 29, ill.; *The Art Journal*, vol. LXVI, 1904, pp. 90 sq., ill.

30 Published four years later in *Evergreen*, vol. I, 1895, p. 27.

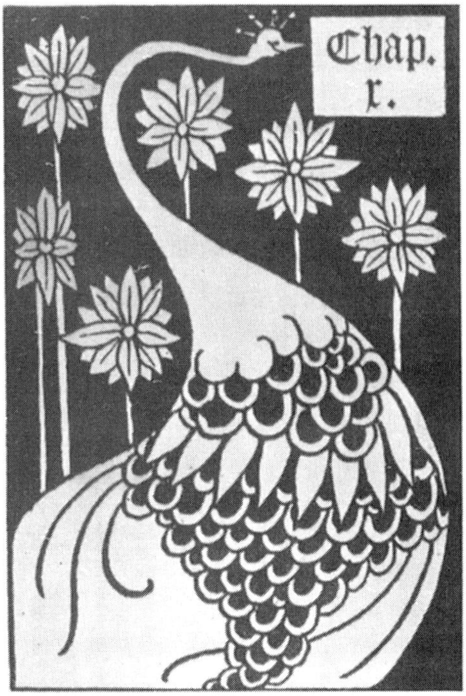

Fig. 133. Beardsley: Illustration from *Morte d'Arthur*. 1892.

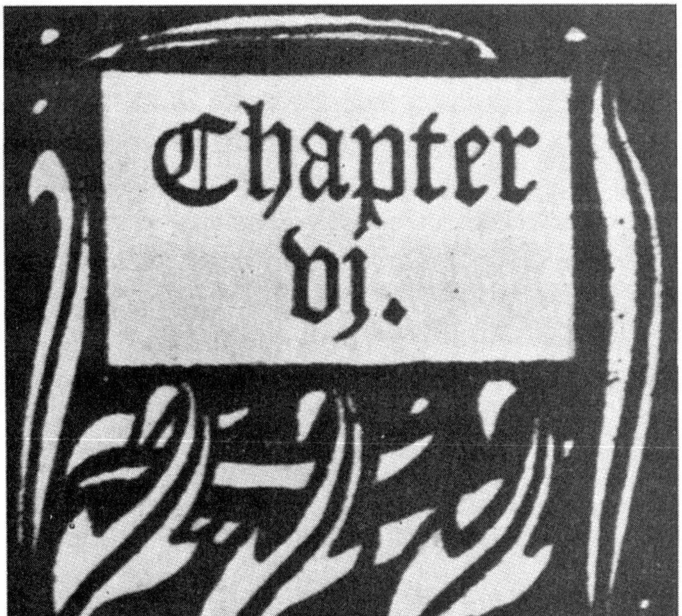

Fig. 134. Beardsley: Illustration from *Morte d'Arthur*. 1892.

the young Glasgow artists. Moreover, Japonism was in vogue, and floral art flourished, intimately associated with the Arts and Crafts Movement, whose principles provided the guiding light for the leader of the Glasgow school, Francis Newbery. It was in this part of Great Britain that the Celtic influence was strongest, and Beardsley's influence on the Glasgow group was already established by his contemporaries.[31] Charles R. Mackintosh's first decorative attempts were naturally rooted in these artistic principles with their emphasis on the two-dimensional, as can be seen in his cat frieze in his studio-bedroom in Denniston,[32] ca. 1890. In this room, on one wall of which hang Japanese prints, can also be found a cabinet designed by himself, with the pronounced and squared terminations we have already seen in the work of Mackmurdo. The cabinet and the fireplace are painted white, and under the ceiling run a row of cats with long thin wavy tails—and between them is a tall thin female figure. Characteristically enough it is only in the pattern design that we find these advanced stylistic features in Mackintosh's work, for in his architectural designs, as has been seen, he oscillates between neo-Gothic and neo-Baroque.

Thomas Howarth, who has written the standard work on Charles Mackintosh, *Charles Rennie Mackintosh and the Modern Movement*, relates how young Mackintosh would choose, for example, ". . . a sonnet for a few lines of poesy—almost invariably of melancholy timbre—and form abstract linear patterns round it, usually finishing the design in wash: purples, yellows and greens predominating." His friend MacNair would for instance take "illustrations of objects which interested him—chairs for example—place tracing paper over them, and try to improve on the original design, or better still, to evolve entirely new forms of his own invention."[33]

At the same time he also worked with symbolistic forms, as in the *Conversazione Programme*, 1894, which depicts "birds bringing harmony to the trees."

His friend Herbert MacNair (1870–)[34] was just as concerned with

31 The Arts and Crafts Exhibition Society, *The Studio*, vol. IX, 1896–97, p. 202.

32 T. Howarth, *Charles Rennie Mackintosh and the Modern Movement*, London 1952, pp. 20 sqq., pl. 5a.

33 The last two quotations, *ibid.*, pp. 17 sqq.

34 Gleeson White, Some Glasgow Designers and their Work, *The Studio*, vol. XI, 1897, pp. 86–100, 227–236, vol. XII, 1898, pp. 147–151, vol. XII, 1898, pp. 12–15; T. Howarth, *op. cit.*, p. 6.

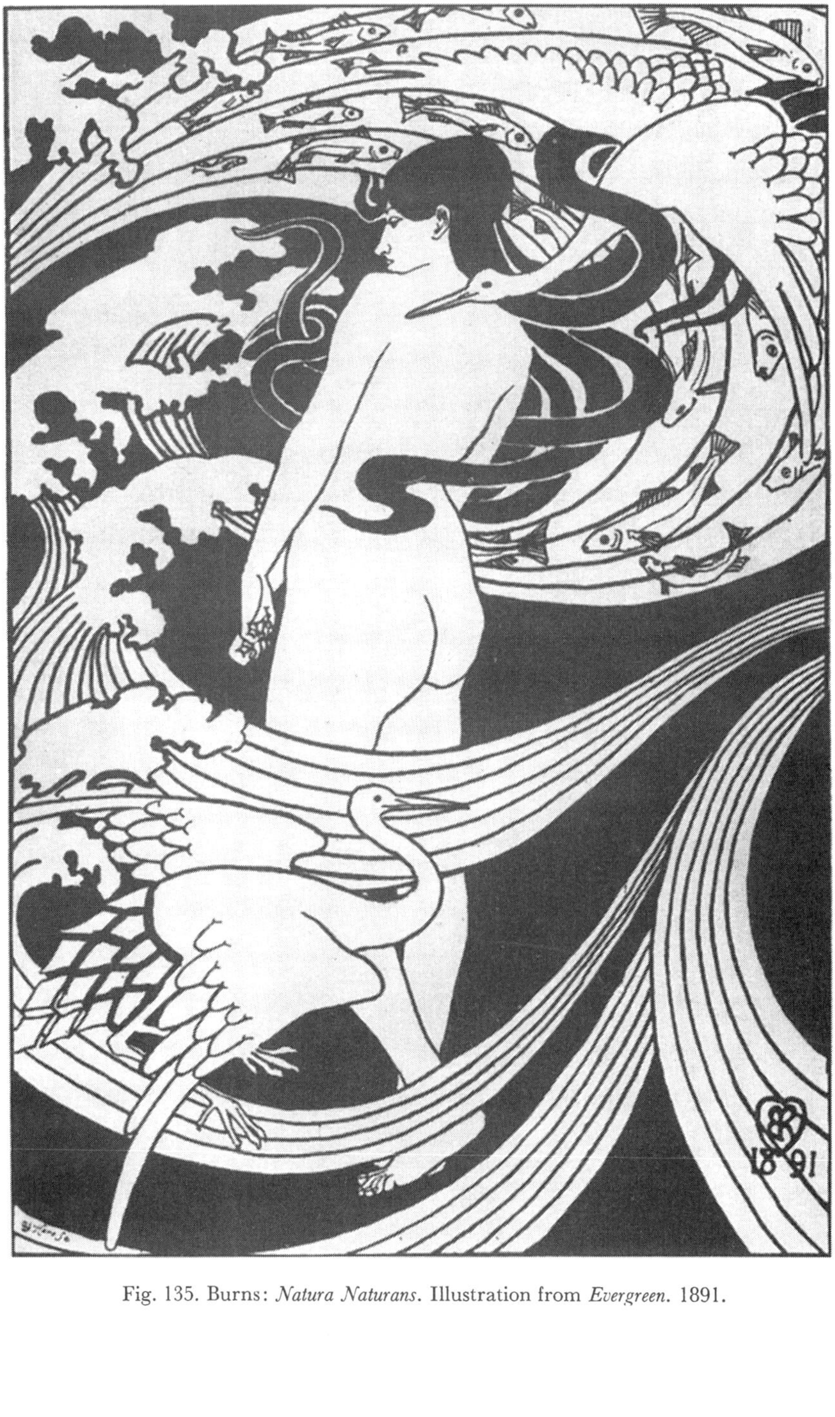

Fig. 135. Burns: *Natura Naturans*. Illustration from *Evergreen*. 1891.

symbolical trends; not a single drawing was made without its purpose, and as often as not the motif had an allegorical meaning. His book illustration in Thomas Howarth's collection[35], interspersed as it is with poems, allegorical symbols, with its sad women and the closed shapes, shows how the literary tendencies in the 1890's find expression in his whiplash linear rhythm, where one plane is enclosed within another—a sort of synthetic symbolism. This is a natural continuation of the English tendencies, corresponding to Continental Symbolism.

*

The importance of the late pre-Raphaelite school can hardly be overestimated as far as the development of proto-Art Nouveau in Great Britain and Art Nouveau in Scotland are concerned. The late pre-Raphaelite linear interest, the preoccupation with floral rhythm, and with tall and narrow com positions, and not least the marked symbolistic tendencies, give the clues to several of the features noted in the development in Great Britain. Even the special interpretation of Woman derives from the pre-Raphaelite school and may partly be explained by the milieu of the Aesthetic Movement.

35 T. Howarth, *op. cit.*, p. 19, ill.

Symbolism - Synthetism

Apart from the attitude to Nature, the interest in symbols was the other important and sustaining idea among the pre-Raphaelites. While Naturalism was gradually transformed into the cult of linearism, symbolism became a deeper and more important part of the spiritual heritage of the movement. The mystic George F. Watts (1817–1904) was the most typical symbolist in English painting in the last quarter of the 19th century, as may be seen in a great many of his literary pictures from 1885–1900.

The symbolism in English painting and in the Glasgow school was part of a contemporary European Symbolism, and though the English movement is somewhat older, thanks to the heritage of the pre-Raphaelites, the trends round about the middle of the 1880's may be regarded as a common West-European cultural expression.

Symbolism in painting is a reaction against Naturalism and Impressionism, just as in literature it represents a reaction against *Parnassus*. It is the triumph of subjectivism over objectivism; it is a return of the significant motif. "Pour toutes les idées claires," as Puvis de Chavannes said, "il existe une pensée plastique qui les traduit . . . . La pensée . . . je la roule, je la roule jusqu'à ce qu'elle soit élucidée à mes yeux et qu'elle apparaisse avec toute la netteté possible. Alors je cherche un spectacle qui la traduise avec exactitude. C'est là du symbolisme, si vous voulez. . . ."[1]

Continental Symbolism is generally said to date from 1885, with Puvis de Chavannes and Gustav Moreau as its forerunners, and with Odilon Redon and Eugène Carrière as its main figures on the one hand, and Paul Gauguin and Vincent van Gogh with their more radical form of expression on the other.

In 1901 the art historian Richard Muther devoted a chapter to the trend which Puvis de Chavannes represents in French Symbolism, and

1 M. Denis, *Théories 1890–1910. Du symbolisme et de Gauguin vers un nouvel ordre classique,* Paris 1920, p. 51. "For all clear ideas there exists a plastic thought which translates them. This thought . . . I work with it (literally: knead) until it is elucidated in my eyes and appears in all possible clarity. Then I try to find a spectacle which exactly translates it. That's symbolism, if you like. . . . ."

called it *Der Sieg der Linie*[2]. He makes no mention of Gauguin, however, nor of the Synthesism nor Cloisonnism of the Pont-Aven school, where *inter alia* the cult of the line was to have a far greater significance both for European painting and decorative art.

Even the painters who developed Synthesism and Cloisonnism could not agree as to who originally created these trends, whether it was Gauguin, Anquetin, Denis, Bernard, or Sérusier.[3] As far as we are concerned it is of little importance whether it was Gauguin or Anquetin who was the first, or whether Gauguin's Martinique series from 1887 should be defined as Synthetism.[4] It is sufficient to establish that Synthetism exists as a conscious trend in the Pont-Aven group in 1888 with Gauguin as its dominant personality.

Gauguin's intention with Synthetism was to achieve a presentation which was purged of details and all non-essentials, and would therefore have a stronger and more expressive effect. The essential was the unity, the synthesis of the motif. This cult of synthesis *per se* is Synthesism. He travelled along the road to Synthesism via line and simplification of plane. The motif was promoted to the foremost plane, in this respect differing markedly from Cézanne's three-dimensional conception of space. Next he abandons light-and-shade effect—and in this respect he differs from the neo-Impressionists—and operates with homogeneous planes. In the draughtsmanship he simplified the general shape, suppressing details and using a powerful limiting outline, so that the surfaces were enclosed as in *cloisonné* enamel. This is what Gauguin called Cloisonnism—essentially it is a pictorial means to achieve synthesis. Paul Sérusier defined it as follows: "Ce qu'on a appelé le cloisonnisme, c'est cette manie d'user de gros cernés bleus foncé pour affirmer la forme."[5]

Gauguin's symbolism, interpreted through his expressive Synthesism, came to light in a number of canvases from 1889, *Jacob lutte avec l'Ange*, *Le*

2 R. Muther, *Ein Jahrhundert französischer Malerei*, Berlin 1901, pp. 287–309.

3 *Mercure de France*, December 1903, January 1904.

4 C. Chassé, De quand date le synthétisme de Gauguin? *L'amour de l'Art*, Paris, vol. XIX, 1938, pp. 127–134.

5 *Idem*, *Gauguin et le groupe de Pont-Aven*, Paris 1921, p. 72. "What has been called Cloisonnism is this craze for using large dark-blue outlines to emphasise the form." According to Emile Bernard, he and Anquetin created Cloisonnism about 1886 under the joint influence of Japanese prints and Cézanne.

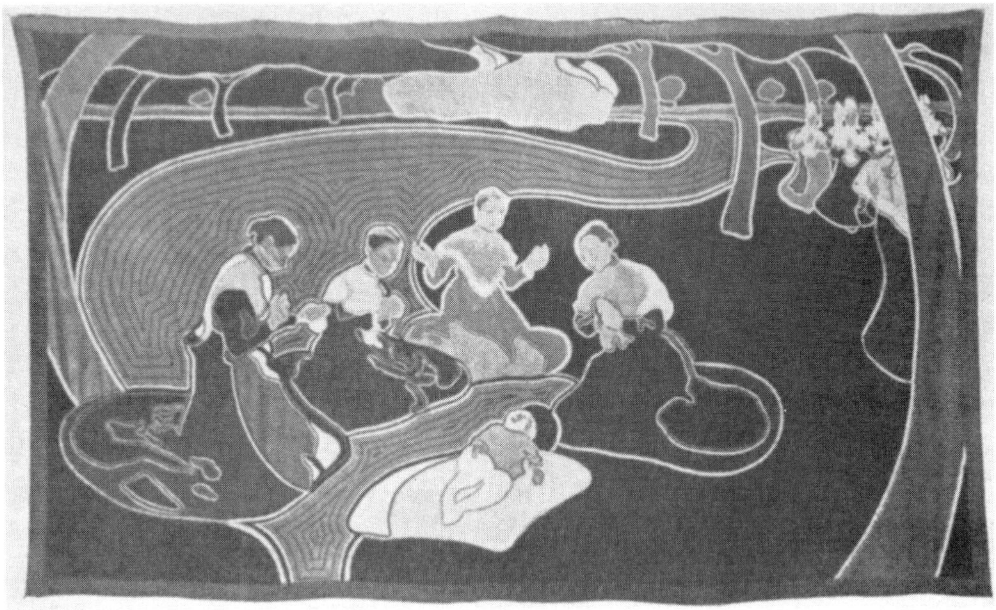

Fig. 136. Van de Velde: Embroidery. 1892.

Christ Jaune, and *La Belle Angèle*, and with his interest in decorative art; we also find designs for a plate from this year,[6] with the characteristic sweep of line and the gentle curves of the swan's neck. Chaplet's vase, which he decorated in the same way, with clear planes, pure surfaces, and firm lines, also belongs to the same year.[7]

The Pont-Aven group soon fused with painters such as Pierre Bonnard, Henri-Gabriel Ibels, Paul Ranson and Edouard Vuillard, and in 1892 *Les Nabis* was founded; here the form-language of Cloisonnism and Synthetism partly lived on.[8]

Neo-Impressionism, too, in its own special way was to contribute to the development. From the beginning of the 1880's it appeared as a continuation of the ideas of Impressionism—Divisionism and Pointillism give some indication of the programme of the trend—but it also represents

6 Lithograph, ill. in A. M. Berryer, Apropos d'un vase de chaplet décoré par Gauguin, *Bulletin des Museés Royaux d'Art et d'Histoire,* No. 1–2, Jan.–Apr. 1944, Brussels, p. 22; C. Chassé, *op. cit.,* vignette at the end of the book.

7 A. M. Berryer, *loc. cit.,* p. 14, ill.

8 A. Humbert, *Les Nabis et leur époque. 1888–1900,* Paris 1955.

a reaction against the disintegration of form of Impressionism, and with Seurat and his compositions in the latter half of the 1880's, *La Grande Jatte*, 1884–86, *Le Crotoy*, 1889, and *Le Cirque*, 1890, among the more important ones, the line once more came into its own, and was restored with all its elegance.

It was these painters whom the radical *Les XX* group invited. Gauguin exhibited there in 1889 and 1890, van Gogh in 1890 and 1891, and in 1892 there was a large memorial exhibition to Seurat with as many as eighteen canvases, apart from drawings, among which were such *chefs-d'oeuvre* as *La Parade* and *Le Cirque*. In the same year the English also exhibited embroidery, designs for stained glass and book-covers,[9] and new life seemed in fact to have been blown into the Brussels exhibitions at that time. This was the milieu that Henry van de Velde longed to enter, and where he hoped to be able to assert himself: "J'ai tant désir de faire bataille avec vous, puisque c'est le seul Encouragement et Honneur que je puisse attendre," he wrote to Octav Maus in 1886–87.[10] At this time van de Velde was a painter, influenced by Seurat. His embroidery from 1893 (fig. 136) was said to have been "exécuté selon la technique néo-impressioniste . . . que van de Velde, peintre encore, continuait d'appliquer à ses tableaux de chevalet."[11] The technique of embroidery has all the qualities of Cloisonnism, so that it can easily be adapted to *appliqué* technique. We recognise the expressiv line from Gauguin and Seurat and to a certain extent von Gogh's painting—it is an embroidery whose precursors are in every respect to be found among the French school of painting.

At about the same time as van de Velde, or possibly a little earlier, Victor Horta had already transformed the same impulses into decorative art. But the entrance door to 6 Rue Paul-Emile Janson, Brussels, 1892–93 (fig. 137), is something more than a translation of ideas from French painting: it is a completely new creation of ornamental art, the first time the

9 O. M. Maus, *Trente Années de lutte pour l'art: 1884–1914*, Brussels 1926, p. 134.

10 *Ibid.*, p. 84. "I have such a great desire to take up the cudgels with you, since this is the only encouragement and honour I can expect."

11 *Ibid.*, p. 147. Also reviewed in: Les Arts Décoratifs au Salon des XX, *l'Art Moderne*, vol. XIII, 1893, pp. 65–66. "Executed according to the neo-impressionist technique . . . that van de Velde, still a painter, continued to use in his easel-paintings."

Fig. 137. Horta: Stained glass window for main entrance. 6 Rue Paul-Emile Janson, Brussels. 1892–93. A. C. L. Brussels copyright.

fully matured new style was used in the field of architecture and ornamental art. Here Horta has devoted himself entirely to the cult of the line for its own sake, and here—in the decoration of the vestibule[12] (fig. 262), the iron construction (fig. 126) and the glass window (fig. 137)—he fully exploited the decorative forms of Art Nouveau. It is interesting to observe that recent research has confirmed the generally held view that this building (fig. 167) by Horta represents the first fully developed essay in the new style.[13]

The lines rise like stalks from a bulbous root, abstracted from the natural form, in places almost rococo, bound to the two-dimensional plane, with the surfaces well defined, and with clear lines as in Cloisonnism. This work had many precursors, the interest in plants[14] and French Synthesism[15] being probably the most important.

Horta was the first on the Continent to translate these impulses into terms of applied art, and this is his most important contribution in the decorative field. But if his contribution is to be seen in the right light, it should be viewed against the background of contemporary illustration, where a corresponding interest in line had gone furthest.

On the cover of the symbolical poet Max Elskamp's *Dominical*, 1892 (fig. 138), the subtitle is *Propitiatoirement orné par Henry van de Velde*. The woodcut has just been carried out with the expressive line of the synthetic school—transformed by a designer.

Georges Lemmen[16] (1865—1916), who at an early date was interested

12 6 Rue Paul-Emile Janson (formerly 12 Rue de Turin) is now occupied by an *Atelier de Haute Couture*, and the decorations have been painted over, though they may still be seen in a favourable light.

13 The style and its relation to architecture and painting are first dealt with by Nikolaus Pevsner in *Pioneers of Modern Design*, New York, 1949. The subject is also dealt with in St. Tschudi Madsen, Horta. Works and Style of Victor Horta before 1900, *The Architectural Review*, London, vol. CXVIII, 1955, pp. 388–92.

14 There are no works by Horta from the years 1888–1891 and we do not know much about his activities during that period, but we know that he took a great interest in the study of plants and flowers. (Information kindly supplied to the author by Madame Horta, May 1953.) For bibliography on Horta see Horta, Belgium, part III.

15 Horta received his first training as a painter, staying for several years in Paris—from 1878—and later at the Academy in Brussels, so we may suppose that the gifted young artist knew of *Les XX* and their exhibitions.

16 Georges Lemmen lived isolated and lonely, he never visited England, a trip to Marseille in 1891 together with the painter Camille Gaspard and the poet Gregoir Le Roy being his only visit to a foreign country. He was a painter, and never designed furniture or ceramics, but some jewellery, metal-fittings, bookbindings and tapestries—Toulouse Lautrec bought one of them—. In the years 1894–97

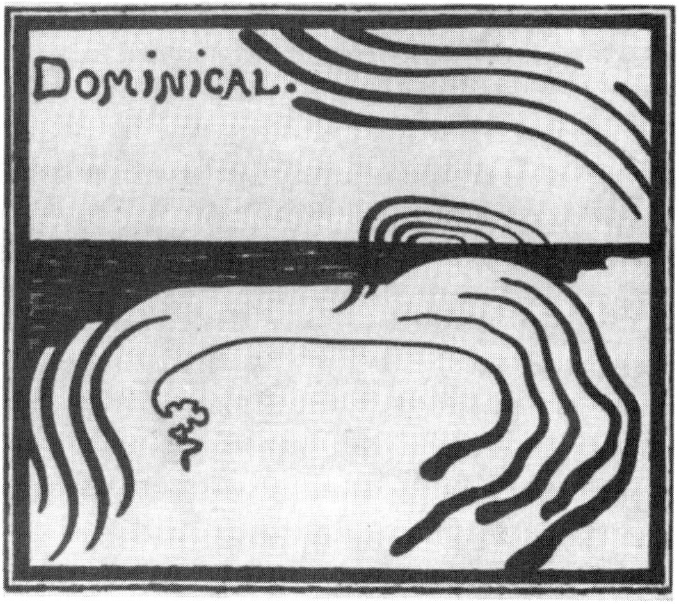

Fig. 138. Van de Velde: Illustration from Max Elskamp, *Dominical*. 1892.

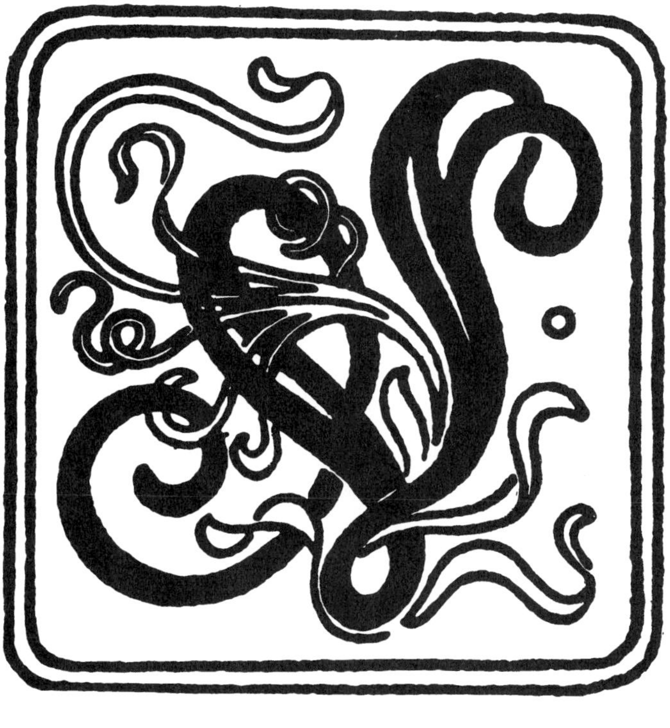

Fig. 139. Lemmen: Initial, *Van Nu en Straks*. 1893.

in Walter Crane,[17] designed in 1893 an initial to *Van Nu en Straks* (fig. 139),[18] which shows all the intricate loops and linear plant-style of the period, strongly reminiscent of Horta's decorations on the staircase of No. 6 Rue Paul-Emile Janson.

Van de Velde continued to work as a book illustrator, gradually developing his style, though he never succeeded in acquiring the light graceful touch to be found in the work of Lemmen: it remained heavy, and gradually approached the completely abstract (fig. 140).[19]

In Holland we find precisely the same tendencies, but the connection with French painting and Symbolism there is not so strong as in Belgium. The Dutch symbolical painting goes back to 1890 with Jan Toorop (1858-1928)[20]; like the leading symbolist in Belgium, Fernand Khnopff, a man of the same age, he married an Irish woman, and their mothers were also of British extraction, but the direct pre-Raphaelite influence is not so noticeable in the work of Toorop, where other and more exotic elements were at work. Toorop spent the first eleven years of his life in Java, and came to Holland in 1869. In 1884 he made his way to England, together with Verhaeren, married in 1886 in Brussels and from 1885 to 1889 spent his time partly in London and partly in Brussels. After passing through a neo-Impressionist phase in 1886–87 he became a symbolist thanks to his friendship with Maeterlinck.

By 1891 he was a fully-developed symbolist, with works like *The Garden of Pain* and *Les Rôdeurs*, in both of which his tender, fair type of woman is

he was associated with van de Velde. Exhibited 1889–92 at *Salon des Indépendants*, Paris, but did not wish to join any group or school, exhibited together with Camille Gaspard, Emile Claus, Georges Morren, Georges Beuysse in *la Vie et Lumière*, Brussels, 1900–10. No traces of Art Nouveau are to be found in any of his 110 works at *Cabinet d'Estampe*, Musées Royaux, Brussels: the only tendencies in that line are in *Deux Têtes de jeunes filles*, 1895, No. II, 89815, Cabinet d'Estampe, M. R. Information given by Camille Gaspard to the author April 1953. See also O. G. Destrée, Georges Lemmen, Die Schmuckkünstler Belgiens, *Dekorative Kunst*, vol. I, 1897–98, pp. 105–11; *ibid.*, vol. IV, 1899, pp. 217–55. Moderne Teppiche von G. Lemmen, *Dekorative Kunst*, vol. I, 1897–98, pp. 97–105.

17 He wrote two articles on Crane in *l'Art Moderne*, March 1st and 15th, 1891.

18 *Van Nu en Straks*, vol. I, No. 6–7, 1893, p. 35.

19 H. van de Velde, *Déblaiement d'Art*, Brussels 1894, p. 33.

20 A. Plasschaert, *Jan Toorop*, Amsterdam 1925; J. B. Knipping, *Jan Toorop*, Amsterdam 1939; Kees von Hoek, *Jan Toorop Herdenking*, Amsterdam 1930; complete biography in H. van Hall's *Repertorium voor de Geschiedenis der nederlandsche Schilder- en Graverkunst*, The Hague, 1936–49, vol. I, No. 8434–8464, vol. II. No. 16782–16931.

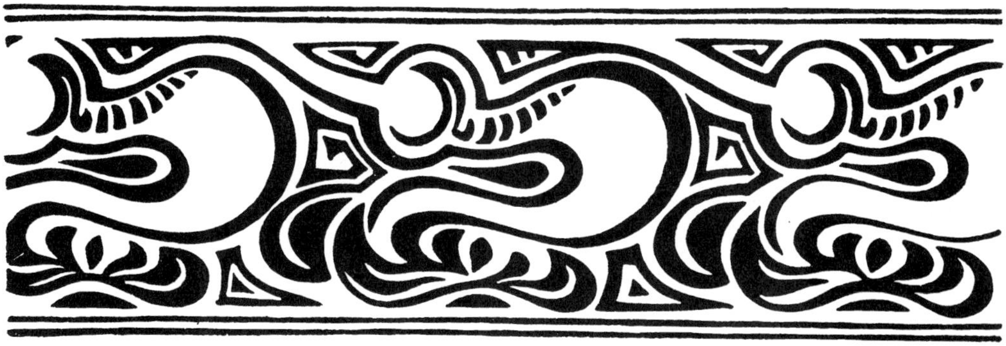

Fig. 140. Van de Velde: Frieze from *Déblaiement d'Art.* 1894.

to be found, surrounded by symbols of death and squalor. In 1892 he carried out a series of symbolical drawings, *Oh, Grave where is thy Victory*, *Apocalypse*, and *Symbolic Drawing*[21] (figs. 141, 142, 143) where the symbolical contents are garbed in linear whiplash rhythm. The following year a drawing of his appeared which characteristically enough was called *Linjenspel.* Lines and surfaces, garments and hair all flow in the same rhythm; especially in *Symbolic Drawing* we can talk of an Art Nouveau rhythm where the long slack curves terminate in abrupt retroflex movements. In 1895 he designed the poster for *Delftsche Slaolie*[22] (fig. 144), where his linear style is fully developed and the similarity with the Glasgow school is obvious, from details such as the expressive movement of the hands to the shape of the face and the hair, and the linear emphasis.

The much-discussed question arises: which way did the impulses run, from the Continent to England, or in the opposite direction? Jessie R. Newbery (1864–), the wife of the leader of the Glasgow school, and herself interested in embroidery, says that "the Four" were acquainted with artists such as Beardsley, Schwabe, and Toorop through *The Studio.* These artists gave an impetus and direction to the work of "the Four",[23] she says, speaking however in 1933, when the passage of years may have

21 W. J. R. Dreesmann, Amsterdam, A. Plasschaert, *op. cit.*, pl. 12, 16.

22 Stedelijk Museum, Amsterdam; collection of posters.

23 *Memorial Exhibition, Charles Rennie Mackintosh,* McLellan Galleries, Glasgow 1933, foreword by Jessie R. Newbery.

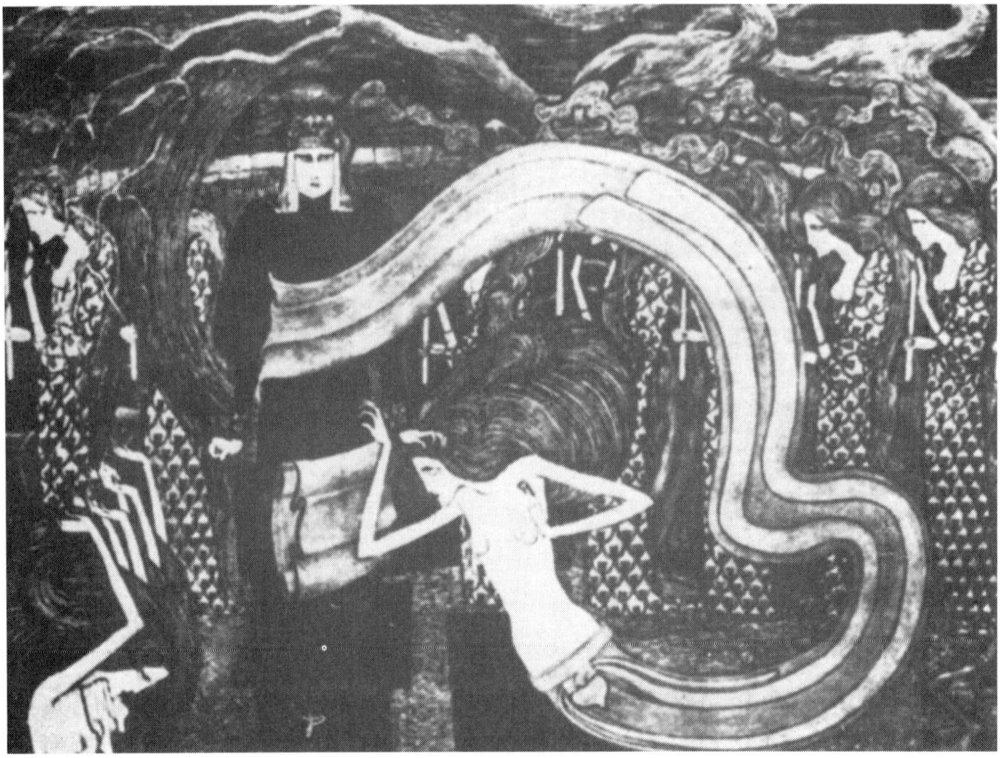

Fig. 141. Toorop: *Apocalypse*. Drawing. 1891–92.
From Plasschaert.

made it difficult for her to have remembered the precise details. *The Studio* was indisputably England's leading art periodical, and was widely read on the Continent, and had excellent contacts there. A small illustrated article on Toorop appeared in 1893,[24] but as Thomas Howarth notes,[25] they saw little more of Toorop, except for a theatre programme published in *The Studio* in 1897, before a number of his paintings were reproduced in *Deutsche Kunst und Dekoration*,[26] just about the year 1900. Francis and Jessie Newbery were, however, in possession of a copy of Zola's *Le rêve* illustrated by Schwabe, and it may have been known by Mackintosh.[27] On the other

24 W. S. Sparrow, Herr Toorop's: Three Brides, *The Studio*, vol. I, 1893, pp. 243 sq.

25 T. Howarth, *Charles Rennie Mackintosh and the Modern Movement*, London 1952, pp. 288 sq.

26 *Deutsche Kunst und Dekoration*, vol. IV, 1899, pp. 541–52.

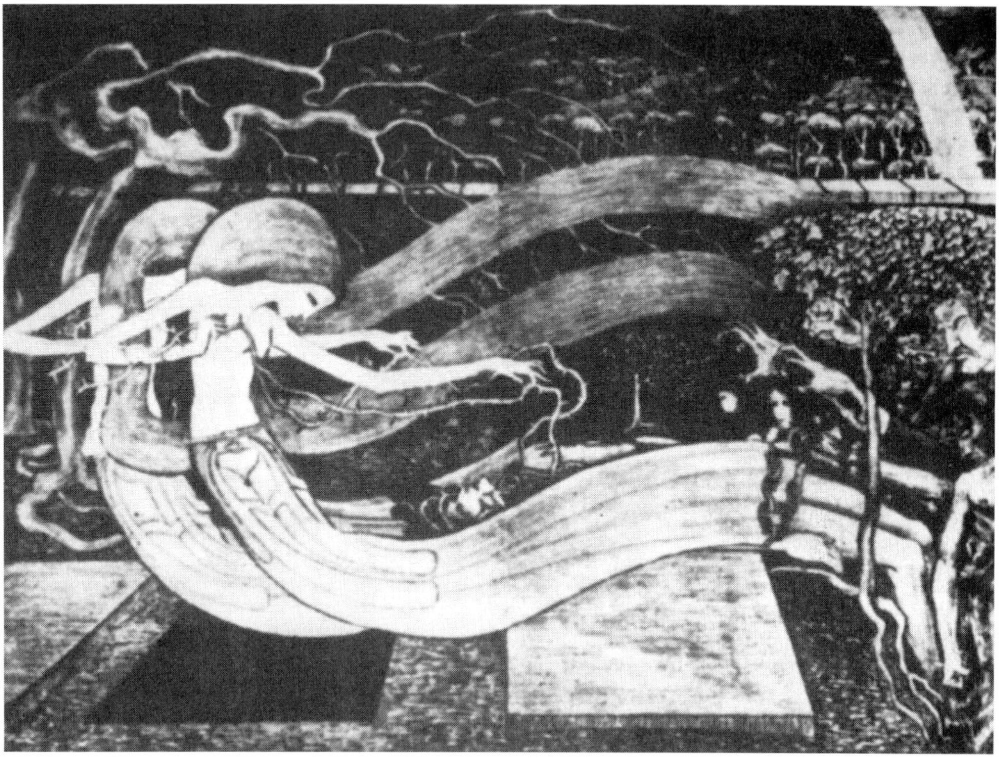

Fig. 142. Toorop: *Oh, Grave where is thy Victory.* 1892.
From Knipping.

hand Herbert MacNair states "... the work of our little group was certainly not in the very least inspired by any Continental movements—indeed we knew little about these until we were well away on our own endeavours."[28] There is no mention of Carlos Schwabe in *The Studio* during these years, except for a drawing which appeared in May 1897.[29]

It seems rather difficult to trace any direct influence on Great Britain from the Continent. For those who prefer the theory of Great Britain as primary source, there is, however, more evidence.[30] We know that

27 For this very interesting information the author is kindly indebted to Thomas Howarth in whose possession the book is now to be found.

28 This statement is given by Herbert MacNair to Thomas Howarth. T. Howarth, *op. cit.*, pp. 264–65.

29 T. Howarth, *op. cit.*, p. 229.

30 See the chapter *The British Influence.*

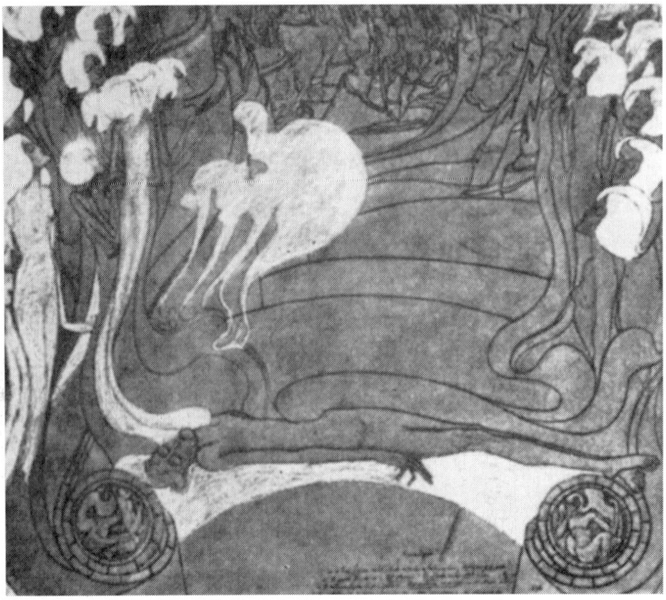

Fig. 143. Toorop: *Symbolic drawing*. 1892.
From Plasschaert.

Toorop as well as Khnopff, and the potter Finch visited Great Britain. In view of the pre-Raphaelite Symbolism and its female type as a background, both with traditions and roots in Great Britain with Beardsley, Burne Jones, Crane, Image and Mackmurdo busy at work, and with proto-Art Nouveau, and the Celtic revival,—it is not easy to explain how a reproduction or two in *The Studio* could suddenly have provided such an impetus.

But instead of considering the question of the two influences, it would, I believe, be more prudent to regard linear Symbolism as the outcome of a great many mutual influences, and as a result of a parallel development with a great measure of formal correspondence. It is interesting to note that recent research has come to the same conclusion.[31] The ideas were "in the air": pre-Raphaelitism and its Symbolism as well as proto-Art Nouveau in Great Britain, the Oriental-inspired Symbolism with Moreau and Redon and their circle, as well as the Pont-Aven group and French expressive Symbolism and Synthetism in this cultural sphere, together with the more literary and mystic Symbolism in Germany, though this had no influence on the development of Art Nouveau.

31 T. Howarth, *op. cit.*, p. 265.

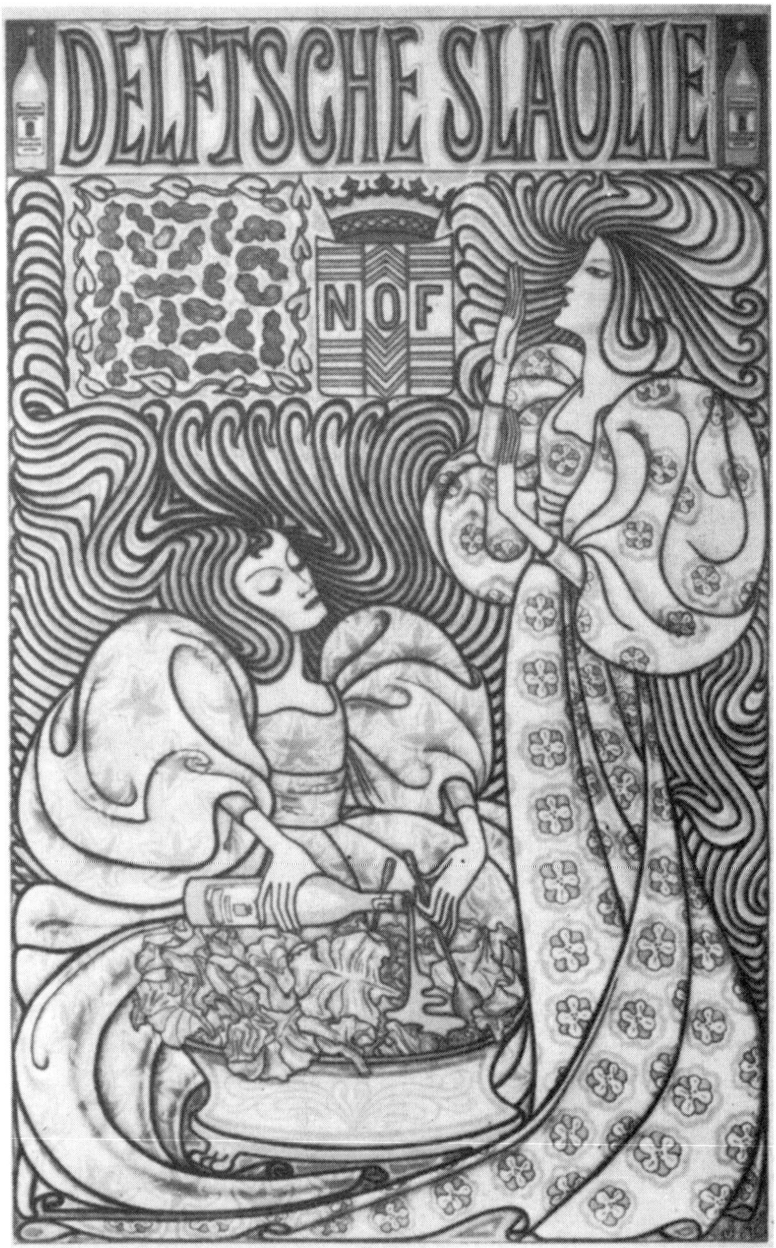

Fig. 144. Toorop: Poster. 1895.
Steedlijk Museum, Amsterdam. Copyright reserved.

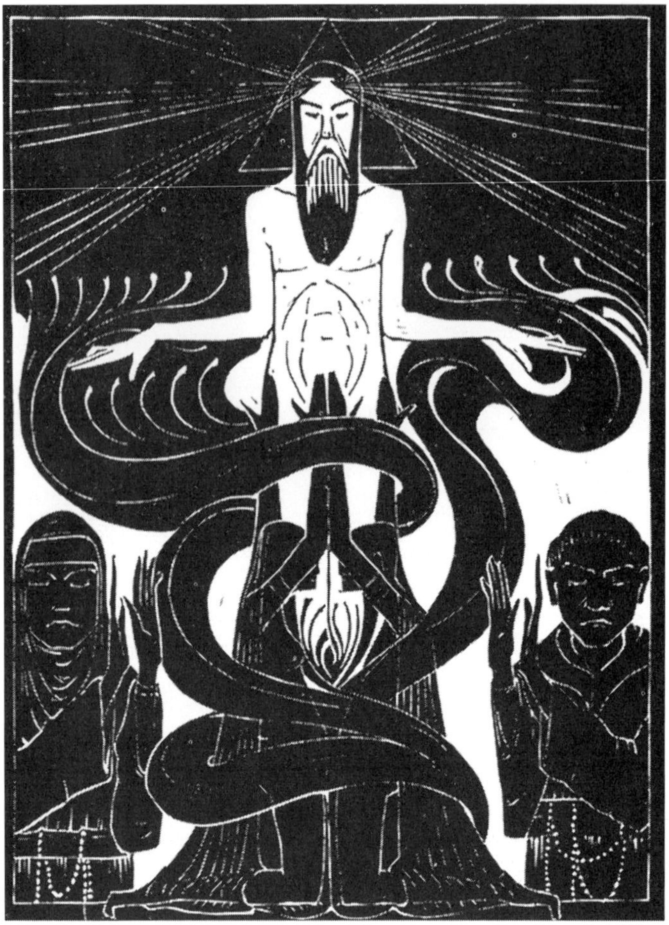

Fig. 145. De Bazel: *The Marriage*. 1894.

In the German-influenced countries the Norwegian Edvard Munch (1863–1944) became the foremost exponent of this expressive and linear symbolical trend, with his important paintings and graphic works in the years 1893–94–95. He cannot, however, be said to have exerted any direct influence on Art Nouveau, as he remained a painter, devoting no time to applied art, and never participating in the struggle for decorative art.

*

Holland and Belgium lay in the direct path of all these intersecting cultural trends, and here contacts with the various streams was intensified by a number of exhibitions and personal contacts, though to a certain extent the attitudes of these two countries are determined by tradition and geography: Belgium was more closely allied with the French culture and Holland with the English.

The Marriage, 1894, a woodcut by the Dutchman de Bazel (fig. 145) is one of the many examples of the Symbolism which in Holland, hand in hand with the Oriental impulses already mentioned, acquired a markedly exotic character. In Scotland the style was just as linear, though less Oriental, as in Mackintosh's *Diploma of the School of Art Club*, 1893, and his *Spring*, 1894, as well as Macdonald's *A Pond*, 1894.[32]

During the three years from 1889 to 1892, which are so important in this connection, an interchange of impulses takes place, which can be fairly well registered, between the various countries and their artists, and this results in an independent but fairly homogeneous stylistic expression—linear Symbolism.

32 Illustrated in T. Howarth, *op. cit.*, pl. 7c, 7a, 7b.

Symbolism in Applied Arts

Expressing symbolism is one thing in painting, and in furniture and design another. The simplest method is by means of an inscription—a text painted on, or inlaid. This had long been the custom in England: the Gothic revivalists in imitation of the medieval fashion would often place an inscription on the ecclesiastical object, e.g. Pugin.[1] But he also used texts on secular objects, and a salt-cellar from about 1848 bears the inscription "*Without me is no savour,*"[2] and a sideboard "*Non in solo pane vivit homo sed in omni verbo quod procedit de ore Dei.*"[3] Bruce J. Talbert followed suit on a sideboard he designed in 1873.[4] The literary-inclined pre-Raphaelites painted a cabinet in 1861 which had been designed by J. P. Seddon, with motifs from King René of Anjou's honeymoon, as related in Walter Scott's *Anne of Geierstein,* and Rossetti, Madox Brown, Burne Jones, and William Morris also assisted in its decoration.[5] The neo-Gothic William Burges (1827–81) wrote "*venez laver*" on a washstand from 1880, as well as the words "*Vita Nova.*"[6] Among the artists of the Arts and Crafts Movement the use of inscriptions was also widespread. Thus Clement J. Heaton (1861–1940) used a line of Shelly on a large cabinet he had made in 1886,[7] while Lewis Day's bellows bore the inscription "*Wind Flowers.*"[8] But it was in the work of Walter Crane that these texts were brought to their full development. If his painting was literary, his design was eloquent. Many of his

1 Chalice from 1851 with the inscription "*Calicem salutaris accipiam et nomen Domini invocabo,*" No. 1328–1951, Victoria and Albert Museum; chalice from 1851, with the same inscription, 1327–1951, Victoria and Albert Museum; candlestick from 1851, inscribed "*Surrexit Dominus vere alleluia,*" St.Cuthbert College, Victoria and Albert Museum, *Catalogue of an Exhibition of Victorian and Edwardian Decorative Arts,* No. C.6.

2 Victoria and Albert Museum, *op. cit.,* C 15.

3 *Ibid.,* C 3.

4 *Ibid.,* H 1; the sideboard is inscribed "*Melius est vocari ad olera cv charitate qua ad vitvlu saginatu cv odio.*" [*sic.*]

5 No. W 10–1927, Victoria and Albert Museum.

6 Victoria and Albert Museum, *op. cit.,* J 3, illustrated, St. Tschudi Madsen, Victoriansk Dekorativ Kunst, *Nordenfjeldske Kunstindustrimuseums Årbok,* 1952, Trondheim, 1953, p. 47.

7 No. G.14, William Morris Gallery, Walthamstow, London.

8 Victoria and Albert Museum, *op. cit.,* M 4.

wallpapers and ceramics from the 1870's and 1880's bear inscriptions,[9] and the same also applies to Heywood Sumner's door on a music cabinet from 1889, where the text "*The Charm of Orpheus*"[10] occurs.

This use of texts on furniture with more or less symbolical and instructive quotations may well be connected with the Gothic revival, though in all probability it is just as much an outcome of the markedly literary and artistic attitude which exerted its influence in England in the latter half of the 19th century. The chair with the Irish warrior on the back and the wolf hounds on the arm-rests is highly eloquent, for the latter carry the inscription "*Gentle when stroked,*" "*Fierce when provoked.*"[11] The chair "*The Day-dreamer*"[12] was decorated as follows: "At the top two winged thoughts—the one with birdlike pinions, and crowned with roses, representing happy and joyous dreams; the other with leathern bat-like wings—unpleasant and troublesome ones. Behind is displayed Hope, under the figure of the rising sun."[13]

In other words the aim is to express the function of the furniture and at the same time to convey a mood. This is one of the fundamental decorative principles of the 19th century, and contrasts markedly with the tendencies of the 20th century, where construction aims to express function. It cannot be said that one principle is better than the other, decoration and construction being both essential parts of a piece of furniture, but one attitude is simply that of another century.

One of the *chefs-d'oeuvre* of Scottish symbolical decorative art is the music-room designed for Fritz Wärndorfer in Vienna, which Mackintosh at the end of the 1890's decorated with motifs taken from Maeterlinck's *Sieben Prinzessinen.* The German art historian Lux says in 1908 on the subject of these decorations that they were "ausdrückliche ornamentale Ausspinnen des Themas die Sieben Prinzessinen," and he goes on to say

9 No. 2292–1932, E.4034, 4028, 4027–1915, E.4041, 4045–1915, Victoria and Albert Museum; Victoria and Albert Museum, *op. cit.,* M.57, 60, 62.

10 Victoria and Albert Museum, *op. cit.,* M.71, 72.

11 *Official Descriptive and Illustrated Catalogue of the Great Exhibition 1851,* London 1851, I–III, No. XIV, 78, Class XXVI.

12 *Ibid.,* No. 187, Class XXVI, ill., N. Pevsner, *High Victorian Design,* London 1951, p. 39; St. Tschudi Madsen, *loc. cit.,* p. 17.

13 *Official Descriptive and Illustrated Catalogue of the Great Exhibition, 1851,* London 1851, vol. II, p. 748.

that "hier schliesst sich der Kreis der buchstäblichen geistigen Befruchtung."[14] The subject was undoubtedly well suited to Mackintosh, in view of the predilection of the Glasgow school for women—both separately and in rows.

In the Glasgow school a symbolical ornamentation developed, independent of the furniture, and consisting essentially of stylised and markedly abstracted hearts, buds, sprouting bulbs, and egg-shaped forms. These ornaments can undoubtedly be regarded as symbols associated with life and growing force. Just as the artists regarded themselves as the germs of a new age and a new style, which was to flourish, it is natural to assume that they expressed this feeling in the symbols they chose. This general basic interpretation is supported by a remark of Meier-Graefe, a man who was well-versed in the symbolical trend, and who was exceptionally alive to the feelings of his age. Of their decoration he says:

"Künstliche Blumen aus farbigem Papier mit Glasknospen dekorierten die Tische; an langen, parallelen Bindfäden hingen die elektrischen Birnen und als Wandschmuck hatte man in regelmässigen Zwischenräumen ausgeblasene, gefärbte Eier, grosse und kleine, aufgehängt, über deren Bedeutung sich die Leute die Köpfe zerbrachen und die mir als durchaus verständliche, ja notwendige Symbole erschienen."[15]

In France the use of inscriptions does not go so far back, as it would hardly agree with the Classical trends of the 1860's and 1870's, but with Emile Gallé the use of inscriptions is introduced, of very high artistic quality, and symbolically profounder than in England, because he demanded that an inscription in itself should be associated with the function of the furniture. As early as 1889 he had exhibited a vase with a floral decoration, which bore a line of verse by Verlaine: "Je récolte en secret des fleurs mystérieuses." (I glean in secret mysterious flowers.)

[14] J. A. Lux, *Die Geschichte des modernen Kunstgewerbes in Deutschland,* Leipzig 1908, p. 66. For further description, L. Hevesi, *Altkunst—Neukunst, 1894–1908,* Vienna 1909, p. 222; T. Howarth, The Wärndorfer Music Room, *op. cit.,* pp. 155–57. "Expressly ornamental elaboration of the theme of the seven Princesses." ". . . here the circle of the literary spiritual fruition is closed."

[15] J. Meier-Graefe, *Entwicklungsgeschichte der modernen Kunst,* I–III, Stuttgart 1904–05, vol. II, p. 621. "Artificial flowers of coloured paper with glass buds decorated the tables; the electric bulbs were suspended from long, parallel connecting wires, and as a mural ornament inflated coloured eggs, large and small, had been hung up at regular intervals. The meaning of these eggs puzzled people, but to me they seemed quite understandable, nay necessary symbols."

A natural consequence of the idea of unity and equality between the arts was the intimate collaboration between symbolical painters and poets, and we find van de Velde cultivating the friendship of Elskamp, Maeterlinck converting Toorop to symbolism, and Gallé associated with Victor Prouvé, who was a close friend of his. Victor Prouvé, too, was highly interested in applied art,[16] and when he was only nineteen years old decorated a vase which had been executed by Gallé in 1877. It was called "*La Nuit*" after Alfred de Musset's poem.[17] In 1889 Gallé asked Prouvé to design the inlay work for a large table on the subject: La Germanie tout entière est separée des Gaules par le Rhin"[18]—a quotation from Tacitus which admirably expressed the patriotic feelings of the people of Lorraine. Writing about the table Gallé says modestly enough of himself: "Moi, j'ai fait un grand effort pour sortir ces pierres précieuses, et faire à votre basson puissant un accompagnement de petite flute modeste comme il convient."[19] Prouvé was also commissioned by Gallé to design the décor of a vase on the subject "Orphée implorant l'ombre d'Euridise."[20] The difference between the English and French use of inscriptions is more apparent when we consider Heywood Sumner's text from the same year, 1889. While Sumner added the text, Gallé and Prouvé created the work of art on the basis of the literary subject, thus establishing a more intimate contact.

At the beginning of the 1890's Gallé created a number of pieces of furniture which bear inscriptions, and from 1893 mention may be made of *La Vigne*, *Les soucis des champs*, *Septembre* and *Octobre*. These are Gallé's so-called *meubles parlants*, with quotations taken specially from Hugo, Verlaine, Baudelaire, Sully Prudhomme, Verhaeren, Maeterlinck, as well as Ruskin and Morris. With his artistic *vue d'ensemble* Gallé regarded a vase as an artistic medium of expression on a par with painting or sculpture, the object of which was to create a medium of communication to which his

16 G. Ducrocq, Victor Prouvé, *Art et Décoration,* vol. I, part 2, 1897, pp. 1–8.

17 Information kindly given by Madeleine Prouvé to the author, April 1953.

18 As note 17. "The whole of Germany is separated from the Gauls by the Rhine."

19 M. Prouvé, Victor Prouvé, MS., kindly lent to the author, p. 64. "I've made a great effort to bring out these precious stones, and provide, as far as possible, a modest little flute accompaniment to your powerful bassoon."

20 *Ibid.,* p. 64. "Orpheus imploring the shade of Euridice."

fellow-mortals would react. In furniture and decorative art the inscription was the means closest at hand, and was of a symbolical nature. "Ma conclusion est donc que le terme de *symbole* est bien près de se confondre avec celui *d'art.* Conscient ou inconscient, le symbole qualifie, vivifie l'œuvre: il en est âme."[21]

Moreover he maintains that the décor must be clearer than the English: "Les symboles sont les pointes où se concrètent les idées."[22] And where is the inspiration to be found? The answer is: "La libre Nature—c'est à dire au symbolisme même."[23] In the same way Nature and symbolism in the works of Gallé fuse to form the foundation for his artistic views.

With van de Velde symbolism in decorative art took an entirely new turn: he too wanted the object to express something beyond itself, and the ornament to symbolise, but not a literary idea, and certainly not Nature.[24] He maintains, as has been seen, that the ornament and its shape should express—symbolise—the object's function and nothing more. Through its shape it should clarify the aim of the object, and allude to its function—always based on reason.[25]

This theory arises from the symbolistic philosophy of the age, but goes beyond ordinary decorative symbolism, pointing the way ahead. At the same time it reminds us of his spiritual predecessors—of the real pioneers, the theoreticians from the middle of the 19th century—an Owen Jones for instance:"The useful must ever be regarded as a vehicle for the beautiful, consequently, that all decoration should arise naturally out of the construction, and that ornamentation should never be purposely constructed."[26]

*

21 E. Gallé, Le Décor Symbolique, lecture delivered May 17 at l'Académie de Stanislas, Nancy, *Ecrits pour l'Art,* Paris 1908, pp. 210–28 (p. 228). "My conclusion then is that the term symbol is almost being confused with art. Consciously or unconsciously the symbol qualifies, enlivens the work; it is the soul of it."

22 *Ibid.,* p. 218. "Symbols are where ideas take concrete form."

23 *Ibid.,* p. 219. "Free Nature—i.e. in symbolism itself."

24 H. van de Velde, *Renaissance im Kunstgewerbe,* Berlin 1901, Neue Ausgabe, p. 94.

25 *Ibid.,* pp. 102 sq. See also H. van de Velde, Ein Kapitel über Entwurf and Bau Moderner Möbel, *Pan,* vol. III, 1897, pp. 260–64.

26 O. Jones, *On the True and the False in the Decorative Arts,* London 1863, vol. I, p. 43.

The Gothic revival and the Arts and Crafts Movement in the various countries, provided a basis on which to start on the long and weary journey away from Historicism, and these trends also contributed to a certain degree to the form-language.

The trends in painting of the 1880's and 1890's are the most recent of the factors contributing to the development of Art Nouveau; they are an essential part of the age itself, and pre-Raphaelitism, Symbolism, and Synthetism are some of the main sources of the style itself.

From the sketchbooks of painters interested in Symbolism, and from the decorated leaves of the illustrated books themselves, sprang a linear, two-dimensional and symbolistic decorative art, filled with reaction against the form-language of Historicism. But there were a great many trends which helped to shape it. The contemporary interest in plants gave the line its sprouting power: theorists developed principles of line, each one more artificial than the other: Japan contributed sophistication, the sense of the asymmetrical, and the idea of an art of flat planes, while neo-Rococo gave some of its ornamental lavishness. As it was translated from the pages of the book to the inkwell and the writing-desk, the new art necessarily became three-dimensional, and the markedly plastic conception of form of neo-Baroque was caught up, giving the line fullness and volume. While all these streams were gathering momentum the Celtic spirit imparted something of its own linearity as well as the *entrelac* motif, and iron grilles bent their bars in sympathy.

Round about 1892–93 all these trends and tendencies merged to produce, not one, but several forms of art, which found varying expressions in different countries and in the works of many different artists. Nevertheless they constituted a comparatively homogeneous conception, with clearly defined characteristics and thus emerged the style now universally recognised as Art Nouveau.

Part III

DEVELOPMENT

Great Britain

Glasgow Style

ENGLAND

The new trends which took place from the 1860's to the 1870's and in the decades that followed, and which emanated from Morris, have formally little connection with Scottish Art Nouveau. The Glasgow school was a Scottish contribution to this new development—a trend contributed by a small independent group—which occupies a position all on its own, apart from the general development away from Historicism in Great Britain. The general development here was rooted in traditional soil. As may be seen in the work of Morris, as well as in the work of architects such as Philip Webb and Richard Norman Shaw, the sound and simple principles of England's older architecture was their *point de départ*, which they developed without effecting any revolutionary break. This is also true of the architects and the designers who followed them: they continued to work in the spirit of innovation which was the basis of the Arts and Crafts Movement.

It can also be assumed too that the interest in folk art and its simple furniture also influenced this stylistic development. Morris's firm used the Sussex type of chair, Charles E. Eastlake concentrated on a simple type of furniture of an almost rustic character in his widely read book *Hints on Household Taste*, from 1868, of which there were four new editions in the following years, followed two years later by Shirley Hilberd's *Rustic Adornments for Homes and Taste*, while the art historian Karl Rosner points out in 1898 that for the first time folk art aroused considerable attention at the World Exhibition in Paris in 1867.[1]

1 K. Rosner, *Am Ende des Jahrhunderts,* Berlin, 1898, p. 77.

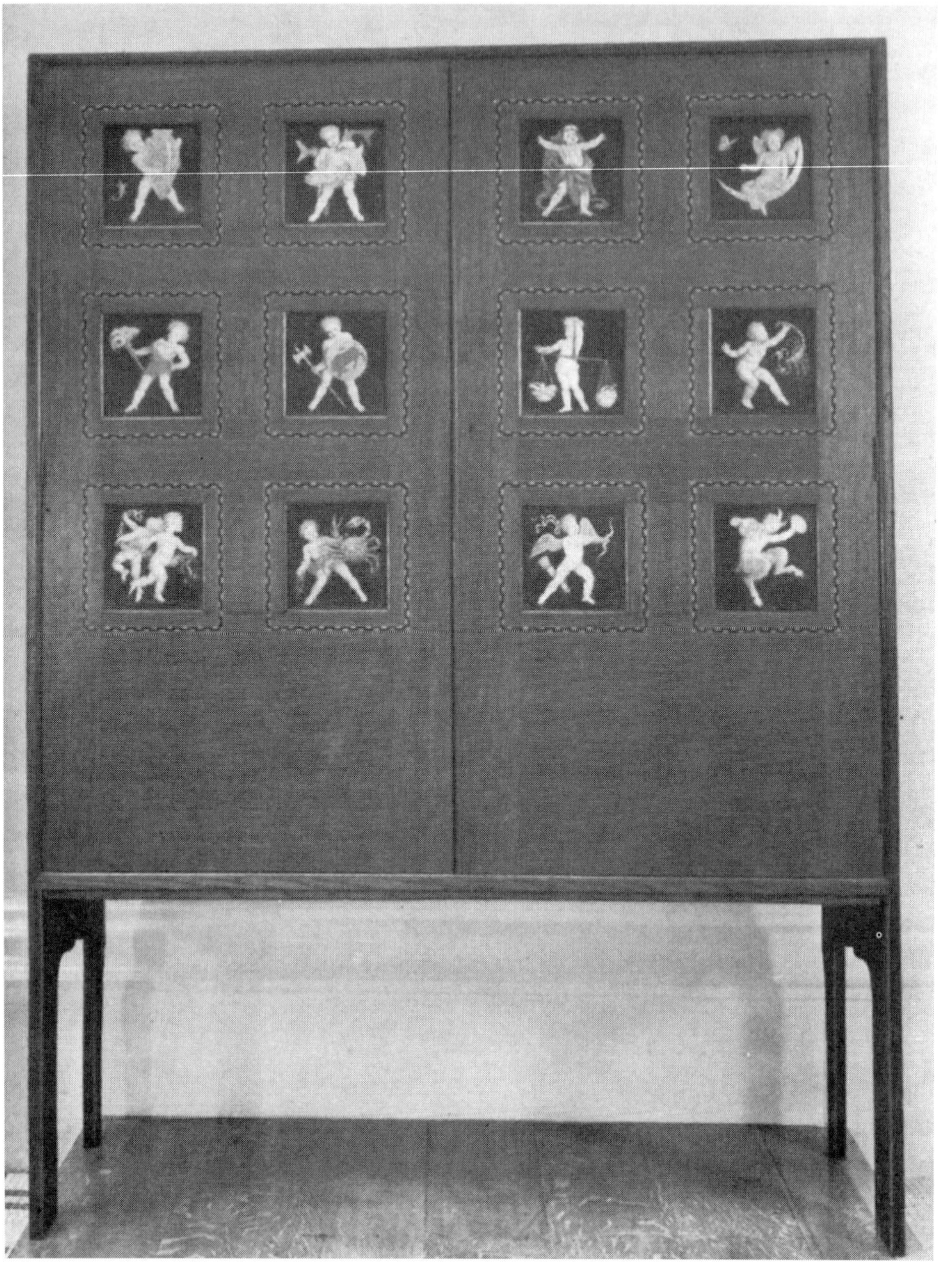

Fig. 146. Day: Cabinet. Oak inlaid with ebony and satinwood. Painted panels. About 1888.
Courtesy of Miss D. M. Ross. Victoria and Albert photo. Crown Copyright reserved.

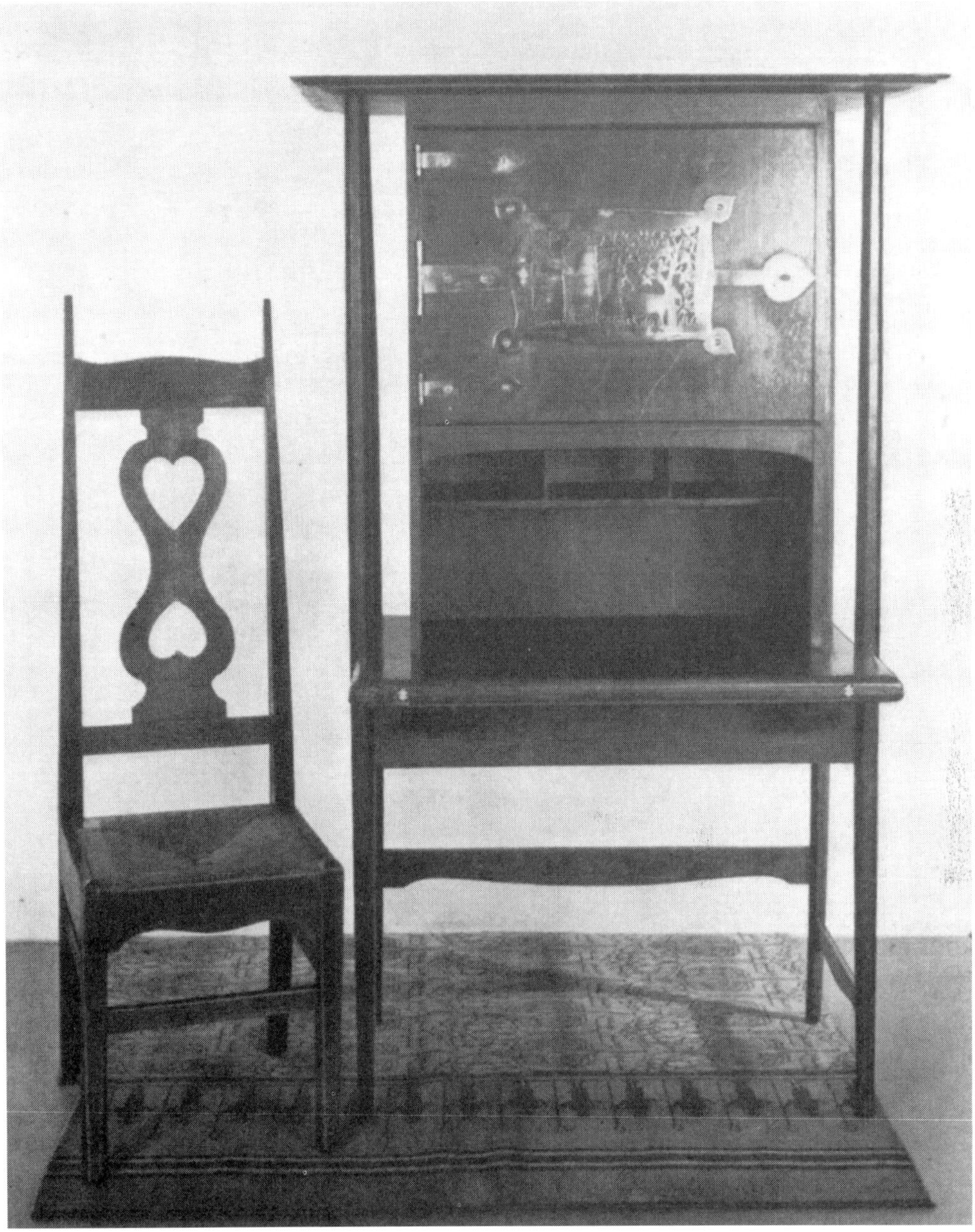

Fig. 147. Voysey: Writing desk and chair. Oak with brass fittings. Designs for desk, February, 1895. Chair. 1899.
Victoria and Albert photo. Crown Copyright reserved.

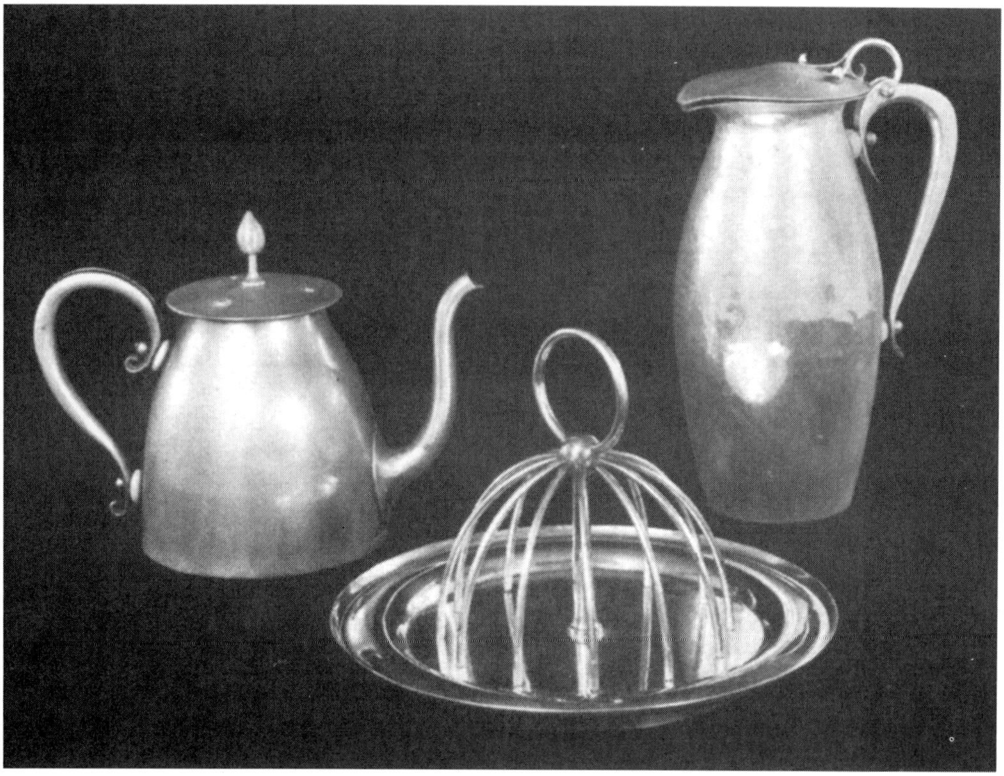

Fig. 148. Voysey: Toast rack, 1900. Jug about 1896. Tea pot about 1896. Rack and jug, silver. Tea pot, brass.
Victoria and Albert photo. Crown Copyright reserved.

This style of furniture, with which the more advanced designers worked, was simple and almost devoid of decoration, with considerable emphasis on all constructive elements and finesses. The structure of the wood is allowed to come into its own, and this, together with the massive and ponderous character which is typical of it, gives it a rustic air. In addition models are also taken direct from rustic furniture. The décor consists essentially of hammered metal and large decorative wrought-iron embellishments. The rectilinear nature of this furniture, and the frequent use of frame and panel give it, together with its lack of decoration, a sober and austere appearance. Another characteristic feature is the use of a prominent projecting cornice, the high back, and the extension of the back posts of the chair. A small heart-shaped panel and a slight curve may be introduced to give liveliness to this austere design. Inlay work is occasionally used in furniture of especially high quality.

These features of furniture design combined to produce a special English style in the 1890's, and it was in this style that the architects who together formed *Kenton and Company* in 1890 also worked. This undertaking only lasted for two years, but a number of the group continued, under the name of the *Cotswold School*. The most important members of this group were all architects—Ernest Gimson (1864–1919),[2] William R. Lethaby (1857–1931),[3] Reginald Blomfield (1856–1942),[4] Ernest (1863–1926) and Sidney Barnsley (1865–1926), and Mervyn Macartney. Both Gimson and Lethaby occasionally show certain neo-Gothic features, but their work is primarily characterised by a respect for the material and profound understanding of the constructive problems involved. Together with a furniture designer such as Ambrose Heal (1872–),[5] and the most important of them all, the architect Charles Francis Annesley Voysey (1857–1941),[6] these were the leading designers before and after the turn of the century (figs. 146, 147, 148). This exceedingly simple, and constructive, style was to prove the most important and novel in English design. Especially in the work of Gimson, Voysey and Heal this Arts and Crafts style assumed a strikingly sober and elegant form. Frank Brangwyn[7] (1867–), who at one time designed for Bing in Paris in 1895–96, was a painter and furniture desig-

2 E. Gimson, *Ernest Gimson. His Life and Work*, London 1924.

3 R. Blomfield, W. R. Lethaby, An Impression and a Tribute, *Journal of R.I.B.A.*, vol. XXXIX, 1931–32, pp. 293–302; N. Rooke, The Drawings of W. R. Lethaby, *loc. cit.*, pp. 31–32; *idem*, The Work of Lethaby, Webb and Morris, *ibid.*, vol. LVII, 1950, pp. 167–75.

4 R. Blomfield, *Leaves from an Architect's Note-book*, London 1929; *idem, Memoirs of an Archit ct*, London 1932.

5 G. Boumphery, The Designers I. Sir Ambrose Heal, *The Architectural Review*, vol. LXXVIII, 1935, pp. 39–40; W. Gleeson White, *A Note on Simplicity of Design in Furniture for Bedrooms*, London 1898; the Conversion of the Bedroom, *The Artist*, vol. XXIII, 1898, pp. 36–41.

6 His most important writings and the most important articles about him are quoted here, C. F. A. Voysey, Domestic Furniture, *The Journal of the Royal Institute of British Architects*, vol. I, 3rd series, 1894, pp. 415–18; Schultz, *The Arts connected with building*, London 1909, pp. 103–37; *idem, Individuality*, London 1911; *idem*, A Catalogue of the works of C. F. Annesley Voysey at the Batsford Gallery 1931, London 1931; C. F. A. Voysey, An Interview with C. F. A. Voysey, *The Studio*, vol. I, 1893, pp. 231–37; J. Betjamin, Charles Francis Annesley Voysey, The Architect of Individualism, *The Architectural Review*, vol. LXX, 1931, pp. 93–96; R. Banham, The Voysey Inheritance, *ibid.*, vol. CXII, 1952, pp. 367–71; G., The Work of Mr. C. F. A. Voysey, *The Studio*, vol. XI, 1897, pp. 16–25. A biography will be published shortly by John Brandon-Jones, Il Balcone, Milan.

7 H. Furst, *The Decorative Art of Frank Brangwyn*, London 1924; P. G. Konody, Frank Brangwyn und

ner who acquired a considerable reputation abroad and was in closer contact with Continental Art Nouveau. It was in Paris that he completed the 180-foot-long frieze on thes ubject of *Le Roi au Chantier*, together with a tapestry, and yet stylistically neither of these works has anything in common with Art Nouveau.[8] Artists such as Lewis Day and Walter Crane, who belonged to the Arts and Crafts Movement, cannot be said to have contributed to this part of the development. Crane's development has already been dealt with: at heart he was a Medieval and Renaissance Romantic, as a designer he was highly receptive, with an open eye to all contemporary trends. Lewis Day was possibly one of the leading designers of the 1880's and 1890's, although he has no original contribution to make in his simple and rather traditional designs. Both Crane and Day in their decorative art, seen as a whole, belong to an older generation, and generally it may be said that the neo-Renaissance was more important to their stylistic development than the work of their mentor William Morris.

In silver work Charles Robert Ashbee (1863–1942),[9] Alexander Fisher (1864–1936),[10] and William Arthur Smith Benson (1854–1924)[11] were among the more outstanding. The two first mentioned tended towards the Art Nouveau style, each in his own way: Ashbee through the thin and serpentine legs which he frequently gives to his objects, Fisher through the Celtic style (fig. 114).[12] Benson, on the other hand, who had been in contact with Morris, regarded the simple unornamented form as so essential that he hardly made contact with the style.

The cup which the Goldsmith's and Silversmith's Company, London,

seine Kunst, *Kunst und Kunsthandwerk*, vol. III, 1900, pp. 317–30; W. Shaw Sparrow, *Frank Brangwyn and his Work*, London 1910.

8 H. Furst, The Decorations for M. Bing's Hotel, *The Decorative Art of Frank Brangwyn*, London 1924, pp. 49–51.

9 A. Miller, *Charles R. Ashbee*, unpublished paper delivered to the Art Workers Guild, May 6, 1949; N. Pevsner, William Morris, C. R. Ashbee und das zwanzigste Jahrhundert, *Deutsche Vierteljahrsschrift für Literaturwissenschaft und Geistesgeschichte*, Halle, vol. XIV, Heft 4, 1936. For his writings see List of Literature.

10 Fred Miller, The Art of the Enameller, and of Mr. Alex. Fisher in particular, *The Journal of Art*, 1898, pp. 263–67.

11 W. A. S. Benson, *Elements of Handicraft and Design*, London 1893; *idem, Drawing. Its History and Uses*, London 1925.

12 The typical Art Nouveau-like form of Fisher is also seen in a Triptych in steel and enamel, ill. in *The Studio*, Special No. The Record of Art, 1898, p. 69.

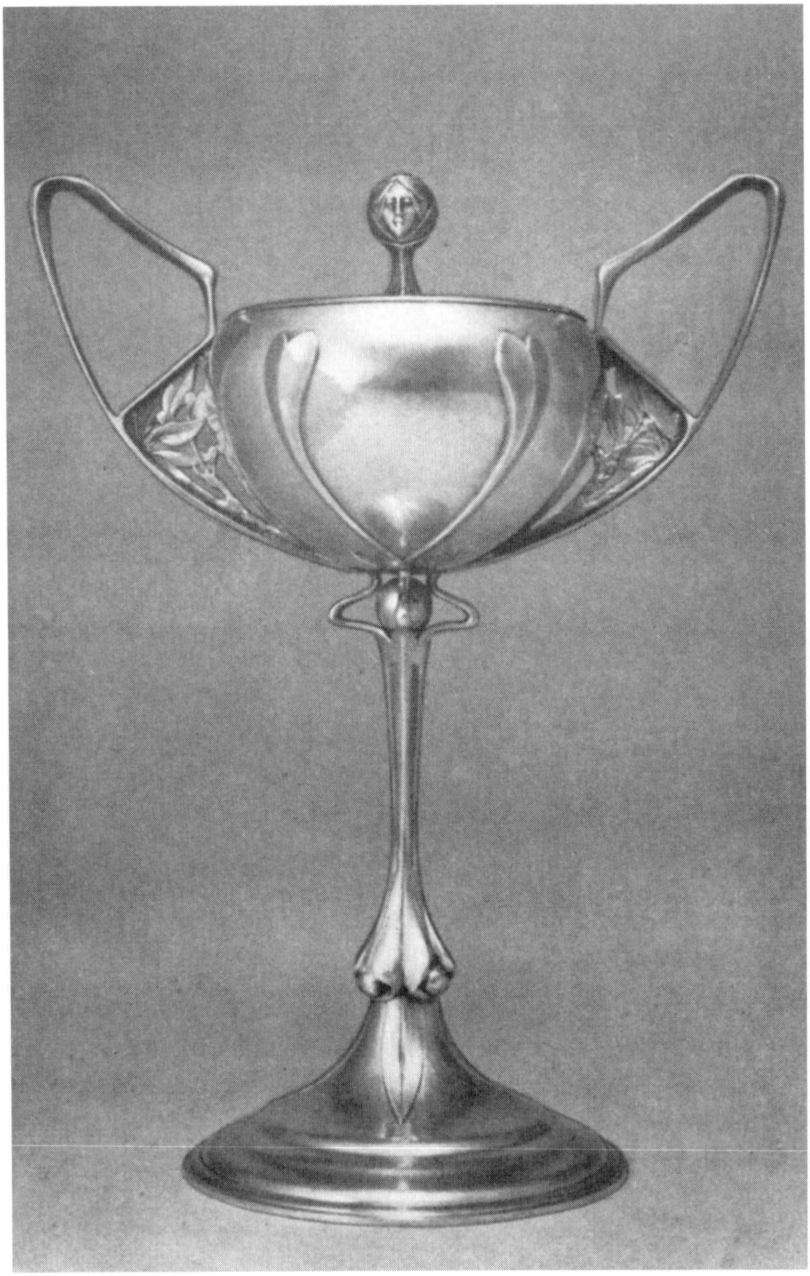

Fig. 149. The Goldsmith's and Silversmith's Company, London. Silver cup. Bought 1900.
Vestlandske Kunstindustrimuseum, Bergen. Copyright reserved.

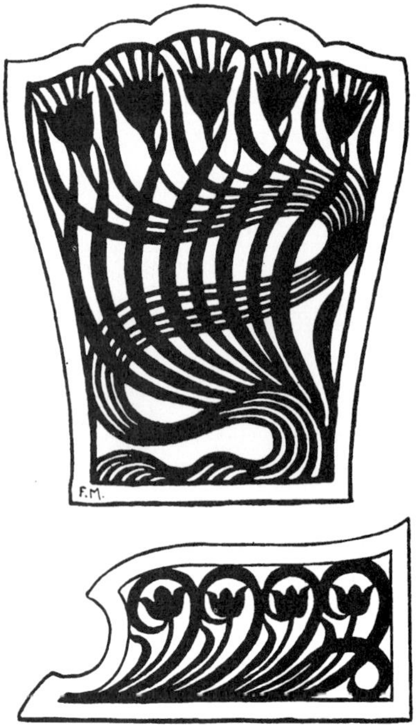

Fig. 150. Miller: Design for chair back. 1899.

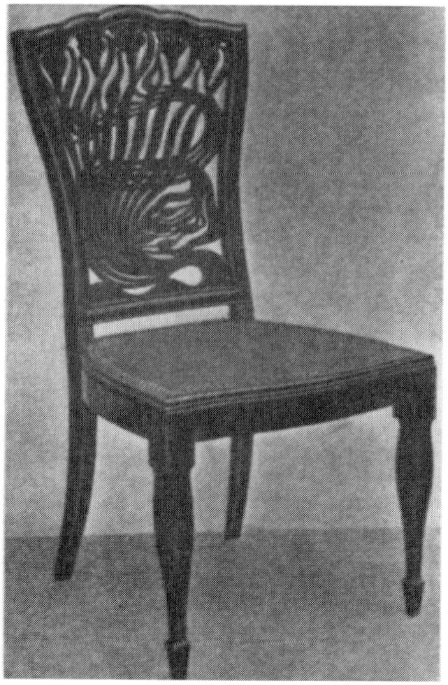

Fig. 151. Mackmurdo: Chair. Designed 1881.

executed in 1900[13] (fig. 149) is one of the works that best illustrate the "British Art Nouveau" as far as work in silver is concerned. The plant-influenced decoration has precisely that elegant, linear, and stem-like appearance, and is in complete harmony with the ideals of the age, both in England and in Scotland. The English never came much closer to the Continental ideals in their special development of style at the end of the 1890's; but at the same time their style also points back towards the English proto-Art Nouveau with its softly shaped, pliant, and unornamented stems.

The style developed by English artists around 1880 undoubtedly had a great deal of influence on what we might call the English version of Art Nouveau. Fred Miller's chair decoration from 1899[14] (fig. 150) is in its design entirely dependent on Mackmurdo's chair from 1881[15] (fig. 151).

13 V.K. 30. 5. 1901. Vestlandske Kunstindustrimuseum. Bergen. Copyright reserved.

14 *Der Moderne Stil,* Stuttgart, vol. I, pl. 99.

15 *The Studio,* vol. XVI, p. 186.

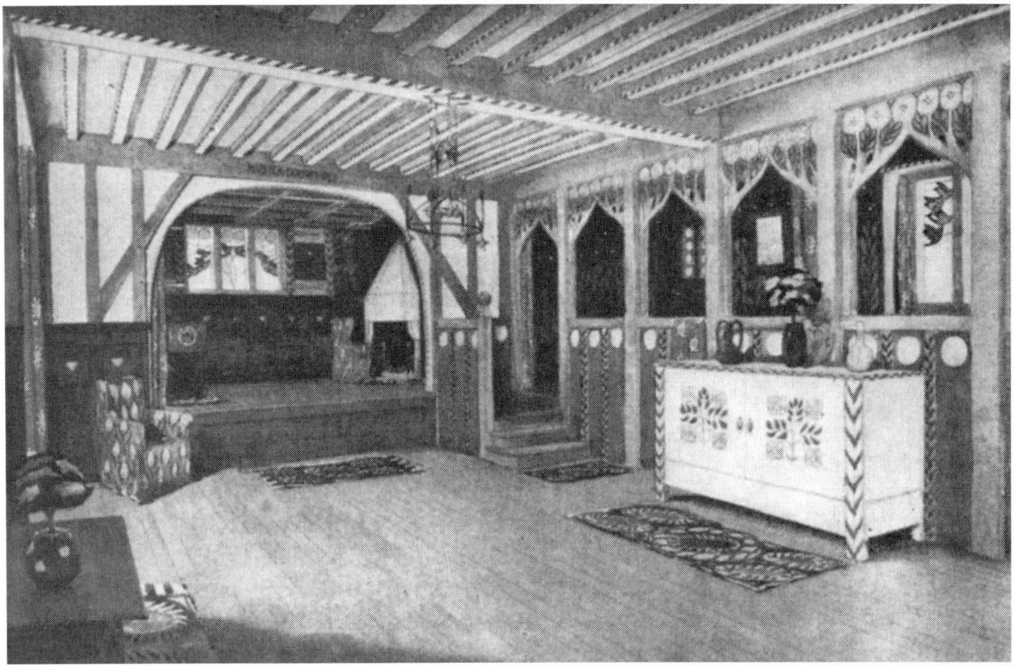

Fig. 152. Baillie Scott: Music room. 1901.

Two artists who to a certain extent may be said to be associated with Art Nouveau are George Walton (1867–1933)[16] and Mackay Hugh Baillie Scott (1865–1945).[17] The first of these was trained at the Glasgow School of Art, and co-operated with Mackintosh, but was always more influenced by the Arts and Crafts, and moved to London in 1897.

Baillie Scott was one of the British architects most in touch with the

16 N. Pevsner, George Walton. His Life and Work, *The Journal of the Royal Institute of British Architects,* vol. XLVI, 1939, pp. 537–48. The chapter "George Walton" in T. Howarth, *Charles Rennie Mackintosh and the Modern Movement,* London 1952, pp. 223 sqq.

17 M. H. Baillie Scott, An Artist's House, *The Studio,* vol. IX, 1896–97, pp. 28–37; *idem,* On the Choice of Simple Furniture, *ibid.,* vol. X, 1897, pp. 152–57; *idem,* A small country House, *ibid.,* vol. XII, 1898, pp. 167–72, p. 177; *idem,* Some Furniture for the New Palace, Darmstadt, *ibid.,* vol. XIV, 1898, pp. 91–97; *idem, Haus eines Kunstfreundes,* with an introduction by H. Muthesius, Darmstadt 1902; *idem, Houses and Gardens,* London 1906; *idem,* Ideals in Building. False and True, Schultz, *The Art Connected with Building,* London 1909, pp. 141–51; J. Betjeman, M. H. Baillie Scott, F.R.I.B.A., *The Studio,* vol. CXXX, 1945, p. 17; W. Fred, Der Architekt M. H. Baillie Scott, *Kunst und Kunsthandwerk,* vol. IV, 1901, pp. 53–73; E. D. Roncole, M. H. Baillie Scott, *Emporium,* vol. XX, 1904, pp. 1–19.

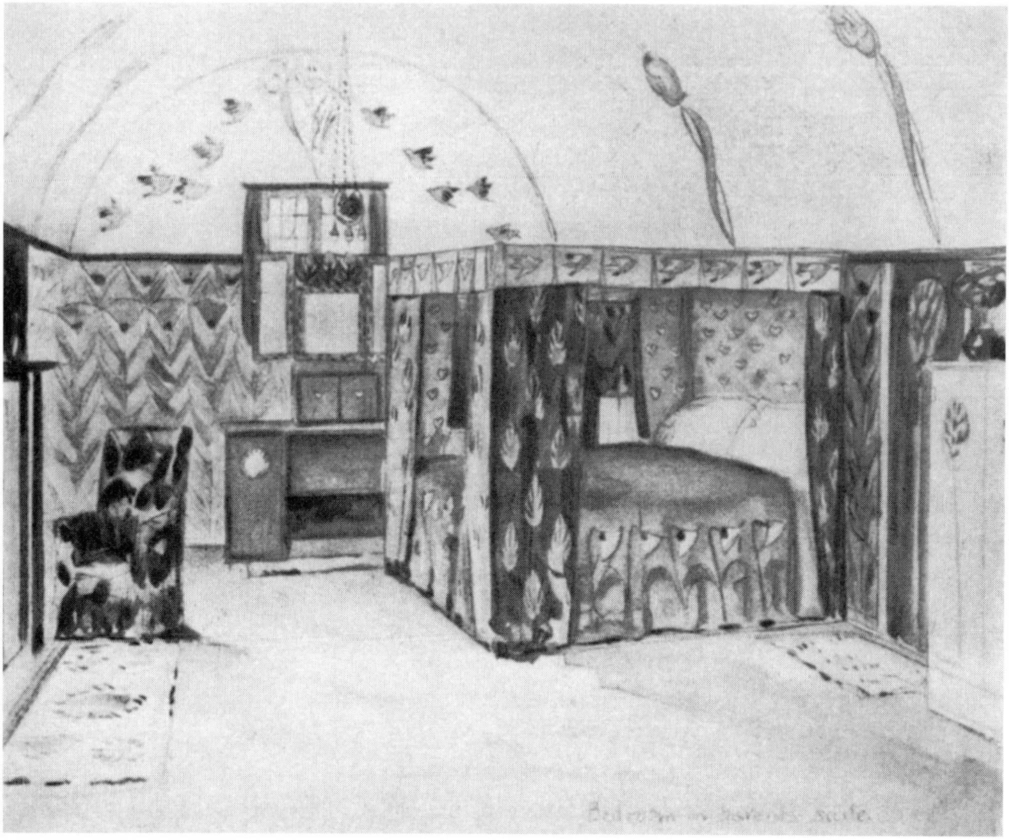

Fig. 153. Baillie Scott: Bedroom. 1901.

Continent. He designed, *inter alia*, furniture for the Grand-Duke of Hesse, at Darmstadt, in 1898, and built a number of houses in Germany, Poland, Russia, and Switzerland, and into the bargain won the competition sponsored by the indefatigable art promoter in Darmstadt, Alexander Koch, in 1900, to design a *Haus eines Kunstfreundes*. Mackintosh won second prize. Comparing the exteriors designed by the two prizewinners one is struck by Baillie Scott's adherence to tradition and period elements and how completely revolutionary Mackintosh is. The same applies to the interiors (figs. 152, 153, 154),[18] where Baillie Scott uses lavishly all sorts of floral

[18] From *Haus eines Kunstfreundes*, I, II, Darmstadt 1902.

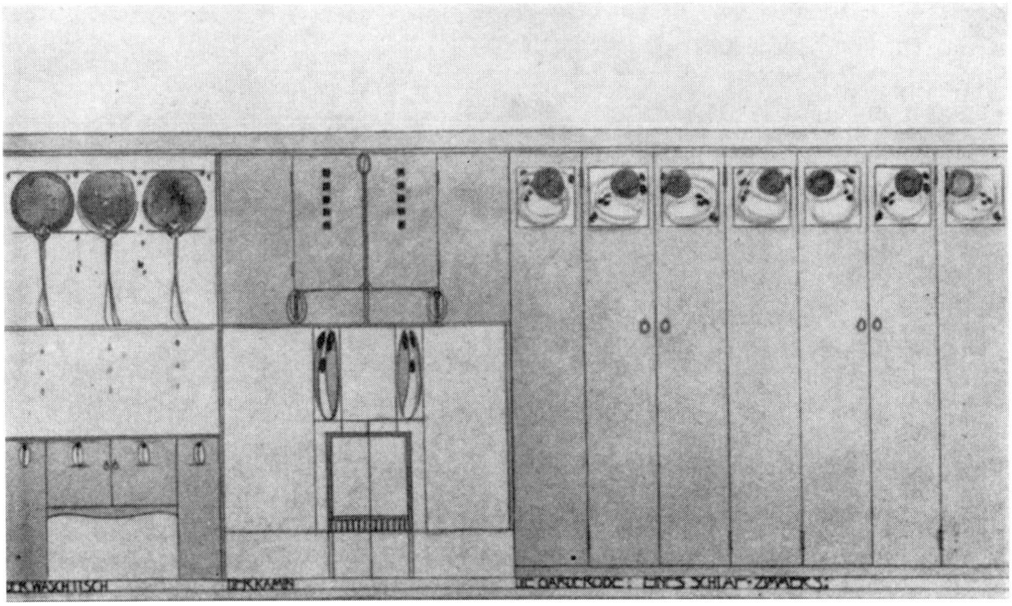

Fig. 154. Mackintosh: Bedroom. 1901.

textiles, in the 19th century manner, all enclosed in a traditionally romantic English setting.

In the details of Baillie Scott's work (fig. 155)[19] we are still on traditional ground: he stylises the flower, and the leaves may be said to show a touch of Art Nouveau rhythm, but the essentials of Art Nouveau are missing: there is no linearity, no growing force vibrant in every coil, and no pliancy of line, or asymmetry. But to those Continental artists who were still dedicated to period styles, this interior decoration was completely new and inspiring—and it was English!

A glance at Baillie Scott is interesting, even though he was not an Art Nouveau architect, because of all English designers he was best known on the Continent, and moreover familiarity with his work helps us to realise what was meant on the Continent when designers constantly spoke of English interior decoration and applied art.

19 Victoria and Albert Museum, *Catalogue of an Exhibition of Victorian and Edwardian Decorative Arts*, London 1952, p. 36.

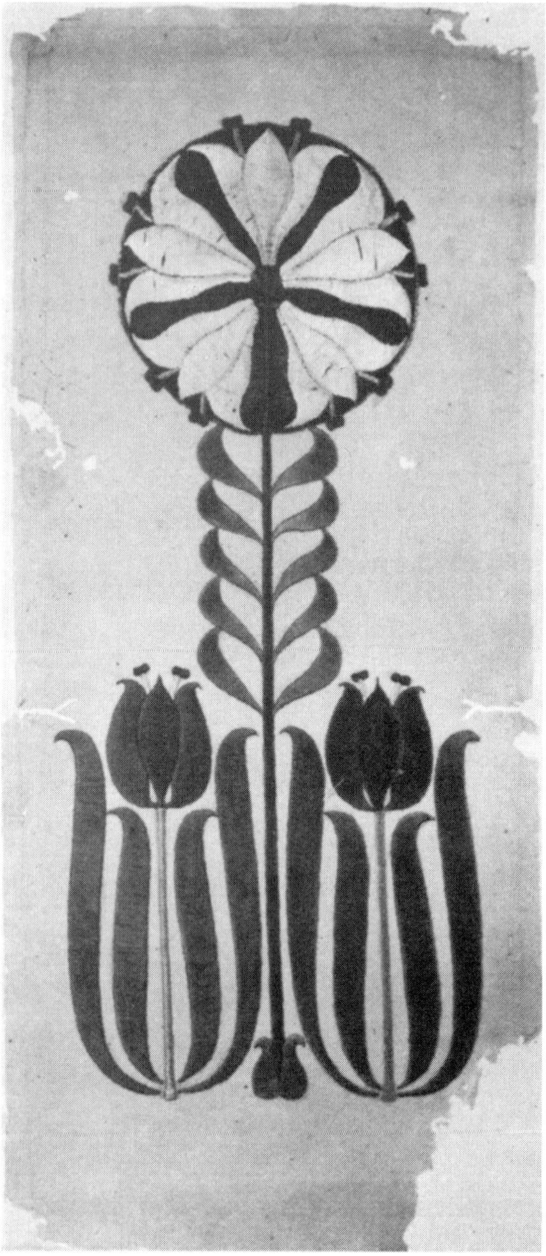

Fig. 155. Baillie Scott: Bed curtain appliqué of silk and embroidery on felt. Courtesy of Mrs. Lister Wallis. Victoria and Albert Museum photo. Crown Copyright reserved.

Only one English architect can really be said to have worked in Art Nouveau, viz. Charles Harrison Townsend (1852–1928).[20] Among his principal works are the *Bishopsgate Institute*, 1892–94, the *Whitechapel Art Gallery*, 1897–99, and *Horniman's Museum*, 1901–02, all in London.

Townsend is dealt with in recent research by both Nikolaus Pevsner in *Pioneers of Modern Design* and by Thomas Howarth in *Charles Rennie Mackintosh and the Modern Movement* in such a way that only a few remarks need be added.

The most interesting point is his use of asymmetrical elements. The Whitechapel Art Gallery was originally conceived as a symmetrical building,[21] but after considerable alterations it now[22] has a reduced tower, instead of two, and a large, gaping

20 Notes and Cuttings by Charles Harrison Townsend, Victoria and Albert Museum; Ch. H. Townsend, "Cliff Towers": A House on the Devonshire Coast, *The Studio*, vol. XIII, 1898, pp. 239–46.

21 Illustrated in *The Studio*, vol. X, 1897, p. 131.

22 Illustrated in N. Pevsner, *Pioneers of Modern Design*, N.Y. 1949, p. 99; T. Howarth, *op. cit.*, pl. 90, D.

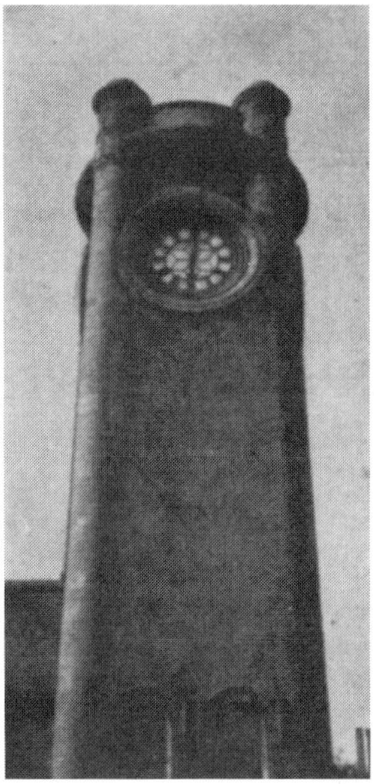

Fig. 156. Townsend: The Tower of Horniman's Museum, London. S.E. 1900–1902.

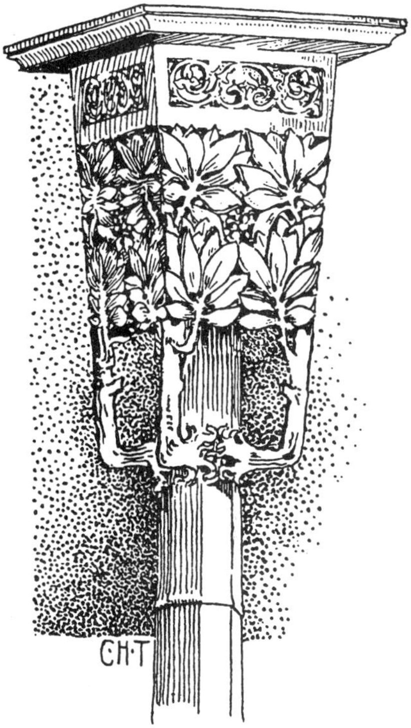

Fig. 157. Townsend: Design for Capital. 1896.

portal, pushed, however, to one side. One would hardly have expected an architect who wrote so conventionally on *Originality in Architectural Design*,[23] to have been responsible for something so novel in character. But the asymmetry is not based on an artistic distribution of masses which produce harmonious balance as a result, such as is found in the works of Mackintosh and Voysey.

In Horniman's Museum (fig. 156) the same asymmetrical striving is in evidence, and the same rounded form, as well as the same plastic fashioning of the architectural elements. Here is an architect whose conception is entirely three-dimensional: this feeling for form agrees wholly with the conception of form of the neo-Baroque of the 1890's, as well as its predilection for overemphasis of certain architectural elements and also for the large, flat arch. The decorative elements are placed flush with the surface, and are quite subordinate to the main shapes, as in the drawing for *Pan*, 1896 (fig. 157).

[23] Ch. H. Townsend, Originality in Architectural Design, *The Builder*, vol. LXXXII, 1902, pp. 133–34.

Townsend's position, however, is that of a lone wolf in England: the leading artists and designers turned their attention in different directions.

It is only in metalwork and the ornamentional mounting among the Arts and Crafts artists that we can find a decoration which really recalls Art Nouveau. The interest in graceful line and undulating contours was inherited by the later Arts and Crafts artists, and fused in their work with the form-language of the Gothic revival, with the result that especially in English ecclesiastical decoration we get an Art Nouveau-like neo-Gothic which clearly bears the mark of the Arts and Crafts Movement. We find this unusually well represented in Comper's two churches, *Holy Trinity*, Latimore Road, 1881, and *St. Cyprian*, Gloucester Gate, about 1905, as well as in *Holy Trinity*, Sloane Street, 1888, by J. D. Sedding. All of these are in London. The best representative, however, is *St. Cuthbert*, Philbeach Gardens, London, 1887–93, designed by W. Bainbridge Reynolds.[24] The Church itself is in the style of pure Gothic revival, but in the choir rails and the lectern Bainbridge Reynolds has given the metal the peculiar and special rhythm. From a Continental point of view it would be out of the question to call this Art Nouveau, and yet it is in metalwork of this nature that the English approached Art Nouveau as far as their tradition and feeling of independence permitted.

In Nottinghamshire Nikolaus Pevsner mentions the Wilbeck Library, the decorations by Henry Wilson, 1896, and calls the inglenook and the fireplace "as charming as anything which that movement of English 'Art Nouveau' or English revolt from period imitation produced."[25]

*

Art Nouveau was, and remained, in Great Britain almost entirely a purely Scottish phenomenon.

Admittedly the periodical *The Studio* endeavoured to stimulate interest

[24] Nikolaus Pevsner says of this church that it has "a charm almost Art Nouveau." N. Pevsner, *London. The Buildings of England,* London 1952, p. 244. The author is indebted to Nikolaus Pevsner for help and information in the question of the relationship between the Arts and Crafts Movement and Art Nouveau.

[25] N. Pevsner, Nottinghamshire, *The Buildings of England,* London 1951, p. 198.

in the decorative arts through the medium of competitions, and gradually, as the Art Nouveau style became an international phenomenon in the latter half of the 1890's, one finds Art Nouveau-inspired designs for applied arts constantly cropping up in this enlightened and wideawake periodical. But in its wider context, and especially in relation to developments on the Continent, this is hardly large enough in its scope to be discussed here.

SCOTLAND

The Glasgow school is the result of a great many intersecting trends: the Arts and Crafts Movement and its striving for renewal, the pre-Raphaelite School and the literary and symbolical tendencies, the refined art of Japan, the Celtic revival with its nationalistic urge, and the formal reaction which was a part of the age. With the appearance on the contemporary scene of an artistic personality of the stature of Mackintosh, Scotland had got an architect who with great creative power seized upon the tendencies of the age, giving them independent form. He and his contemporaries helped to mould what we are justified in calling a separate trend or school—the Glasgow school, the Scottish Art Nouveau.

The reason why Glasgow became its centre may be explained, as Thomas Howarth points out, by the fact that at this time there was a great deal of artistic activity in Glasgow. The Glasgow Art Institute was founded in 1879, and at the beginning of the 1880's an active group of painters emerged, the so-called "Boys from Glasgow," and in 1885 the young and energetic Englishman Francis H. Newbery (1854–1946)[1] was appointed headmaster of the Glasgow School of Art. He had been trained in South Kensington in London, and naturally was acquainted with the Arts and Crafts Movement in the beginning of the 1880's. He taught among other subjects applied arts.[2]

1 T. Howarth, *Charles Rennie Mackintosh and the Modern Movement,* London 1952; *Who was Who,* vol. IV, 1941–50, London 1952.

2 ". . . this season they (Newbery's lectures) will deal more with the Arts and Crafts." Notice in *The Studio,* vol. II, 1894, p. 73.

Thomas Howarth has dealt with the Glasgow school, its leading artist, Charles Rennie Mackintosh (1868–1928), and the school's links with the Continent, in such a way that there is little or nothing to add. But for the sake of continuity, and in order to present a *vue d'ensemble*, it might be as well to recapitulate briefly the most important events. This review will essentially be based on Thomas Howarth's book, *Charles Rennie Mackintosh and the Modern Movement.*

Mackintosh was working as an architect in 1889. The two others in the group who formed the inner circle were the sisters Margaret and Frances Macdonald (1865–1933, 1874–1921), the first of whom married Mackintosh, while the other married Herbert MacNair, who forms the fourth in this group. The sisters were mentioned for the first time in the annals of the school in 1891; and in 1893–94 "the Four" were hard at work with their linear drawings and posters. If we add the name of Jessie Newbery (1864–), the wife of Francis Newbery, and a teacher in embroidery from 1894–1908, one gets an idea of how intimately associated they were. More apart and less important is Talwin Morris (1865–1911).

The painters of the Glasgow school had close contacts with Germany and Austria, as well as Belgium, but not with France, and when the Glasgow School of Art was invited by *l'Oeuvre Artistique* in 1895 to take part in an exhibition in Liége, three crates of exhibition material were sent over in that year, comprising all the sections of the school. The furniture design of the school was at this time primarily influenced by the simplicity of the Arts and Crafts Movement, and showed the characteristic use of heavy mountings, and plain undecorated surfaces, occasionally relieved by an ornament which was modest in its scope but unerringly placed.

The exhibition was well received in Belgium, and we are fortunate in having the opinion of one of Belgium's leading architects of the 1890's, Paul Hankar, on the exhibition. He writes:

"Le règne de la sacro-sainte Renaissance n'est plus. . . . Cette impression se dégage surtout fortement de l'envoi considérable (110 pièces) de l'Ecole des Beaux Arts de Glasgow, dirigé par M. Francis Newbery. Dessins d'architecture, tissus, papiers peints, affiches, vitraux, tapis, ouvrages en metal, sortis de l'observation personnel des arts du passé et surtout de la nature. Enseignement éminemment pratique. Les élèves concourent tous les ans pour l'exécution d'une affiche annonçant l'exposition de leurs œuvres. Il y en a deux exemples devant lesquels je défie le passant de ne pas s'arrêter. . . . Il serait vraiment à désirer que l'on envoyât étudier cette exposition par tous les directeurs de ces usines à poncifs que nous appelons en Belgique Académie des Beaux-Arts."[3]

Hankar's appreciation is characteristic, not least his outburst on the subject of the posters. There were also a number of Englishmen exhibiting, among them Burne Jones, Ashbee, Crane, William Morris, Townsend, and Heywood Sumner. The criticism in this case was more mixed, and of Crane Hankar says, "Il reste un peu trop illustrateur"—"Ses peintures sont d'un ton bien désagréable et bien fatiguées."[4]

In the following year the Scottish group exhibited with far less success in the Arts and Crafts Exhibition Society's exhibition in London.[5] The Newberys, the Macdonald sisters, and Mackintosh were represented, the three last mentioned showing metalwork, while Mackintosh included a hall settle.[6] Mackintosh's metalwork carried typical inscriptions, thus a panel in beaten brass bore the legend: "Art and Literature seeking Inspiration at the Tree of Knowledge and Beauty,"[7] and on one of the panels it is possible to read "Part seen, imagined Part."[8] These inscriptions are highly indicative of the contemporary symbolism and the feeling of the unity of the arts.

3 P. Hankar, Exposition d'art appliqué, Mai 1895, *l'Emulation,* vol. XX, 1895, col. 65–69. "The reign of the sacred Renaissance is no longer. . . . This impression emerges with great force from the considerable contribution (110 pieces) of the Glasgow School of Art, of which Mr. Francis Newbery is the head. Architectural drawings, materials, painted paper, posters, window-panes, tapestries, metalwork, resulting from personal observation of the arts of the past and especially of Nature. Eminently practical teaching. The pupils compete every year in working out a poster advertising an exhibition of their work. There are two examples of these before which I defy the passer-by not to stop. . . . It would be highly desirable if this exhibition could be studied by all the heads of the "drawing factories" which in Belgium are known as Academies of Fine Arts."

4 *Ibid.,* "He remains a little too much of an illustrator"—"His paintings are very disagreeable in tone and very tiresome."

5 The Arts and Crafts Exhibition, *The Studio,* vol. IX, 1896–97, pp. 50–62, 117–34, 189–204, 262–85.

6 *Arts and Crafts Exhibition Society, Catalogue 1896,* London 1896, No. 509, ill., *The Studio,* vol. IX, 1896–97, p. 205.

7 *Arts and Crafts Exhibition Society Catalogue, 1896,* London 1896, No. 504.

8 *Ibid.*. No. 589.

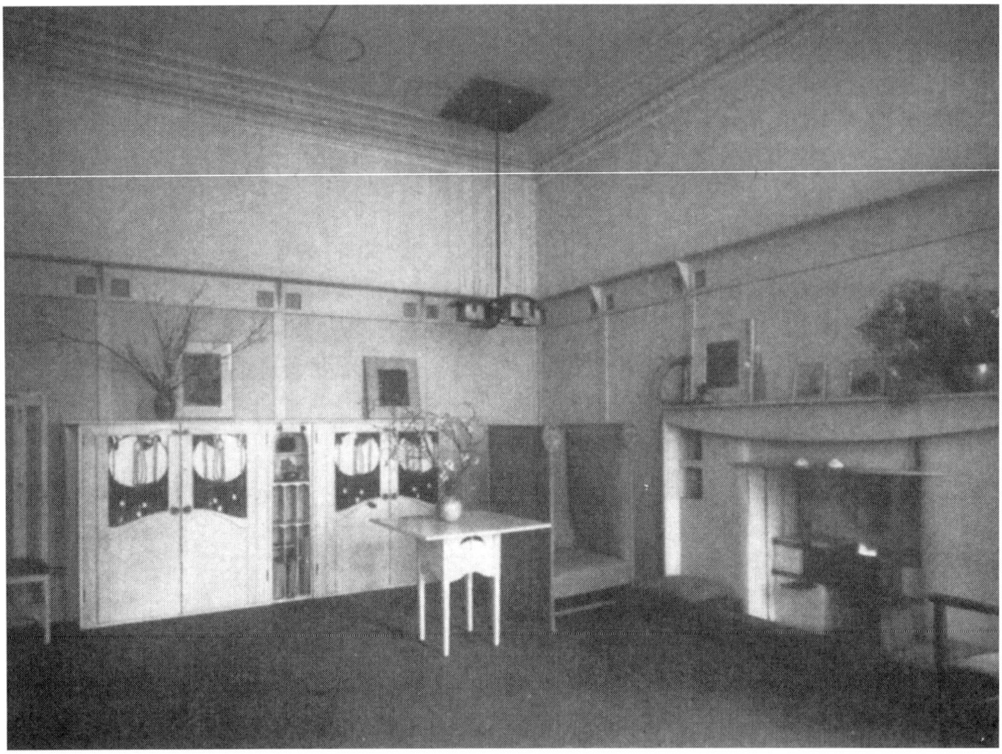

Fig. 158. Mackintosh: The drawing room. 120 Mains Street, Glasgow, 1900.

"The Four" constituted in the middle of the 1890's a distinct group, with a personal form-language, and well into the 1890's they still remained an isolated phenomenon—a Scottish phenomenon—exercising very little influence on the general development in the rest of Great Britain. Even Gleeson White's four very positive articles in *The Studio* in 1897 hardly appear to have inspired anyone in England to follow the example of the Scottish School.

In the following years Mackintosh carried out his decorative *chefs d'oeuvre*, Miss Cranston's tearooms—The Buchanan Street Tearoom—together with George Walton, 1896–97; the Argyle Street Tearoom in 1897, also with Walton, while the Ingram Street Tearoom, 1901, and the Willow Tearoom in Sauchiehall Street, 1903–04, were entirely his own work, as

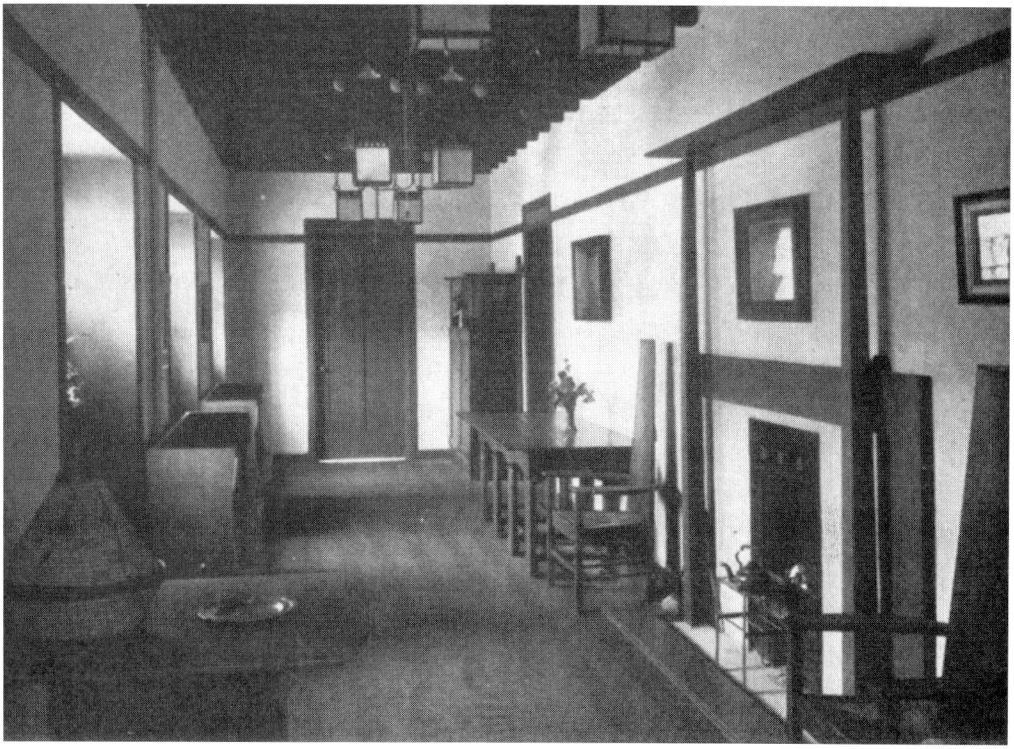

Fig. 159. Mackintosh: The Hall, Windy Hill. 1899–1901.

were the designs for *Haus eines Kunstfreundes* in 1901 and the music room for Wärndorfer, in Vienna, at the end of the 1890's. His architectural *chefs d'oeuvre* are the Glasgow School of Art, Glasgow, 1897–99, 1907–09, Windy Hill, Kilmacholm, 1899–1901, and the Hill House, Helensburgh, 1902–03.

In the decorative *chefs d'oeuvre* one appears to be faced with a stylistic dualism: Mackintosh moved with great ease and confidence from the brittlest linear rhythm, which literally hovers in a world of olive-green and ivory white harmonies, to the most ponderous cubes which constitute integral elements in a system of rectilinear surfaces of dark-green and black.

The spritely linear style is familiar to us from *Haus eines Kunstfreundes*, and it also appears fully in his own flat in 120 Mains Street, Glasgow, 1900 (fig. 158). The general impression which the room gives is one of light and airiness, the result of choice of colour and furnishing: the walls were pale grey, the floor was covered with a pale grey carpet; the ceiling, the friezes, the fireplace, the two tables, the bookshelf, and several of the chairs were white. The decorative accent was provided by the small square panels in rose-coloured gesso: the Scottish School never allows the decoration to overflow and take possession of the entire object, as is done in Continental Art Nouveau. As with the English artists, this is one of their foremost decorative principles, and is a natural result of the relentless struggle of the Arts and Crafts Movement to achieve a simple, austere decoration. Once the victory had been achieved, and furniture had been pruned of the extravagances of Historicism, ornament was limited to a strictly "bound" and restrained form.

We can see also how Mackintosh follows up his principle from the first tearooms, combining furniture and decorative elements to produce a unified impression. The critics have discussed the origin of the light-coloured tones, and wondered from whom it was introduced.[9] In this connection Voysey's use of pale hues can hardly be overestimated, but the changed attitude to colour goes back originally to William Morris, who broke away so radically from the principles of his age, for instance going so far as to paint furniture and part of the interior in the Red House white. We should also take into account the importance of Japanese influence in Mackintosh's use of light and airy furnishing. There is direct evidence of this in his drawingroom, with the many Japanese prints on the walls, as well as in the oriental style of flower arrangements.

The panel, which in the typical fashion of the 1890's stretches a good way up the wall, is composed of vertical and horizontal elements. When Mackintosh designed a room the main accent characteristically enough was provided by the interplay between verticals and horizontals. The faintly arched lines are subordinate to a fixed rectilinear frame, in the table just as much as in the mantelpiece and the bookshelves. Only in a few places does he give free rein to ornament, e.g. in the cupboard doors with their oval white panels, but here, too, the décor is framed in a network of horizontals and verticals. In each corner four cubic lamps hang from thin vertical wires.

9 *Journal of the Royal Institute of British Architects,* vol. IL, 1942, pp. 94–95.

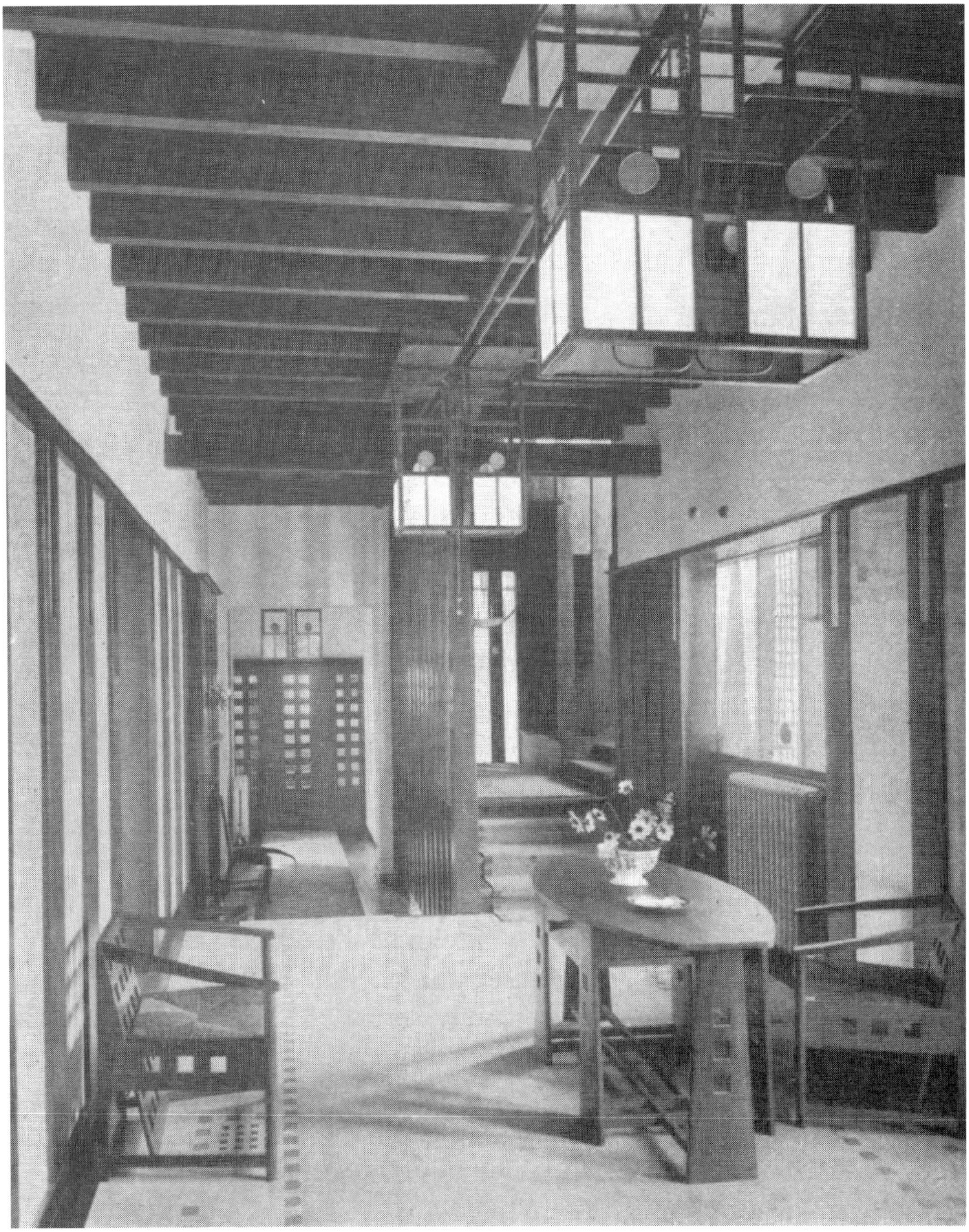

Fig. 160. Mackintosh: The Hall, Hill House, Helensburgh. 1902–1903.

The ornament has been restrained and subordinated to the general impression, no longer existing for its own sake, but as part of a larger whole. Mackintosh, the poster artist and fanciful designer, is here playing second fiddle to Mackintosh the architect and interior decorator. The development of the two-dimensional to the three-dimensional is complete.

But Mackintosh is also capable of striking deeper and darker chords in his interior decoration, and at the same time of working in an entirely rectilinear style. The dining room of his own house, for example, has dark brown panels with stained black and bees-waxed furniture. "Mackintosh's objective here was to create a sombre mysterious setting for what to him was a most important ritual—eating and drinking."[10] It is only a short step to Symbolism from here. There is one thing, however, which is identical in both rooms: the unity of the interior, both having their special function and mood—and every detail being subordinate to it.

The hall in Windy Hill, 1899–1901 (fig. 159), shows how much he can accomplish in the sober undecorated arts and crafts style, while the hall in the Hill House, 1902–03 (fig. 160), shows that rectilinearism in itself had become an end. Rectilinearism is no longer merely sober and simple, but has become an essential decorative element. The bedroom, on the other hand (fig. 70), is conceived in the pale and softer style, though here too, the rectilinear element plays an important role.

This interesting dualism in no way indicates any split in Mackintosh's art. In his mature style the slight curve and the pliant line, as well as all the other decorative features we have seen, are only elements of a larger entity, with the emphasis on the practical and the relevant, and combined with an unerring interplay between ornament and surface.

One of the most striking features about Mackintosh is that he is not only one of Great Britain's most revolutionary architects in the 19th century, and a pioneer of the Modern Movement, but at the same time the most sophisticated decorator and interior designer in Great Britain in the1890's (fig. 161).

It is easy for the architect to sidestep the problems of interior decoration and few men excel in this field: some subordinate it to the constructive element or merely follow fashion, others are content to pass on the responsi-

[10] T. Howarth, *Charles Rennie Mackintosh and the Modern Movement,* London 1952, p. 45, pl. 15 A.

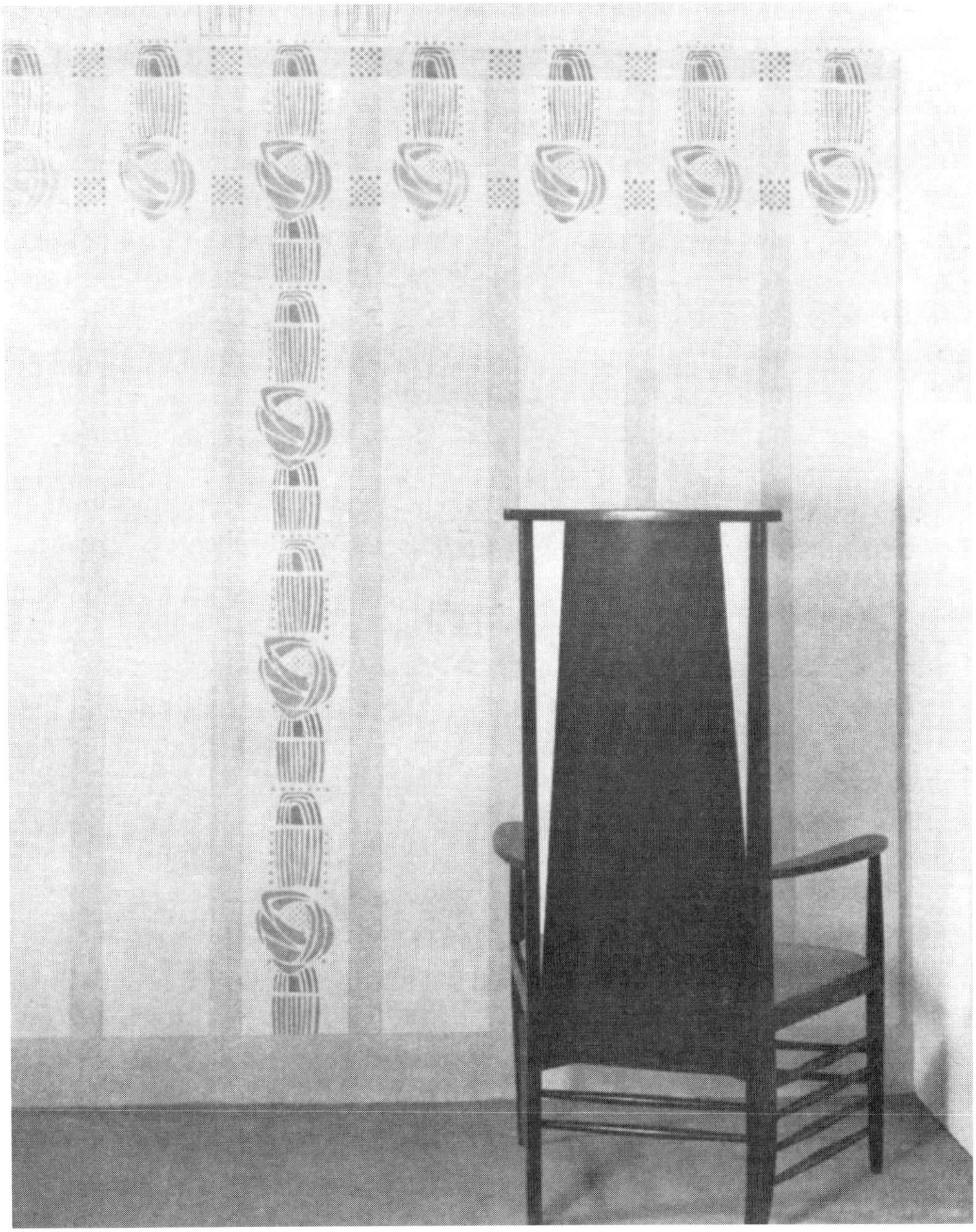

Fig. 161. Mackintosh: Chair and decoration for the Hill House, Helensburgh. 1902–1903.
Pattern: Olive, light grey and pink on white. Victoria and Albert Museum photo. Crown Copyright reserved.

bility to self styled "interior decorators" or commercial firms. Mackintosh, however, was more successful probably than any of his contemporaries, and he mastered the art.

The Glasgow School of Art (fig. 162) and its importance in architecture have been dealt with at great length by Thomas Howarth, and it is interesting to note that the decoration is of secondary importance, though all the small touches are in evidence. The main entrance is asymmetrically constructed, a feature which may possibly be traced back to the Gothic revival with its conception of the rational element of medieval architecture: we can see how the staircase and window are placed. The markedly plastic treatment of the building itself can probably best be explained by the neo-Baroque conception of form typical of the age, and Mackintosh, too, has a large Baroque-like arch on the first floor.

The work of the other members of the group (fig. 163) is of secondary importance, compared to Mackintosh. The most prominent were the Macdonald sisters, who were especially noted for their metalwork (figs. 164a, b). Mention has already been made of the elongated willowy figures of weeping women, the expressive movements of the hands, the symbolical contents, the text, etc., neatly framed in the panel, and characterised by rows of thin vertical lines. A painting by Margaret makes the picture of their two-dimensional art clearer (fig. 165). It was this art which caused Meier-Graefe to exclaim: "In Glasgow verlor die englische Kunst das Hermaphroditentum. Sie ging in die Hände der Frauen über."[11]

In 1898 Jessie Newbery formulated her decorative principles in eleven maxims, which might also be said to apply to the other women in the School: "I believe in everything being beautiful, pleasant, and if need be, useful. To descend to particulars, I like the opposition of straight lines to curved, of horizontal to vertical; of purple to green, of green to blue. I delight in correspondence and the inevitable relation of part to part."[12]

[11] J. Meier-Graefe, *Entwicklungsgeschichte der modernen Kunst,* I–III, Stuttgart, 1904–05, vol. II, p. 620. "In Glasgow English art was no longer hermaphrodite but passed into the hands of women."

[12] G. White, Some Glasgow Designers, Part III, *The Studio,* vol. XII, 1898, p. 48. There is nothing especially new in her maxims, but it is interesting to see the decorative principles of the time, so clearly put into words, particularly her feelings for opposition of straight lines to curved, which contrasts with Chr. Dresser's view. See "Cult of plant and Line," note 26.

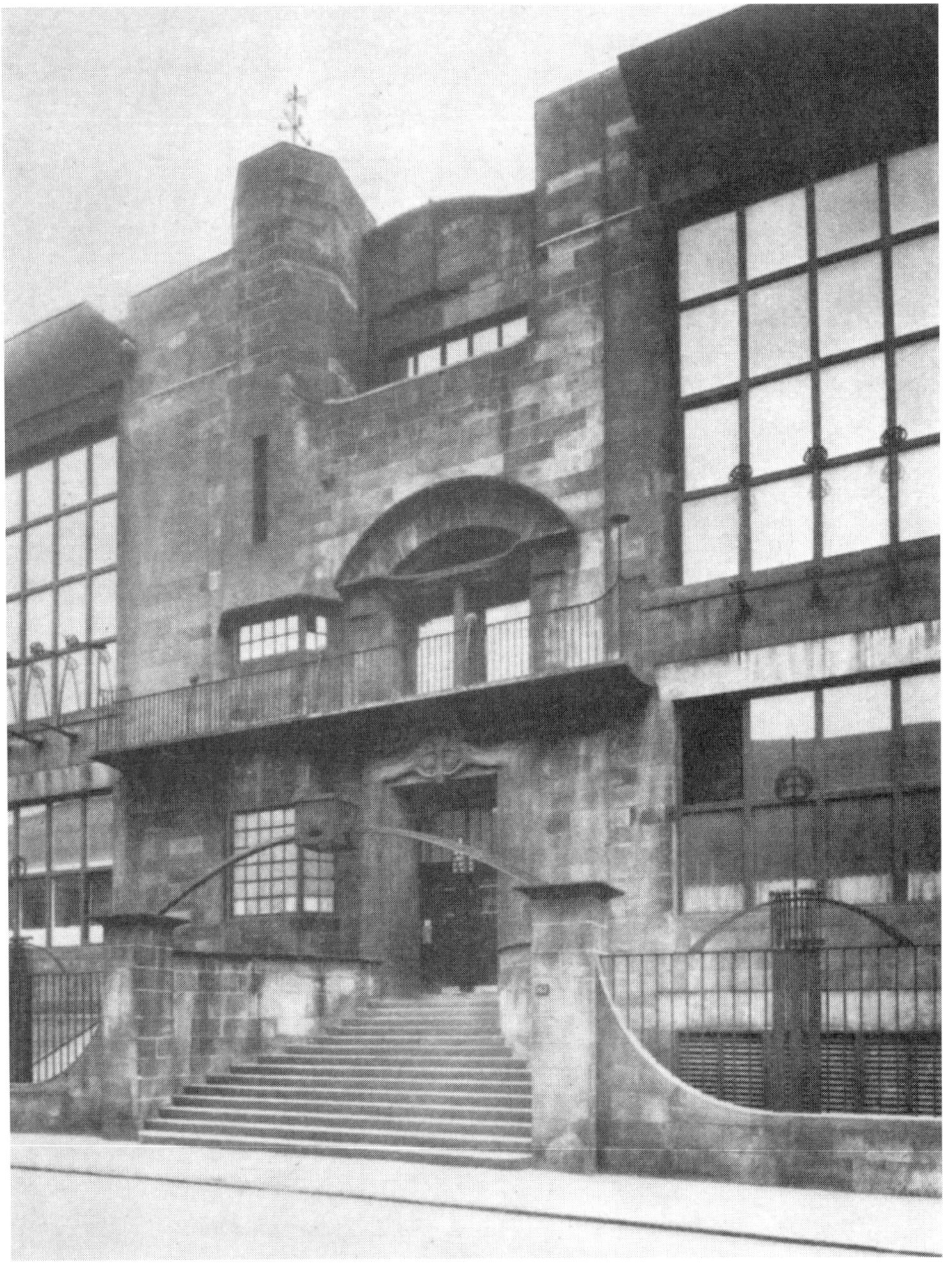

Fig. 162. Mackintosh: Glasgow School of Art. North facade and main entrance. 1897–99.

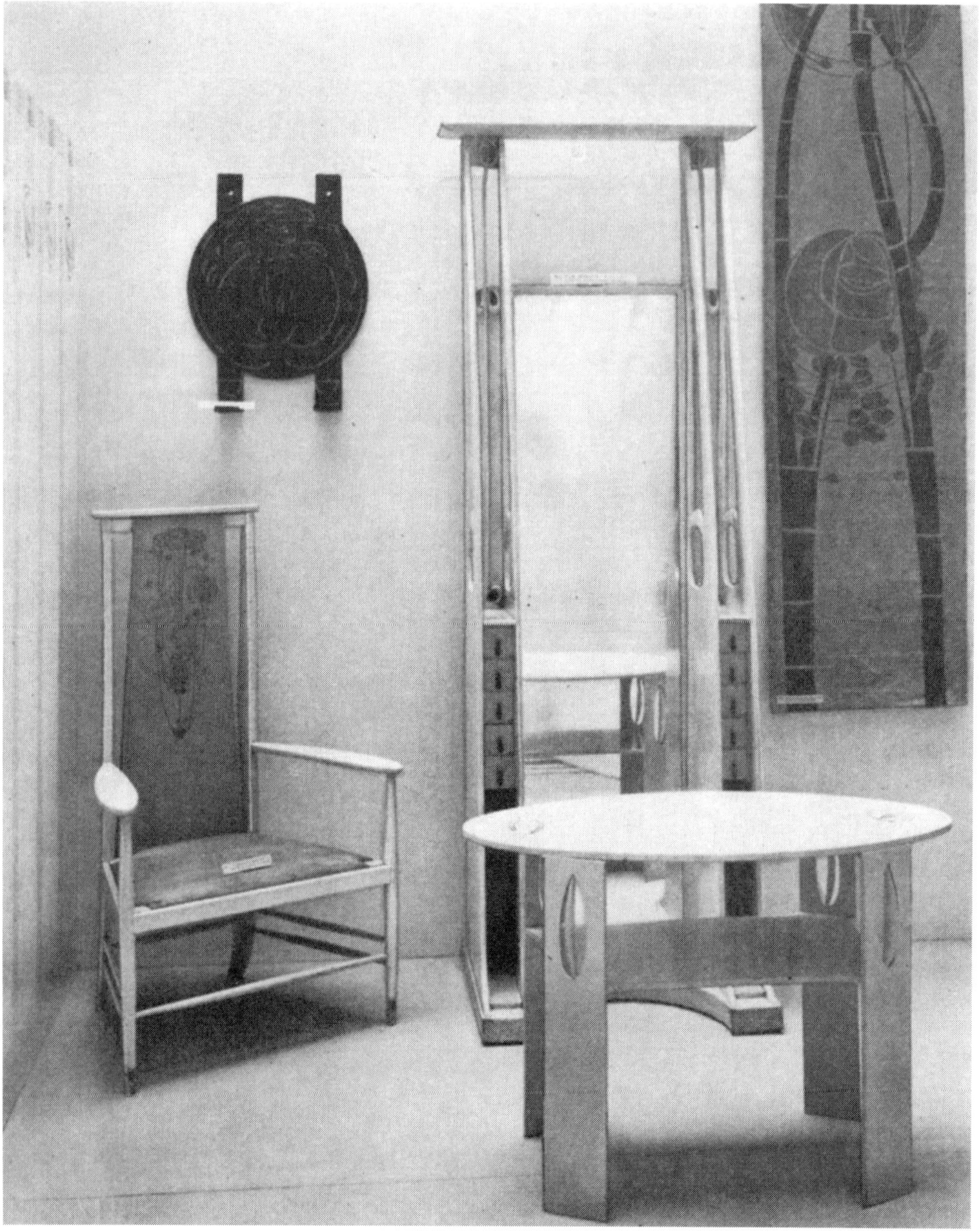

Fig. 163. Furniture made by the Mackintosh Group. 1896–1903.
Victoria and Albert Museum photo. Crown Copyright reserved.

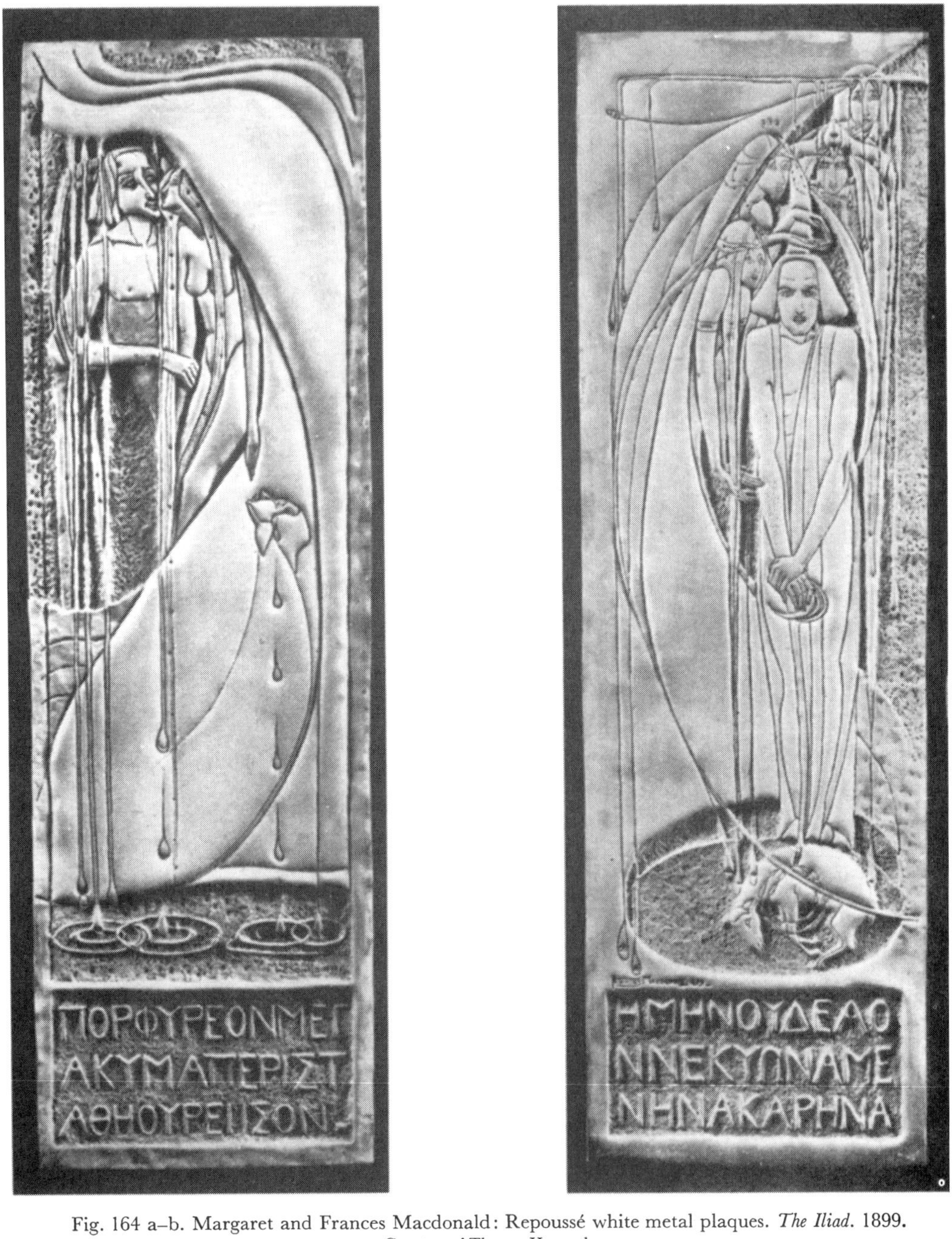

Fig. 164 a–b. Margaret and Frances Macdonald: Repoussé white metal plaques. *The Iliad*. 1899.
Courtesy of Thomas Howarth.

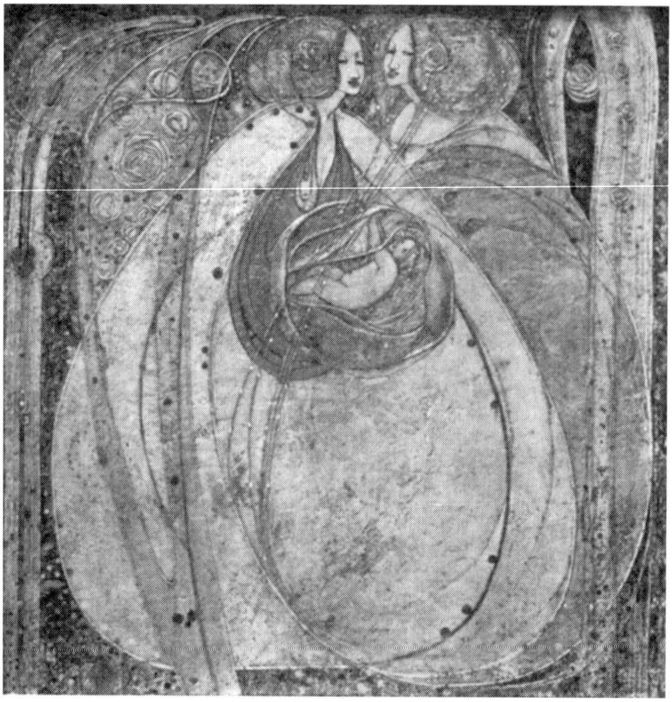

Fig. 165. Margaret Macdonald: Panel. Painted gesso. 1902. The Glasgow School of Art, Glasgow.
Victoria and Albert Museum photo. Crown Copyright reserved.

Talwin Morris represents a more masculine aspect, and one closer to the Arts and Crafts (fig. 166).

As far as the use of the square and the rectangle is concerned, and their decorative value, the natural tendency is to regard them as a development based on the linear play of construction. The interest of the Arts and Crafts Movement in the constructive—in frames and panels—has also probably been a contributing factor as far as furniture design is concerned, together with the rectangularity of Japanese work. Austrian artists, who had close contacts with the Scottish School, adopted this style, and in the hands of Josef Hoffmann it developed into a most cherished motif in the years around 1900.

The Glasgow school was known relatively late on the Continent. In November 1898 the works of "the Four" were published for the first time in a foreign periodical, in an article in *Dekorative Kunst*, Munich, and in May of the subsequent year their work was once more discussed in the same

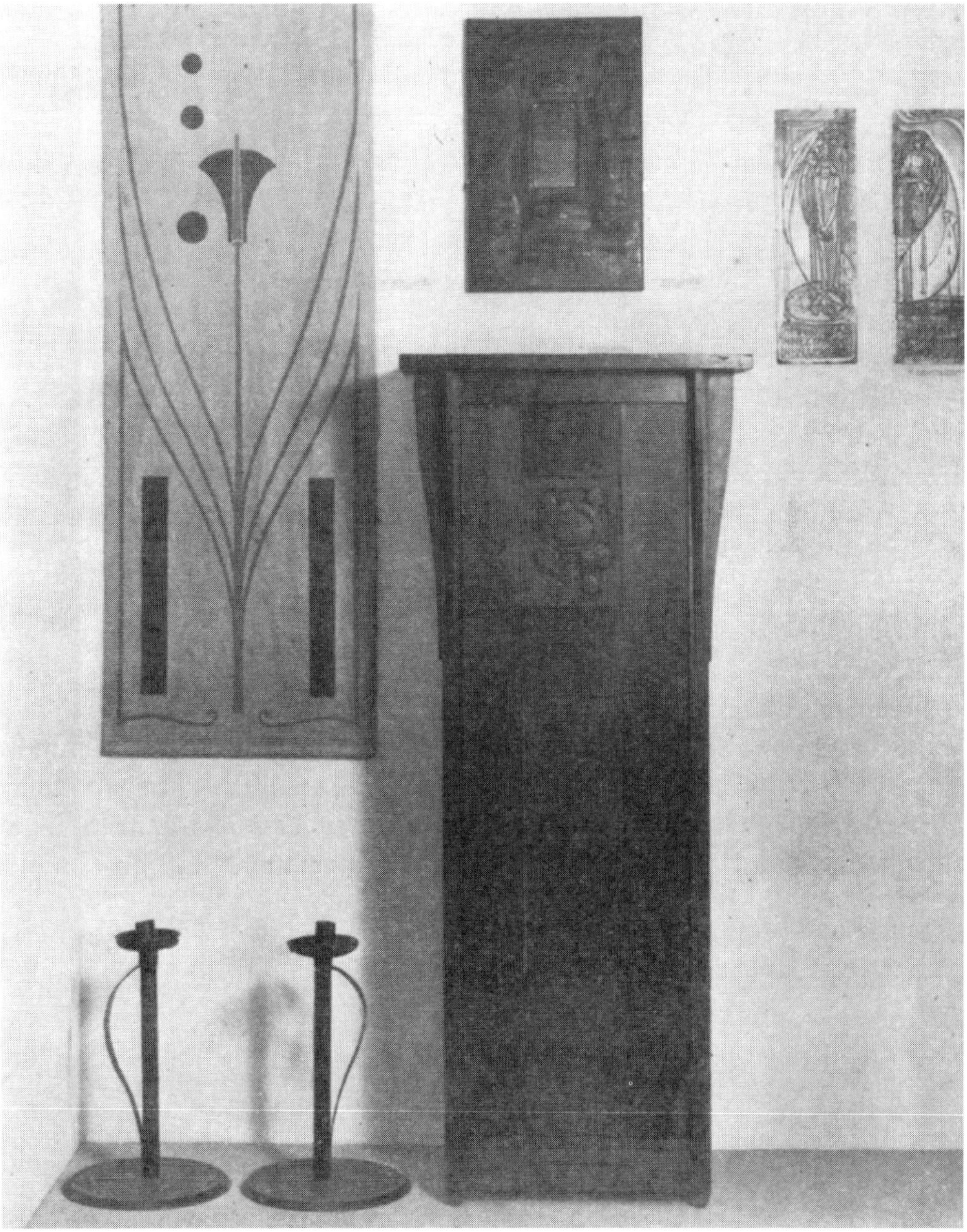

Fig. 166. Talwin Morris: Cupboard, mirror and blind.
Glasgow Museum and Art Gallery. Victoria and Albert Museum photo. Crown Copyright reserved.

periodical. In 1900 they participated with great success in the Viennese Exhibition, in 1901 in Dresden, and in the subsequent year we find them in Turin, as successful as ever, to be followed in a short space of time by exhibitions in Venice, Budapest, and Dresden once again, the last exhibition being probably in the year 1903. According to Thomas Howarth they also visited Berlin shortly afterwards.[13] After an interval of several years there also seems to have been an exhibition in Moscow in 1913.

They never came to France, nor did they exert any influence on French design. *L'Art Décoratif* contained an article on the group in 1898,[14] but the Scottish style was not suitable to Paris. In his book *De la Tamise à la Sprée. L'Essor des Industries d'Art*, 1905, B. E. Kalas specifically mentions this.

The importance of the group gradually decreased for a great many reasons. As Thomas Howarth points out Mackintosh was after all no real leader, and as a writer he lacked distinction. The group had no clear programme, no common goal, and there was no intellectual personality capable of assisting them. For this reason they never started any "movement" in the real sense of the word, such as we find in Belgium, Germany, and Austria.

Besides, battle had been joined, and just after the turn of the century the development in Germany and Austria had proceeded so far that the role of Art Nouveau had already been played out: the decorative play of the Glasgow school was already *passé* among those in the forefront of the battle, and in architecture the Modern Movement had gone much further on the Continent.

But how was it that Mackintosh's style exercised no real influence on the development in England itself, and that it never received an *entrée* into Continental Art Nouveau?

13 T. Howarth, *op. cit.*, p. 168. See also *Dictionary of National Biography*, 1922–30, London 1937. (P. Morton Shand.) 1903 seems most likely, when Baillie Scott also exhibited in Berlin.

14 *L'Art Décoratif*, vol. I, 1898, pp. 53–54, 71–77, 18 ills.

ECLIPSE

While Mackintosh was acclaimed in Austria, Germany, and Italy, in England itself forces arrayed themselves against this style: so effective was the attack that was launched against it, and so numerous the many important artists to be found in the van, that, whatever chances the style might have had of establishing itself, it was now clearly doomed.

In the year 1900, when Art Nouveau was enjoying its greatest triumphs at the Paris Exhibition, the position in England was as follows: that year the Englishman George Donaldson was acting as vice-president of the jury in Class 69—furniture—at the Paris Exhibition. On June 28 he wrote to the Victoria and Albert Museum, offering a gift of several thousand pounds. In the letter in which this offer was made, he wrote:

"I am, therefore, in a position to state, that in my opinion, the New Art Movement has taken a firm hold in Europe, and that in most cases, superior ingenuity and taste are displayed than that shown in our own production.

"However much this New Art may conflict with our Classical standards or ideas of architectural basis, I am forced to the conclusion that we are in the presence of a distinct development. Where it will lead to none can foretell. But, in these competitive days, . . . it occurs to me that it is of great importance to our people that the best models of the style called 'New Art' should be purchased and placed before them."[1]

The directors accepted this generous offer, little realising, no doubt, the complications which were to ensue. In the course of December 1900 most of the furniture had been acquired: it was a considerable collection, comprising about twenty French pieces of furniture, the work of leading designers and firms. Apart from these a further ten pieces—some of them Hungarian and some of them Norwegian—subsequently arrived.

It was soon decided to exhibit the new acquisitions, and in the middle of the summer of 1901 Englishmen for the first time had a chance of getting

[1] Victoria and Albert Museum, Registry 1900. File No. 130.

a glimpse of Continental Art Nouveau through the medium of an exhibition arranged in the Victoria and Albert Museum. But even before the exhibition was opened opposition to it came to light, and as so frequently happens when the English feel that one of their dearest traditions is seriously menaced, recourse was had to the columns of *The Times*. On April 15, 1901, the following letter to the editor appeared in this venerable daily:

To the Editor of The Times,

Sir,—It is much to be regretted that the authorities of South Kensington have introduced into the Museum specimens of the work styled "l'Art Nouveau."

This work is neither right in principle nor does it evince a proper regard for the material employed. As cabinet maker's work it is badly executed. It represents only a trick of design which, developed from debased forms, has prejudicially affected the design of furniture and buildings in neighbouring countries.

In its present position it is in danger of being looked upon as a recognised model which has received the approval of the authorities for study by students and designers, and the harm it may thus produce on our national art cannot be easily gauged.

We, the undersigned, desire publicly to protest against its importation at South Kensington, and most strongly against its recommendation by the authorities to the notice of furniture makers and others.

We are, Sir, Yours faithfully,

John Belcher, A.R.A.
Reginald Blomfield
Mervyn Macartney
Edward S. Prior

The opposition could not have revealed itself more clearly, but in the meantime a number of institutions had become interested in the exhibition, among them the Museum of Science and Art in Edinburgh, the Science and Art Institutions in Dublin, and at a subsequent date the Birmingham Industrial Polytechnic Exhibition; and the idea was to allow the exhibition to tour England.

The Board of Education, South Kensington, which had formally accepted the gift, regarded themselves as obliged on July 12 to issue a memorandum to the various bodies destined to receive the exhibition, which contained the following:

"Much of the modern Continental furniture however exhibits a style which is not consistent with the teaching at Art Schools of the United Kingdom. It is therefore necessary that students inspecting the examples in this collection should be guided, in forming an opinion as to their merits and obvious faults, by instructors who have given attention to such subjects as Historic Ornament, Principles of Ornament, and Architecture."

Young students, so it appeared, must not be corrupted, and the collection seems after a while to have been regarded more or less as a sort of travelling warning. At the same time, too, the technical journals launched an attack on the exhibition and the style of furniture it represented. *The Builder* said: "It is a gift of worse than doubtful value. Hitherto the modern English School of furniture design has kept free from these extravagances, . . . Now the examples of the bad and tawdry stuff which is called 'New Art' furniture receive the *imprimatur* [*sic*] of the National Art Museum; . . ."[2] *The Journal of Decorative Art*, which had not been particularly sympathetic to the Art Nouveau style at the Paris Exhibition the year before, rallied to the support of its colleague with the following: "No greater disservice has been done to the cause of true art education for a long while past in this country than the acceptance by the authorities at South Kensington of the gift by Mr. George Donaldson."[3]

It is more than understandable that the generous George Donaldson felt a little hurt at the way in which his gift had been received, and the editor of *The Magazine of Art* came to his defence in a letter to *The Times* on August 14, in which the noble nature of Mr. Donaldson's intentions was praised, intentions which Donaldson himself had formulated as follows:

"I venture to think that this selection of 'New Art' furniture demonstrates at least that there are forms and combinations of line, colour, and materials not hitherto dreamt of in the philosophy of English designers

2 *Ibid.*
3 *The Journal of Decorative Art,* vol. XXI, 1901, p. 197.

and producers of furniture, and I have performed what I felt to be a duty in placing these things before them."[4]

Understanding for the donor and the style was shown, e.g. in the *Morning Leader*,[5] but with leading artists and critics forming a compact and influential mass there was no chance of the style being popularised. Walter Crane was not particularly well disposed towards the style, which he describes as this "strange decorative disease known as 'l'Art Nouveau', which some writers have actually asserted was the offspring of what properly considered was really its antithesis—the Morris school of decoration."[6] "I see rather a kind of invention in this than a new interpretation of nature, . . ." he says somewhere else.[7] Lewis Day tells us that "when we speak in this country of the 'new Art' it is with an inflection of irony in our voice;" and he continues, "It shows symptoms not of too exuberant life, but of pronounced disease."[8] Lewis Day repeats his attack on the style in *Macmillan's Magazine* and *The British Architect* (June) of the following year.[9] Everywhere reaction is encountered, and Beardsley's friend Arthur Symons calls the style "a feeble dilettante in bric-à-brac,"[10] and in Waring and Gillow's *Our Homes and How to Beautify Them*, 1902, it received a fearful broadside in the chapter entitled "l'Art Nouveau on the Continent."

Against such compact resistance Art Nouveau had little chance of gaining popularity, the more so as its linear rhythm was well known and tested in proto-Art Nouveau, without finding much response. This was hardly likely to stimulate interest in an age when everything had to be "something new."

But the deepest reason is to be found—as is obvious from the opinions quoted—in the actual developments of the English Arts and Crafts. A great deal of trouble had been taken to move away from Historicism, and a simple sober style of furniture had been evolved, on traditional grounds,

4 G. Donaldson, Gift of "New Art" furniture for circulation, *The Magazine of Art,* vol. XXV, 1900, pp. 466–71 (471).

5 *The Journal of Decorative Art,* vol. XXI, 1901, p. 237.

6 W. Crane, *William Morris to Whistler,* London 1911, p. 232.

7 *Idem,* Moot-Points, London, 1903, p. 82 sq.

8 L. F. Day, l'Art Nouveau, *The Art Journal,* October 1900, pp. 293–317 (295).

9 *Idem,* The New Art, *Macmillans Magazine,* November 1901, No. 505, pp. 19–23.

10 A. Symons, The Decay of Craftmanship in England, *Studies in Seven Arts,* London 1906, pp. 175–88.

and based on sound simple constructive principles, partly of a rectilinear nature. It is easy, therefore, to understand that the Continental Art Nouveau, with its floral decoration, its soft lines, and the French apparent lack of construction, found no ready response and failed to gain admittance.

*

England had helped to provide the precursors of this style, and to prepare the ground, and on the Continent the English influence was considerable, but the Continental fruit was clearly not for consumption in England.

THE BRITISH INFLUENCE

"The whole of our movement," says Herman Muthesius in 1904, "is based on the results England achieved from 1860 and up to the middle of the 1890's"[1]—and on the Continent Herman Muthesius was the one most familiar with the situation, both as far as the development in England was concerned and its associations with the Continent.

Names such as the *Modern Style*, *Style Liberty*, and *Stile Inglese* show us that this influence was generally recognised, and an art critic writing after his return from Italy in 1901 says ". . . the great source of its (Stile Inglese) inspiration unblushingly is confessed to be the *Studio Magazine*."[2] *The Studio* was the first of that wave of periodicals which swept across the countries during the following years, achieving a circulation and influence on the Continent which it is difficult for us to understand today. But the country which probably had the closest cultural connections with England during the 1880's and 1890's was Belgium.

The internationally-minded Whistler had exhibited with *Les XX* every year from 1884, and Octave Maus says that the contact with Anglo-Saxon artists and Whistler's influence found their expression not only in art but also in interior decoration and even in dress.[3] In 1892 the English exhibited

1 H. Muthesius, *Das Englische Haus,* I–III, Berlin 1904–05, vol. I, p. 179.

2 *The Journal of Decorative Art,* vol. XXI, 1901, p. 237.

3 O. Maus, *Trente Années de Lutte pour l'Art. 1884–1914,* Brussels 1926, p. 41.

in Brussels for the first time; in 1893 Ford Madox Brown was represented, in 1894 Ashbee, Image, Heywood Sumner, William Morris, and Beardsley; the latter had twelve drawings from *Salomé* and *Morte d'Arthur*. In the same year Crane also exhibited in the *Circle Artistique*,[4] and the next year, 1895, we find precisely the same group, with the addition of Voysey and Crane, exhibiting with *Les XX*—now transformed to *La Libre Esthétique*—as well as the Glasgow School at Liége. In 1897 we once more find Voysey, Fisher, and Morris's furniture designer George Jack (1855–1932), as well as the potter William de Morgan (1839–1917) exhibiting at *La Libre Esthétique*. Artists who were interested in the Arts and Crafts Movement, contributed every time, as well as others who had to a certain extent worked in proto-Art Nouveau. In 1896 van de Velde exhibited what he called "une salle de five o'clock."[5] The English contact was clear enough!

In 1881 Paul Dietrich and Joseph Schwarzenberg opened their art shop in Brussels, where they sold aquarelles and prints. This was the first *Librairie d'art* in Belgium. The proprietors frequently visited England, purchasing and arranging the sale of works by artists such as Heywood Sumner, Walter Crane, and Frank Brangwyn, and it is hardly surprising that in 1893 the firm became the representatives of *The Studio* when this periodical commenced publication.[6]

As Belgium's two leading art periodicals, *l'Art Moderne*, founded 1881, and the architectural periodical *l'Emulation*, 1874, clearly show, the interest in the pre-Raphaelites and William Morris was very strong; and at the beginning of the 1890's we find a number of articles on these subjects. Several articles were written on William Morris,[7] and the interest in these subjects reaching a climax in 1893. Thus in 1893 G.M., writing in *l'Emulation* on the subject of *Les Préraphaelites anglais*, says: "De toutes les influences extérieures que nous subîmes depuis vingt-cinq ans, celle de l'Angleterre apparaît la plus manifeste."[8]

4 *L'Art Moderne,* vol. XIV, 1894, p. 397.

5 Where other sources have not been given, the information is taken from O. Maus, *op. cit.* See also H. Liebaers, William Morris in Vlaanderen, *De Vlaamsche Gids,* 1946, pp. 592–97.

6 Information kindly given by Jean Schwarzenberg to the author, April 1953.

7 *L'Emulation,* vol. XVIII, 1893, cols. 136–37; *ibid.,* vol. XIX, 1894, cols. 129–36; J. Lahore, William Morris et l'art décoratif en Angleterre, *Revue Encyclopédique,* No. 89, 1894.

Finch, Toorop and Khnopff visited England, and van de Velde's studies of the English movement and his repeated recognition of the fundamental importance of Ruskin and Morris are familiar to us.[9] Already in 1893 and 1894 he had written articles on English wallpapers—where the proto-Art Nouveau emerged most clearly—and in these he evinced an excellent knowledge of English decorative art.[10]

This marked interest in England during the first half of the 1890's can also be noticed in France, where we have ample evidence that the artists themselves realised it. Henri Toulouse-Lautrec answering Henri Nocq's question about a new style declares: "Je crois qu'il n'y a qu'à regarder William Morris, pour avoir une réponse à toutes vos questions, malgré le préraphaelisme et les *reminiscences* nombreuses—cet homme a produit des livres qu'on peut lire et des objets dont on peut se servir."[11] The designer Ernest Duez says of the English influence: "D'ici quelques années, tout les intérieurs seront décorés à la mode anglaise . . . c'est n'est pas la perfection, mais, c'est déjà un progrès sur ce que nous avions jusqu'à présent."[12] Félix Régamey also expresses the same idea.[13] The use of the expression "home," which we frequently find in the work of Octave Uzanne, is also symptomatic.[14] This anglomania was so pronounced that in 1897 the writer Charles Genuys declares that the time has come to shake it off.[15]

8 *Ibid.*, vol. XVIII, 1893, cols. 168–70. "Of all outside influences which we have received during the last twenty-five years, the influence from England seems the strongest.

9 H. van de Velde, William Morris, Artisan et socialist, *L'Art Moderne*, vol. XVIII, 1898, p. 137; *idem, Renaissance im Kunstgewerbe*, Berlin 1901, Neue Ausgabe, pp. 50–57, p. 68, pp. 92 sq.; *idem, Page de Doctrine*, Brussels 1942, pp. 7–27.

10 *Idem*, Artistic Wall Papers, *l'Art Moderne*, vol. XIII, 1893, pp. 193–95, 202–204; *idem*, Essex and Co.'s Wall Papers, *ibid.*, vol. XIV, 1894, pp. 254–55.

11 H. Nocq, *Tendances Nouvelles. Enquête sur l'évolution des industries d'art*, Paris 1896, p. 46. "I believe we have only to look at William Morris to find an answer to all your questions—despite pre-Raphaelism and countless relics—this man has produced books which can be read and objects which can be used."

12 *Ibid.*, p. 37 sqq. "A few years hence all interiors will be decorated in the English fashion. . . . It is not perfection, but it is already an advance on what we have had so far."

13 *Ibid.*, p. 55 sq.

14 O. Uzanne, Notes sur le goût intime, et la décoration personelle de l'habitation moderne, *l'Art et l'Idée*, vol. II, 1892, pp. 257–76.

15 Ch. Genuys, A propos l'Art Nouveau, *Revue des Arts Décoratifs*, vol. XVII, 1897, pp. 1–6.

In 1901 France's William Morris, Jean Lahore,[16] stated that Ruskin and Morris are the precursors of Art Nouveau,[17] and speaks of an English Art Nouveau at the exhibition of 1878 more or less in the same way as Englishmen talked of a French Arts and Crafts Movement in 1896.[18]

Naturally enough Art Nouveau was considered in the same light as the Arts and Crafts Movement, and as far as France was concerned it seemed for a while at least as if Art Nouveau was precisely the solution needed to solve problems of design at the end of the century.

In Holland there is not so much written evidence of English influence, Dutch artists being less theoretical, but there was special interest in Walter Crane at the beginning of the 1890's, an interest that in the case of Dijsselhof started in 1893.[19] In the same year Jan Veth wrote his *Kunst en Samenleving naar Walter Crane.* Though written sources are not so abundant, the furniture design of this period speaks its unmistakable language. Intimately associated with that of England as it had been for centuries, advanced furniture design in the 1890's was entirely influenced by Arts and Crafts Movement, as we can see in the work of designers such as Berlage, Dijsselhof, and the pupils of Cuypers: de Bazel and Lauweriks. The main difference that can be noticed is that Dutch designers rely more on Renaissance and Medieval traditions, which is hardly surprising when we consider how strong was the position of the neo-Renaissance in Holland.

So far English influence has predominated, but in Austria and Germany the importance of the Scottish group is just as great. In 1901 Fritz Minkus writes that the English influence in Austria was greater than in any other country on the Continent; it was noticeable in social etiquette, the training of children, sport, as well as ordinary behaviour and taste and fashions generally, and, he continues, when the stagnation set in at the end of the century in Austria, the simple and practical English interior decoration and English furniture design came more and more to the fore.[20] In 1897,

16 Th. Walton, A French Disciple of William Morris "Jean Lahore," *Revue de Littérature comparée*, Paris, vol. XV, 1935, pp. 524–35.

17 J. Lahore, *L'Art Nouveau. Son histoire. L'art nouveau étranger à l'exposition. L'art nouveau au point de vue social*, Paris 1901.

18 For reference see the chapter "Name and Conception," footnote 36.

19 J. de Jong, G. W. Dijsselhof, *Nieuwerichting in de Kunstnijverheid in Nederland,* Rotterdam 1929.

20 Fritz Minkus, Oesterreich, *Die Krisis im Kunstgewerbe,* Leipzig 1901, pp. 52–61.

for instance, there was an exhibition featuring the best English furniture design.[21] The Scottish connection with Vienna is dealt with by Thomas Howarth, and has already been mentioned, as well as Mackintosh's mission in Vienna for Fritz Wärndorfer. In 1900 "the Four" participated in the Eighth Secessione Exhibition, where they were greatly admired and discussed at considerable length in such periodicals as *Ver Sacrum* and *Das Interieur.*

As far as Germany was concerned the position was more or less the same. In his book *Die Geschichte des modernen Kunstgewerbes in Deutschland*, 1908, Joseph Lux describes Ruskin and Morris's movement and the "highly peculiar and influential" art of the Mackintoshes as two of the three forerunners responsible for the renewal of Arts and Crafts in Germany. The third precursor he mentions is van de Velde. He repeatedly emphasises the importance of the Glasgow School to Germany,[22] which he declares arrived via Vienna.

Richard Graul, who was an equally prominent connoisseur of German applied art, declares that the anglomania set in in earnest after the Chicago Exhibition of 1893 "—kurz, der 'englische Stil' hat im Sinne des gesunden Menschenverstands für grössere Sachlichkeit und dekorative Einfachheit plädiert."[23] As the Germans were gradually caught up in the European Movement they were quick to introduce English art into their periodicals. In *Pan* in 1896 we find an article on *Englische Kunst im Hause*,[24] with the emphasis on artists such as Townsend, Voysey, and Crane. In the same number there is also an article on *Das englische Buch*,[25] as represented by artists such as Burne Jones, Crane, and Beardsley, and as in Austria we are frequently coming across articles on Walter Crane, who at that time was the English artist best known on the Continent. In the *Zeitschrift für Innendekoration* we also find in the years before the turn of the century a number of articles on English art, especially on Baillie Scott, Ashbee, and Crane.[26]

21 The Art Revival in Austria. Special Summer Number, *The Studio*, 1906.

22 J. A. Lux, *Die Geschichte des modernen Kunstgewerbes in Deutschland*, Leipzig 1908, p. 60, pp. 68 sq.

23 R. Graul, *Die Krisis im Kunstgewerbe*, Leipzig 1901, pp. 39–51. "In short, the 'English-style' has pleaded in the spirit of sound common sense for greater realism and decorative simplicity". (40)

24 E. von Bodenhausen, Englische Kunst im Hause, *Pan*, vol. II, 1896–97, pp. 329–36.

25 *Idem*, Das englische Buch, *ibid*, pp. 337–40.

26 *Zeitschrift für Innendekoration*, vol. IX, 1898, pp. 177–84, 186–87, vol. X, 1899, pp. 1–8, vol. XIII, 1902, pp. 177–200, vol. XIV, 1903, pp. 165–74.

*

English influence was noticeable all over the Continent, while the Scottish influence was perhaps strongest in Austria and Germany. All the time we find the same little group of artists repeatedly mentioned—Walter Crane, Burne Jones, Heywood Sumner, and Image, Voysey, Baillie Scott, Ashbee, and Townsend, as well as "the Four"; and nearly all these artists have in some way or another been in contact with English proto-Art Nouveau. But the most striking feature is that the constructive and sober principles of the Arts and Crafts Movement, and not the decorative, proved of interest, and were to prove of such fundamental importance to the development of architecture and applied art on the Continent.

This gives us an important key to the understanding of the development on the Continent just after the turn of the century—and a clue to the fate of Art Nouveau. After the British had provided the impetus for the whole of this new movement on an evolutionary basis, and contributed to the development of ornamentation, Continental artists first turned their attention to ornament, and in so doing believed that they had got hold of a style. Gradually, however, the sober, rational, and constructive principles were realised, they were assiduously cultivated, and developed until they became revolutionary ideas, and meanwhile decorative problems were relegated to a subordinate position.

Belgium

Native Soil

Belgian architecture in the 1870's and 1880's was dominated by three architects—Joseph Poelaert (1817–79), François Beyaert (1823–94), and Alphonse Balat (1818–95)—and on the whole it was markedly influenced by neo-trends, primarily neo-Baroque, often Flemish in appearance, and by a polychrome Italian neo-Renaissance. Towards the end of the century neo-Gothic had already played its role, but Dutch sandstone Renaissance was still alive.

Style trends in decorative art differed somewhat from those in architecture: in the 1870's the neo-Renaissance dominated—as in architecture—while from 1880–90 neo-Rococo exerted a powerful influence in minor applied art, entirely dominating the scene around 1890. In the following years neo-Rococo became more and more floral, showing a strong admixture of stalks and reeds, about 1893–94 the rippling undulating contours of neo-Rococo take on a more rigid appearance, and flowers disappear to be replaced by sinuous stems forming a closed shape. Here Art Nouveau emerges from neo-Rococo and the interest in plants, as is clearly shown for example in 150 drawings from the beginning of the 1890's carried out by Belgium's leading goldsmith, Philippe Wolfers.[1] In 1894–95 Art Nouveau was fully developed in applied art.

But while these trends, confined to the imitating of styles, proceeded, rational and constructive forces were also at work. In 1872 Belgian architects formed the *Société Centrale d'Architectes de Belgique*, and in 1874 they started their own mouthpiece, *l'Emulation*, which was to prove a forum for architectural discussions in Belgium, and which set the tone with a radical note. In one of the first numbers we read: "Ce que nous voudrions rencontrer dans l'architecture du XIXe siècle, c'est cet esprit de raisonnement que nous admirons dans toutes les découvertes. . . ."[2]; and Poelaert

1 Philippe Wolfers drawings, 1–50, 1001–1100, kindly put at the disposal of the author by M. Marcel Wolfers, April 1953.

2 *L'Emulation,* 1st January 1875, vol. I, 1875, col. 27. "What we should like to encounter in the architecture of the 19th century is the spirit of reasoning which we admire in all discoveries."

was attacked in 1878 for "draping" iron: "Il ment à son œuvre, car il emploie des matériaux auxquels il donnera un aspect tout différent de leur nature."[3]

There was a tremendous reaction against period styles, and an intense search for something new. In 1881 *l'Art Moderne* was started, in 1884 *Les XX* banded together, in 1892 *l'Association pour l'Art* was founded with the object of working for art exhibitions, in the same year the English crossed the Channel and exhibited for the first time, in 1894 *Pour l'art* was started to promote applied arts, in the same year *Les XX* were changed to *La Libre Esthétique*, and in 1894, too, *l'Association pour le progrès des arts décoratifs* was formed. In order to stimulate interest a number of organisations arose which dealt with the sale and purchase of art; Dietrich and Schwarzenberg's association from 1881 has already been mentioned, and *La Société Nouvelle* art organisation from 1884 might also be mentioned in this connection. In 1891 the *Maison du Peuple* received its art organisation, *Section d'art*, in 1894 *La Société l'anonyme de l'art* was founded, and on December 29th of the same year *La Maison d'art de la Toison d'or* opened its doors.

This artistic activity was followed up by a number of art periodicals, of which—*l'Emulation* and *l'Art Moderne*—where the two most important. In addition to these were *La Wallonie*, published from 1886–92, *La Basoche, Revue littéraire et artistique*, from 1884–86, *Le Reveil, Revue mensuelle de littérature et d'art*, which started publication in 1891, and *Van Nu en Straks*, which corresponds more or less to the Century Guild's *Hobby Horse*, started in 1893.

This was the position in art circles, in architecture, and in applied arts, in a country where impulses were so many and so varied. With so much going on, and with so many tendencies "in the air," it was hardly surprising that Art Nouveau should present several aspects. First we have Horta with his plant-inspired abstractions and his neo-Baroque conception of form, to which certain Louis XV and Gothic features are added; beside him stands the interior architect Gustave Serrurier-Bovy, influenced by the English school, with his simple arts-and-crafts-inspired furniture. Between these

[3] *Ibid.*, vol. IV, 1878, col. 28. "He lies in his work, because he uses materials to which he gives an aspect foreign to their nature."

two, from the point of view of form, stands Henry van de Velde, with his rational ideas and his abstract ornaments, and his English-inspired furniture design. Paul Hankar, next to Horta, is one of the leading experimental architects in the 1890's in Belgium, and in his work we find all the outstanding tendencies of the age—as well as Orientalism and polychromy.

VICTOR HORTA

Victor Horta (1861–1946)[4] was the son of a cobbler, and travelled to Paris at the age of seventeen—against his parents' wishes. He was armed with the knowledge he had gained during two years at the Academy in Ghent, the town where he was born. It is not known how long Horta stayed in Paris, but there is no doubt that these years were of the greatest importance to him.

Back again in his own country, Horta continued his training at the *Académie des Beaux Arts* in Brussels, where he was an outstanding student, leaving in 1881. It was not difficult for him to obtain a position in the office of the architect to King Leopold II, the serious-minded classicist, Alphonse Balat, best known for his *Musées Royaux des Beaux Arts* in Brussels, 1880.

Victor Horta's first commission—apart from a few minor works[5]—involved three buildings in Rue des Douze Chambres in his native town

4 C. Conrady, l'Oeuvre de Victor Horta, *Architecture,* Brussels, May–June 1948, pp. 81–85; A. Courtens, Victor Horta, *Le Document,* Brussels, 1946–47, No. 4, pp. 69–79; Jean Delhaye, Hommage à mon maître, *l'Appartement d'aujourd'hui,* Liège 1946, pp. 9–17; S. Pierron, Victor Horta, *Savoir et Beauté,* vol. IV, 1924, pp. 193–202; A. Dumont, Hommage à Victor Horta, *l'Emulation,* February 1946, No. 4, pp. 1–2; *idem,* l'Evolution de l'Architecture en Belgique. Victor Horta, *Revue des Arts Décoratifs,* vol. XIX, 1899, pp. 273–290; W. J. G. Godwin, Mackintosh, Victor Horta and Berlage, *Architectural Association Journal,* vol. LXV, February 1950, pp. 140–45; St. Tschudi Madsen, Horta. Works and Style of Victor Horta before 1900, *The Architectural Review,* vol. CXVIII, 1955, pp. 388–92; *idem,* Stilskaperen Victor Horta, *Byggekunst,* Oslo, No. 1, 1954, vol. XXXVI, pp. 8–12;—*Architecture—Urbanisme—Habitation,* Nov. 1947, No. 11, pp. 165–67; *Art et Décoration,* vol. I, No. 1, 1897, pp. 11–18; No. 2, p. 23; *ibid.,* vol. XI, 1902, pp. 72–75; *Art et Technique,* Brussels, July-August 1913; *Der Baumeister,* vol. I, 1903, pp. 9 sqq., 133 sqq.; *Cicerone,* Leipzig, vol. XV, 1923, pp. 160–204; *Deutsche Kunst und Dekoration,* vol. XI, 1903, No. 1, pp. 148 sqq.; *l'Emulation,* vol. XX, 1895, p. 187, pl. 39–43; *Die Kunst,* vol. II, 1900, pp. 206 sqq. For a complete list of his works up to 1910, see St. Tschudi Madsen, *loc. cit.*

5 Memorial for Lambeau, a classicist temple, Parc Cinquantenaire, Brussels, 1886–87, and a memorial, at Ghent, representing a recumbent young girl, 1884. The author would like to express his indebtedness to Jean Delhaye, J. J. Eggericx and C. Alexandre especially for the chapter about Victor Horta.

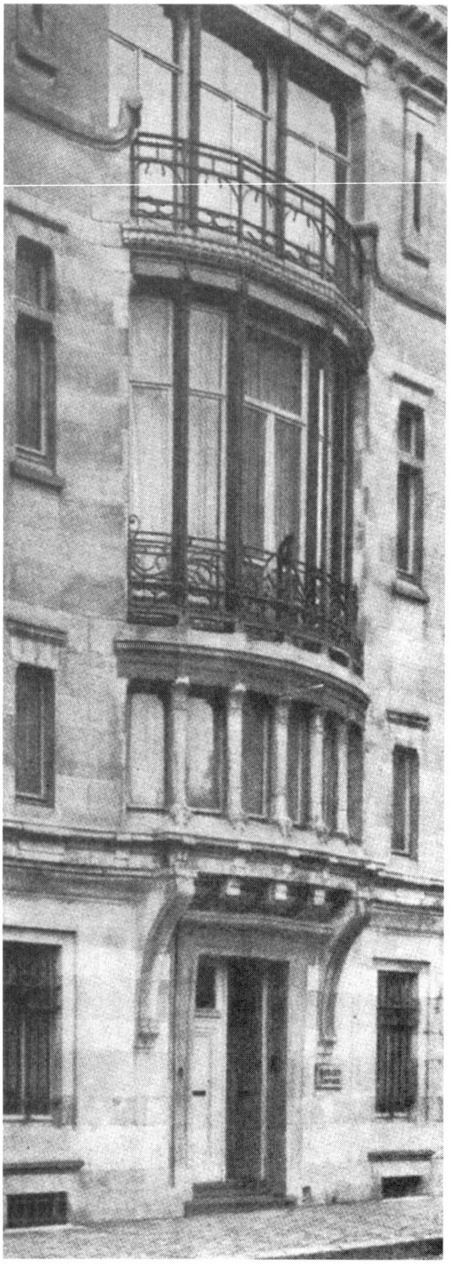

Fig. 167. Horta: 6 Rue Paul Emile Janson, Brussels. 1892–93. Courtesy of A. C. L. Brussels.

of Ghent, executed in an exceedingly sober and almost unornamented neo-Renaissance style in 1885.

After this commission Horta returned to Balat's office for a short time, also travelling in the years 1884–86. The years 1886–90 are perhaps the most interesting in Horta's development; but unfortunately we know very little about him during these years, except that he did not build any houses; but he wrote a certain amount, especially during the years 1888–89.

After Balat died he assumed charge of his office for some years. But in the year 1892 he had already designed a house for Professor Tassel, in one of the more quiet streets near Avenue de Louise, at that time No 12 Rue de Turin, today No 6 Rue Paul Emile Janson, Brussels. The house was finished in 1893 (fig. 167).[6]

This was the first continental Art Nouveau monument, with reminiscences of neo-Gothic, neo-Rococo and plant forms (figs. 126, 137, 262). It is

[6] Usually dated to 1893. Octave Maus in his detailed description mentions that the house was actually under construction in 1892. O. Maus, Habitations Modernes, *l'Art Moderne*, vol. XX, 1900, pp. 221–23. The information about his youth from St. Tschudi Madsen, Horta. Works and Style of Victor Horta before 1900, *The Architectural Review*, vol. CXVIII, 1955, pp. 388–92, 17 illustrations. The three following illustrations of Horta from W. Rehme, *Die Architektur der neuen freien Schule*, Leipzig 1902.

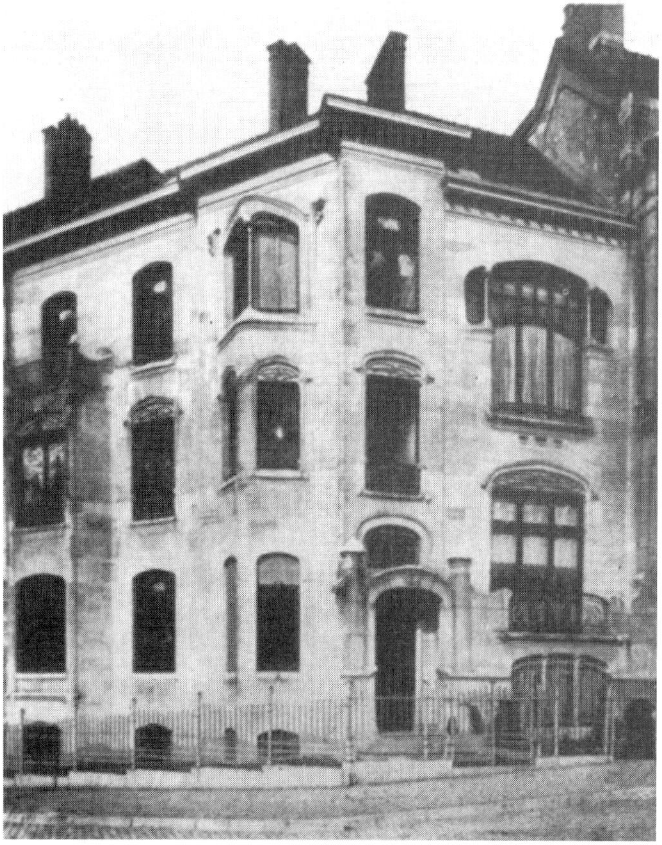

Fig. 168. Horta: 2 Avenue Palmerston, Brussels. 1895–96.

a four storeyed, narrow-fronted house, the facade in stone and cast iron. The iron girder, exhibited naked and unashamed, veritably boasts of its honesty. The use of iron in the construction enabled the architect to produce a surprisingly open ground-floor plan. It differs from the traditional Belgian scheme by a less restricted space for the staircase, and by the introduction of the circular hall.

The next house he designed was for Frison, 37 Rue Lebeau, Brussels, 1893–94. in duo-chrome bluish sandstone. The Gothic elements have been dispensed with, but instead we find his favourite motif, the ornament which merges with the stone. Otherwise the facade is unadorned.

The next important work he carried out was the Hotel Winssingers, 66 Rue des Monnaies, Brussels, 1895–96. Here once again we find columns in front with Gothic-like capitals springing out in a flamelike ornament. Every tiny detail here has been meticulously worked out, and has received the same Art Nouveau form-language: radiator ventilators, keyhole fittings, and window-frames, but the actual opening of the window is medieval in shape.

A characteristic house from this period is the Hotel van Eetvelde, 2 Avenue Palmerston, Brussels, 1895–96 (fig. 168). The house has the asymmetric treatment of the facade favoured by Art Nouveau artists: the actual facade plane is plastically treated and the surface is practically devoid of ornament; this is confined to the windows, and wherever it occurs independently it creeps discreetly and quickly into the wall as soon as it deviates from its fixed position. The columns have a number of Gothic touches.

Hotel Solvay, 224 Avenue Louise, Brussels, also dates from these years, started in 1895, finished 1900, and it is interesting to note that these houses with all their ornaments were ready on Horta's drawing board in 1895 even before Sigfried Bing opened his shop in Paris. Horta continued throughout the 1890's in his dual task, the creation of a new idiom of form and the search for a logical and clearly expressed architectural solution to constructional problems. The first task had been achieved in Tassel's house, 1892–93, the second found a completely satisfactory solution in the *Maison du Peuple*, 1896–99, Place Emile van de Velde, Brussels, the first facade in Belgium consisting mainly of iron and glass. It is of importance to the history of architecture owing to its construction, but from the point of view of Art Nouveau it is mainly interesting because of its grilles.

In 1898 Horta designed two houses for himself, 23 Rue Américaine, Brussels (fig. 169). In the first of these, which was his own residence, he worked, characteristically enough, more closely in the Belgian tradition, with bow windows and other traditional details, while in the second, which contained his studio, iron construction is freely exposed. The elements of Art Nouveau are found only in the iron grille and the consoles.

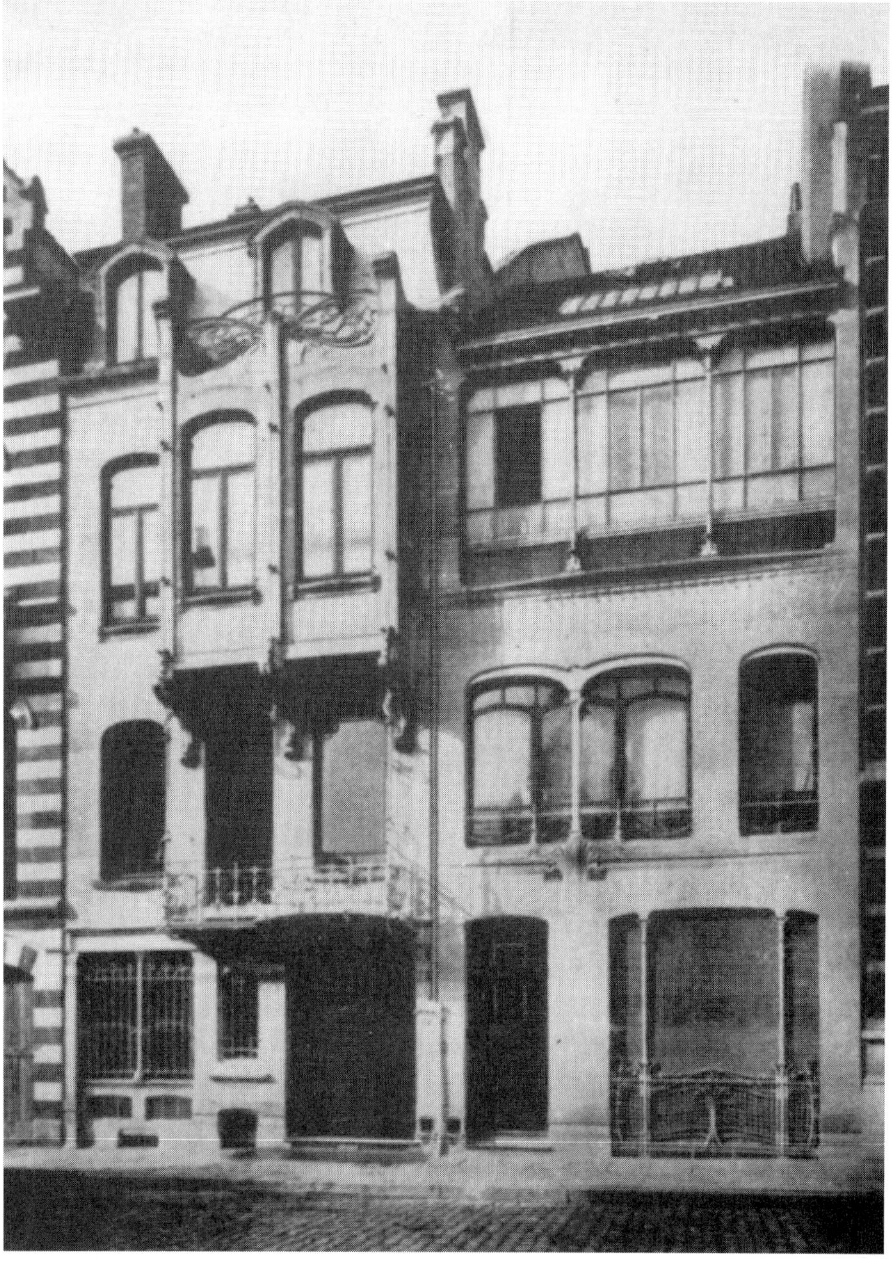

Fig. 169. Horta: 22–23 Rue Américaine, Brussels. 1898.

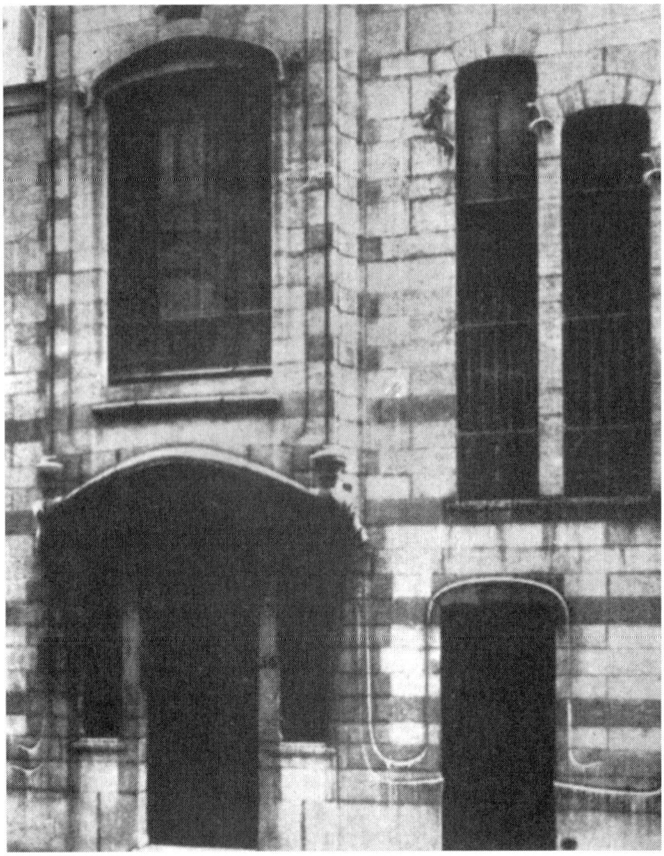

Fig. 170. Horta: Detail of 34 Avenue Palmerston, Brussels. About 1900.

In 34 Avenue Palmerston, Brussels, approx. 1900 (fig. 170), it is possible to see how his mature Art Nouveau style develops. The decorative line runs with the utmost discretion along the plinth of the building, helping to link the various parts together, and finally merging with the surface of the wall. A number of small ornaments are placed with great refinement near the windows.

It is far more difficult to realise the limitation of ornament, to use it sparingly and place it elegantly in relation to surface, than to eliminate it entirely, which was done with a great deal of ostentation by the following generation. Horta used ornaments, and succeeded in doing so to perfection.

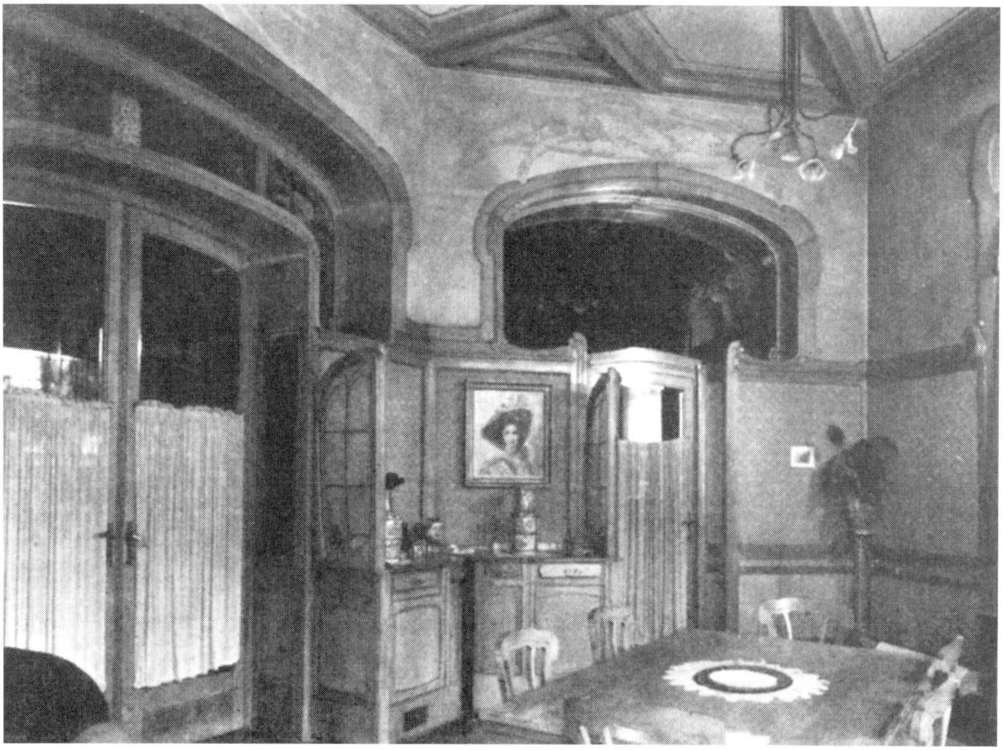

Fig. 171. Horta: Dining room. Hotel Aubecq, 520 Avenue Louise, Brussels. 1900.
Copyright A. C. L. Brussels.

Apart from the entrance door, which clearly shows a neo-Baroque feeling for form, the facade is decoratively and plastically restrained.

An interior from the dining-room of the Hotel Aubecq, 520 Avenue Louise, Brussels, 1900 (fig. 171), shows the degree of calmness he achieved about the turn of the century. The room breathes an air of Louis XV—or neo-Rococo—with a few Gothic touches, and, as can be seen in all his exteriors, the slight arch in door and windows is one of the most characteristic features. In 1902 he won first prize at the Turin Exhibition with a rather ponderous suite of furniture.

*

Horta's simplification of style was, however, to be pushed still further, e.g. in 85 Rue Washington, Brussels, 1906, which is very firm and simple.

In time his constructive striving and rational attitude to architecture became far more important than the decorative elements. In the large building designed for Philippe Wolfers, 11–13 Rue d'Arenberg, Brussels, 1906, there are no longer any traces of Art Nouveau. His youthful aim, to create a personal form language and to cast off the shackles of Historicism, had long been achieved—his pliant, abstract, and dynamic décor, created without any regard for the actual structure and qualities of the material, had become an international style. Just after the turn of the century he abandoned it himself, leaving others to vulgarise it.

GUSTAVE SERRURIER-BOVY

"Nature robuste, généreuse et sainement équilibrée, ayant horreur des conventions et soif de nouveauté raisonnée,"[7] was the way in which the Symbolist Charles Delchevalier described his friend Gustave Serrurier-Bovy (1858–1910).[8]

The son of a building contractor, he made up his mind at an early age to become an architect, and started training at the *Académie des Beaux Arts*, Liége, devoting himself especially to the study of Gothic. The only building he designed, however, was a small chapel at Chettyfontaine, 1882. In about 1884 he abandoned his study of architecture, set off on his travels, and arrived in England, where he fell under the spell of William Morris,[9] and devoted himself on his return home to interior decoration. Little is known of his activities for practically a decade thereafter until in 1894 he

7 Ch. Delchavelier, Gustave Serrurier-Bovy, *Clarté*, Brussels, 1930, No. 5, p. 18. "Robust, generous, and soundly-balanced nature, with a horror of convention and a thirst for reasoned novelty."

8 G. Serrurier-Bovy, *Album d'intérieur*, Liége, n.d.; Ch. Delchevalier, Gustave Serrurier-Bovy, un précurseur dans l'art de la décoration moderne, *Clarté*, Brussels, 1930, No. 5, pp. 18–21; R. Dulong, Les Arts d'Ameublement aux Salons, *Art et Décoration*, vol. VI, 1899, pp. 42–47; G. Soulier, Serrurier-Bovy, *ibid.*, vol. IV, 1898, pp. 78–85; *idem*, L'art dans l'habitations, *ibid.*, vol. VII, 1900, pp. 105–17; H. van de Velde, Gustave Serrurier-Bovy, *Zeitschrift für Innendekoration*, vol. XIII, 1902, pp. 41–68; Ouvrages de Dames, *Art Décoratif*, vol. VI, 1904, pp. 138–44; Gustave Serrurier-Bovy, *De Bouwgids*, Antwerp, May 1911, pp. 95–105.

9 *Ibid.*, p. 19.

exhibited in the *Libre Esthétique* as a fully-fledged furniture designer. Writing about the domestic study which he showed at that exhibition he says:

"Ich betrachte als erste Kundgebung des modernen Mobiliars, von meiner Seite, das Ensemble, das im Jahre 1894 im ersten Salon der 'Libre Esthétique' ausgestellt war. Ich hatte schon früher einige, aber sehr wenig zahlreiche Versuche gemacht, aber abgesehen davon, dass es nur vereinzelte, und an sich wenig interessante Gegenstände waren, standen sie andererseits zu sehr unter dem klassischen oder englischen Einfluss, um irgend einen Wert zu haben. Ich betrachte dies Arbeits-Zimmer, das im Jahre 1894 ausgestellt wurde, als gänzlich frei von den Reminiszenzen des alten und des englischen Stils. Jetzt, wo ich nach acht Jahren seine Pläne wiedersehe, versichere ich Ihnen, ohne irgend welche Eitelkeit, dass ich noch heute ebenso zufrieden damit bin, wie am ersten Tage, und wenn ich seitdem auch Besseres geschaffen habe schuf ich nichts, was mir mehr oder ebenso grosse Freude gemacht hätte. Es wurde mir gesagt und geschrieben, dass der englische Einfluss sich in meinen Schöpfungen zu sehr bemerkbar mache; ich glaube aber, dass das vollkommen falsch ist, denn dieses Ensemble als erster Versuch weist es aufs Entschiedenste zurück."[10]

If we consider the drawings from this year (fig. 172), the English influence, will be apparent: the simple unpainted wood, the complete absence of decoration, apart from the powerful fittings, and the marked emphasis of framework and panels, as well as the floral decoration in the background. But there is one feature which is more marked in his work than

10 Part of a letter from Gustave Serrurier-Bovy. H. van de Velde, Gustave Serrurier-Bovy, *Zeitschrift für Innendekoration*, vol. XIII, 1902, p. 50. "From my point of view I consider the first signs of a modern style of furniture to be the *ensemble* which was exhibited in the year 1894 in the first salon of the Libre Esthétique. I had already made a number of earlier, but not very numerous, attempts, but apart from the fact that these were only a few and not very interesting objects, they were also too much under Classical or English influence to be of any worth. I consider the study that was exhibited in the year 1894 as being entirely free from the reminiscence of old and English style. Now, on seeing its plain surfaces again after eight years, I can assure you, without in any way boasting, that to this day I am just as pleased with it as I was on the first day, and though I may have created better things since, I never made anything which gave me so much pleasure. People told me and wrote to tell me that the English influence was too noticeable in my creations; but I believe that that is completely wrong, for this *ensemble*, as a first attempt, emphatically contradicts it." The following illustrations are also from this article.

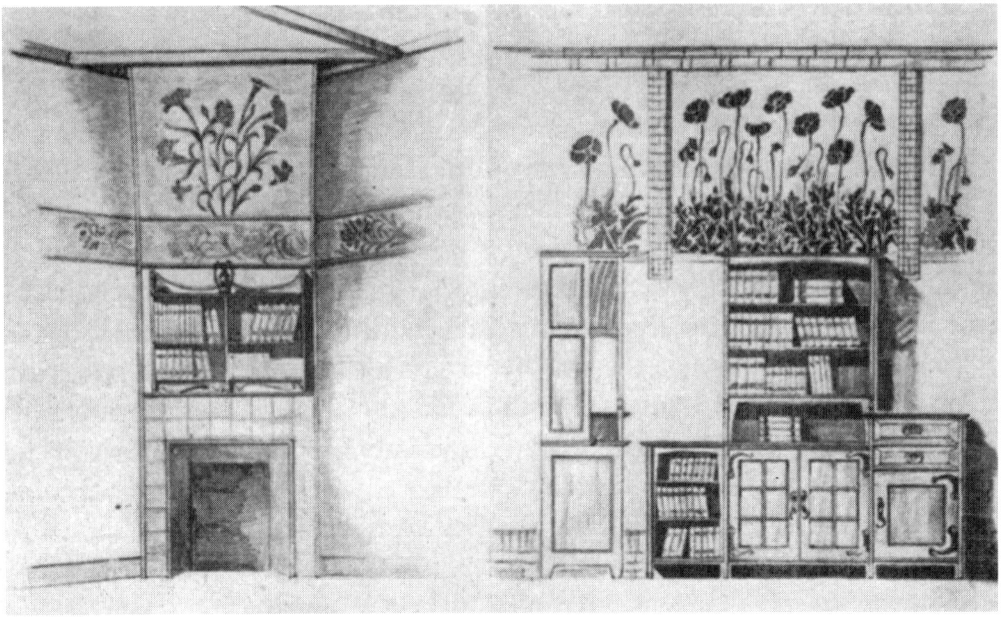

Fig. 172. Serrurier-Bovy: Design for library. 1894.

in that of the English artists: the asymmetry. This feature—though the Japanese inspiration is clear enough—is so typical of Serrurier-Bovy that it might be said that the unerring and well-balanced shape of this motif is his most important contribution to the furniture design of Art Nouveau. It may also be seen in his furniture designs from 1895 and 1899 (figs. 173, 174). And yet one of his most outstanding pieces of furniture in this respect is to be found in the Musée des Beaux Arts in Liége. One practical aspect of this asymmetry is that it enables him to combine several pieces of furniture in one and the same construction.

Later in the 1890's his style becomes lighter, the surface of the furniture being broken up into a number of vertical slats, giving a distinct elegance reminiscent of contemporary English furniture (fig. 175). A specifically Belgian feature is to be found in the slightly arched trusses which run above the panels, and could not possibly have been borrowed from the English. This feature may be ascribed entirely to Serrurier-Bovy and van de Velde.

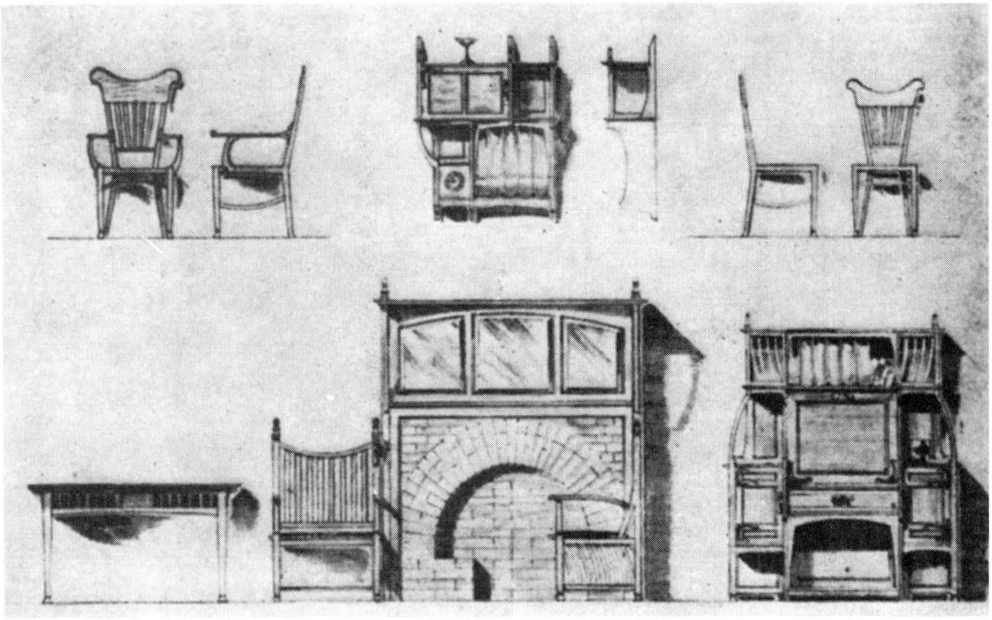

Fig. 173. Serrurier-Bovy: Furniture for study-room. 1895.

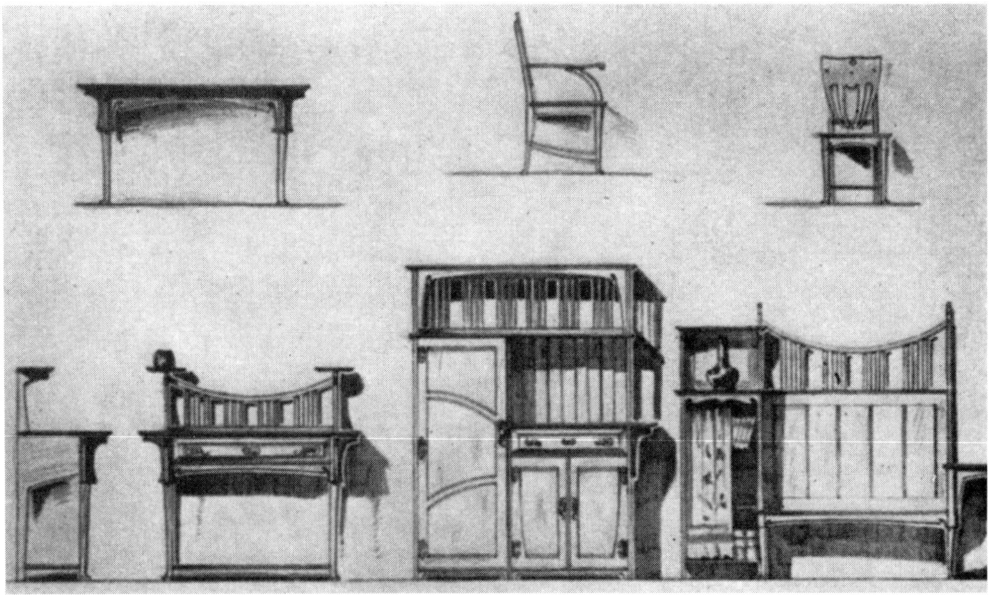

Fig. 174. Serrurier-Bovy: Furniture for dining room. 1895. Modified 1899.

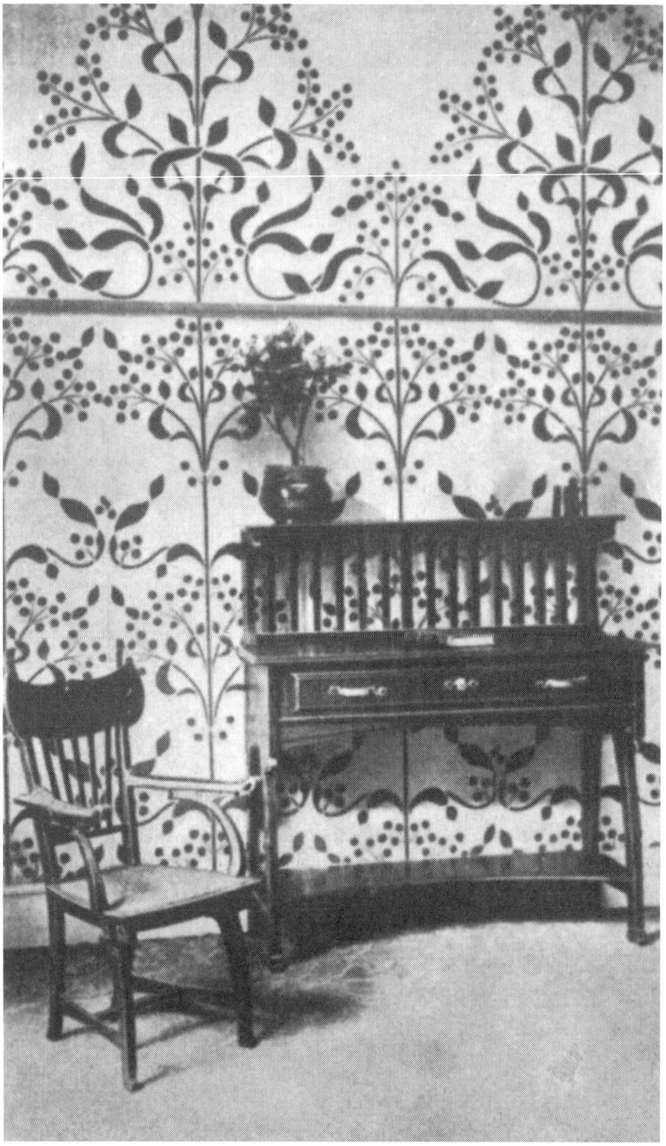

Fig. 175. Serrurier-Bovy: Sideboard. 1898.

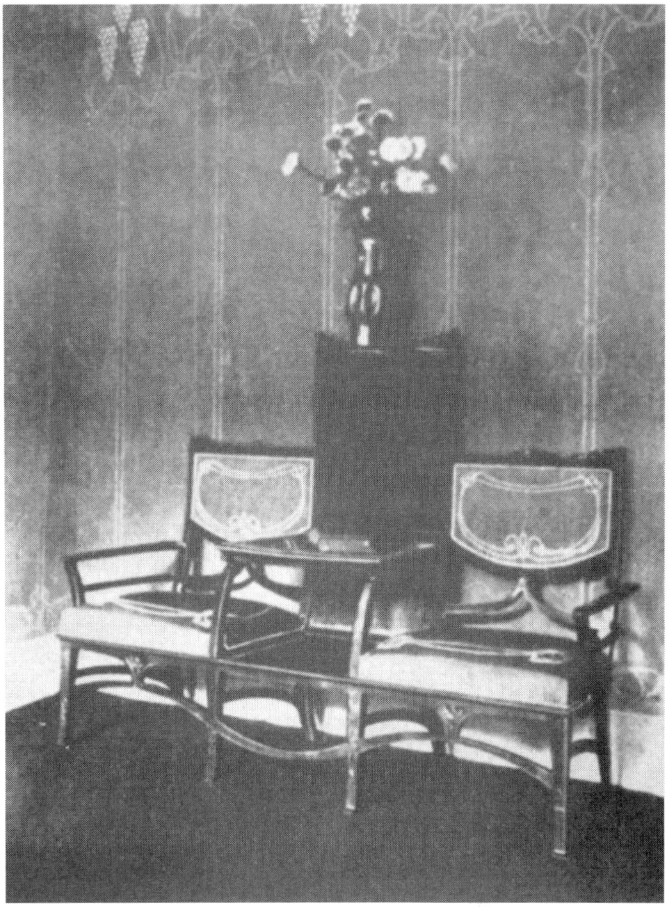

Fig. 176. Serrurier-Bovy: Joined table and chairs.

The slightly arched trusses, which are both less constructive than elegant and not in harmony with the qualities of the material, were to become one of the outstanding characteristics of Belgian Art Nouveau.

A fairly typical piece of furniture by Serrurier-Bovy from 1900 is the combined chair-table-shelf piece shown in fig. 176. The various parts are linked together by an undulating rhythm to form a whole—even all the constructive parts are bent.

At the beginning of the 20th century his decorative style undergoes a straightening, as we can see from his ornament design[11]: the square and

11 Ouvrages de Dames, *Art Décoratif,* vol. VI, 1904, pp. 138–44.

the rectangle gradually assume a more important role. It is natural to consider this simplification as a consequence of the influence of the Austrian School in the years immediately after the turn of the century.

In the years preceding Serrurier-Bovy's death in 1910 it is difficult to find any significant traces of his influence. He ran a large furniture-manufacturing business in Liége, and judging by his sales catalogue the firm specialised in period furniture. There is no mention of furniture designed in Serrurier-Bovy's own style.

Serrurier-Bovy's influence on his contemporaries was very considerable. Max Osborn writes: "G. Serrurier-Bovy übernahm die verdienstvolle Rolle des Vermittlers. Ihm gehört der Ruhm, zuerst die neuen dekorativen Formen von London nach Brussel gebracht zu haben."[12] Van de Velde pays him due credit in his article about him in the *Zeitschrift für Innendekoration* in 1902; in another connection he says that Serrurier-Bovy ". . . . unstreitbar der erste Künstler auf dem Kontinent war, der die Bedeutsamkeit des englischen Kunstgewerblichen Stils begriff und der den Mut hatte, ihm bei uns einzuführen und einzubürgen."[13] This is a charming tribute from a fellow-artist who was striving to reach the same goal. Serrurier-Bovy's role could hardly have been defined with greater clarity.

*

Victor Horta launched the dynamic Art Nouveau, but Serrurier-Bovy introduced the English Arts and Crafts style: the use of oak and unpainted wood, sparingly decorated sometimes with celtic-inspired metal fittings. But to this he added Horta's principle of subjecting different materials to one and the same decorative law. Furthermore he introduced Japanese asymmetry and the "Belgian curved truss." Thus he created the Belgian Art Nouveau style of furniture.

[12] *Zeitschrift für Innendekoration,* vol. XI, 1900, No. 1. "G. Serrurier-Bovy took over the valuable role of intermediary. It was to his credit that he was the first to bring the new decorative forms from London to Brussels."

[13] H. van de Velde, *Renaissance im Kunstgewerbe,* Berlin 1901, Neue Ausgabe, p. 63. ". . . was unquestionably the first artist on the Continent who realised the importance of the English Arts and Crafts style, and had the courage to introduce it to us and to defend it."

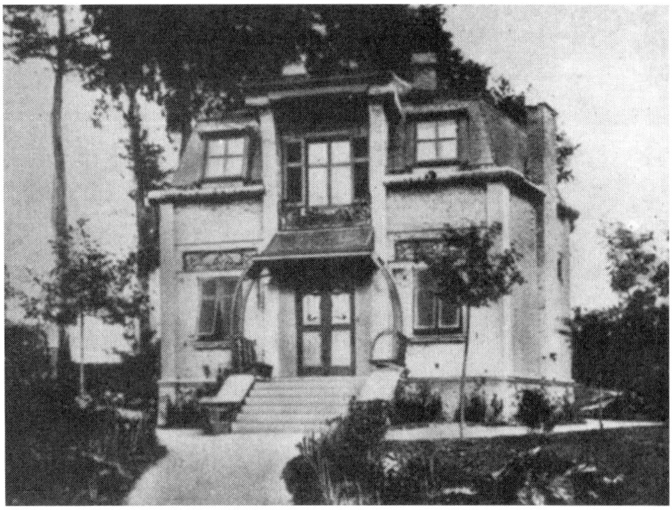

Fig. 177. Van de Velde: The Artist's house, Uccle near Brussels. 1896.

HENRY VAN DE VELDE

With Henry van de Velde (1863–)[14] the style acquired an ardent protagonist. After giving up his career as a painter, and making his debut as a decorative artist in 1893, he wrote a great deal during the years that followed, setting forth his ideas at some length. In 1895 he started to plan his new house at Uccle near Brussels, which was completed by 1896 (fig. 177). The praise of contemporary art historians has invested this building with a significance to which it is hardly entitled from the point of view of architectural history. The exterior is very simple and of no architectural interest. Voysey's and Mackmurdo's architecture at the end of the 1880's, Horta's houses in Ghent from the middle of the 1880's, as well as all the simple and unpretentious villas from about the same time, help to place this building in its proper historical context. Here too, as in many of the

14 For his own writings see Bibliography. M. Casteels, *H. van de Velde,* Brussels; J. Meier-Graefe, Henry van de Velde, *l'Art Décoratif,* vol. I, No. 1, 1898, pp. 1–48; (*Dekorative Kunst,* vol. III, Special Number, 1898, pp. 1–44) M. Osborn, Henry van de Velde, Brussels, *Zeitschrift für Innendekoration,* vol. XI, 1900, pp. 1–11; K. E. Osthaus, *van de Velde, Leben und Schaffen des Künstlers,* Hagen 1920; K. Scheffler, Henry van de Velde und der neue Stil, *Kunst und Künstler,* vol. IX, 1911, pp. 119–33; *idem, Henry van de Velde,* Berlin 1913 (four essays).

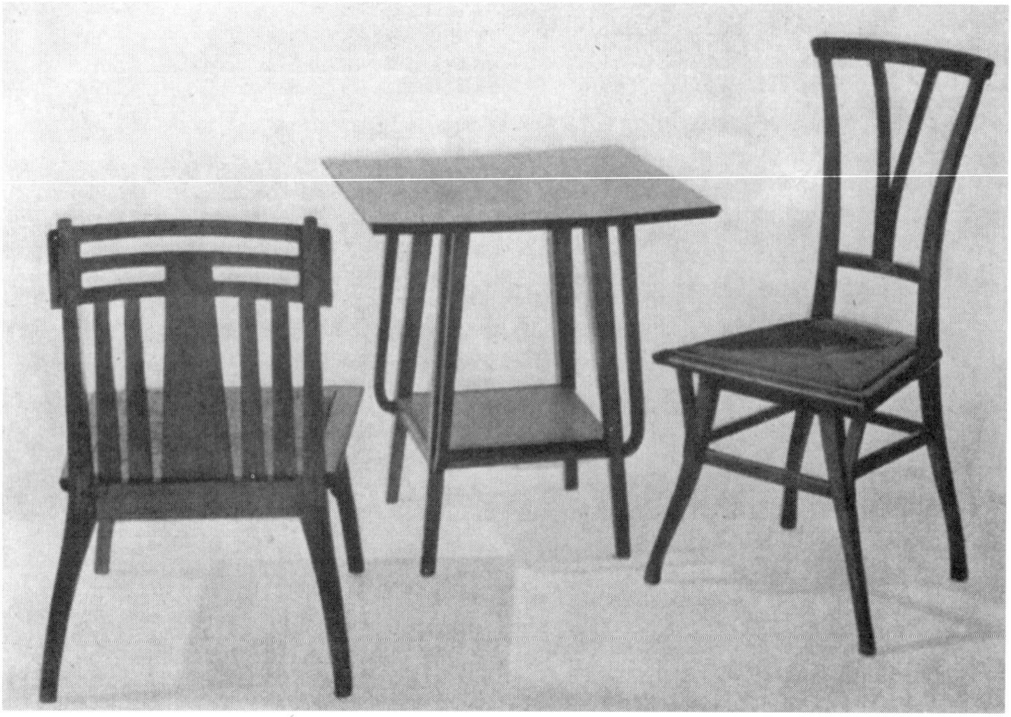

Fig. 178. Van de Velde: Furniture for the Artist's house. 1896.
From *Um 1900.*

buildings designed by Horta, we find the iron beam lying clearly visible; apart from this Serrurier-Bovy's characteristic arch is one of the essential peculiarities of the interior and the exterior. Van de Velde also uses, as Serrurier-Bovy himself had done in 1894–95, the light slat-like furniture (fig. 178). It is however fairly certain that these interiors, as a whole, differed considerably from ordinary ideas of taste in Belgium. In their simplicity they seem to have been less floral than Serrurier-Bovy's, and every single detail seems to be the result of a conscious and logical striving—even though, as the Frenchman Maurice Joyant puts it, this "se sentait tout de même un peu trop."[15] But to do any good it was necessary to demonstrate the new ideas—to go the whole hog—as, indeed, did Henry van de Velde.

[15] M. Joyant, *Henri de Toulouse-Lautrec 1864–1901,* I–II, Paris 1926, vol. I, p. 167. "All the same could be felt (in French also "smelt") a little too much."

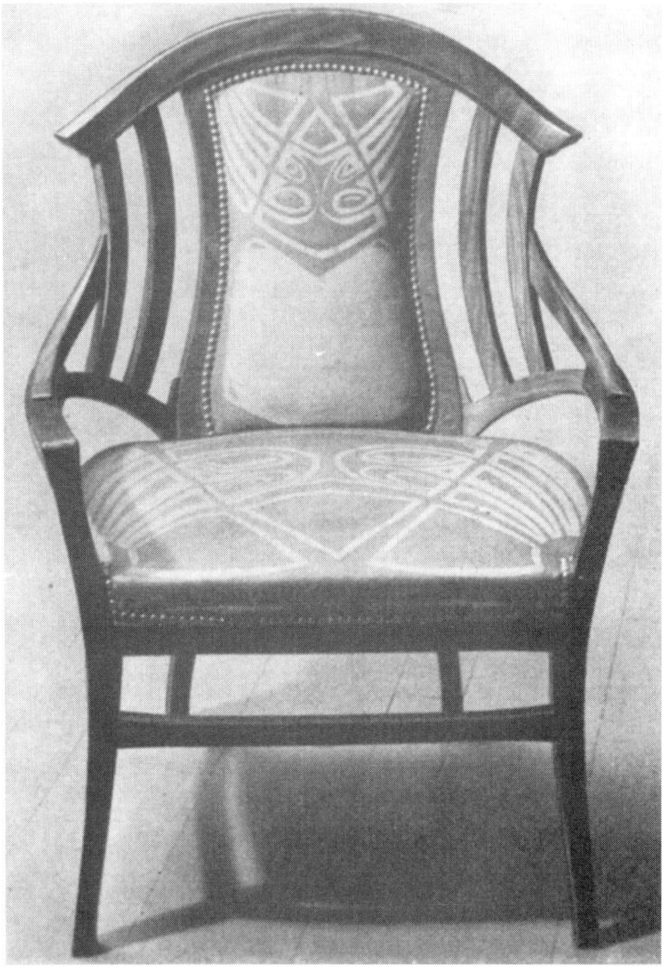

Fig. 179. Van de Velde: Writing-desk chair. 1896.
Nordenfjeldske Kunstindustrimuseum, Trondheim. Copyright reserved.

S. Bing and J. Meier-Graefe visited van de Velde in 1895 or 1896[16] and were both enthusiastic; van de Velde's French guests, however, were not always equally kind in their judgement, and Toulouse-Lautrec's remark has become a classic: "Inouï, hein! mais au fond, il n'y a que la salle de bains, les cabinets de toilette et la nursery peints en ripolin blanc qui soient tout à fait bien."[17]

16 1896 is given in the sources available; it might as well have been 1895.

17 *Ibid.*, vol. I, p. 168. "Unheard of, eh? But at heart only the bathroom, the lavatories, and the nursery painted in white ripolin are really good."

In Uccle van de Velde started a sort of applied arts centre by enlisting the services of the village craftsmen, who worked according to his own and other people's designs. The Dutch painter Johan Thorn Prikker, and the two Belgians, the painter George Lemmen, and the potter Alfred William Finch, also submitted designs over a short period of time, or carried out work, but Lemmen's main interest was in painting, and Finch—who had been in England in 1891—could hardly be said to have turned out anything in this period which could be termed Art Nouveau.[18] In 1897 he made his way to Finland, and took up employment with the Iris workshops in Borgå. His colouring, however, in the 1890's was typical Art Nouveau: his glass is often greenish, with touches of violet; his pottery is brownish, beige, and warm in its colouring.

In 1895 or 1896 Bing commissioned van de Velde to decorate four rooms in his new shop *Art Nouveau*, which the architect Bonnier had designed for him in 22 Rue de Province, Paris. Here he exhibited together with artists such as the French potters Delaherche and Dammouse, the English painter Brangwyn, the craftsmen and artists from Nancy, Gallé and Majorelle, as well as the painters Denis and Vuillard.

The writingdesk-chair from 1897 (fig. 179),[19] a type which in fact he used right up to 1903–04, shows his style at this time, with the bent laths in the Serrurier-Bovy tradition. The cover of the chair is by the Dutchman Thorn-Prikker. In the spring of 1897 he exhibited in Dresden, and his five interiors were received by an enthusiastic press, and were considered a veritable salvation in Germany. His lamp and door fitting a year or two later (figs. 180, 181) show a more Horta-like and dynamic stalk style. In 1899 Meier-Graefe founded the *Maison Moderne*, for which van de Velde executed the interiors, and at the same time the German art-historian introduced him to the *Pan* circle in Berlin; the result was a great many commissions in Germany. In the same year he visited Berlin, and spent the winter of 1900–01 travelling round Germany lecturing on the subject

[18] No. A.M. 340–397, Musée Cinquantenaire, Brussels; only one of these, No. A.M. 352 may be said to be Art Nouveau. For Finch's part in the history of Belgian ceramics, see J. Helbig, Notes sur l'évolution de la céramique en Belgique 1850–1950, *Revue Belge d'Archéologie et d'histoire de l'art,* Brussels, vol. XIX, 1950, pp. 213–18.

[19] N.K. 144–1900. Nordenfjeldske Kunstindustrimuseum, Trondheim.

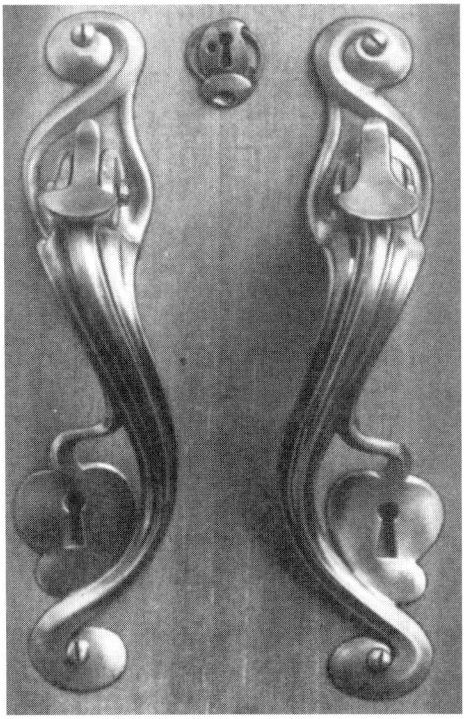

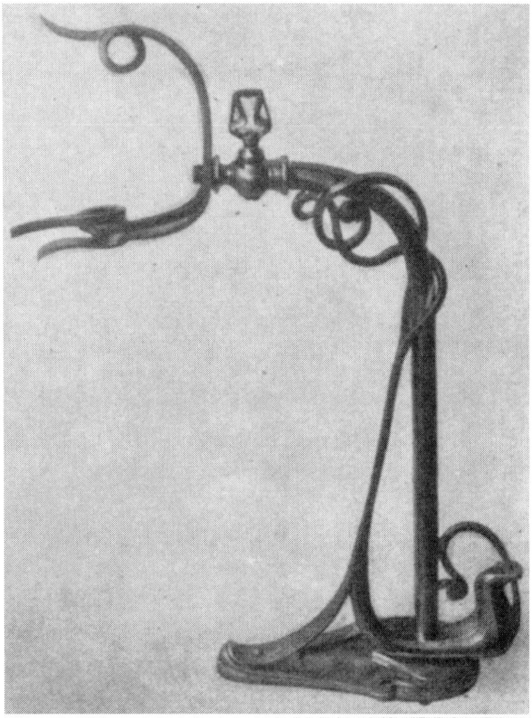

Fig. 180. Van de Velde: Door mounting, brass. P.ph. Fig. 181. Van de Velde: Lampstead, brass. P.ph.

of *Prinzipielle Erklärungen*, published in 1902 under the title of *Kunstgewerbliche Laienpredigten*. In the years 1899–1902 he carried out the following notable commissions: interiors for the Habana Compagnie, a cigar store, 1900; Hohenzollern Kunstgewerbehaus, 1899; Haby Barbershop, 1900—all these in Berlin—as well as his *magnum opus* the Folkwang Museum, Hagen, in 1902, in a plastic Art Nouveau with neo-Baroque features.

In 1902 his furniture style was considerably more mature (fig. 182).[20] Where his line had formerly run rhythmically and softly it now acquires a rectilinear break, while the contours still show the slight arch. In the following year he continued his work in Germany, designing Esche Haus, Chemnitz, 1903; Hohenhof, Eppenhausen, Hagen, Weimar, 1904 (fig. 183); Leuring House, Scheveningen, Holland, 1904; and the School of Applied

20 *Zeitschrift für Innendekoration*, vol. XIV, 1903, p. 263. The Cabinet was made for Dr. F. Kiel.

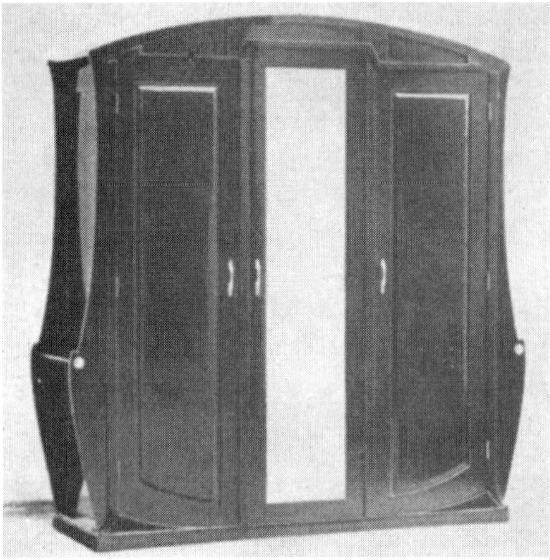

Fig. 182. Van de Velde: Wardrobe. 1902

Art in Weimar, 1905, to which he had been invited by the Grand Duke in 1902. With his room for the Dresden Exhibition in 1906 van de Velde's first stylistic phase comes to an end, a phase in which he attempted to combine the wavy line with a logical form of construction—a problem which was of necessity bound to remain unsolved, because the wavy line is not always logical. His next two phases are from 1906–14, and from 1918 on. His contribution, however, in these periods comes outside the scope of this work.

*

The result of any evaluation of van de Velde's work is bound to be that his contribution as a fruitful medium of his own and other people's ideas is far more important than his purely artistic production. In three spheres he stands out as an independent thinker within the realm of the theory of decorative art: in his reaction against Naturalism, in his search for structural ornamental form, based on reason, and in his special symbolism, alluding to the object's function. As a theoretician he is among the outstanding men of the 1890's.

As a decorative artist he is at his best in minor metal work (fig. 184). As a furniture designer he is eclectic, and an excellent representative of the

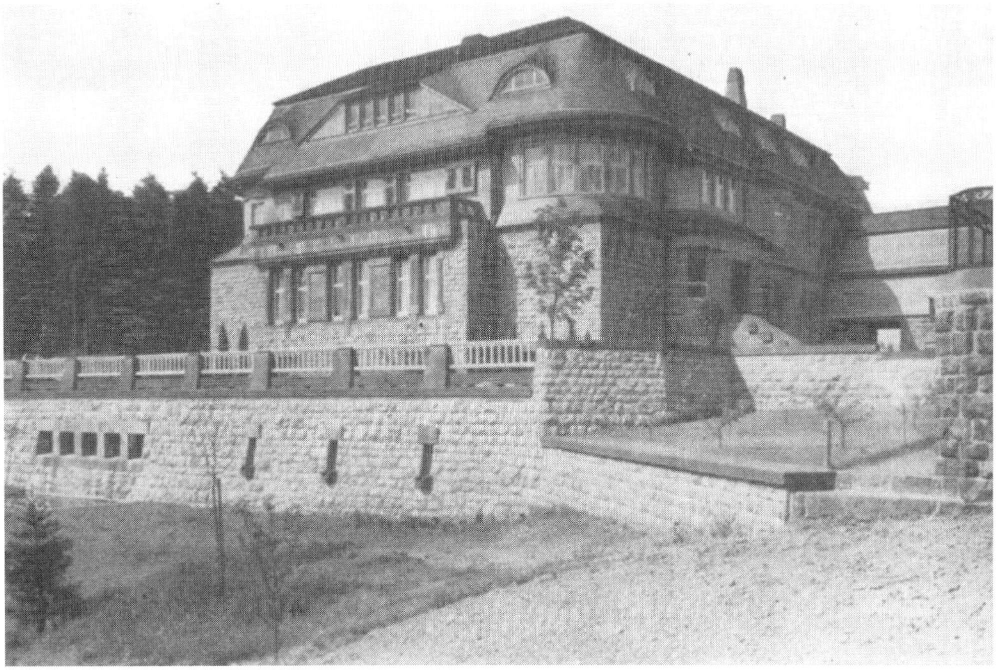

Fig. 183. Van de Velde: "Hohenhof," Eppenhausen, Hagen, Weimar. 1904. P.ph.

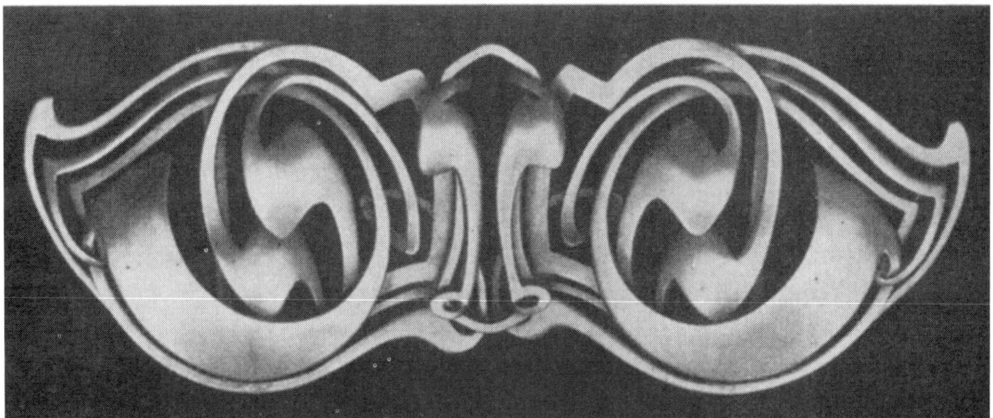

Fig. 184. Van de Velde: Belt clasp, silver. About 1900. P.ph.

swift development of style which was taking place from 1892–1893 to 1902 and 1903. His furniture is often rather too "logical"—"Se sent tout de même un peu trop"— and heavy in its shape, and never achieves the lightness of English work, nor the elegant sophistication of the French.

As an architect he fell short of his specially trained colleagues: the buildings he designed are in no way revolutionary in the history of European architecture, and do not bear comparison with the work of men such as Mackintosh, Horta, Voysey, Perret, Garnier, and his advanced German and Austrian colleagues.

Van de Velde has inevitably been elevated to a position in the history of art which his work clearly does not deserve. But his strength as a theorist and his ardent campaign to create a new basis for applied art can hardly be overestimated, and from the point of view of art history his importance to Germany—but only to Germany—is very considerable. The fact that German art-historians, until recently, were the only ones to investigate the stylistic traits of this period, may have resulted in some overestimation.

PAUL HANKAR

The most important architect in Belgium in the 1890's, beside Horta, was Paul Hankar (1859–1901)[21] (fig. 185). In his work Orientalism played a more important role than in the work of contemporary architects, both in exteriors and interiors. In decorative art, in common with the other Belgian artists, he was also greatly influenced by the English School. In his own

21 O. Maus, Habitations Modernes, Paul Hankar, *l'Art Moderne,* vol. XX, 1900, pp. 229–231; Obituary, *l'Emulation,* vol. XXVI, 1901, cols. 6–8. Information kindly given by Miss Yvonne Hankar to the author, March 1953. Thanks to the help of J. J. Eggericx, it has been possible to make a list of most of his works, all of them in Brussels.

1889	83, Chausée de Charleroi.	1898–1900	151, Avenue Tervueren.
1893	71, Rue de Facqz.	1898–1900	128, Rue de la Loi.
1895	Barber's shop, Ixelles.	1898–1900	21, Rue Ruysbroech.
1897	48–50, Rue de Facqz.	1898–1900	13, Rue Royale.
1898	7, Rue Antoine Bréart.	1900	Villa Wolfers, La Hulpe.
1898–99	383–85, Avenue Louise.	1901	23, Rue Paul-Emile Janson.
1899	76–78, Rue de la Croix de Pierre.		

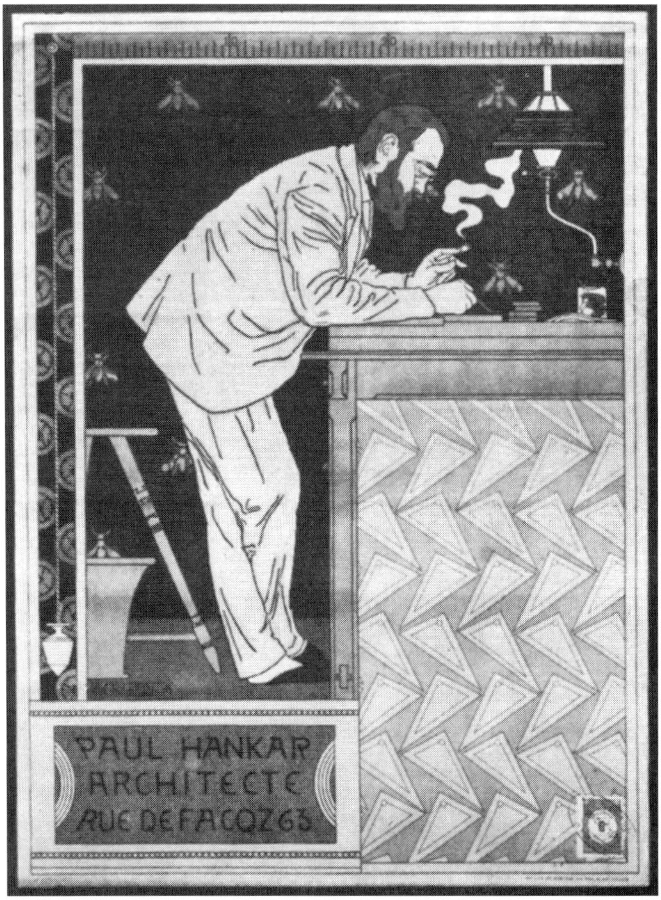

Fig. 185 Crespin: Poster for Paul Hankar. 1894.
Courtesy of Miss Y. Hankar.

home he had Japanese furniture, and in his studio the wallpaper had been designed by Walter Crane.[22]

Hankar's first building, 83 Chaussée de Charleroi, Brussels, 1889[23] (detail fig. 125), was a relatively ordinary house in a simple neo-Renaissance style, built of brick, with light bands of sandstone and the traditional bay window. After his marriage in March 1891 he applied himself with great enthusiasm to the task of designing furniture for his new home, and in 1891–92 his first furniture saw the light of day. It is very simple, with a

22 Information kindly given by Miss Y. Hankar to the author, March 1953.
23 Ill., *l'Emulation,* vol. XVII, 1893, pl. 33–35.

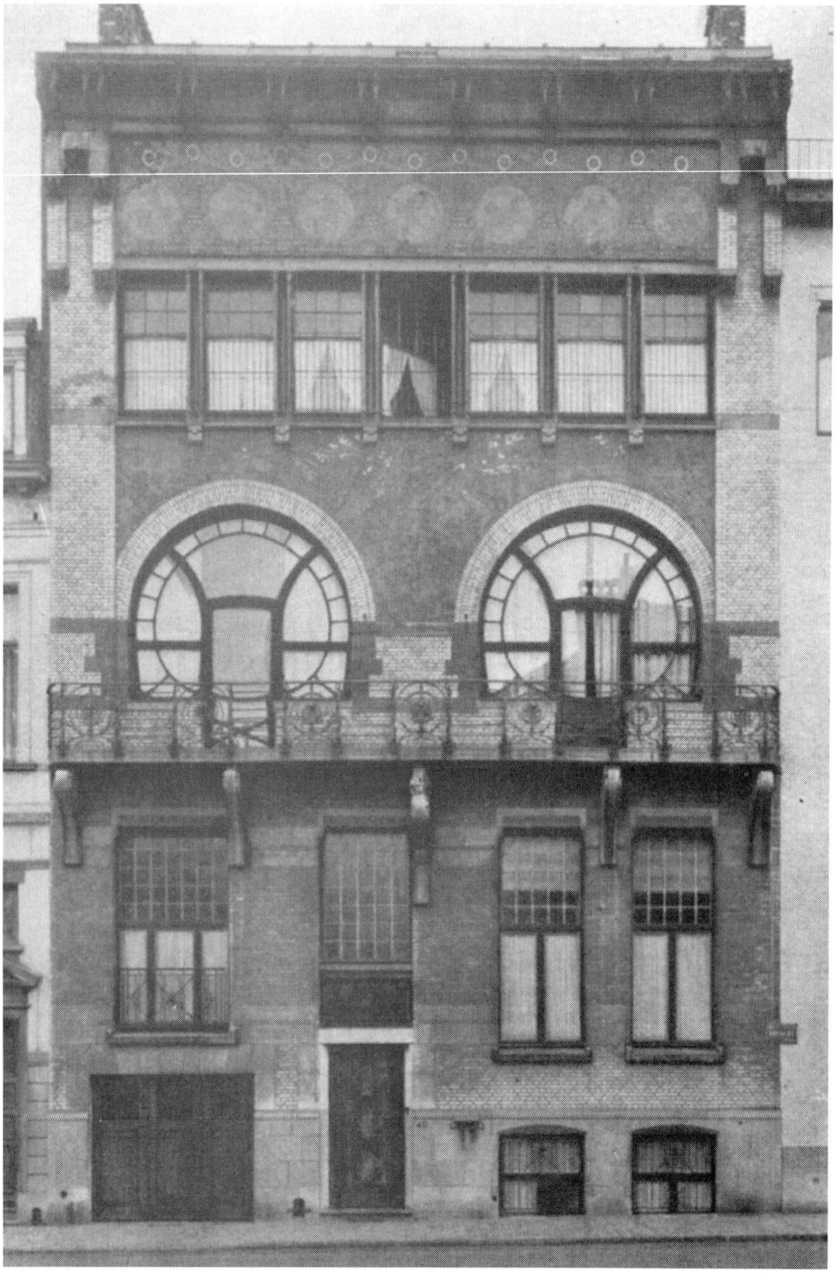

Fig. 186. Hankar: 48 Rue de Facqz, Brussels. 1897.
Copyright A. C. L Brussels.

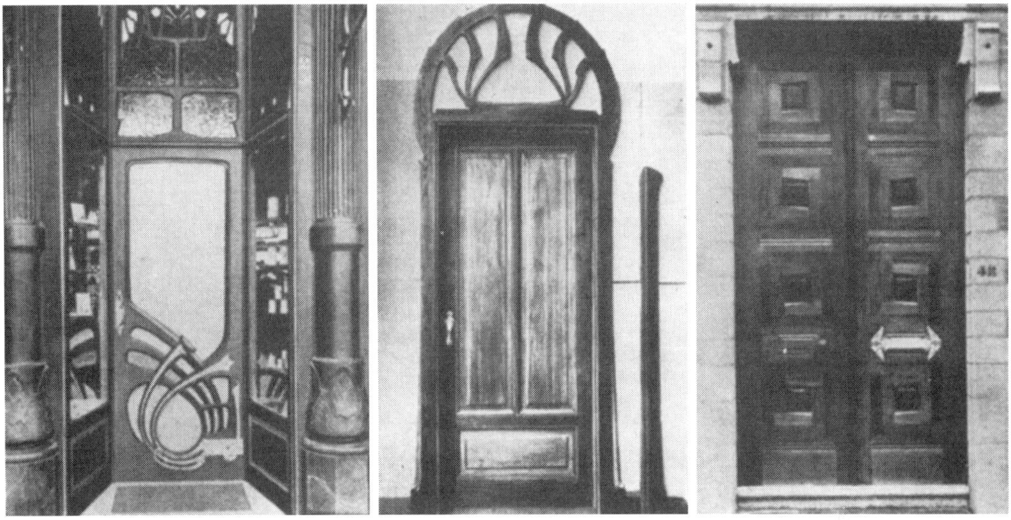

Fig. 187 a–c. Hankar: a. Shop door. Brussels. About 1900. b. Door. 42 Rue de Facqz, Brussels. About 1898. c. Main entrance door. 48 Rue de Facqz, Brussels. 1897.

somewhat ponderous neo-Renaissance character, revealing a very decided interest in new constructive solutions.[24]

In 1893 he designed a table which in its construction and shape is Japanese in feeling [25] and in the same year his own house in 71 Rue de Facqz, Brussels,[26] was ready. The exterior is original in its striving for new effects, and with its polychrome facade in white, red, and blue tiles, as well as the inscriptions *Jour*, *Nuit*, *Matin*, and *Soir*, is fairly typical of the tendencies of the 1890's. The cornice, which projects very markedly, is a feature showing neo-Renaissance influence. But what is most interesting is the striking simplicity in the interior derived from Japan, with a distinct predilection for straight constructive elements.

For some time Hankar was associated with his friend Crespin, the man who had designed his poster, and together they decorated a barber's shop in Ixelles, completed before 1896 in plain Art Nouveau.[27]

24 Photos in the possession of Miss Y. Hankar, Brussels.

25 In the possession of Miss Y. Hankar, Brussels.

26 Ill., *l'Emulation,* vol. XX, 1895, pl. 14–17.

27 Ill., *The Studio,* vol. VIII, 1896, p. 178.

His next work was the house he designed for the painter Ciamberlani, also in the Rue de Facqz, 1897(fig. 186), a side road to the Avenue Louise, the fashionable street in Brussels during the 1890's. This house has Art Nouveau consoles on the top floor, polychrome sgrafitto, and the large horseshoe-shaped arch with the arched crossbars which are so typical of Serrurier-Bovy and Hankar. This feature often combined with "broken" slats (fig. 187)[28] can also be seen in his design. The large arch which was to become such an essential part of Art Nouveau interior and furniture design was made popular in the work of these two artists, and the Oriental source is clearly shown in Hankar's art. Just as typical, however, is his striving for austerity, as can be seen in the door to 48 Rue de Facqz (fig. 187 c). Fig. 187 a shows a ponderous asymmetric Art Nouveau style fully developed.

*

The Art Nouveau features are not the most important ones in Hankar's work, which so clearly reflects the tendency of the 1890's. It shows the influence of Orientalism, and his striving for austerity, which became part and parcel of the further development. Furthermore his Orientalism seems to illustrate how this trend could be one of the sources of the rectilinear and square form elements which were to become such an essential part of the new trends that eventually replaced Art Nouveau.

PHILIPPE WOLFERS

The firm of Wolfers in Brussels[29] represents the main line in the development of Belgian silver- and gold-work during the last hundred years. Louis Wolfers extended the already existing firm in 1850, and in the middle of the 1880's his son Philippe Wolfers (1858–1929)[30] began to make his mark as a designer and sculptor. He had studied under Isidore de Rudder, a

28 The three doors from W. Rehme, *Ausgeführte moderne Bautischler-Arbeiten,* Leipzig 1902, pls. 10, 17, 33.

29 Photos and the extensive archives of the firm, as well as information most kindly given by Marcel Wolfers to the author, April and May 1953.

30 S. Pierron, Philippe Wolfers, *Revue des Arts Décoratifs,* vol. XXI, 1900, pp. 153–60; P. Serrure, Philippe Wolfers, *Le Bijou,* vol. I, 1933, pp. 17–23, 35–37; V. Pica, Philippe Wolfers, *Emporium,* vol. XXVII, 1908, pp. 1–23; *idem, Philippe Wolfers,* Milan, 1926; J. E. Whitby, The Artistic Jewellery of M. Wolfers, *The Magazine of Art,* Sept. 1899, pp. 515–19.

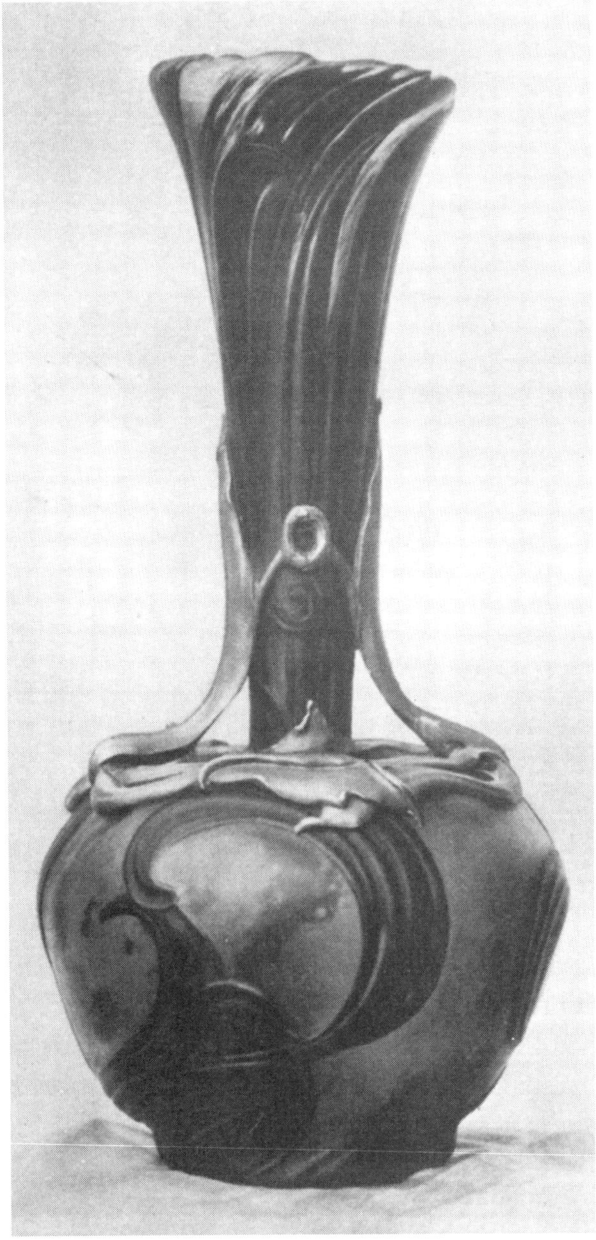

Fig. 188. Wolfers: *Lys du Japon.*
Crystal vase mounted with silver gilt. 1896.
Courtesy of M. Wolfers, Brussels.

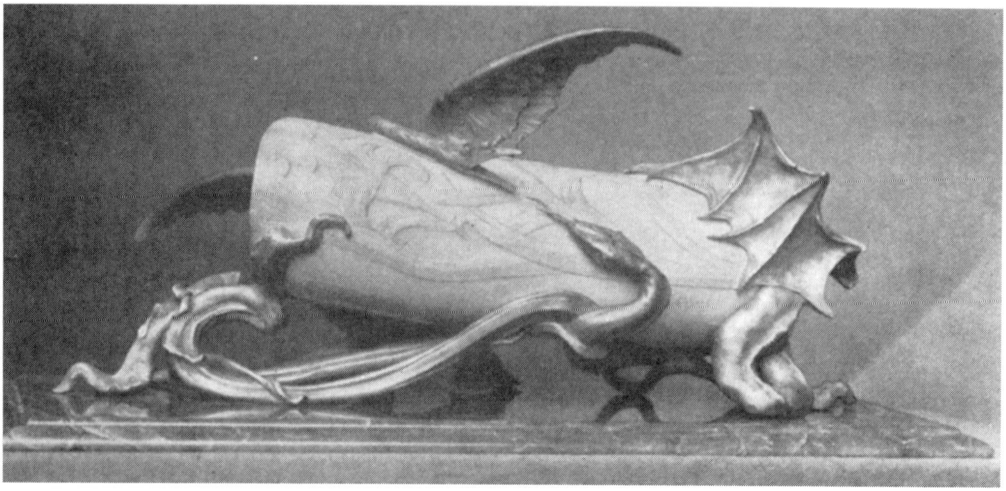

Fig. 189. Wolfers: *Civilisation et barbarie*. Ivory, silver on marble. 1896–97.
Courtesy of M. Wolfers, Brussels.

close friend of Paul Hankar and the designer Crespin. Philippe Wolfers is an excellent exponent of decorative art trends in Belgium in the 1880's and 1890's and is the leading Art-Nouveau artist within his branch.

After the neo-Renaissance of the 1870's had run its course, young Philippe Wolfers was just on the threshold of his career, and born and bred as he was in a milieu entirely influenced by the Louis XV style, it came natural to him to work in neo-Rococo, which throughout the 1880's was the dominant style in his branch. Though both Japanese and neo-Renaissance influences are in evidence in his work in the 1880's, neo-Rococo gradually took the upper hand, and flourished especially in the years 1889–92, becoming more floral and plant-like in the beginning of the 1890's, until in 1895 the transformation to Art Nouveau is complete. During this development he was constantly absorbed in a study of flowers and plants in great numbers, so that it is quite natural that his Art Nouveau should be of a floral and plant-like character (fig. 188).

The material in highest favour among the Belgian goldsmiths in the 1890's was ivory, of which the Belgian Congo provided abundant supplies. Wolfers's work, *Civilisation et barbarie*, approx. 1896–97 (fig. 189), is characteristic both in its choice of material, and in its symbolism.

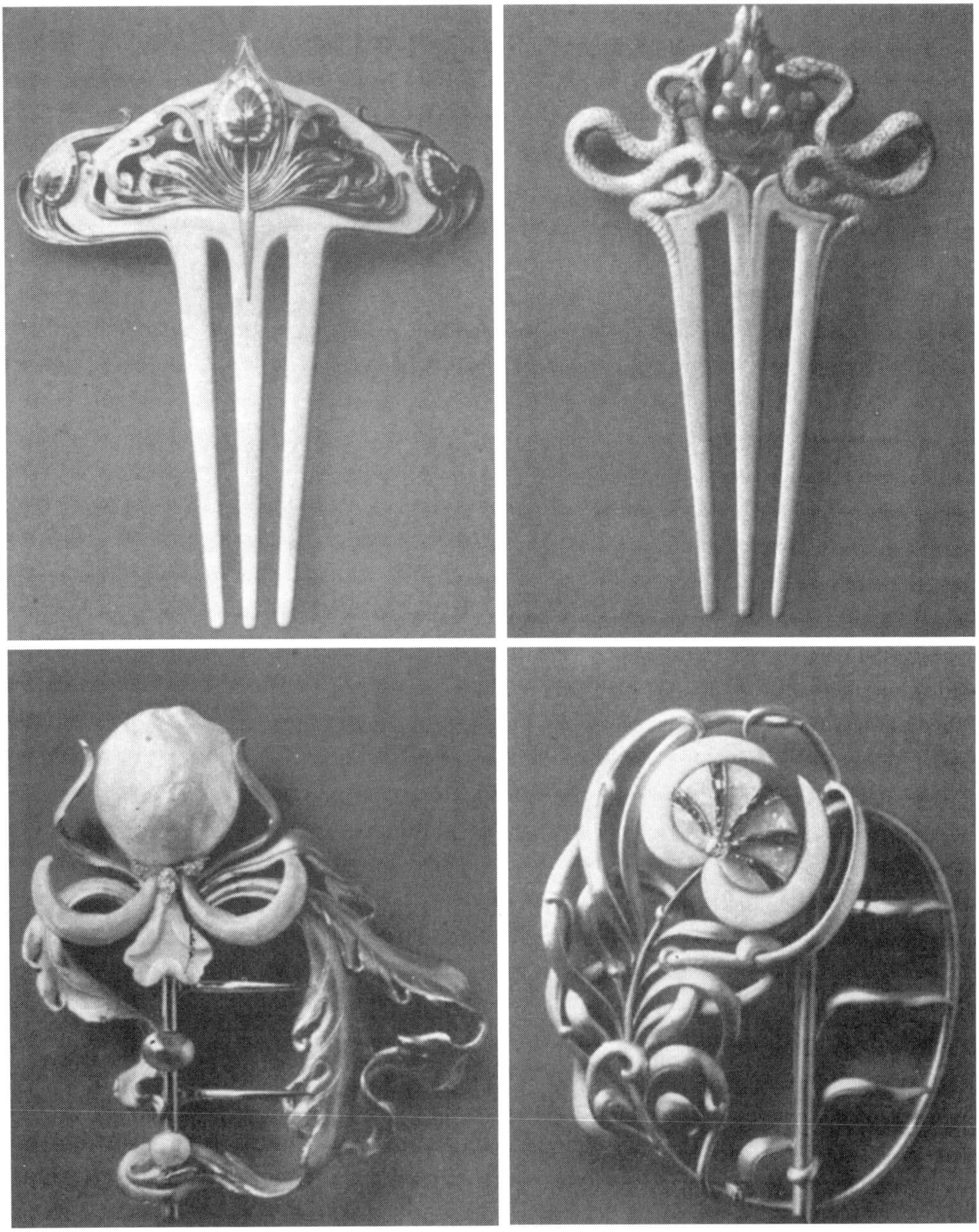

Fig. 190 a–d. Wolfers: a. Comb. Ivory, amethyst, pearls and enamel. 1899. b. Comb. Ivory, gold and enamel. 1899. c. Broach. Gold, pearls and opal. 1898. d. Broach. Gold rubies and enamel. 1898.

Courtesy of M. Wolfers, Brussels.

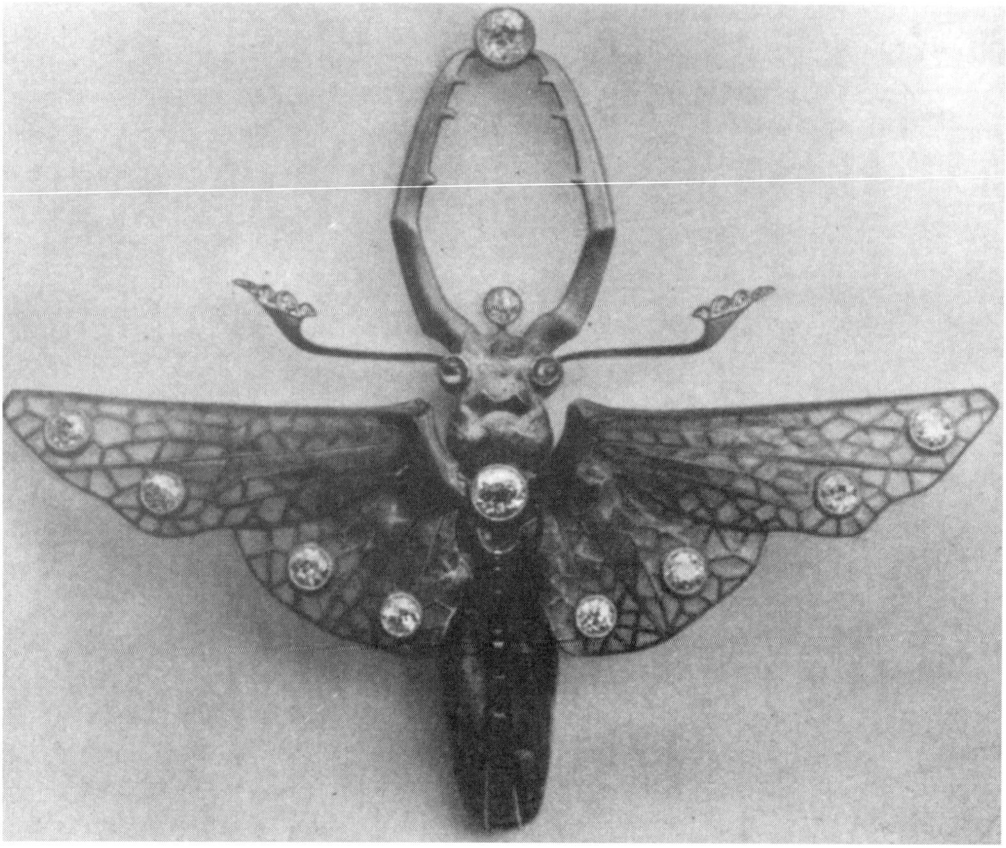

Fig. 191. Wolfers: Broach. About 1900.
Courtesy of M. Wolfers, Brussels.

His jewellery is outstanding in its style, fanciful in its elegant asymmetry, refined in the treatment of material, and of high technical quality (figs. 190 a–d). Philippe Wolfers is the René Lalique of Belgium, and his development corresponds in many ways to that of his French colleague, though the latter's effects were at times even more exquisite. Both frequently used insects as motifs in their jewellery design (fig. 191), as was often the case among Art Nouveau artists. This was a motif which previous ages had not exploited, but which was peculiarly appropriate to the times.[31]

31 E. Millot, l'Entomologie appliquée au décor, *La Lorraine*, vol. XX, 1902, pp. 113–16; M. P. Verneuil, *l'Animal dans la Décoration*, with an introduction by E. Grasset, Paris 1898. Grasset here points to

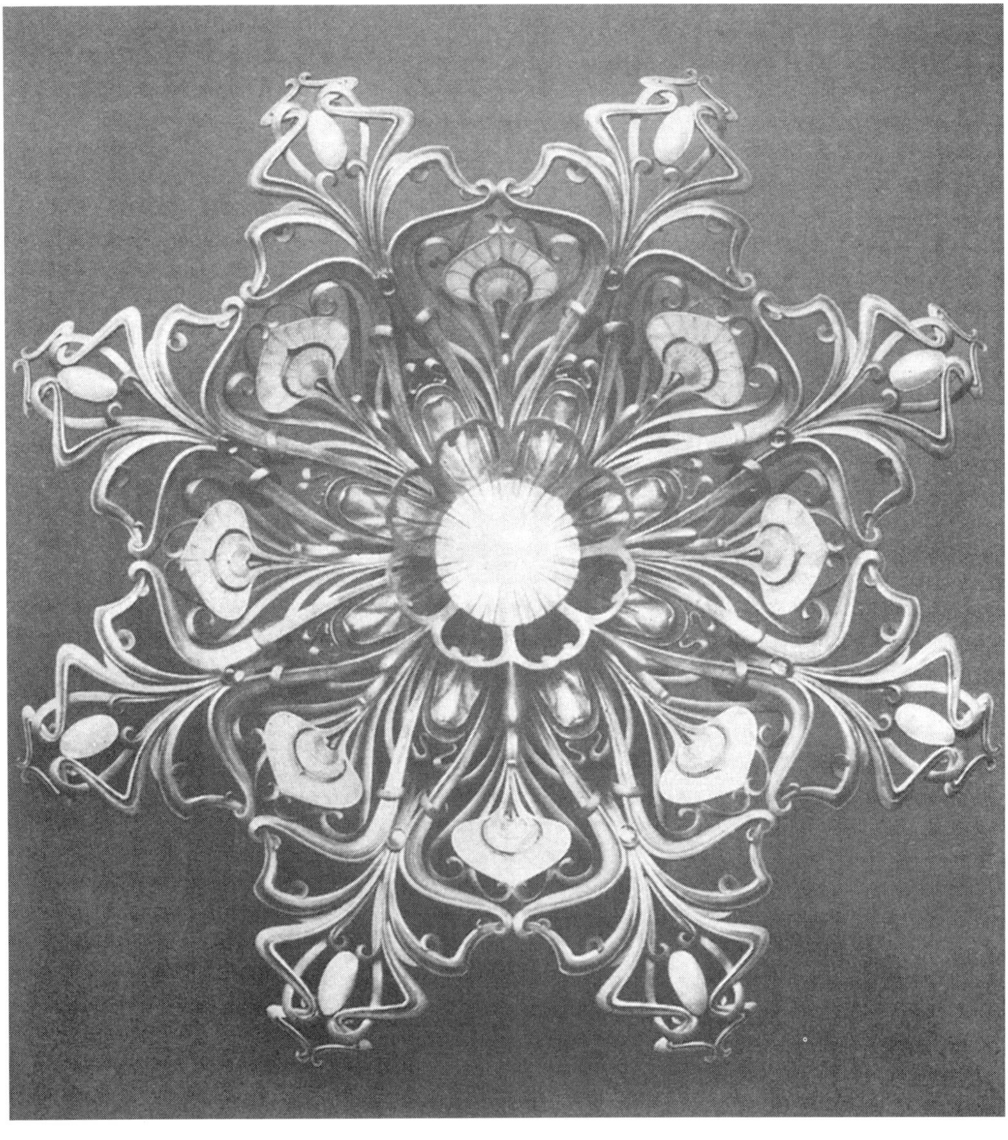

Fig. 192. Wolfers: Holder for a vase, seen from above, silver and enamel. 1897.
Courtesy of M. Wolfers, Brussels.

Oriental art as a source. M. P. Verneuil, The Insect in Decoration, *The Craftsman*, vol. V, 1903–04, pp. 563–74. The elegant treatment of this motif belongs to the French sphere, and plays no part in England.

Towards the end of the century Wolfers' Art Nouveau style becomes gradually less floral and plant-like, and more abstract (fig. 192), after which it changes in harmony with the general development in the first years of the 20th century: the actual ornament is limited to a single field, and is no longer allowed to occupy the entire object; at the same time the interplay between surface and decoration has as a result become more important. After 1905 we find no more Art Nouveau in Wolfers' work.

*

Architects of secondary importance working in the Art Nouveau style in Belgium include Paul Saintenoy, who designed Old England House, as well as 81 Avenue Louise, 1902–03, the latter more in a blend of neo-Rococo and Art Nouveau; furthermore Blerot, floral and influenced by French style, who designed 1 Rue Vilain XIV, 1902, 3 Rue Vilain XIV, 1901, 428 Avenue Louise, 1903, 97 Boulevard Militaire and 28 Rue de Belle Vue; the Horta imitator Seeldrayers, who was responsible for 52 Rue Morris; Peerboom, who designed 14 Place Louis Morichar; and Rysselberghe, who for a short while was associated with van de Velde, and designed and carried out 48 Rue Livourne. All the houses mentioned above are situated in Brussels.

*

Belgium is the only country where it is possible to speak of Art Nouveau architecture, but, both in architecture and in decorative art, this style was short-lived. Van de Velde left the country in 1899, and subsequently played no further role there; Hankar died in 1901, and Serrurier-Bovy in 1910, while the leading artists, including both Horta and Wolfers, abandoned the style in about 1905.

France

Art Nouveau

THE NANCY SCHOOL

About the year 1890 neo-Rococo was the dominant style-trend in the decorative art of France, with a noticeable floral streak of a Naturalistic kind.[1] Emile Gallé's (1846–1904)[2] debut in 1878 and his breakthrough at the Exhibition in 1889 must be considered against this background. Gallé studied first philosophy and botany, was then trained at the glassworks in Meissenthal, 1870, volunteered in the war of 1870–71, and went to England in 1872. Gallé had already worked as an artist in glass from the beginning of the 1870's in his father's pottery-works, which were extended in 1874 to include the faience workshop of Saint Clément. At its largest, about the year 1900, Gallé's workshop employed approximately 300 workers, who were engaged in furniture and glass production. When Gallé died there was no artistic leader capable of running this business, and the workshop gradually declined, being finally dissolved in 1913.[3] As far as Gallé's furniture is concerned he always remained, to a certain extent, in the French stylistic tradition. The constructive nature and the total effect of his furniture are almost always linked up with period style: large cupboards are designed in the Renaissance style, desks mostly in Louis XV, and chairs in Louis XVI.[4] But a feature common to most of his furniture, especially smaller pieces, is the fact that the constructive elements—the actual struc-

1 V. Champier, *Les industries d'art à l'exposition universelle de 1889,* Paris 1890; R. Max, *La décoration et l'art industriel à l'exposition universelle de 1900,* Paris 1903; A. Picard, Rapport général de l'exposition de Paris 1889, I—II, Paris 1889; *l'Art décoratif à l'exposition universelle de 1889,* Paris 1889.

2 L. de Fourcauld, *Emile Gallé,* Paris 1903; L. Gillet, Emile Gallé, Le Poème de Verre, *La Revue Hebdomadaire,* Paris, vol. XIV, 8th of October, 1910, pp. 153–72; B. Karageorgevitsch, A Master of Glass, *The Magazine of Art,* vol. II, 1904, pp. 310–14; G. Varenne, La Pensée et l'Art d'Emile Gallé, *Mercure de France,* 1st of July 1910; G. Gros, Poetry in Glass. The Art of Emile Gallé 1846–1905, [*sic*] *Apollo,* London, New York, vol. LXII, 1955, pp. 134–36.

3 Information kindly given by Madame Perdrizet Gallé to the author, April 1953.

4 L. de Fourcauld, *Emile Gallé,* Paris 1903, Renaissance: Cabinet, *La Montaigne,* p. 63, cabinet, *Heureux les pacifiques,* p. 53. Louis XV: *La Forêt Lorraine,* p. 26, *Orchidées Lorraines,* p. 61, both writing tables. Louis XVI: *Le Merisier de Sainte Lucie,* p. 56, Canapé, p. 66.

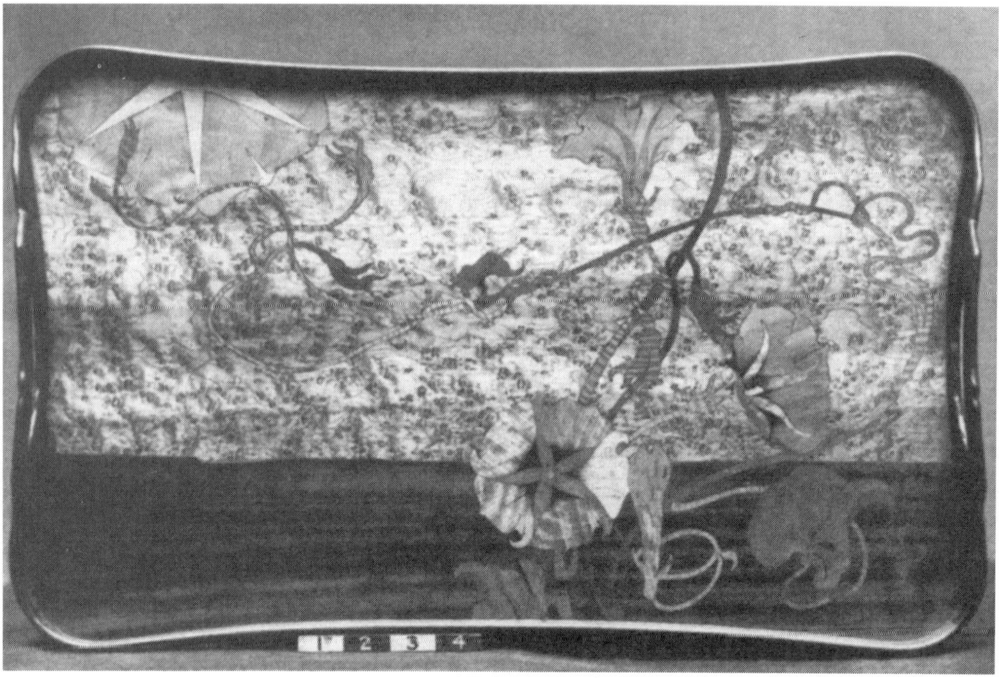

Fig. 193. Gallé: Tray of carved walnut inlaid with marquetry of maple, pear and satinwood. 1900. Victoria and Albert Museum. Crown Copyright reserved.

ture—is transformed into stalks or branches emanating from constructive points. The decoration, both the inlay work and the carving, is floral in character, and blossoms freely all over the surface of the furniture (fig. 193).[5] In this way the furniture appears to be transformed into a living thing, enclosed in its own world of flowers and plants.

In his glasswork, however, Gallé's main forms show a greater degree of unconventionality. In this medium he felt entirely at home, and was able to develop freely. His contribution rests on three techniques which he appropriated, and the mastery of which is a feature of all his work.

The most important technique is probably the *gravure à la roue,* as he called it (fig. 194).[6] This technique is executed with the help of fairly small emery-wheels which grind the glass away, leaving the decoration in relief—

[5] Cat. No. 1983–1900, Victoria and Albert Museum, London.

[6] Cat. No. 1900–43, Vestlandske Kunstindustrimuseum, Bergen.

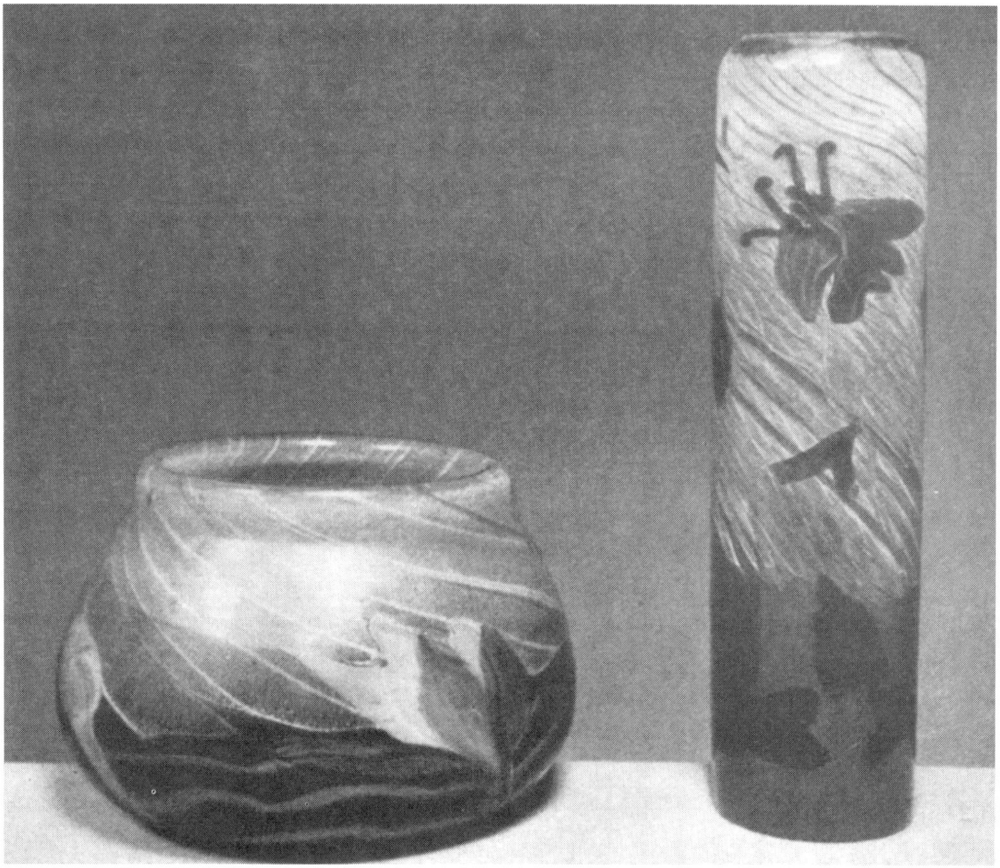

Fig. 194. Gallé: Two vases. Signed Gallé. 1900.
Vestlandske Kunstindustrimuseum, Bergen, Copyright reserved.

in other words, precisely the opposite effect of that usually achieved in glass. In this way the surface acquires life—"patchy"—owing to the traces of the wheel, and the effect is the same as in his carved work, where the traces of the knife are always visible. This is bound up with his view of technique and material, which demands that a work of art should never tell a lie, but should bear witness to the craftsman's work which produced it.

The second technique, which was not quite so exacting, was the *gravure à l'acid*, or the acid treatment of glass. Certain parts of the glass were covered with wax, and were therefore proof against corrosion. In this way

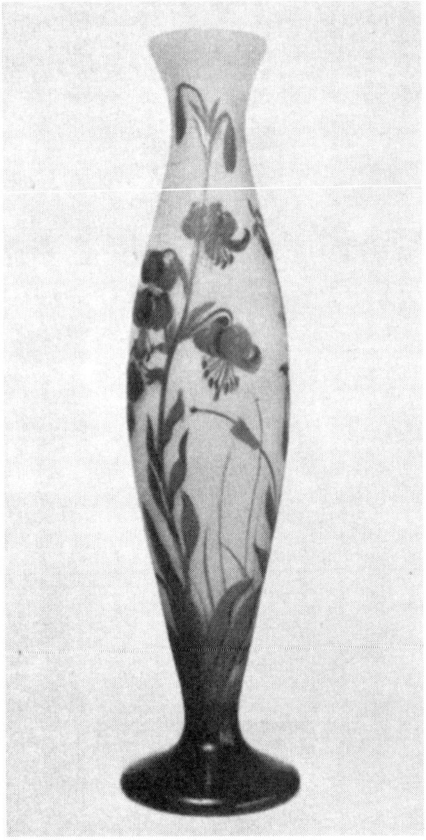

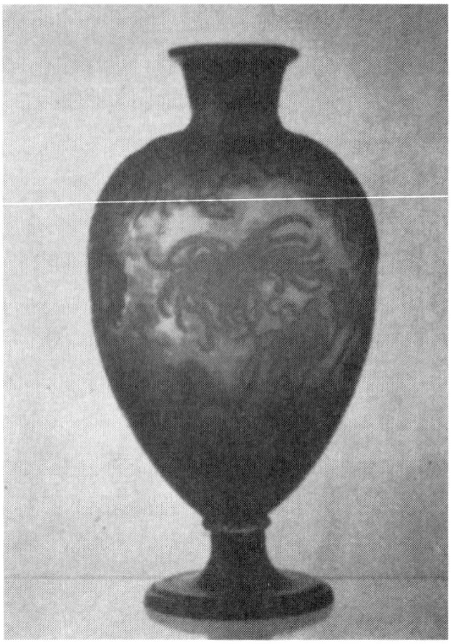

Fig. 196. Gallé: Vase. 1897.
Nationalmuseum, Stockholm. Copyright reserved.

Fig. 195. Gallé:
Vase. Signed Gallé. About 1900.
Malmö Museum. Copyright reserved.

he was able to achieve a smooth unetched relief against a matt-etched background (fig. 195).[7] He often combined these two techniques.

The third technique consisted of laying glass of various colours on top of one another, *verre doublé*, thus obtaining rich deep colour-effects. When the glass was cut away, Gallé obtained shades in different hues, against a background, usually red-brown or milky, which was opaque, transparent, or frosted (fig. 196).[8]

Gallé mastered these three techniques more skilfully than any of his contemporaries, and to a large extent his reputation is based on his work

7 Cat. No. 32.281, Malmö Museum, Malmö.
8 Cat. No. 71.1897. Nordiska Museet. Stockholm.

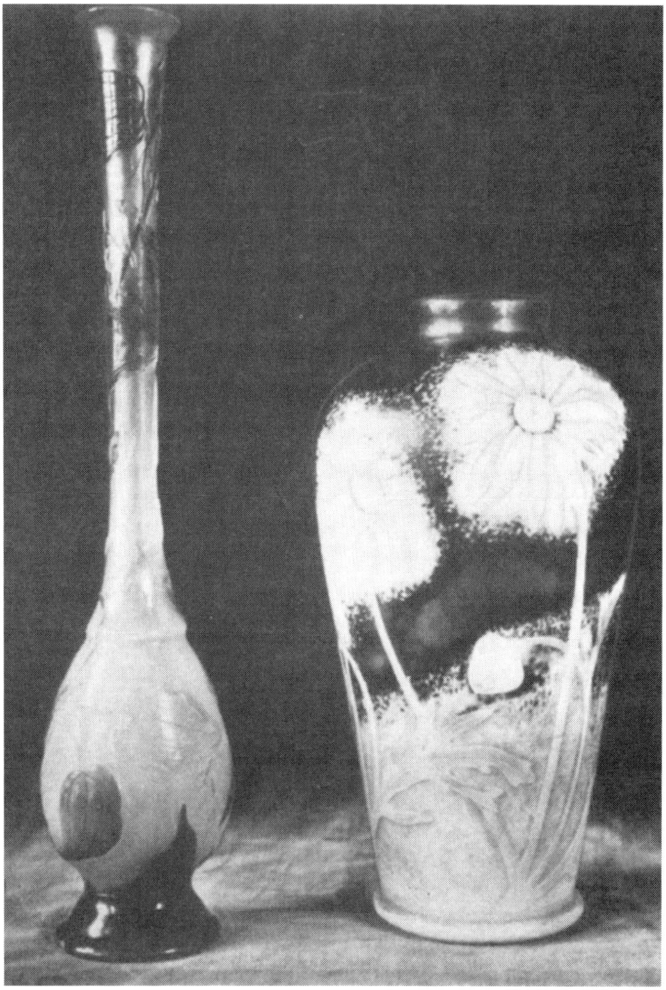

Fig. 197. Daum: Two vases. Signed Daum. About 1900. Malmö Museum. Copyright reserved.

with glass, and on these three techniques which he frequently called *"marqueterie de verre."*

The actual shape of the vase will vary considerably: in the 1870's and at the beginning of the 1880's he was still bound by the traditional shape, with the *corpus* frequently divided into sections by horizontal grooves. But in the 1890's he showed far less constraint: his vases are often long-necked and thin, with imaginative floral openings, or they may be squat and angular. The colours he chooses are mother-of-pearl, apple-green, rose, violet, orange, and especially the reddish-brown which frequently shows saturated and full-bodied nuances. His work is always signed, and the signature, which is part of the decoration itself, is frequently braided in a pattern of flower and plant stalks.

By comparison with the work of the master, the glass designed and produced by the other Nancy craftsmen is bound to appear insipid. They adopted Gallé's techniques and his decoration, and occasionally achieved results which may seem fairly comparable. Here in fact it is possible to speak of a school, in the real sense of the word. In this connection we need only mention Auguste Daum (1854–1909),[9] and his brother Antonin (fig. 197).[10] They are less extravagant than Gallé, and their decoration is frequently confined to poppies and snowdrops, the corpus is frequently more traditional, and the technique as a rule coarser. Furthermore, they did not use inscriptions in the same way as Gallé, and more seldom signed their names on the glass itself. The decoration, too, is sometimes confined to separate fields on the corpus, to horizontal rings, a decorative principle which Gallé himself never made use of. In his work the flower takes possession of the whole vase.

Among furniture designers in Nancy, Louis Majorelle (1859–1926)[11] may be assigned a position which corresponds to that of Gallé in art-glass. After attending the *Académie des Beaux Arts* in Paris from 1877, and studying under Millet, he returned to his native Nancy in 1879 in order to take over the business of his father, Auguste Majorelle, on the latter's death. He soon turned his hand to furniture design, and in the 1880's he produced work in the Louis XIV, Louis XV, and Louis XVI styles. It was not until the end of the 1890's, after he had worked mainly in neo-Rococo, that he gradually adopted, in 1897–98, Gallé's floral shapes (fig. 198).[12] In 1898

9 E. Nicolas, Les Verreries et christaux d'art de MM. Daum, *La Lorraine*, vol. XX, 1902, pp. 258–63; La Verrerie d'art de MM. Daum Frères, *La Lorraine*, vol. XVIII, 1900, pp. 97–99, 106–09, 120; Lampes en verrerie d'art par Daum Frères, *La Lorraine*, vol. XIX, 1901, pp. 135–38.

10 Cat. No. 4270 and 2740, Malmö Museum, Malmö.

11 F. Jourdain, La Villa Majorelle à Nancy, *La Lorraine*, vol. XX, 1902, pp. 242–250; P. Juyot, *Louis Majorelle. Artiste décorateur – maître ébéniste,* Nancy 1926; *Majorelle Frères et Cie. Meubles d'art,* Nancy n.d. Information and archives kindly put at the disposal of the author by Jean Majorelle, Nancy, April 1953.

12 No piece of furniture in Art Nouveau has so far been found before that date, according to Louis

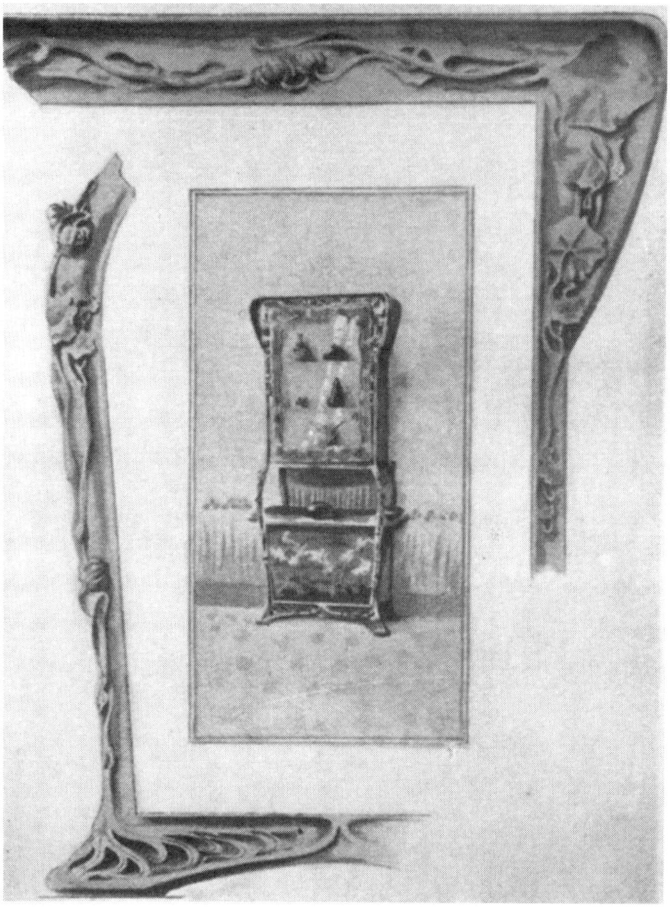

Fig. 198. Majorelle: Design for furniture. Watercolour. 1898. (From *Documents d'Atelier.*)

the firm, with its 30 employees, moved to 6 Rue Vieil-Aître, and it was here that Art Nouveau production commenced.

As a furniture designer Majorelle followed in Gallé's footsteps, the constructive elements were often transformed into stalks which spring up and develop into a floral decoration (fig. 199).[13] Majorelle, however, is less bound by tradition in his construction, and more plastic in his *décor*. Hardly any Art Nouveau artist treated iron as freely and plastically as he

Majorelle's assistant, Alfred Levy, April 1953. His first Art Nouveau motifs are found in V. Champier, *Documents d'atelier,* Paris 1898, pl. XIV.

13 Cat. No. 1999–1900, Victoria and Albert Museum, London.

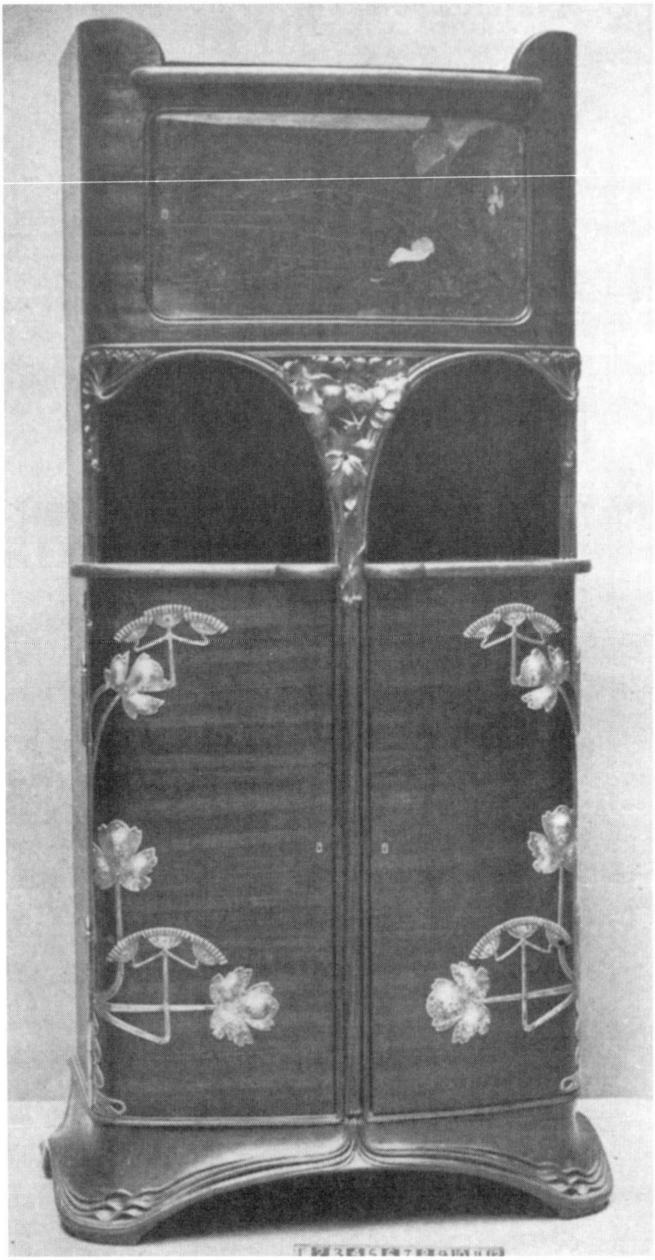

Fig. 199. Majorelle: Cabinet of wood veneered with marquetry of various woods. Signed L. Majorelle. Nancy. 1900.
Victoria and Albert Museum. Crown Copyright reserved.

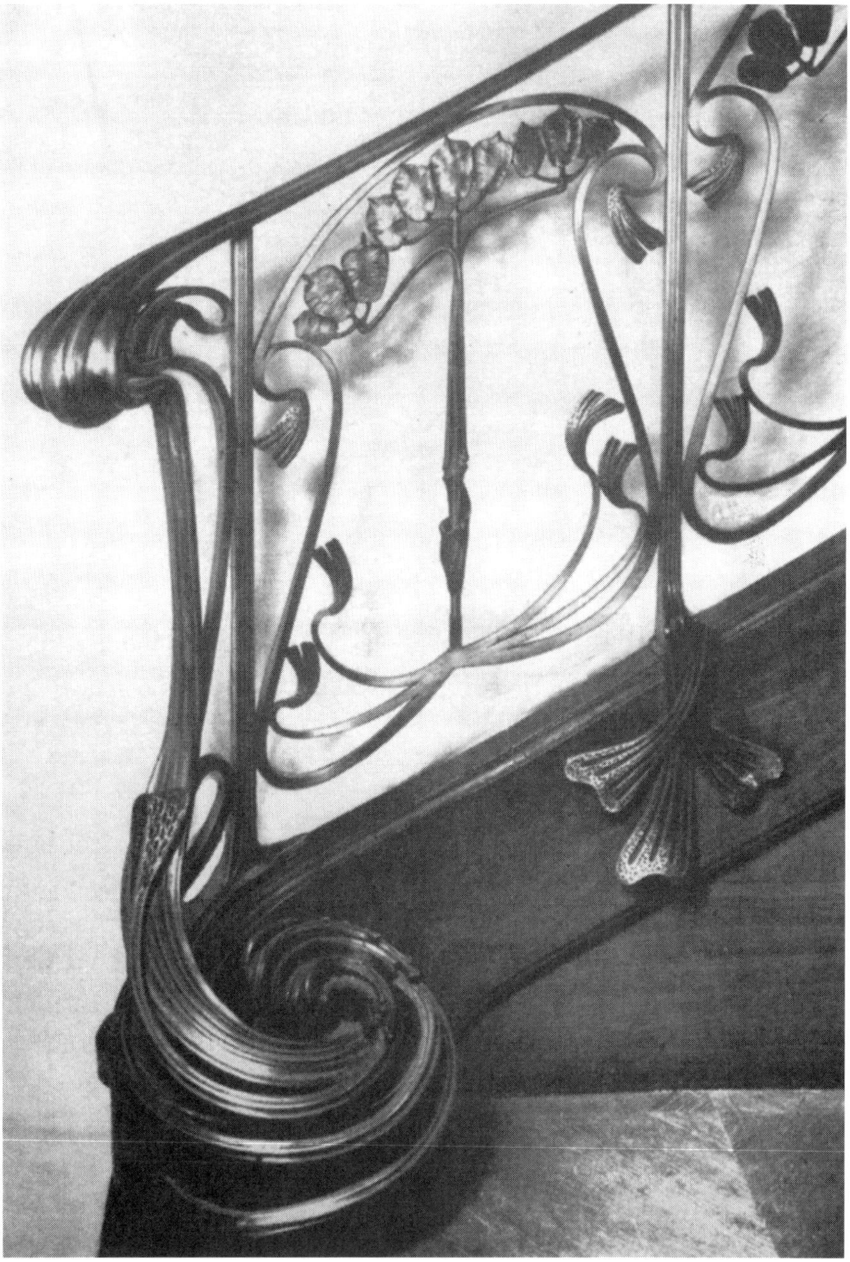

Fig. 200. Majorelle: Bannister. Forged iron. About 1900.
Musée des Arts Décoratifs, Paris. Copyright reserved.

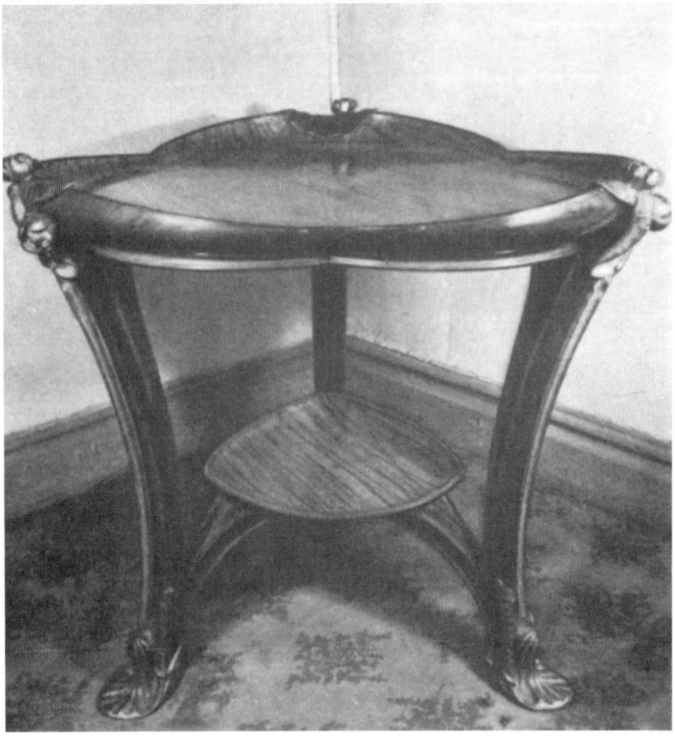

Fig. 201. Majorelle: Table. Mahogany and tamarind. 1900.
Musée des Arts Décoratifs, Paris.
Copyright reserved.

did, not even Horta (fig. 200).[14] His *chef d'oeuvre* in this respect is the iron stair-rail in the Galerie La Fayette, Paris.

In the field of furniture design his work was just as plastic, and in common with several of the Nancy artists, he first modelled his decorative forms and his most important furniture in clay[15] (fig. 201).[16] But Majorelle achieved his best work when he put the emphasis less on form, removing the external neo-Rococo and neo-Baroque details, and allowing the undulating and dynamic flow of the line to dominate the entire character of his furniture. His armchair (fig. 202),[17] with the discreetly restrained decoration and the graceful lines, may be said to be among the most exquisite achieve-

14 Musée des Arts Décoratifs, Louvre, Paris.
15 Information kindly given by Alfred Levy, Nancy, to the author, April 1953.
16 Cat. No. A. 10317, Musée des Arts Décoratifs, Louvre, Paris.
17 Cat. No. 2001–1900, Victoria and Albert Museum, London.

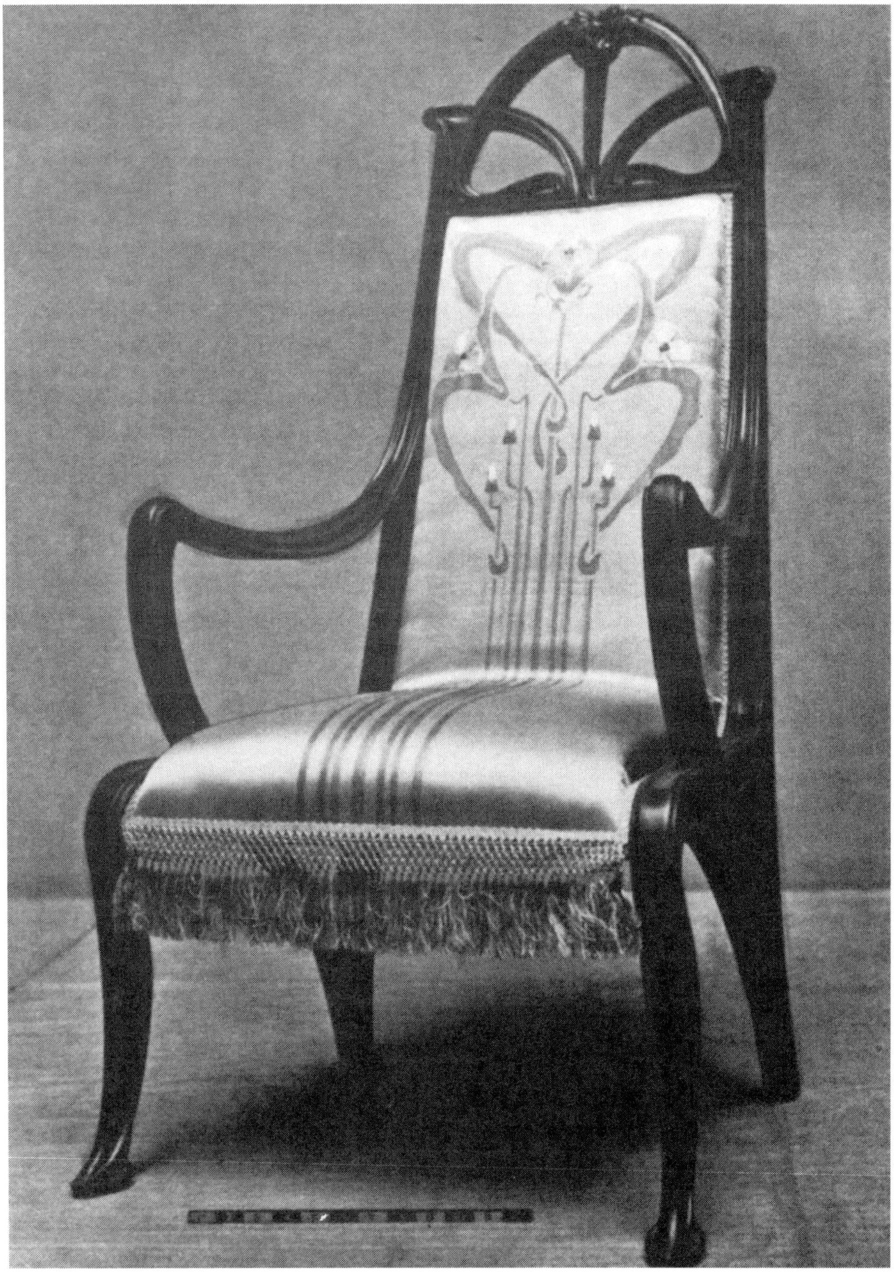

Fig. 202. Majorelle: Armchair. Walnut, stained green, fitted with embroidered and painted mauve satin. 1900.

Victoria and Albert Museum. Crown Copyright reserved.

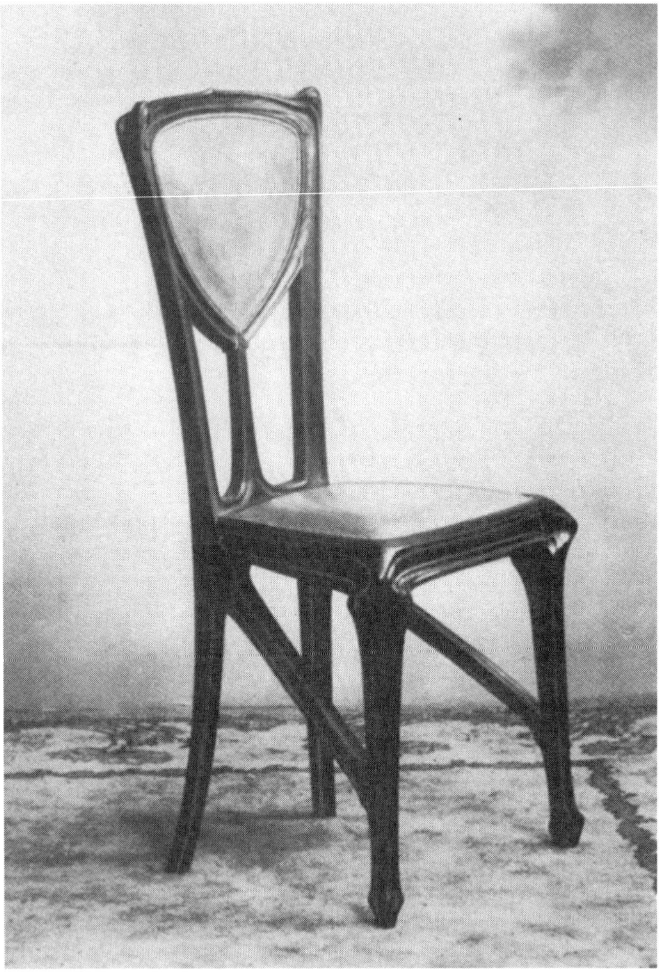

Fig. 203. André: Chair. Mahogany. 1900. Courtesy of J. André, Nancy.

ments of French Art Nouveau—or even of European furniture design around the turn of the century.

During the first few years after 1900 the style seems to flow more smoothly: suites such as *La Vigne* and *Orchidées*,[18] with their ponderous Art Nouveau shapes, disappear, giving way to a simple, sober and more international style, with large and smooth surfaces and a more abstract decoration, which is confined to certain places. But in his fittings and when

18 *Majorelle Frères & Cie. Meubles d'art*, Nancy n.d., pl. 35, 74.

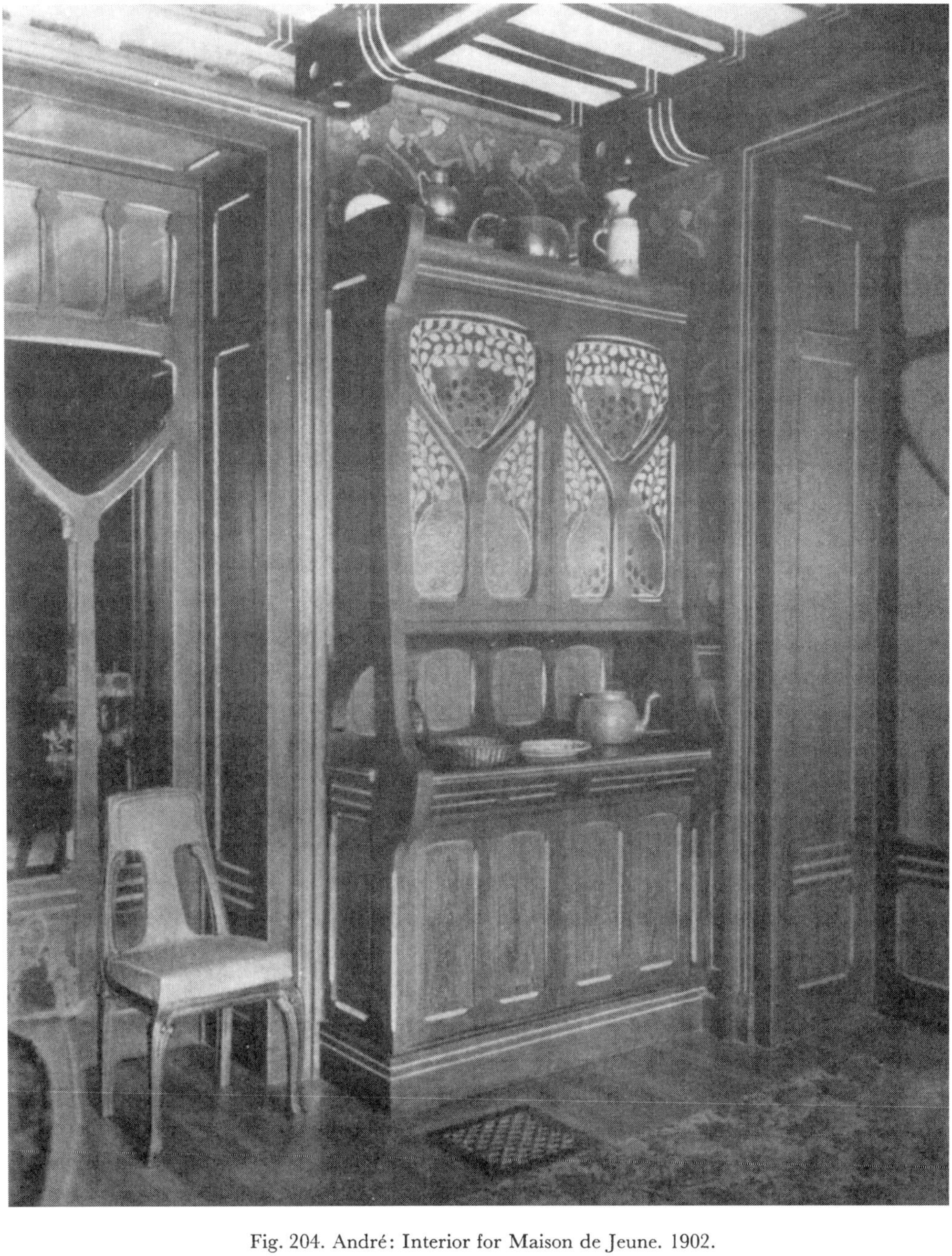

Fig. 204. André: Interior for Maison de Jeune. 1902.
Courtesy of J. André, Nancy,

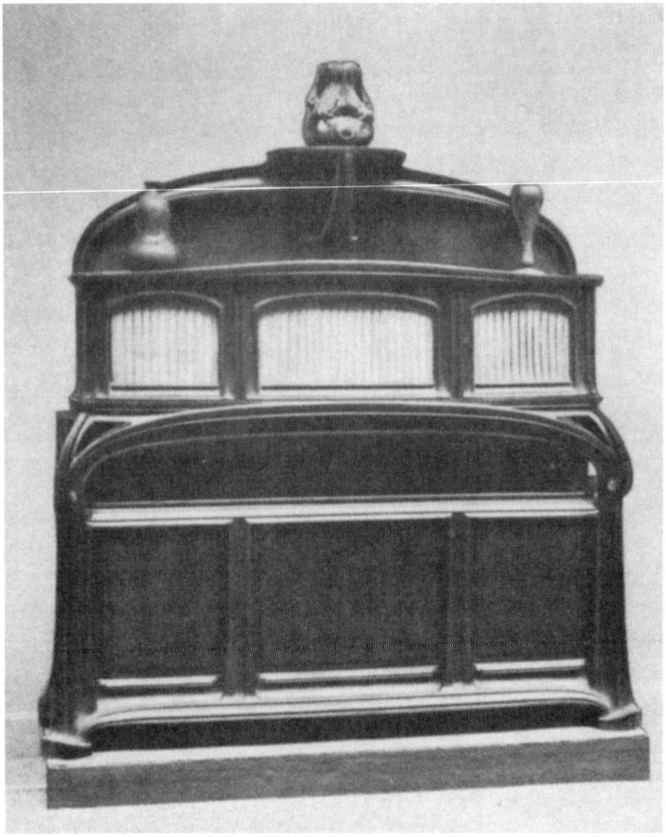

Fig. 205. Vallin: Furniture to conceal radiator. Two vases by Daum, and one by Bussière. About 1900.

he touches a period style, he remains essentially French. Rustic features, which occur so frequently among the experimental artists of Europe at that time, are not in evidence in Nancy, and hardly at all in France.

The other furniture designers of the Nancy school had all been trained as architects. Among the outstanding members were Emile André (1871–1933)[19] and Eugènc Vallin (1856–1925),[20] as well as Jaques Gruber,[21] who was notably influenced by the Louis XV style. Artists of secondary

19 E. Nicolas, l'Architecture et le mobilier architectural modernes à Nancy, *La Lorraine,* vol. XX, 1902, pp. 163–68, 177–81. Information also kindly given by Jacques André, Nancy, to the author, April 1953.

20 E. Nicolas, *loc. cit.; idem,* Un cabinet de travail, *La Lorraine,* vol. XX, 1902, pp. 276–81.

21 E. Nicolas, Les Vitraux de M. Gruber, *La Lorraine,* vol. XXI, 1903, pp. 222–33; Les Meubles de Gruber, *ibid.,* vol. XIX, 1901, pp. 99–110.

importance, who all worked more or less in Gallé's and Majorelle's style, included Camille Gauthier[22] and Poinsington,[23] who later on both specialised in hotel furniture.

The chair with the triangular back (fig. 203)[24] seems to be a particularly typical product of Nancy. The motif is often used by Nancy craftsmen, and with its tree-like form is excellently adapted to the floral decoration. Emile André, who was the leading architect at Nancy at this time, adopted in the years just after 1900 a simpler and less ornate style (fig. 204) and finally abandoned Art Nouveau completely about the year 1905–06.[25]

Eugène Vallin, two years senior to Majorelle, was more closely associated with him, and in his furniture design he reminds us more than any of the others of Majorelle. He has the same sculptural and dynamic form-language based on floral and neo-Baroque inspiration, but subsequently he abandoned the floral elements, and used the curvature of the structure as a decorative element of his furniture (fig. 205)[26]—in other words he adopted abstract decoration or he used no decoration at all. This style, which was less extravagant, lasted somewhat longer, to disappear almost imperceptibly just before the First World War.[27]

*

The Nancy school, which grew up around the year 1890, under the leadership and inspiration of one man, reached the summit of its artistic development about 1900.[28] In the following year *l'Ecole de Nancy, Alliance Provinciale des Industries d'Art* was founded with the object of "favoriser la renaissance et le développement des métiers d'art en province" (promoting the rebirth and the development of arts and crafts in the province), to

22 E. Nicolas, Meubles de Camille Gauthier, *La Lorraine,* vol. XIX, 1901, pp. 249–50.

23 *Idem,* Les Meubles de MM. Gauthier et Poinsington, *La Lorraine,* vol. XXI, 1903, pp. 101–05.

24 Photo from the archives of Jacques André, Nancy, taken 1900. Next photo, fig. 200 taken 1902.

25 Maison Bichaton, 1902, Maison Lejeune, 1902, Maison Lombard, 1903, are all in a sort of Art Nouveau-Gothic with high-pitched gables. In Banque Renaud, Rue St. Jean, 1908, all traces of Art Nouveau have disappeared, but medievalism and Louis XV touches are still there.

26 Musée des Beaux Arts, Nancy.

27 Information kindly given to the author by Auguste Vallin, Nancy, April 1953.

28 L'Exposition de l'Ecole de Nancy, Paris 1900.

quote from a paragraph in the statutes of the school. But only a few years later, in 1904, the man who had inspired the whole movement and whose initiative had been responsible for the founding of the school, died, and the Ecole de Nancy disappeared from the limelight, and returned to the province's own Louis XV tradition.

PARIS

Like Walter Crane, Eugène Grasset (1841–1917)[29] was one of the artists who worked essentially in an Art Nouveau-like style before Art Nouveau, and who were of much greater importance to its origins than its development. Grasset commenced his training as an architect in Lausanne, but made his way to Egypt in 1869, reaching Paris after the end of the war in 1871. Here he studied Viollet-le-Duc and Japanese art assiduously, working as a decorator and typographical draughtsman, and published *inter alia Ornements Typographiques* in 1880, where his interest for both Japan and the Middle Ages found expression in a series of vignettes in a very typical proto-Art Nouveau.[30] In 1883 *Histoire des quatre Fils Aymon* appeared, which Octave Uzanne described as ". . . classé incontestablement parmi les premiers beaux livres du siècle."[31]

Grasset's interest in two-dimensional art found complete expression in poster design, which was emerging as an art at the end of the 1880's and the beginning of the 1890's, and of which Grasset was to prove one of the founders. Poster art[32] is scarcely one of the sources of Art Nouveau, as

29 G. Mourey, Eugène Grasset, *Art et Décoration,* vol. XIII, 1903, p. 1; O. Uzanne, Eugène Grasset. Illustrateur, Architect, Décorateur, *l'Art et l'Idée,* vol. II, 1892, pp. 193–220; *idem,* Eugène Grasset and Decorative Art in France, *The Studio,* vol. IV, 1894, pp. 37–47; Eugène Grasset, *La Plume,* May 1894, pp. 175–228 (Special Number); Eugène Grasset, *La Plume,* 1900, pp. 1–63 (Special Number).

30 In 1869 he had already designed a composition for a wallpaper in Egyptian style, where the lines and curves remind one very much of proto-Art Nouveau designs. Ill. in *Revue des Arts Décoratifs,* vol. XVII, 1897, p. 184.

31 O. Uzanne, Eugène Grasset. Illustrateur, Architect, Décorateur, *l'Art et l'Idée,* vol. II, 1894, p. 196, "indisputably classed among the outstanding beautiful books of the century."

32 A. Alexandre, *The Modern Poster,* N.Y., 1895; Ch. Hiatt, *Picture Posters,* London 1895; E. McKnight Kauffer, *The Art of the Poster,* London 1924; E. Maindron, *Les Affiches illustrées,* Paris 1886; C. M. Price, *Posters,* N.Y., 1913; L. Sponsel, *Das Moderne Plakat,* Dresden 1897.

has been maintained, but became a *genre* in which Art Nouveau artists naturally expressed themselves, not surprisingly when we consider how many of them were decorators. Large surfaces, homogeneous colour planes, powerful contours, and a two-dimensional effect, are essential to this *genre*, and these qualities had all been developed in painting with Synthetism. The first precurser is naturally painting, and poster art reflects it in an extreme way.

As a furniture designer Grasset never showed Art Nouveau influence, his furniture being rectilinear, shorn of *décor*, asymmetrical, and constructive—all features derived from Japanese influence and Medievalism.

Grasset's attitude to Art Nouveau was not particularly positive: he was averse to it not least on social grounds, as he considered that this kind of art was not democratic. A return to an imitation of period styles—even Empire—was impossible: there was only one solution left—"consulter l'usage présent, l'utilité des objets et les orner au moyen des formes puisées dans la nature, en tenant compte de la matière employée."[33]

Like Crane, Grasset too objects to the actual Art Nouveau style, and just as the English kept to their tradition on a basis of austerity, Grasset and Gallé adhered in their furniture design to the French stylistic tradition, while covering it with a lavish and fanciful naturalistic decoration. The English designers, too, undoubtedly showed an interest in Nature in their decoration, but they were less fanciful, more stylised and restrained, and the Arts-and-Crafts artists gradually abandoned the use of ornament altogether where furniture was concerned. An entirely different principle applied in the case of the French designers: they considered decoration necessary—the important thing was simply to find a suitable form for it.

The general stylistic development in France from the 1880's and right up to the end of the century was entirely influenced by the country's own traditional styles, to which artists constantly returned. In the art of the silversmith and the goldsmith neo-Rococo—Louis XV—predominated, and in the case of furniture the general rule applied that each piece of

[33] E. Grasset, L'Art Nouveau, *Revue des Arts Décoratifs,* vol. XVII, 1897, p. 186, "consult present usage, the utility of the objects, and decorate them by means of forms taken from Nature, while having regard for the material employed."

furniture and each room demanded its own style: Renaissance for a study, library, and sometimes a bedroom; Louis XV for a salon and a lady's bedroom; Louis XIV for a hall and living-room; and Louis XVI for the drawing-room. But on the whole Louis XV strikes the dominant note as far as taste generally went in the decades before the year 1900.

Since France was the country where Art Nouveau became most firmly established and lasted longest, it might be practical to consider the development chronologically, while at the same time dealing with the individual artists. In so doing we can concentrate on Paris, which was the main centre of the international movement, with Sigfried Bing and his shop as its focal point.

The exhibition of 1889 had aroused a considerable amount of feeling: it was clear that there was something brewing. At the *Salon de Champs de Mars* in 1891 applied art was subsequently exhibited for the first time side by side with painting. The artists' struggle for equality between the various arts had borne fruit, and this was continued during the subsequent years; in 1893 the example was followed by the *Salon des Champs Elysées*. In 1892 Octave Uzanne founded his periodical *L'Art et l'Idée*, in which decorative art was given a central position. France also had a number of talented writers who followed events with interest, and who actively supported Art Nouveau. Among these were Gabriel Mourey, Jean Schopfer, and Charles Genuys, while Victor Champier adopted a more expectant attitude, and Arsène Alexandre and Eugène Grasset were definitely in opposition. But the decisive bomb exploded when Sigfried Bing, on Thursday, December 26, 1895,[34] opened his doors to Europe's connoisseurs of art in his shop at the corner of the Rue de Province and the Rue Cauchat. Sigfried Bing the art collector[35]—small and squat, a native of Hamburg and of Jewish descent—

[34] 1896 is usually given as the date of the opening by most authors, e.g. by H. Lenning in *Art Nouveau*, The Hague, 1951, p. 51. Sometimes the year 1897 is given, René Puaux gives the date 26th of December 1891, *Deutsche Kunst und Dekoration*, vol. XII, 1903, p. 313, which obviously must be a misprint for 26th of December 1895. Bing himself says 1895, L'Art Nouveau, *The Craftsman*, vol. V, 1903–04, p. 1. There can be no doubt whatsoever about this date, because A. Alexandre wrote his article about the opening of the shop in *Le Figaro*, Paris, the 28th of December 1895.

[35] There has been some confusion about his first name, usually he is only called S. Bing. K. Osborn who gives a vivid description of the man in his book about van de Velde, calls him J. Bing; H. Lenning calls him Samuel in his book *Art Nouveau*. His name was most probably Sigfried Bing. He must not be confused with Marcel Bing either, who was also a connoisseur of Japanese art.

was already well known for his publications on Japanese art. During the years 1888–91 he published *Japon artistique*, a monthly illustrated journal, edited in London as *Artistic Japan*.

The inaugural exhibition included paintings by Vuillard, Besnard, Denis, and Brangwyn, interiors by van de Velde, and applied art by such craftsmen as Ranson and Conder. The reception was mixed, and just as Englishmen invariably turn to the columns of *The Times* to vent their wrath, so Arsène Alexandre turned to *Le Figaro*, where, among other things, he declared: "Tout cela sent l'Anglais vicieux, la Juive morphinomane ou le Belge roublard, ou une agréable salade de ces trois poisons."[36] The editor of *La Revue des Arts Décoratifs*, Victor Champier, and the leader of *l'Union Centrale des Arts Décoratifs*, were more open in their attitude, but simply noted that the new experiment was so radical that it might well repel artists, and that one ought perhaps to think of allowing an imitation of period styles once more.[37]

But as usually happens with sensational openings of this kind, when the public are attracted by the outcry which is raised, the success of the venture was assured.

During the years that followed Bing gathered around him a number of the younger artists, men who were to make their name as the foremost representatives of Art Nouveau. The three most prominent who worked for Bing were Georges de Feure (1868–1928),[38] known for his drawings in *Le Courrier Français* and *Le Boulevard*, Eugène Gaillard, about whom little more is known except that he wrote a book called *A Propos du Mobilier*, but who was nevertheless one of the foremost Art-Nouveau artists; and finally the potter and furniture designer Eugène Colonna. Mention should also be made of the potter Auguste Delaherche,[39] who was associated with Bing at various times.

36 A. Alexandre in *Le Figaro*, Saturday, the 28th of December 1895. All this seems to have an air of the vicious Englishman, the Jewess addicted to morphine, or the Belgian spiv, or an agreable mixture of these three poisons.

37 V. Champier, Les Expositions de l'Art Nouveau, *Revue des Arts Décoratifs*, vol. XVI, 1895–96, pp. 1–6.

38 T.B., Georges de Feure, *Zeitschrift für Innendekoration*, vol. XIII, 1902, pp. 5–7, figs. 208, 209, 212 from this article; G. Mourey, Georges de Feure, *The Studio*, vol. XII, 1898, pp. 95–102; R. Puaux, *Georges de Feure*, Paris n.d.; *idem*, Georges de Feure, *Deutsche Kunst und Dekoration*, vol. XII, 1903, pp. 313–48; O. Uzanne, Georges de Feure, *Art et Décoration*, vol. IX, 1901, pp. 77–88.

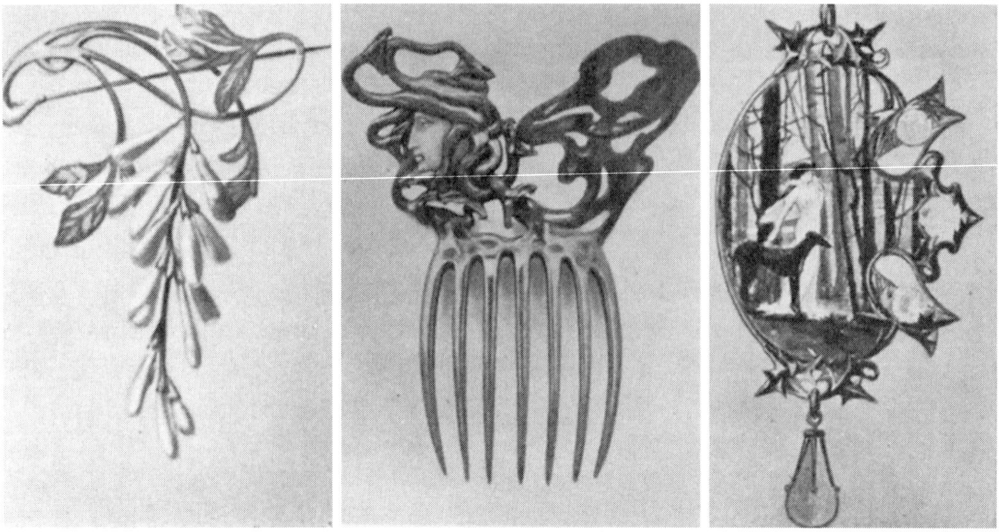

Fig. 206 a–c. Lalique: a. Brooch. About 1900. Østerreichisches Museum für angewandte Kunst, Vienna. b. Comb. From *Art et Décoration*, vol. VII, 1899. c. Design for jewellery, *loc. cit.*

Long before Bing opened his shop—from as far back as 1892–93—a number of artists had mooted the idea of joining battle in more organised fashion, and in the same year that Bing opened his shop, the sculptors Alexandre Charpentier (1856–1909),[40] Jean Dampt (1854–1946),[41] the decorator and designer Felix Aubert (1866–?),[42] as well as the architect Tony Selmersheim (1871–?),[43] and the potter Moureau-Nélaton joined forces and formed the group *Les Cinq*, which had its first exhibition that

39 It has been quite impossible to trace any biographical information about Gaillard and Colonna. Auguste Delaherche (1857–?); A. Delaherche, *Catalogue de l'Exposition de ses oeuvres au Musée des Arts Décoratifs, 1907,* Paris 1907; R. Koechlin, *Le Pavillon de l'Union Centrale des Arts Décoratifs*, 1900, Paris 1900, p. 12; G. Mourey, Auguste Delaherche, *The Studio,* vol. XII, 1898, pp. 112–18; G. Lecomte, *A. Delaherche,* Paris 1922; O. Uzanne, Auguste Delaherche, *l'Art et l'Idée,* vol. I, 1892, pp. 81–90.

40 O. Grautoff, "Alexandre Charpentier"; Thieme, Becker, *Allgemeines Lexikon bildender Künstler,* Leipzig, vol. VI, 1912, pp. 405–06; G. Mourey, An interview on "Art Nouveau" with Alexandre Charpentier, *The Architectural Record,* vol. XII, 1902, pp. 121–25.

41 Illustrations of his furniture in *Revue des Arts Décoratifs,* vol. XVI, 1896, p. 226; *ibid.,* vol. XVII, 1897, p. 28.

42 G. Geffroy, "Felix Aubert"; Thieme, Becker, *op. cit.,* vol. II, 1908, pp. 225–26.

43 F. Jourdain, Tony Selmersheim, *Art et Décoration,* vol. XVI, 1904, pp. 189–98; G. Soulier, Charles Plumet et Tony Selmersheim, *Art et Décoration,* vol. VII, 1900, pp. 11–21.

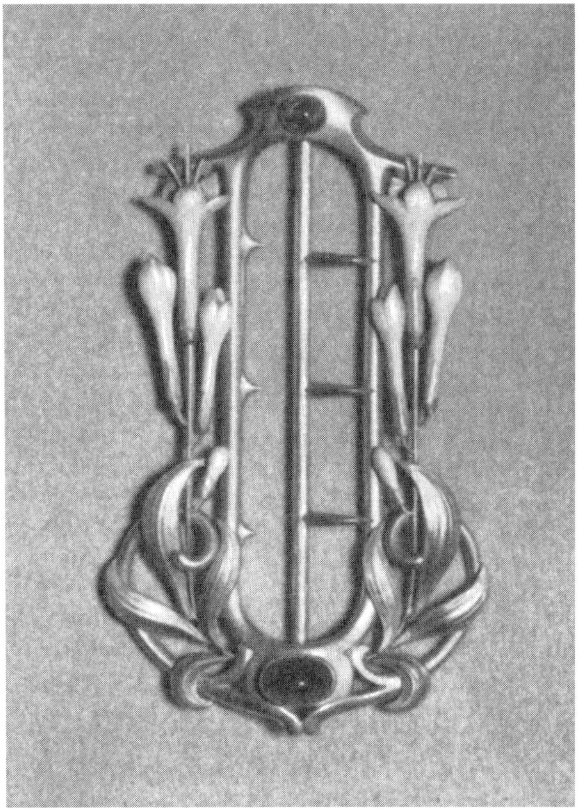

Fig. 207. Maison Vever: Brooch. Gold, enamel and semi-precious stones. 1900. Vestlandske kunstindustrimuseum, Bergen.

year. During the next year the architect Charles Plumet (1861–1925)[44] also joined the group, and its name was changed to *Les Six.*[45] That year, too, they exhibited their applied art in the *Galerie des Artistes Modernes* in the Rue Vavin—the second centre of advanced applied art in Paris. The development was now gathering momentum, and criticism was favourable. In 1897 the group was further extended, and now comprised, apart from those mentioned above, the sculptor Henri Nocq (1866–?), who was keenly interested in applied art and who had already launched his celebrated investigation in the *Journal des Artistes* in the autumn of 1894, as well as the

44 G. Soulier, *op. cit.*, C. Plumet, *Art Français contemporain. Maisons de rapport de Charles Plumet,* Paris 1928; Une nouvelle construction par C. Plumet, *L'Art Décoratif,* vol. III, part 1, pp. 154–64.

45 G. Mourey, Decorative Art in Paris: The Exhibition of "the Six," *The Studio,* vol. XIII, 1898, pp. 83–91.

architect Henri Sauvage (1873–1932).[46] Every year they exhibited under the name of *L'Art dans Tout*; in 1897 the German art critic Julius Meier-Graefe opened his shop *Maison Moderne*, 2 Rue de la Paix, so that now in the middle of Paris's artists' quarter there were three centres for artists interested in Art Nouveau.

Apart from the artists mentioned there were a number of architects working in the Art Nouveau style. Most prominent among them was Hector Guimard (1867–1942),[47] as well as Louis Bonnier, who redecorated Bing's house in 1895,[48] Xavier Schollkopf, who designed Yvette Guilbert's house, as well as Louis Sorel and Louis Bigauz, who occasionally worked in the Art Nouveau style. Among those who worked in silver and gold the outstanding Art Nouveau artists were first of all René Lalique (1860–1945)[49] (figs. 206 a–c), after whom came the Maison Vever[50] (figs. 94, 207), under the leadership of Ernest Vever who withdrew in 1880 and handed over to Paul Vever (1851–1915) and Henri Vever (1854–1942). Finally we have the Maison Christofle, where the younger generation took over after Charles Christofle in 1863. The management of the firm was then in the hands of Paul Christofle (1838–1907) and his cousin Henri Bouilhet (1830–1910), especially known for his writings on French silver. Both these firms adopted practically the same attitude to Art Nouveau, remaining discreetly in the background to start with, but, as neo-Rococo gradually

46 F. Jourdain, Hôtel et Café moderne, *Revue des Arts Décoratifs,* vol. XX, 1900, pp. 33–40; G. Mourey, Sauvage, *Les Albums d'Art Druet,* Paris 1928; G. Soulier, Henri Sauvage, *Art et Décoration,* vol. V, 1899, pp. 65–75.

47 H. Guimard, Le Castel Béranger, Paris 1899, foreword by M. G. d'Hastingue; H. Guimard, An Architect's opinion on the Art Nouveau, *The Architectural Record,* vol. XII, 1903, pp. 127–33; G. Baus, Les Gares du Metropolitain de Paris, *L'Art Décoratif,* vol. VII, 1900, pp. 38–40; V. Champier, Le Castel Béranger, *Revue des Arts Décoratifs,* vol. XIX, 1899, pp. 1–10 (some biographical notes); H. Frantz, "Castel Béranger"—the "New Art" in Architectural Design, *The Magazine of Art,* vol. XXV, 1900–01, pp. 85–87; F. Mazade, An "Art Nouveau" Edifice in Paris, *The Architectural Record,* vol. XII, 1902, pp. 53–66; G. Soulier, *Etudes sur le Castel Béranger,* Paris 1899. Drawings and photographs in Avery Library, Columbia University.

48 Dekorative Kunst, vol. I, 1897–98, pp. 28–31.

49 L. Bénédite, *René Lalique,* Paris n.d.; G. Geffroy, *René Lalique,* Paris 1922; R. Marx, René Lalique, *Art et Décoration,* vol. VII, 1899, pp. 13–22. The jewellery: Musée des Arts Décoratifs, Louvre, Paris.

50 Information about the firm and its activities during the turn of the century kindly given by G. Vever to the author, June 1953. The Illustrated Brooch. Cat. No. 30.5.1901. Vestlandske Kunstindustri-museum, Bergen.

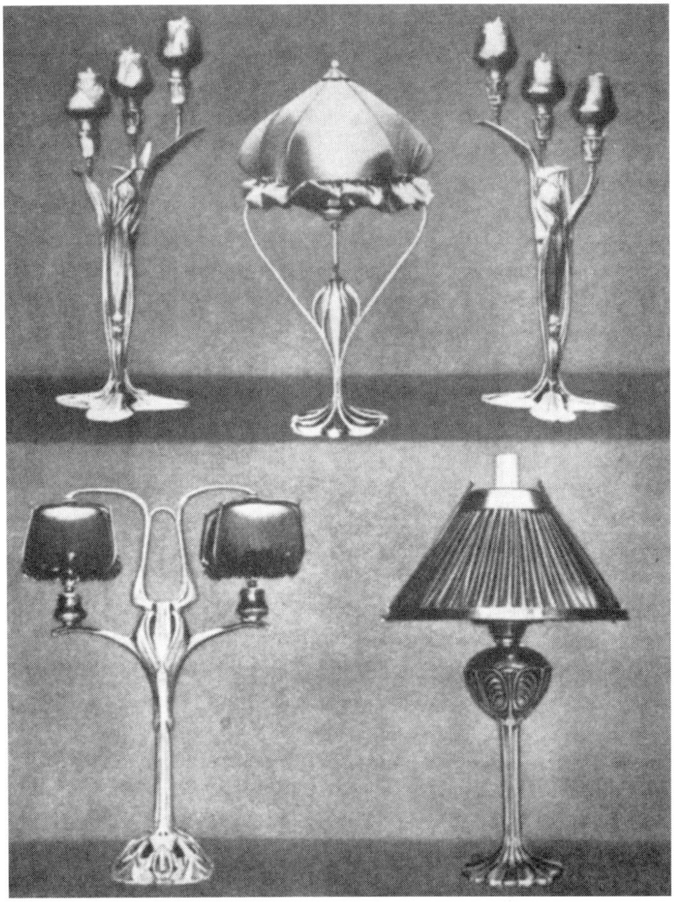

Fig. 208. De Feure: Lamps. Before 1902.

became more and more floral, allowing the style a considerable measure of latitude around the year 1900.

If the word "feminine" can be used at all about applied art, then it can aptly be used to describe the work of Georges de Feure. Not only does he place his slender graceful female forms on posters and screens, and anywhere else he can put them, but his neat objects are designed so gracefully and so airly as though they were all intended for a female hand (fig. 208). He uses pastel-like and pale colours, with a special penchant for the most delicate shades of grey. Up to 1900 his form-language is always derived from plants and flowers (figs. 209 a–d) with the stalks—always elegantly

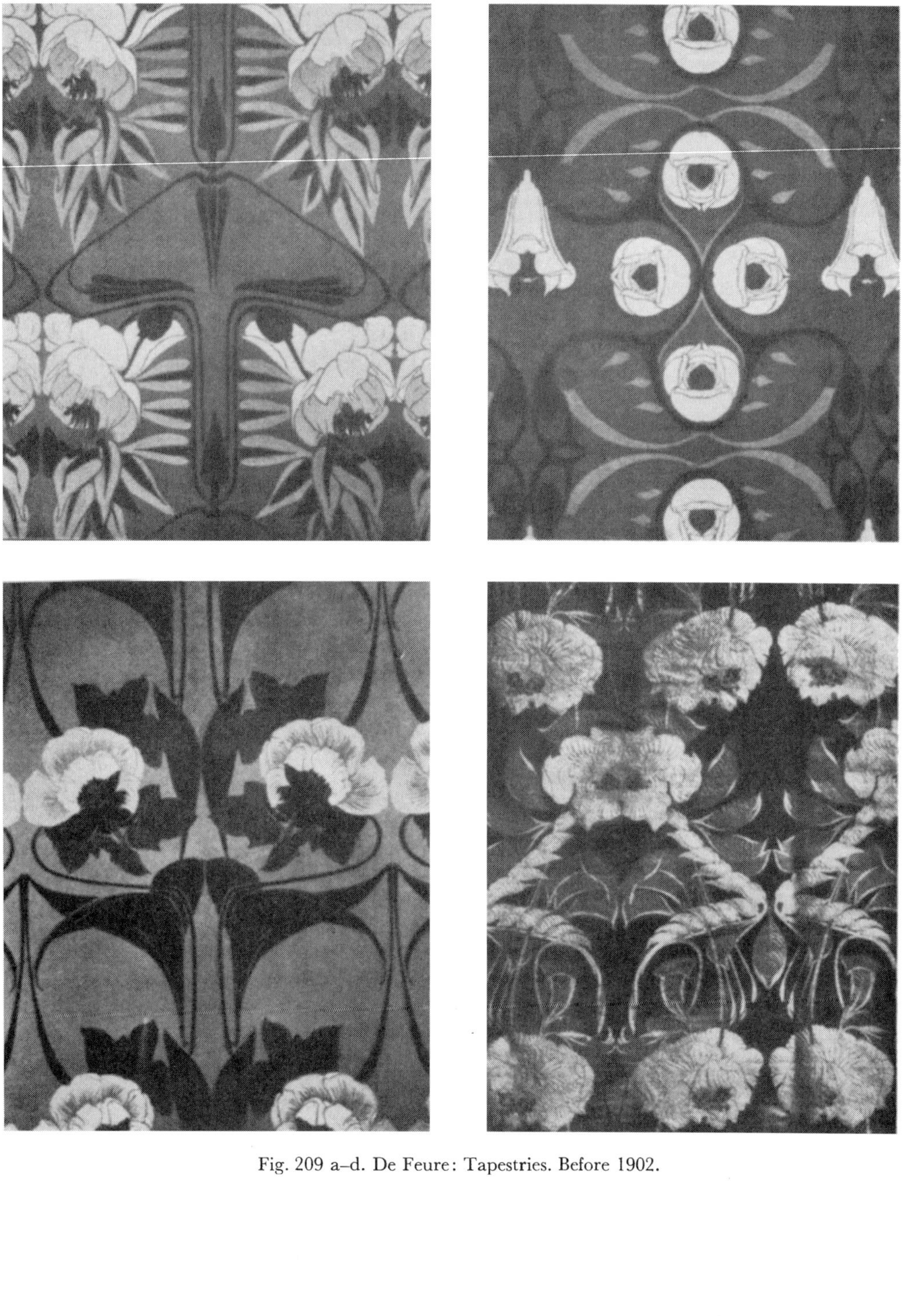

Fig. 209 a–d. De Feure: Tapestries. Before 1902.

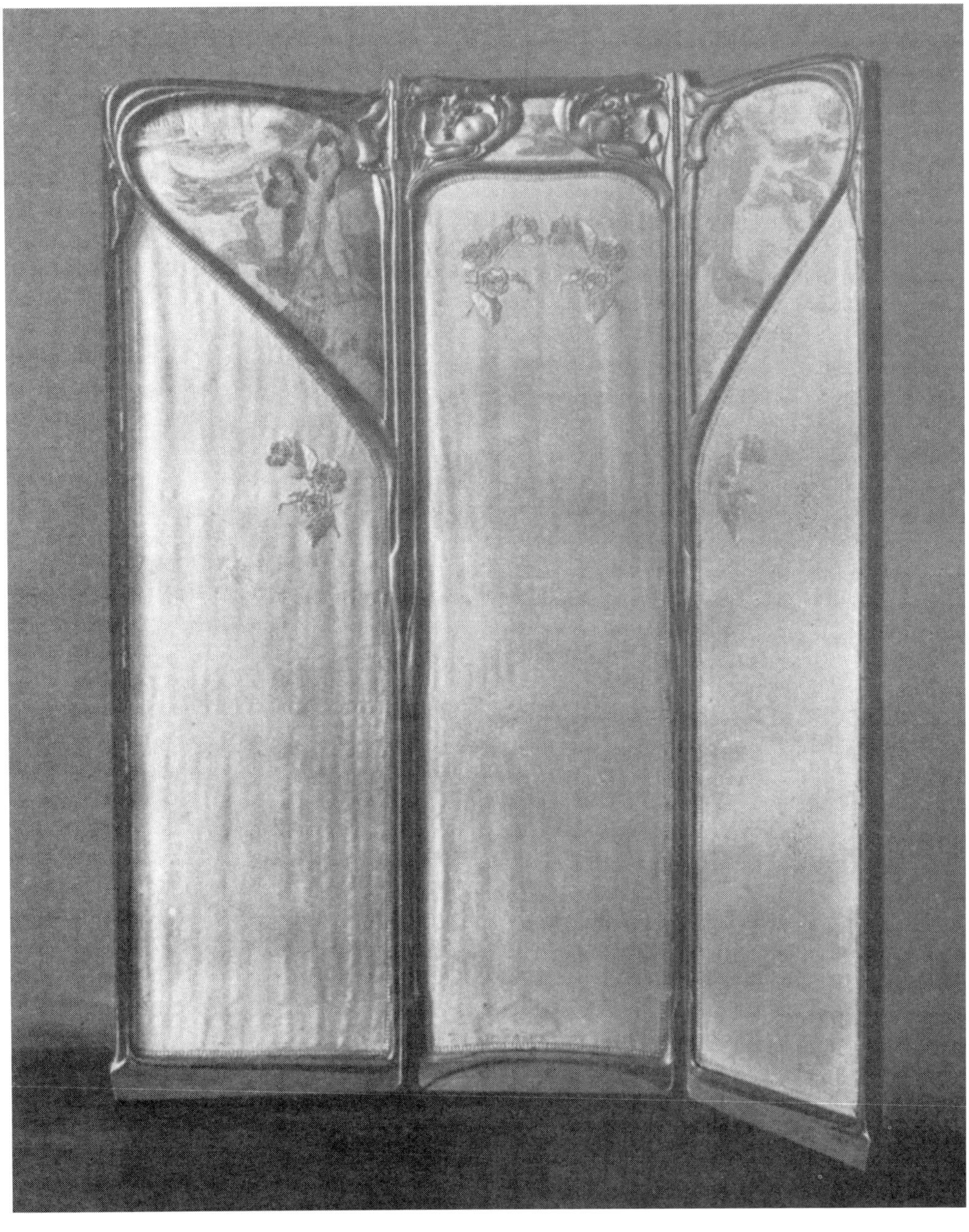

Fig. 210. De Feure: Screen. Gilted wood and embroidered silk. 1900.
Musée des Arts Décoratifs, Paris. Copyright reserved.

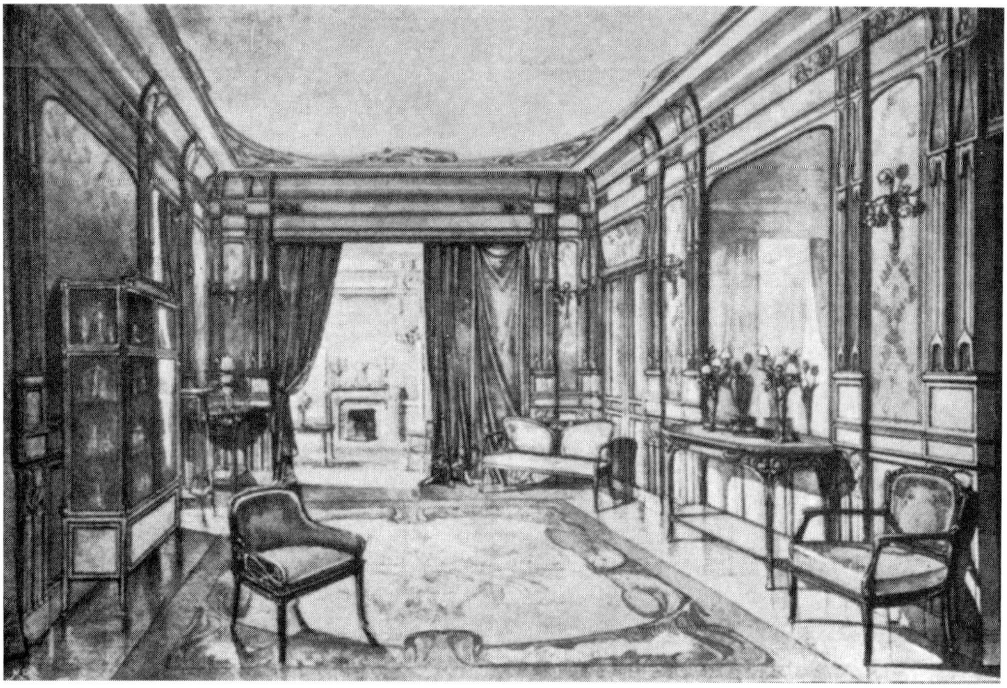

Fig. 211. De Feure: Design for interior. About 1900.
From Puaux.

and delicately executed—forming the constructive elements (fig. 210).[51] But besides his stylised plant shapes, there was at the same time a factor of a more traditional nature: his furniture is certainly Art Nouveau, but not least on account of the gilding he always applies they assume a French traditional character. A Louis XVI chair could without any difficulty at all harmonise perfectly with one of his interiors (fig. 211).

De Feure, however, went the way of all the other Art Nouveau artists: after the success of 1900 they beat a retreat when faced with the excesses of the style, and imperceptibly returned to a restrained form of Art Nouveau, which was more closely allied to French period furniture, but which at the same time had a grace of its own, a grace which can only be explained through the pliant and muted form-language of Art Nouveau (fig. 212). Like the ordinary stylistic development, this muted final phase—and not

51 Musée des Arts Décoratifs, Louvre, Paris. Exhibited 1900 at L'Art Nouveau Bing.

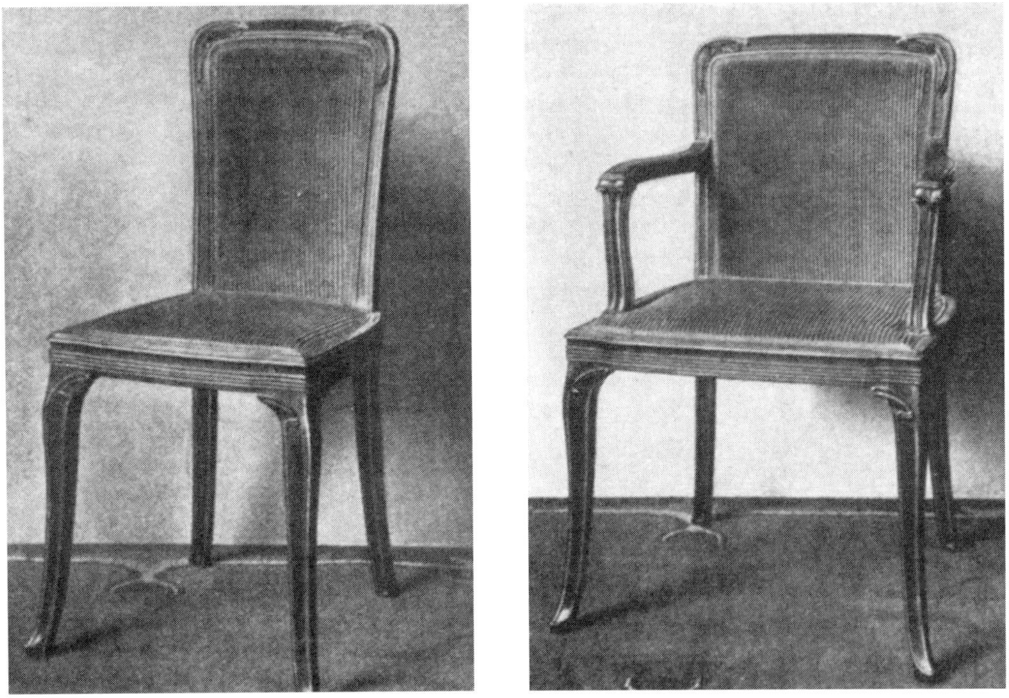

Fig. 212 a–b. De Feure: Two chairs. Before 1902.

the experimental striving of the early period or the violent expansion in which the style culminated—now seems to have attained the noblest results. The development occurred so swiftly that the artist does not appear to have arrived at a harmonious solution until the very moment when the whole style has reached its culminating point.

Eugène Gaillard is a far more virile artist, in his plastic and dynamic decoration more closely akin to Majorelle and Vallin (fig. 213).[52] While de Feure's contact with French tradition was Louis XVI, that of Eugène Gaillard was Louis XV. At Bing's Art Nouveau exhibition in 1900 there were six rooms, of which de Feure—as might be supposed—had designed the dressing-room and the boudoir, while Gaillard was responsible for the vestibule, the bedroom, and the dining-room, and Colonna for the drawing-

52 Cat. No. M.A.D. 14801, Musée des Arts Décoratifs, Louvre, Paris.

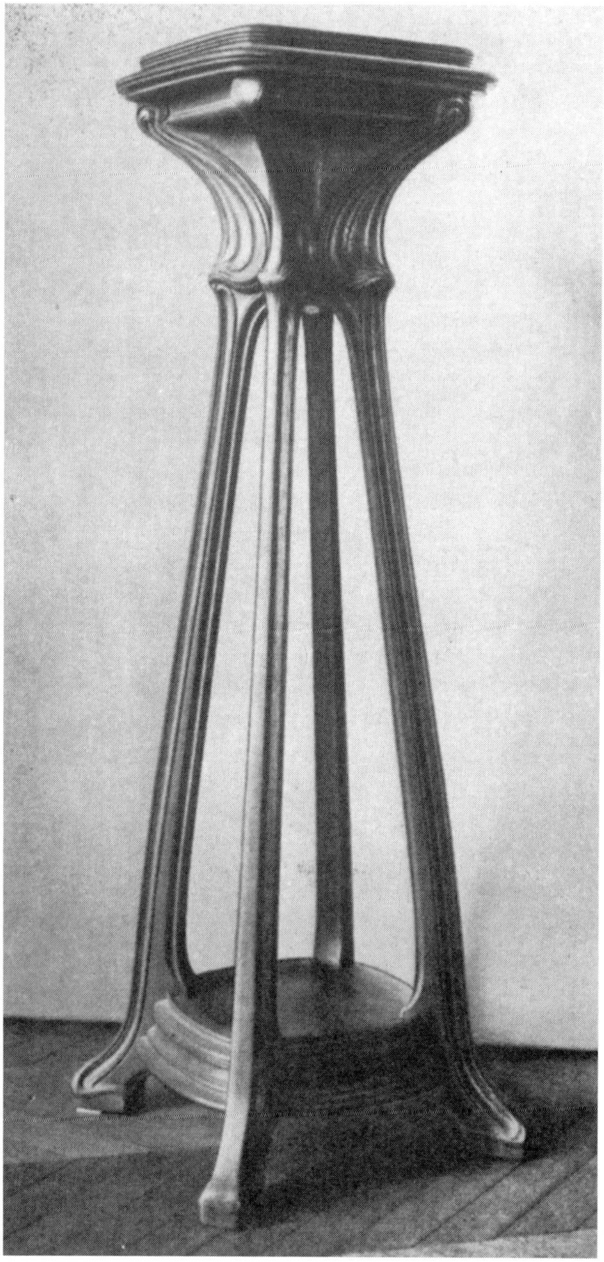

Fig. 213. Gaillard: Flower stand. Mahogany. About 1900.
Musée des Arts Décoratifs, Paris. Copyright reserved.

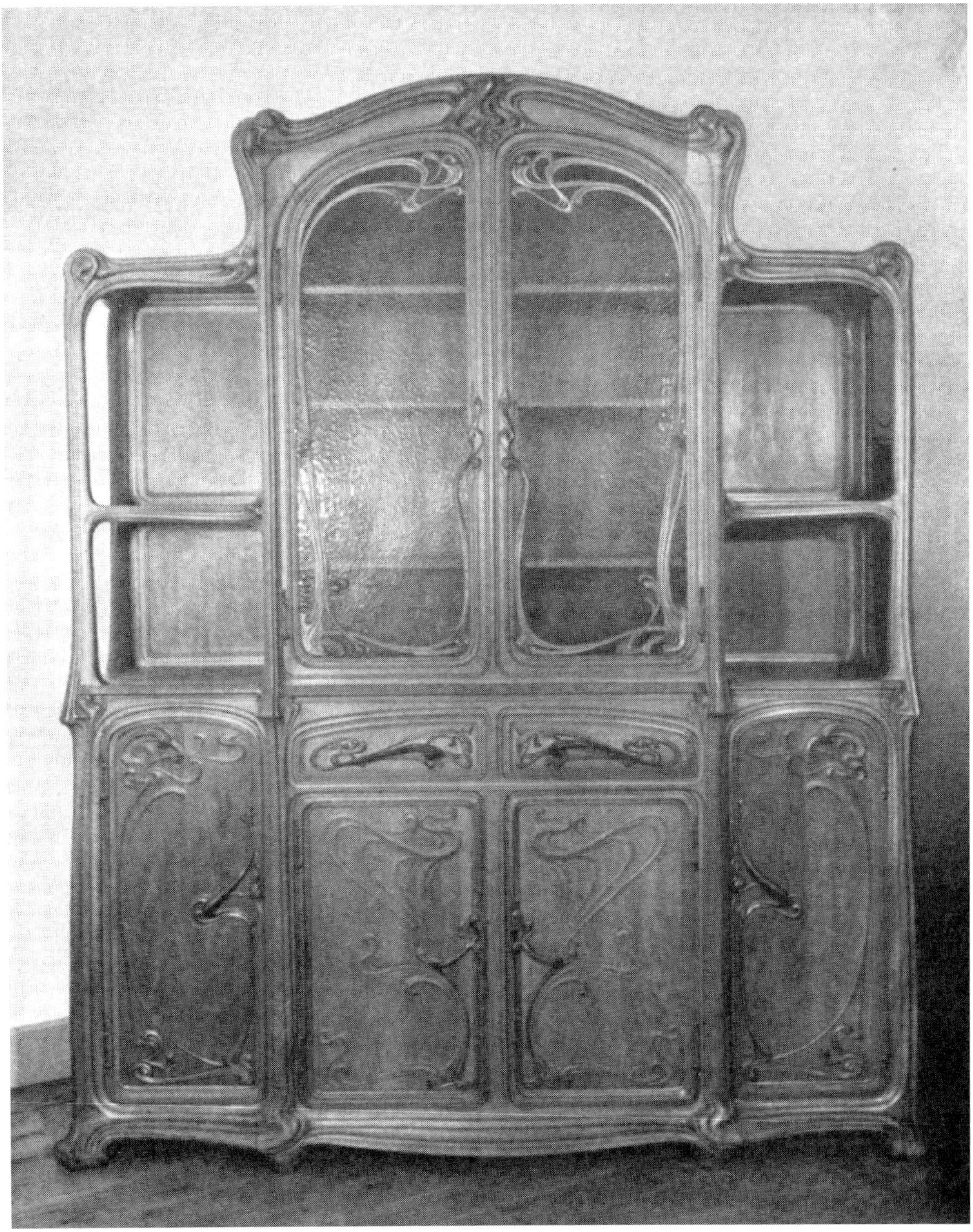

Fig. 214. Gaillard: Buffet. Nut with bronze fittings. 1900.
Det Danske Kunstindustrimuseum, Copenhagen. Copyright reserved.

room. Gaillard's furniture, especially his tables and chairs, was rather ponderous; one of his main pieces was the large cabinet (figs. 214, 215),[53] where his decoration is entirely abstract and plastic, and characterised by the dynamic and forceful countermovement.

Bing's Art Nouveau was a brilliant success at the Exhibition in 1900: the critics were enthusiastic, and perhaps the most eulogistic was Gabriel Mourey.[54] The French artists had no rivals, as neither van de Velde nor the Scots were represented, while the Germans were clearly ill-prepared, and Art Nouveau was generally regarded as a French phenomenon, an expression of French elegance and extravagance.

As a furniture designer Eugène Colonna takes his place midway between the two above-mentioned. He is less dynamic than Gaillard, and shows the best features of de Feure's elegance, as well as being calmer and more austere in his decoration than either of them (fig. 216).[55] De Feure and Colonna worked in textiles as well as in porcelain (fig. 217).[56]

But even Gaillard tended to become more rigid in his style after the exhibition. The chair which he designed a few years later (fig. 218)[57] shows that the *décor* has been pushed more into the background, while the furniture as a whole has become lighter and the lines straighter. This is still more clearly shown in the wardrobe from 1910 (fig. 219)[58], where the surfaces have become large and flat, where the rectilinear structure dominates, and the Art Nouveau decoration has been relegated to the keyholes. It might be of interest to see what Gaillard himself says about the principles of furniture design a few years after the exhibition. His views are based on five main rules[59]:

1. A piece of furniture shall as far as possible express its function.
2. Respect for the nature of the material.
3. No unnecessary constructive elements.
4. In wood an arch is only to be regarded as a decorative element.

53 Cat. No. 1009, Det Danske Kunstindustrimuseum, København.

54 G. Mourey, The House of the Art Nouveau Bing, *The Studio,* vol. XX, 1900, pp. 164–80.

55 Cat. No. 149, 1901, Victoria and Albert Museum, London.

56 The four objects belong to Musée des Arts Décoratifs, Louvre, Paris.

57 Cat. No. 14802, Musée des Arts Décoratifs, Louvre, Paris; acquired 1908.

58 Photo kindly provided by Musée des Arts Décoratifs, Louvre, Paris.

59 E. Gaillard, *A Propos du Mobilier,* Paris 1906, pp. 21 sqq.

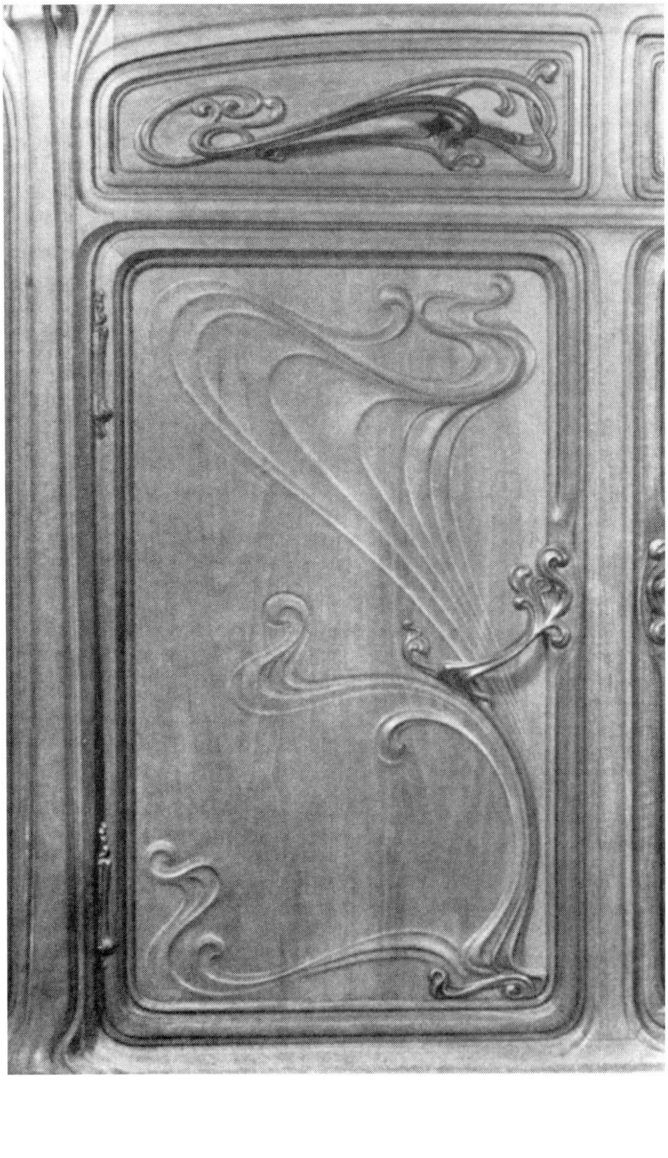

Fig. 215. Gaillard: Detail of buffet. 1900.
Det Danske Kunstindustrimuseum, Copenhagen. Copyright reserved.

5. The ornament should be abstract.

These principles are sound enough, and as far as his attitude towards the arch and the constructive parts are concerned, this must be regarded as a reaction against Belgian excesses in this direction. Gaillard, too, took exception to the style in general in the years immediately after 1900.

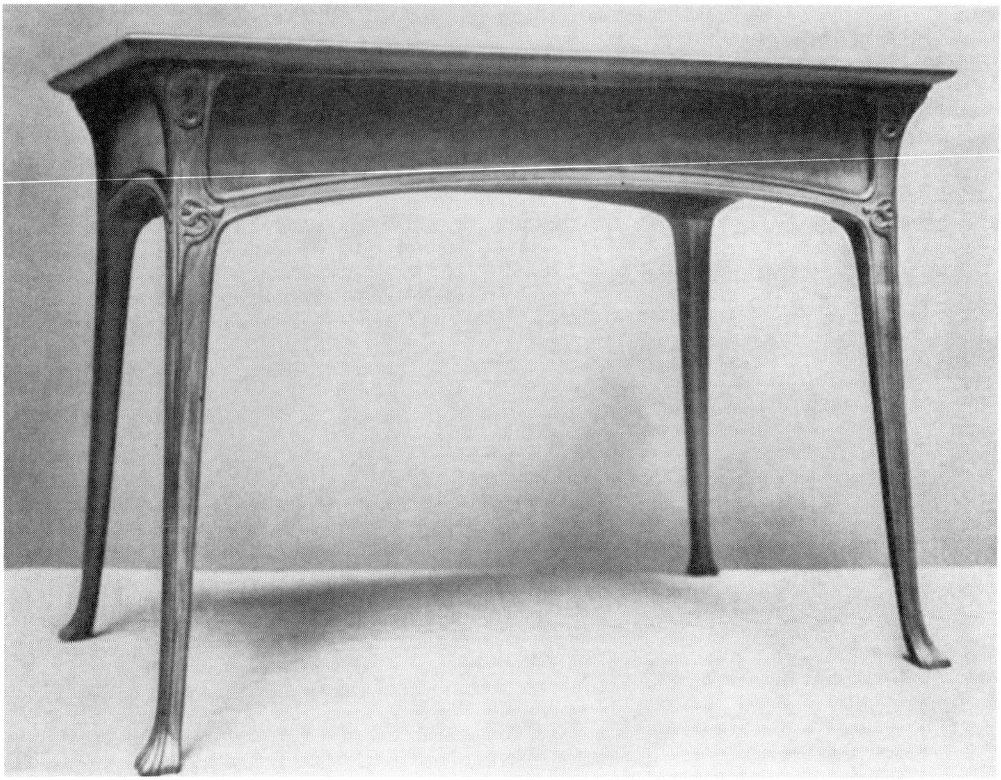

Fig. 216. Colonna: Table of oak, ash and pearwood. 1900.
Victoria and Albert Museum. Crown Copyright reserved.

Bing's intention in opening *Art Nouveau* and associating himself with these artists was naturally not to create a style but to assist French applied art. Both Bing and the *l'Art dans Tout* group adopted the same principles, which might be formulated as follows: emphasis on organic structure, honesty in every detail, avoidance of excessive ornaments and lastly: function of the object and nature of the material determine the form. These ideals had been expressed by the group in 1897 in a manifesto, and Bing himself had clearly formulated his intentions by opening the shop, some years later.[60]

60 A. D. F. Hamlin, The Art Nouveau. Its Origin and Development, *The Craftsman,* vol. III, 1902–03, p. 137. Recently commented in J. Grady, Nature and the Art Nouveau, *The Art Bulletin,* vol. XXXVII,

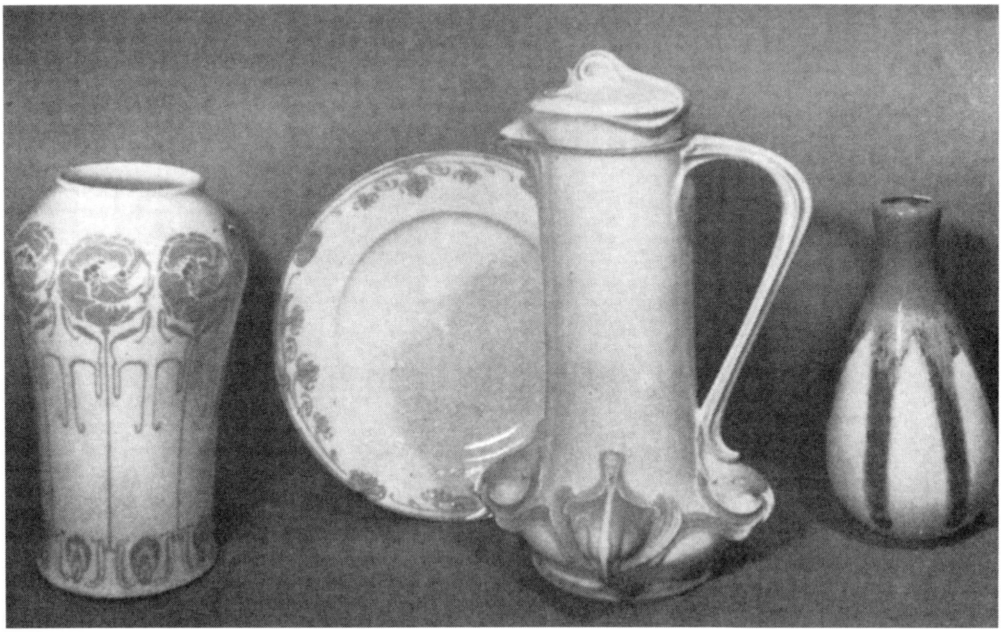

Fig. 217. Pottery made for Bing. 1898–1904. From left to right: Colonna, Colonna, De Feure, Delaherche.
Musée des Arts Décoratifs, Paris. Copyright reserved.

These basic principles, which were to be decisive for the 20th century, were if not born, at any rate bred, in this milieu of Art Nouveau artists. It is almost incredible that they should have followed these principles to such a slight degree—but this also gives us some indication of the influence that the Art Nouveau cult of line exercised over them. Even an artist with such an unusually clear and forceful intellect as van de Velde never succeeded in bringing practice into line with theory.

The leading Art Nouveau architect in France was undoubtedly Hector Guimard. We have already considered Castel Béranger[61] (figs. 6–9), but his *chef-d'oeuvre* stylistically is nevertheless *Humbert de Roman's public hall and school* in Rue St. Didier, Paris, completed in 1902.[62] Here we find fanciful

No. 3, p. 187. Bing's intentions are expressed in R. Puaux, *Georges de Feure,* Paris, n.d., p. 2 sq. The book is probably edited in, or shortly before, 1902.

61 See note 47.

62 Discussed and illustrated in F. Mazade, An Art Nouveau Edifice in Paris, *The Architectural Record,* vol. XII, 1902, pp. 52–66.

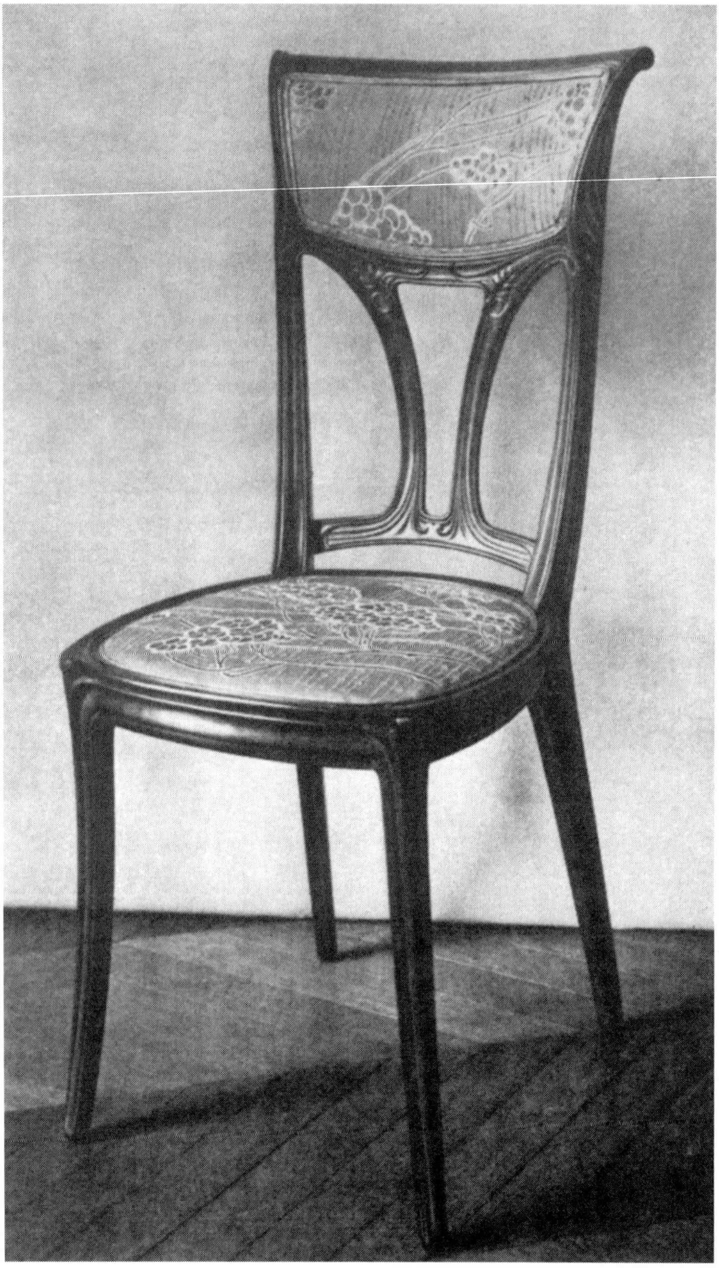

Fig. 218. Gaillard: Chair. A few years after 1900.
Musée des Arts Décoratifs, Paris. Copyright reserved.

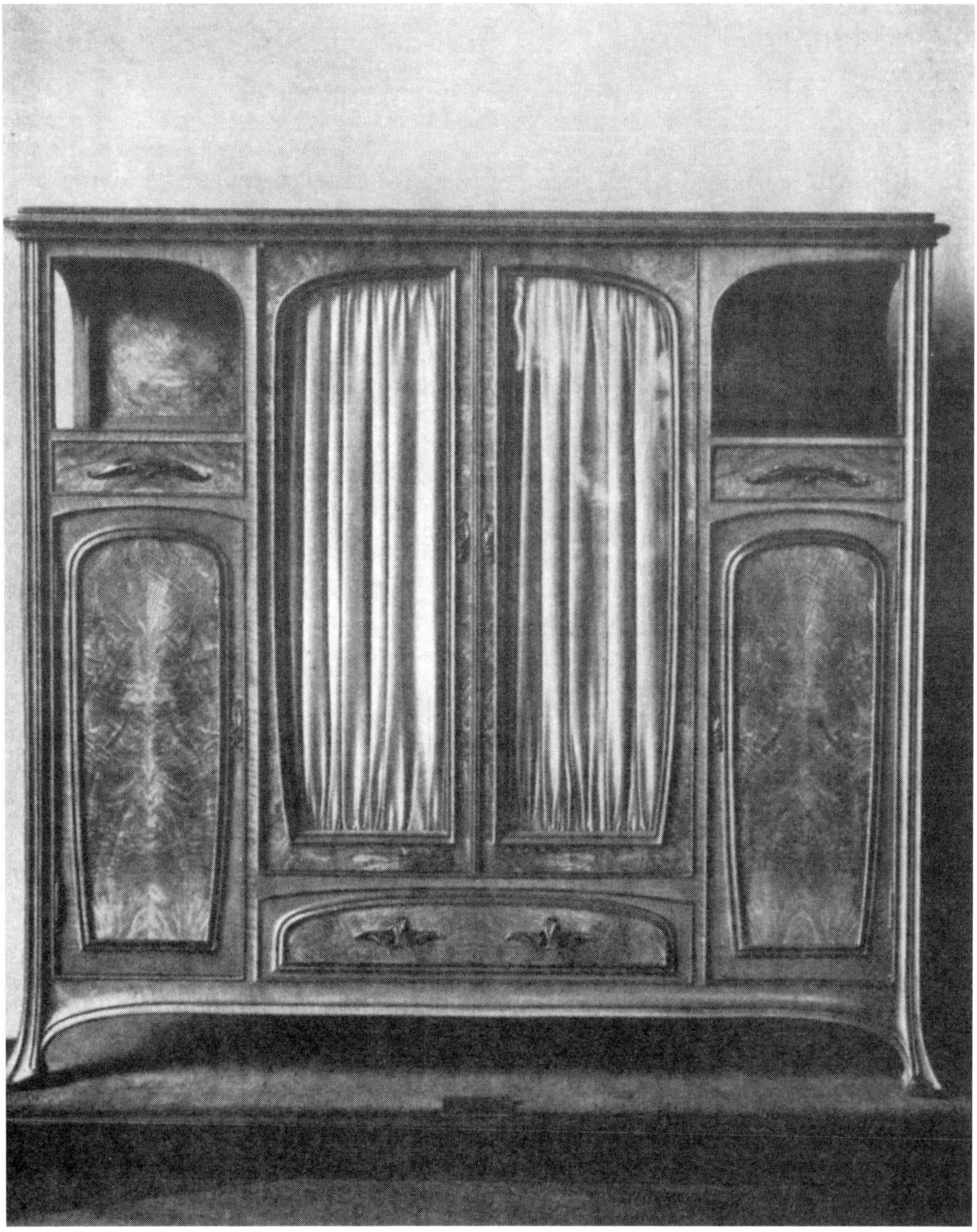

Fig. 219. Gaillard: Wardrobe. 1910.
Musée des Arts Décoratifs, Paris. Copyright reserved.

asymmetry, a Baroque feeling for form, Gothic-like construction, Art Nouveau in iron and abstract ornaments—all presented with his enthusiasm for various colours and a variegated material effect.

Hector Guimard has three principles which he has personally formulated and which, as he says, determined his three masterpieces in Art Nouveau: *Castel Béranger*, 1894–98, the *Metropolitain in Paris*, 1900, and the *Humbert de Roman Building*, 1902; and these principles have been derived from Nature:[63]

1. Logic—construction taking account of all the conditions in question.
2. Harmony—construction into full accord.
3. Sentiment—the complement of both which leads by emotion to the highest expression of art.

A glance at his Metro stations in Paris (fig. 220)[64] explains what he means by "construction into full accord." His conception of harmony is clearly influenced by a symbolical plant conception, where the bearing elements not only correspond to the quality of iron, but also grip intersecting points like the roots of plants, or claws. There is no doubt that the *décor* brilliantly illustrates the function of the construction—and this was precisely what was aimed at. A work of art must be judged by what it aims to express, and not according to the principles of the 1930's, 1940's, or 1950's. This would be just as unfair as to judge Rococo according to the ideals of the Empire style.

His furniture expresses the same search for harmony (figs. 221, 222, 223).[65] Every piece of furniture is a sophisticated play of details placed with great refinement and supple curves, wrapped in a veil of mystery. Why he really intended to give an illusion of cascading silk in wood decoration remains a riddle, and if we are to judge this work according to his own principles the logic of it appears somewhat confused.

Alexandre Charpentier's furniture is simple and rectilinear, and clearly Arts and Crafts influenced, early in the 1890's. Round about the year 1900, however, he adopts the whole gamut of abstract form-language of Art

63 H. Guimard, An Architect's opinion of "l'Art Nouveau," *The Architectural Record,* vol. XII, 1902, pp. 127–33.

64 W. Rehme, *Architektur der neuen freien Schule,* Leipzig 1902, pl. 100.

65 Photos kindly provided by Musée des Arts Décoratifs, Louvre, Paris.

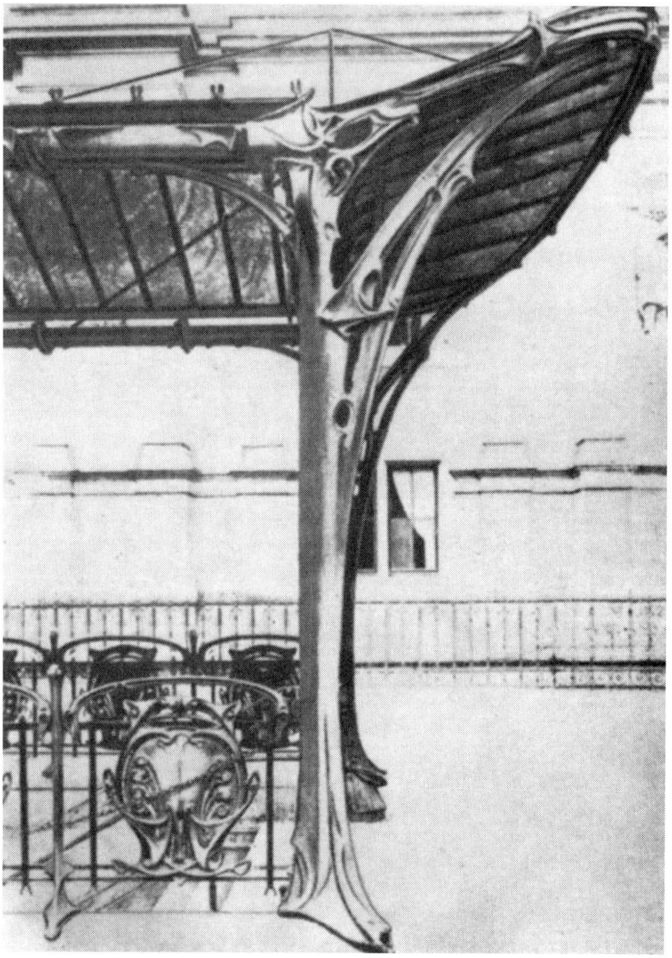

Fig. 220. Guimard: Metropolitan Underground in Paris. Cast iron. 1900.

Nouveau (fig. 224),[66] without, however, exercising any real influence on the development or trend of the style. As a sculptor he frequently adds his low reliefs with naked women wherever he can do so, whether the piece of furniture in question is a music cupboard or a sideboard.[67]

After the style had become *mondain* in 1900, it was naturally adopted by all and sundry, and from this moment it becomes part of the history of fashion.

66 Musée des Arts Décoratifs, Louvre, Paris.

67 G. Mourey, A decorative Modeller: Alexandre Charpentier, *The Studio,* vol. X, 1896, pp. 157–65.

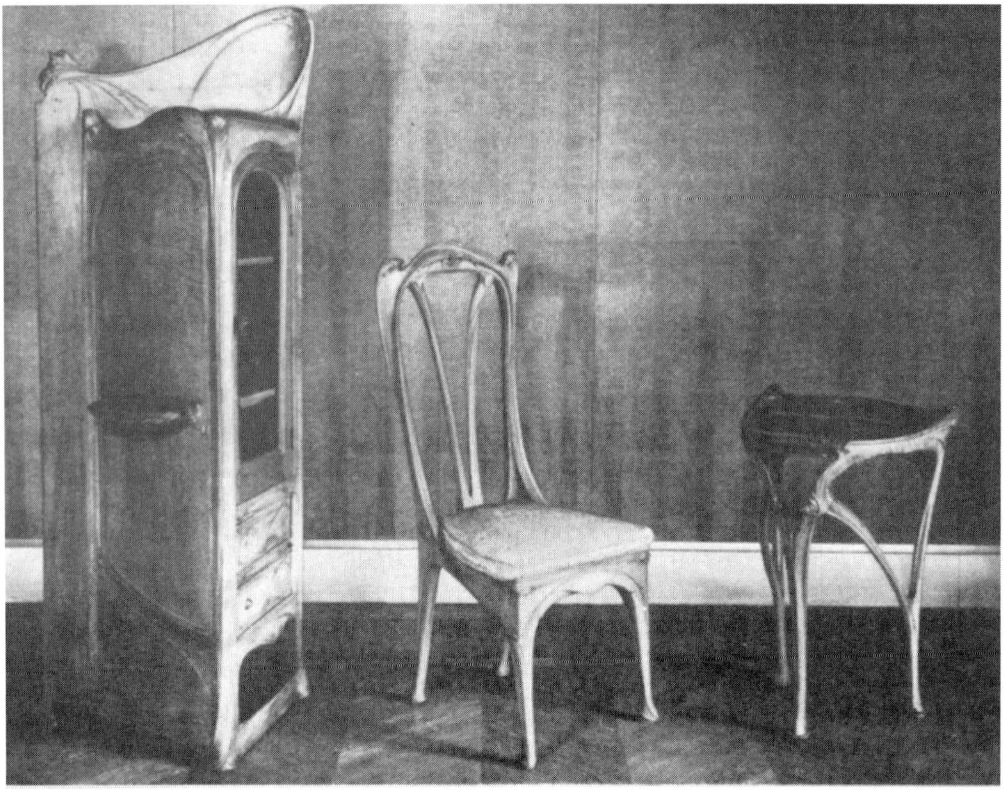

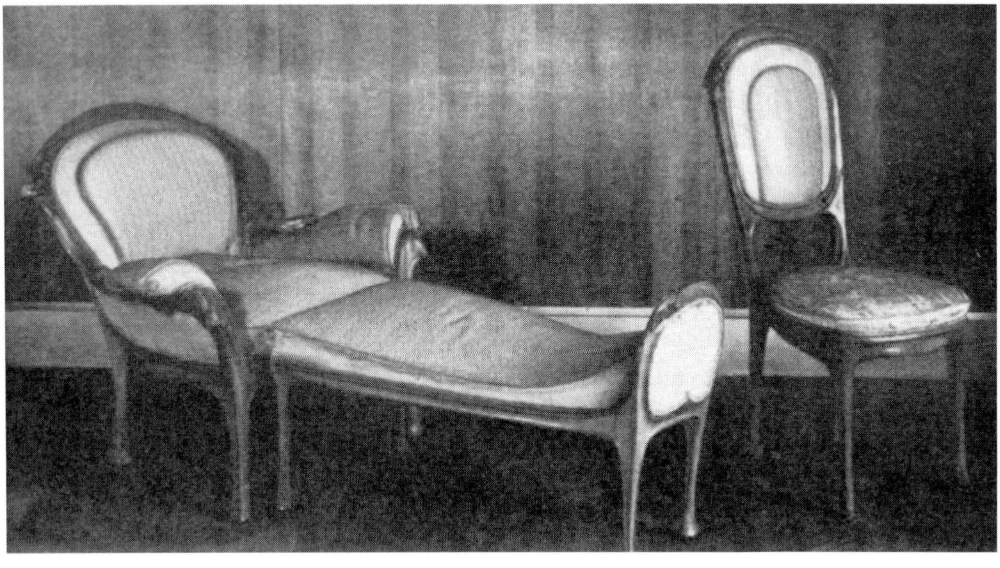

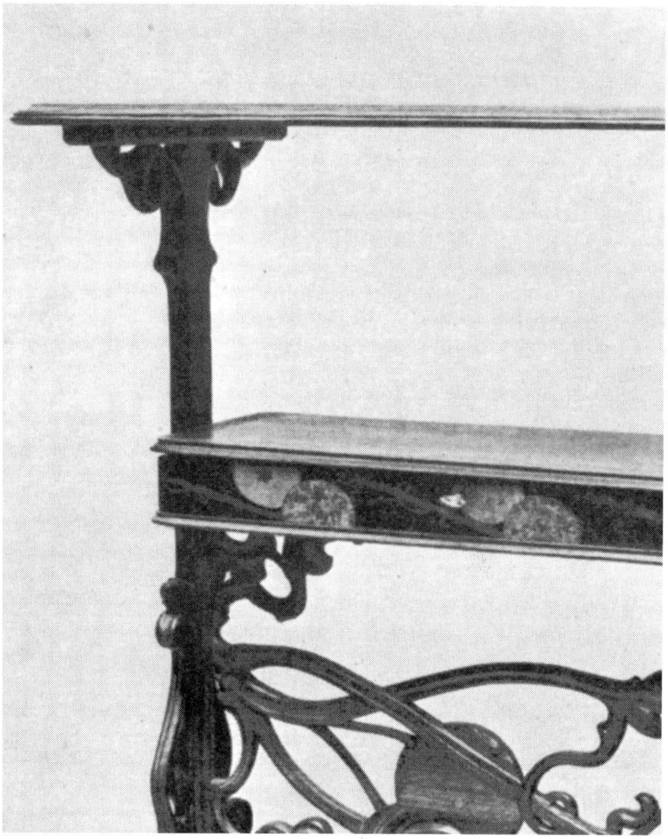

Fig. 221. Guimard: Furniture. 1900.
Musée des Arts Décoratifs, Paris. Copyright reserved.

Fig. 222. Guimard: Furniture. 1900.
Musée des Arts Décoratifs, Paris. Copyright reserved.

Fig. 223. Guimard: Cabinet. 1900.
Musée des Arts Décoratifs, Paris. Copyright reserved.

One of the many furniture-designing firms which represented this style at its best, was Perol Frères, who worked more or less in a style influenced by the Nancy school (fig. 225).[68]

The Union Centrale des Arts Décoratifs decided to prepare for the exhibition in 1900 in an entirely different way: an advanced Naturalism, of the kind which the potter and architect George Hoendschel had launched (fig. 226),[69] was chosen. Here there is not the slightest attempt at stylisation—and the experiment made by this institution in 1900 must be regarded

68 Cat. No. 1992–1900, Victoria and Albert Museum, London.

69 G. Hoendschel, *Le Pavillon de l'Union Centrale des Arts Décoratifs à l'Exposition Universelle de 1900,* Paris 1900; R. Koechlin, *Le Pavillon de l'Union Centrale des Arts Décoratifs à l'Exposition Universelle de 1900,* Paris 1900. The room is now in Musée des Arts Décoratifs, Louvre, Paris.

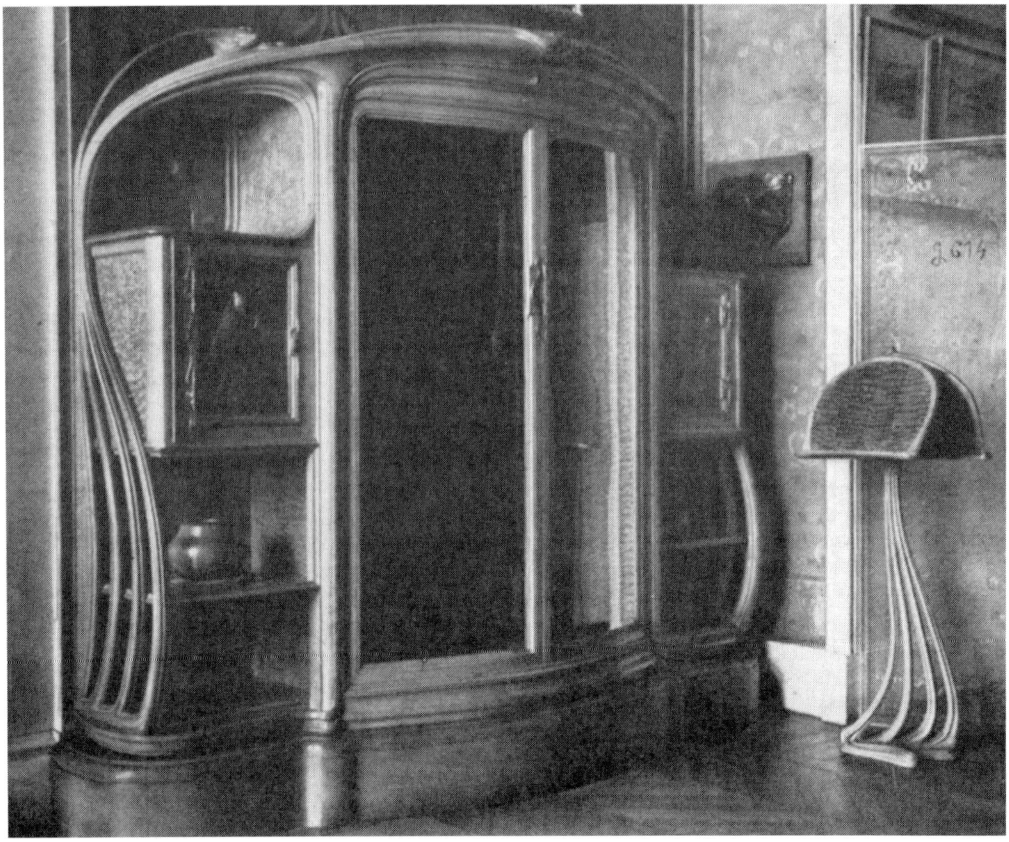

Fig. 224. Charpentier: Music cabinet and music stand. 1900.
Musée des Arts Décoratifs. Paris. Copyright reserved.

as the last frenzied attempt to apply Nature pure and simple as a solution to the style problem of the 19th century.

At the Turin Exhibition in 1902[70] France was represented by Gallé and Majorelle from the Nancy school, Tony Selmersheim, Charles Plumet, and Henri Sauvage—apart from René Lalique—as well as de Feure, Gaillard, and Colonna from Bing's Art Nouveau. The only one who showed any advance on 1900, was de Feure: his furniture was somewhat simpler than previously, but just as elegant. The others continued with their plastic effects, but by now all flowers and floral elements had been abolished.

70 V. Pica, *L'Arte Decorativa all'esposizione di Torino del 1902*, Turin 1903.

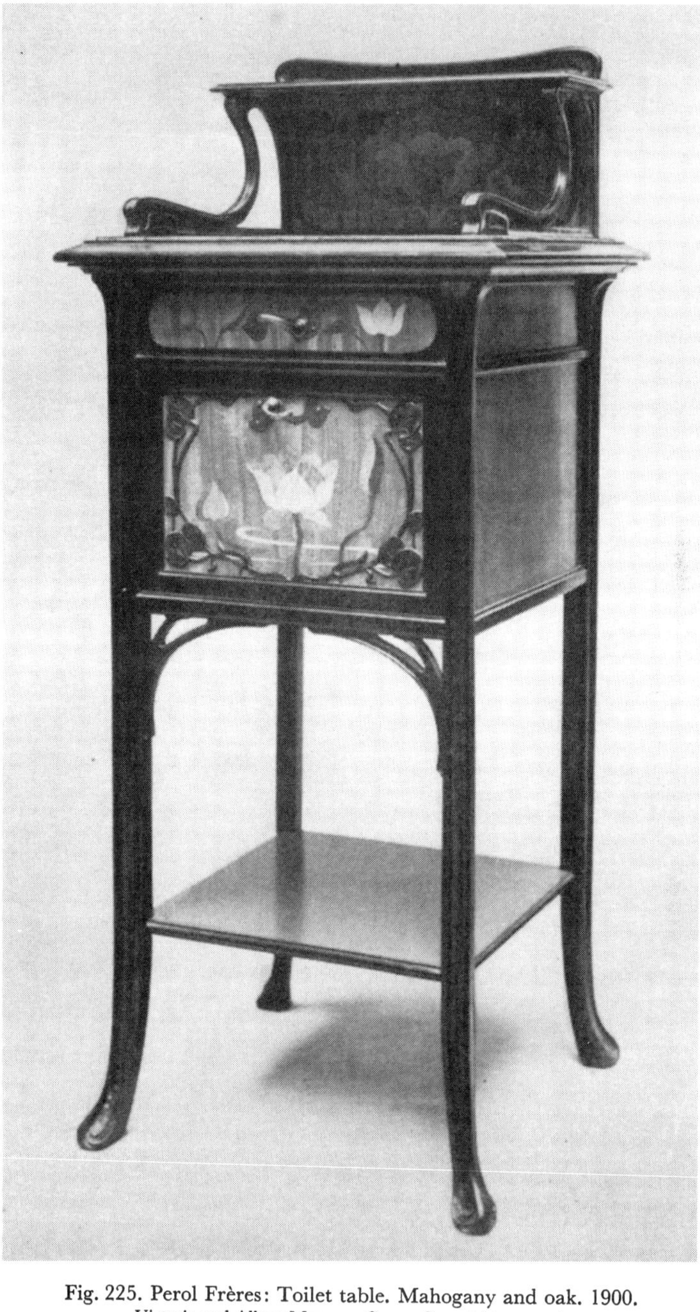

Fig. 225. Perol Frères: Toilet table. Mahogany and oak. 1900.
Victoria and Albert Museum. Crown Copyright reserved.

In 1902 the situation was an interesting one: the French, who were now no longer unopposed as they had been at the exhibition in 1900, ran up against a number of rivals, men such as Voysey, Townsend, Crane, Day, and Ashbee from England, "the four Macs" from Scotland, Horta, van de Velde, Serrurier-Bovy, Hobe, and Crespin from Belgium, Hoffman and Hammel from Austria, together with Behrens, Pankok, Paul, Koepping, and Olbrich from Germany—and on this occasion the Germans were clearly better prepared.

The milieu was by no means Parisian—the Art Nouveau artists were far more at home in Bing's intimate showcase in 1900. Raymondo d'Aronco's mighty neo-Baroque Art Nouveau Rotunda was hardly the form of Art Nouveau to which the Parisians were accustomed. Besides, the French were not particularly adept at exhibition technique: their furniture was mainly ranged in rather uninspiring fashion along the walls, while the other nations were far more successful in creating interiors. But in France no attempt had been made in 1902 to compose furniture as part of a room. The Frenchmen—and especially the Nancy school—regarded a piece of furniture as a work of art in itself.

Furthermore in Turin the French were face to face with artists who exceeded them even in refinement, and in this respect Mackintosh's room was unchallenged. But what was more important, here they were competing face to face with rooms designed by artists such as Olbrich and Hoffman, who had hardly any decoration at all, rooms and furniture being entirely simple and yet devoid of the rustic features of the Arts and Crafts Movement. The Austrians and Germans, who were late arrivals on the battlefield against "stylistic tyranny," had approached the problem from an angle which differed entirely from that of the French—they had simply abandoned the decoration.

In 1905 the French stayed at home and did not join in with the other nations at Liége. In the course of these few years we have seen how each one of the French artists seemed to lose the "first fine careless rapture" of Art Nouveau, and strike a more resigned note. At the same time a feeling of tradition asserted itself more and more, especially in the direction of Louis XVI and Empire, and during the London Exhibition of 1908 Art

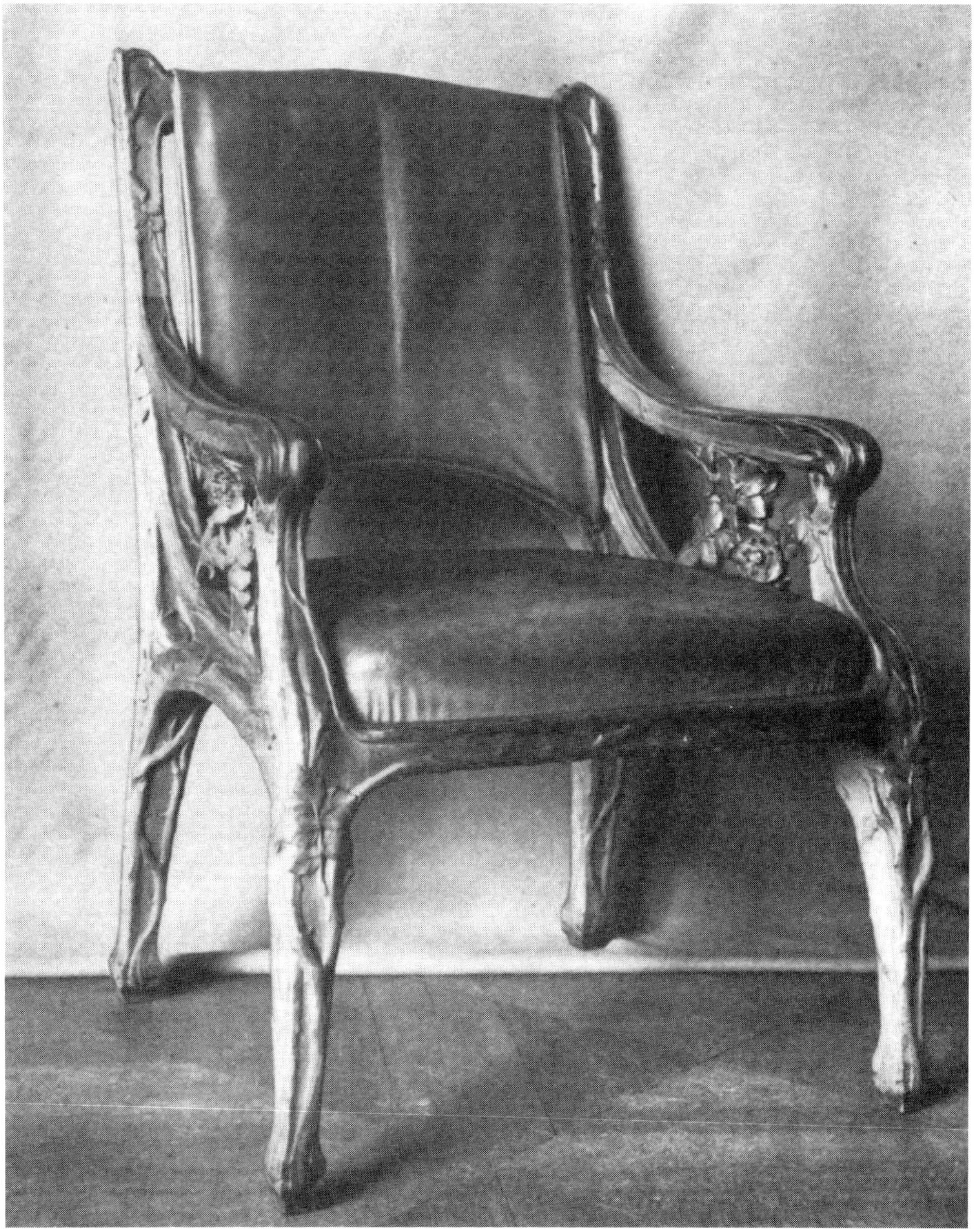

Fig. 226. Hoendschel: Chair. 1900.
Musée des Arts Décoratifs, Paris. Copyright reserved.

Nouveau was completely eclipsed. "La note dominante et même à peu près exclusive de la section française de l'ameublement, était reconstitution des styles anciens, principalement du XVIII siècle."[71]

In 1909 Edouard Dévérin[72] asked a number of prominent critics and artists, in a series of interviews which were later published, why the promising and experimental period at the beginning of the 1890's had not borne fruit. Franz Jourdain, René Lalique, and Louis Majorelle, as well as Roger Marx, evaded the question, and admitted that all the hopes which had flourished in 1899 and 1900 had faded, and they all noted that once again the trend was towards Classicism. In 1911 André Blum's *La Crise des Arts Industriels en France* was published, yet another sign of the times.

*

The development in France seemed clear: from 1889 to 1900, with flowers and subsequently stalks as the main source of inspiration, the development had run from Naturalism in the direction of stylisation, reaching full abstraction in decoration in Paris, after which a phase of simplification set in, with the introduction of straight lines, and clearly defined planes, after the turn of the century. Before 1905 this movement seems to have lost impetus, after which there was a return to a simplified and modernised Classicism.

The artists and critics who had been asked for their views failed to explain the reasons for this, but the explanation is probably that another development was brewing which was not decorative in nature, and was not rooted in flowers or plants—a trend that completed the programme the Art Nouveau artists had proclaimed—a trend which in contrast to Art Nouveau was intimately associated with architecture. This movement took place in Germany and Austria, and solved the stylistic problem of the 19th century, in an entirely different, and more radical, manner.

In France the disappointment was all the greater, because Art Nouveau had promised so much, and people had pinned their hopes on the style.

71 Exposition Franco–Brittanique de Londres 1908. Rapport général de Yves Guyot et G. Roger Sandoz, vols. I–II, Paris 1908, vol. I, p. 245. "The dominant, in fact almost the only, note struck by the French furniture section showed an emphasis on the revival of period styles, especially those of the 18th century."

72 E. Dévérin, La Crise de l'art décoratif en France, *La Revue,* Paris, 15th of June, 1909, pp. 433–52.

Holland

Books and Batiks

The general stylistic development in Holland during the last quarter of the 19th century follows in the main the same general lines as can be traced for the rest of Europe, with a few marked differences. For national and traditional reasons the neo-Renaissance occupied a more prominent position, at the expense of neo-Baroque. From the 1880's and beyond two trends can be traced within architecture: one a pastiche-like and picturesque Dutch neo-Renaissance, and the other based on Viollet-le-Duc's theories, with the emphasis on a sound use of material and constructive simplicity. While the former predominated in secular architecture throughout the 1880's, the latter asserted itself at the beginning of the 1890's. Although Holland's greatest period architect, P. J. H. Cuypers (1827–1921)[1], would appear to be a child of pure Historicism, it would be more correct to regard him as a father of the rationalistic trend. He had worked for two years with Viollet-le-Duc, was intensely interested in rational architectural solutions, and re-introduced brick as a building material in Holland. There is an unbroken line from him to T. Nieuwenhuis, Lion Cachet, J. L. M. Lauweriks and de Bazel, who were all among his many pupils. At the beginning of the 1890's the period aspect is gradually discarded as the artists turn more and more to pure, undecorated, and simple architectural solutions, and go back to the old architecture of Egypt and the Near East for inspiration. Thus about the year 1900 a sober, unornamented, and monumental style of architecture developed, and it was along this road that Holland moved towards the Modern Movement. In ecclesiastical architecture, however, neo-Gothic survives to the very end of the century.[2]

H. P. Berlage (1856–1934)[3] reflects this development in architecture

[1] J. Th. J. Cuypers, *Het werk van Dr. P. J. H. Cuypers, 1827–1917,* Amsterdam 1917; *idem, Album met reproducties naar bouw- en andere werken van P. J. H. Cuypers.* Complete bibliography in: *Repertorium betreffende Nederlandsche Monumenten van Geschiedenis en Kunst 1901–1940,* The Hague, 1940–43, vol. I, pp. 47–48.

[2] J. van Haaren, De Situatie van de neo-gothiek in Nederland, *Honderd Jaar Religieuze Kunst in Nederland 1853–1953,* Utrecht 1953, pp. 21–23, 45–47.

[3] J. Gratama, *Dr. H. P. Berlage Bouwmeester,* Rotterdam, 1925; M. Eisler, De Bouwmeester H. P. Berlage,

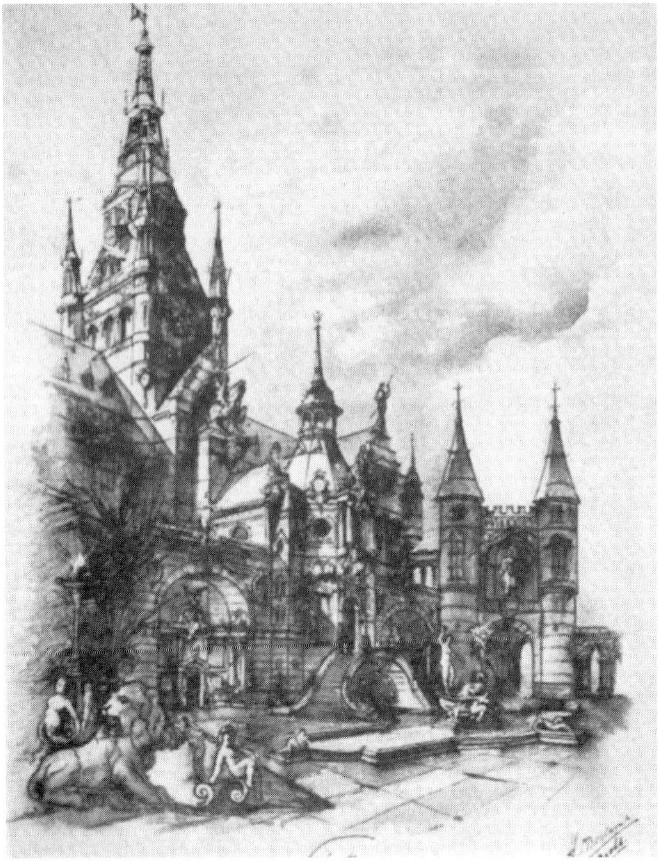

Fig. 227. Berlage: Sketch. 1888. From Gratama.

in his earlier work. A typical example is his fanciful sketch from 1888, showing Historicism in a setting which is not only typically Dutch but unusually lavish (fig. 227). In 1897 he submitted the first draft design for the Damrak Stock Exchange, Amsterdam (fig. 228 a), with its choir-like main entrance, the whole building being designed in a neo-Norman style. The same year he produced his second design (fig. 228 b), which shows a marked simplification: the number of gables has been reduced from ten to six, the "choir" has been abandoned, and the contours of the tower are far more se-

Vienna 1919; T. Landré, H. P. Berlage, *Onze Kunst,* vol. XVII, 1910, pp. 73–101, are the most important references. Complete bibliography in *Repertorium betreffende Nederlandsche Monumenten van Geschiedenis en Kunst, 1901–1940,* The Hague 1940–43, vol. I, pp. 44–46.

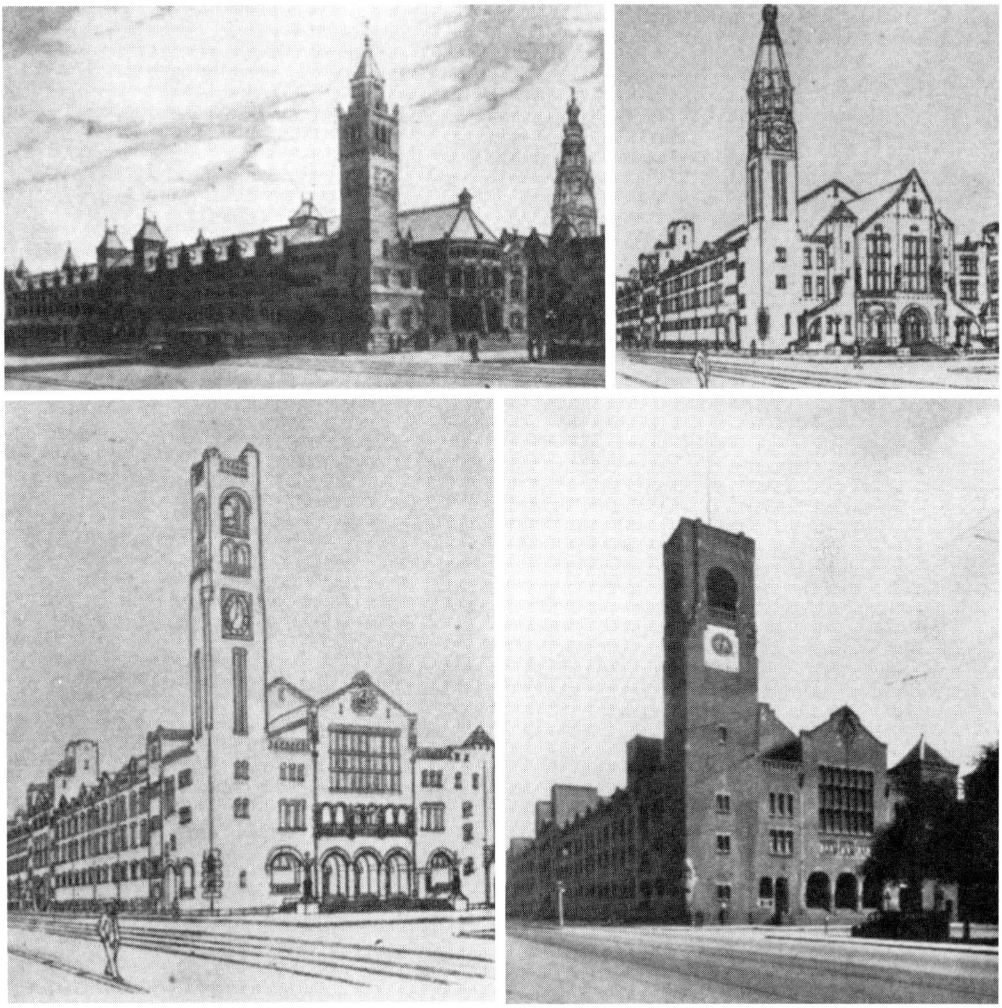

Fig. 228 a–d. Berlage: a–c. Designs for the Exchange at Damrak, Amsterdam. 1897.
d. The Exchange 1898–1903.
Courtesy of Rijksmuseum, Amsterdam.

vere. The next design (fig. 228 c) represents yet a further step in the direction of a still more simple solution, and a firmer architectural poise. The tower has been further simplified, and the process of elimination has borne fruit almost in every detail. The stairs have been built into the actual block itself, and the whole facade has been straightened out. This gives a far more

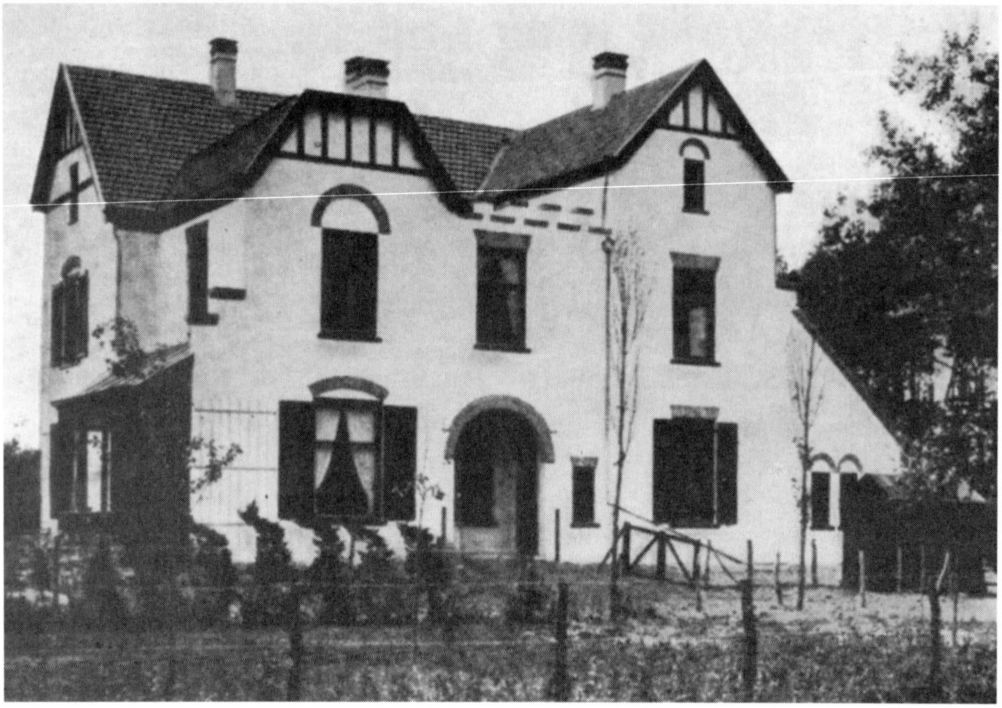

Fig. 229. Berlage: Villa, Bussum. 1893.
From Gratama.

immediate impression of the architectural mass, while at the same time the Romantic piecemeal treatment of the facade has disappeared.

By comparison the completed work (1898–1903) (fig. 228 d) reminds us in appearance of an Assyrian temple: the edifice stands there firm and clearcut, shorn of all inessentials, a composition consisting entirely of masses, blocks, and proportions rhythmically distributed. Berlage has now liberated himself from imitation, and created Holland's first piece of modern architecture.

It should be noted, however, that Berlage had evolved a simpler conception of architecture several years earlier, as can be seen in his villa, Bussum, 1893 (fig. 229). Only a Voysey could have produced anything like it at this period of time. As a furniture designer his work is similar in character and paralleled only by that of artists working in the English Arts

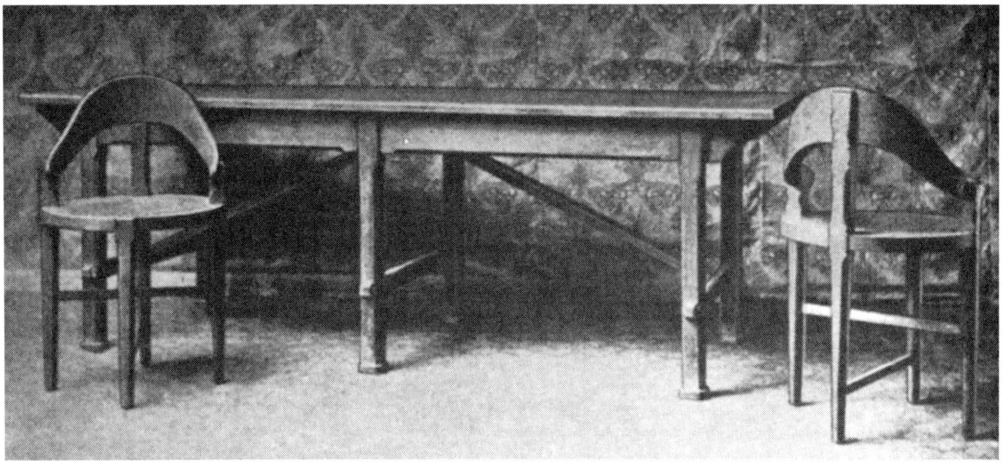

Fig. 230. Berlage: Furniture for an office, Kerkplein, The Hague. 1895. Very much like the furniture he made for *Arti et Amititiae,* Spui, Amsterdam. 1893. From Gratama.

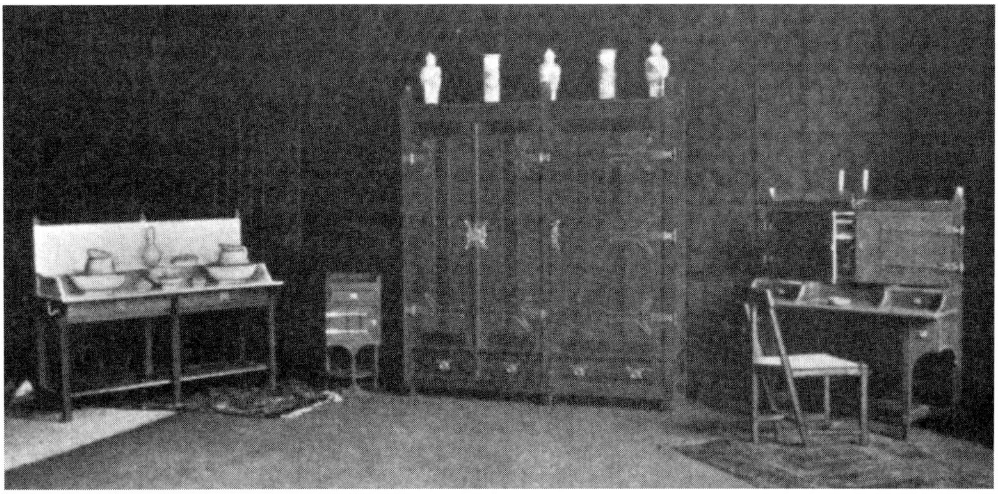

Fig. 231. Berlage: Bedroom furniture. 1895. From Gratama.

and Crafts Movement (figs. 230, 231). Here too a number of Medieval features indicate in their modest way where the source of inspiration is to be found.

Berlage's style remained more or less the same till the end of the century: neither in his architecture nor in his furniture design was Art

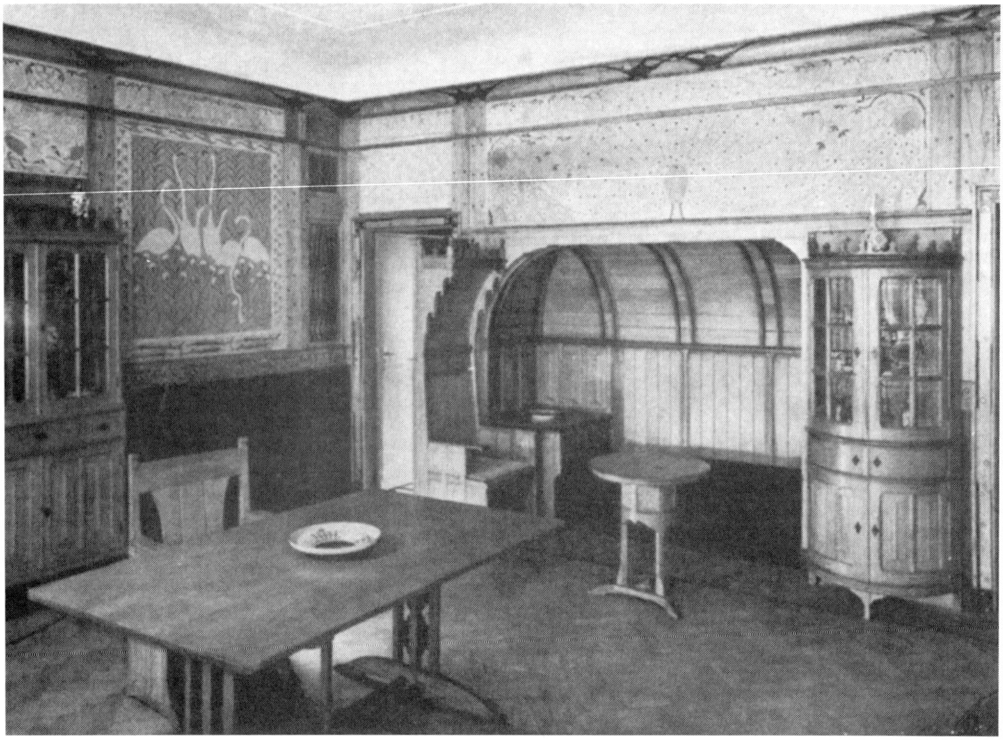

Fig. 232. Dijsselhof: Interior. 1890–92.
Gemeentemuseum, The Hague. Copyright reserved.

Nouveau in evidence, the constructive problems, and not the decorative, determining his entire development.

The architect in whose work Art Nouveau is most evident is Willem Kromhoult (1864–1934).[4] In his American Hotel, Amsterdam, 1896–1901, the Romanesque Berlage style is above all noticeable, but in the shape of the tower, with its soft rounded form and asymmetrical composition Art Nouveau influences emerge clearly.

It is characteristic of the development in Holland that Art Nouveau only appears in purely decorative work, but, as though to make up for this, it makes its appearance here earlier than anywhere else. In architecture, under the leadership of Berlage, the main development was entirely un-

[4] Architect W. Kromhoult, B.N.A., *Bouwkundige Weekblad,* vol. LIV, 1934, p. 169.

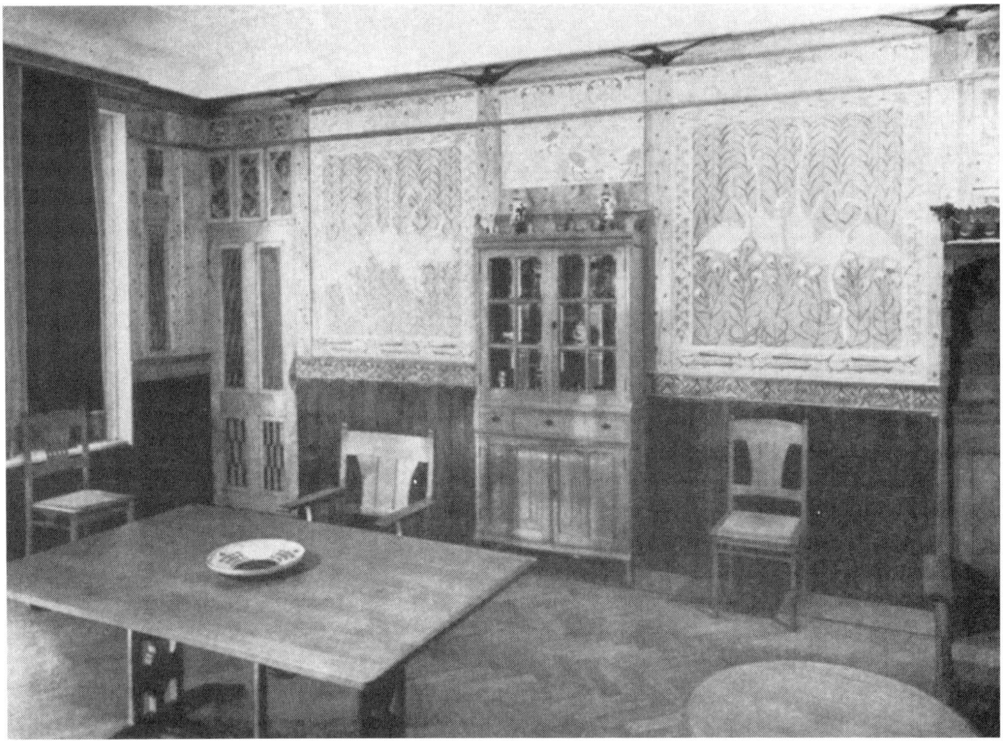

Fig. 233. Dijsselhof: Interior. 1890–92.
Gemeentemuseum, The Hague. Copyright reserved.

touched by the style; there are no traces of Art Nouveau either in K. P. C. de Bazel (1869–1923)[5] or in the work of Jacob van den Bosch (1868–?).[6] The same was true of furniture. Even the architects who were most influenced by Art Nouveau seemed to concentrate on constructive elements.

In applied art the first steps towards a change of outlook were taken in the 1870's. In 1876 J. R. de Kruyff wrote *De Nederlandsche kunstnijverheid in verband met den internationalen wedstrijd bij gelegenheid van de in 1877 te Amsterdam te houden Tentoonstelling van kunst, toegepast op Nijverheid*, and in the following year the government appointed a committee with the precise task of in-

5 K. P. C. de Bazel, *De houtsneden van K. P. C. de Bazel,* Amsterdam 1925; C. W. Nijhoff, K. P. C. de Bazel, *Onze Kunst,* vol. XIII, 1908, pp. 220–30, vol. XIV, 1908, pp. 17–32.

6 H. Ellers, Jacob van den Bosch (1868–), *Onze Kunst,* vol. XIV, pp. 199–206, 237–48.

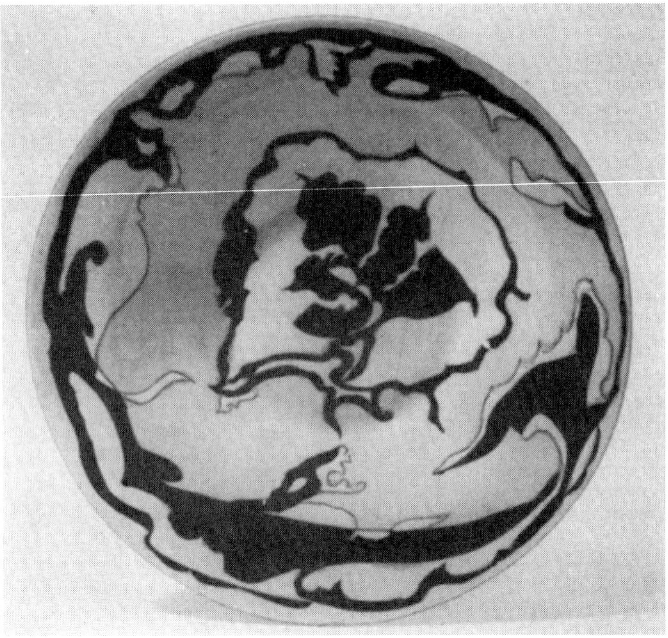

Fig. 234. Colenbrander: Plate.
Gemeentemuseum, The Hague.
Copyright reserved.

vestigating Dutch applied art, with de Kruyff as secretary. In 1884 the *Nederlandsche Vereeniging tot bevordering der Kunstnijverheid* was founded.

The leading designer in the sphere of applied art in the 1890's was Gerrit Willem Dijsselhof (1866–1924),[7] and in his work the special batik-inspired Dutch Art Nouveau made its appearance. The decorative *chef-d'oeuvre* in the style is the so-called Dijsselhof Room, now in the Gemeentemuseum at The Hague (figs. 232, 233).[8] This room was executed in the years from 1890–92 for Dr. van Hoorn of Amsterdam, and the textiles were also designed in the same period, viz. 1890–92. Some of the articles, however, were produced somewhat later by Dijsselhof, though for the same room, viz. the table in the middle appeared in 1896, and all the cupboards are from the same year. The rest is from 1890–92.

In the early 1890's, too, the results achieved by book illustrators and painters clearly indicate the artists' attempt to discover a new, untried style:

7 Complete bibliography in H. van Hall, *Repertorium voor de Geschiedenis der nederlandsche Schilder- en Graverkunst,* The Hague, 1936–49, vol. I, No. 8815–8826, vol. II, No. 4762–4765.

8 *Meddelingen,* II, 1931, Gemeentemuseum, The Hague.

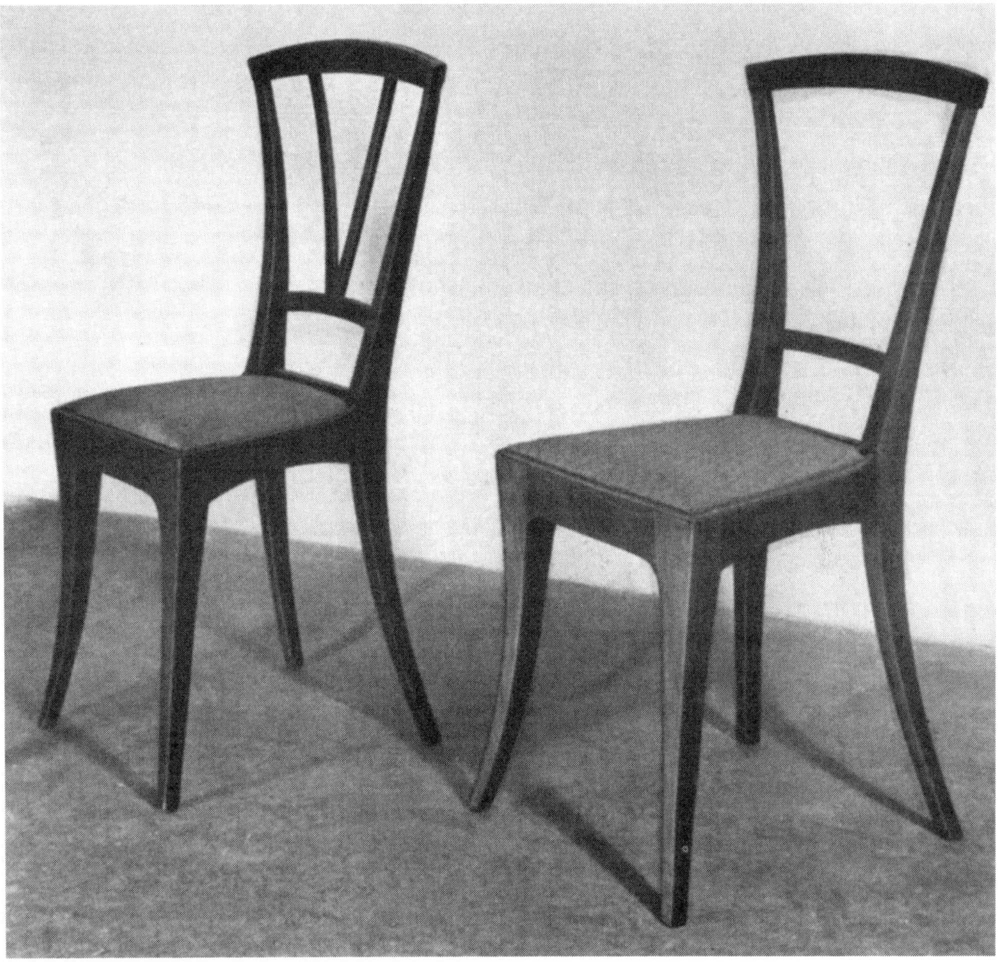

Fig. 235. Thorn Prikker: Chairs. 1900.
Gemeentemuseum, The Hague. Copyright reserved.

thus among the book illustrators Art Nouveau tendencies are recognisable in the work of Niewenhuis (1866–?)[9]; the most outstanding after Dijsselhof was, however, T. A. C. Colenbrander (1841–1930),[10] who specialised

[9] N. van Harpen, T. Nieuwenhuis, *Maandblad voor Beeldende Kunsten,* vol. I, 1924, pp. 75–80; T. Nieuwenhuis, *Afbeeldingen van Werken naar ontwerpen van T. Nieuwenhuis,* Amsterdam 1911. Introduction by A. Schendel.

[10] W. J. d. G., In Memorium Th. A. C. Colenbrander 1841–1930, *Elseviers,* vol. LXXX, 1930, p. 143.

in textiles and pottery in his peculiar batik-inspired style (fig. 234).[11] Mention should also be made of Lion Cachet (1864–1945),[12] who had learnt his batik technique from Dijsselhof, while among glass designers Chris Lebeau was outstanding.

Among illustrators, apart from Lemmen and Toorop, were artists such as Anton der Kinderen and Roland Holst. The painter Johan Thorn Prikker (1868–1932)[13] was more versatile, producing not only batik-inspired textiles for wallpapers and designs for marquetry, but also turning his hand to furniture design. His furniture was simple, with arched stretchers in the style of van de Velde (fig. 235).[14] He also worked with van de Velde in the Haus Leuring, where Thorn Prikker was responsible, among other things for the mural decorations from 1900–02. Here, along the ceiling there is a frieze in Art Nouveau style.[15] Shortly afterwards, in 1904, Prikker settled in Germany, where he spent the rest of his life.

The interest in Egyptian art which was particularly strong in Holland, in architecture as well as in applied art, was best expressed in the work of Johannes L. M. Lauweriks (1864–1932).[16] Like de Bazel he executed a number of woodcuts in the 1890's in a style clearly influenced by Egypt, as well as furniture with a number of Egyptian features. Traces of Art Nouveau in his work, however, are to be seen in silverwork, but they are late, sporadic examples (figs. 236 a–b).[17]

In considering Dutch Art Nouveau—or what one might be tempted to call lack of Art Nouveau, if it is considered in its general European context—one is struck by its simple and two-dimensional aspect. The paucity

11 Gemeentemuseum, The Hague.

12 J. Gratama, En interieur in het huis van Th. G. Dentz van Schaik te Amsterdam, *Onze Kunst,* vol. XVII, 1910, pp. 158–70; C. A. Lion Cachet, Geweven en genkoopte stoffen van C. A. Lion Cachet, *Maandblad vor beeldende Kunsten,* vol. I, 1924, pp. 16–21; *idem,* Voorwerpen van gebatikt perkament, *ibid.,* vol. I, 1924, pp. 108–13.

13 J. Thorn Prikker, *Brieven van Johan Thorn Prikker,* Amsterdam 1897, introduction by Henri Borel; M. Creutz, *Johan Thorn Prikker,* Munich n.d. Complete bibliography in H. van Hall, *op. cit.,* vol. I, No. 16704–16738, vol. II, No. 8388–8394.

14 Cat. No. M.A. 1121–22, Gemeentemuseum, The Hague.

15 Ph. Zilcken, Johan Thorn Prikker, *Elseviers,* July–December, vol. XXIV, 1902, pp. 147–60.

16 Blaauw, J. L. M. Lauweriks, *Bouwkundig Weekblad,* vol. LIII, 1932, p. 142; Joop Pot, J. L. M. Lauweriks, *ibid.,* vol. LIII, 1932, p. 141; J. de Meijer, J. L. M. Lauweriks, *Wendingen,* vol. X, 1929, pp. 2–28; Files in the Cabinet of Prints and Drawings, Rijksmuseum, Amsterdam, No. 15 Z and 15 F. 28.

17 File Lauweriks, 15 F. 28, Rijksmuseum, Amsterdam.

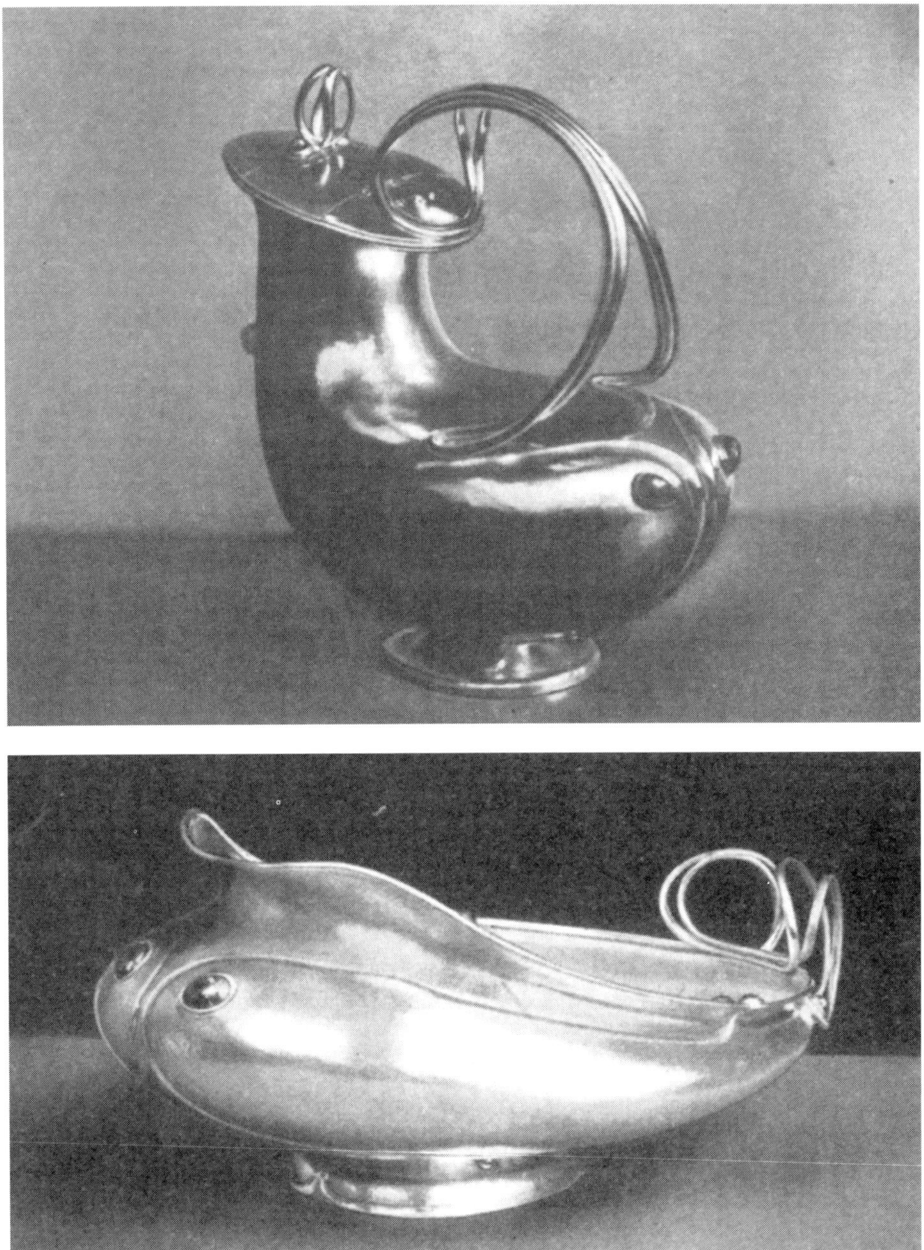

Fig. 236 a–b. Lauweriks: Silver jug and fruit bowl. 1911–12.
Rijksmuseum, Amsterdam. Copyright reserved.

of examples of this style is due to the constructive line of Dutch architecture. The reason for this seems to be on the one hand the close relationship with French rationalism, and on the other hand the fact that Historicism promoted architectural ideals which had essentially more to give. Moreover, Dutch Historicism rested on a more sober foundation than was the case in neighbouring countries, while at the same time a sound neo-Gothic—at least where furniture design is concerned—resulted in a healthy development which in many ways resembles that in England. It would, however, be difficult to decide just how much this was due to influences from England, with whom Holland had always enjoyed close relations in the realm of furniture design.

A feature which applies particularly to Holland, and which may explain in part the lack of Art Nouveau, is that neo-Baroque, as already mentioned, exerted no important influence. And it must be remembered that the form-conception of Art Nouveau is to quite a large extent based on neo-Baroque, and the absence of this style may explain why the essential conditions necessary for the other were not available. It is also characteristic that such Art Nouveau as is to be found is markedly two-dimensional. This is in part due to the influence of batik, but must also be ascribed to the stylistic trends in Holland generally, and the traditional dislike of excesses. Dutch Art Nouveau is also far more symmetrical in conception than that of other countries: Fanciful and asymmetrical details, Rococo in origin, are almost non-existent, while ornament clearly defined in its limits and unerringly placed was a feature of furniture in Holland as early as the middle of the 1890's. It is natural to assume that this, too, is because neo-Rococo played a far less important role here than it did in other countries.

*

Even during the Art Nouveau period, while other nations were addicted to fantasies of an international kind, Dutch architecture and decorative art, as well as applied art, retained those characteristic features on which it has always been able to pride itself, and which it shares with the island kingdom to the west—a simple, austere, but unerring and expert treatment of the whole, as well as of the separate parts.

Austria

Viennese Secessionists

The development in Austria was of such a kind that what corresponds to the Art Nouveau style merely became an interlude on a two-dimensional plane. The general development of style in Austrian architecture in the 1890's was entirely bound by tradition, and yet, beneath the Classical surface, a radical architecture developed which was to prove of European importance.

Otto Wagner (1841–1918)[1] was working at the beginning of the 1890's in what was almost a Florentine neo-Renaissance style, his more plastic shapes occasionally suggesting the neo-Baroque spirit. His interiors varied from neo-Rococo to neo-Renaissance. Towards the end of the century a Classical tendency was noticeable in his work, with simple wholesome lines, relieved by a number of light and delicate Louis XVI touches—a phenomenon which is undoubtedly part of the general tendency round about the year 1900, as we have noted also in France. Only occasionally does Wagner adopt a chance Art Nouveau motif, as in the Nussdorfer Nadelwehr, 1897.

While Wagner remained lighter in his style than other neo-Baroque architects, the latter developed round about 1900 into an independent Austrian movement. The plastic neo-Baroque form-conception was maintained, but most of the ornamentation was abandoned, to be replaced by long and narrow fluting, or the surfaces were allowed to remain almost unadorned. Frequently the plinth of the building has a pronounced outward curve near the ground. This gives the architecture its characteristic look: the building seems to *rest* on the ground, and the plastic effect appears more pronounced than usual because all external frippery has been removed. At the same time the building appears lighter, because the decoration which has been maintained is, as a rule, vertical and austere by nature. With this in view several of the features of Austrian Art Nouveau can be under-

[1] O. Wagner, *Einige Skizzen und Ausgeführte Bauwerke von Otto Wagner,* Vienna, vol. I, 1892, vol. II, 1897, vol. III, 1906; *ibid., Aus der Wagner Schule,* Vienna 1900; *ibid.,* Wagnerschule 1901, Vienna 1902; *ibid., Wagnerschule 1902–03 und 1903–04,* Leipzig 1905; *ibid., Das Oesterreichische Postsparekassenamt,* Vienna, n.d.; J. A. Lux, *Otto Wagner,* Munich 1914; H. Tietze, *Otto Wagner,* Vienna 1922.

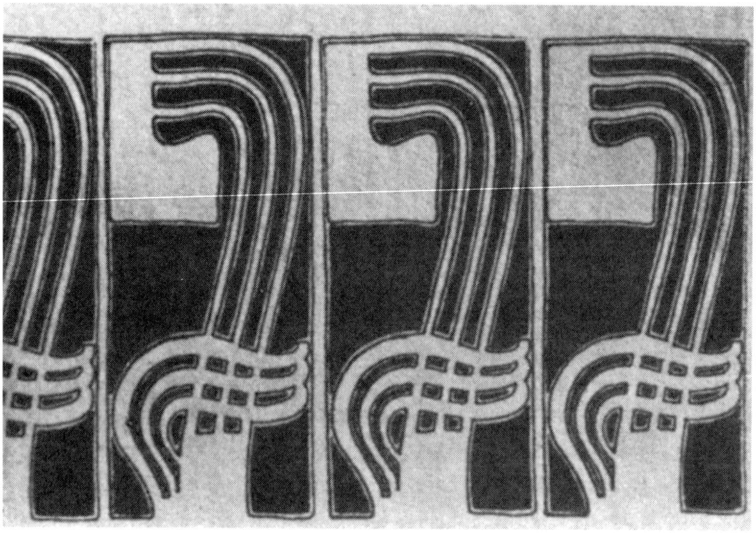

Fig. 237. Hoffmann: Vignette for *Ver Sacrum.* 1898.

stood, e.g. Hoffmann's neo-Baroque design (fig. 64), and certain Louis XVI details which unexpectedly crop up.

Nevertheless the movement away from the archeological and historical attitude to style proceeded unabated. In Wagner's opinion the archeological attitude prevented any new creation in the realm of decorative art.[2] He had personally provided the most important theoretical contribution to a solution of the question in his book *Moderne Architektur,* which he had written in 1895, and which by 1902 had run through three editions. The struggle of the Viennese painters to revive painting resulted in 1897 in the formation of the Secession group, but in Austria only a few painters joined in the struggle to emancipate applied art. The architects led the way, architects trained in Otto Wagner's rational school. Furthermore the intimate contact with England during the 19th century meant that the ideals of the Arts and Crafts Movement exercised a far greater influence on the Austrians than for example the French floral experiments or the Belgian Art Nouveau. Both Josef Hoffmann (1870–)[3] and Joseph Olbrich (1867–1908)[4] were

[2] O. Wagner, Die Kunst im Gewerbe, *Ver Sacrum,* vol. III, 1900, pp. 21–23.

[3] J. Hoffmann, Einfache Möbel, *Das Interieur,* vol. II, 1901, pp. 193–208; M. Dreger, Skizzen, Studien und ausgeführte Entwürfe von Josef Hoffmann, *Ver Sacrum,* vol. III, 1900, pp. 67–82; F. Khnopff, Josef Hoffmann, *The Studio,* vol. XXII, 1901, pp. 261–67; L. Kleiner, *Josef Hoffmann,* Berlin 1927; A. Weiser,

members of the group, and both were keen to start entirely anew in common with Belgians and Frenchmen, and not on traditional grounds like the English. "It was for this reason that the pure square and the use of black and white as dominant colours specially interested me," writes Josef Hoffmann, "because these clear elements had not appeared in former styles."[5]

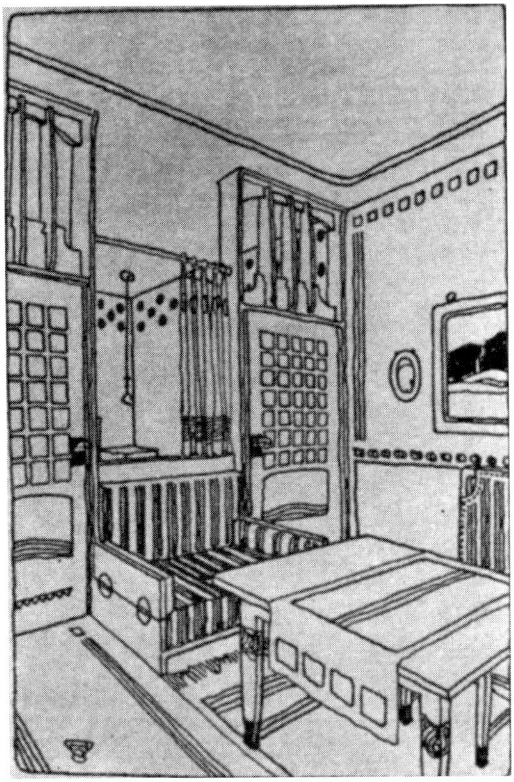

Fig. 238. Hoffmann: Design for interior. 1898.

As a book illustrator Hoffmann had ample opportunity to develop his ornaments in black-and-white vignettes for *Ver Sacrum*, and it is here that his characteristic ornamentation is created in the years just before 1900 (fig. 237).[6] This is remarkable for its straight lines, intersecting whiplash curves, and the lavish use of squares. Here, too, he learnt the art of placing his ornament to best effect and to treat it as a subordinate factor. In this respect both Hoffmann and Olbrich differ from Germans and Frenchmen, and have much more in common with their English contemporaries.

When Hoffmann introduced his squares and straight lines into the realm of furniture design the transition was so much the easier, as the

Josef Hoffmann, Geneva 1930, J. A. Lux, Innenkunst von Prof. Josef Hoffmann, Vienna, *Zeitschrift für Innendekoration,* vol. XIII, 1902, pp. 129–32, *Wendingen,* Amsterdam, Special Number, August-September, No. 8–9, 1920.

4 J. Olbrich, *Ideen von Olbrich,* Vienna 1900, *Architektur von Professor Joseph Olbrich,* vols. I–III, Berlin 1905; *J. Olbrich's Zeichnungen für Baukunst und Kunstgewerbe,* Berlin 1912, J. A. Lux, *Josef Maria Olbrich,* Berlin 1919; G. Veronesi, *Josef Maria Olbrich,* Milan 1948.

5 Letter to the author of the 10th of September 1954.

6 *Ver Sacrum,* vol. I, September 1898, p. 25.

Japanese style and the Arts and Crafts Movement had already blazed the way; already by the end of the 1890's the square had become his favourite motif (fig. 238).[7] Subsequently this motif was to become immensely popular in Vienna and large parts of Europe in the decade that followed—squares on floors, squares on mantelpieces, squares in the upper section of the window, where they seemed to thrive for some reason or other—squares on mouldings and inlay work, or as a single brick—or in twos and threes—placed in the middle of a facade, or in rows horizontally or vertically on walls.

J. M. Olbrich also started his career as a book illustrator, and developed his style assiduously in the columns of *Ver Sacrum*. He adopted the circle as his favourite motif (fig. 239)[8]—the circle as an oriflame, monochrome circles, circles in rows, and circles in clusters—and he, too, learnt to place and limit his motif. From the pages of a book these two artists transferred their motifs to other surfaces, in interior decoration, and occasionally in furniture design.

Formally the square and the circle represent the diametrical opposite of Art Nouveau ideals, and yet these simple geometrical shapes which the Austrians developed at the end of the 1890's, are—as Hoffmann himself says—undoubtedly part of a reaction and a search for an entirely new form. But precisely because Hoffmann and Olbrich were architects in Wagner's school—and did not remain illustrators—they were more concerned with architectural and constructional problems than with the ornament, and when they did use ornament its function was in a way the same as in a book, viz. it was there merely as an effective vignette. And this brings us to the core of the Secession style in interior decoration and furniture design: it represents a striving to escape from period styles, and is based on rational and constructive principles, with a sparing use of elegantly placed geometrical ornaments in an entity consisting of simple planes.

With the Secession style we move away from what is generally associated with the conception of Art Nouveau, because the solution of the style problem was in this case so different. But because the Secession style is a

7 *Ibid.*, vol. III, 1900, p. 65.
8 *Ibid.*, vol. I, January 1898, p. 13.

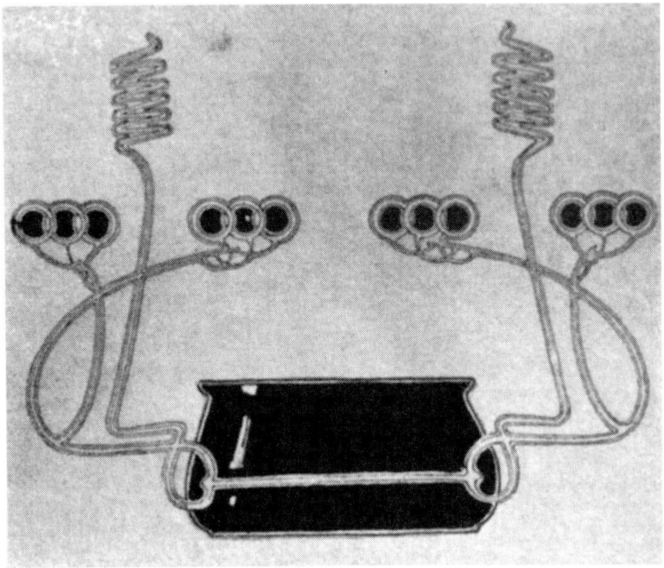

Fig. 239. Olbrich: Vignette for *Ver Sacrum*. 1898.

parallel trend, containing elements of Art Nouveau, it seems appropriate at least to place it in this context.

The Viennese school's conception of interior decoration agrees astonishingly well with that of the Scottish school. If, for example, one compares Mackintosh's staircase hall, the headmaster's appartment, *The Glasgow School of Art*, 1897, with Hoffmann's hall for *Haus Moser*, Vienna, 1902 (figs. 240–241), or Mackintosh's hall for *Hill House*, 1902–03 (fig. 160), with Hoffmann's contemporary hall for Director K. in Vienna (fig. 242),[9] it will be seen that there is a striking likeness, a likeness which as early as the autumn of 1898 was commented on quite generally in *Dekorative Kunst.*

But what was the actual relationship between Glasgow and Vienna? This question was first thoroughly dealt with by Nikolaus Pevsner in *Pioneers of Modern Design,* and latterly by Thomas Howarth, who has studied this question very closely. He comes to the conclusion that the resemblance is due rather to a development which proceeded independently in the two countries, although a mutual knowledge of the schools of painting in the respective countries has undoubtedly accelerated this development as far

9 *Zeitschrift für Innendekoration,* vol. XIII, 1902, p. 152.

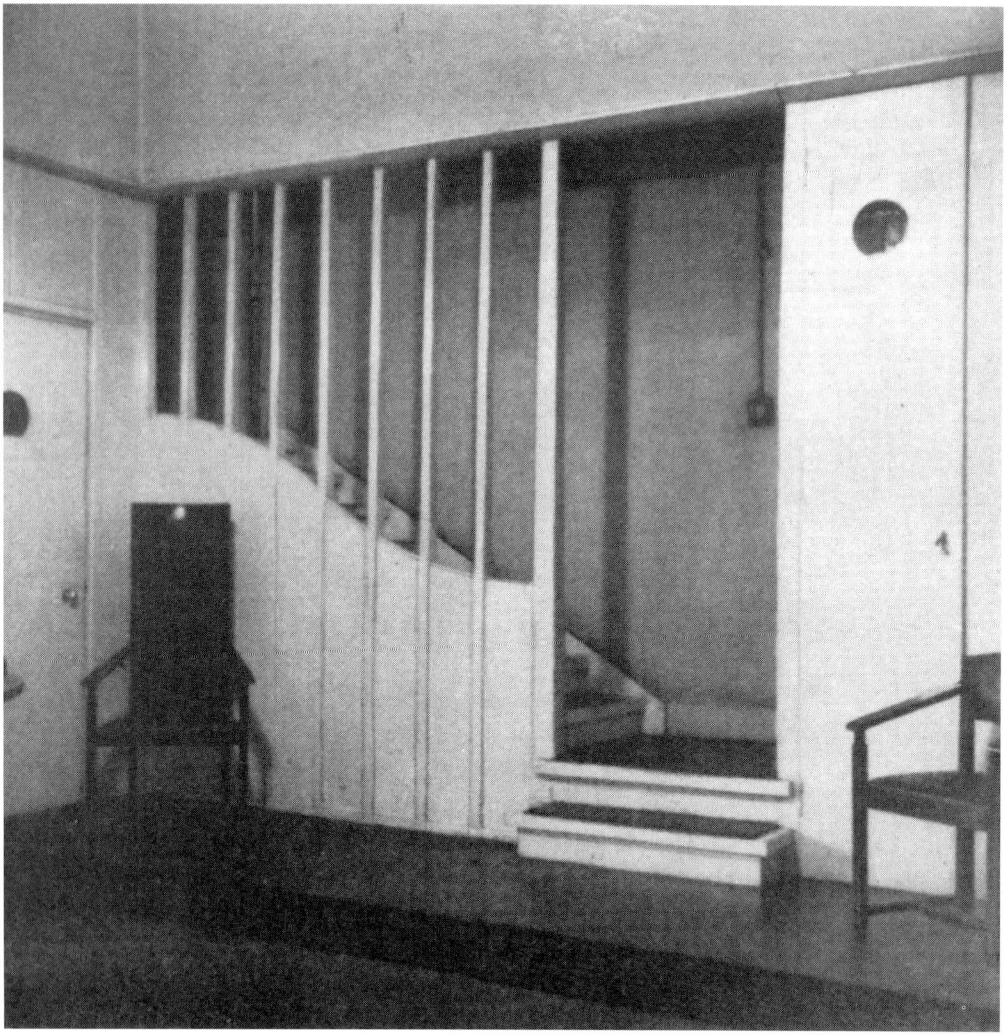

Fig. 240. Mackintosh: Headmaster's room with staircase. 1897–99.
Courtesy of T. Howarth.

as purely external forms of expression are concerned. Thomas Howarth has undoubtedly got to the core of the problem in this respect. The architectural development has undoubtedly proceeded independently in the two countries, as well as the development of certain decorative elements. That both Mackintosh and Hoffmann in 1897–98 use the quadrangle and similar

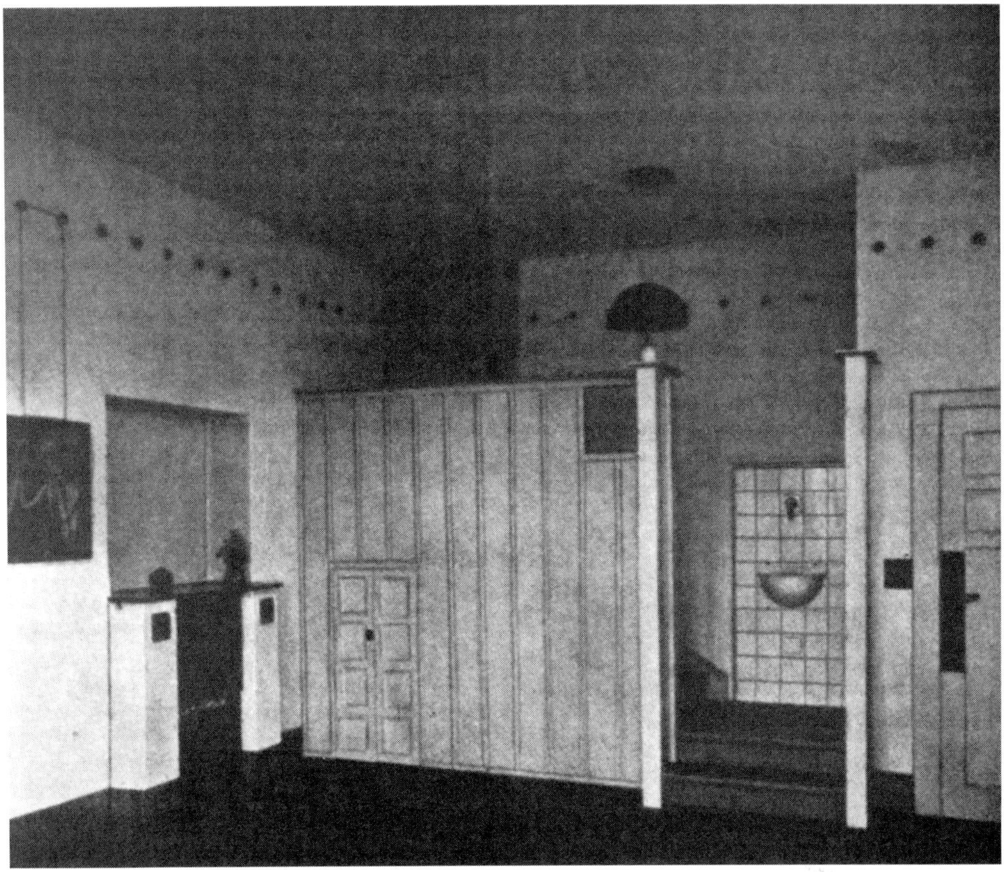

Fig. 241. Hoffmann: The Hall at Haus Moser. 1902.

colours: black and white, does not necessarily mean that one has influenced the other. Two of the most advanced architects at the time may have arrived at the same solution. Such influence as the Glasgow school may have had was probably more in the nature of a stimulus to the Viennese school than of a purely direct kind.

The first exhibition of applied art in the Viennese Secession took place in 1898, and for the occasion Josef Hoffmann had designed the exhibition hall in his characteristic style,[10] while Olbrich, more in keeping with

10 Illustrated in *Ver Sacrum,* May-June, vol. I, 1898, p. 7. For the exhibition, see also *Deutsche Kunst und Dekoration,* vol. III, 1898, pp. 197–219.

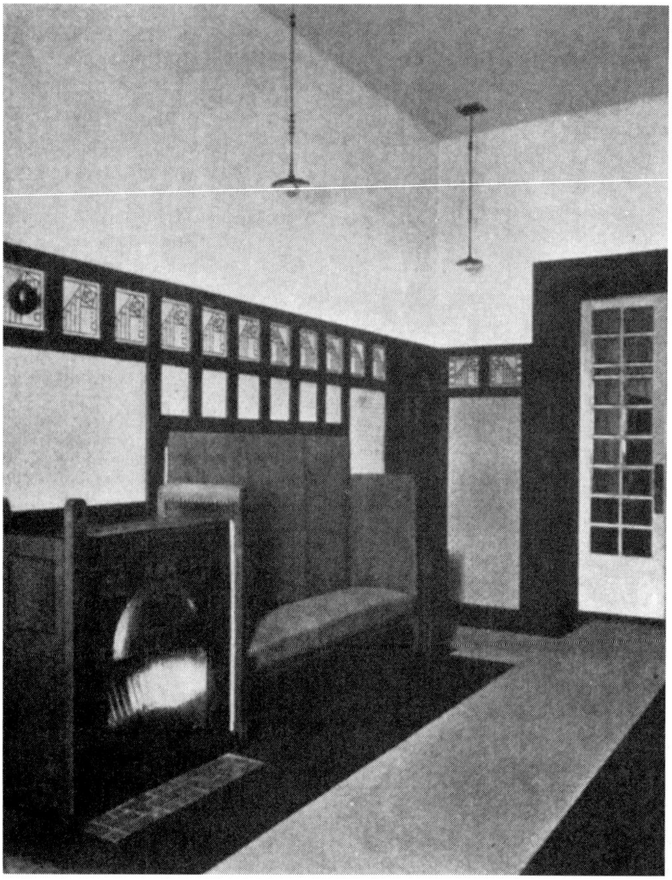

Fig. 242. Hoffmann: The hall in Mr. K.'s house. About 1902.

Vienna's tradition of lavishness, used a stylised floral scheme of decoration, with a tendency to geometrical patterns. At the exhibition in the subsequent year[11] both these designers were well to the fore with furniture notable for the refinement of its proportions rather than for its decoration (figs. 243, 244).[12] "... (they) appeared very sober and refined alongside the writhing voluptuous forms affected on this occasion by van de Velde and Pankok,"[13] Thomas Howarth writes, and he emphasises specially the relationship

11 Folnesics, Das Moderne Wiener Kunstgewerbe, *Deutsche Kunst und Dekoration,* vol. V, 1899–1900, pp. 253–81.

12 *Deutsche Kunst und Dekoration,* vol. V, 1899–1900, pp. 260–61.

13 T. Howarth, *Charles Rennie Mackintosh and the Modern Movement,* London 1952, p. 267.

between Hoffmann's furniture and the design of the English artists by declaring: "In this piece of furniture he achieved the simplicity of Voysey and the originality of Mackintosh without emulating the stylistic mannerisms which so often date the work of both British designers."[14] In Paris in 1900 Hoffmann exhibited an entire suite of furniture (fig. 245)[15] without any traces of Art Nouveau.

In view of the fact that Austria also had an architect such as Adolf Loos (1870–1933),[16] who as early as 1898 was drawing much more simply than Olbrich or Hoffmann (fig. 246), it is easier to understand why Art Nouveau

14 *Ibid.*, p. 267.

15 *Zeitschrift für Innendekoration*, vol. XI, 1900, p. 127.

16 A. Loos, *Ins Leere gesprochen, 1897–1900*, Berlin 1921; *idem, Trotzdem*, Innsbruck, 1930; H. Kulka, *Adolf Loos. Das Werk des Architekten*, Vienna 1931; F. Glück, *Adolf Loos*, Paris 1931; R. Lanyi, *Adolf Loos*, Vienna 1931; A. Marilaun, *Adolf Loos*, Vienna 1922; B. Markalaus, *Adolf Loos*, Vienna 1931.

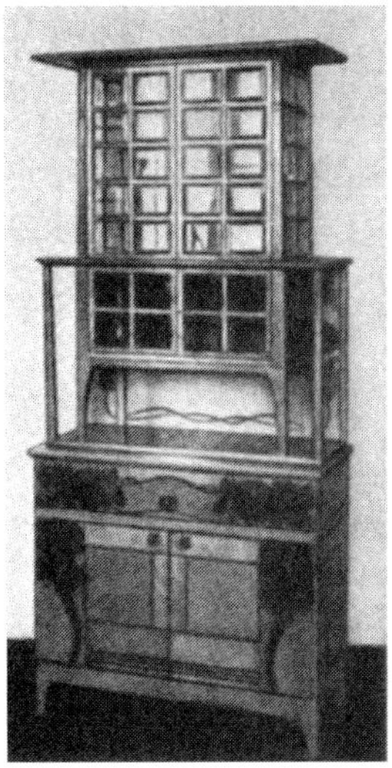

Fig. 243.

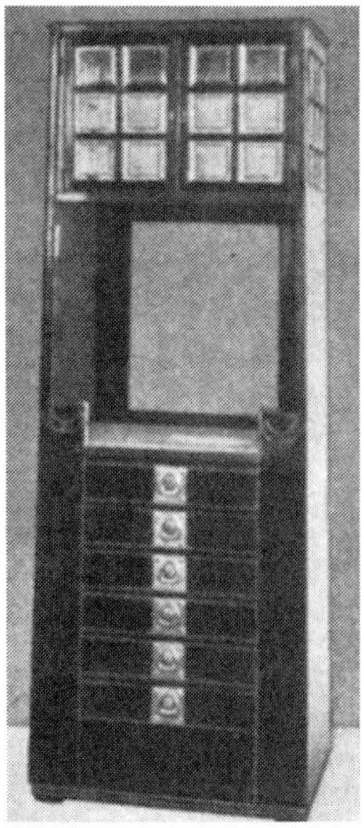

Fig. 244.

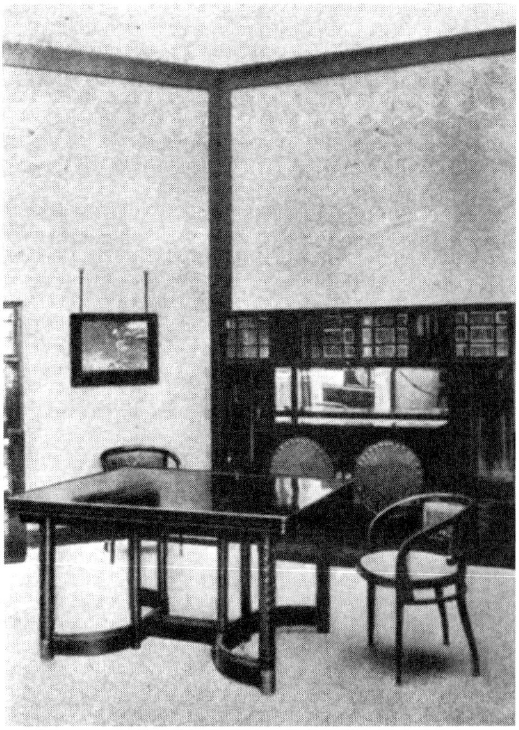

Fig. 245.

Fig. 243. Olbrich: Cabinet. Beech with inlay work. 1899.

Fig. 244. Hoffmann: Cabinet. Mahogany. 1899.

Fig. 245. Hoffmann: Dining-room for the Paris Exhibition. 1900.

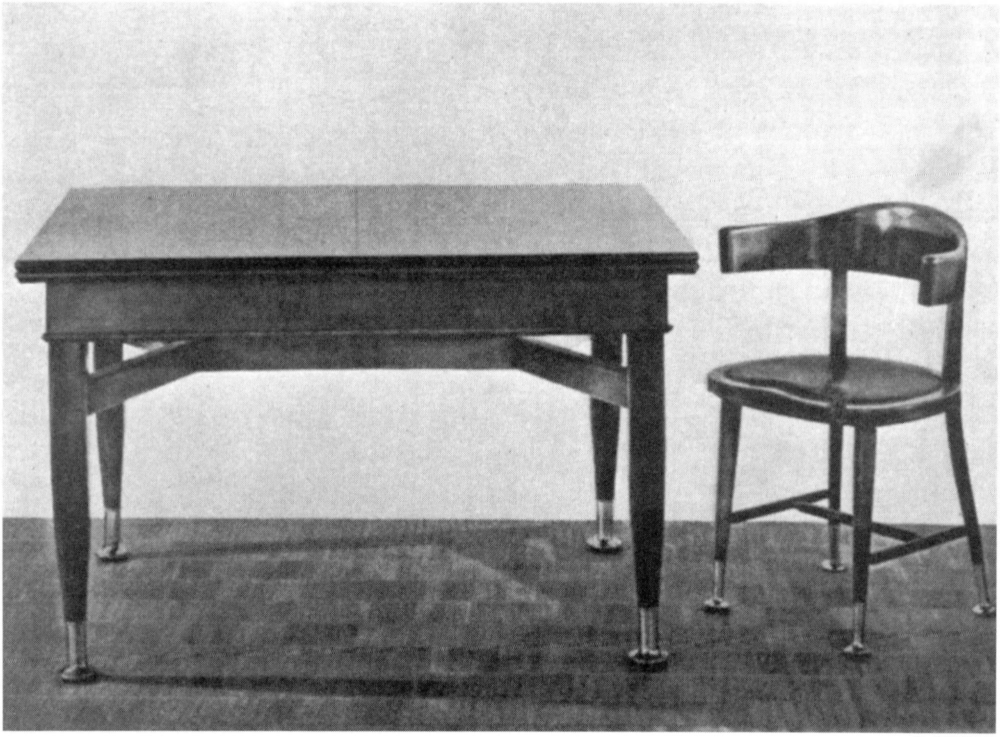

Fig. 246. Loos: Table and chair. 1898.
From *Um 1900.*

only represented a relatively unimportant deviation from the general development, and why it was possible as early as 1901 for Mackintosh to be described by the Viennese as "recht dekadent"[17] (quite decadent). Loos, and also Auguste Perret and Tony Garnier, play an important part in the development of modern architecture, but it has not been possible to trace any Art Nouveau in their work, either in object or in detail, "Ornament is a crime,"[18] he used to say.

Among artists influenced by the Art Nouveau style at the turn of the century can be mentioned Koloman Moser (1868–1916),[19] who, in common with Hoffmann and Olbrich, also devoted himself to teaching.

17 L. Abels, Die Kunstgewerbe-Ausstellung der Secession, *Das Interieur,* vol. II, 1901, pp. 17–23.

18 T. Howarth, *op. cit.,* p. 282. Outburst of Loos, according to Behrendt.

19 Koloman Moser, *Dekorative Kunst,* vol. VII, 1900–01, pp. 227–31.

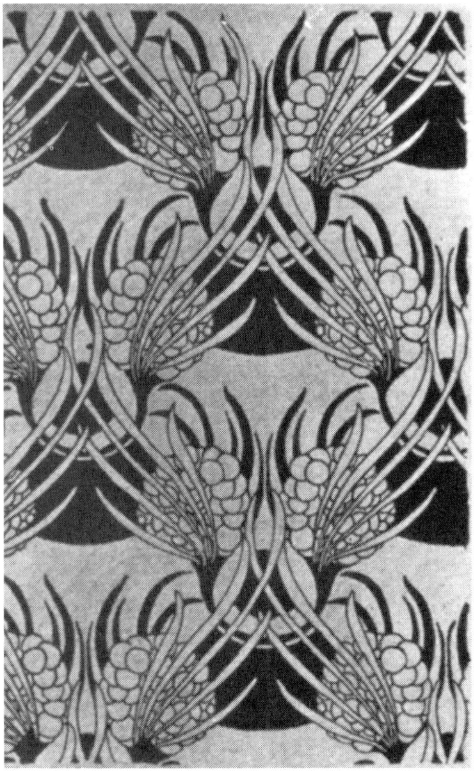

Fig. 247. Moser: Design for textile. *Abimelech*. 1899.

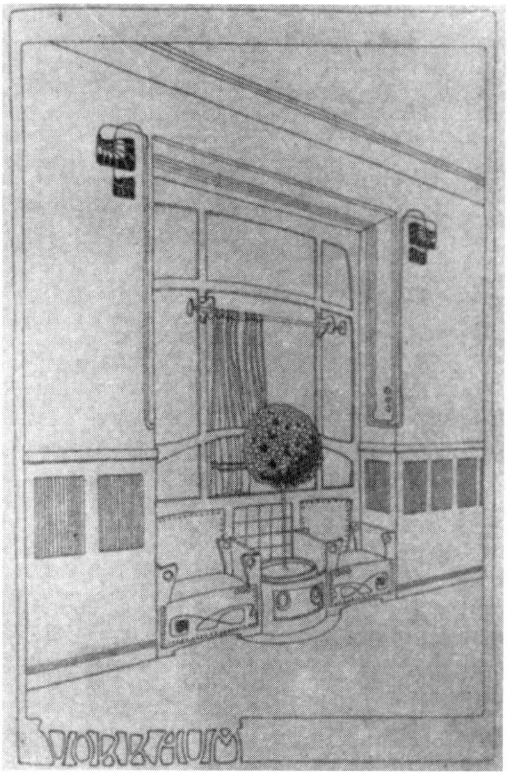

Fig. 248. Prutscher: Design for interior. 1900.

Moser was originally a painter, and instead of taking up furniture design and architecture reserved his energies for two-dimensional art (fig. 247).[20] These three had a number of pupils, and it is evident from the pages of *Ver Sacrum* that Leopold Bauer, Moser's pupil Max Benirschke, and—especially in the later numbers—J. M. Auchentaller, continued their master's work. In furniture design there is a trend which is often called the Hoffmann school, with Leopold Bauer and Otto Prutscher (fig. 248),[21] as well as Marcell Kammerer—who was more noticeably influenced by Olbrich—among the more prominent designers. But most important of them all was the painter Gustav Klimt (1862-1918), one of the founders of

20 *Ver Sacrum*, vol. II, 1899, 3, p. 14.

21 *Das Interieur*, vol. I, 1900, pl. 14.

the *Sezession*, although dependent on earlier Art Nouveau artists as late as 1897, as Nikolaus Pevsner states.[22]

Apart from the above mentioned there were a great many less important artists, who varied their Art Nouveau-influenced poster style from imitations of Mackintosh in silver and applegreen, to Olbrich-inspired decorations composed of circles, Beardsley women seen from behind in long party frocks with trains, Mucha girls— more scantily clad and seen more from the front—as well as trivial squares à la "quadratel Hoffmann" (Hoffmann square) ad infinitum.[23]

In architecture, too, we also find a poster-like use of Art Nouveau motifs. The Viennese periodical *Der Architekt* contains a number of examples in the years just before and after 1900.

*

In its essence what can be called Art Nouveau in Austria is very closely allied to the surface and to the two-dimensional, which strengthens the assumption that its origins are to be found in book illustrations. From here it spread to other surfaces, and to interior decoration. Because the development occurred so late, the symbolical, floral, and stalk-abstracted forms used in the rest of Europe were by-passed, and the decoration was based on geometrical figures. This form-language corresponds quite logically to the constructive search and the desire for an agreement with the material: herein lies the key to its popularity and its widespread application.

Thus Austria found her own style, a new style which had no formal connection with Art Nouveau. This style—which was to have the greatest importance to architecture and decorative art in Europe—is the main reason for the absence of a strong Art Nouveau movement in Austria.

It can be shown that even before 1900 the road ahead had been mapped out in Austria, a road which by-passed Art Nouveau and was to lead directly to the Modern Movement; and which, as far as applied art was concerned, resulted in entirely new stylistic ideals, which were to spread across Austria and Europe through the *Wiener-Werkstätte*.

22 N. Pevsner, *Pioneers of Modern Design*, N. Y. 1949, p. 104.

23 *Die Flaeche*, Vienna, 1902–04. Ca. 6–700 patterns and designs of the best known artists of the time.

Germany

Jugendstil[1]

The World Exhibition in Vienna in 1873 and the exhibition in Munich in 1876, where applied art for the first time was accorded a place of its own, helped to establish the position of the neo-Renaissance in Germany. This style flourished from the 1870's to the 1880's, but towards the end of the 1880's merged imperceptibly into neo-Baroque on the one hand and a lighter Renaissance of a Florentine character on the other. Leopold Gmelin's account of the position of German applied art in 1893 contains the following observation: ". . . . no important artistic-industrial institution engaged in the construction of furniture or fittings for rooms, can limit its activity to one style only, or exclude either of the other styles." Apart from neo-Rococo and neo-Renaissance there was in Germany especially an interest in folk art, in simple rustic furniture, eagerly supported by art historians such as Sammler and Mielke. "The complete painting of pieces of furniture in various coloured dye-lac, a tendency now flourishing particularly in Munich and Dresden, originated in accession to the imitation of peasants' furniture; . . . ."[2]

At the beginning of the 1890's the floral style made its influence felt in Germany as in other countries, but without appreciable Art Nouveau tendencies.

After the Chicago Exhibition of 1893 the "kunstgewerbliche Anglomanie"[3] set in, and the three years from 1895 to 1898 witnessed an almost

[1] From the point of view of art history, the Germans have dealt more thoroughly with the problems of their Art Nouveau—the Jugendstil—than any other country, and this chapter will to some extent be based upon the following research works: Fr. Ahlers-Hestermann, *Stilwende. Aufbruch der Jugend um 1900,* Berlin 1941; W. C. Behrendt, *Der Kampf um den Stil im Kunstgewerbe und in der Architektur,* Berlin 1920; J. A. Lux, *Die Geschichte des modernen Kunstgewerbes in Deutschland,* Leipzig 1908; E. Michalski, Die Entwicklungsgeschichtliche Bedeutungen des Jugendstils, *Repertorium für Kunstwissenschaft,* vol. XLVI, Berlin 1925, pp. 133–49; F. Schmalenbach, *Jugendstil. Ein Beitrag zu Theorie und Geschichte der Flächenkunst,* Würzburg 1934; F. Schumacher, *Strömungen in deutscher Baükunst seit 1800,* Leipzig 1936.

[2] L. Gmelin, *Deutsche Kunstgewerbe zur Zeit der Weltausstellung in Chicago 1893,* Munich 1893. Two last quotations pp. 26 sq.

[3] R. Graul, Deutschland, *Die Krisis im Kunstgewerbe,* Leipzig 1901, pp. 39–51 (40). Anglo-mania in applied art.

unbelievable spate of activity in applied art in Germany. This sudden upheaval was in the main due to three factors, which were peculiar to Germany: in the first place Germany was permeated by a marked national consciousness and a desire for national assertion; secondly Germany possessed, thanks to her leading position in art research, a great many competent art historians and art critics who devoted themselves with great intensity to the problems of applied art; and finally there was the fact that Germany had a great deal of leeway to make up in the development in architecture and applied art, in order to keep abreast of the times. Compared to England, Belgium, and France, Germany arrived on the scene rather late, and now at last the Germans awoke from their neo-Renaissance dreams and their isolation—they had, for instance, not been represented at any exhibition in Paris since 1867. While the Japanese had exhibited in London since 1861, the first Japanese exhibition was arranged in Berlin in 1882.[4] "Seit fünf oder sechs Jahren erst sprechen wir in Deutschland von einer modernen Bewegung in Kunstgewerbe," wrote Richard Graul in 1901.[5] Another of Germany's contemporary experts in the field of applied art, Joseph A. Lux, expresses more or less the same idea: "Das Jahr 1898, gleichsam das Revolutionsjahr, darf man daher als das offizielle Geburtsjahr der modernen Bewegung in Deutschland bezeichnen."[6]

In the years just preceding 1900 the Germans now seized on van de Velde and his style with great delight, not only because he proved so popular among young designers, and had already made a name for himself as a writer, but also because he undoubtedly appealed to the German mentality with his clear and unambiguous theoretical doctrines. In short he was just the kind of leader they were looking for. The quality of his art was not always of the highest, he had no training as an architect, and his applied art frequently deviated from his own theories. At the time, however, these were minor considerations.

4 G. Brandes, Japanesisk og impressionistisk Kunst, *Berlin som tysk Rigshovedstad,* Cph. 1885, pp. 530–39, The author is here indebted to Oscar Thue.

5 R. Graul, *op. cit.,* p. 39, "it is only during the last five or six years that we in Germany have talked of a modern movement in applied art."

6 J. A. Lux, Deutsche Werkstätter, *Die Geschichte des modernen Kunstgewerbes in Deutschland,* Leipzig 1908, pp. 116–36. "The year 1898, as well as being a year of revolution, may be described as the official birthday-year of the Modern Movement in Germany."

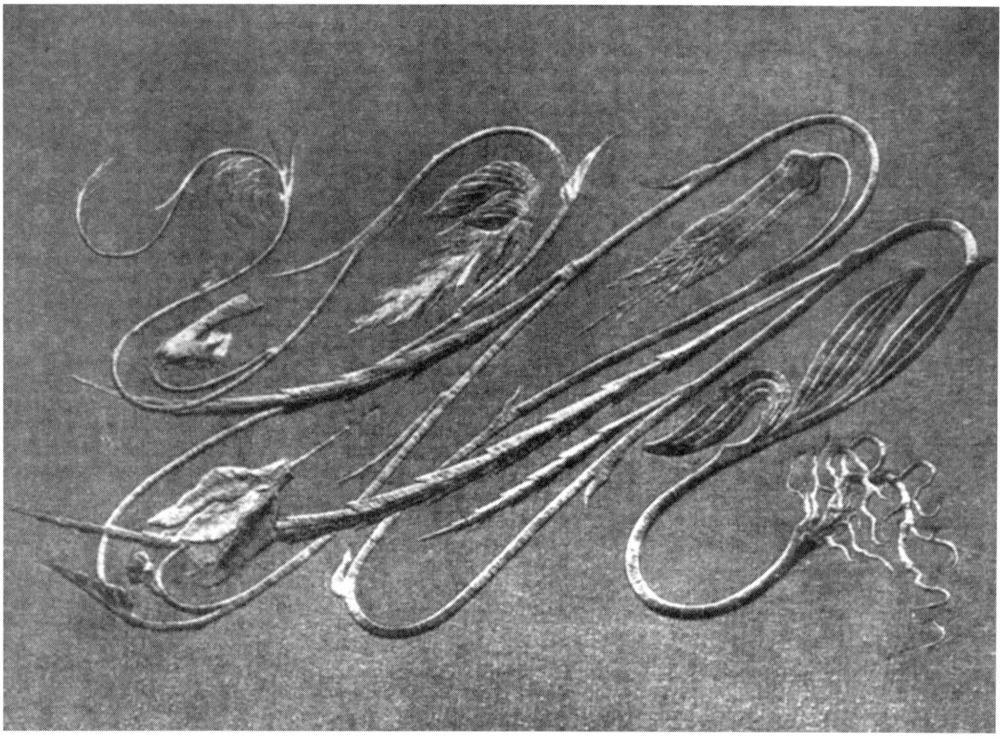

Fig. 249. Obrist: Embroidery. Probably 1892–94.
Historisches Stadtmuseum, Munich.

What, then, was the historical development in these few but eventful years? After Julius Meier-Graefe had started *Pan* in 1895 with the object of "transforming the foreign doctrine in accordance with the national spirit," Germany had opened the first window on Europe. In the same year the director of the Krefelder Museum, Friedrich Deneker, invited Henry van de Velde to deliver a lecture at Krefeld, and at the same time the Belgian artist designed some brocade patterns for the silk firm Deuss & Oetker.[7] This was his first contact with Germany, and it was also typical of Germany's willingness to embrace new ideas and impulses. In 1897 Obrist, Pankok, Paul, and Riemerschmid founded the *Münchener Vereinigte Werkstätten für Kunst im Handwerk*, and in the following year a similar

[7] K. Osthaus, Van de Velde, *Leben und Schaffen des Künstlers,* Hagen 1920, p. 16.

organisation, the *Dresdener Werkstätte für Handwerkskunst*, started in Dresden under the management of Karl Schmidt. Both organisations aimed to create a national German art, independent of stylistic imitation, and on a sound constructive basis, through the medium of co-operation between artist and artisan. In the spring of 1897 van de Velde held his exhibition in Dresden, and thereby contact was firmly established. During these years a number of periodicals containing a great many articles on foreign subjects, with the emphasis on England and Austria, were also started. The periodical *Jugend*, founded in 1896, had no particular associations with applied art, but with its light and cheerful tone, and its up-to-date attitude, it reflected in a popular way contemporary trends in verse, humour, and drawing. As many as four art journals were started in the year 1897, viz. *Kunst und Handwerk*, *Dekorative Kunst*, *Deutsche Kunst und Dekoration*, and *Kunst und Dekoration*, of which the first two were published in Munich, where *Jugend* and *Simplicissimus* also saw the light of day, while the two last-mentioned were published in Darmstadt, where *Zeitschrift für Innendekoration* had been published since 1889. It was no coincidence that Darmstadt should have been the centre of so much activity, for it was here that the Grand-Duke Ernst Ludwig of Hesse had his residence, and under his patronage the arts blossomed. His motto was: "Mein Hessenland blühe und in ihm die Kunst." (May my Hessenland flourish and with it the arts.)

In 1899 van de Velde made his way to Berlin, and Olbrich was summoned to Darmstadt. On March 24, 1900, the foundation stone of the *Ernst Ludwig Haus* was laid, and in the following year the *Künstlerkolonie* at Mathilde-Höhe was established, while in the same year the exhibition "*Dokument deutscher Kunst*" was opened, and seven artists moved into the new quarters which the Grand-Duke had so generously provided, and which they had had a free hand in decorating.

In these two towns of Munich and Darmstadt, which played such a prominent part in the development, the Jugend style was to enjoy a brief golden age before it was abandoned by the leading artists and became hackneyed in the hands of the less capable men.

The characteristic features of the development in Germany were the sudden and intense activity, and the ardent *desire* to solve problems which

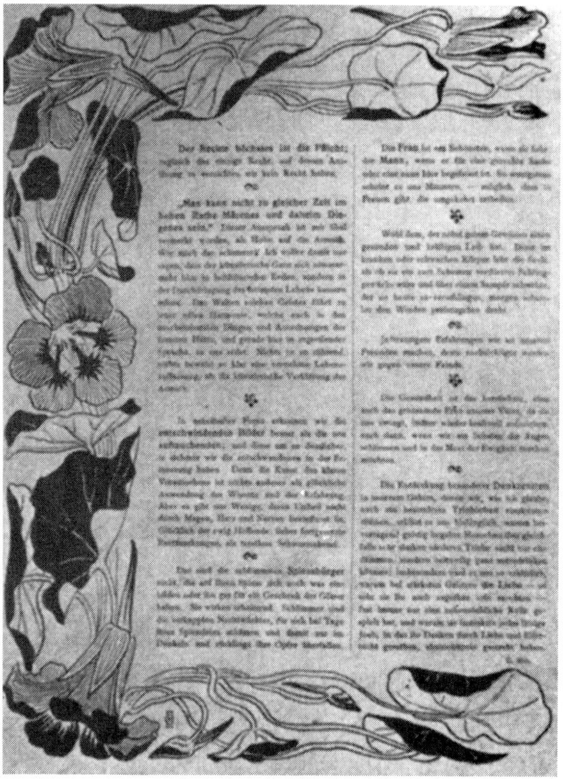

Fig. 250. Eckmann: His first illustration for *Jugend*. 1896.

lay at the root of the movement. "Der Wille zu Reform des Kunstgewerbes war da, und dort wo ein Wille ist, ist auch ein Weg."[8] In order to find a way the shrewd policy was adopted of enlisting the aid of leading artists from abroad, and as a result a great many—and sometimes conflicting—impulses operated. Apart from the influences which were generally felt on the Continent—e.g. from England and Scotland, and all the styles of Historicism, Floralism, etc., as well as Symbolism and Syntethism—one might have expected to find features directly imported from Austria and Belgium, but this was not so.

The first two artists in Germany to create decorative motifs with a

[8] R. Graul, *op. cit.*, p. 41. "The desire for a reform of applied art was there, and where there's a will there's a way."

linear rhythm which might be called Jugend, were Hermann Obrist (1863–1927)[9] and Otto Eckmann (1865–1902).[10] As a young man Obrist studied geology and chemistry, but after attending the *Karlsruhe Kunstgewerbeschule* from 1888 he devoted himself to applied art, and in 1892 founded an embroidery workshop in Florence, which he moved to Munich in 1894, the year he held his exhibition in the *Odeonplatz* in Munich, where his thirty-nine embroideries were on show. He had studied Nature assiduously, and his motifs were derived from Nature. Nature had been transformed into an ornament by giving it symmetry. In this way blades of grass, flowers, and leaves were linked together in regular stars, patterns, and wheels, retaining their naturalistic freshness even in strictly ornamental shapes. This was Obrist's important contribution. At the same time his embroidery had a great deal of the refinement of Japanese art (fig. 249).

With these patterns, which he designed at the beginning of the 1890's, we probably encounter the first linear Jugend rhythm in Germany, plainly derived from natural forms. The ever-watchful *Pan* published whole series of his embroideries in its fifth volume. Stylistically he occupies a similiar position to Crane in England and Grasset in France, and in common with these two he stuck mainly to the two-dimensional plane.

After working chiefly as a landscape painter Eckmann in 1894 executed the symbolical *chef d'oeuvre*, *Die Lebens-Alter* in six parts, and here we encounter his first Jugend-like linear and undulating movement in the smoke rising up from the vessel.[11] The painting has none of Toorop's or Crane's rhythm throughout, but only a few traces. During the years that followed Eckmann devoted himself to an intensive study of Nature, and when *Pan*

9 H. Obrist, Luxuskunst oder Volkskunst, *Dekorative Kunst,* vol. IX, 1901–02, pp. 81–99; *idem,* Wozu über Kunst schreiben, *ibid.,* vol. V, 1900, pp. 169–97; *idem,* Die Zukunft unserer Architektur, *ibid.,* vol. VII, 1901, pp. 329–48; *idem, Neue Möglichkeiten in der Bildenden Kunst, Aufsätze von 1896–1900,* Leipzig 1903; W. Bode, Hermann Obrist, *Pan,* vol. II, 1895–96, pp. 326–28; *idem,* Special edition of *Pan* 1896; G. Fuchs, Hermann Obrist, *Pan,* vol. II, 1895–96, pp. 318–25; K. Scheffler, Hermann Obrist, *Kunst und Künstler,* January 8, 1910, pp. 555–59; Fred W., A chapter on German Arts and Crafts with Special Reference to the work of Hermann Obrist, *The Artist,* New York, vol. XXXI, 1901, pp. 17–26.

10 O. Eckmann, *Neue Formen, Dekorative Entwürfe für die Praxis,* Berlin 1897; M. Osborn, *Neue Arbeiten von Otto Eckmann,* Berlin 1897; E. Zimmermann, Prof. O. Eckmann, Berlin, *Deutsche Kunst und Dekoration,* vol. VI, 1900, pp. 305–32. Special publication of *Berliner Architekturwelt,* Berlin 1901.

11 Illustrated in *Deutsche Kunst und Dekoration,* vol. VI, 1900, p. 309.

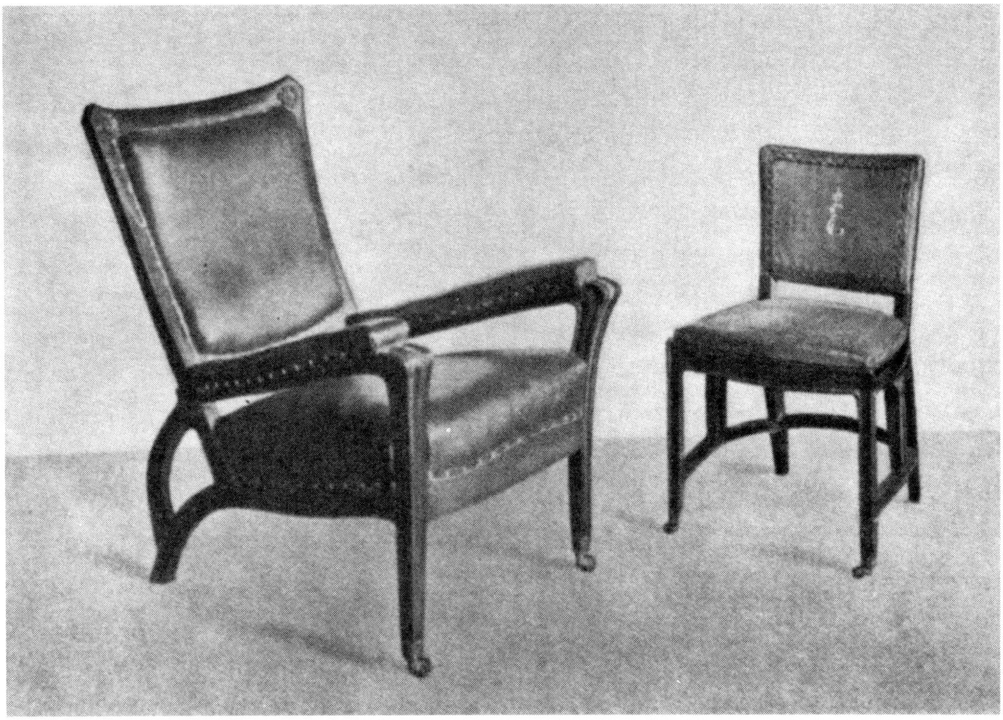

Fig. 251. Eckmann: Chairs made for the Grand-Duke of Hesse. 1899.

started publication he found in its columns a splendid stamping-ground for his floral and plant fantasies, and from 1896 the pages of *Jugend* were also available (fig. 250).[12] From the point of view of art history Eckmann's work in the naturalistic style is not a novelty, as Carlos Schwabe had carried out book illustrations some four or five years before which bear a striking similarity to it (fig. 96), but Eckmann's importance lies in the fact that he introduced tension and energy in the run of line by the sudden and clearly marked thickening at the bends. This is a detail which is not so often encountered in Belgium or Holland, and scarcely in Scotland, but is more typically German, and may perhaps originate in Eckmann's stylised plant forms. It is the artist's method of transferring the Belgian–French dynamic and explosive interplay to the two-dimensional plane.

[12] *Jugend*, vol. I, 1896, No. 1–2, p. 26.

Eckmann's furniture (fig. 251)[13] is remarkable for its delicacy and almost classical rigidity, as well as the constructive search in its wealth of superfluous ribs, struts, and the like, such as we have seen in the Belgian school in the work of Serrurier-Bovy and van de Velde.

Quite apart stands the glass designer Karl Koepping (1848–1914); in a great many glasses of extreme delicacy, he exploited the possibilities of his material almost to breaking point in straw-like forms (fig. 252).[14]

Both Eckmann and Obrist worked in Munich, and belonged to the group of seven artists who are usually called the Munich school. The other five members were Richard Riemerschmid (1868–),[15] Bernhard Pankok (1872–),[16] Bruno Paul (1874–),[17] August Endell (1871–1925),[18] and Peter Behrens (1868–1940)[19]—the last-mentioned subsequently settled in the other centre of applied art and architecture in Germany about the year 1900, viz. Darmstadt.

Common to all the members of the Munich group is a markedly constructive attitude: all furniture is abundantly furnished with joints and struts, the constructive elements are usually slightly arched, as well as the top and bottom of the main shape, otherwise planes and edges are rectilinear. In this way there is a characteristic interplay of angles between straight lines and slight curves, which helps to give the style a slightly heavy accent.

13 *Deutsche Kunst und Dekoration,* vol. V–VI, 1899–1900, p. 334.

14 Det Danske Kunstindustrimuseum, Copenhagen. Several glasses illustrated in *Pan,* vol. II, 1896–97 p. 252. Etchings by the artist.

15 M. Thiersch, *Wir fingen einfach an,* Munich 1954; *Dekorative Kunst,* vol. VIII, 1901, pp. 329–76.

16 K. Lange, Bernhard Pankok's Eheschliessungszimmer in Dessau, *Dekorative Kunst,* vol. XI, 1902–03, pp. 321–51; H. Obrist, Luxuskunst oder Volkskunst, *Dekorative Kunst,* vol. IX, 1901–02, pp. 81–99.

17 J. Popp, *Bruno Paul,* Munich, n.d.; G. Habich, Bruno Paul als Dekorativer Künstler, *Zeitschrift für Innendekoration,* vol. XII, 1901, pp. 199–208; W. Michel, Bruno Paul als Innenkünstler, *ibid.,* vol. XVIII, 1907, pp. 48–54; Bruno Paul, *Dekorative Kunst,* vol. IX, 1901–02, pp. 60–68.

18 A. Endell, Architektonische Erstlinge, *Dekorative Kunst,* vol. VI, 1900, pp. 297–317; *idem,* Formenschönheit und dekorative Kunst, *Dekorative Kunst,* vol. II, 1898, pp. 119–25; *idem,* Möglichkeiten und Ziele einer neuen Architektur, *Deutsche Kunst und Dekoration,* vol. I, 1897–98, pp. 141–53; *idem, Um die Schönheit. Eine Paraphrase über die Münchner Kunstausstellung 1896,* Munich 1896; G. F., "Das Bunte Theater" von August Endell, *Deutsche Kunst und Dekoration,* vol. IX, 1901–02, pp. 275–89, *Dekorative Kunst,* vol. VI, 1900, pp. 297–317.

19 P. Behrens, *Feste des Lebens und der Kunst,* Jena 1900; F. Hoebber, *Peter Behrens,* Munich 1913; K. Breysig, Das Haus Peter Behrens, *Deutsche Kunst und Dekoration,* vol. IX, 1901–02, pp. 133–94; G. Fuchs, Die Vorhalle zum Haus der Macht und der Schönheit, *ibid.,* vol. XI, 1902–03, pp. 1–44; K. Scheffler, Das Haus Behrens, *Dekorative Kunst,* vol. IX, 1901–02, pp. 1–48.

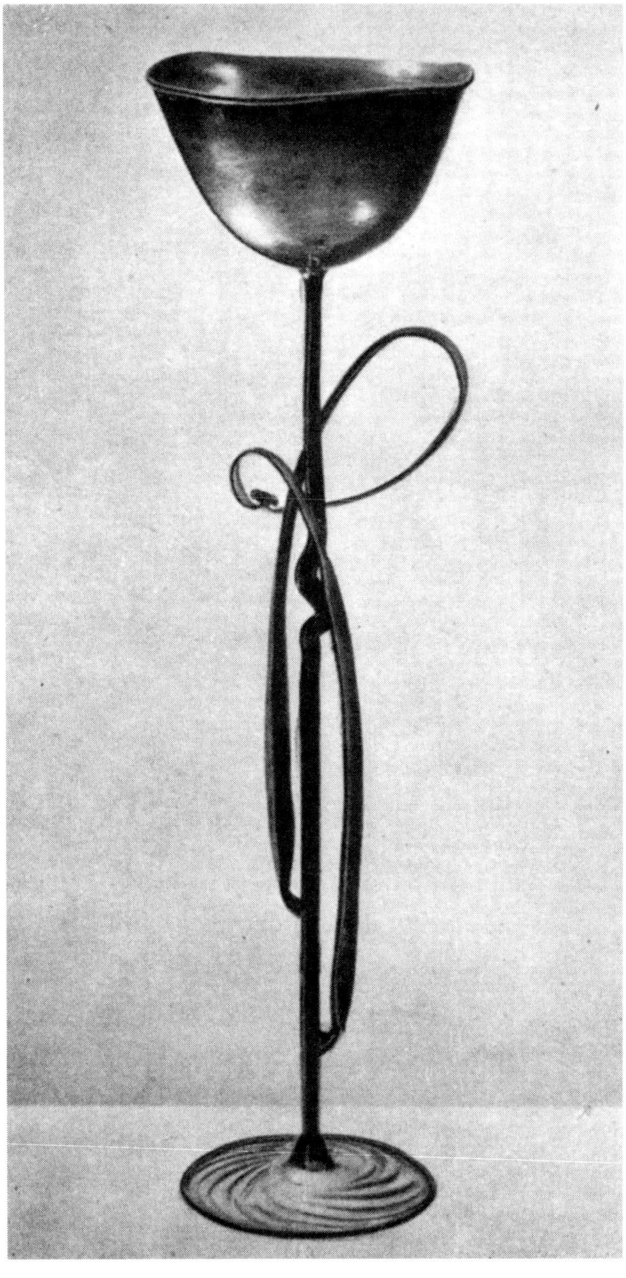

Fig. 252. Koepping: Glass. About 1895–96.
Det Danske Kunstindustrimuseum, Copenhagen. Copyright reserved.

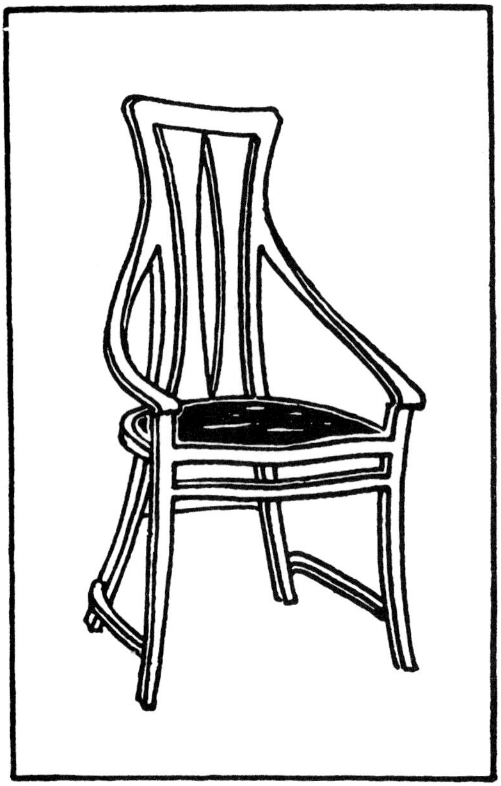

Fig. 253. Behrens: Lady's chair for the dining-room in *Haus Behrens*. 1900.

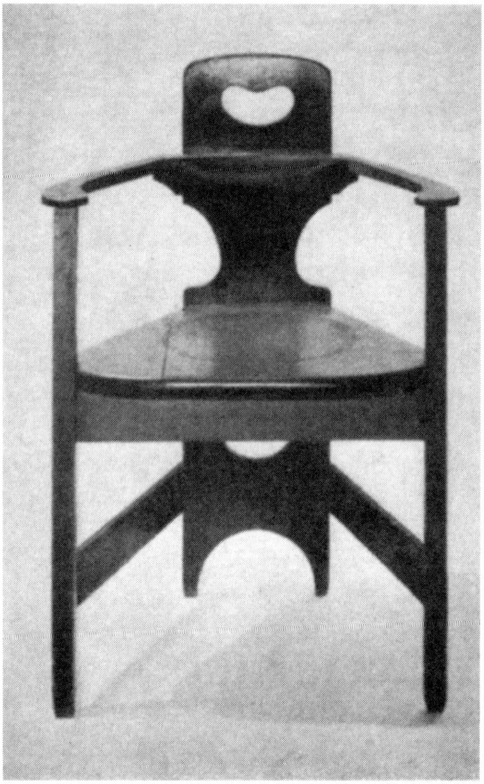

Fig. 254. Riemerschmid: Armchair, painted red. About 1900. From *Um 1900*.

A special feature is the chair back which tapers towards the top (fig. 259). The decoration is two-dimensional, firmly placed and clearly limited. It is as a rule floral, or else an abstract play of bent parts, straight lines, and slight curves. The similarity with Serrurier-Bovy's and van de Velde's furniture is striking (fig. 253).[20]

Riemerschmid, who is referred to as a painter right up to 1898 reflects the shifting interplay of style round the change of the century, before the Germans had evolved their own style. His furniture is sometimes so simple and so modern in appearance, that it is apt to be mistaken for types from the 1940's, e.g. his chairs for the Paris Exhibition in 1900 (fig. 34), and the

[20] *Deutsche Kunst und Dekoration,* vol. IX, 1901–02, p. 148.

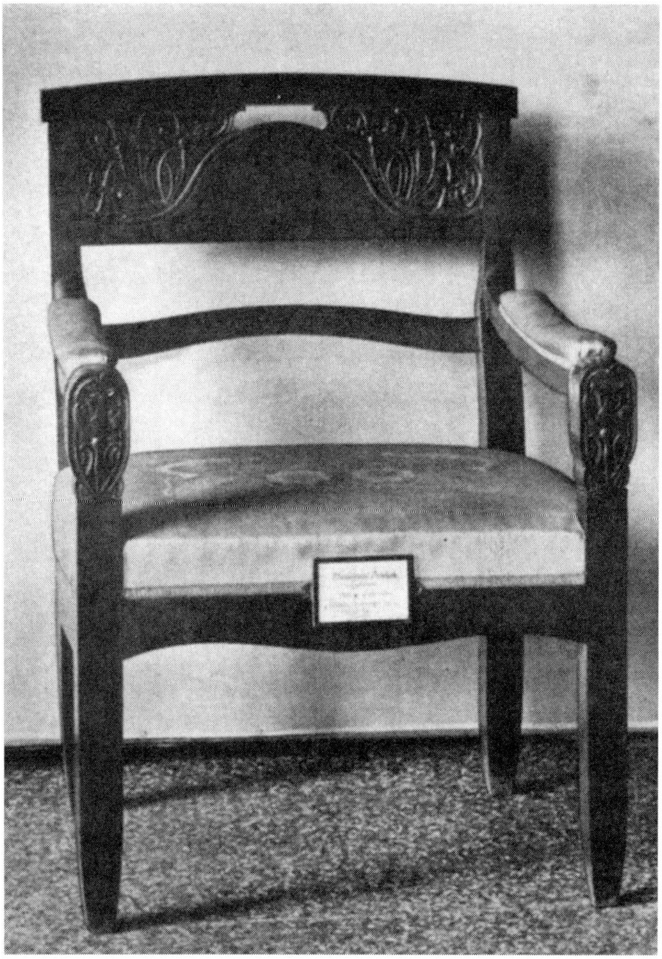

Fig. 255. Pankok: Chair. Pearwood. 1897.
Det Danske Kunstindustrimuseum, Copenhagen, Copyright reserved.

furniture for his music room,[21] exhibited in Dresden in 1899. At the same time he shows distinct neo-Baroque features, for example in the *Münchener Schauspielhaus*, 1900, where the columns in a few places merge with the wall as in Horta's work. He also reflects influence from the Arts and Crafts Movement in England (fig. 254).

Riemerschmid is typical of the age. In his art all traces of Jugend seem to have been swept away, two or three years later; such was the speed of

21 Illustrated in *Deutsche Kunst und Dekoration*, vol. IV, 1899, p. 529.

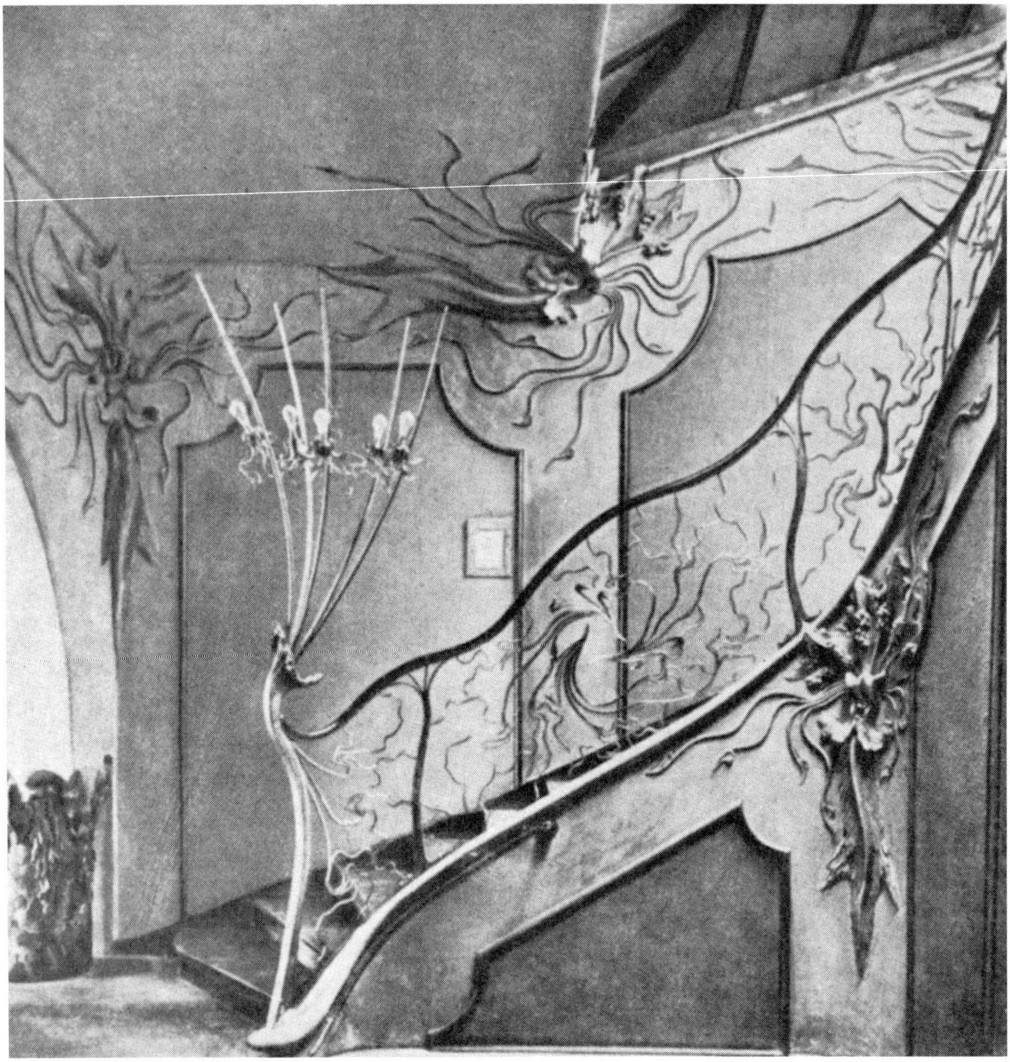

Fig. 256. Endell: Stairway for Atelier Elvira. Munich. Forged iron.
Executed by J. Müller. 1898.

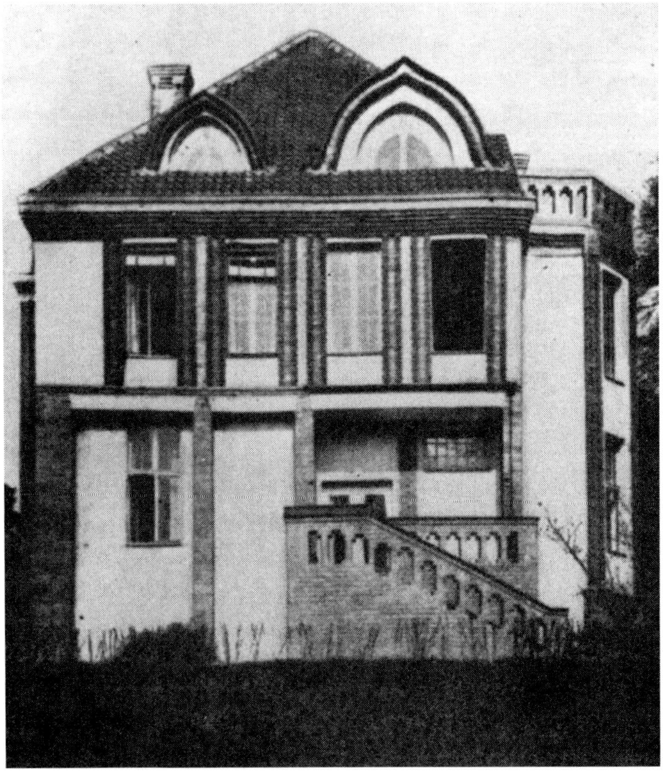

Fig. 257. Behrens: The Artist's house. Darmstadt. 1900–01.

the development in Germany. The same is more or less true of the other Munich artists. Even Pankok's chair from 1897 (fig. 255)[22] is not what we should call Jugend, and in the house he designed for Lang, we can hardly talk of Jugend nor in Paul's furniture. Here a new style is gaining ground, a style whose chief characteristics are austerity, few but unerringly-placed ornaments, and an interplay of straight lines and distinctive angles, shaped as though in reaction to the supple form-language of Art Nouveau.

In a somewhat different category comes the aesthetic theoretician August Endell, whose two *chefs-d'oeuvre* in the Jugend style are the *Atelier Elvira,* 1898, and the *Sanatorium auf Föhr,* 1900. Like all the other build-

22 Cat. No. 1004–1900, Det Danske Kunstindustrimuseum, Copenhagen. The same chair illustrated in *Pan* in 1897.

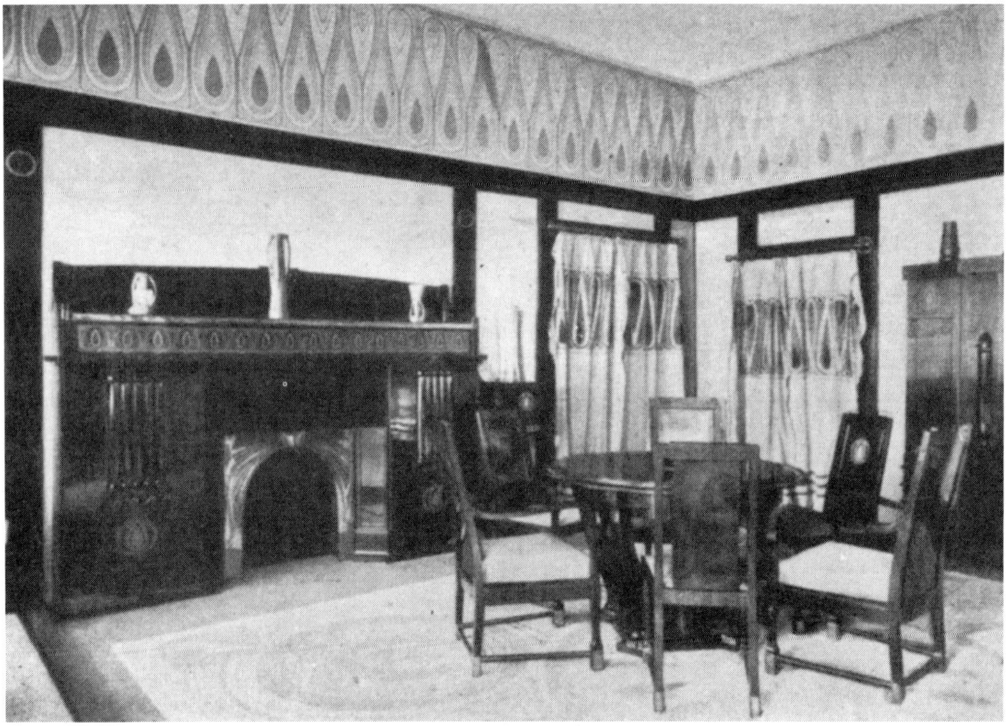

Fig. 258. Behrens: Living room for Ludwig Alter. Exhibited Turin 1902.

ings they have no trace of Jugend in the main conception of the exterior, which is simple enough: it is in its iron decoration that Endell gives free rein to his Obrist-like and Japan-inspired ornamentation, filled with root-fibres and breaking wave-tops; here he allows it free play (fig. 256).[23]

Peter Behrens was the central figure in this group of architects, and with his removal to Darmstadt, and his summons from the Grand-Duke of Hesse in 1899, he bridges the gap to the other school. Behrens, too, started as a painter, and in a painting such as *Storm*, from the end of the 1890's,[24] he has a certain Jugend linear rhythm. But if one considers his first *chef d'oeuvre*, the artist's own house in Darmstadt, and the interior for L. Alter

23 *Dekorative Kunst*, vol. VI, 1900, p. 301.

24 Illustrated in F. Hoebber, *Peter Behrens,* Munich 1913, pl. 3.

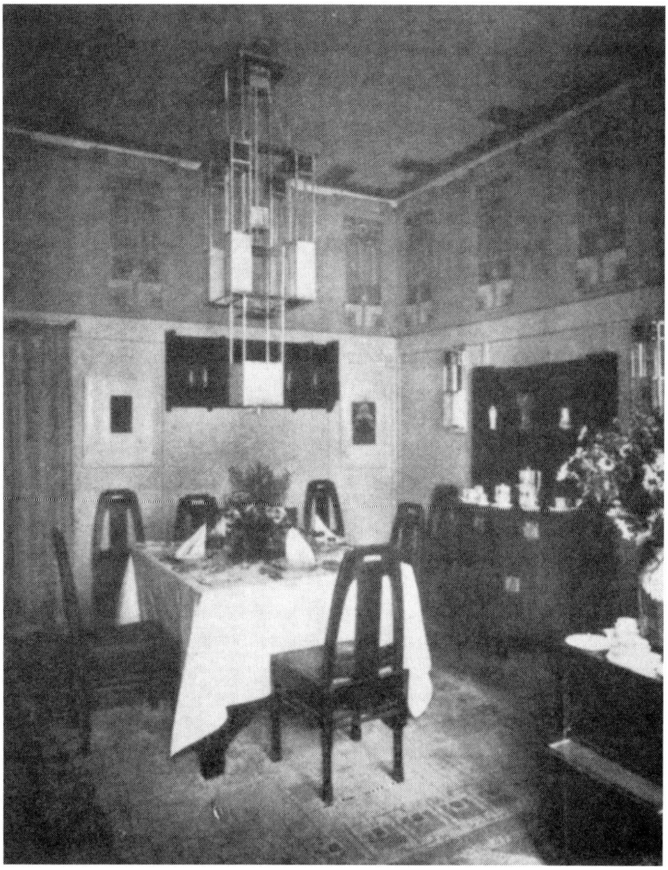

Fig. 259. Behrens: Dining-room. 1902.

(figs. 257, 258),[25] it is clear that there is little Jugend left. Here, on the other hand, we find the germ of what was later to be called the "*Style Munichois.*" By 1903 all traces of the young painter's fluent linear rhythm had disappeared (fig. 259).[26]

With *Die Darmstädter Künstler-Kolonie,*[27] and its two leading exponents, Behrens and Olbrich, the Jugend style moves still further afield. Here, too,

25 Fig. 257: W. Rehme, *Architektur der neuen freien Schule,* Leipzig 1902, pl. 77. Fig. 258: *Deutsche Kunst und Dekoration,* vol. XI, 1902, p. 39.

26 *Zeitschrift für Innendekoration,* vol. XIV, 1903, p. 6.

27 K. Scheffler, von der Darmstädter Künstler-Kolonie, *Dekorative Kunst,* vol. VIII, 1901, pp. 289–308, 417–49; Die Darmstädter Künstler-Kolonie, *Deutsche Kunst und Dekoration,* vol. IV, 1899, pp. 412–23; Die Darmstädter Künstler-Kolonie, *ibid.,* vol. VI, 1900, pp. 333–72.

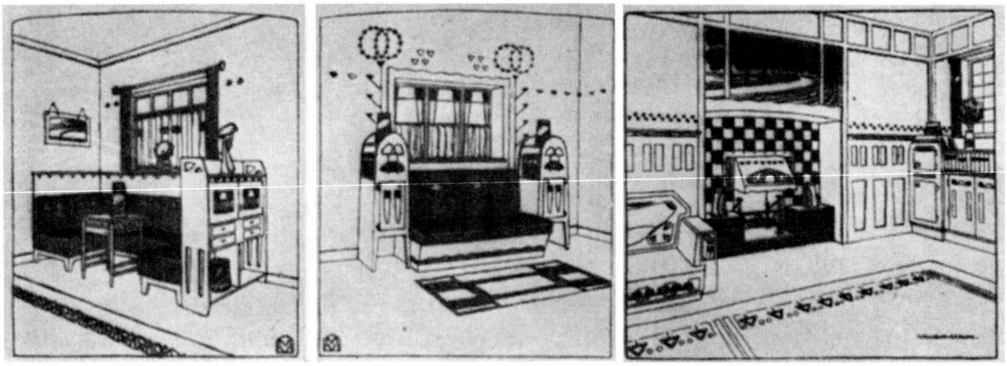

Fig. 260. Mink: Designs for interiors. 1901–02.

the group originally consisted of seven artists, the five others being the designer Hans Christiansen,[28] the architect and interior designer Patriz Huber (1878–1902),[29] the sculptors Ludwig Habich (1872–),[30] and Rudolf Bosselt (1871–),[31] and the painter Paul Bürck (1878–).[32]

It is natural that two significant artists such as Olbrich and Behrens should set the tone for this group. Huber developed on lines very similar to Olbrich; and Valentin Mink (fig. 260)[33] was also a typical Olbrich pupil, clearly showing the Austrian predilection for the geometrical, while Behrens's influence is more in evidence in architecture. But quite naturally we also find reflexes from other contemporary trends. The sculptors made work executed in precious metals with a Jugend-style *décor*, women with Jugend locks and closed eyes, and a few pieces by Bosselt in simple *entrelac*, but on the whole Habich and Bosselt himself—as long as they are working within decorative art—stick to the two-dimensional art which is so different

[28] H. Christiansen, *Neue Flachornamente,* Berlin 1898; H. Schliepmann, Hans Christiansen, *Deutsche Kunst und Dekoration,* vol. II, 1898, pp. 289–99; *idem,* Christiansen's Kunst-Verglasungen, *ibid.,* vol. V, 1899–1900, pp. 205–10; Isarius, Hans Christiansen und sein Haus, *ibid.,* vol. IX, 1901–02, pp. 49–88.

[29] F. Commichau, Patriz Huber, *Deutsche Kunst und Dekoration,* vol. VIII, 1901, pp. 545–73; E. W. Bredt, Patriz Huber, *Dekorative Kunst,* vol. VIII, 1901, pp. 457–77; Patriz Huber und die moderne Wohnungs-Einrichtung, *Zeitschrift für Innendekoration,* vol. XI, 1900, pp. 41–46; Patriz Huber und die Heimat-Kunst, *ibid.,* vol. XII, 1901, pp. 61–67.

[30] F. Commichau, Ludwig Habich, *Deutsche Kunst und Dekoration,* vol. IX, 1901–02, pp. 1–24.

[31] *Idem,* Rudolf Bosselt, *Deutsche Kunst und Dekoration,* vol. IX, 1901–02, pp. 93–108.

[32] Paul Bürck, *Deutsche Kunst und Dekoration,* vol. IV, 1899, pp. 341–44 (64 illustrations).

[33] *Zeitschrift für Innendekoration,* vol. XIII, 1902, p. 48.

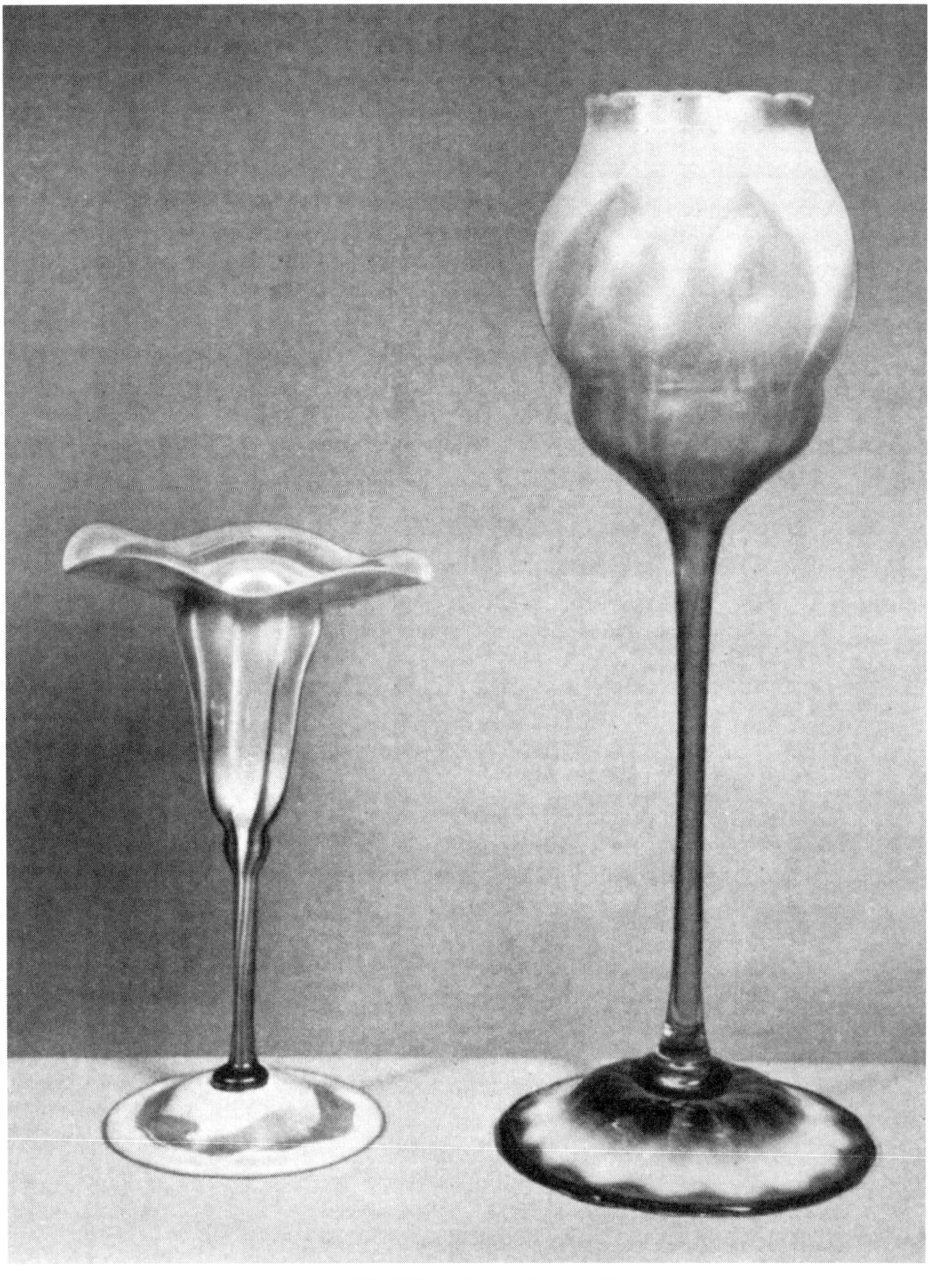

Fig. 261. Tiffany: Two glasses. 1900.
Vestlandske Kunstindustrimuseum, Bergen. Copyright reserved.

from the Frenchmen's and Belgians' plastic conception of form at this time. Bürck's furniture from this brief period resembles more than anything work by van de Velde.

These fifteen to twenty artists represent the leaders of Germany's applied art, and they all abandoned the Jugend style a few years after the turn of the century, as is clearly shown by the participation at the Turin Exhibition in 1902,[34] while a critic describing the interior decoration exhibition in St. Louis in 1904 declares that "Die Jugendstilsünden waren zur Gänze überwunden."[35] F. Schmalenbach also mentions a number of quotations from the years 1900–05 by various artists, which prove that the style was considered *passé*.[36]

As a matter of course a number of artists adopted the style, and continued using it right up to the years preceding the First World War, but this lies outside the main artistic development.

The Jugend style was conceived in the two-dimensional plane: it is in the columns of *Pan* and *Jugend* that its noblest emanation was found, and here artists such as Ernst H. Walther, Richard Grim, and T. Onasch, continued Eckmann's tradition. But as *Pan*'s importance gradually waned—after its mission had been fulfilled, and other periodicals carried on the work some three or four years after it had been founded—the elegant *Jugend* also disappeared. German commercial excesses in bronze, copper, and pewter lie outside the field of pure applied art, but in glass the Germans created a number of interesting forms and new colour nuances, often with a touch of refined greenish and mauvish hues, occasionally blended with gold, but seldom achieving the quality of Tiffany's Art Nouveau glass (fig. 261).[37]

This popularisation and simplification of style, which took place both in Belgium and France, but especially in Germany, was instrumental in bringing the Jugend style into disrepute in the succeeding generation.

*

34 V. Pica, *L'Arte Decorativa all Esposizione de Torino,* Bergamo 1903.

35 J. A. Lux, *Die Geschichte des modernen Kunstgewerbes in Deutschland,* Leipzig, 1908, pp. 209. "The sins of the Jugend style had been completely overcome."

36 F. Schmalenbach, *Jugendstil. Ein Beitrag zu Theorie und Geschichte der Flächenkunst,* Würzburg 1935, p. 74.

37 Cat. No. 30.5. 1901 a–b. Vestlandske Kunstindustrimuseum, Bergen.

In Germany the Jugend style, more than Art Nouveau anywhere else, was an intermezzo—a two-dimensional intermezzo. Through the artists who were summoned to Germany, and thanks to the shrewd judgment with which their programme was adopted, the Jugend style was swiftly transformed into what its theoreticians—first and foremost van de Velde—had intended it should be. The Germans cut through the pastry and pastiche of this style, seizing the essentials far more quickly than other nation, a phenomenon which can be explained by the fact that the Germans arrived so late on the scene, that it was possible for them to see more clearly the outlines of a more radical and more fruitful development. It was the young generation, not more than twenty-five to thirty years old at the end of the 1890's, who were to carry the development on in the 1900's. They had been trained in an atmosphere of strife, in opposition to the stylistic development of the 19th century; the theoretical premisses were patently at hand, and they had the psychological support and strength of the conviction that they would open the new century. This alert generation could exploit to the full the experience of their predecessors—their struggles and their failures—and for them the Jugend style became merely a wanton and ephemeral *Ereignis der Jugend.*

Summing up

Art Nouveau is essentially a European style of decoration which developed a number of national variants from about 1892 to 1902–03, but with precursors further back in the 19th century. Its main feature is an unusual emphasis upon the ornamental value of the line, a line of undulating movement and rhythmic force, often enhanced by a counter movement filled with tension. Art Nouveau is asymmetrical in nature, as is evident in the tiniest movement of a single line as well as in the composition of an actual ornament. Such asymmetry extends to the disposition of flat surfaces and to distribution of masses.

In two-dimensional decoration the line is everything, the contour soft and clear; in three-dimensional decoration the form is closed and softly rounded.

One of the most important characteristics of the style is the well balanced relation between ornament and surface, while at the same time the ornament appears to fuse with the structure of the object it ornaments. Consequently the various elements in a design seem to flow into one another.

In the field of interior decoration, the style is applied with absolute consistency. From details to the whole it represents a search for synthesis of form. Applied to metal and fittings the style appears in a claw or tongue-like shape, which binds the various parts together, both in fact and symbolically. The colour-range of the style varies somewhat from one country to another, as well as its form-pattern—but here, too, various common features may be observed. Pastel shades are those most used: silver-grey, pale grey, pale green, pale blue, pale red, pale violet, mauve, pink, and a predilection for olive-green, cream, greyish-pink and milky white.

There is throughout the style an emphasis on purely aesthetic values; certain formal qualities are cultivated which entail a complete revaluation of the attitude to interior decoration and applied art as a whole. The result can be traced in its further development, and is clearly noticeable right up to the present day.

The development of the style was more or less parallel in the various countries of Western Europe, emerging suddenly and with precocious maturity, bursting the bonds of the two-dimensional plane, and establishing itself in furniture design, pottery, and minor metal work. It reached its climax at the Paris Exhibition of 1900, never really extending its hegemony to architecture, and culminating in the following years, and then, round about 1902–03, being absorbed by Classicistic and Rationalistic trends, after which it still enjoyed a stylistically insignificant existence in a commercialised version until 1910, surviving in some places right up to the First World War.

These are the general international features of the style. The fewer the formal elements present, the less appropriate is the term Art Nouveau; in contemporary English style, for example, so few of these characteristics appear, that it is hardly possible to talk of Art Nouveau in an international context.

It is possible, nevertheless, to distinguish four different main aspects, which to a certain extent are conditioned by nationality: an abstract and plastic conception of form especially widespread in Belgium; a linear and symbolic aspect, notably in Scotland; a floral and markedly plant-inspired style in France; and a constructive and geometrical one in Germany and Austria.

*

In its fully developed form the Art Nouveau style was the outcome of a great many circumstances—one might almost be tempted to call it the culmination of certain artistic tendencies evident in the latter half of the 19th century. During this period, all over Europe an intense desire sprang up to revitalise the industrial arts, the result mainly of industrialism and the decline of accepted aesthetic norms. The last shred of aesthetic sensibility, such as existed in earlier times, was lost, or so it seemed, and had not yet been replaced by a new scale of values.

Romanticism proved a stimulus to historical research; this in turn aroused a new interest in the history of art, which then led naturally to Historicism. The Medieval—or rather the Gothic style—was the first period style to be adopted. But the Gothic revival had two aspects, a purely romantic retrospective one, and a rationalistic one. The latter embodied an architectural, ornamental, and constructive aestheticism which was to provide a basis for the forces of renewal. England, which at this period, and during the subsequent decades, possessed the leading art theoreticians naturally assumed a leading position in the work of renewal. The Arts and Crafts Movement was a natural result of the rationalist tendencies of the Gothic revival, intimately associated with native traditions and on an entirely national basis. An offshoot of this movement was proto-Art Nouveau, a term which consequently cannot be applied to a specific period in the history of English style, but merely describes stylistic forms and tendencies common to a number of the leading artists in the Arts and Crafts Movement. This proto-Art Nouveau does not appear to have exercised any direct influence on the development either at home or abroad, but is a specifically English phenomenon created by a number of experimental designers, who were influenced by the rhythmic linear play of the late pre-Raphaclites.

Formally Art Nouveau inherited little from the Gothic revival and the Arts and Crafts Movement, but the underlying idea of the style—the idea of revitalising industrial arts by a return to stricter aesthetic demands and a higher level of craftsmanship—had been inherited from these English movements.

One of the features which nevertheless may be said to have played a direct role in Art Nouveau was the medieval use of inscriptions; not least owing to the symbolistic trends this peculiarly literary trait was adopted by industrial art, not least in France, where the literary and symbolistic interest was undoubtedly the most important reason.

Great Britain's fundamental role—with the pre-Raphaelite Movement, the aesthetic writings of British theoreticians, the Gothic revival, the Arts and Crafts Movement, and the Celtic revival—in the emergence of Art Nouveau cannot be exaggerated. And yet the importance of the British Isles was not so much formal as preparatory. As far as the pre-Raphaelite Movement is concerned, however, it is possible to speak of a more direct influence, as Robert Schmutzler's recently published article "The English

Origins of Art Nouveau," in the *Architectural Review*, London, February 1955, shows.[1]

That Art Nouveau was never firmly established in England was due to the fact that native designers had already made considerable progress in their own new style. On the firm basis of tradition a form-language and a stylistic conception had been achieved, which covered not only the decorative arts, but at the same time expressed a more comprehensive view, including architecture. Contemporary designers and critics fully realised England's dominant position, and it is easy to understand that the British were chary of accepting what, to them, must have appeared a Continental pursuit of fashion. They had, as well, passed through the period of proto-Art Nouveau, and in the contemporary quest for something new there was little point in establishing a form-language whose problems had already been investigated by leading designers some ten to fifteen years previously.

British influence on the Continent during this period is obvious enough, creating as it did the basis for Art Nouveau, though without making any direct contribution. Artists such as C. F. A. Voysey, M. H. Baillie Scott, Walter Crane, and Frank Brangwyn were well known on the Continent—some of them had foreign commissions entrusted to them—but their reputation had nothing to do with Art Nouveau.

*

An examination of the origin of Art Nouveau in conjunction with the English, and also the entire European development during the latter half of the 19th century, makes it clear that it partly arose as a positive reaction, and partly as a further development of the interest in Nature. But many designers tended rather to look back into the past in order to decide what to avoid, rather than forwards to discover what was needed. The style was thus partly an "anti"-movement, reacting not only against Historicism as a phenomenon in itself, but also against its formalistic conceptions.

On this basis it is possible to explain a great many form-elements. The spiky sprawling decorative form-language of the 1860's, '70's and '80's

1 It has proved impracticable to incorporate Schmutzler's findings in this work, but it is gratifying to note that his results largely agree with those of the author.

was replaced by the compact and closed; the jagged contour was replaced by the firm. Meanwhile the colour-scale changes from the dark harsh hues of the earlier period to light pastel shades.

In view of the intimate co-operation existing between painters and applied artists in the 1880's and 1890's, it is also natural to consider many of the formal elements of Art Nouveau as part of the development which came in the wake of Impressionism. In the widest sense Art Nouveau reflects the latest phase in a movement away from Naturalism and Impressionism via neo-Impressionism—to Symbolism and Synthetism in France—towards Expressionism in the Germanic cultural sphere.

In view of the reaction against period styles it is interesting to see to what extent form-elements from period styles were adopted. The external contributions of neo-Gothic were in themselves of minor importance, while neo-Rococo and Japanese influence contributed to the asymmetrical conception, and there are reasons for believing that the Celtic revival was also an important, though perhaps not direct, factor in shaping Art Nouveau, providing if nothing else a spur. The use of the *entrelac* motif seems at any rate to be associated with this movement.

But among the most important factors of all must be placed the interest in Nature. Already from the middle of the century Nature had played a highly important role as a source of inspiration, in painting, sculpture, and decorative art. Ornaments reproduced the world of flowers with the most minute attention to naturalistic detail. But just as in pictorial art mere imitation was gradually abandoned, so decorative art followed suit, passing via stylisation to simplification. But most of the Art Nouveau designers constantly regarded Nature as their main source of inspiration and renewal. In reality, however, this attitude to Nature was a typical mid-Victorian idea, of which John Ruskin was the most consistent exponent.

The plant world of Art Nouveau, however, differs considerably from that of earlier ages: it is concerned just as much with the stem as with the flower, e.g. verbena, snowdrops, all sorts of creepers, the lily, tall slim reeds and rushes, and not least the water-lily, Egyptian lilies, and other rushlike water plants. Although the use of plants as a decorative element was not new, the plant world of Art Nouveau was certainly new and original enough! The animal world of Art Nouveau was far less varied, and was mainly confined to insects.

In itself this choice of plants is characteristic, and brings us to an essential feature of the actual *Zeitgeist:* the designer was attracted not by demure wild flowers—unless of course the stem was particularly suitable for his purpose—nor did he turn his attention to dignified and cultivated garden plants: it was the exotic species, creeping stem plants and the like, which stimulated his imagination, not because they were beautiful, but because they were peculiar, unfamiliar, and had not previously been used. The last-mentioned reason was in itself sufficient to popularise them in the 1890's. Usually they were plants with colourless flowers, carrying a message of aesthetic delight, sophisticated and languid.

The flower was discarded, and the stem and leaf were cultivated. The gay hues from the luxuriant floral world of the 1870's and 1880's gave way to the cool evening mood of the 1890's, by the shores of a placid pool, where the lilies lie at rest, and the dragon-fly glides softly by.

*

A glance at the English background and at the European precursors has thus shown how many of the formal elements, and how much of the origin, of the style, are to be found in the 19th century. But where and when did Art Nouveau emerge fully-fledged?

The cultural cockpit, the meeting place of the most important trends in Europe at this time, was Belgium, with its wideawake metropolis of Brussels. Its fashionable avenues reflected a great deal of Paris, and in artistic circles French trends were eagerly assimilated. Thanks to Octave Maus, *Les XX*, and *La Libré Esthétique*, artists such as Cézanne, Gauguin, Toulouse-Lautrec, Seurat, and Signac were familiar names in Belgian art circles. Expressionism, Cloisonnism, Gauguinism, and Synthetism were well-known terms. But apart from these trends, Belgium had its own native Symbolism, under the leadership of Khnopff, while Holland to the north enjoyed a flourishing Symbolism, primarily under the auspices of Toorop. These two artists, however, also had strong ties with England, and knew the British Isles, and the late pre-Raphaelitism. But these were not the only links with Great Britain: in Belgium and Holland Morris was probably better known than anywhere else on the Continent; furthermore Selwyn Image, Walter Crane, and a great many other Englishmen had exhibited in Brussels, and the Glasgow school had its first Continental exhibition in Belgium. Though this exhibition probably did not exert any influence, it was to a large extent symptomatic of the Belgian watchfulness. Besides, designers and decorative artists were in the habit of visiting England, while the architects in search of rationalistic solutions read Viollet-le-Duc and made their way to Paris.

The cultural milieu, in fact, was open to every wind that blew, and it was in this very milieu that fully-fledged Art Nouveau first emerged in Victor Horta's house designed for Professor Tassel, in 6 Rue Paul Emile Janson, 1892–93, in one of Brussels' fashionable quarters. The exterior of this house reveals a quest for rationalism in a neo-Gothic guise. Beneath the dainty colours of the interior in what is now a fashion-house (fig. 262) it is still possible to trace Horta's bold, abstract decorations with their elegant and forceful lines, while the iron construction in the roof bears its eloquent testimony to the age.

At the beginning of the 1890's Belgium had a great many competent and questing artists, who formed the break-through. Unlike their contemporaries in England they aimed more consciously to devise something entirely new, quite unhampered by any tradition. On the Continent where everything happened much more suddenly, the intention was to create a real *naissance.* In England, on the other hand, the development was rather a *renaissance,* rooted in native soil.

In Belgium there was a Victor Horta, who instead of indulging in theorising developed a dynamic art sprung from an artistic mind full of vigour and vitality; then there was van de Velde, sure of himself, formulating theories based on his wide reading, inspired by an ardent desire to renew, and full of ideas which he was at all times ready to champion. In his hands construction became ornament, and ornament construction. And then we have Gustave Serrurier-Bovy, with his own independent furniture design, inspired by the Arts and Crafts Movement; young Paul Hankar, whose rational quest was to a large extent inspired by Japanese influence, and lastly Philippe Wolfers. All five, each in his own way, fused the various

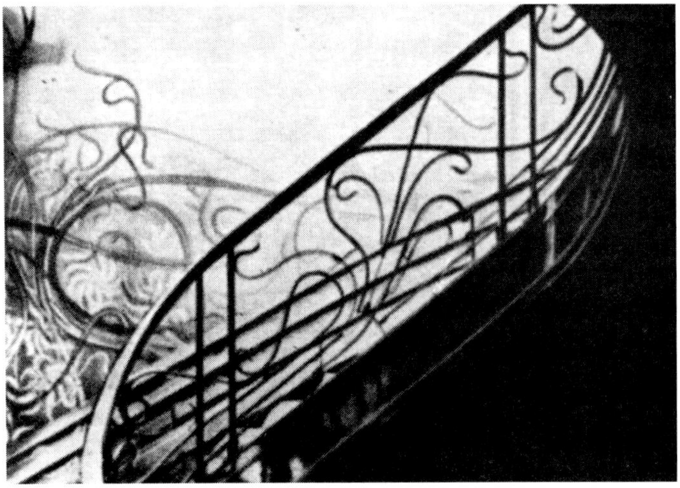

Fig. 262. Horta: Staircase. 6 Rue Paul Emile Janson, Brussels. 1892–93.

trends of the age to create a personal, but nevertheless common, form-language. Very characteristic of Belgian and French Art Nouveau is the plastic conception of form, directly derived from interest in sculptural problems. Modelling of the object was thus a common feature, and may be seen as an expression of the neo-Baroque trend.

The position in Scotland was really different. With Charles Rennie Mackintosh as the undisputed artistic leader, "the Four" developed a style which, in the European context, enjoys a place apart, as a highly sophisticated version of international Art Nouveau. Towards the end of the 1890's, approximately in 1897, Mackintosh evolved a form-language which in some ways contrasted with the style of the Glasgow school, but which was nevertheless just as artistic. In his quest for a solution to the rational problems of architecture he controlled decoration, exploiting in his rectangular style the square and the circle for ornamental purposes, but rarely dispensing entirely with the softly flowing curve.

The Glasgow school had contacts with the Continent—not only in Belgium, but also in Austria, where their style appears to have proved eminently suitable to the Viennese of the time. There is not necessarily any direct plagiarism by the Secessionists of the Glasgow school, as a result of this association; but in this connection it is characteristic that the Austrian Josef Hoffmann adopted the same ornaments and strove to attain the same simple style as Mackintosh during the years immediately preceding 1900. Both Mackintosh and Hoffmann were attempting to reach the same goal, and at times they used remarkably similar ornamentation.

In Holland Art Nouveau remained on the two-dimensional plane. The country's leading architect, H. P. Berlage, a figure of European importance, never created anything that might be called Art Nouveau; he represented a reaction against Historicism, working in the direction of simplification. In his case the result is modern architecture of fundamental significance, and not Art Nouveau. The same was also true of most of the leading architects in France, Germany, and Austria. The most interesting figures in Holland, as far as we are concerned, are the interior designer G. W. Dijsselhof, T. A. C. Colenbrander, a potterist and textile designer, and the all-round artist Th. Nieuwenhuis, all more or less inspired by batik technique. These three artists, together with men such as Lion Cachet, J. L. M. Lauweriks, and K. A. C. de Bazel, created the specifically Dutch version of Art Nouveau, which got under way at such an early stage, compared to the other countries in Europe, but which never developed into a really mature style, probably because on traditional and emotional grounds these artists felt more attracted to England than to any other country as far as furniture design was concerned, and because, in decorative art, Dutch designers struck out on a road of their own.

In France Emile Gallé, that lover of Nature and warm-hearted artistic personality, was the founder of the Nancy school. With his wide literary interests, and his penetrating technical experience and skill, Gallé is one of the most fascinating of all the Art Nouveau designers. No work, be it furniture or glass, that came from his hand ever bore the hallmark of mediocrity.

With the firmly-rooted Rococo tradition of the town and milieu, and with Gallé as leader, the Nancy school was bound to develop as it did.

Less interesting, but among the most typical of Art Nouveau personalities, is Nancy's other great furniture designer, Louis Majorelle. While Gallé was committed to a great many branches of art industry, Majorelle confined himself to furniture. Eugène Vallin, whose work may at times be confused with that of Majorelle, adopted the same style. Just as Majorelle, Vallin, and André continued Gallé's furniture tradition, so the Daum brothers continued his work in the art of glass. Thus Gallé succeeded in creating a milieu in Nancy, as well as founding a school of industrial art, but when the force of his inspiration was no longer present, the school gradually broke up.

The group in Paris had a shrewd businessman and art patron as its leading figure and, with the opening in 1895 of the shop "l'Art Nouveau," got a centre. Here artists such as the sophisticated George de Feure, whose work always showed a touch of Louis XVI, the more dynamic Eugène Gaillard, and the moderate Art Nouveau designer Colonna, would meet. Outside the Sigfried Bing group, were France's Walter Crane, Eugène Grasset, an elegant designer with a touch of Art Nouveau, and the imaginative Hector Guimard, with his whimsical and riotous inventions in metal, a man full of theoretical ideas of which it is difficult to find any trace in his art. France had its group: "Les Quatre G.," Gallé, Gaillard, Guimard, Grasset, just as Scotland had its "Four Macs," but the analogy, as far as France is concerned, is confined to the phonetical. There was really only one school in France, viz. the Nancy school. The other artists were entirely individual personalities, each with his own conception of Art Nouveau.

Austria and Germany had one thing in common: both were late in joining the new movement. In Austria Art Nouveau artists emerged from the advanced group of painters—the Secessionists—but on the whole, as far as applied art was concerned, Austria was firmly rooted in its Classical traditions. Germany had been more isolated, devoting herself more to national traditions. The exertions, especially in Germany, were markedly conscious. To an even greater extent than in Belgium, designers seemed determined, with German thoroughness and consistency, to create a style. But even earlier than in other countries leading artists abandoned the style, following other rational trends latent in the period. Already in the latter half of the 1890's designers started to leave Munich, and in 1902 not a single one of the original seven was left. The same was true of Darmstadt: of the original group only two were left when the colony held its second exhibition in 1904. In 1906 Habich left, and in 1908 Olbrich died.

Austria had Josef Hoffmann and Joseph Olbrich, whose Art Nouveau in both cases originated in book illustration, and found expression on paper rather than in practice. As we have already mentioned, Hoffmann's development ran parallel with that of Mackintosh—and, it is reasonable to suppose, they developed independently of each other. Austria's importance to the development round about the year 1900 is confined to refined and rational development of furniture design and architecture, in the work of the two architects already mentioned, and also in that of Adolf Loos.

Germany on the other hand acquired its popular, commercial Jugend style, with its two aspects: on the one hand inspired by Otto Eckmann's and Hermann Obrist's floral Jugend, and on the other hand the abstract design of van de Velde's pupils.

Among leading designers the Jugend style was merely a brief intermezzo, and important architects such as Peter Behrens, Richard Riemerschmid, and Bernhard Pankok, adopted a simpler and firmer form-language as early as 1900.

*

Apart from Spain, the other countries in Europe made no contribution to the development of Art Nouveau, nor have they produced any versions of the international picture beyond what was of purely national interest. Scandinavia is possibly an exception, with those salient aspects of the Celtic revival, Sweden and Norway's dragon style, which formed a symbiosis with Art Nouveau. Owing to the special nature of the material, it is natural to impose a geographical boundary, based on the countries we have dealt with. Neither Italy—with her blend of Art Nouveau, Naturalism (fig. 263), and the furniture design inspired by the Arts and Crafts Movement called the "Stile Liberty"—nor the Balkans (especially Hungary, with her lavishly

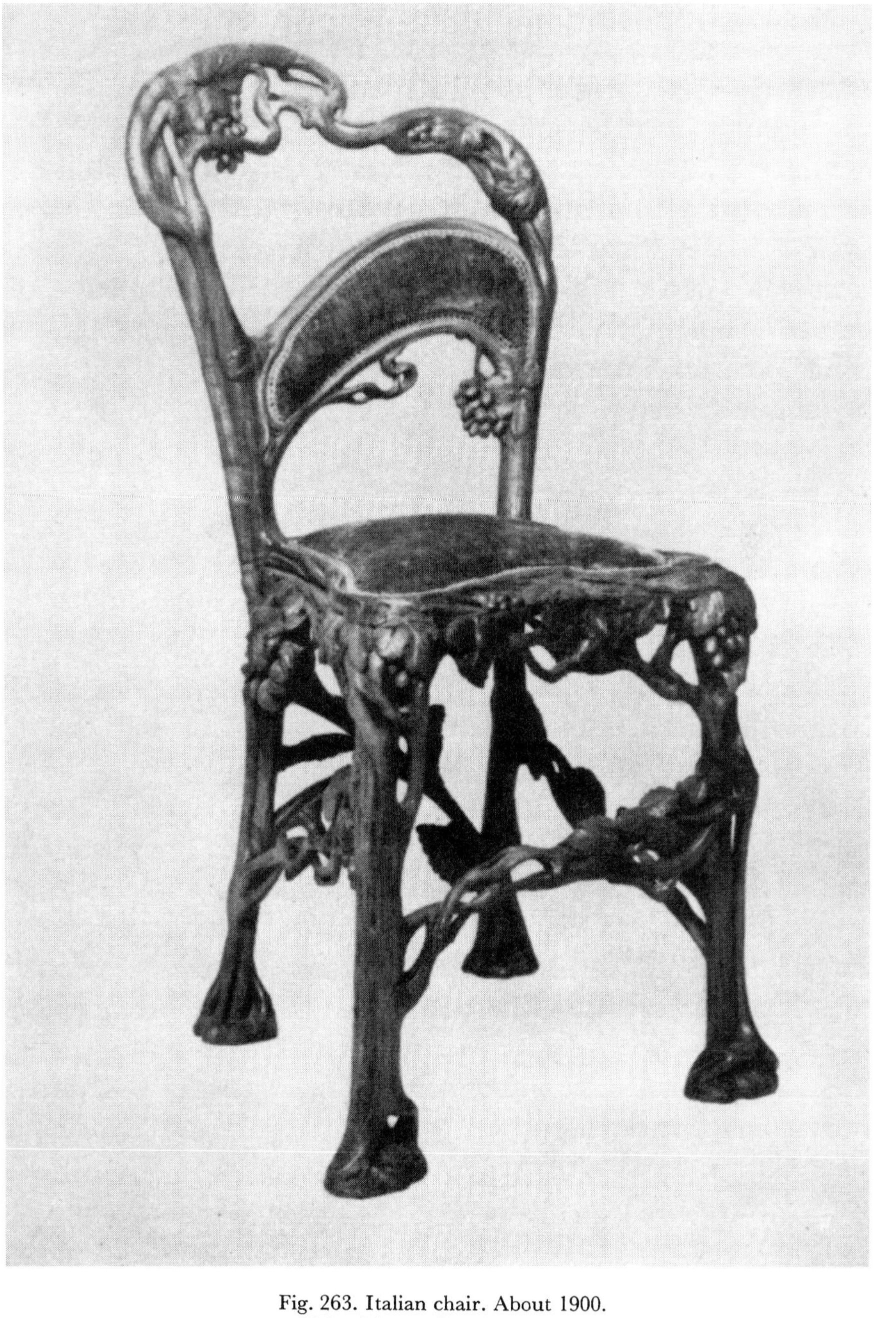

Fig. 263. Italian chair. About 1900.
Malmö Museum. Copyright reserved.

decorated style of this period) are of anything like the same importance as the art of the countries we have dealt with. As far as Russia is concerned, it is difficult to procure the necessary literature and to make any real contrast with this cultural sphere, but there does not appear to have been an Art Nouveau in Russia to the same extent as in Western Europe.

America, on the other hand, made her contribution, in the work of Tiffany, but so far it has not been possible to determine whether the country played any part in the origins of this style. On the lines we have followed even interiors in Sullivan's Auditorium Building, Chicago, 1888, do not fall within the framework of what we might call Art Nouveau, however original and interesting they may be.

*

But how, when, and why did the Art Nouveau style come to an end? If we can answer the first two questions, the solution of the third should follow.

Some of the artists died in the early nineteen hundreds—Hankar in 1901, Eckmann in 1902, Gallé in 1904, Olbrich in 1908, Auguste Daum and Charpentier in 1909, and Serrurier-Bovy in 1910. But this in itself would not have brought the movement to a close.

The popularity enjoyed by the style in Paris in 1900 declined in the two following years. In Turin in 1902 it was clear to everybody that the style had reached its climax, and was on the decline. In turn each one of the artists abandoned it, altering his form-language, and tending towards simplicity, a more practical approach, and less emphasis on decoration. After the turn of the century Mackintosh and the Austrians modified their decorations; these now became more geometrical. As stated the leading Germans had abandoned the style some years before, both in Darmstadt and in Munich, and stimulated by the work of the tireless writer Hermann Muthesius thereafter worked more on the lines of contemporary English designs. In France the Nancy school declined in importance after the death of its inspiring leader, and the style of the individual artists calmed down, assuming a more traditional Louis XV or classic expression. Not only in Nancy, but in Paris too, Art Nouveau gradually fused with a soft

Louis XVI version which de Feure and Colonna found quite natural; and Gaillard, too, moderated his style. Like his colleagues in England Grasset turned his back on Art Nouveau, Serrurier-Bovy had already produced conventional types of furniture before his death, whilst Horta moderated his form-language, and van de Velde struggled desperately in an attempt to adapt his style to his theories.

Already in 1902–03 Art Nouveau may be said to have played out its role, and in 1910 only commercial remnants were left. Art Nouveau lived on only in a petrified form in small but aptly framed and discreetly placed decorative fields.

It seems clear that Art Nouveau started earlier than one was formerly inclined to admit, and that it also came to a conclusion earlier than generally supposed. The style reached full fruition during the decade from about 1892–93 to 1902–03, and was in general followed by a return to Classicism.

*

In the enthusiasm and faith of the 1890's the fact that Art Nouveau belonged in several ways to the 19th century, was not recognised—today it is easy for us to see what is derived from the 19th century, and to see that Art Nouveau constituted an interlude, but for those who believed in the style in the 1890's, and saw that for the first time for generations it was possible to create a new and independent style, it was probably not so easy to realise its weaknesses.

Another factor, less tangible, but which has nevertheless played an important role, was the purely psychological. Changing style was someting which for decades had involved no more trouble than a change in clothes.

But it is much easier to don clean clothes at the beginning of the week: it is on Mondays that people are full of good intentions and hope for a new start—and how much easier when a new *century* was looming up. All of a sudden the new style was there—like a new shining Sunday suit, newly arrived from Brussels or Paris. But it was a suit that proved impossible to work in on a weekday.

It proved a great disappointment to all who had believed so much and given so much. Disappointment was especially great in France, and during the years that followed a wave of resignation set in, and designers turned in their need to Classical traditions.

Nearly all the leading artists were men born in the years just before and just after 1860, and by 1900 had reached their prime, with the energy and the talent to perceive the weaknesses of the style;—and the new trends were latent in the age. In the first decade of the century a rational architecture took shape in the German, Gallic, and Anglo-American cultural spheres, and once again architecture unobtrusively assumed the lead as the art which set the tone and provided the inspiration.

Art Nouveau did not fulfil the general European desire for a lasting international style: it failed to solve the common problems which new materials and social tasks posed. Furthermore, Art Nouveau, despite its international character, was a markedly national style, born of strong national desires and hopes. Few styles have acquired such an essentially individual and national expression. At the very end of the 19th and the beginning of the 20th century strong nationalistic tendencies were at work in European politics and literature. Barrès, Maurras, and Corradini were among the leading personalities. Just as every country, during the last decades of Historicism, had clung to the style it considered its own, so Art Nouveau was given as national an aspect as possible, and in this it belongs far more to the development of the 19th than to the development of the 20th century.

All the formal elements which Art Nouveau inherited from Historicism also link it to the 19th century, but the most important consideration is that it was to a large extent the style of the individual artist, demanding manual work and skill for the construction of all its arched elements and asymmetrical details. In attempting to renew craftsmanship and furniture design the designer relied on the work of men's hands, and not on the machine. Apart from moulded elements nothing, in fact, produced in the Art Nouveau style could be manufactured.

Art Nouveau represents a final vigorous return to the handmade article: it was the 19th century's final reaction against the machine and its aesthetic norms. In England, with theoreticians and designers such as Charles Ashbee and John Sedding, this stage had already been passed, but on the Continent artists and designers still continued to base their work on William Morris's idea that a renewal was dependent on the work of the hand, and the craftsman's delight in doing this work.

*

But, nevertheless, the style influenced the 20th century. First of all the imitations of period styles was brought to an end. Designers went to the roots of their problems, thus preparing the ground for the stylistic developments that followed. Secondly the feeling for unity in interior decoration was re-established: unity and consistency replaced the varied and the picturesque in the attitude to interior design; light replaced darkness. In this way Art Nouveau was of fundamental importance to the subsequent generation, while the realisation that it was possible to create a form-language independent of period styles, must have increased the designer's confidence and self-assurance.

An important heritage from Art Nouveau is the markedly aesthetic approach to the problem of applied arts. To-day it is difficult to assess the real value of this contribution, as its influence still seems to be at work. In the same way it is too early to make a correct and impartial final estimate of the influence of Art Nouveau on pictorial art, although it may be said that Spain is one of the most important sources of inspiration. Quite clear, however, is the direct influence exerted by Gaudí on Surrealism. The question of the relationship between Art Nouveau and non-figurative art has not as yet been dealt with, but should provide an interesting and fruitful field of study.

It is especially interesting to note the importance of Art Nouveau to architecture. The interest in structure as expression was a part of Art Nouveau, of importance both to furniture and architecture—through the style this tendency was developed both theoretically and practically. The Art Nouveau conception of treating the different elements as a whole—

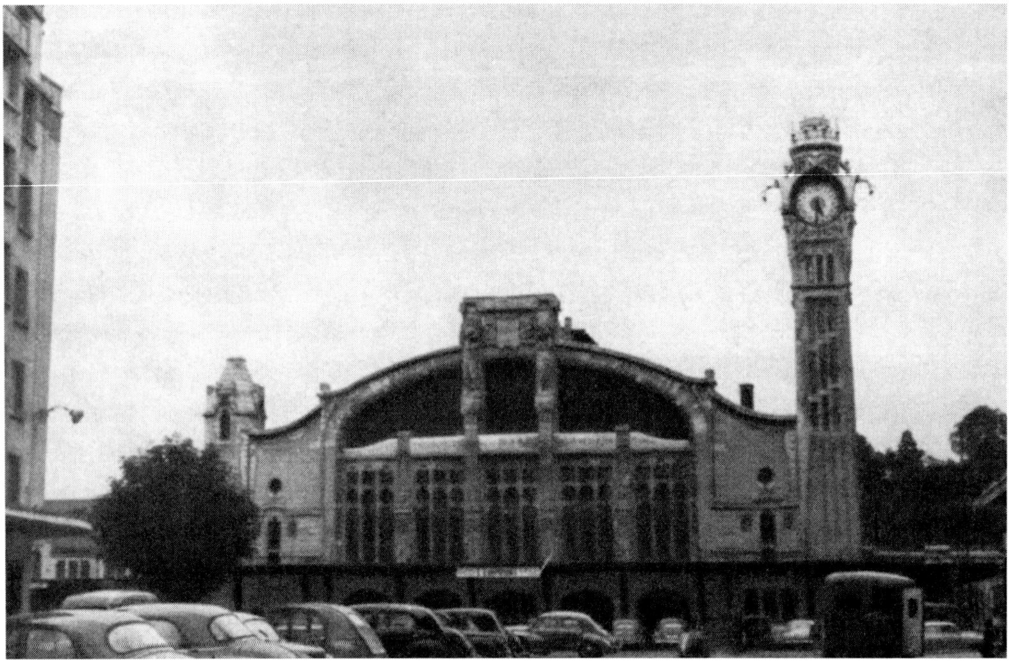

Fig. 264. Derveaux: The Railway station, Rouen. 1928.
Courtesy of Andreas Bugge.

the unity of expression—may also be said to have influenced architecture. Art Nouveau also developed the refined use—and placing—of architectural details.

The style also proved important to the external form-language: the only spanning element which had not been employed to any marked extent in earlier styles was the gently flattened arch which was slightly rounded off at its base. This was the arch most used in Art Nouveau. But this arch was not entirely new: in addition to medieval use, Schinkel had already used it for the windows in the *Bau-Akademie* in Berlin, 1836, though it had sharp corners at its base; and this very type of window-opening, with the gently curving arch above it, was exploited to a considerable extent in late Classicism, establishing itself as early as the 1840's. Baroque, too, also makes use of a softly rounded and at times gently curving arch. It is quite conceivable that the Art Nouveau designer may have drawn inspiration from it, together with the other Baroque impulses he received. On a large scale, however, the influence of iron construction has also determined the form. But owing to the peculiar nature of the Art Nouveau arch, it would be most reasonable to consider it as one of the independent and original contributions made to the form-language of architecture.

In the subsequent neo-Baroque trend in architecture, which set in with renewed force after the turn of the century, this arch constituted one of the most important features. In the years around 1900 neo-Baroque seems to enter on a new phase: the more classical forms of the 1870's and 1880's give way to a markedly asymmetric distribution of mass, often with towers, and containing the soft rounded arch of Art Nouveau, but in a sort of Baroque setting. The arch is now no longer an architectural detail, but an important part of the architectural structure.

This form of Art Nouveau-Baroque was exceedingly persistent, especially in France, where Adolph Derveaux's railway station in Rouen, from 1928 (fig. 264), is undoubtedly one of its last off-shoots.

The asymmetrical architectural distribution of mass is a feature which belongs to the architectural conception of Romanticism, but Art Nouveau, too, cultivated asymmetry. Whether we assume that it was the form-conception of Art Nouveau which influenced the last phase of neo-Baroque architecture, or that neo-Baroque asymmetry was a case of Romantic tradition living on, and thus influencing Art Nouveau, is a moot point. The problem is in reality only another version of cause and effect.

But the most reasonable solution may be to regard the asymmetry of Art Nouveau as an independent creation of tendencies to be found in Romanticism, neo-Rococo, and the asymmetry of Japanese art. It may also be assumed that the neo-Baroque architecture of the early 20th century —derived from retrospective and Romantic conceptions—received important impulses from the style which had just enthroned asymmetry as a formal principle. Art Nouveau thus accelerated a general development of greater importance, and certainly stimulated, as well, an unconventional and well-balanced treatment of masses.

*

In decoration—the art which Art Nouveau so completely dominated—the style resulted in a renewed understanding of the value of ornament and its relation to the surface. As far as interior design is concerned—the sphere in which a striving for unity was most apparent—the conception of the room and its contents as a unified whole was once more restated according to consistent aesthetic principles. In architecture—the sphere which Art Nouveau never seriously affected—it helped to enrich the architectural form-language, and contributed by its expression of structure to the development of modern architecture.

Part IV

SOURCES

RECENT EXHIBITIONS

Le Décor de la Vie sous la IIIe République de 1870–1900. Pavillon de Marsan, Louvre, Paris. April–July 1933.

In Holland staat en huis. Stedelijk Museum, Amsterdam. July–October 1941.

L'Ecole de Nancy. Musée des Beaux Arts, Nancy. 1947.

Um 1900. Art Nouveau und Jugendstil. Kunstgewerbemuseum der Stadt Zürich. June–September 1952.

Victorian and Edwardian Decorative Arts. Victoria and Albert Museum, London. October 1952–February 1953.

Reine Victoria, Roi Leopold Ier et leur temps. Musées Royaux d'Art et d'Histoire, Brussels. February–April 1953.

Jugend 1900–1914. Stedelijk Museum, Amsterdam. Summer 1953.

Honderd Jaar Religieuze Kunst in Nederland 1853–1953. Utrecht. May–June 1953.

Catalogues

In Holland staat en huis. Stedelijk Museum, Amsterdam 1941.

Ville de Nancy. Galeries Poirel. Musée de l'Ecole de Nancy. Nancy 1947.

H. Curjel, *Um 1900. Art Nouveau und Jugendstil. Kunst und Kunstgewerbe aus Europa und Amerika zur Zeit der Stilwende.* Kunstgewerbemuseum der Stadt Zürich. Zürich 1952.

Catalogue of an Exhibition of Victorian and Edwardian Decorative Arts. Victoria and Albert Museum, London. London 1952.

Catalogue de l'exposition Reine Victoria, Leopold Ier et leurs temps. Musées Royaux d'Art et d'Histoire. Brussels 1953.

J. B. Knipping, a.o., *Honderd Jaar Religieuze Kunst in Nederland 1853–1953.* Utrecht 1953.

CONTEMPORARY CATALOGUES

In chronological order

Official Descriptive and Illustrated Catalogue of the Great Exhibition, vols. I–III, London 1851.

The Art Journal Illustrated Catalogue of the Great Exhibition, *The Art Journal,* 1851, London 1851.

The Illustrated Catalogue of the Exhibition of Art Industry in Dublin 1853, *The Art Journal,* 1853. London 1853.

Exposition des Produits de l'Industrie de toutes les Nations. Catalogue Officiel. Paris 1855.

Official Catalogue, Industrial Department. International Exhibition. London 1862.

Illustrated Catalogue of the International Exhibition of 1862, vols. I–IV. London 1862.

Complete Official Catalogue. Paris Universal Exhibition 1867. English version. London 1867.

The Illustrated Catalogue of the Universal

Exhibition Paris 1867, *The Art Journal,* 1867. London 1868.
Catalogue de produits et d'objets d'art Japonais. Paris 1868.
Official Catalogue of the International Exhibition of 1871. London 1871.
Official Catalogue of the International Exhibition of 1872. London 1872.
Official Catalogue of the International Exhibition of 1873. London 1873.
L'Exposition Universelle de Vienne, *Journal Illustré.* Vienna 1873.
Die Kunstindustrie auf der Wiener Weltausstellung 1873. Vienna 1873.
Official Catalogue of the International Exhibition 1874. London 1874.
Catalogue général officiel de l'exposition universelle international de 1878. Paris 1878.
The Art Journal Illustrated Catalogue of the Paris Universal Exhibition 1878, *The Art Journal* 1878. London 1879.
Le Japon à l'exposition universelle de 1878. Paris 1878.
Arts and Crafts Exhibition Society. *Catalogues of Exhibitions.* London 1888–1906.
Catalogue Général officiel. Exposition universelle international de 1889 à Paris. Lille 1889.
L'Art décoratif à l'Exposition universelle de 1889. Paris 1890.
Les Industries d'art à l'exposition universelle de 1889. Paris 1903 (Victor Champier).
La décoration et l'art industriel à l'exposition universelle de 1889. Paris 1890 (Roger Max).
Rapport général de l'exposition de Paris 1889, vols. I–II. Paris 1889 (Alfred Picard).
Internationale Kunstausstellung Berlin 1896. Munich 1896.
Catalogue illustré de l'exposition International de Bruxelles. Paris 1897.
Catalogue général officiel. Exposition international universelle de 1900. Paris 1900.
La Décoration et les Industries d'art à l'exposition universelle de 1900. Paris 1900 (Roger Max).
Les Industries artistiques françaises et etrangères à l'exposition universelle de 1900. Paris 1900 (Gustave Geffroy).
Les industries d'art à l'exposition universelle de 1900. Paris 1902 (Victor Champier).
L'Art Décoratif moderne. L'Exposition Universelle de 1900. Paris n.d. (Theodore Lambert).
Le Pavillon de l'Union Centrale des Arts Décoratifs à l'exposition de 1900. Paris 1900 (Raymond Koechlin).
Meubles de Style Moderne. L'Exposition Universelle de 1900. Paris 1900.
L'Arte decorativa all'Exposizione di Torino. Mobili alla prima exposizione internazionale d'arte decorativa moderna, vols. I–IV. Turin 1903 (Vittore Pica).
Exhibition international de Milan 1906. Paris 1906.
Rapport Général de l'exposition universelle de Liége 1905. Liége n.d.
Exposition Franco-Britannique de Londres 1908. Rapport Général, vols. I–II. Paris 1908.
Exposition française. Art Décoratif Copenhague 1909. Rapport Général. Paris 1909.

CONTEMPORARY ARTICLES

The most important contemporary articles about Art Nouveau

Bing, Sigfried: l'Art Nouveau, *The Architectural Record,* New York, vol. XII, 1902, pp. 279–85.
— l'Art Nouveau, *The Craftsman,* New York, vol. V, 1903–04, pp. 1–15.
Champier, Victor: Les expositions de l'Art Nouveau, *Revue des Arts Décoratifs,* Paris, vol. XVI, 1896, pp. 1–16.
Croly, Herbert: The New World and the New Art, *The Architectural Record,* New York, vol. XII, 1902, pp. 135–53.
Day, Lewis F.: l'Art Nouveau, *The Art Journal,* London, 1900, pp. 293–97.
— "The New" Art, *Macmillans Magazine,* London, 1901, No. 505, Nov., pp. 19–25.

Fendler, F.: Jugendstil, *Berliner Architektur-Welt,* Berlin 1901.

Genuys, Charles: A Propos de l'Art Nouveau, *Revues des Arts Décoratifs,* Paris, vol. XVII, 1897, pp. 1–6.

— La Recherche d'un Style Nouveau, *Revue des Arts Décoratifs,* Paris, vol. XV, 1894–95, pp. 353-55.

Gleichen-Russwurm, A.: Jugendstil, Ästhetische Plauderei, *Die Woche,* vol. IV, 1902, No. 2.

Grasset, Eugène: l'Art Nouveau, *Revue des Arts Décoratifs,* Paris, vol. XVII, 1897, pp. 129–44, 182–200.

— l'Art Nouveau, *La Plume,* Paris, Special Number, May 1894.

Guimard, Hector: An Architect's opinion on the Art Nouveau, *The Architectural Record,* New York, vol. XII, 1902, pp. 127–33.

Hamlin, A. D. F.: The Art Nouveau. Its Origin and Development, *The Craftsman,* New York, vol. III, 1902–03, pp. 129–43.

Hermann, Georg: Die Jugend und ihr Künstlerkreis, *Zeitschrift für Bücherfreunde,* Leipzig, 1900–01, vol. IV, No. 1, pp. 57–77.

Jacques, G. M.: l'Art Nouveau Bing à l'Exposition de 1900, *L'Art Décoratif,* Paris, vol. II, 2, 1900, pp. 88–91.

Locke, Josephine C.: Some Impressions of l'Art Nouveau, *The Craftsman,* New York, vol. II, 1902, pp. 201–04.

Melani, Alfredo: The Art Nouveau at Turin, *The Architectural Record,* New York, vol. XII, 1902, pp. 585–99, 735–50.

Mourey, Gabriel: l'Art Nouveau Bing, *Revue des Arts Décoratifs,* Paris, vol. XX, 1900, pp. 257–68, 278–84.

— The House of the Art Nouveau Bing, *The Studio,* London, vol. XX, 1900, pp. 164–80.

— An interview on "Art Nouveau" with Alexandre Charpentier, *The Architectural Record,* New York, vol. XII, 1902, pp. 121–25.

Muthesius, Herman: Kunstgewerbe, Jugendstil und bürgerliche Kunst, *Die Rheinlande,* vol. VII, 1903–04, p. 53.

Osborn, Max: S. Bing's Art Nouveau auf der Welt Ausstellung Paris 1900, *Deutsche Kunst und Dekoration,* Darmstadt 1900, vol. VI, pp. 550–69.

Puaux, René: l'Art Nouveau Bing. Paris, *Deutsche Kunst und Dekoration,* Darmstadt, vol. XII, 1903, pp. 308–12.

Sargent, Irene: The Wavy Line, *The Craftsman,* New York, vol. II, 1902, pp. 131–42.

Schopfer, Jean: The Art Nouveau: An Argument and Defence, *The Craftsman,* New York, vol. IV, 1903, pp. 229–38.

Schulze, Otto: Jugendstil-Sünden, *Kunst und Handwerk,* Munich, 1901–02.

Schultze-Naumburg, P.: Der „Sezessionsstil," *Der Kunstwart,* Munich, vol. XV, 1901–02, 1. part, p. 326.

CONTEMPORARY PERIODICALS

America

Architects and Builders Magazine. New York. 1899–1911.

The Architectural Record. New York, London. 1891–.

The Craftsman. New York. 1901–16.

Forms and Fantasies. Chicago. 1898–99.

Interior Decorator. Chicago. 1891–94.

Interiors. New York. 1888–.

Poster. New York. 1896.

Austria

Der Architekt. Vienna. 1895–1914.

Das Interieur. Vienna. 1900–15.

Kunst und Kunsthandwerk. Vienna. 1898–1924.

Ver Sacrum. Vienna. 1898–1903.

Wiener Bauindustrie Zeitung. Vienna. 1883–1904.

Belgium

Art Belge. Brussels. 1902.

l'Art et la Vie. Brussels. 1902–.

l'Art Moderne. Brussels. 1881–1914.

La Basoche. Revue Littéraire et Artistique. Brussels. 1884–86.

l'Emulation. Publication mensuelle de la Société Centrale d'Architecture de Belgique. Brussels. 1874–.

La Pléiade. Journal littéraire mensuel. Brussels. 1889–.

Le Reveil. Revue mensuelle de littérature et d'art. Ghent. 1891–.

La Société Nouvelle. Brussels. 1884–1914.

Van Nu en Straks. Brussels, Antwerp. 1892–1901.

La Wallonie. Brussels. 1886–92.

Great Britain

The Architect. London. 1869–1926.

The Architectural Record. New York, London. 1891–1938.

The Architectural Review. London. 1896–.

Architecture. London. 1896–98.

Art Annual. London. 1884–1915.

Artistic Japan. London. 1888–91. (English edition of *Japon Artistique*.)

The Art Journal. London. 1839–1912.

The Art Workman. London. 1873–82.

The Arts and Crafts Exhibition Society. Papers and Transactions. London. 1888–1906.

Arts and Crafts. London. 1896–.

The Cabinet Maker. London. 1880–1936.

Decoration in Painting, Sculpture, Architecture and Manufactures. London. 1881–.

The Decorator and Furnisher. London. 1882–94

Evergreen. Edinburgh. 1895–97.

The Furniture Gazette. London. 1873–93.

Furniture and Decoration. London. 1894–99.

The Furniture Record. London. 1899–1928.

The Hobby Horse. London. 1883–93.

The House. London. 1897–1903.

The Journal of Decorative Art. London. 1881–.

The Journal of Dublin Arts and Crafts Society of Ireland. Dublin. 1896–1901.

The Journal of the Royal Institute of British Architects. London. 1893–.

The Journal of Design and Manufactures. London. 1849–52.

The Magazine of Art. London. 1878–1904.

The Modern Style. London. 1902-.

The Poster and Art Collector. London. 1898–1901.

Posters Collector's Circular. London. 1899.

The Savoy. London. 1896.

The Studio. London. 1893–.

The Yellow Book. London. 1894–97.

France

l'Ameublement. Paris. 1870–1902.

l'Architecture. Paris. 1888–1912.

Art Appliqué. Paris 1903–05. (French ed. of *Moderne Stil*.)

Art et Décoration. Paris. 1897–.

l'Art Décoratif. Paris. 1898–1914.

l'Art et l'Idée. Paris. 1892.

l'Art et l'Industrie. Paris. 1877–81.

l'Art et les Artistes. Paris. 1905.

l'Art pour Tous. Paris. 1861–1906.

Le Bijou. Paris. 1874–1914.

Construction Moderne. Paris. 1885–.

Crocquis d'Architecture. Paris. 1866–98.

La Décoration ancienne et moderne. Paris. 1893–1906.

La Gazette des Beaux Arts. Paris. 1859–.

Japon Artistique. Paris 1888–91.

La Lorraine Artistique. Nancy. 1900–1914.

Nancy-Artiste. Nancy. 1882–1900.

La Plume. Paris. 1889–1913.

La Revue des Arts anciens et modernes. Paris. 1897–.

La Revue des Arts Décoratifs. Paris. 1880–1902.

La Revue Blanche. Paris. 1891–1903.

La Revue de la Bijoutérie. Paris. 1900–.

La Revue des Deux Mondes. Paris. 1831–1911.

La Revue Encyclopédique. Paris. 1895–1905.

Germany

Architektonische Rundschau. Stuttgart. 1885–1915.

Die Architektur des XX. Jahrhunderts. Berlin. 1901–14.

Baumeister. Munich. 1902–.

Bayerischer Kunstgewerbe-Verein. Munich. 1887–97.

Dekorative Kunst. Munich. 1897–1929.

Dekorative Vorbilder. Stuttgart. 1889–1915.

Deutsche Bauzeitung. Berlin. 1867–1902.

Deutsche Kunst und Dekoration. Darmstadt. 1897–1934.

Die Insel. Berlin, Leipzig. 1899–1902.

Jugend. Munich. 1896–1914.

Die Kunst. Munich. 1899–.

Das Kunstgewerbe. Dresden. 1890–95.

Kunstgewerbeblatt. Leipzig. 1885–1916.

Kunst und Dekoration. Darmstadt. 1897–1912.

Kunst und Handwerk. Munich. 1850–1932.

Kunst und Künstler. Berlin. 1902–07.

Die Kunst unserer Zeit. Munich. 1889–1912.

Der Kunstwart. Munich. 1887–.

Moderne Bauformen. Stuttgart. 1902–.

Der Moderne Stil. Stuttgart. 1899–1905.

Pan. Berlin. 1895–1900.

Simplicissimus. Munich. 1896–.

Zeitschrift für Bauwesen. Berlin. 1869–.

Zeitschrift für Innendekoration. Darmstadt. 1889–.

Holland

De Architect. Amsterdam. 1890–1907.

Architectura et Amicitia. Maasluis. 1893–1904.

Arti et Industriae. The Hague. 1892–.

Bouw en Sierkunst. Harlem. 1898–1902.

De Bouwmeester. Amsterdam. 1885–95.

Bouwkundig Weekblad. Amsterdam. 1881–1917.

Elsevier's Weekblad. Amsterdam. 1890–.

Het Huis. Amsterdam. 1903–04.

De Kunstwereld. Amsterdam. 1894–97.

Kunst en Industrie. Amsterdam. 1878.

Maandblad voor Beeldende Kunsten. Amsterdam. 1924–.

Onze Kunst. Amsterdam & Antwerp. 1902–29.

Tweemaandelijk Tijdschrift. Amsterdam. 1894–.

Italy

Annuale dei Lavori Publici. Rome. 1862–.

l'Arte. Rome. 1898–1901.

Arte Italiana Decorativa e Industriale. Rome & Venice. 1890–1914.

l'Edilizia Moderna. Milan. 1892–.

Emporium. Bergamo. 1895–.

BIBLIOGRAPHY

Articles from contemporary periodicals are not included, except for those written by the artists. A useful list, though not complete, is to be found in Henry F. Lenning, *The Art Nouveau,* The Hague, 1951, pp. 132–35. For assistance in preparing this bibliography I am indebted to James Grady, whose article "A Bibliography of the Art Nouveau" is published in *Journal of the Society of Architectural Historians,* Crawfordsville, Indiana, vol. XIV, No. 2, pp. 18–27.

Abbot, Thomas K.: *Celtic Ornaments from the Book of Kells*. London 1892–1895.

Addison, Agnes: *Romanticism and the Gothic Revival*. New York 1938.

Ahlers-Hestermann, Friedrich: *Stilwende. Aufbruch der Jugend um 1900*. Berlin 1941.

Alexandre, Arsène: *The Modern Poster*. New York 1895.

Appia, Adolphe: *La Mise en Scène de Drame Wagnérien*. Paris 1895.

l'Architecture en Belgique. 1872–76. Paris–Liége–Berlin 1876.

Architektur des Auslandes. Vienna 1905.

l'Art et la Vie en Belgique. 1830–1905. Brussels 1921.

l'Art en Belgique du moyen-age à nos jours. Brussels 1939. (Paul Fierens *et alii*).

Art Nouveau. Papiers de Fantaisie. Paris n.d.

Arts and Crafts Essays. London 1893. (Preface by William Morris.)

Ashbee, Charles R.: Challenge Cups, Shields, and Trophies, *The Art Journal*, London, vol. L, 1898, pp. 230–32.

— *Craftmanship in Competetive Industry*. Camden 1908.

— *An Endeavour towards the teaching of John Ruskin and William Morris*. London 1901.

— An Experiment in Cast-iron Work, *The Studio*, London, vol. XIV, 1898, pp. 253–56.

— *A Few Chapters on Workshop Reconstruction and Citizenship*, London 1894.

— *Modern English Silverwork*. London 1909.

— *Should we stop teaching Art*. London 1911.

— A short History of the Guild and School of Handicraft, *Transactions of the Guild and School of Handicraft*, London, vol. I, 1890, pp. 19–31.

— On Table Service, *The Art Journal*, London, vol. L, 1898, pp. 336–38.

Baaren, H., Schubad, G. C.: *Het meubel en het interieur in de negentiende en twintigste euw*. Deventer 1951.

Bahr, Herman: *Sezession*. Vienna 1900.

Baillie Scott, Mackay H.: An Artist's House, *The Studio*, London, vol. IX, 1896–97, pp. 28–37.

— *Haus eines Kunstfreundes. Meister der Innen-Kunst I*. London 1902.

— *Houses and Gardens*. London 1906.

— Ideals in Building, False and True, Schultz: *The Arts connected with Building. Lectures on Craftmanship*. London 1909, pp. 141–51.

— On the Choice of simple Furniture, *The Studio*, London, vol. X, 1897, pp. 152–57.

— A Small Country House, *The Studio, London*, vol. XII, 1898, pp. 167–72, 177.

Bajot, Edouard: *L'Art Nouveau—Décoration et Ameublement*. Paris 1898.

Banham, Reyner: The Voysey Inheritance, *The Architectural Review*, London, vol. CXII, 1952, pp. 367–71.

Bayard, Emile: *Le Style Moderne. l'Art de reconnaître les Styles*. Paris 1919.

— *Le Style Moderne*. Paris 1919.

Bazel, K. P. C. de: *De Houtsneden van K. P. C. de Bazel*. Amsterdam 1925.

Beardsley, Aubrey: *The Early Works of Aubrey Beardsley*. London 1899.

— *The Later Works of Aubrey Beardsley*. London 1900.

Behrendt, Walter C.: *Modern Building. Its Nature, Problems and Forms*. New York 1937.

— *Der Kampf um den Stil im Kunstgewerbe und in der Architektur*. Berlin 1920.

Behrens, Peter: *Feste Lebens und der Kunst*. Jena 1900.

— *Ein Dokument Deutscher Kunst: die Ausstellung der Künstler-Kolonie in Darmstadt, 1901*. Munich 1901.

Bell, Malcolm: *Edward Burne-Jones. A Record and a Review*. London 1892.

Bénédite, Léonce: *René Lalique*. Paris n.d.

Benn, R. Davis: *Style in Furniture*. New York 1904.

Benson, William A. S.: *Elements of Handicraft and Design*. London 1893.

— *Drawing. Its History and Use*. London 1925.

Berlage, Hendrik Petrus: *Gedanken über den Stil in der Baukunst*. Leipzig 1905.

— *Grundlagen und Entwicklung der Architektur*. Berlin 1908.

— Over Architectuur, *Tweemaandlijk Tijdschrift*, Amsterdam, vol. II, part 1, 1896.

Berryer, Anne-Marie: A Propos d'un vase de Chaplet décoré par Gauguin, *Bulletin des Musées Royaux d'Art et d'Histoire*, Brussels, No. 1–2, April 1944, pp. 13–27.

Betjamin, John: Charles Francis Annesley Voysey. The Architect of Individualism, *The Architectural Review*, London, vol. LXX, 1931, pp. 93–96.

Bing, Samuel: *Artistic Japan: Illustrations and Essays*. London 1888–91. Ed. Paris, *Japon Artistique*, Paris 1888–91.

— *Salon de l'Art Nouveau*. Paris 1896.

Blanche, Jacques-Emile: *Portraits of a Life Time. The Late Victorian Era. The Edwardian Pageant. 1870–1914.* New York 1938.

Blomfield, Paul: *William Morris.* London 1934.

Blomfield, Reginald: W. R. Lethaby. An Impression and a Tribute, *The Journal of the Royal Institute of British Architects,* London, vol. XXXIX, 1931–32, pp. 293–302.

— *Leaves from an Architect's Note-Book.* London 1929.

— *Memoirs of an Architect.* London 1932.

— *Richard Norman Shaw.* London 1940.

Boada, I. Piug: *El Templo de la Sagrada Familia.* Barcelona 1952.

Bode, Wilhelm: „Hermann Obrist." Special edition of *Pan.* Berlin 1896.

— *Kunst und Kunsthandwerk am Ende 1900 Jhrh.* Berlin 1901.

Bornstein, P.: *Am Ende des Jahrhunderts.* Berlin 1898.

Bott, Allan: *Our Fathers.* London 1931.

Bouilhet, André M. Henry: L'Exposition de Chicago, *Revue des Arts Décoratifs,* Paris, vol. XIV, 1893–94, pp. 66–79.

— *L'Orfèvrerie française aux XVIIIe et XIXe siècles,* vol. I–III. Paris 1908–13.

— *L'Orfèvrerie française au XXe siècle.* Paris 1941.

Boumphery, Geoffrey: The Designers I, Sir Ambrose Heal, *The Architectural Review.* London, vol. LXXVIII, 1935, pp. 39–40.

Bracquemond, J. M.: *Du Dessin et de la Couleur.* Paris 1885.

Brandes, Georg: *Berlin som tysk Rigshovedstad.* Copenhagen 1885.

Brenna, Arne: *Form og Komposisjon i nordisk granittskulptur 1909–1926.* Oslo 1953.

— Jugendstilen i norsk og europeisk skulptur. Lecture delivered for M.A. at the University of Oslo, 1951. MS.

Brenna, Arne and Madsen, Stephan Tschudi: *Vigelands Fontenerelieffer.* Oslo 1953.

Briggs, Martin Shaw: Sir Gilbert Scott, *The Architectural Review,* London, vol. XXIV, 1908, pp. 92–100, 147–52, 180–85, 290–93.

Buchert, J.: *Fleurs de Fantaisies.* Paris n.d.

Buckley, J. Hamilton: *The Victorian Temper.* Cambridge. U.S. 1951.

Burdett, Osborn: *The Beardsley Period.* London 1925.

Burges, William: *The Architectural Designs of William Burges,* vols. I–II, London 1883.

— *Architectural Drawings.* London 1870.

Bury, Adrian: *Shadow of Eros. Alfred Gilbert.* London 1952.

Butterfield, Lindsay P.: *Floral Forms in Historic Design.* London 1922.

Bøe, Alf: *From Gothic Revival to Functional Form. A Study in Victorian Theories of Design,* Oslo. In Print.

Cachet, Lion C. A.: Voorwerpen van gebatikt perkament, *Maandblad voor beeldende Kunsten,* Amsterdam, vol. I, 1924, pp. 108–13.

Calzada, André: *Historia de la Arquitectura Española.* Barcelona 1933.

Carter, E.: Arthur Mackmurdo, *Journal of the Royal Institute of British Architects,* London, vol. IL, April 1942, pp. 94–95.

Casson, Hugh: *An Introduction to Victorian Architecture.* London 1948.

Casteels, Maurice: *Henry van de Velde.* Brussels 1932.

— *The New Style. Architecture and Decorative Design.* London 1931.

Caw, James L.: *Scottish Paintings 1620–1908.* London 1908.

Chambers, Frank P.: *The History of Taste.* New York 1932.

Champier, Victor: *Documents d'atelier. Art décoratif moderne.* Paris 1898.

— *Les Industries d'art à l'exposition universelle de 1889.* Paris 1890.

— *Les Industries d'art à l'exposition universelle de 1900.* Paris 1902.

Chassé, C.: *Gauguin et le groupe de Pont-Aven.* Paris 1921.

— De quand date le synthétisme de Gauguin? *L'amour de l'art,* Paris, vol. XIX, 1938, p. 127–34.

Chavance, René: *Le papier peint et le décor de la maison.* Paris n.d.

Cheney, Sheldon: *The New World Architecture,* London, New York 1930.

Chennevières, Philippe de: *Souvenirs d'un directeur des Beaux-Arts,* vols. I–II, Paris 1885.

Cherbuliez, Victor: *L'Art et la Nature.* Paris 1892.

Cheronnet, Louis: *Paris vers 1900.* Paris 1932.

Christiansen, Hans: *Neue Flachornamente.* Berlin 1898.

Cirici-Pellicer, P., see Pellicer, Cirici P.

Cirlot, Juan Eduardo: *El Arte de Gaudi.* Barcelona 1950.

Clark, Kenneth: *The Gothic Revival.* London 1928.

Clephane. Irene: *Our Mothers.* London 1932.

Clouzot, Henry: *Des Tuileries à Saint Cloud. l'Art décoratif du second empire.* Paris 1925.

— *Le Style Louis-Philippe Napoleon III.* Paris 1939.

Cobden-Sanderson, T. J.: *The Arts and Crafts Movement.* London 1905.

Cole, Henry: *Fifty Years of Public Work,* vols. I–II. London 1884.

Cook, Theodore A.: *The Curves of Life.* New York 1914.

Cornell, Elias: *De store Utställningarnas historia.* Stockholm 1952.

Crane, Lucy: *Art and the Formation of Taste.* London 1882.

Crane, Walter: The Art of Walter Crane, Notes by the Artist, *The Art Journal,* The Easter Art Annual, London 1898.

— *An Artist's Reminiscences.* London 1907.

— *The Basis of Design.* London 1898.

— *The Claims of Decorative Art.* London 1892.

— Design in Relation to the Use and Material, *National Association for the Advancements of Art.* London 1889, pp. 202–12.

— *Ideals in Art.* London 1905.

— *Line and Form.* London 1900.

— *Moot-Points. Friendly Disputes upon Art and Industry between Walter Crane and Lewis Day.* London 1903.

— Of Wall Paper, *Arts and Crafts Essays,* London 1893, pp. 52–62.

Crane, Walter: *Of the Decoration of Public Buildings.* London 1897.

— *William Morris to Whistler.* London 1911.

Cremona, Italo: Discurso Sullo Stile Liberty, *Sele Arte,* Florence, No. 3, Nov./Dec., 1952, pp. 15–22.

Creutz, M.: *Johan Thorn Prikker.* Munich n.d.

Crow, Gerald H.: William Morris. Designer, *The Studio,* Special Winter Number. London 1934.

Cuypers, J. Th. J.: *Het werk van dr. P. J. H. Cuypers 1827–1917.* Amsterdam 1917.

Dali, Salvador: The Terrifying and Comestible Beauty of the "Modern Style," *Minotaure,* Paris 1932, No. 3–4. pp. 69–76.

— Apparitions aérodynamiques des êtres objets, *Minotaure,* Paris 1935, No. 6, pp. 33–34.

Day, Lewis F.: l'Art Nouveau, *The Art Journal,* London, 1900, pp. 293–97.

— An Artist in Design, *Magazine of Art,* London, vol. X, 1886–87, pp. 95–100.

— *Everyday Art: Short Essays on the Arts Not-Fine.* London 1882.

— Fashion and Applied Art, *National Association for the Advancements of Decorative Arts, 1889,* London 1890, pp. 218–28.

— Machine Made Art, *The Art Journal,* London, 1885, pp. 105–110.

— *Nature in Ornament.* London 1892.

— the New Art, *Macmillans Magazine,* London, No. 505, Nov. 1901, pp. 19–23.

— *Some Principles of Every-Day Art.* London 1890.

— William Morris and his Decorative Art, *The Contemporary Review,* London, vol. LXXXIII, 1903, pp. 787–96.

Delchavelier, Charles: Gustave Serrurier-Bovy, *Clarté,* Brussels 1930, No. 5.

Delhaye, Jean: *l'Appartement d'aujourd'hui.* Liége 1946.

Denis, Maurice: *Thèories 1890.1910.* Paris 1920.

Destréé, Olivier G.: *Les Pré-Raphaelites; notes sur l'art décoratif et la peinture en Angleterre.* Brussels 1894.

Dresser, Christopher: The Work of Christopher Dresser, *The Studio,* London, vol. XV, 1898, pp. 104–114.
— Art Industries, *Penn Monthly,* London, January 1877.
— *The Art of Decorative Design.* London 1862.
— *Development of Ornamental Art.* London 1862.
— *Japan: Its Architecture, Art, and Art Manufactures.* London 1882.
— *Modern Ornamentation.* London 1886.
— On Decorative Art, *The Planet,* London, No. 1, January 1862, pp. 123–35.
— *Principles of Decorative Design.* 3. ed. London 1880.
— *Studies in Design.* London 1876.
— Principles in Design, I–XI, *The Technical Educator,* London, vol. I, 1870.
— *Rudiments of Botany.* London 1859.
— *Unity in Varity.* London 1859.
Dumond-Wilden, L.: *Fernand Khnopff.* Brussels 1907.
Duthuit, Georges: *Chinese Mysticism and Modern Painting.* Paris 1936.
Dutton, Ralph: *The English Interior, 1500. 1900.* London 1948.

Eastlake, Charles: *Hints on Household Taste.* London 1868.
— *A History of the Gothic Revival.* London 1872.
Eckmann, Otto: *Neue Formen. Dekorative Entwürfe für die Praxis.* Berlin 1897.
— *Der Weltjahrmarkt. Paris 1900.* Berlin 1900.
Ehmig, Paul: *Das Deutsche Haus,* vols. 1.111. Berlin 1916.
Eisler, Max: *Gustav Klimt.* Vienna 1921.
Endell, August: Architektonische Erstlinge, *Dekorative Kunst,* Munich, vol. VI, 1900, pp. 297–317.
— *Die Schönheit der Grossen Stadt.* Stuttgart 1908.
— Formenschönheit und dekorative Kunst, *Dekorative Kunst,* Munich, vol. II, 1898, pp. 119–25.
— Möglichkeiten und Ziele einer neuen Architektur, *Deutsche Kunst und Dekoration,* Darmstadt, vol. I, 1897–98, pp. 141–53.
Endell, August: *Um die Schönheit. Eine Paraphrase über die Münchner Kunstausstellung 1896.* Munich 1896.
Evans, Joan: *Pattern. A Study of Ornament in Western Europe, 1180–1900,* vols. I–II, Oxford 1931.
Evers, Henri: *Het Orientalisme in de Westersche Architektuur.* Rotterdam 1894.

Falke, Jakob von: *Geschichte des modernen Geschmacks.* Vienna 1866.
— *Aesthetik des Kunstgewerbes.* Vienna 1883.
Farmer, A. J.: *Le mouvement esthétique et décadent en Angleterre.* 1873–1900. Paris 1931.
Federmann, Arnold: *Johann Heinrich Füssli, Dichter und Maler, 1741–1825.* Zurich 1927.
Fegdal, Charles: *Félix Valloton.* Paris 1931.
Feldegg, Ferdinand: *Leopold Bauer.* Vienna 1918.
Fendler, F.: Um Wiener-Sezession, Special issue of *Berliner Architektur-Welt,* Berlin 1901.
Fierens, Paul: *Theo van Rysselberghe.* Brussels 1937.
— *Essai sur l'Art Contemporain.* Paris 1897.
— *Nouveaux Essais sur l'Art Contemporain.* 2nd edition revised. Paris 1903.
— *La Tristesse Contemporaine.* Paris 1899.
— La Belgique et l'architecture moderne, *La Vie Artistique,* Brussels, 1937, pp. 509–18.
— *et alii: l'Art en Belgique du moyen age à nos jours.* Brussels 1939.
Fischel, O., Boehn, M. von: *Modes and Manners of the Nineteenth Century,* vols. I–IV. London 1927.
Die Flaeche. Vienna 1902–04.
Fleischmann, Benno: *Gustav Klimt. Eine Nachlese.* Vienna 1946.
Flouquet, Pierre-Louis: Surréalisme et architecture. A propos Gaudi y Cornet, *La Maison,* Brussels, vol. VIII, 1952, No. 11, pp. 340–44.
Flower, Margaret: *Victorian Jewellery.* London 1951.
Fontainas, André: *Mes souvenirs du Symbolisme.* Paris 1924.
Formenwelt aus dem Naturreiche. Leipzig n.d.

Fourcauld, Louis de: *Emile Gallé.* Paris 1903.
Fraipont, G.: *La Fleur et ses Applications décoratives.* Paris n.d.
Fuchs, Georg & Newberry, F. H. I.: *Internationale Ausstellung für Dekorative Kunst in Turin, MDCCCCII.* Darmstadt, Leipzig 1903.
Furst, Herbert: *The Decorative Art of Frank Brangwyn.* London 1924.

Gaillard, Eugène: *A propos du Mobilier.* Paris 1906.
Gallé, Emile: *Ecrits pour l'art.* 1884.89. Paris 1908.
— *Exposition de l'Ecole de Nancy à Paris. 1ere série. Le Mobilier.* Paris 1901.
— *Le Décor Symbolique,* discours de réception, Académie Stanislas. Nancy 1900.
— Le Salon du Champs de Mars, *Revue des Arts Décoratifs,* Paris, vol. XII, 1891–92, pp. 332–35.
Garczynski, Edward R.: *Auditorium.* Chicago 1890.
Garnier, Charles: *La Nouvelle Opéra.* Paris 1881.
— Le Style Actuel, *l'Emulation,* Brussels, vol. XVIII, 1893, cols. 161–67.
Garnier, Tony: *Une Cité Industrielle.* Paris n.d.
Gaunt, William: *The Aesthetic Adventure.* London 1945.
— *The Pre-Raphaelite Tragedy.* London 1942.
Geffroy, Gustave: *Les industries artistiques françaises et etrangères à l'exposition universelle de 1900.* Paris 1900.
— *René Lalique.* Paris 1922.
Giedion, Sigfried: *Bauen in Frankreich. Bauen in Eisen. Bauen in Eisenbeton.* Berlin 1928.
— *Mechanization takes Command. A Contribution to anonymous History.* New York 1948.
— *Space, Time and Architecture. The Growth of a New Tradition.* Cambridge U.S.A. 1941.
Gillet, Louis: Emile Gallé: Le Poème du verre, *La Revue Hebdomadaire,* Paris, vol. XIX, 1910, pp. 153–72.
Gimson, Ernest: *Ernest Gimson. His Life and Work.* London 1924.
Gloag, John: *A History of Cast Iron in Architecture.* London 1948.
Glück, Franz: *Adolf Loos.* Paris 1931.
Gmelin, Leopold: *Das Deutsche Kunstgewerbe zur Zeit der Weltausstellung in Chicago 1893.* München 1893.
Godwin, Edward: *Art Furniture.* London 1877.
Goodhart-Rendel, H. S.: *English Architecture since the Regency: An Interpretation.* London 1953.
Grady, James: A Bibliography of the Art Nouveau, *Journal of the Society of Architectural Historians,* Crawfordsville, Indiana, vol. XIV, 1955, No. 2, pp. 18–27.
— Nature and the Art Nouveau, *The Art Bulletin,* Princeton, New Jersey, vol. XXXVII, 1955, No. 3, pp. 187–94.
Grasset, Eugène: l'Architecture moderne jugée par Eugène Grasset, *l'Emulation,* Brussels, vol. XXI, 1896, cols. 58–59.
— l'Art Nouveau, *Revue des Arts Décoratifs,* Paris, vol. XVII, 1897, pp. 129–44, 182–200.
— *Histoire des Quatre Fils Aymon.* Paris 1883. (illustrations for).
— *Méthode de composition ornementale,* vols. I–II. Paris 1905.
— *Ornements Typographiques.* Paris 1880.
— *La plante et ses applications ornementales.* Paris 1899.
— *Plants and their Application to Ornament.* London 1896–1900.
— Eugène Grasset, *La Plume,* Paris, vol. VI, 1894, pp. 175–228.
— Eugène Grasset, *La Plume,* Paris, vol. XII, 1900, pp. 1–63.
Gratama, J.: *Dr. H. P. Berlage Bouwmeester.* Rotterdam 1925.
Graul, Richard: *Die Krisis im Kunstgewerbe.* Leipzig 1901.
Grautoff, Otto: *Die Entwicklung der modernen Buchkunst in Deutschland.* Leipzig n.d.
Gray, Nicolette: *XIXth Century Ornamented Types and Title Pages.* London 1938.
Gropius, Walter: *The New Architecture and the Bauhaus.* London 1935.

Gros, Gabriella: Poetry in Glass. The Art of Emile Gallé, 1846–1905, *Apollo,* London, New York, vol. LXII, 1955, pp. 134–36.

Guerinet, Edouard: *La décoration et l'ameublement à l'exposition de 1900.* Paris 1901.

— *L'Exposition de l'Ecole de Nancy.* Paris 1900.

Guiffrey, J., see Sandoz, Roger G.

Guimard, Hector: An Architect's Opinion of "l'Art Nouveau," *The Architectural Record,* New York, vol. XII, 1902, pp. 127–33.

— *Le Castel Béranger.* Paris 1899.

Haack, Dr. Friedrich: *Die Kunst des XIX. Jahrhunderts.* Esslingen n.d.

Hamilton, Walter: *The Aesthetic Movement in England.* London 1882.

Hamlin, A. D. F.: *A History of Ornament,* vols. I–II. New York 1916–23.

Hankar, Paul: l'Oeuvre Artistique. Exposition d'art appliqué. Liége, mai 1895, *l'Emulation,* Brussels, vol. XX, 1895, cols. 65–69.

Hannover, Emil: *Rundskue over Europas Kunsthaandværk paa Verdensudstillingen i Paris 1900.* Copenhagen 1900.

Harbron, Dudley: *Amphion or the Nineteenth Century.* London 1930.

— *The Conscious Stone. The Life of Edward William Godwin.* London 1949.

Helbig, J.: Notes sur l'evolution de la Céramique en Belgique. 1850–1950, *Revue Belge d'Archéologie et d'Histoire de l'Art,* Brussels, vol. XIX, 1950, pp. 212–18.

Hevesi, Ludwig: *Acht Jahre Sezession. 1897. 1905.* Vienna 1906.

— The Art Revival in Austria. Special Summer number, *The Studio,* London 1906.

— *Altkunst - Neukunst. Wien 1894–1908. Vienna* 1908.

— *Österreichische Kunst im 19. Jahrhundert,* Part II. Leipzig 1903.

— *Die Pflege der Kunst in Österreich. Vienna 1848–1898.* Vienna 1900.

— *Wiener Totentanz.* Stuttgart 1899.

Hiatt, Charles: *Picture Posters.* London 1895.

Hichens, Robert: *The Green Carnation.* New York 1894.

Hilberd, Shirley: *Rustic adornments for Homes and Taste.* London 1870.

Hirth, Georg: *Das Deutsche Zimmer.* Munich, Leipzig 1899.

Hitchcock, Henry-Russell: Early Cast Iron Facades, *The Architectural Review,* London, vol. CIX, 1951, pp. 113–16.

— *Early Victorian Architecture in Britain,* vols. I–II. New Haven 1954.

— *Modern Architecture, Romanticism and Reintegration.* New York 1929.

Hoeber, Fritz: *Peter Behrens.* Munich 1913.

Hoek, Kees van: *Jan Toorop Herdenking.* Amsterdam 1930.

Hoendschel, Georges: *Le Pavillon de l'Union Centrale des Arts Décoratifs à l'Exposition Universelle de 1900.* Paris n.d.

Hoffmann, Josef: Einfache Möbel, *Das Interieur,* Vienna, vol. II, 1901, pp. 193–208.

Hoffmann, Julius: *Bilderschatz für das Kunstgewerbe.* Stuttgart 1892.

— *Der Moderne Stil,* vols. I–VII. Stuttgart 1899–1905.

Hope, Henry R.: The Sources of Art Nouveau. Thesis for D.Ph., Harvard University, 1943, MS.

Hopstock, Carsten and Madsen, Stephan Tschudi: *Stoler og Stiler.* Oslo 1955.

Howarth, Thomas: *Charles Rennie Mackintosh and the Modern Movement.* London 1952.

Horta, Victor: *Considération sur l'art moderne.* Brussels 1925.

— *l'Enseignement architectural et l'Architecture Moderne.* Brussels 1926.

— *Le Sky-scraper.* Extract from *Bulletin des Commissions Royales d'Art et d'Archéologie,* vol. LXIII. 1929. Brussels 1930.

Humbert, Agnès: *Les Nabis et leur époque. 1888–1900.* Paris 1955.

Husarski, Vaslav: *Le Style romantique.* Paris 1931.

Hyde, H. Montgomery: Oscar Wilde and his Architect, *The Architectural Review,* London, vol. CIX, 1951, pp. 175–76.

Image, Selwyn: On Art and Nature, *The Hobby Horse*, London, vol. I, 1884, pp. 16–18.
— *Selwyn Image Letters*. Edited by A. H. Mackmurdo. London 1932.
Ironside, Robin: *Pre-Raphaelite Painters*. London 1948.

Jackson, Frank G.: *Theory and Practice of Design*. London 1903.
Jackson, Holbrook: *The Eighteen Nineties*. London 1913.
— *William Morris*. London 1926.
Joel, David: *The Adventure of British Furniture. 1851–1951*. London 1953.
Jong, J. de: *De Nieuwerichting in de kunstnijverheid in Nederland*. Rotterdam 1929.
Joseph, David: *Geschichte der modernen Baukunst*, vols. I–IV. Leipzig 1912.
— *Geschichte der Baukunst des 19. Jahrhunderts*, vols. I–II. Leipzig 1910.
Josephson, R.: Svensk 1800-tals arkitektur, *Arkitektur* 1922, appendix to *Teknisk Tidsskrift*, Stockholm, vol. LII, 1922, pp. 1-64.
Joyant, Maurice: *Henri de Toulouse-Lautrec. 1864–1901*, vols. I–II. Paris 1926–27.
Juynboll, H. H., see Rouffaer, G. P.
Juyot, Paul: *Louis Majorelle. Artiste décorateur. Maître ébéniste*. Nancy 1926.

Kalas, B.-E.: *De la Tamise à la Sprée. l'Essor des Industries d'Art*. Reims 1905.
Kauffer, E. McKnight: *The Art of the Poster*. London 1924.
Kaufman, Edgar, Jr.: Tiffany, Then and Now, *Interiors*, New York, vol. CXIV, No. 7, 1955, February, pp. 82–85.
Keller, Alfred: *Le Décor de la Plante*. Paris n.d.
Kielland, Thor B.: *Den nye verdensstil*. Oslo 1938.
— L'art Nouveau 1895–1925, *Fransk Møbelkunst*. Oslo 1928.
Kleiner, Leopold: *Josef Hoffmann*. Berlin 1927.
Klingender, F. D.: *Art and the Industrial Revolution*. London 1947.
Knipping, J. B.: *Jan Toorop*. Amsterdam 1945.
Koch, Alexander: *Darmstadt, eine Stätte moderner Kunstbestrebungen*. Darmstadt 1905.
— *Handbuch Neuzeitlicher Wohnungs-Kultur*. Darmstadt 1912.
— *Kochs Monographien*. Darmstadt n.d.
Koechlin, Raymond: *Le Pavillon de l'Union Centrale des Arts Décoratifs à l'Exposition de 1900*. Paris 1900.
— l'Art français moderne n'est pas "munichois," *l'Art Français Moderne*, Paris, January 1916, pp. 1–36.
Konody, P. G.: *The Art of Walter Crane*. London 1902.
Kulke, Heinrich: *Adolf Loos*. 1931.
Kuyck, Hugo van: *Modern Belgian Architecture*. New York 1948.

Laborde, Léon de: *De l'Union des arts et de l'industrie*, vols. I–II. Paris 1856.
Ladd, Henry Andrews: *The Victorian Morality of Art*. New York 1932.
Lahore, Jean: *l'Art Nouveau: Son histoire, l'art nouveau à l'Exposition, l'art nouveau au point de vue social*. Paris 1901.
— *l'Art pour le Peuple à défaut de l'art par le peuple*. Paris 1902.
— *Les Habitations à bon marché et un art nouveau pour le peuple*. Paris 1904.
— *William Morris et le mouvement nouveau de l'art décoratif*. Geneva 1897.
Lambert, Théodore: *l'Art décoratif moderne. l'Exposition universelle*. Paris n.d.
— *Escaliers et Ascenseurs*. Paris 1898.
— *Nouvelles Constructions*. Paris 1900.
— *Meubles et ameublement de style moderne*. Paris n.d.
— *Meubles de style moderne. Exposition universelle, 1900*. Paris n.d.
Lancaster, Clay: Japanese Buildings in the United States before 1900, *The Art Bulletin*, New York, vol. XXXV, No. 3, 1953, pp. 217–225.
— Oriental Contribution to Art Nouveau, *The Art Bulletin*, New York, vol. XXXIV, 1952, pp. 297–310.
— Oriental Forms in American Architecture 1800–70, *The Art Bulletin*, New York, vol. XXIX, 1947, pp. 183–93.

Lanyi, Richard: *Adolf Loos.* Vienna 1931.
Larroument, Gustave: *Documents d'Atelier.* Paris 1898.
— *L'Architecture au XXe Siècle,* vols. I–II. Librairie Centrale d'Art et d'Architecture. Paris n.d.
"L'Art Décoratif." *Histoire Générale de l'Art Française de la Révolution à Nos Jours.* Paris 1922.
Laurent, Marcel: *L'Architecture et la Sculpture en Belgique.* Brussels, Paris 1928.
Lecomte, Georges: *A. Delaharche.* Paris 1922.
Lenning, Henry F.: *The Art Nouveau.* The Hague 1951.
— The Movement in Europe—van de Velde, Horta and Guimard, *World Review,* London, Jan. 1953, pp. 33–38.
Léon, Paul: La Querelle des classiques et des gothiques, *La Revue de Paris,* Paris, vol. XX, July 1913, pp. 361-86.
— La Renaissance de l'Architecture Gothique, *La Revue de Paris,* Paris, vol. XX, July 1913, pp. 115–133.
Lethaby, William Richard: *Philip Webb and his Work.* London 1925.
— *William Morris as Workmaster.* London 1902.
Liberty & Co. Ltd.: *Handbook of Sketches.* London 1890.
— *Cymric Silver.* London 1900.
Lichten, Frances: *Decorative Art of Victoria's Era.* London 1950.
Lichtwark, Alfred: *Makartbouquet und Blumenstrauss.* Munich 1894.
Lilley, A. E. V.: *A Book in Plant Form, with Some Suggestions for Their Application to Design.* London 1907.
Lindahl, Göran: *Högkyrkligt Lågkyrkligt Frikyrkligt i svensk arkitektur 1800–1950.* Stockholm 1955.
Loos, Adolf: *Ins Leere gesprochen (1897.1900).* Berlin 1925.
— *Trotzdem (1900–1930).* Innsbruck 1931.
Lowry, John: The Japanese Influence on Victorian Design. Lecture given at Victoria and Albert Museum, London. December 1952. MS.
Ludovici, A.: *An Artists Life in London and Paris 1870–1925.* London 1926.
Luthmer, F.: *Blühenformen als Motive für Flachornament.* Berlin 1893.
Lux, Joseph August: *Josef Maria Olbrich.* Berlin 1919.
— *Die Moderne Wohnung und ihre Ausstattung.* Vienna, Leipzig 1905.
— *Das neue Kunstgewerbe in Deutschland.* Leipzig 1908.
— *Otto Wagner.* Berlin 1919.

Macallister, Isabel: Alfred Gilbert. London 1929.
Mackail, J. W.: *The Life of William Morris,* vols. I–II. London 1899.
Mackintosh, Charles Rennie: *Memorial Exhibition.* McLellan Galleries, Glasgow. 4th–27th May 1933.
Mackmurdo, Arthur H.:
Wrens City Churches. London 1883.
— The Guild Flag's unfurling, *The Hobby Horse,* London, vol. I, 1884, No. 1, pp. 2–13.
— History of the Arts and Crafts Movement. MS.
— Nature in Ornament, *The Hobby Horse,* London, vol. VII, 1892, pp. 62–68.
— The Presidential Address, *National Ass. for the Advancement of Art,* London 1890, pp. 158–71.
Madsen, Stephan Tschudi: Dragestilen. Honnør til en hånet stil, *Vestlandske Kunstindustrimuseums Årbok 1949–50,* Bergen 1952, pp. 19–62.
— Fem franske visitter. Stiltendenser i Europa omkring 1905, *Bonytt,* Oslo, vol. XV, 1955, pp. 105–10.
Madsen, Stephan Tschudi and Brenna, Arne: *Gustav Vigelands Fontenerelieffer.* Oslo 1953.
— Horta. Works and Style of Victor Horta before 1900, *The Architectural Review,* London, vol. CXVIII, 1955, pp. 388-92.
— Romantikkens arkitektur. En almeneuropeisk oversikt med særlig henblikk på nygotikken. Thesis for M.A., University of Oslo. MS.